S0-BKN-711

PUBLIC INTERNATIONAL LAW

SECOND EDITION

Other books in the *Essentials of Canadian Law Series*

Intellectual Property Law
Income Tax Law
Immigration Law
International Trade Law
Family Law
Copyright Law
Individual Employment Law
The Law of Equitable Remedies
Administrative Law
Ethics and Canadian Criminal Law
Public International Law
Environmental Law 2/e
Securities Law
Youth Criminal Justice Law
Computer Law 2/e
The Law of Partnerships and Corporations 2/e
Media Law 2/e
Maritime Law
Criminal Law 3/e
Insurance Law
International Human Rights Law
Legal Research and Writing 2/e
The Law of Evidence 4/e
The Law of Trusts 2/e
Franchise Law
The Charter of Rights and Freedoms 3/e
Personal Property Security Law
The Law of Contracts
Pension Law
Constitutional Law 3/e
Legal Ethics and Professional Responsibility 2/e
Refugee Law
Mergers, Acquisitions, and Other Changes of Corporate Control
Bank and Customer Law in Canada
Statutory Interpretation 2/e
The Law of Torts 3/e
National Security Law: Canadian Practice in International Perspective
Remedies: The Law of Damages 2/e

ESSENTIALS OF
CANADIAN LAW

PUBLIC INTERNATIONAL LAW

SECOND EDITION

JOHN H. CURRIE

Faculty of Law, Common Law Section
University of Ottawa

Public International Law, second edition
© Irwin Law Inc., 2008

All rights reserved. No part of this publication may be reproduced, stored in a retrieval system, or transmitted, in any form or by any means, without the prior written permission of the publisher or, in the case of photocopying or other reprographic copying, a licence from Access Copyright (Canadian Copyright Licensing Agency), 1 Yonge Street, Suite 800, Toronto, ON, M5E 1E5.

Published in 2008 by

Irwin Law Inc.
14 Duncan Street
Suite 206
Toronto, ON
M5H 3G8

www.irwinlaw.com

ISBN: 978-1-55221-139-7

Cataloguing in Publication data available from Library and Archives Canada

The publisher acknowledges the financial support of the Government of Canada through the Book Publishing Industry Development Program (BPIDP) for its publishing activities.

We acknowledge the assistance of the OMDC Book Fund, an initiative of Ontario Media Development Corporation.

Printed and bound in Canada.

3 4 5 6   15 14 13

SUMMARY
TABLE OF CONTENTS

DETAILED
TABLE OF CONTENTS

CHAPTER 3:

SOURCES OF INTERNATIONAL LAW *80*

PREFACE
TO THE FIRST EDITION

The field of public international law is vast, comprising an entire legal system governing the rights and obligations of states in their relations with one another and, increasingly, with non-state actors. The area has undergone explosive growth in the past half-century and so, accordingly, has its pervasive influence on international relations and domestic legal systems alike. Canada in particular has been a leader in this area such that, today, there is virtually no aspect of Canadian law that has not in some way or another been influenced by international law. International law has therefore ceased to be an arcane and specialized topic, of interest only to a small group of academics and lawyers in government practice. It has entered the legal mainstream and yet is still little known by many practitioners, judges, and students.

This book is therefore intended as a systematic introduction to this complex and increasingly important area of the law. It describes and places in context the fundamental elements of the international legal system — the subjects of international law, its key institutional structures, its sources, its interaction with domestic legal systems — and reviews some of its most important substantive topics — including the law of treaties, the relationship between states and territory, the law of the sea, state jurisdiction and jurisdictional immunities, international human rights law, and the fundamental rules of state responsibility. While the sheer reach and diversity of modern international law place an exhaustive treatment of every one of its numerous substantive topics beyond the scope of this introductory text, the contents of this book have been chosen for their fundamental importance to an understanding of international law more generally and to further study in specialized areas. It is hoped that, in assisting readers to acquire a basic understanding of the international legal system, this work may also encourage their more active and effective participation in its future development.

Many people have had a hand in bringing this project to fruition. I am particularly grateful to my colleague Don McRae for devoting much time to reviewing and commenting upon the manuscript, as well as for his encouragement throughout the project; Christine Johnson, LL.B. (Ottawa)/M.A. (Carleton) candidate, for truly superlative research and editorial assistance; my assistant, Debra Lemieux, for her valuable editorial comments on early drafts; colleagues Ruth Sullivan for planting the idea of the book in my mind (thereby distracting me during our squash game) and Bill Kaplan for his subsequent leap of faith in enthusiastically embracing the proposal; my editor, Jo Roberts, for her meticulous eye; Jeff Miller of Irwin Law for his patient guidance and support throughout the endeavour; and my family and many friends and colleagues for their encouragement and understanding over the past year. I am also indebted to the Foundation for Legal Research and the Law Foundation of Ontario for their generous financial support of this undertaking.

John H. Currie
Ottawa
August 2001

PREFACE
TO THE SECOND EDITION

As chance would have it, the final, revised page proofs for the first edition of this book left my desk in August, 2001. A scant few weeks later, the September 11, 2001 terrorist attacks on New York and Washington shocked global public consciousness. For some, the attacks and their aftermath called into question the appropriateness or even the relevance of existing international legal regimes concerning transnational terrorism, the maintenance of international peace and security, and the protection of human rights. Some doubted the international legal system's capacity to adapt to the "new realities" of global terrorist networks, asymmetrical warfare, and the proliferation of weapons of mass destruction. Some—abetted by an American administration seemingly sceptical of the value of international law (or the rule of law more generally) and keen to assert the United States' now-dominant "hard" power—even predicted (at times exultantly, one suspects) the demise of international law itself.

In retrospect, it would be difficult to deny the profound geopolitical repercussions of the events of September 11, 2001. So too would it be difficult to overstate the heinous nature of the attacks or the tragedy of their consequences. However, it seems that their negative significance for the relevance, adaptability, or survival of the international legal system has been greatly overstated. International terrorism, threats to international peace and security by non-state actors, and the spread of weapons capable of causing mass casualties were concerns already well-known to international law in 2001. Complex treaty networks addressing each, overlaid with customary international legal obligations and institutional frameworks, were already in place. This perhaps explains why some of the most immediate responses to the attacks assumed international legal form, such as United Nations Security Council resolutions under Chapter VII of the *Charter of the United Nations*, declarations by the North Atlantic Treaty Organization (NATO) under the *North Atlantic Treaty*, or the invocation of the time-worn international legal right of states to use armed force in self-defence, to name but a few. Certainly the occurrence of the attacks highlighted the need for some adjustments or additions to existing legal regimes. But here again the actions of states underscored their faith in the ability of the international legal system to adjust, as illustrated in their negotiation and conclusion of new anti-terrorism treaties, or even in the United States' call, in its 2002 National Security Policy, for "adaptation" of the law of self-defence.

As for the potential demise of international law, whether in the face of terrorism or state violations of its most fundamental precepts, its very nature makes this extremely unlikely. As we shall see in this book, international law is an organic phenomenon. Its content is essentially dictated by the actions and views of states. If such actions and views reveal widespread antipathy to existing international legal rules, the result is not to "break" the system but rather to amend its rules. As such, the normative content of international law will be as rich or impoverished, progressive or retrograde, robust or anaemic, as states generally will it to be. It is difficult to see, however, how they could will it out of existence altogether. In any case, far from abandoning the *concept* of international law, states (including the United States, albeit somewhat inconsistently) have if anything reaffirmed their commitment to it in response to the unsettling events of the early twenty-first century. As to whether in doing so, they have strengthened or weakened its substantive content, that will remain difficult to judge for some years to come, although some tentative conclusions in this regard are offered in relevant places in the pages that follow.

It is this persistent relevance, adaptability, and resilience of international law that continues to animate this book. International law has continued to evolve, as it must, and to grow in significance for our daily lives, as it should. And while the idea of international law has impinged upon the public consciousness in new and urgent ways in the past few years, it remains poorly understood by many. The manuscript for this second edition was prepared throughout the summer and fall of 2007, and occasional references to "the time of writing" refer to this period. Where possible, further updates have been made during the final production process with a view to having the text reflect factual and legal developments to the end of 2007. In addition to these overall updates and revisions, many of the discussions found in the first edition have been considerably expanded in this second edition. Several new topics or issues have also been introduced. In particular, given the centrality of the topic to the structure of the modern international legal system, an entirely new chapter on the use of force in international relations has been added.

As ever, I am thankful to the Law Foundation of Ontario for its ongoing support of my research. I also owe a debt of gratitude to the team at Irwin Law, particularly Jeff Miller, Alisa Posesorski, and Heather Raven, for their professionalism and guidance throughout the project. Special thanks also go to the many colleagues and students who provided critical commentary and feedback on the first edition of this book. Many of the improvements in this second edition are attributable to them, although any errors or shortcomings remain mine alone. Finally, I am profoundly grateful for the unflagging support of my family, without whose affectionate indulgence and forbearance this work would not be what it is.

John H. Currie
Ottawa
January 2008

CHAPTER 1

INTRODUCTION: NATURE AND ORIGINS OF PUBLIC INTERNATIONAL LAW

A. NATURE OF PUBLIC INTERNATIONAL LAW

1) General Character and Distinction from National Law

Public international law is not so much an area or topic of the law as it is an entire legal system that is conceptually distinct from the national legal systems that regulate daily life within states. It comprises a whole set of formal rules and customary practices that together define the legal rights and obligations, and govern the interactions, of international legal subjects. Traditionally, only states have enjoyed the status of international legal subjects and as we shall see this is still largely the case today.[1] This explains the term "international law," which of course denotes "law between nations."[2] It is also why international law is often described as the "law of nations."[3]

Thus, public international law exists outside of and apart from national legal systems.[4] It may be useful to think of it as a legal system that

---

1 But see further Chapter 2, where we explore in greater depth the modern dimensions of international legal personality.

2 See J. Bentham, *An Introduction to the Principles of Morals and Legislation*, 1789 (London: W. Pickering, 1823), c. XVII at para. 2.

3 See H. Grotius, *Three Books Treating of the Rights of War and Peace, Book I: Of the Rights of Peace and War*, 1625 (London: M.W. for Thomas Basset, 1682) at 5 [*Three Books*].

4 This is not meant to suggest that international and national legal systems do not interact, nor to prejudge the nature of their relationship. In fact, they intersect

applies where national legal systems leave off: while the latter govern relations of persons within states, international law essentially governs relations between states themselves. Moreover, unlike the multiplicity of national legal systems that exist worldwide, there is one universally applicable international legal system regulating the entire international community.[5]

International lawyers and judges use a variety of terms to describe national law, the most common of which are "domestic," "internal," or "municipal" law. All of these are meant to emphasize its distinct character when juxtaposed with international law. As a concrete example, the entire Canadian legal system (including the Canadian Constitution; all federal, provincial, and municipal laws and regulations; the common law; and all Canadian legal structures and institutions) would be described by international lawyers as a national (or "domestic," "internal," or "municipal") legal system. So too would the Russian or Costa Rican legal systems, for example. In contrast, the law governing Canada's relationship with Russia or Costa Rica or any other state would be described as international law.

As we shall see further below, the substantive scope of international law has grown since the mid-twentieth century to include many subject-areas that traditionally were considered to be of concern only to domestic legal systems.[6] Along with this substantive expansion have come new players in the international legal system, some—for instance, the United Nations and other international organizations—with formal capacities within that system, and others—such as individuals and non-governmental organizations—with more limited or informal roles.[7] As a result, it is no longer accurate to think of international law solely in terms of the mutual legal rights and obligations of states. Rather, it now includes rules and mechanisms governing the relations of states, international organizations and, in a limited number of areas of concern to the international community generally, individuals and

---

in many ways (see, for example, Chapter 3, Section C(4), as well as Chapters 6, 8, and 9) but are nevertheless generally considered to be distinct systems.

5   Although it should be noted that within that system are a number of regional sub-systems focused on particular areas of international law of particular interest to certain groupings of states: see, for example, Chapter 5, Section D and Chapter 10, Section C. Such regional sub-systems are built, however, on the common substratum of the universally applicable international legal system.

6   The most prominent example of this is probably the advent of international human rights law: see Chapter 10.

7   We explore the international legal personality of various players in the international legal system below in Chapter 2.

other non-state actors.[8] It nevertheless is still the case that the international legal system—whether examined from the perspective of its sources, its major institutions, its functional objectives, or its dominant subjects—remains fundamentally distinct from those operating within states.

2) Public International Law Distinguished from Private International Law

Another important distinction frequently confused by first-time students of international law is the difference between public international law and so-called "private international law." Public international law, as described above, is the legal system primarily governing the rights, duties, and relations of states. Private international law, by contrast and notwithstanding its somewhat misleading designation, is really an area of national or domestic law.[9] Each national legal system has a set of rules governing how it will treat legal problems with a "foreign element"—that is, a potential connection to another national legal system.[10] For example, the law of France will determine whether a French court has jurisdiction over a traffic accident occurring in Germany but involving French tourists. German law will also have a set of rules governing the same question, which may or may not be consistent with those prescribed by French law. These and similar rules make up the private international law of France and Germany respectively.

The fact that each national legal system has its own rules of private international law gives rise to the potential for clashes between those rules. This is why private international law is an area often referred to as "conflict of laws." The important point for present purposes, however, is that private international law is not essentially concerned with the rights, duties, and relationships of or between states and other international legal subjects as such. It is, rather, an area of domestic law, the content of which varies from state to state, and which determines the way each domestic legal system will treat, for its own purposes, issues that have connections with other domestic legal systems.

---

8   See J.G. Starke & I.A. Shearer, *Starke's International Law*, 11th ed. (London: Butterworths, 1994) at 3.

9   See *Case Concerning the Payment of Various Serbian Loans Issued in France* (1929), P.C.I.J. Ser. A, No. 20 at 41; M.N. Shaw, *International Law*, 5th ed. (Cambridge: Cambridge University Press, 2003) at 1–2.

10 See, generally, J-G. Castel, *Introduction to Conflict of Laws*, 4th ed. (Markham, ON: Butterworths, 2002).

It is important to note, however, that there are areas of overlap between the two disciplines of public and private international law. For example, states sometimes resort to public international law—for example, in the form of treaties—to harmonize their respective rules of private international law.[11] Further, as we shall see below,[12] public international law imposes certain constraints on the ability of states to apply their domestic law to foreign transactions or events, constraints that often have an effect on the formulation of domestic rules of private international law.

In keeping with common practice, "international law" will be used throughout this book to refer to public, as opposed to private, international law.

3) A Decentralized Legal System—Or No Legal System At All?

One of the first questions that arises when considering a universally applicable legal system that exists "above" or "beyond" domestic legal systems is its source. Where did the international legal system come from in the first place? How and by whom is international law made? Who runs the system?

The workings of each domestic legal system can usually be traced to a constitution or some other definitive source of authority or legitimacy. The processes by which law is made are usually clearly defined. A variety of established institutions have clear authority to make, administer, and enforce the law.

The greatest challenge in understanding the international legal system, however, is that it possesses virtually none of this certainty and structure. It is, to borrow a frequently used term, a "decentralized" system. This euphemism is meant to convey that, unlike most domestic legal systems, international law has very little hierarchical organization. It has no formal or written constitution establishing general law-making or law-enforcing institutions or otherwise distributing powers

---

11   See, for example, the *Vienna Convention on Contracts for the International Sale of Goods*, 11 April 1980, Can T.S. 1992 No. 2, 1489 U.N.T.S. 3 (in force 1 January 1988). This *Convention* is one of many produced by the Hague Conference on Private International Law, a treaty-based organization located in The Hague and tasked with the development of treaties that foster greater harmonization between the private international law of participating states: see *Statute of the Hague Conference on Private International Law*, 9–31 October 1951, 220 U.N.T.S. 121 (in force 15 July 1955).

12   See Chapter 8, Section C.

of governance.[13] Indeed, the international legal system is primarily characterized by the absence of any centralized governance or even effective coordination. Thus, international law is the product of diffuse, decentralized, and non-hierarchical law-making processes.[14] Further, in comparison with domestic systems, it exists in a relative institutional vacuum in which the dominant players are its own subjects.[15] As a result, it has no generally available means of enforcement, no coercive measures that can be brought to bear on its subjects for breaches of the law.[16] Rather, international law largely depends, for its enforcement, on consensual dispute resolution mechanisms and political or economic pressure brought to bear on the offending state by other states or the international community as a whole.

These features of the international legal system have led some to reject its characterization as a true system of law at all. Certain critics charge that, absent effective means of coercive enforcement, international law in reality amounts to little more than a voluntary moral or ethical code of conduct.[17] Such a view clearly depends on certain pre-conceived notions as to the necessary attributes of a legal system. More subtly, various international relations theorists prefer to analyze the relations of states in behavioural terms and are sceptical of the relevance or accuracy of applying legal theory in this context.[18]

Some aspects of this debate will be explored more fully below,[19] but for present purposes it perhaps suffices to observe that even states, which one might expect to be most hostile to the idea of legal constraints on their freedom of action, universally concede the existence and binding force of international law. While they frequently differ as to its content and tend to resist the creation of coercive compliance

---

13   On the limited role and powers of the United Nations and its various organs, see Chapter 2, Section D, Chapter 3, Section A, and Chapter 11, Section D(2)..

14   See A. Cassese, *International Law*, 2d ed. (Oxford: Oxford University Press, 2005) at 5–6. See also Chapters 3–5.

15   See further Chapter 2.

16   A notable but narrow exception is the United Nations Security Council's power to enforce the maintenance of international peace and security pursuant to Chapter VII of the *Charter of the United Nations*, 26 June 1945, Can. T.S. 1945 No. 7 (in force 24 October 1945) [*UN Charter*]. See further Chapter 11.

17   See, for example, J. Austin, "The Province of Jurisprudence Determined" in *Lectures on Jurisprudence or the Philosophy of Positive Law*, vol. 1 (London: John Murray, 1873) 82 at 232. See further Chapter 3, Section B.

18   An accessible review of international relations theory and its approach to international law is provided by A-M. Slaughter, "International Law and International Relations Theory: A Dual Agenda" (1993) 87 A.J.I.L. 205.

19   See further Chapter 3.

measures, states incessantly affirm through their behaviour and statements the existence of legal rights and duties that are not merely voluntary but obligatory. Even in seeking to evade the consequences of their internationally wrongful acts, states tend to defend themselves by relying upon rules of international law which they characterize as definitive and binding.[20]

If for no other reason than this, therefore, it becomes necessary to examine and understand the international legal system that states themselves appear to take for granted. Although, as we shall see, that system may differ in many respects from most domestic legal systems, studying it may ultimately provide some insights into what law itself is all about.

B. ORIGINS AND DEVELOPMENT OF INTERNATIONAL LAW

In order to better understand the nature and scope of modern international law, it is necessary to return to its origins and to trace, at least in outline, its subsequent development. Only then can most of its peculiar attributes and fundamental characteristics be fully appreciated.

Fortunately (but also somewhat surprisingly), this requires no great reach into the ancient past. It is probably the case that human societies have recognized rules of interaction ever since they became aware of one another's existence, many of which have provided the foundations for our current system of international law.[21] However, conventional theory is that the international legal system as we know it today has its origins in the sixteenth and seventeenth centuries, and that its birthplace was Europe.[22]

---

20 See, generally, H. Kelsen, *Principles of International Law*, 2d ed. by R.N. Tucker (New York: Holt, Rinehart and Winston, 1966); L. Henkin, *How Nations Behave: Law and Foreign Policy*, 2d ed. (New York: Columbia University Press for the Council on Foreign Relations, 1979).

21 See, for example, Shaw, above note 9 at 13–22.

22 It should be noted that there are several competing theories and differing historical accounts of the origins of modern international law. For example, Soviet scholarship analyzed the stages of development of international law in terms of successive class societies: see, for example, T.A. Taracouzio, *The Soviet Union and International Law* (New York: Macmillan, 1935); see also J.A. Cohen & H. Chiu, *People's China and International Law: A Documentary Study* (Princeton: Princeton University Press, 1974). For entirely different accounts, see, for example, Whilhelm Grewe, *The Epochs of International Law*, trans. by M. Byers (Berlin: de Gruyter, 2000); M. Zimmermann, "La crise de l'organisation

1) The Peace of Westphalia (1648)[23]

Most international lawyers point to the Peace of Westphalia of 1648, which put an end to the Thirty Years' War in Europe, as the essential turning point that witnessed the birth of the current international legal system.[24] While it is somewhat arbitrary to choose such a discrete event to explain what was, in reality, an evolutionary process, the Peace of Westphalia conveniently marks the confluence of several critical developments in Europe at about this time.

One of these was the culmination of the gradual emergence of strong, centralized political units, usually under monarchical authority, which increasingly asserted their authority over defined territories and populations. Some of these exploited the wealth of the so-called New World in order to further consolidate their own military, economic, and political positions. With increased military and economic might came a willingness, and the means, to challenge existing political and social structures, some of which were medieval in origin and pan-European in scope.

At roughly the same time the Renaissance had flowered throughout much of Europe, followed closely by the Reformation, definitively marking the end of the medieval period and signalling the decline in power and influence of the Catholic Church. The concomitant resurgence of secular scholarship, which borrowed many of its ideas from ancient Greek philosophy, sparked a renewed interest in theories of natural law. From this there emerged a contingent of scholars, the most famous of whom was Hugo Grotius,[25] intent on applying natural law theories to describing, and even prescribing, a system of law governing the interactions of the increasingly autonomous polities in Europe. Given its importance to understanding the modern source of binding

---

internationale à la fin du moyen-âge" (1933-II) 44 Rec. des Cours 319; R. Ago, "Pluralism and the Origins of the International Community" (1978) Ital. Y.B. Int'l L. 3.

23   See J.H. Currie, C. Forcese, & V. Oosterveld, *International Law: Doctrine, Practice and Theory* (Toronto: Irwin Law, 2007) at 19–25; Cassese, above note 14 at 22–25, and Shaw, above note 9 at 22–24.

24   See, for example, A. Nussbaum, *A Concise History of the Law of Nations*, rev. ed. (New York: Macmillan, 1962) at 115; Currie *et al.*, *ibid.* at 22; Cassese, *ibid.* at 22-25; Shaw, *ibid.* at 25.

25   (1583–1645), and the author of the 1625 work "*De Jure Belli ac Pacis*" ("On the Law of War and Peace"): see *Three Books*, above note 3. In recognition of his pioneering work, some have dubbed Grotius the progenitor of international law: see, for example, H.M. Kindred & P.M. Saunders, eds., *International Law: Chiefly as Interpreted and Applied in Canada*, 7th ed. (Toronto: Emond Montgomery, 2006) at 3.

obligation in international law, the work of these scholars will be explored in greater detail below.[26] The important point in the present context, however, is that such a body of scholarship instilled in European thought the idea that a system of law regulating an international community was a natural and inevitable phenomenon.

In this political and intellectual climate, the Peace of Westphalia proved to be a threshold event. The Thirty Years' War was chiefly the result of religious rivalries between Catholic and Protestant members of the Holy Roman Empire, and it eventually engulfed most of Europe. At the time it began, most European nations remained subject to a number of "supranational" — that is, external — sources of authority. One of the most important of these was the Catholic Church. Though considerably weakened by growing challenges to its authority by Protestant countries, the supranational character of ecclesiastical law and the authority of the Pope nevertheless permitted the Catholic Church to maintain considerable sway over countries which remained faithful to it. Indeed, such countries were regarded by the Church as the only ones having a "legitimate" government or even existence. Other sources of external authority included the Holy Roman Empire itself, of which most central European countries were members, as well as the powerful "trade guilds" which controlled considerable aspects of economic activity throughout Europe. As a result, most European countries prior to the Thirty Years' War did not have exclusive jurisdiction over their own affairs but were, rather, subject to various external sources of power.

The peace treaties concluding the Thirty Years' War, signed in the two Westphalian towns of Münster and Osnabrück, struck decisive blows against some of these external sources of power. First, the treaties recognized the existence and legitimacy of Protestant states, effectively breaking the necessary link between allegiance to the Catholic Church and legitimate statehood. Second, most members of the Holy Roman Empire gained the power to conclude treaties with or wage war against foreign powers, effectively granting them most of the attributes of external sovereignty and presaging the eventual demise of the Empire.

In short, the Peace of Westphalia announced the emergence of a new form of political organization in Europe, one premised upon states' essential independence from external authority. The forebears of truly sovereign nation-states, self-contained political units owing allegiance only to themselves and thus governing their own internal affairs to the exclusion of all others, had been conclusively established. It is

---

26   See Chapter 3, Section B.

this essentially autonomous conception of the state—the "sovere ꜜ state"—that remains at the core of the structure of international society, and hence international law, today.

In Europe, the vacuum left by the displacement of papal and imperial authority required the elaboration of a new system that could regulate, or at least describe, the ways in which an international society populated by sovereign states should interact. Building on the earlier work of Grotius and his contemporaries, a new generation of international legal scholars, of which the most influential was likely Emmerich de Vattel,[27] took up this task. Modern international law is very much the product of the work of such writers, as adopted and refined by the newly sovereign states of which they were writing. Thus, the emergence of the modern, sovereign state is the very *raison d'être* of the modern international legal system.

However, it is in these origins that one also finds the seeds of the most fundamental paradox of international law, one that explains its "decentralized" nature but also continues to this day to dog its legitimacy as a "true" system of law: If modern states are by definition sovereign, meaning not subject to external sources of authority, how is it possible to conceive of a system of law that will regulate their conduct? Can there be such a thing as international law truly "governing" sovereign states? The matter is not readily resolved, and provides the most fundamental tension in the international legal order even today. Due to its vital importance to the very existence or reality of international law, this issue and the various ways in which it is addressed by international lawyers will be considered at greater length later in this book.[28] For present purposes, however, a broad outline of the principal developments in international law following the Peace of Westphalia is in order.

2) The Growth of "European International Law": The Seventeenth to Nineteenth Centuries[29]

The seventeenth to nineteenth centuries confirmed the establishment in Europe of a system of international law premised on the sovereign

---

27 See E. de Vattel, *Le Droit des Gens: The Principles of Natural Law as Applied to the Conduct and to the Affairs of Nations and of Sovereigns*, 1758, vol. 3, ed. by J.B. Scott, trans. by C.G. Fenwick, Classics of International Law Series (Washington, DC: Carnegie Institution of Washington, 1916). See further Chapter 3, Section B.

28 See Chapter 3, Section B.

29 See Currie *et al.*, above note 23 at 25–29; Cassese, above note 14 at 25–34; Shaw, above note 9 at 24–29.

independence of states. Most of the fundamental elements of that system, including the sources of the law, the principal rights and obligations of states (particularly those reinforcing their sovereignty), and rules governing their various interactions, were established during this period. This process coincided with and was facilitated by the rise of positivism in both domestic and international legal scholarship in Europe and America. Positivism's empirical focus on conduct and consent as the bases of law permitted the articulation of rules of international law while preserving, and indeed reinforcing, the notion of the sovereignty of the state.[30]

In positivist theory, whenever states interacted, their conduct was a potential source of legal rules governing their future conduct. As contact among European states[31] was particularly pronounced during this period, the content and shape of international law, already European in its origins, came to be dominated even further by European political and legal values. By the nineteenth century, the result of this was the emergence of a system of international law heavily oriented towards the interests of an exclusive club consisting of the "Concert of Europe" and other states based on a European, and Christian, model. While treaties were occasionally concluded with some of the more prominent non-Christian states, such as the Ottoman Empire, China, Japan, Persia, and Siam, these tended to be on an unequal footing. Most of these states thus remained on the periphery of the European system of international law until they ultimately, albeit reluctantly, adopted its basic precepts in the late nineteenth and early twentieth centuries. Other less powerful non-Christian nations had by then succumbed to European expansionism and been folded into the European colonial empires. Indeed, European international law was so constructed as to legitimize these acts of conquest and appropriation.

Thus, by the early twentieth century, a system of international law largely constructed by Europeans and based on European political theory and social structures had effectively, by one means or another, become universalized. This process explains why the core of the modern international legal system, which is today universally accepted and applied, still bears the distinct imprint of European values and

---

30   See further Chapter 3, Section B. Positivism in general eschews the notion that law is pre-ordained or inherent in the natural order of things. Rather, it asserts that law is simply whatever a particular society authoritatively accepts or establishes as such at any given time: see, generally, D. Lloyd, *The Idea of Law* (Markham, ON: Penguin Books, 1981) c. 5.

31   As well as the United States beginning in the late eighteenth century and Latin American states in the nineteenth century.

traditions. This fact — the global application of an essentially F international legal system — is the source of a second fundam_ sion in modern international law.

3) The First and Second World Wars[32]

The end of the First World War heralded the gradual decline, throughout the twentieth century, of European dominance in international society and world affairs. This led, eventually, to a certain levelling of the international playing field and, consequently, a more truly global system of international law — albeit one still heavily imbued with European traditions.

In part, this process was catalyzed by the perceived need to restructure international society in the wake of the First World War. That conflict, while European in its origins, had ultimately involved most of the world and had awakened a form of global self-consciousness. The idea of a truly global international community — one populated by many sovereign states, all juridically equal as opposed to subordinate to European or Christian states — took root. This led to a process of rethinking much of the content of international law and of the structure of the international community that was to continue well past the middle of the twentieth century, and indeed continues in various ways today.

Aside from the emergence in international law of the principle of the formal equality of states, two key events during the inter-war period are usually identified as crucial to subsequent developments in international law. The first is the rise of the Soviet Union and socialism following the Bolshevik revolution in Russia in 1917. Altogether aside from its political and military significance to the global balance of power, the Soviet Union was one of the earliest states to challenge many of the fundamental precepts of international law that had previously been elaborated by mainly Western European states. "Soviet international law" espoused radical new principles.[33] It was among the first to assert the right of peoples, whether national or ethnic groups within states or colonized nations, to self-determination.[34] It advocated rules of international law designed to foster the substantive, rather than the merely formal, equal-

---

32 See Cassese, above note 14 at 34–39; Shaw, above note 9 at 30–33.

33 See, for example, E. Korovin, "Soviet Treaties and International Law" (1928) 22 A.J.I.L. 753, reviewed in Cassese, *ibid.* at 57–60. See also G.I. Tunkin, *Theory of International Law*, trans. by W.E. Butler (Cambridge: Harvard University Press, 1974); and H.W. Baade, ed., *The Soviet Impact on International Law* (Dobbs Ferry, NY: Oceana, 1965).

34 See further Chapter 2, Section C.

ity of states. Perhaps most radically of all, it proclaimed the doctrine of socialist internationalism, which included a purported right of socialist states to assist the struggle of the working class in any other state.

All these doctrines represented fundamental challenges to the well-established principle of the sovereignty of states. While not all were successfully advanced, and the Soviet Union did not wholly reject the existing international legal order, its dissent sowed the seeds for re-thinking international legal rules and the structure of the international community throughout the twentieth century.

The second major development of the inter-war period was the establishment of the League of Nations in 1919. The League, with its goal of promoting "international co-operation and ... international peace and security,"[35] signalled a new theme in international law: the need to foster cooperation and friendly relations between states and to curb their resort to the use of force. Some moves had already been made in this direction as early as 1815 in the wake of the Napoleonic Wars.[36] However, the establishment of the League and other permanent international institutions intended to foster the peaceful settlement of disputes, such as the Permanent Court of International Justice,[37] marked an institutional as well as a legal commitment to these principles. Unhappily, the functioning of such institutions and the respect of these commitments depended on voluntary self-restraint by states. Such arrangements proved wholly inadequate to contain the forces that ultimately led to the Second World War. However, the international legal foundations for the eventual outlawing of the use of force in international relations had been laid.

Other, more sinister, developments of the inter-war period included the growth in some states of ethnic nationalism and the concomitant rise of fascism. These and other factors eventually led to the collapse of the international legal order and a global descent into conflict in the Second World War. Yet from those cataclysmic events arose another turning point in the development of modern international law, probably the most significant since its birth in Westphalia in the mid-seventeenth century.

---

35 *Covenant of the League of Nations Adopted by the Peace Conference at Plenary Session, April 28, 1919* (1919) 13 A.J.I.L. Supp. 128, Preamble. For a fascinating account of the establishment of the League, see M. MacMillan, *Paris 1919: Six Months that Changed the World* (New York: Random House, 2002) at 53–106.

36 The Treaties of Paris of 26 September 1815 and 20 November 1815 committed the parties to cooperation and friendship through measures of multilateral diplomacy and collective security: see Cassese, above note 14 at 29–30.

37 *Statute of the International Court of Justice*, 26 June 1945, Can. T.S. 1945 No. 7 (in force 24 October 1945) [*ICJ Statute*].

4) The Post–Second World War Period[38]

It became clear during the Second World War, particularly in light of technological "advances" in the capacity of states to carry out mass destruction, that the new imperative on the post-war international legal agenda had to be the establishment of effective constraints on the international use of armed force. As suggested above, this development had its seeds in the League of Nations experiment. The failure of that experiment, with its appalling consequences, lent new urgency to the project and provided some valuable lessons in how it might be more effectively implemented.

The international community's response to that challenge at the end of the Second World War was the establishment of the United Nations in June 1945.[39] The United Nations was conceived as a permanent international organization, membership of which was to be open to "all peace-loving states."[40] Its overriding purpose was to maintain international peace and security, and to do so through developing friendly relations, fostering international cooperation, and harmonizing the international efforts of states.[41] Its founding principles were the sovereign equality of all states and a general forbearance from the unilateral use of force in international relations.[42]

Much of this is similar to the scheme set forth in the ultimately unsuccessful *Covenant of the League of Nations* and yet, as suggested above, the establishment of the United Nations ranks as the most significant event in modern international law since the Peace of Westphalia. This is so for a number of reasons.

First, the *UN Charter* is premised upon an outright rejection of the unilateral use of force,[43] rather than the *Covenant*'s commitment not to resort to "war," a narrower legal concept. Second, the *UN Charter* provides a mechanism for the enforcement of the ban on the use of force in the form of the United Nations Security Council, essentially an executive body composed of permanent and periodically elected members.[44] Membership in the United Nations involves, in effect, delegation to the Security Council of the power to take measures, including military ac-

---

38   See Cassese, above note 14 at 39–45; Shaw, above note 9 at 33–41.
39   *UN Charter*, above note 16.
40   *Ibid.*, Article 4(1).
41   *Ibid.*, Article 1.
42   *Ibid.*, Article 2.
43   *Ibid.*, Article 2(4). See further Chapter 11, Section C(3)(a).
44   *Ibid.*, Chapter V.

tion, to maintain or restore international peace and security.[45] This is the so-called "collective security" mechanism established in the *UN Charter*. Third, membership in the United Nations has since its inception been almost universal, in contrast to the League of Nations which had only a limited sustained membership. This has meant a generalized embrace by most of the world's states of the foregoing obligations and enforcement mechanisms.

In short, the founding of the United Nations effectively moved the ban on the use of force by states to the very core of international law, except in certain tightly defined circumstances.[46] Although, sadly, this has not led to the eradication of the use of armed force in international affairs, there is now no doubt that states acknowledge its general illegality and seek to justify their military actions in terms of exceptions to the general ban. Further, while the system of collective security envisaged in the *Charter* has often been stymied by the realities of power politics, particularly during the Cold War era, it has on occasion been effectively, if controversially, invoked.[47]

The United Nations has had other profound influences on the shape of international law in the post-Second World War era as well. Chief among these is that it has provided a permanent and universal forum, particularly but not exclusively through the General Assembly, for on-going contact, discussion, and debate between member states. This has not only served the intended purpose of fostering communication and cooperation among all states on a formally equal footing, but has also

---

45   *Ibid.*, Chapter VII. This should not be mistaken for the establishment of a form of international policing authority with jurisdiction to enforce compliance with international law generally. The Security Council's coercive powers are confined to threats to international peace and security, and ultimately depend on the cooperation of member states for their implementation. See further Chapter 11.

46   For example, when acting in self-defence (*UN Charter*, above note 16, Article 51) or pursuant to collective measures of enforcement sanctioned by the Security Council pursuant to its Chapter VII powers. See further Chapter 11.

47   For example, in response to the North Korean invasion of the Republic of Korea in 1950: SC Res. 82(1950), UN SCOR, 5th Year, UN Doc. S/1501 (25 June 1950) (declaring a breach of international peace and security) and SC Res. 83(1950), UN SCOR, 5th Year, UN Doc. S/1511 (27 June 1950) (authorizing collective measures). See L.M. Goodrich, *Korea: Collective Measures Against Aggression*, International Conciliation Series No. 494 (New York: Carnegie Endowment for International Peace, 1953). A more recent example is the Security Council's response to the invasion of Kuwait by Iraq in 1990: SC Res. 660(1990), UN SCOR, 45th Year, UN Doc. S/RES/660(1990) (2 August 1990) (determining breach of international peace and security) and, *inter alia*, SC Res. 678(1990), UN SCOR, 45th Year, UN Doc. S/ RES/678(1990) (29 November 1990) (authorizing collective measures). See further Chapter 11.

led directly to a prodigious growth in output of new intern?
in a wide range of subject-areas. As a result, modern internatiν.
ranges far beyond rules concerning diplomatic and other contacts between states. Rather, international law now deals, in one way or another,
with most aspects of human endeavour, including trade and commerce,
human rights, culture and heritage, conservation and the environment,
labour law, intellectual property, criminal law, and so on.[48]

Particularly instrumental in this substantive growth has been the
rise in prominence of multilateral "law-making" treaties, broad-based
agreements between states codifying whole areas of international law.[49]
Also significant has been the establishment of a multitude of secondary
international organizations, which in turn have fostered further expansion in the scope of international law.

One of the most important concomitant institutional developments
was the establishment, also in 1945, of the International Court of Justice as the "principal judicial organ" of the United Nations. This Court,
in fact the continuation of the Permanent Court of International Justice
established in the League of Nations era, has general jurisdiction to
resolve international legal disputes submitted to it on consent by states.
It may also render advisory opinions on legal questions referred to it by
various organs of the United Nations. The judgments of the Court have
therefore also contributed to certainty and growth in the content of
international law.[50] The Court further provides an authoritative mechanism by which states may resolve their disputes peacefully, fostering
the emergence of a rules-based, rather than a power-based, system for
regulating international affairs.

Thus, the mere existence of the United Nations and its satellite
institutions has facilitated substantial growth and clarification in the
content of, and increased respect for, international law in the twentieth
and twenty-first centuries.

In addition to these institutional developments, moreover, the end
of the Second World War also ushered in political changes having far-
reaching implications for the structure of international society and the
content of international law.

Of fundamental importance was the eventual collapse, beginning
in the 1950s and stretching into the 1970s and 1980s, of the great Euro-

---

48   In fact, so vast is the modern coverage of modern international law that it
     would be quite impossible to introduce readers to all or even most of its aspects
     in this book. Thus, this book of necessity has the more modest goal of introdu-
     cing readers to the essentials of the international legal system itself.
49   See further Chapter 4.
50   See further Chapter 3.

pean colonial empires. The seeds of the doctrine of self-determination sown by the Soviet Union in the inter-war period[51] came to fruition as colonized peoples, primarily in Africa and southeast Asia, asserted their right to join the community of nations as sovereign equals.[52] In keeping with parallel international legal developments recognizing certain fundamental human rights, including the right to self-govern-ance, these calls were heeded with the result that scores of newly in-dependent states arrived on the international scene. From the roughly fifty or so states that emerged from the Second World War, membership in the international community had nearly quadrupled by the end of the twentieth century.

This radical and sudden change in the composition of the inter-national community had an almost immediate impact on the nature and focus of international legal discourse. Given the fundamental prin-ciple of the sovereign equality of states, each such newly independent state was entitled to membership in the United Nations and to a seat, and a vote, in the United Nations General Assembly. The international legal agenda was thus dramatically refocused from exclusive attention to the priorities and aspirations of developed nations to those of the predominantly developing, newly independent states. Global economic development, domestic control of natural resources, and exploitation of the global commons (for example, the high seas) are only a few of the areas in which the numerically powerful newly independent states made their presence known in international law.[53] Several of the result-ing developments will be examined in greater detail below.[54]

Yet a further fundamental development in the post-Second World War era was a far-reaching change in the position of the individual in international law. As we have seen, international law by its very na-ture developed in response to the need for a system of law to regulate states. As states were its only true "subjects," there was little room or

---

51   And, arguably, by the United States through President Wilson's "Fourteen Points": see MacMillan, above note 35 at 10–13.

52   See further Chapter 2, Section C.

53   See R.P. Anand, ed., *Asian States and the Development of Universal International Law* (Delhi: Vikas Publications, 1972); T.O. Elias, *Africa and the Development of International Law* (Leiden: A.W. Sijthoff, 1972); S-C. Leng & H. Chiu, *Law in Chinese Foreign Policy: Communist China and Selected Problems of International Law* (Dobbs Ferry, NY: Oceana, 1972); H. Bull & A. Watson, eds., *The Expansion of International Society* (Oxford: Clarendon Press, 1984).

54   See, for example, Chapter 2, Section B(5)(b), on state succession; Chapter 7, Section C(2)(h), on the deep seabed; Chapter 7, Section E, on outer space and celestial bodies; Chapter 8, Section D, on the treatment of aliens; and Chapter 10, on the international protection of human rights.

need to accommodate the existence of individuals. The regulatio..
their rights, obligations, and conduct was considered a purely domestic
matter best dealt with by national legal systems. There was thus little
justification for the recognition of rights and duties of individuals as a
matter of international law; indeed this would have been perceived as
an impermissible incursion into the domestic jurisdiction of sovereign
states.

However, the atrocities committed during and before the Second
World War, often by states against their own nationals, outraged international public opinion and drove the topic of the basic protection of
human rights onto the international agenda. The Nuremberg trials
following the Second World War confirmed the already nascent notion that individuals, and not only states, could be held accountable
as a matter of international law for certain acts considered fundamentally inimical to the international legal order.[55] The corollary proposition—that international law might also confer certain fundamental
protections for individuals, in addition to imposing fundamental obligations on them—proved irresistible in light of the magnitude of the
abuses witnessed during the war. Thus, notwithstanding their seeming
unsuitability in a system of law initially designed only to define the
rights and obligations of states, international human rights emerged as
a fundamental pillar of post-war international law.

The subsequent development of international human rights law
will be described in greater detail in a later chapter,[56] but for now its
importance is that it marks the dilution of international law's former
character as nothing more than a "law of nations." Not only does the
development illustrate the diversification (albeit piecemeal) of the subjects of international law,[57] it also typifies the expansion of traditional
international law, in the post-Second World War era, into countless
new substantive areas.

More recent developments have included increased Security Council activity since the collapse of the Soviet Union and the end of the
Cold War; dramatic growth in international trade and economic global-

---

55 The texts of the Nuremberg Judgments may be found in the *Trial of the Major
    War Criminals before the International Military Tribunal*, Nuremberg, 14 Novem-
    ber 1945–1 October 1946, Official Documents (1947). The Nuremberg princi-
    ples were affirmed in *Affirmation of the Principles of International Law Recognized
    by the Charter of the Nuremberg Tribunal*, UNGA Res. 95(1), UN GAOR, 1st Sess.,
    UN Doc. A/64/Add.1 (1946). See, generally, G. Ginsburgs & V.N. Kudriavtsev,
    eds., *The Nuremberg Trial and International Law* (Boston: M. Nijhoff, 1990).
56 See further Chapter 10.
57 See further Chapter 2.

ization; the establishment of various international criminal justice mechanisms, including the permanent International Criminal Court; the multiplication of other judicial or quasi-judicial fora applying international law in a variety of subject-areas; and the emergence of aggressive new doctrines of self-defence and other uses of force in the wake of the September 11, 2001 terrorist attacks on New York and Washington. It is difficult to assess the long-term impact or significance of these and other developments on the continuing evolution of the international legal system, but on the whole they seem at least to bear witness to the fact that the system is dynamic and more firmly entrenched in the reality of day-to-day international, as well as domestic, life than ever. Moreover, international law continues to evolve and grow at a relentless pace. This may suggest that the international legal system has either reached or is approaching a point of "critical mass"—from beginnings of dubious legitimacy and uncertain effectiveness, international law has progressed to the point where it affects, practically, daily, and in innumerable circumstances, all of our lives. This is particularly true in states, such as Canada, which have been active participants in its development. It will likely be truer still as international law continues to develop and as an already small world continues to shrink.

As such, it is no longer realistic to deny the existence or effectiveness of international law. Rather, it has become indispensable to understand it and to participate, whether as lawyers, judges, students, or simply citizens, in its further and more just development. The goal of this book, therefore, is to help readers acquire a basic understanding of the international legal system so that they may become more effective participants, in any of these capacities, in its future development.

FURTHER READING

ARBOUR, J-M. & PARENT, G., *Droit international public*, 5ᵉ éd. (Cowansville, QC: Yvon Blais, 2006) at 1–62 («Introduction générale»)

ALLOTT, P., "The Concept of International Law" in M. Byers, ed., *The Role of Law in International Politics: Essays in International Law and International Relations* (Oxford: Oxford University Press, 2000) 88

CASSESE, A., *International Law*, 2nd ed. (Oxford: Oxford University Press, 2005) c. 1–3

CURRIE, J.H., FORCESE, C., & OOSTERVELD, V., *International Law: Doctrine, Practice and Theory* (Toronto: Irwin Law, 2007) c. 1

EMANUELLI, C., *Droit international public: contribution à l'étude du droit international selon une perspective canadienne*, 2ᵉ éd. (Montréal: Wilson & Lafleur, 2004) at 1–42 («Introduction»)

FALK, R., *The Status of Law in International Society* (Princeton: Princeton University Press, 1970)

GREEN, L.C., *International Law: A Canadian Perspective* (Agincourt, ON: Carswell, 1984) c. 1

GREWE, W., *The Epochs of International Law*, trans. by M. Byers (Berlin: de Gruyter, 2000)

HENKIN, L., *How Nations Behave: Law and Foreign Policy*, 2d ed. (New York: Council on Foreign Relations, 1979)

JOHNSTON, D.M., *The Historical Foundations of World Order: The Tower and the Arena* (The Hague: Martinus Nijhoff Publishers, 2007)

KINDRED, H.M. *et al.*, eds., *International Law: Chiefly as Interpreted and Applied in Canada*, 7th ed. (Toronto: Emond Montgomery, 2006) c. 1

KOSKENNIEMI, M., *The Gentle Civilizer of Nations: The Rise and Fall of International Law 1870–1960* (Cambridge: Cambridge University Press, 2002)

MACDONALD, R. ST. J. & JOHNSTON, D.M., eds., *The Structure and Process of International Law* (Boston: Kluwer Law International, 1983)

NUSSBAUM, A., *A Concise History of the Law of Nations*, rev. ed. (New York: Macmillan, 1962)

SHAW, M.N., *International Law*, 5th ed. (Cambridge: Cambridge University Press, 2003) c. 1–2

SHENNAN, J.H., *The Origins of the Modern European State, 1450–1725* (London: Hutchinson, 1974)

STARKE, J.G. & SHEARER, I.A., *Starke's International Law*, 11th ed. (London: Butterworths, 1994) c. 1

STRAYER, J.R., *On the Medieval Origins of the Modern State* (Princeton: Princeton University Press, 1970)

WILLIAMS, S.A. & DE MESTRAL, A.L.C., *An Introduction to International Law: Chiefly as Interpreted and Applied in Canada*, 2d ed. (Toronto: Butterworths, 1987) c. 1

DE VISSCHER, C., *Theory and Reality in Public International Law*, trans. by P.E. Corbett, rev. ed. (Princeton: Princeton University Press, 1968), Book 1

CHAPTER 2

INTERNATIONAL LEGAL PERSONALITY: THE SUBJECTS OF INTERNATIONAL LAW

A. RELEVANCE AND DEFINITION OF "SUBJECTS"

Perhaps no topic more readily illustrates the sharp distinction between international and domestic legal systems than that of "subjects." A sustained discussion of who or what constitutes a subject of the law would likely seem quite curious to most domestic lawyers, as the application of the law to all individuals and other legal persons (such as corporations) is a virtual given in most domestic legal systems founded upon the rule of law. Moreover, the law in most domestic legal systems applies primarily to individuals and only secondarily, in accordance with the rules establishing and regulating them, to artificial or corporate legal persons.

Precisely the opposite is true in the international legal system. From its inception (and indeed by definition) international law has applied not to real persons at all but almost exclusively to a surprisingly small number of artificial, politico-legal entities known as states. It is for this reason that international law has often been referred to as the "law of nations"[1]—law that governs the rights and obligations of nations or states.

---

1   See, for example, Hugo Grotius, *Three Books Treating of the Rights of Peace*, 1625 (London: M.W. for Thomas Basset, 1682), ed. by J.B. Sco

While, as we shall see below, there has been some evolution in the range of subjects to which international law now applies, states remain its primary subjects. Even with the dramatic changes in the composition of the international community since the end of the Second World War, this means that the international legal system still largely applies only to a select club of less than 200 subjects or so.

However, caution is in order here. There are no firm rules of international law that necessarily limit the classes of its potential subjects. While it is true that states were at one time the sole, and remain today the principal, subjects of international law, states as we shall see are also in a very real sense the authors of international law.[2] Thus, to the extent that states permit international law to evolve so as to encompass potential new classes of subjects (as indeed they have over the past sixty years or so), it becomes necessary to evaluate the international legal personality of such new classes. It may accordingly be helpful to think of states as "primary" subjects of international law—that is, subjects by definition or as of right—and to think of other international legal subjects as "secondary" subjects—that is, subjects of international law only to the extent and for the purposes permitted by its primary subjects, states.[3]

Once it is conceded that entities other than states may emerge as secondary subjects of international law, it becomes important to define what is meant by an international legal subject. What are the attributes of an international legal subject? What privileges and obligations are associated with such status? The International Court of Justice, in its landmark Advisory Opinion in the *Reparations Case*,[4] addressed these questions in defining the criteria for international legal personality. A subject of international law, wrote the Court, is "capable of possessing international rights and duties, and … has capacity to maintain its rights by bringing international claims."[5] While this definition may be somewhat circular, it is generally considered to reflect the essence of what it means, in effect, to enjoy international legal personality.

F. Kelsey, Classics of International Law Series (Oxford: Oxford University Press, 1925); J.L. Brierly, *The Law of Nations*, 6th ed. by H. Waldock (Oxford: Clarendon Press, 1963).

2   See Chapters 3–5.

3   A. Cassese, *International Law*, 2d ed. (Oxford: Oxford University Press, 2005) at 71. On this distinction, see further Section D, below in this chapter, in particular the *dicta* of the International Court of Justice in the *Reparations Case* concerning the "lesser" personality of international organizations when compared to that of states, below note 4.

4   *Reparation for Injuries Suffered in the Service of the United Nations*, Advisory Opinion, [1949] I.C.J. Rep. 174 [*Reparations Case*].

5   *Ibid.* at 179.

With this in mind we turn now to consider various candidates for international legal subject status and the extent of their international legal personality—starting of course with the most obvious candidate of all, states.

B. STATES AS PRIMARY INTERNATIONAL LEGAL SUBJECTS

1) Introduction

As observed above,[6] international law as a legal system evolved in response to the emergence of a new form of societal organization in Europe —the modern nation-state. Along with these new entities came a need for a legal system to regulate their mutual rights, obligations, and interactions. Thus, from the outset, states have been the very *raison d'être* of the international legal system and thus its principal (and until recently, its sole) subjects.

In this section we will examine the generally accepted criteria for statehood—that is, how one knows if a particular entity is a state and thus entitled to the full range of rights and subject to all the duties of statehood established by international law. We will then consider some of the basic rights and obligations of states in international law, as well as various legal issues surrounding the birth, life cycle, and demise of states.

2) Criteria for Statehood

Although the criteria for statehood have been established in customary international law through long usage,[7] a convenient and frequently cited restatement of those criteria is found in the so-called *Montevideo Convention*.[8] Article 1 of the Convention provides as follows:

> The state as a person of international law should possess the following qualifications: (a) a permanent population; (b) a defined terri-

---

6   See Chapter 1.
7   See Chapter 5.
8   *Convention on the Rights and Duties of States*, 26 December 1933 (entered into force 26 December 1934), (1934) 28 AJ.I.L. Supp. 75. Although a regional treaty arrangement between the United States of America and a number of Latin American states, it is generally considered to reflect a universally applicable—if not wholly satisfactory—definition of statehood.

tory; (c) government; and (d) capacity to enter into relations with the other states.

This definition, as useful as it may be, must be treated with caution. This is because, as in much of international law, there is no centralized agency with the authority to establish these criteria or to apply them to candidates for statehood.[9] In other words, the foregoing definition is an inferential one—it is derived from an examination of the principal attributes common to those entities that have tended to be treated as states in international law. As such, there will be exceptional instances where one or more of the foregoing requirements of statehood may be absent or in abeyance, at least for a period of time, and yet where an entity is nevertheless treated as a state. Similarly and as we shall see further below, there may be situations where all of the foregoing criteria are met but where the entity in question is nevertheless not generally recognized as a state, at least for a period.

a) Permanent Population

The minimalist requirement of a permanent population clearly speaks to the basic need for some form of stable human community capable of supporting the superstructure of the state.[10] In particular, the requirement of permanence suggests the viability of the community over time, although it does not imply that any particular longevity or extended pedigree is required before a population can be considered sufficiently permanent to form the basis for a state. Nor does international law postulate any requirements in terms of minimum population; indeed, there are several examples of states with very small populations.[11]

Similarly, there is no requirement of homogeneity, ethnic or otherwise, for a qualifying population, and in fact the population need not even comprise nationals of the state in question, as long as that population maintains a relatively permanent residence on defined territory.[12]

---

9 However, as membership in the United Nations is limited to states and admission as a member requires approval of the General Assembly and the Security Council, such admission to membership is generally taken as conclusive evidence of statehood: Articles 3–4, *Charter of the United Nations*, 26 June 1945, Can. T.S. 1945 No. 7 (entered into force 24 October 1945) [*UN Charter*].

10 I. Brownlie, *Principles of Public International Law*, 6th ed. (Oxford: Oxford University Press, 2003) at 70.

11 Some of the least populous states of the world include Vatican City (under 1,000), Tuvalu (under 11,000), and Nauru (under 12,000).

12 See J. Crawford, *The Creation of States in International Law*, 2d ed. (Oxford: Oxford University Press, 2006) at 52–53. Vatican City may be seen as an exception to the requirement of a permanent population in residence: *ibid.* at 222–23.

b) Defined Territory

The existence of defined state territory is one of the most essential attributes of statehood. International law always exacts actual and effective possession or control of a defined piece of land territory as the critical precondition of statehood. Indeed the concept of sovereignty, as it evolved in European and European-derived societies and influenced the mainstream of international law, is tightly linked to the notion of exclusive control of territory within fixed boundaries.[13]

Beyond the requirement of actual and effective control, however, international law places no detailed strictures on the nature of the territory that will suffice as the foundation for a state.[14] As with population, international law requires no particular minimum area or type of terrain.[15] The territory in question need not be "continuous," in the sense that it may be composed of several separate and even far-flung pieces.[16] It need not possess a coastline.[17]

The requirement of a "defined" territory should not be misunderstood, either, as a need for any clear demarcation of borders or an absence of disputes as to the precise extent of the territory under the state's sovereignty.[18] Such a requirement would be far too onerous and would not reflect the fact that a large number of states, which are clearly acknowledged to exist as such, nevertheless have significant ongoing border disputes with their neighbours. The essential condition is that *some* territory be unquestionably under the control of the putative state, even if its precise extent is uncertain or varies over time.[19]

The nature of the relationship between states and territory is explored more fully in a later chapter.[20]

---

13   See *Island of Palmas Case* (1928), 2 R.I.A.A. 829 at 839; Crawford, *ibid.* at 56.

14   Crawford, *ibid.* at 46–47.

15   For example, the territories of Vatican City, Monaco, and Nauru cover less than one, two, and twenty-one square kilometres respectively.

16   For example, the territory of the United States of America includes Alaska and Hawaii.

17   Some of the world's inland states include Hungary, Zambia, and Paraguay.

18   See, for example, *Deutsche Continental Gas-Gesellschaft v. Polish State* (1929), 5 I.L.R. 11 at 14–15 (German-Polish Mixed Arb. Trib.); *North Sea Continental Shelf Cases*, [1969] I.C.J. Rep. 3 at 32; *Case Concerning the Territorial Dispute (Libyan Arab Jamahiriya v. Chad)*, [1994] I.C.J. Rep. 6 at paras. 44 and 52 [*Libya/Chad*].

19   Crawford, above note 12 at 49–52. But see R. Higgins, *The Development of International Law Through the Political Organs of the United Nations* (London: Oxford University Press, 1963) at n. 20, suggesting that serious doubts as to boundaries can undermine claims of statehood.

20   See Chapter 7.

c) Government

While it is generally accepted that a state requires some administrative structure capable of governing its population, effectively controlling its territory, and representing it internationally, there are instances where this requirement appears not to be essential, at least for a period of time. In other words, the existence of an effective government can provide good evidence of the stable human community and sovereign control of territory referred to above, and thus of the existence of a state. However, its temporary absence appears not necessarily to be fatal to statehood.

On occasion, newly emergent states have been recognized as such by the international community before the establishment of fully organized or effective central governments. This was the case, for example, with the emergence of the sovereign states of Poland in 1919 or of Burundi and Rwanda in 1961.[21] On the other hand, extensive civil strife or an ongoing lack of effective central control over territory can undermine a new state's claim to full status as such in the international community.[22] Which of these two positions prevails may depend on whether the putative new state seeks such status in circumstances where its international legal right to do so is clearly and broadly recog-

---

21   See Brownlie, above note 10 at 71. Another example that could be cited is the admission of the Republic of the Congo to membership in the United Nations in 1960 in spite of an arguable lack of effective local government: see SC Res. 142 (1960), UN SCOR, 15th Year, UN Doc. S/RES/142 (1960); *Admission of the Republic of the Congo (Leopoldville) to Membership in the United Nations*, GA Res. 1480(XV), UN GAOR, 15th Sess., Supp. No. 16, UN Doc. A/RES/1480(XV) (1960); and see, generally, Crawford, above note 12 at 56–58. Such flexibility is reminiscent of international law's traditional recognition of the limited international legal personality of insurgency movements which manage to establish a degree of control over territory within a state: see M.N. Shaw, *International Law*, 5th ed. (Cambridge: Cambridge University Press, 2003) at 219–20; Brownlie, *ibid.* at 63; H. Lauterpacht, *Recognition in International Law* (Cambridge: Cambridge University Press, 1947) at 494–95; Sir A. McNair, *The Law of Treaties* (Oxford: Clarendon Press, 1961) at 676.

22   For example, Finland declared independence in 1917, formed a new Diet and promptly descended into civil war. The country was disorganized and rife with civil conflict to such an extent that the police and the armed forces were divided. The Diet, forced from the capital, was unable to govern and could not maintain control without the assistance of Soviet troops. In 1920, the Council of the League of Nations appointed a Commission of Jurists to render an opinion on a dispute between Finland and Sweden over the Aaland Islands, and one of the preliminary questions was the date on which Finland became a state. Based on the foregoing facts, the Jurists concluded that Finland was not an independent state until a stable political organization emerged after 1918: *Aaland Islands Case* (1920), L.N.O.J. Special Supp. (No. 3) at 3.

nized, or is rather adverse to the international legal rights of another established state.[23]

Generally, the attitude of the international community in the face of a temporary breakdown in domestic governmental control within an already well-established state is more flexible. This relatively permissive approach to the requirement of government can be illustrated by considering, for example, the situation of Somalia since 1992. At that time virtually all semblance of central governmental authority in Somalia disintegrated, leaving the country in a state of near anarchy.[24] Rather than deem the state of Somalia no longer to exist, however, the international community through the instrumentality of the United Nations (UN) Security Council mounted a humanitarian aid effort.[25] Following withdrawal of the UN mission in 1995, other intergovernmental efforts have been made to restore a central government capable of sustaining Somalia's statehood in the longer term. While these efforts have met with limited success and effective, central government control over most of Somalia remains either non-existent or contested, it is not generally doubted that Somalia's statehood nevertheless persists.[26]

Similarly, the temporary "dislocation" of a government from its territory and population has, on occasion, been tolerated by the international community. The experience of governments in exile during the Second World War[27] demonstrates that under certain exigent circumstances, the ordinary rules requiring the convergence of population, territory, and government will be relaxed. However, this tolerance is likely limited to situations where it can realistically be anticipated that the dislocation will be temporary and that all three elements will eventually be reunited.[28]

---

23 Crawford, above note 12 at 58–59.
24 Letter from the Secretary General to the President of the Security Council, UN Doc. S/24868 (29 November 1992) at 2.
25 SC Res. 794 (1992), UN SCOR, 47th Year, UN Doc. S/RES/794 (1992). On the events leading to this resolution, see, generally, B.F. Burmester, "On Humanitarian Intervention: The New World Order and Wars to Preserve Human Rights" (1994) Utah L. Rev. 269 at 313–17.
26 For a more complete picture of the governmental situation in Somalia at the time of writing, see the Report of the [UN] Secretary General on the Situation in Somalia, U.N. Doc. S/2007/381 (25 June 2007), online: www.securitycouncilreport.org/atf/cf/%7B65BFCF9B-6D27-4E9C-8CD3-CF6E4FF96FF9%7D/SOMALIA%20S2007381.pdf; see also subsequent reports.
27 For example, the governments of Poland and France.
28 For example, the international community withheld recognition of the Beijing authorities long after they had established effective control over mainland China, viewing the Chiang Kai-Shek government in Taiwan as representative of the state of China. However, when it became clear that there was no possibility

As with population and territory, moreover, the content of the requirement of government is relatively modest. In particular, international law has not traditionally prescribed or required any particular form of government, democratic or otherwise. A premium has traditionally been placed by international law on the so-called principle of effectiveness[29]—that any government able in effect to govern the population, control the territory, and carry on the state's international relations, regardless of the means employed for such purposes and as long as international law is otherwise respected, will suffice. As such, international law has not generally inquired into the political or moral legitimacy of governments, at least when it comes to satisfying the basic criteria of statehood.[30]

As we shall see further below in considering the topic of recognition, however, there are recent signs that segments of the international community may now require that a candidate for statehood demonstrate some elements of governmental "legitimacy" before being endorsed as a new state. For example, a commitment to respect for basic human rights and even democratic principles has on occasion been demanded.[31] However, until greater state practice consolidates or confirms such developments, the demands of international law in terms of standards of government, at least for purposes of confirming statehood, will likely remain quite moderate.[32]

d) Capacity to Enter into Relations with Other States, or Independence

This, like territory, is a decisive criterion.[33] Its essential feature is that the candidate for statehood be in a position to exercise its will free-

---

of the return of that government to Beijing, recognition of the new mainland government followed: A.P. Rubin, "Recognition Versus Reality in International Law and Policy" (1998) 32 New Eng. L. Rev. 669 at 671. For a detailed discussion of the legal status of Taiwan, see Crawford, above note 12 at 198–221.

29 See Crawford, *ibid.*, c. 2 generally and at 46 particularly.

30 *Ibid.* at 131.

31 See further Section B(3), below in this chapter.

32 Crawford characterizes state practice on this topic as "scanty" (see above note 12 at n. 107) and concludes that neither respect for fundamental human rights nor adherence to democratic principles is at present a criterion for statehood (*ibid.* at 148–55). By contrast, he concludes that "an entity may not claim statehood if its creation is in violation of an applicable right to self-determination": *ibid.* at 131. See also, generally, B.R. Roth, *Governmental Illegitimacy in International Law* (Oxford: Clarendon Press, 1999).

33 See Brownlie, above note 10 at 71. Crawford considers "capacity to enter into relations with other states" a conflation of the requirements of government and

ly, within the bounds of international law, in order to interact with other states as an equal. This in turn requires that the putative state be able to exercise its political, economic, and legal will free from control by other states. In other words, to be a true state on the Westphalian model an entity must represent the sole sovereign authority over a particular population and territory, subject only to the strictures imposed by international law itself.[34]

To satisfy this criterion it will clearly be important for the candidate to display the attributes of sovereign statehood and the institutional capacity to participate fully in international life. However, formalities will be insufficient if in fact foreign control is being exercised behind the scenes. In such cases, notwithstanding the outward appearance of independence, the international community is unlikely to treat the putative state as an equal entitled to the various attributes of statehood. By way of example, notwithstanding the South African apartheid regime's attempt to clothe the so-called Transkei Homeland with the outward appearances of independence in 1976, in fact most of its policies, economic and otherwise, were controlled by South Africa. This resulted in condemnation of its so-called independence by the international community as illegal and repudiation of its alleged status as a sovereign state.[35]

If independence is to be evaluated substantively and not based on outward appearances, it remains necessary to distinguish true foreign control from mere international pressure brought to bear on a state in order to influence its exercise of will.[36] At least in considering the criteria for statehood, international law merely requires that an entity have a will of its own to be exercised—not that it do so in a vacuum, uninfluenced by various pressures that may be brought to bear by other

---

independence, the latter of which is "the central criterion for statehood": Crawford, *ibid.* at 62.

34 See, for example, *Customs Régime Between Germany and Austria, Advisory Opinion* (1931), P.C.I.J. (Ser. A/B) No. 41 [*Austro-German Customs Case*] at 45–46; *Island of Palmas Case*, above note 13 at 838.

35 On 26 October 1976, the UN General Assembly strongly condemned the creation of such homelands. The Assembly declared the independence of the Transkei invalid and called upon all governments to refrain from recognizing or dealing with that government: *Policies of Apartheid of the Government of South Africa*, GA Res. 31/6, UN GAOR, 31st Sess., Supp. No. 39, UN Doc. A/RES/31/6 (1976) at 10. On state practice concerning the personality of the various "homelands" (or "bantustans") created pursuant to apartheid policies, see Crawford, above note 12 at 338–48.

36 Crawford, *ibid.* at 76.

states intent on preserving or advancing their own interests.[37] Thus, a state which bows to even intense outside pressure does not thereby lose the independence which is a necessary attribute of its statehood. Rather, its choice to comply, if choice there ultimately was, is in fact a demonstration of its independent, sovereign will. Ultimately, the question comes down to whether the state in fact had the capacity to choose as it did, even if based on an assessment of its best interests in light of its relations with certain other states.[38]

Similarly, it is necessary to distinguish a lack or loss of independence from a situation where the state has agreed either to limit its own freedom of action or to allow another state to exercise some of the normal attributes of statehood on its behalf. For instance, a state will on occasion enter into an agreement with another state whereby the latter agrees to conduct aspects of the foreign relations of the former on its behalf. For example, in the 1920s Switzerland acted on behalf of Liechtenstein in respect of that country's diplomatic relations.[39]

Similarly, states will sometimes extend, by way of treaty, their "protection" to another state. This was the arrangement between France and Morocco pursuant to the 1912 *Treaty of Fez*.[40] Under the treaty, France undertook to represent Morocco internationally in various matters. Notwithstanding the fact that the powers thus assumed by France comprised a critical element of Morocco's status as an independent state—its capacity to conduct foreign relations—the International Court of Justice concluded in 1952 that the *Treaty of Fez* had left Morocco's sovereign status as a state intact.[41]

---

37 A separate issue is whether foreign pressure, even if insufficient to compromise a state's essential independence, may nevertheless amount to an unlawful interference in that state's internal affairs. See further Section B(4), below in this chapter.

38 Brownlie articulates a high threshold for loss of independence through foreign control, requiring "foreign control overbearing the decision-making of the entity concerned on a wide range of matters of high policy and doing so systematically and on a permanent basis": Brownlie, above note 10 at 72.

39 In 1921, Liechtenstein and Switzerland concluded an agreement for the administration of Liechtenstein's postal and telegraph services by the Swiss authorities. After 1924, the countries formed a customs union and Switzerland generally represented Liechtenstein in diplomatic relations; see, for example, the *Extradition Treaty* with the United States signed by Switzerland on behalf of Liechtenstein, 183 L.N.T.S. No. 4235. See W.S.G. Kohn, "The Sovereignty of Liechtenstein" (1967) 61 A.J.I.L. 547.

40 *Protectorate Treaty between France and Morocco (Treaty of Fez)*, 30 March 1912, (1912) 6 A.J.I.L. Supp. 207.

41 *Case Concerning Rights of Nationals of the United States of America in Morocco (France v. United States of America)*, [1952] I.C.J. Rep. 176 at 185 and 188. It

The key to reconciling these seeming paradoxes is to look for evidence of consent, agreement, or genuine agency in the establishment of the relationship. If in fact the "represented" state has agreed to and continues to support the arrangement, that in itself is an exercise of its independence and a display of its statehood. In other words, a consensual arrangement, even one where one state assumes elements of the day-to-day displays of statehood of another, is fully compatible with the independence required to maintain statehood.[42]

The distinction between situations of subordination or dependence on the one hand, and consensual arrangements binding a state to legal obligations on the other, was clarified by Judge Anzilotti of the Permanent Court of International Justice in the *Austro-German Customs Union Case*.[43] The case involved a request to the Court from the Council of the League of Nations for an advisory opinion on whether a proposed customs union was compatible with the *Treaty of Saint Germain-en-Laye*,[44] concluded in 1919 in the wake of the First World War. Pursuant to Article 88 of the *Treaty*, Austria agreed "to abstain from any act which might directly or indirectly … compromise her independence", unless a contrary arrangement had the consent of the Council of the League of Nations. In 1931, Germany and Austria entered into a treaty purporting to establish a customs union between them. The treaty would have had the effect of constraining Austria's ability to impose customs duties on imports from Germany (and vice versa). Thus, the question arose as to whether the customs treaty constituted an alienation by Austria of its independence, in contravention of the *Treaty of Saint Germain-en-Laye*.

A majority of the Court found that it did not,[45] for reasons perhaps best expressed by Judge Anzilotti in his separate, concurring opinion:

---

should be noted that this conclusion has been hotly debated given evidence that the relationship between France and Morocco went far beyond that of sovereign equals engaged in a treaty relationship and indeed approximated one of colonial domination. One observer at the time predicted that the French would gradually acquire a "veiled suzerainty" over Morocco: N.D. Harris, "The New Moroccan Protectorate" (1913) 7 A.J.I.L. 245 at 267. See, generally, "The Debate on French Imperialism, 1960–1975" in H.L. Wesseling, *Imperialism and Colonialism: Essays on the History of European Expansion*, Contributions in Comparative Colonial Studies Series No. 32 (Westport: Greenwood Press, 1997). On the legal status of protectorates more generally, see Crawford, above note 12 at 286–320.

42 See, generally, Crawford, *ibid.* at 69–70.

43 *Austro-German Customs Case*, above note 34.

44 *Treaty of Peace Between the Allied and Associated Powers and Austria*, 10 September 1919 (Saint Germain-en-Laye), [1919] B.T.S. No. 11.

45 A majority of the Court (8 to 7) held, however, that the proposed union would be incompatible with the terms of the 1922 *Geneva Protocol No. 1* to the *Treaty of Saint Germain* (relating to the post-war reconstruction of Austria). Of this

... [T]he legal conception of independence has nothing to do with a State's subordination to international law or with the numerous and constantly increasing states of *de facto* dependence which characterize the relation of one country to other countries.

It also follows that the restrictions upon a State's liberty, whether arising out of ordinary international law or contractual engagements, do not as such in the least affect its independence. As long as these restrictions do not place the State under the legal authority of another State, the former remains an independent State however extensive and burdensome those obligations may be.[46]

Thus, the important point is made that the requirement of independence refers to independence from the will or authority *of other states*, and not independence from the strictures of international law itself, whether contained in a treaty (such as the one establishing the customs union) or otherwise.

Finally, as with the criterion of government, it is important to have regard to surrounding factual and legal circumstances in assessing whether a true, albeit temporary, loss of independence does indeed compromise statehood. In particular, a *de facto* loss of independence brought about by an internationally unlawful foreign intervention is not generally treated as bringing about the legal extinction of the victim state.[47] Rather, the state losing its factual independence in such circumstances is entitled, as a matter of international law, to its return.[48] Independence can thus be seen, in this sense, as both a criterion and an entitlement of statehood which, once established, international law strives to protect. However, unlawful usurpation of independence for a sufficiently lengthy period of time may eventually, on grounds of effectiveness, undermine an entity's claim to continuing statehood.[49] Just how this may come about requires an understanding of the role played by other states in applying the traditional criteria of statehood, which is the topic of the next section.

---

majority of eight judges, only a minority of six would have found incompatibility with the *Treaty* itself. Judge Anzilotti would have found the union incompatible with both instruments.

46   *Austro-German Customs Case*, above note 34 at 58.

47   Crawford, above note 12 at 132.

48   *Ibid.* at 73–74, citing the Israeli and Syrian invasions of Lebanon, the Vietnamese invasion of Cambodia, the Soviet invasions of Czechoslovakia and Afghanistan, and the United States' invasions of Grenada, Panama, Afghanistan, and Iraq (2003).

49   *Ibid.* at 74.

3) Recognition

a) Recognition of States

It was suggested above that fulfilling all of the foregoing criteria for statehood may not, in some circumstances, be sufficient in itself to bring a state effectively into existence. In fact, this is implied in the fourth criterion of statehood, the capacity to enter into relations with other states. Even if an entity satisfies all other criteria and is able and willing to engage in international relations, what happens if other states are not willing to enter into international relations with it? Indeed, what is the entity's status if other states are not even willing to recognize its existence as a state?

These questions are important because, as seen above, there is no central international legal authority with a general duty or power to pronounce upon the status of candidates for statehood. Historically, this function has fallen to individual states, which decide for themselves, in the exercise of their sovereignty, whether or not they recognize another entity as a state and thus as an equal on the international legal plane.[50] As membership in the United Nations is limited to states, admission to such membership might inferentially be considered a modern-day substitute for this decentralized process.[51] However, admission to UN membership is a highly politicized matter, and while successful admission is generally taken as conclusive evidence of statehood, the converse is not necessarily true. Thus, it still remains the case that granting or withholding recognition of statehood *per se* is es-

---

50   See Lauterpacht, above note 21 at 55.

51   United Nations members vote, in the General Assembly, on the admission of new members to the Organization: see above note 9. In 1992, the UNGA took the highly unusual step of declaring that the Socialist Federal Republic of Yugoslavia, then a member of the Organization, no longer existed and that the rump Yugoslavia (calling itself the Federal Republic of Yugoslavia, or Serbia and Montenegro) was a new state that would have to apply for admission to the Organization: *Recommendation of the Security Council of 19 September 1992*, GA Res. 47/1, UN GAOR, 47th Sess., Supp. No. 49, UN Doc. A/RES/47/1 (1992) at 12. In fact, it was admitted to membership on 11 November 2000: SC Res. 1326, UN SCOR, 55th Sess., UN Doc. S/RES/1326 (2000); *Admission of the Federal Republic of Yugoslavia to Membership in the United Nations*, GA Res. 55/12, UN GAOR, 55th Sess., Supp. No. 49, UN Doc. A/RES/55/12 (2000). More recently, Montenegro seceded from the Federal Republic of Yugoslavia and was admitted to UN membership in its own right, leaving Serbia to continue the UN membership of the Federal Republic: see *Resolution on the Admission of New Members*, UNSC Res. 1691, UN SCOR, UN Doc. S/RES/1691 (2006); *Admission of the Republic of Montenegro to Membership in the United Nations*, UNGA Res. 60/264, UN GAOR, 60th Sess., UN Doc. A/RES/60/264 (2006).

sentially a bilateral process, coming within the sovereign discretion of each individual state.[52]

Of course the practical implications of this are considerable. In order to truly enjoy the benefits of statehood, it will usually be necessary for a candidate for statehood (or states friendly to its cause) to engage in a considerable lobbying effort to convince foreign governments to recognize its existence as a state. The more such recognition an entity receives, the greater are its chances of ultimately enjoying the day-to-day entitlements of statehood, by the sheer force of public international opinion. Conversely, a failure to attract considerable international support for one's statehood can be fatal to one's claim, as illustrated by the cases of Southern Rhodesia in 1965 and of Taiwan to this day.[53]

Apart from these practical considerations, the question that remains is whether the act of recognition has any legal significance or whether it is merely a political fact which only has implications for an entity's *de facto* ability to be treated as a state, as distinct from its *de jure* existence as one. The question is not purely theoretical, but has import-

---

52   In Canada, recognition is generally considered a political matter governed by Canada's national interests and is thus exercised by the federal government as an aspect of the royal prerogative power over the conduct of foreign affairs: see J.A. Beesley & C.B. Bourne, eds., "Canadian Practice in International Law During 1971 as Reflected Mainly in Public Correspondence and Statements of the Department of External Affairs" (1972) 10 Can.Y.B. Int'l L. 287 at 308–9. Note that while the majority of opinion considers the act of recognition to be discretionary, some writers view it as an obligation wherever the four criteria of statehood exist: see S.A. Williams & A.L.C. de Mestral, *An Introduction to International Law: Chiefly as Interpreted and Applied in Canada*, 2d ed. (Toronto: Butterworths, 1987) at 80–81.

53   Southern Rhodesia's unilateral declaration of independence from the United Kingdom in 1965 was ignored by the international community until Zimbabwe was established in 1980 with the cooperation of the United Kingdom. Taiwan also presents a striking example of an entity possessing a stable population, a defined territory, an effective government, and *de facto* independence, but which is not generally treated by the international community as a state. While its government (styling itself the government of the Republic of China) has diplomatic relations with approximately two dozen small and/or developing states, the vast majority of states do not recognize its statehood. In part this may be attributable to the Taiwanese government's own failure clearly to assert separate statehood from the People's Republic of China, preferring to promote a "one China" policy with itself as legitimate government of the whole of China. The Taiwanese government nevertheless engages in more or less formal relations with many states and some international organizations, through such agencies as the Taipei Economic and Cultural Office. See L. Chen, "Taiwan's Current International Legal Status" (1998) 32 New Eng. L. Rev. 675. For a detailed review of the history and legal status of Taiwan, see Crawford, above note 12 at 198–222.

ant implications for the entity's rights and obligations at international law pending its recognition by other states.

On this matter there are two main schools of thought, known respectively as the constitutive and the declaratory theories of recognition.

The constitutive theory holds that recognition by other states is an essential prerequisite—a fifth criterion, as it were—of statehood.[54] In this model, the act of recognition by other states creates, or is "constitutive" of, a new state. One consequence of this is that the entity in question would presumably have neither the rights nor the obligations of a state, notwithstanding satisfaction of the four objective criteria identified above, until it is constituted as such by sufficient acts of recognition.

There are many difficulties with this theory, not least of which is determining the number of acts of recognition that would be required before a state came into existence.[55] Further, would the candidate's legal status, and thus its rights and obligations at international law, be effective only for recognizing states? Would its statehood commence at differing times vis-à-vis different states, depending on the timing of their acts of recognition?[56] More theoretically, but just as importantly, is subjecting a state's very existence to the discretionary, political decisions of other states consistent with the principle of the sovereign equality of states?[57] There is also a concern that placing such a constitutive power in the hands of states, to be exercised in a discretionary manner according to their own national interests, would be a return to the late nineteenth century when European states, along with the United States of America, largely controlled membership (and quality of membership) in the family of nations.[58]

Proponents of the constitutive theory have attempted to address some of these concerns by positing a correlative obligation on states to extend recognition to entities fulfilling the four criteria reviewed above,[59] although state practice discloses little evidence of the existence of such an obligation and it is difficult to see how it might be enforced.[60]

54　See, for example, Lauterpacht, above note 21 at 55; L. Oppenheim, *International Law: A Treatise*, 8th ed. by H. Lauterpacht, vol. 1 (London: Longmans, Green, 1955) at 544, §209.

55　Brownlie, above note 10 at 88.

56　As suggested by H. Kelsen, "Recognition in International Law: Theoretical Observations" (1941) 35 A.J.I.L. 605 at 609.

57　Crawford, above note 12 at 21.

58　See A. Cassese, *International Law in a Divided World* (Oxford: Clarendon Press, 1986) at 38–43.

59　See, for example, Lauterpacht, above note 21 at 74 and 77–78.

60　See Williams & de Mestral, above note 52 at 81; Crawford, above note 12 at 22.

It is also question-begging, for how can states owe obligations of an international character to a state which does not yet exist?[61]

The declaratory theory, by contrast, attributes no significant legal consequence to the act of recognition.[62] According to this theory, an entity that satisfies the four criteria described above would by that fact alone be a state in international law. Thus, recognition would play no role in constituting a state, but would simply be a declaration of a pre-existing legal state of affairs and would at most play a diplomatic or political role.

However, the declaratory theory, while more generally endorsed in the literature and in the practice of states, also poses some difficulties. Its chief shortcoming is that it seems to give no prominence at all to what is, in fact, a vitally important step in the process of accession to full statehood. How can a capacity and even a willingness to enter into legal relations have any meaning if other states are not willing to take up the offer? It also ignores the fact that, absent a duly authorized body with authority to determine statehood, the attitudes of individual states remain the ultimate — indeed the only — definitive test of a new state's viability as a player on the international playing field.

In the end, however, the practice of states appears to endorse the essence of the declaratory theory.[63] Brownlie observes that even those states that refuse to recognize the statehood of certain entities nevertheless make various claims against them that can only be sustained if those entities are states.[64] In other words, even states that withhold express recognition nevertheless treat the entities in question as though they were already fully constituted states subject to obligations at international law.[65]

There have nevertheless been some recent indications that could be interpreted as a contrary trend. In particular, the dissolution of the former Yugoslavia and the disbanding of the USSR in the early 1990s demonstrated that certain influential states were willing to withhold recognition pending satisfaction of certain conditions by the new can-

---

61 Lauterpacht was aware of this difficulty, but attempted to circumvent it by positing an obligation of recognition owed to the international community of states collectively: above note 21 at 74–75 and 191–92.

62 See, for example, T-C. Chen, *The International Law of Recognition*, ed. by L.C. Green (London: Stevens, 1951); Brierly, above note 1.

63 Crawford, above note 12 at 23–26.

64 Brownlie, above note 10 at 87, citing the example of claims by some Arab states against Israel, or by the United States of America against North Vietnam in 1964–65.

65 See also Crawford, above note 12 at 26.

didates for statehood. These conditions, imposed by the European Community and the United States of America, largely related to the candidates' ability and willingness to abide by basic human rights norms and democratic principles—or, more generally, the dictates of international law—thus going well beyond the traditional four criteria for statehood.[66] In the end, however, recognition was extended notwithstanding dubious evidence of compliance with these additional requirements, casting doubt upon their potential role in other contexts. Moreover, even prior to recognition, entities emerging from the former Yugoslavia tended to be treated as states.[67] These developments nevertheless demonstrate that some states may be willing to use the act of recognition as a means of influencing the nature of the state thus recognized, suggesting perhaps a quasi-constitutive role.

Taking account of both the practical realities of international life and the actual behaviour of states, some authors suggest there are elements of truth to both the declaratory and constitutive theories.[68] Recognition is essentially declaratory in the sense that it is treated as such by most states and either follows the candidate's fulfilment of the four objective criteria of statehood as a matter of course or, if not, is considered irrelevant to the candidate's rights and duties as a state under international law. However, it is quasi-constitutive in the sense that even an entity fulfilling all four objective criteria of statehood will find it very difficult to give effect to its statehood until some states at least are willing to recognize and treat it as such. It may also serve, as a practical matter, to clarify the status of entities whose satisfaction of the objective criteria of statehood is uncertain or ambiguous.[69]

b) Recognition of Governments

A distinct legal matter is the largely historic practice, now in decline, of recognition of governments. The practice required states to monitor other states for unconstitutional changes in government. A recognizing state would then issue a statement either granting or withholding recognition of the new government, based largely on its own national interests.

---

66 See K. Knop, "The 'Righting' of Recognition: Recognition of States in Eastern Europe and the Soviet Union" in Y. LeBouthillier, D.M. McRae, & D. Pharand, eds., *Selected Papers in International Law: Contribution of the Canadian Council on International Law* (The Hague: Kluwer, 1999) 261; C. Hillgruber, "The Admission of New States to the International Community" (1998) 9 E.J.I.L. 491.

67 Crawford, above note 12 at 25.

68 Williams & de Mestral, above note 52 at 81; C. de Visscher, *Problèmes d'interprétation judiciaire en droit international public* (Paris: A. Pédone, 1963) at 191.

69 Crawford, above note 12 at 27.

As we will see below, changes in government, even if unconstitutional, do not in general affect the international legal personality of the state.[70] Thus there is little if any international legal significance attached to the act of recognition of a new government, as opposed to a new state. What little political purpose may be served by the practice is probably accomplished in any event through a state's decision either to establish, maintain, or break off diplomatic contact with another.[71] Moreover, granting or withholding recognition of governments, regardless of how they have come to power, is arguably inconsistent with a state's duty not to interfere in the domestic affairs of other states.[72]

For these reasons, the practice of recognition of governments has been on the wane. Canada abandoned the practice in 1988,[73] following the lead of most of its closest allies, including the United States of America, the United Kingdom, and France.[74] In its place, these and many other states have adopted the so-called Estrada doctrine, so named for the foreign minister in 1930 of Mexico, the first state to entirely abandon the practice of recognition of governments.[75] Mexico declared that it would no longer take any position on the validity of new governments in other states, as this was perceived to be unjustified interference in their domestic affairs. Rather, the doctrine calls for states to limit their acts of recognition to states and not their governments.

4) Principal Rights and Duties of States

Although we have examined the manner in which statehood is evidenced and acknowledged, the essence of statehood is difficult to grasp without also referring to its most important incidents. These have already been foreshadowed[76] and will be enlarged upon in following chapters, but for now certain core rights and duties of states should be noted.

---

70   See Section B(5)(a), below in this chapter.
71   See Crawford, above note 12 at 152. On diplomatic relations more generally, see Chapter 9, Section C.
72   See Chapter 1, and Section B(4), below in this chapter.
73   E.G. Lee, ed., "Canadian Practice in International Law at the Department of External Affairs in 1988–89" (1989) 27 Can. Y.B. Int'l L. 373 at 387–88.
74   See, generally, L.T. Galloway, *Recognizing Foreign Governments: The Practice of the United States* (Washington: American Enterprise Institute, 1978); C. Warbrick, "The New British Policy on Recognition of Governments" (1981) 30 I.C.L.Q. 568.
75   "Estrada Doctrine of Recognition," *Boletín Oficial de la Secretaría de Relaciones Exteriores*, Estados Unidos Mexicanos, Sept. 1930, vol. LV, No. 9 at 9.
76   See Chapter 1.

Undoubtedly the most important "right" of a state is eignty.[77] Sovereignty in this context essentially means excl or jurisdiction over territory and population, fettered only by quirements of international law.[78] It does not mean that a state is above international law, but merely beyond the power or jurisdiction of other subjects of international law.[79]

Closely related to the sovereignty of states is their formal equality.[80] This concept is enshrined in the UN Charter[81] and in fact flows as a necessary result of the existence of multiple sovereign entities. If states were not formally equal it would merely be a matter of time before the sovereignty of the "less equal" would be usurped by the "more equal." Of course, formal, legal equality does not necessarily entail equality in terms of military power, economic might, or political stature. All it ensures is that from the standpoint of international law, every state possesses the same basic legal rights and obligations.[82] One obvious purpose of asserting such a system is to foster the development of a rules-based system rather than a power-based system of interaction between states. If all states have the same basic legal rights and duties regardless of their economic or military power, even the smallest state can, at least in theory, assert its rights on the international legal plane.

Closely linked to the sovereign equality of states, as we have seen in considering the criterion of independence above, is the right of states to be free from intervention in their domestic affairs, most especially by other states.[83] Of course, the necessary corollary of such a right is a corresponding duty to refrain from intervening in the domestic affairs of other states. The right and duty of non-intervention has many facets, but it is generally agreed that it does not mean that states must be treated as

---

77 See International Law Commission, "Draft Declaration on Rights and Duties of States," Articles 1–2, in *Report of the International Law Commission on the Work of its First Session*, [1949] II Yearbook of the International Law Commission 277 at 287 [*Draft Declaration*].

78 *Island of Palmas Case*, above note 13 at 838.

79 Starke describes sovereignty as the "*residuum* of power which [a state] possesses within the confines laid down by international law": J.G. Starke & I.A. Shearer, *Starke's International Law*, 11th ed. (London: Butterworths, 1994) at 91.

80 *Draft Declaration*, Article 5, above note 77 at 288.

81 *UN Charter*, above note 9, Article 2(1).

82 See the *Declaration on Principles of International Law Concerning Friendly Relations and Co-operation among States in Accordance with the Charter of the United Nations*, GA Res. 2625 (XXV), UN GAOR, 25th Sess., Supp. No. 28, UN Doc. A/8028 (1971), Principle 6 [*Friendly Relations Declaration*].

83 See, for example, Articles 3–4 and 8–11 of the *Draft Declaration*, above note 77 at 287–88; Articles 2(1), (4), and (7) of the *UN Charter*, above note 9; *Friendly Relations Declaration*, ibid., Principles 1, 3, and 6.

though they exist in a vacuum. International law in fact contemplates that states will interact and even attempt to influence one another.

What is impermissible, however, is any attempt to undermine another state's free exercise of its sovereign will. For example, aggression or the use or threat of force against the territorial integrity or political independence of another state is categorically outlawed in the *UN Charter*[84] and customary international law.[85] This particular prohibition is so central to the entire international legal system in the post–Second World War period that it is considered a "peremptory norm" of international law—that is, a rule so fundamental that it cannot be set aside even by agreement between states.[86] Beyond the use of force, any other form of interference, whether economic, political, or otherwise, which is aimed at subverting another state's ability freely to exercise its sovereign rights (as opposed to merely influencing its exercise of such rights) is also illegal.[87]

Other fundamental rights and duties of states, including the obligation to fulfill international legal obligations in good faith, respect international human rights, and so on will be illustrated in the chapters that follow. For now it suffices to bear in mind that the principal hallmark and advantage of statehood is the concept of sovereign equality and its necessary corollary, the right—and duty—of non-interference in the domestic affairs of other states.

5) State Continuity and Succession

a) State Continuity

State continuity refers to the basic principle that once a state has come into existence, it continues to exist as one and the same international legal person until it is extinguished by one of the processes recognized by international law.[88] The doctrine is most important in considering the effects of changes in government on a state's international legal personality, and more particularly on its continuing rights and obligations at international law.

---

84 *UN Charter, ibid.*, Article 2(4).

85 See, for example, the *Friendly Relations Declaration,* above note 82, Principle 3; *Corfu Channel Case (Merits) (United Kingdom v. Albania)*, [1949] I.C.J. Rep. 4 at 34; *Case Concerning Military and Paramilitary Activities in and against Nicaragua (Nicaragua v. United States of America)*, [1986] I.C.J. Rep. 14 at 106–10.

86 For more on the prohibition of the use of force in modern international law, see Chapter 11.

87 See above note 85.

88 Discussed in Section B(5)(b), below in this chapter.

We have already seen that, once established, a state usually benefits from a presumption of continued existence even through periods when it may temporarily lack internal governmental authority.[89] As it turns out, that benefit comes with a concomitant burden: as a general rule, changes in government within a state, whether by (domestically) legal, illegal, unconstitutional, or even violent means, do not affect the continued identity of the state on the international legal plane. Thus, even where the new government has not been recognized by other states,[90] the state itself continues to exist, to possess rights, and also to accumulate obligations in international law.

This effect of the doctrine of state continuity was well-illustrated in the *Tinoco Arbitration*.[91] In 1917 the Costa Rican Secretary of War, Frederico Tinoco, led a successful military *coup d'état* in Costa Rica and assumed power. His regime called an election, in which he was elected president, and established a new constitution. His government, however, was short-lived. When Tinoco visited Europe in 1919 for health reasons, his government fell within a month, the old constitution was restored, and new elections held. The new government then set about trying to undo much of what the Tinoco regime had done. As part of this program, the new government enacted a law nullifying many of the transactions entered into by the Tinoco government on behalf of Costa Rica, including obligations transacted with foreign entities such as the Royal Bank of Canada.

Great Britain brought an international claim on behalf of its nationals that were thus affected.[92] The issue that therefore arose was the ability, as a matter of international law, of the (domestically) illegal Tinoco government to bind the state of Costa Rica internationally.

The sole arbitrator, William H. Taft, observed that changes in government or of governmental policy do not affect the state's position in international law. This is because international obligations are owed by the state, not by any particular government. Such obligations remain those of the state regardless of the nature of the governmental authority actually and effectively conducting the affairs of the state at any given time. Moreover, the domestic illegality of the government is of no consequence in international law, as long as the government purporting to represent the state at any given time is in fact, effectively, in a position to do so.

---

89 See Section B(2)(c), above in this chapter.

90 In the case of states still practising recognition of governments in the formal sense discussed above.

91 *Aguilar-Amory and Royal Bank of Canada Claims* (*Great Britain v. Costa Rica*) (1923), 1 R.I.A.A. 375 [*Tinoco Arbitration*].

92 At the time, Great Britain conducted Canada's foreign relations on its behalf.

This illustrates the essentially *laissez-faire* approach of international law when it comes to matters of domestic governmental legitimacy.[93]

It is also interesting to note that in *Tinoco*, Great Britain had refused to recognize the legitimacy of the Tinoco government during its tenure. However, this was not held to bar it from relying on the *de facto* governmental control exercised by that regime to bind Costa Rica as a state.

Thus, international legal rights and obligations attach to the state and not to its government at any particular time. This means that the state will continue to be bound by international obligations assumed from time to time by its government, even where that government has come to power by domestically illegal, unconstitutional, or even violent means.[94]

This, however, says nothing of the situation where a state's government is replaced through *international* illegality. While a state which is subject, for example, to an internationally illegal foreign occupation will generally continue to exist, it appears that obligations incurred by the occupying state or by a government unlawfully installed by it may not be considered those of the occupied state. Rather, the state guilty of unlawful occupation may be held accountable for such obligations.[95] The position may, however, be different if an initially illegal occupation is subsequently "regularized", for example by way of a binding UN Security Council resolution adopted pursuant to Chapter VII of the *UN Charter*.[96]

---

93   In the end, Taft concluded that the British claim had to be rejected because the transactions in question had been concluded in violation even of Costa Rican law as it existed under the Tinoco regime.

94   See also *Velásquez Rodríguez Case* (Judgment of 29 July 1988), Inter-Am. Ct. H.R. (Ser. C) No. 4 (1988) at paras. 182–85.

95   While state practice on the matter is sparse, Brownlie cites the example of Austria, which was not held accountable for foreign obligations incurred on its behalf by the German authorities during the internationally illegal Anschlüss of 1939–45: above note 10 at 81–82. Consider also the illegal invasion by Iraq of Kuwait in 1990, in connection with which Iraq has been held accountable for international obligations incurred on behalf of Kuwait during the period of occupation. On 29 October 1990, the Security Council reminded Iraq "that under international law it is liable for any loss, damage or injury arising in regard to Kuwait and third States, and their nationals and corporations, as a result of the invasion and illegal occupation of Kuwait": SC Res. 674 (1990), UN SCOR, UN Doc. S/RES/674(1990) at 26.

96   For example, it is arguable that the Coalition Provisional Authority and Governing Council established in Iraq shortly following the US- and UK-led invasion of March 2003 had authority to bind Iraq on the international stage due to condonation of their authority in a series of UN Security Council resolutions: see, for example, UNSC Res. 1483, UN SCOR, UN Doc. S/RES/1483 (2003); UNSC Res. 1500, UN SCOR, UN Doc. S/RES/1500 (2003); and UNSC Res. 1511,

b) State Succession

i) Introduction

State succession, in contrast to state continuity, deals with the situation where a state (rather than a government) as an international legal person is extinguished, comes into existence, or is transformed into a new state. State succession therefore involves a change in sovereignty, and not merely government, over territory. As such, it concerns changes of international legal personality.

The international legal mechanisms by which such changes come about will be examined in a subsequent chapter,[97] but for now it suffices to say that succession can take many forms. Among the most common are:

- separation or dissolution: the total dismemberment and disappearance of a state followed by the emergence of one or more wholly new state(s);[98]
- secession: the partial dismemberment of a state, leaving it with less territory, and the emergence of a new state on the seceding territory;[99]
- decolonization: the severance of colonial ties between a metropolitan power and its colony, giving rise to the emergence of a newly independent state;[100]
- merger: the joining of two or more states to form a single new state;[101]
- absorption: the complete assimilation of one state by another;[102] and
- cession or annexation: the transfer of territory from one existing state to another.[103]

UN SCOR, UN Doc. S/RES/1511 (2003). See also T.D. Grant, "The Security Council and Iraq: An Incremental Practice" (2003) 97 A.J.I.L. 823.

97 See Chapter 7, Section B(2).

98 For example, the dissolution of Czechoslovakia into the Czech Republic and Slovakia on the eve of 1993, or the break-up that began in 1991 of the Socialist Federal Republic of Yugoslavia (SFRY) into the new states of Slovenia, Croatia, Bosnia-Herzegovina, Macedonia, and the Federal Republic of Yugoslavia (none of which were deemed to be the continuation of the SFRY).

99 For example, the secession of Norway from Sweden in 1905, or of Montenegro from Serbia and Montenegro (formerly the Federal Republic of Yugoslavia) in 2006, leaving Serbia as the continuation of the former Serbia and Montenegro.

100 For example, the dissolution of the former British Empire, as exemplified by the independence of India in 1947.

101 For example, the merger of Syria and Egypt in 1958 to form the short-lived (until 1961) United Arab Republic.

102 For example, the absorption of the German Democratic Republic (East Germany) by the Federal Republic of Germany in 1990.

103 For example, the purchase of Alaska by the United States of America from Russia in 1867, or the transfer of Alsace-Lorraine from Germany to France following the First World War.

Whatever the form of succession, an important issue that arises is the fate of the international legal rights and obligations of the predecessor state. In particular, are these rights and obligations extinguished along with the predecessor state, or are they transmitted by operation of law to the successor state?

It would be very difficult to offer a comprehensive treatment of this issue here, given that the rules tend to vary with the nature of the right or obligation under consideration, and sometimes with the form of succession.[104] Moreover, this area of international law has undergone significant upheaval in the wake of the massive decolonization experience of the 1950s and 1960s, such that considerable legal uncertainty has been introduced. Nevertheless, as we will now see, it is possible to discern fairly broad agreement on some rules applicable in the area of succession to treaty rights and obligations, given that this is the area where these issues most frequently arise. We will also touch briefly on the much less certain area of succession to public property and public debts.

Before examining the law of succession to treaties, however, it should be noted that many of the problems potentially posed by state succession are often resolved by predecessor states, their successors, and third party states through agreement or acquiescence.[105] It is not uncommon for parties contemplating a change of sovereignty to provide, usually by treaty, for the succession of various rights and responsibilities. This occurred in the *Treaty of St. Germain* of 1919,[106] by which the public debt of the former Austro-Hungarian Empire was divided among various successor states. Similarly, the five successor states to the former Socialist Federal Republic of Yugoslavia (SFRY) concluded an *Agreement on Succession Issues* in 2001 dealing *inter alia* with succession to the public property and debts of the SFRY.[107] The United Kingdom adopted a practice, during its decolonization process, of concluding devolution agreements with former colonies in order to clarify which pre-existing treaty regimes would continue to apply to the newly independent state.[108] Essentially the same result can be reached by means of a unilateral declaration of entitlement by the successor

---

104 For an overview of the range of issues that can arise, see Brownlie, above note 10 at 623–38.

105 See Shaw, above note 21 at 862–63; Brownlie, *ibid.* at 635–36.

106 Above note 44.

107 *Agreement on Succession Issues* (Bosnia-Herzegovina, Croatia, Macedonia, Slovenia, Federal Republic of Yugoslavia), 29 June 2001, (2002), 41 I.L.M. 3 [*Yugoslav Succession Agreement*].

108 A. Aust, *Modern Treaty Law and Practice* (Cambridge: Cambridge University Press, 2000) at 309–10; Shaw, above note 21 at 883.

state followed by agreement or acquiescence by other interested states. This occurred in 1958 when the newly formed United Arab Republic declared its succession to all treaties concluded by its predecessor states, Syria and Egypt, a declaration that was generally acquiesced in by other states parties to those treaties.[109]

While these consensual or quasi-consensual arrangements can provide a practical solution to many of the problems posed by changes of sovereignty, such arrangements are not always possible, pursued, or respected. The question that therefore remains is, in the absence of an effective consensual arrangement, what results flow, by operation of law alone, from changes of sovereignty?

ii) Succession to Treaties

aa. General Rule: Non-Transmissibility

As a general rule, it would now appear to be generally accepted that a new state does not inherit the treaty rights or obligations of a predecessor state.[110] Similarly, where no new state is created but territory merely changes hands, as in the case of cession or annexation, treaties formerly applicable in the ceded or annexed territory do not generally continue in force in that territory, although those in force for the acquiring state generally do.[111]

Thus, the general rule of state succession in respect of treaties is that of the non-transmissibility of treaty rights and obligations, also known as the "clean slate" doctrine. In other words, successor states are not as a general rule burdened by a predecessor's treaty commitments by operation of law alone. This is a double-edged sword, however, in that a successor does not automatically have the benefit of the predecessor's treaty rights either.

This position is in fact quite consistent with the fundamentally contractual nature of international treaties.[112] It would be somewhat surprising if states, having entered into treaty relations with a particular state, suddenly found themselves in treaty relations with another due

---

109 See, generally, Brownlie, above note 10 at 622.
110 See McNair, above note 21 at 655; Aust, above note 108 at 307–8; Brownlie, *ibid.* at 633; Shaw, above note 21 at 875.
111 Shaw, *ibid.* at 878; Aust, *ibid.* at 308.
112 In fact, the rules of state succession operate without prejudice to treaty law in general, which may provide for different outcomes depending on the circumstances. The only rules under consideration here are those that determine whether a treaty relationship does or does not *ipso jure* survive the fact of state succession. Even if it does, the law of treaties may nevertheless furnish grounds for termination of the treaty relationship: see further Chapter 4.

to the extinction of the original party and the emergence of a successor. This would contradict the essentially consensual nature of treaty law that permits states to establish legal relations of a particular type only with other states of their choice.

The general rule of non-transmissibility is mainly evidenced in the practice of states following the Second World War. In the pre-war period, state practice was predominantly to the contrary.[113] For example, the progress towards independence of the British Dominions, including Canada, was characterized by the continuation in force of the various treaties negotiated by the British government on their behalf. Indeed, many of Canada's current treaty relations continue to be governed by treaties concluded by the United Kingdom on Canada's behalf.[114] This presumed transmissibility of treaty obligations was seemingly acquiesced in by other states.

The post-war period, however, witnessed the massive decolonization process in which the former (mostly European) metropolitan powers relinquished their colonies abroad, which in turn emerged as so-called "newly independent states," ultimately quadrupling the number of states worldwide. These new international legal persons in general rejected the notion that they necessarily, by operation of law, inherited the treaty obligations previously negotiated on their behalf by the colonial powers, and most other states accepted this position. This is not to say that newly independent states automatically rejected all prior treaties. Rather, they reserved the right to decide for themselves whether they were willing to assume those treaty obligations.[115]

In fact, the decolonization process saw a number of differing approaches to the issue of succession to treaty rights and obligations. Nigeria, for example, implicitly accepted all pre-existing treaty rights and obligations, which acceptance was in turn acquiesced in by most other parties to the treaties in question. By contrast, Malawi announced that it would respect pre-existing treaties for a trial period to be followed by a declaration of acceptance or rejection by it of each treaty. Yet other

---

113 Aust, above note 108 at 309.
114 For example, the *Jay Treaty* between Great Britain and the United States: *Treaty of Amity, Commerce and Navigation (Jay Treaty)*, 19 November 1794, 8 US Stat. 116 (entered into force 28 October 1795). This is also the case of Canada's membership in the *Hague Conventions*, for example the *Convention for the Pacific Settlement of International Disputes (Hague I)*, 29 July 1899, reproduced in J.B. Scott, *The Hague Peace Conferences of 1899 and 1907*, vol. II (New York: Garland, 1972) at 80; and *Convention Respecting the Laws and Customs of War on Land (Hague IV)*, 18 October 1907, reproduced in *ibid.* at 368.
115 See Shaw, above note 21 at 881–84.

states made general declarations of policy with respect to pre-existing treaties.[116]

This variation in state practice, its concentration in the decolonization process, and the fact that it differed markedly from the preponderance of pre-war practice, led some states and scholars to suggest that different rules of succession might apply to newly independent states—that is, states emerging from a period of colonial domination—than to states in general. In its extreme form, the suggestion was that newly independent states should not only be free to reject pre-existing treaties, but also free to accept them unilaterally with binding effect, regardless of the wishes of other states parties to those treaties.

Such a rule would of course undermine much of the theoretical basis of treaty law, which as noted above is essentially contractual and thus *mutually* consensual in nature. In any event, such an extreme interpretation of state practice is not widely accepted. Indeed the entire notion that treaty succession rules may differ for newly independent states does not have much currency in international law and is not reflected either in the actions or attitudes of the great majority of states. Recall that one of the fundamental principles of international law is the formal equality of states, such that doctrines purporting to grant more favourable legal treatment to certain classes of states tend to be resisted by states themselves.

The failure of the majority of states to accept a distinction between newly independent and other states for purposes of succession to treaty rights and obligations explains also the relative failure of the 1978 *Vienna Convention on the Succession of States in Respect of Treaties*.[117] This Convention was drafted by the International Law Commission with a view to clarifying some of the legal confusion that resulted from changing state practice following the Second World War. While much of the Convention appears to reflect customary international law, by far its

---

116 See S.A. Williams, *International Legal Effects of Secession by Québec*, York University Constitutional Reform Project Study No. 8 (North York, ON: York University Centre for Public Law and Public Policy, 1992) at 30–35; Aust, above note 108 at 309–11. For a general discussion of African state practice, see also Y. Makonnen, *International Law and the New States of Africa* (Addis Ababa: Ethiopian National Agency for UNESCO, 1983); and T. Maluwa, "Succession to Treaties in Post-Independence Africa: A Retrospective Consideration of Some Theoretical and Practical Issues with Special Reference to Malawi" (1992) 4 Afr. J. Int'l & Comp. L. 791.

117 *Vienna Convention on the Succession of States in Respect of Treaties*, 23 August 1978, 1946 U.N.T.S. 3 (entered into force 6 November 1996) [*Convention on the Succession of States*]. See, generally, M.G. Maloney, "Succession of States in Respect of Treaties" (1979) 19 Va. J. Int'l L. 885.

most controversial provisions are Articles 16, 17, and 34. These articles, which are at the heart of the general scheme of the Convention, provide essentially for the non-transmissibility of treaties for newly independent states, subject to an option to succeed unilaterally to multilateral treaties.[118] By contrast, succession in a non-colonial context would be subject to a general rule of transmissibility of treaty rights and obligations.[119]

This distinction and, as a result, the Convention have been soundly rejected by states. The Convention only came into force in 1996 upon attaining the minimum number of ratifications required for this purpose, and still has only twenty-one states parties.[120] Articles 16, 17, and 34 are therefore of limited guidance as to the generally applicable customary international law of succession to treaty rights and obligations, although the remainder of the Convention's provisions are relatively uncontroversial.

Thus, the majority of state practice and opinion supports a general rule of non-transmissibility of treaty rights and obligations, without regard to distinctions between decolonization and other forms of state succession.[121]

bb. Exceptions to the General Rule of Non-Transmissibility
Along with the general rule of non-transmissibility of treaty rights and obligations come certain generally recognized exceptions. The two most important of these relate to treaties creating so-called "objective regimes", and boundary treaties.

The first of these concerns a class of treaty which creates or governs rights and obligations relating to the use of territory. Such treaties are generally presumed to be transmissible; that is, to pass to and bind successor states.[122] The types of rights and obligations typically referred to

---

118 *Convention on the Succession of States*, *ibid.*, Articles 16 & 17.
119 *Ibid.*, Article 34.
120 Of the early signatories only Ethiopia, Iraq, and the former Yugoslavia became parties to the Convention, which was later acceded to by Cyprus, Dominica, Ecuador, Egypt, Estonia, Liberia, Morocco, Saint Vincent and the Grenadines, the Seychelles, Tunisia, and Ukraine. Following the dissolution of the former Yugoslavia, Bosnia and Herzegovina, Croatia, Slovenia, Macedonia, the Federal Republic of Yugoslavia (in 2001, now Serbia) and Montenegro (in 2006) "succeeded" to the Convention (by depositing notices to this effect, in which other states parties appear to have acquiesced). The Czech Republic and Slovakia became parties after the dissolution of Czechoslovakia, which was only a signatory at that time.
121 See Williams, above note 116 at 72; Brownlie, above note 10 at 633–34; Shaw, above note 21 at 875 and 880.
122 McNair, above note 21 at 655–64; Shaw, *ibid.* at 874; Aust, above note 108 at 307. But see Brownlie, *ibid.* at 634, who "considers that there is insufficient

in this regard include rights of transit, navigation, economic exploitation (such as fishing rights), military use, and so on. "Territory" in this context may be misleading in that the concept of an objective regime applies to rivers, lakes, and similar types of territory as well as land territory.[123]

The underlying theory of the exception is that treaty rights or obligations relating to territory and its permissible uses somehow "attach" to the territory and should therefore "travel" with it when it changes sovereign hands.[124] The regime created is "objective" in the sense that it does not depend critically on the identity of the international legal persons establishing it, but rather on the territory to which it attaches. From a policy perspective there is clearly an element of territorial stability at issue and perhaps even an element of preservation of the rights and expectations of third parties as to the continued use of territory.

The chief difficulty with applying this exception to the clean slate rule is to determine its extent. As illustrated above, there is a considerable lack of precision when it comes to the definition of an objective regime. It is particularly difficult to distinguish between treaty rights and obligations that "attach" to territory and those that do not.

Any doubt that this ambiguity may raise as to the existence or validity of the exception has probably been dispelled, however, by the International Court of Justice in the *Gabčíkovo-Nagymaros* case.[125] The case concerned a 1977 treaty between Hungary and Czechoslovakia. The treaty provided for the joint construction and operation by the two states of a system of locks on the Danube River. Hungary, citing various environmental and economic concerns, abandoned performance of the project in 1989 and notified Czechoslovakia of its termination of the treaty in May of 1992. Czechoslovakia, for its part, dissolved into two new states in January, 1993, the Czech Republic on the one hand and Slovakia on the other. The now-abandoned project fell within the territory of Slovakia and thus one of the issues to be resolved in the ensuing dispute between Hungary and Slovakia was whether Slovakia had inherited the rights of Czechoslovakia under the treaty or whether these had been terminated pursuant to the general non-transmissibility rule.

---

evidence in either principle or practice for the existence of this exception to the general rule."

123 On the broad international legal concept of "territory", see Chapter 7.

124 The relevant article of the *Convention on the Succession of States*, above note 117, Article 12, refers to obligations "considered as attaching to the territories in question." For the customary status of the provisions of Article 12, see the *Case Concerning the Gabčíkovo-Nagymaros Project (Hungary v. Slovakia)*, [1997] I.C.J. Rep. 7 at para. 123 [*Gabčíkovo-Nagymaros*].

125 *Gabčíkovo-Nagymaros, ibid.*

The Court did not find it necessary to confirm the general non-transmissibility doctrine, holding that in any event the objective regime exception to any such rule applied here. The Court characterized the 1977 treaty as clearly "territorial" in nature, relying on the view expressed by the International Law Commission (ILC) that "treaties concerning water rights or navigation on rivers are commonly regarded as candidates for inclusion in the category of territorial treaties."[126] In finding that the 1977 treaty thus qualified as an objective regime and was therefore transmissible to Slovakia, the Court also noted that the treaty contemplated the construction and operation of installations on parts of the territories of the two states, established a navigational regime for a major international shipping route, and affected the interests of third states.[127] Thus, concluded the Court, the treaty "created rights and obligations 'attaching to' the parts of the Danube to which it relates," was not affected by the succession between Czechoslovakia and Slovakia, and was therefore automatically binding upon Slovakia from the time the latter came into existence.[128]

The second major exception to the clean slate rule, much more certain in scope, is with respect to treaties establishing international boundaries. This exception is firmly rooted in widespread state practice and is explained by the obvious policy concern to foster stability through encouraging the permanence of international boundaries once established.[129] This same concern animated application of the so-called *uti possidetis* doctrine, by which internal, administrative boundaries between colonial units governed by a single metropolitan power achieved the status of international boundaries upon decolonization.[130] A similar approach has more recently been taken, outside the colonial context, in order to transform internal federal, administrative, or provincial boundaries into international boundaries upon the break-up of a state.[131] In all of these cases, the approach has been, in the interests of

---

126 *Ibid.* at 72, citing the ILC commentary in United Nations Conference on the Succession of States in Respect of Treaties, *Official Records, Volume III: Documents, 1977–78*, 2nd Sess., UN Doc. A/CONF.80/16/Add.2 (1978) at 33.

127 *Gabčíkovo-Nagymaros, ibid.* at 71–72.

128 *Ibid.* at 72.

129 Shaw, above note 21 at 872–74.

130 For a review of the origins and basis of the *uti possidetis* doctrine and of its continuing relevance in the post-colonial context, see *Case Concerning the Frontier Dispute (Burkina Faso v. Mali)*, [1986] I.C.J. Rep. 554 at paras. 19–26. See also generally S. Lalonde, *Determining Boundaries in a Conflicted World: The Role of Uti Possidetis* (Montreal: McGill-Queen's University Press, 2002).

131 For example, in the case of dissolution of the USSR in 1991 or of Czechoslovakia in 1993; see Shaw, above note 21 at 872–73.

avoiding conflict and instability, to take existing territorial boundaries (whether internal or international) as a given. The boundary treaty exception to the clean slate doctrine is driven by this same overriding policy concern. Thus, treaties establishing international boundaries are transmissible to successor states.

The existence in customary international law of this exception to the clean slate rule has been confirmed by the International Court of Justice in the *Case Concerning the Territorial Dispute (Libyan Arab Jamahiriya v. Chad)*, where the Court held that states have an "obligation to respect pre-existing international frontiers in the event of a state succession."[132] This rule is also restated, in essence, in Article 11 of the *Convention on the Succession of States*, which provides that state succession "does not as such affect a boundary established by a treaty" or "obligations and rights established by a treaty and relating to the regime of a boundary."[133]

The cautious wording used in Article 11 may suggest that it is not so much the treaty as it is the boundary (along with rights and obligations relating to it) that survives succession. Indeed this is the view taken by some authors.[134] While it is not clear that much turns on the distinction, this is likely an overly restrictive view. It is true that in *Libya/Chad* the Court noted that a "boundary established by treaty ... achieves a permanence which the treaty itself does not necessarily enjoy."[135] However, it is important to appreciate the context in which the Court made this observation. In particular, the Court stressed that "the Parties have not exercised their option to terminate the Treaty" while adding that "whether or not the option be exercised, the boundary remains."[136] That the Court considered the Parties to have an "option to terminate the Treaty" clearly implies that there was a treaty to be terminated—that is, that the treaty itself had survived the succession of states in that case. The Court's cautionary note about the relative non-permanence of a boundary treaty, as compared with the boundary itself, therefore had nothing to do with non-transmissibility of the boundary treaty upon succession. Rather, the Court was simply alluding to the fact that the law of treaties furnishes various grounds upon which treaties may be terminated by the parties to them.[137] The point was that, whether or not a boundary treaty, *having survived succession*, is subsequently termin-

---

132 *Libya/Chad*, above note 18 at 23.
133 *Convention on the Succession of States*, above note 117, Article 11.
134 Shaw, above note 21 at 873–74.
135 *Libya/Chad*, above note 18 at para. 73.
136 *Ibid.*
137 See above note 112.

ated by one of the parties to it in accordance with the law of treaties, the boundary established by the treaty nevertheless persists. In other words, properly read, *Libya/Chad* is authority *both* for the transmissibility of boundary treaties *and* for the permanence of international boundaries even where the treaties by which they are established are subsequently terminated.

This of course does not mean that it is impossible to change international boundaries once they have been agreed upon. What is required, however, is a new treaty reflecting the consent of all relevant parties to the territorial change.[138] A simple change in the international legal personality of one or more of the parties to a boundary treaty will not of itself suffice to set it, or the underlying boundary, aside.

Other "exceptions" to the clean slate doctrine are sometimes cited. For example, it is sometimes said that treaty rules that reflect customary international law are binding on a successor state.[139] However, it is probably more accurate to think of this in terms of continuation of the customary international legal obligations *themselves*, rather than continuation of the treaty rules. Similarly, it has been argued that certain multilateral human rights treaties are transmissible upon succession, on the basis that such treaties set out certain "acquired rights" of individuals that do not depend upon the identity of the state enjoying sovereignty over a given piece of territory from time to time.[140] There is little if any support for this particular view in state practice[141] although, again, essentially the same result may flow (at least substantively) given that many of the rights set out in human rights treaties exist as a matter of customary international law as well.[142] As we shall see in a subsequent chapter, it is generally the case that all states, including newly-formed ones, are bound by the rules of customary international law in existence from time to time.[143]

---

138 *Libya/Chad*, above note 18 at para. 73.

139 See, for example, Brownlie, above note 10 at 634.

140 See, for example, R. Mullerson, "The Continuity and Succession of States, by Reference to the Former USSR and Yugoslavia" (1993) 42 I.C.L.Q. 473 at 490–92; M.T. Kamminga, "State Succession in Respect of Human Rights Treaties" (1996) 7 E.J.I.L. 469.

141 See Aust, above note 108 at 308.

142 See further Chapter 10.

143 For the parallel existence of treaty and customary obligations, and the universal character of the latter, see Chapter 5.

iii) Succession to Public Property and Debts

In general, the rules governing the passing of public property and debts from predecessor to successor states are less settled than those concerning the passing of treaty rights and obligations. The lack of certainty is particularly acute in the case of debt. This uncertainty flows in part from the habitual practice of states, which is to deal with such practical matters by agreement. This tends to forestall the clear emergence of rules that would apply decisively in the absence of such agreement.

The International Law Commission has attempted to provide some guidance in this area through elaboration of the *Vienna Convention on the Succession of States in Respect of State Property, Archives and Debts, 1983.*[144] However, while many of its provisions would appear to reflect state practice, its attempt to introduce a distinction between the rules applicable in the colonial and non-colonial contexts has doomed the Convention's chances of attracting widespread support.[145]

As for public or state-owned property, the general customary rule appears to be transmissibility on a territorial basis. That is, title to public property goes with the territory on which it is situated.[146] Thus, where a predecessor state survives the succession, title to public property remaining on its territory or under its control (such as naval vessels at sea, military or other property such as embassies held abroad) remains with it. Likewise, title to state property located on the territory or otherwise under the effective control of the successor state passes to it. It is also probable that title to "local" public property—that is, property previously owned or destined for local use by a seceding territorial unit (for example, public property either belonging to or dedicated for use in a province prior to secession), vests in the new state that emerges from the successful secession. Where no predecessor state

---

144 *UN Conference on Succession of States in Respect of State Property, Archives and Debts,* Final Act, UN Doc. A/CONF.117/15 (1983); *Vienna Convention on the Succession of States in Respect of State Property, Archives and Debts,* 8 April 1983, UN Doc. A-CONF.117-14 (not yet in force) [*Property, Archives and Debts Convention*].

145 Indeed, twenty-four years after its adoption it has only been acceded to by seven states (Croatia, Estonia, Georgia, Liberia, Macedonia, Slovenia, and the Ukraine) and has yet to come into force. Further, the text of the Convention was only adopted by a vote of fifty-four states in favour and eleven against (including Canada, the United States of America, and nine others), with eleven abstentions. See P.K. Menon, "The Succession of States and the Problem of State Debts" (1986) 6 Boston Coll. T.W.L.J. 111.

146 See, for example, *Appeal from a Judgment of the Hungaro-Czechoslovak Mixed Arbitral Tribunal (The Pèter Pázmány University v. The State of Czechoslovakia)* (1933), P.C.I.J. (Ser.A/B) No. 61 at 237. This rule is also set out in Article 14 of the *Property, Archives and Debts Convention,* above note 144.

survives the succession, the public property is generally to be divided on an equitable basis among the successor states.[147] These general rules are, with minor variations, reflected in the *Property, Archives and Debts Convention* and are consistent with recent state practice surrounding the break-up of the former Soviet Union and the former Yugoslavia.[148] Of course, all such rules are provisional only and subject to contrary agreement by the relevant parties.

As suggested above, there appears to be greater uncertainty concerning succession to public debt. Based on the preponderance of state practice, there might be said to be a general obligation for the relevant parties to reach a negotiated solution.[149] Beyond this, some authors take the view that, where succession extinguishes the predecessor state entirely, the successor state remains liable for the predecessor's debt.[150] Difficulties of apportionment arise, however, when there are two or more successor states. It may be that apportionment between successor states on an equitable basis (taking into account the property and rights that each successor inherits as a result of the succession) would provide an appropriate default rule in such cases.[151]

By contrast, where a predecessor state remains in existence, the difficulty is in apportioning the overall debt between the predecessor and successor states. There appears to be some consensus that customary international law recognizes that "local" debt[152] at least should pass to the corresponding successor state,[153] and it is arguable that the same holds true for "localized" debts — for example, debts previously incurred by the central government of the predecessor state on behalf of a seceding territorial unit.[154] On the other hand, the presumptive starting point with respect to the "national" or "federal" debt appears

---

147 See, generally, Williams, above note 116 at 43–44; Brownlie, above note 10 at 624–25.

148 See Shaw, above note 21 at 895–97. See also C. Stahn, "The Agreement on Succession Issues of the Former Socialist Federal Republic of Yugoslavia" (2002) 96 A.J.I.L. 379.

149 See Williams, above note 116 at 78–80. This, indeed, was the approach taken by the successor states to the former Soviet Union, the former Czechoslovakia, and the former Yugoslavia: see Shaw, *ibid.* at 896–97 and 904.

150 See Brownlie, above note 10 at 625; Shaw, *ibid.* at 901. This is generally consonant with the rule set out in Article 39 of the *Property, Archives and Debts Convention*, above note 144.

151 Shaw, above note 21 at 903–4.

152 That is, any debt incurred directly by a seceding unit, such as a province, prior to secession.

153 See Williams, above note 116 at 78; Shaw, above note 21 at 901.

154 K. Zemanek, "State Succession after Decolonization" (1965-III) 116 Rec. des Cours 181 at 255–70.

to be that it remains, in the absence of agreement to the contrary, with the predecessor state.[155] Some authors, however, advocate apportionment of the whole of the predecessor's debt on some equitable basis between predecessor and successors.[156] Possible bases of apportionment might include the ratio of territory or population of the predecessor and successor states. As this approach has not yet been widely reflected in non-consensual state practice, however, the default position in customary international law likely remains the non-transmissibility of the national debt where the predecessor state remains in existence.[157]

The *Property, Archives and Debts Convention* nevertheless proposes that, in the absence of agreement otherwise, state debt should as a general principle be transmissible. This general principle would be subject to reduction of the portion of the debt transmitted to any one successor state according to certain equitable considerations, the principal such considerations being the amount of property, rights, and other interests the successor state acquires by succession.[158] While appealing on grounds of fairness and consistency, this likely departs, as indicated above, from the current state of customary international law. Likewise, the Convention's stipulation that no debt at all is transmissible to a newly independent state in the absence of its agreement[159] introduces a distinction that is not reflected in customary practice and will thus be of dubious relevance to non-parties to the Convention.[160]

In short, the essential point with respect to succession to public debt is that the rules remain either highly uncertain or contingent. This means, as a practical matter, that the general principles identified above and in the Convention tend not to be dispositive of the issue at all but rather act as mere starting points for negotiations between the relevant parties in order to achieve an agreed outcome.

iv) Conclusion

The area of state succession is complex and as yet riddled with uncertainty. There are in fact many other facets to this question than have been examined here, including issues relating to the transmissibility of nationality, state responsibility, membership in international organizations, and so on. The vastness of the topic is not surprising given that the continued existence of states, while generally favoured by the

---

155 Shaw, above note 21 at 902–3.
156 For example, Williams, above note 116 at 79–80.
157 Shaw, above note 21 at 902–3.
158 *Property, Archives and Debts Convention*, above note 144, Articles 36–37 and 39–41.
159 *Ibid.*, Article 38.
160 Shaw, above note 21 at 904; Brownlie, above note 10 at 625–26.

structure of international law, is far from assured, such that states frequently disappear to be replaced by new ones. It is also not surprising given that, as we have seen, states are the primary subjects of the international legal system. Thus, their extinction (or birth) necessarily generates issues that call into play virtually all aspects of the international legal system which has been devised to regulate their very existence. It is therefore likely that this is an area of international law that will continue to evolve significantly as the life cycle of states pursues the course charted for it by circumstance and high politics.

C. PEOPLES SEEKING SELF-DETERMINATION

1) The Concept of Self-Determination

Turning now from our discussion of states as the primary subjects of international law, consideration must be given in light of twentieth century developments to other potential candidates for international legal subject-status. This is because states themselves, in the twentieth century, permitted the development of new rules of international law that clearly confer rights and obligations on entities other than states. It therefore becomes necessary to evaluate the extent of the international legal personality thus bestowed by states on these entities.

One of the most significant developments in this regard has been the emergence of the idea that "peoples"—as distinct from states—have a right of self-determination protected by international law. The precise genesis of this doctrine is somewhat unclear although it would appear to be linked to the same process that led to the development of human rights as a well-recognized body of international law.[161] American president Woodrow Wilson liberally advocated "self-determination", without clearly defining the concept, during the peace negotiations following the First World War.[162] The Soviet Union was an early proponent of a right of self-determination of peoples as part of its new conception of international law, put forward after the Bolshevik revolution in Rus-

---

161 See Chapter 10. International human rights law tends to focus on the rights of individuals (although it does recognize certain group rights such as cultural identity, etc.), whereas self-determination is specifically focused on rights held by a "people," typically an ethnic or other minority within an existing state.

162 See M. MacMillan, *Paris 1919: Six Months That Changed the World* (New York: Random House, 2002) at 10–13.

sia.[163] In any case, the massive decolonization process of the post-war period gave considerable impetus to the concept.

The notion that some entity other than the state can enjoy international legal rights was controversial enough when it first emerged. However, that such an entity could enjoy a right as potentially destabilizing to established states as self-determination was particularly contentious. Thus, many states and scholars openly doubted for many years that the doctrine had attained the status of a rule or principle of international law at all.[164] Now, however, in light of substantial state and UN practice lending at least qualified support to the principle, most commentators accept that a right of self-determination of peoples exists as a matter of international law.[165] The International Court of Justice has also, in a series of judgments, expressly endorsed the existence of a right of self-determination, characterizing it as "one of the essential principles of contemporary international law."[166]

Thus, it becomes necessary to consider how and when conferral of such a right also entails conferral on a "people" of a degree of international legal personality. The ramifications are serious because recognizing a "people" as an international legal subject with international

---

163 See, for example, G.I. Tunkin, *Theory of International Law*, trans. by W.E. Butler (Cambridge: Harvard University Press, 1974) at 60–69.

164 See, for example, J.H.W. Verzijl, *International Law in Historical Perspective*, vol. 1 (Leyden: A.W. Sijthoff, 1968) at 324: "The 'right of self-determination' has … always been the sport of national or international politics and has never been recognized as a genuine positive right of 'peoples' of universal and impartial application, and it never will, nor can be so recognized in the future…."

165 See, for example, K Knop, *Diversity and Self-Determination in International Law* (Cambridge: Cambridge University Press, 2002); A. Cassese, *Self-Determination of Peoples: A Legal Reappraisal* (Cambridge: Cambridge University Press, 1995); C. Tomuschat, ed., *Modern Law of Self-Determination*, Developments in International Law Series No. 16 (Boston: M. Nijhoff, 1993); M. Koskenniemi, "National Self-Determination Today: Problems of Legal Theory and Practice" (1994) 43 I.C.L.Q. 241; M.N. Shaw, *Title to Territory in Africa: International Legal Issues* (Oxford: Clarendon Press, 1986) at 59–144; T.M. Franck, *Fairness in International Law and Institutions* (Oxford: Clarendon Press, 1995) at 140–69; R. Higgins, *Problems and Process: International Law and How We Use It* (Oxford: Oxford University Press, 1994) at 111–28; Starke & Shearer, above note 79 at 113; Brownlie, above note 10 at 553–55; Crawford, above note 12 at 107–31.

166 *Case Concerning East Timor (Portugal v. Australia)*, [1995] I.C.J. Rep. 90 at para. 29 [*East Timor*]. See also *Legal Consequences for States of the Continued Presence of South Africa in Namibia Notwithstanding Security Council Resolution 276 (1970)*, *Advisory Opinion*, [1971] I.C.J. Rep. 16 at paras. 52–53 [*South West Africa*]; *Western Sahara*, *Advisory Opinion*, [1975] I.C.J. Rep. 12 at paras. 54–58; *Legal Consequences of the Construction of a Wall in the Occupied Palestinian Territory*, *Advisory Opinion*, [2004] I.C.J. Rep. 136 at paras. 155–62 [*Israeli Wall*].

ts may entail applying those rights against the competing
a state—traditionally the supreme entity in international
.aw.

It is important to note at the outset, however, that recognition of
the right of peoples to self-determination is not tantamount to granting
any sub-national group the right to break away from its current state
and to establish its own, independent state at will.[167] If anything, the
development of the so-called right of self-determination of peoples has
been very tightly circumscribed so as to preserve as much as possible
the integrity of existing states. Thus, understanding the true extent of
the right requires examination of at least three matters:

1) who qualifies as a "people"?
2) under what conditions does a people's right to self-determination
   arise? and,
3) what are the permissible consequences of the exercise by a people
   of its right to self-determination?

In examining these questions and the restrictive answers they
receive in international law, it may be helpful to bear in mind a distinction frequently drawn by states and international lawyers between
"internal" self-determination and "external" self-determination. Internal self-determination generally refers to the right of all segments of a
state's population to participate meaningfully, or at least without discrimination, in its own self-government. In other words, peoples have
a right to determine how they will be governed within the existing
structure of the state in which they live. By contrast, external self-determination is a concept traditionally associated with the sovereignty
of states. States as sovereign entities determine, free from foreign interference but within the confines of international law, how to govern
themselves.

Peoples seeking self-determination challenge this categorization
and pose the following difficult problem: in what circumstances will
a people's right of self-determination transcend its traditional, internal
dimension to become a right of external self-determination, usually reserved to states? The solution to this problem depends on the answers
developed to date by international law to the three questions outlined
above.

---

167 Crawford, above note 12 at 127.

2) "Peoples"

While many international instruments refer to the principle or right of self-determination of "peoples," none provide any definition of the term. In some cases, it may be that the term was intended as a synonym for "state" or "nation" in describing the concept of external self-determination,[168] but in many others there would appear to be a distinction and even an opposition between "states" and "peoples" and a recognition that each may have distinct rights and interests.[169] It has generally been accepted that the use of this distinct terminology clearly connotes that a "people" refers to a portion of the population of an existing state.[170] Were it otherwise, the numerous references to the rights of self-determination of peoples would merely be unnecessary repetitions of the already well-established rights of sovereign states to non-intervention.[171]

What appears certain, based on the preponderance of state practice in the twentieth century, is that the inhabitants of a colonized or other non-self-governing territory constitute a people in the relevant sense.[172] The concept of people is necessary in such a context in order

---

168 For example, Article 1(2) of the *UN Charter*, above note 9, identifies one of the purposes of the United Nations as being "To develop friendly relations among nations based on respect for the principle of equal rights and *self-determination of peoples* ..." [emphasis added]; see also *UN Charter, ibid.*, Article 55.

169 For example, Article 73 of the *UN Charter, ibid.* (imposing duties on states with respect to "territories whose peoples have not yet attained a full measure of self-government"); the *Declaration on the Granting of Independence to Colonial Countries and Peoples*, GA Res. 1514(XV), UN GAOR, 15th Sess., Supp. No. 16 at 66, UN Doc. A/4684 (1961) [*Colonial Declaration*] (referring to "dependent peoples" and peoples "subject to alien subjugation, domination and exploitation"); the *Friendly Relations Declaration*, above note 82 at 121 (clearly distinguishing in Principle 5 between the rights of "peoples" and the duties of "States." See also, for example, the *International Covenant on Civil and Political Rights*, 16 December 1966, 999 U.N.T.S. 171 (entered into force 23 March 1976, except Article 41 on the Human Rights Committee, which entered into force 28 March 1979), Article 1; *International Covenant on Economic, Social and Cultural Rights*, 16 December 1966, 993 U.N.T.S. 3 (entered into force 3 January 1976), Article 1; World Conference on Human Rights, *Vienna Declaration and Programme of Action*, 25 June 1993, UN Doc. A/CONF.157/23 at para. 2; *Declaration on the Occasion of the Fiftieth Anniversary of the United Nations*, GA Res. 50/6, UN GAOR, 50th Sess., Supp. No. 49, UN Doc. A/RES/50/6 (1995) at para. 1; *African Charter of Human and Peoples' Rights*, OAU Doc. CAB/LEG/67/3 rev. 5 (1982), 21 I.L.M. 58 (in force 21 October 1986).

170 See, for example, *Reference re Secession of Québec*, [1998] 2 S.C.R. 217 at 281.

171 *Ibid.*

172 See *South West Africa*, above note 166 at para. 52; *Western Sahara*, above note 166 at paras. 55 and 57; Shaw, above note 21 at 231.

to distinguish between the colonizing state, which as an international legal entity subsumes the colony itself, and the colonized portion of its population.

Beyond the colonial context, however, there is little by way of conclusive guidance on what would constitute a people. Authors have suggested that a people would be recognizable based on a number of objective and subjective criteria. Objectively, a people probably requires a reasonable degree of homogeneity or at least some relatively common characteristic that distinguishes it from the remainder of the population of the state it inhabits.[173] Indicia of such homogeneity or common identity might include any or all of a common:

- ethnicity,
- language,
- religion,
- cultural heritage, or
- history of persecution.

Subjectively, it is likely necessary that the people in question conceive of itself as a distinct group. Such self-conception as a people might be evidenced by means of a plebiscite or other political or popular manifestation of intent to be treated as a distinct grouping.

However, even if a sub-national group achieves recognition as a distinct people, further criteria must be fulfilled before international law grants such a people any standing to assert a right of external self-determination.

3) Conditions Giving Rise to the Right

By far the most successful examples of the exercise of a right of external self-determination by sub-national groups have been in the colonial context.[174] The great preponderance of instruments referring to the right of self-determination, and the jurisprudence of the International Court of Justice to date, all clearly and unambiguously support the

---

173 For example, Brownlie, above note 10 at 553, refers to "cohesive national groups." By contrast, Crawford largely eschews the role of "peoples" as the central criterion, preferring instead to refer to "self-determination units" which are defined in terms of territory rather than population: see above note 12 at 115–18.

174 See Cassese, above note 165 at 334.

right of colonial and other non-self-governing peoples to full external self-determination.[175]

It is also widely recognized that the colonial experience can be generalized to situations where a people is subject to alien subjugation, domination, or exploitation outside of the colonial context.[176] This would extend, for example, to a situation of foreign occupation.[177]

A possible theoretical basis for conferring a right of external self-determination in all these cases might be the notion that such is necessary in order to restore sovereignty wrongly usurped.[178] In other words, these cases may be less about undermining the integrity of the state in favour of sub-national peoples and more about affirming that the sovereignty of those peoples ought never to have been interfered with in the first place.

Beyond these clear cases, however, there remains an as yet unresolved set of circumstances in which a right to external self-determination may or may not arise. The disagreement among commentators here is rooted in whether it is permissible to generalize from the colonial and alien-subjugation contexts, for which there is clear support in state practice, to a broader set of circumstances, for which arguably there is not. For example, do indigenous peoples, such as Canada's aboriginal peoples, have an international legal right of self-determination? The position of indigenous peoples certainly has been the subject of considerable international legal attention in recent years, culminating in adoption by the UN General Assembly, in 2007, of a *United Nations Declaration on the Rights of Indigenous Peoples*.[179] The *Declaration*, the product of more than a decade of negotiation, recognizes that "[i]ndigenous peoples have the right to self-determination"[180] but ap-

---

175 See, in particular, Principle 5 of the *Friendly Relations Declaration*, above note 82, which provides for the separate and distinct status of colonies and non-self-governing territories and the right of the peoples of such territories to exercise their right of self-determination.

176 *Ibid.*, declaring that "the subjection of peoples to alien subjugation, domination and exploitation constitutes a violation of the principle [of equal rights and self-determination]"; see also the *Colonial Declaration*, above note 169 at para. 1; *Reference re Secession of Québec*, above note 170 at 285.

177 *Israeli Wall*, above note 166 at para. 118. See also Cassese, above note 165 at 334.

178 Cassese, *ibid.* at 334.

179 *United Nations Declaration on the Rights of Indigenous Peoples*, UNGA Res. 61/295, UN Doc. A/RES/61/295 (13 September 2007). Canada was one of only four states (along with Australia, New Zealand, and the United States) to vote against the *Declaration* in the General Assembly, citing concerns with ambiguous or overly restrictive language on issues related to self-government, lands, and resources.

180 *Ibid.*, Article 3.

pears to limit the scope of that right to "autonomy or self-government in matters relating to their internal and local affairs."[181] In other words, the essential thrust of the *Declaration* appears to be elaboration of the right to *internal*, rather than *external,* self-determination of indigenous peoples. This suggests a rather cautious approach by states to the potential generalization or expansion of a right of self-determination in any way that might compromise the territorial integrity of existing states.[182]

Nevertheless, the question remains: are the colonial occupation and alien subjugation contexts exhaustive of the circumstances giving rise to the right of external self-determination? Or is it possible to infer from those cases a more general rule to the effect that any people effectively denied the meaningful exercise of its right of internal self-determination has, as a last resort, a right of external self-determination?

There is considerable support for such a proposition. For example, most of the international instruments referred to above define peoples' right to self-determination as encompassing the right "freely to determine their political status and freely pursue their economic, social and cultural development."[183] Many of the same instruments refer to the obligation of states to represent the interests of "the whole people belonging to that territory without distinction as to race, creed or colour."[184] Total frustration of these aspects of the right to internal self-determination would also appear to be one of the primary effects

---

181   *Ibid.*, Article 4. See also Articles 5, 8–14, 16, 18–20, 23, 26–28, 30, and 32–34, all of which appear to recognize various degrees of autonomy in relation to indigenous institutions, traditions, customs, and traditional lands, but all within the greater context of the state in which they live. Note also Article 46, which cautions that "[n]othing in this Declaration may be … construed as authorizing or encouraging any action which would dismember or impair, totally or in part, the territorial integrity or political unity of sovereign and independent States."

182   It should be noted that the *Declaration* was only adopted following amendments addressing concerns expressed by members of the African Group of States over the *Declaration's* provisions on self-determination and their implications for territorial integrity: see Assembly of the African Union, *Decision on the United Nations Declaration on the Rights of Indigenous Peoples*, AU Doc. Assembly/AU/Dec.141(VIII) (30 January 2007).

183   *Friendly Relations Declaration*, above note 82, Principle 5. Essentially the same wording is repeated in, for example, the *Colonial Declaration*, above note 169 at para. 2; the *International Covenant on Civil and Political Rights* and the *International Covenant on Economic, Social and Cultural Rights*, above note 169, Article 1.

184   *Friendly Relations Declaration, ibid.*, Principle 5. See also, for example, the *Vienna Declaration and Programme of Action*, above note 169 at para. 2, which requires that governments represent "the whole people belonging to the territory without distinction of any kind."

of colonization or alien subjugation.[185] Thus, it has been argued that the colonial and alien subjugation contexts are but specific instances of the more general principle that any conditions depriving a people of its right to internal self-determination trigger its right to seek external self-determination.[186] External self-determination might thus be considered a form of international legal remedy for total frustration or denial of a people's right of internal self-determination.

The arguments arrayed against such a generalization of the right are also strong, however. Virtually all references to the right of self-determination in the international instruments and judgments discussed above caution that the right is not to be exercised in a manner that impairs the territorial integrity of states.[187] There is thus a clear concern on the part of states that too loose a characterization of the circumstances in which a right to external self-determination of peoples arises will lead to a plethora of secessionist claims or movements. This, it is feared, would seriously undermine global stability and jeopardize several centuries of international legal developments which have placed the state at the centre of the international legal system.

Further, while the right to maintain territorial integrity is generally conditioned, in the international instruments, on a state's respect of its peoples' right to internal self-determination, there is little if any state practice supporting the general principle described above outside of the colonial or alien subjugation contexts.[188] Perhaps the closest example of the recognition of a right of self-determination in a non-colonial or alien subjugation context is the international community's treatment of Croatia's, Slovenia's, Macedonia's, and Bosnia-Herzegovina's unilateral declarations of independence from the then Socialist Federal Republic of Yugoslavia in 1991. However, international recognition of the right to

---

185 *Reference re Secession of Québec*, above note 170 at 286.

186 Crawford, above note 12 at 127, refers to "territories forming distinct politico-geographical areas, whose inhabitants are arbitrarily excluded from any share in the government either of the region or of the State to which they belong, with the result that the territory becomes in effect, with respect to the remainder of the State, non-self-governing."

187 For example, Principle 5 of the *Friendly Relations Declaration*, above note 82, provides that "Nothing in the foregoing paragraphs shall be construed as authorizing or encouraging any action which would dismember or impair, totally or in part the territorial integrity or political unity of sovereign and independent States conducting themselves in compliance with the principle of equal rights and self-determination of peoples …."

188 A useful review of state practice can be found in N. Finkelstein, G. Vegh, C. Joly, "Does Québec Have a Right to Secede at International Law?" (19(Can. Bar Rev. 225 at 242–48.

secede in those cases was generally withheld until evidence emerged of military aggression, widespread atrocities, and ethnic cleansing. Thus, their utility as precedents is compromised given that conditions ultimately approximated those of alien oppression or occupation, arguably bringing them within the well-established "alien subjugation" category.

The international community's reaction to the Kosovo crisis since 1999 is also indicative of the extreme caution with which states view the right of self-determination of peoples, even those who are clearly being denied their right to participate in their own internal self-government without discrimination. While NATO countries and ultimately the United Nations intervened directly in the Serbian province in order to halt human rights abuses by Serb authorities against the predominantly ethnic Albanian population, the international community has until very recently studiously refrained from supporting the Kosovar people's secessionist claims. For several years, the focus of the UN-led mission in Kosovo was to establish conditions in which the ethnic Albanian population of Kosovo might once again enjoy its right to internal self-determination, perhaps through a degree of local self-government, while preserving the territorial integrity of Serbia.[189] Only in the face of the complete failure of negotiations to this end did the UN Secretary-General and his Special Envoy on Kosovo's future status ultimately recommend to the UN Security Council that Kosovo be granted independence.[190] The Security Council has not acted on this recommendation at the time of writing, but it is plain that such an outcome is only reluctantly being considered, and is seen as an exceptional measure of last resort rather than a clear and present legal entitlement of the Kosovar people, let alone of secessionist movements more generally.

Thus, there is a tension between the international legal right of states to maintain their territorial integrity and the rather exceptional international legal right of peoples to external self-determination. The only clear cases where the latter has prevailed are in the colonial and alien subjugation contexts. The existence of a third category of cases, or rather a generalization of the first two categories encompassing such a right in all situations where a people is effectively denied its right to internal self-determination, awaits further confirmation through state practice.

---

189 See UNSC Res. 1244 (10 June 1999), UN SCOR, UN Doc. S/RES/1244 (1999).

190 See *Report of the Special Envoy of the Secretary-General on Kosovo's Future Status*, UN Doc. S/2007/168 (26 March 2007); *Report of the Secretary-General on the United Nations Interim Administration Mission in Kosovo*, UN Doc. S/2007/395 (29 June 2007); and *Report of the Secretary-General on the United Nations Interim Administration Mission in Kosovo*, U.N. Doc. S/2007/768 (3 January 2008).

4) Permissible Consequences

Finally, even if a people succeeds in being recognized as such and as coming within the relatively narrow conditions in which a right to external self-determination may arise, the ways in which such a right may be exercised remain to be examined. While it is reflexive to think in terms of independence and accession to full statehood, in fact other possibilities exist. Here at least some certainty has been provided, again by a number of persuasive international instruments[191] as well as judgments of the International Court of Justice.[192]

The three main outcomes of the exercise of the right of external self-determination are:

- emergence as a sovereign, independent state;
- free association with an independent state; and
- integration with an independent state.[193]

This is by no means an exhaustive catalogue of possibilities.[194] What is of primary importance, however, is that the choice between these various alternatives or remedies be made freely by the people in question.[195] Frequently this will require a plebiscite or some other form of popular consultation which can guarantee that the right of external self-determination, in those relatively rare cases where it arises, is in fact exercised by the people to whom it belongs.[196]

5) Summary and Conclusions

We have seen that, while states have been prepared to recognize the existence of sub-national groups or "peoples" clothed with certain international legal rights, such recognition has been somewhat grudging. Only in extreme cases of the complete denial of internal self-deter-

---

191 See the instruments listed above notes 82 and 169.

192 For example, the *Western Sahara* case, above note 166 at paras. 57–58.

193 *Ibid.*

194 For example, Principle 5 of the *Friendly Relations Declaration,* above note 82 also provides for "the emergence into any other political status freely determined by a people."

195 This was particularly emphasized by the Court in the *Western Sahara* case, above note 166 at paras. 57–58; see also Crawford, above note 12 at 127–28.

196 This was the approach taken by the UN in the case of East Timor: following a plebiscite in 1999 in which an overwhelming majority of East Timorese favoured independence from Indonesia (prompting a violent retributive campaign orchestrated by the Indonesian military), East Timor acceded to statehood as Timor-Leste in 2002.

mination, such as in the colonial or foreign occupation contexts, have peoples in fact succeeded in asserting and exercising an international legal right of external self-determination. While these developments may eventually culminate in the clear recognition of a general right of external self-determination for all peoples denied meaningful exercise of their right of internal self-determination, the very powerful interest of states in maintaining their territorial integrity suggests that such further development will be slow and piecemeal.

In the context of our examination of international legal personality, moreover, it can be seen that the existence of a people seeking self-determination as an international legal person will generally be a relatively rare and fleeting phenomenon. With the dismantlement of the colonial empires of the past, clear-cut instances of peoples entitled to external self-determination will not be numerous.[197] Among those, exercise of the right will normally lead either to the transformation of the people into a new state or to its integration within or free association with an existing state.[198] Thus, the international legal personality of the people in question will, ultimately, be transformed into or subsumed by the traditional personality of the state.

D. INTERNATIONAL (INTERGOVERNMENTAL) ORGANIZATIONS

In addition to piercing the shell of the state so as to grant some degree of international legal personality to some sub-national groups, international law in the twentieth century also began to contemplate the potential international legal personality of supranational entities, usually taking the form of groupings or associations of states.

---

197 A current clear-cut instance is the people of the Western Sahara, who have yet to express their wishes in a long-delayed UN referendum (although this may now be overtaken by the resumption of settlement negotiations under UN auspices: see *Report of the Secretary-General on the Situation Concerning Western Sahara*, S/2007/619 (19 October 2007) and UNSC Res. 1783 (31 October 2007), UN SCOR, UN Doc. S/RES/1754 (2007). Another such instance is the Palestinian people in the Occupied Palestinian Territory: see *Israeli Wall*, above note 166 at para. 118.

198 The people may even choose to reintegrate the state of origin if conditions permitting its meaningful exercise of internal self-determination are re-established.

To understand this development, it is necessary to recall[199] that states in the late nineteenth century began to move from mainly bilateral, *ad hoc* diplomatic contacts to more coordinated and sustained forms of international consultation and even, at times, collaboration.[200] The occurrence of both world wars in the early half of the twentieth century illustrated quite starkly the need for enhanced international dialogue and cooperation, galvanizing the establishment of permanent international fora for the maintenance of such contact. As a result, the establishment in 1919 of the League of Nations inaugurated a new era of enhanced multilateral diplomacy, the development of broad-based and even universal international legal regimes and, perhaps most significantly, the establishment of permanent supranational institutions through which such initiatives could be nurtured.

Thus, alongside traditional bilateral diplomatic contact and *ad hoc* diplomatic conferences, there emerged permanent international (or "intergovernmental") organizations, often equipped with their own executive and administrative organs. With the *de facto* emergence of such institutions, the prime example of which is the United Nations, the legal issue that arose was their status in international law.[201] Although such institutions are almost always established by treaty between the various states participating in them,[202] do they nevertheless thereby acquire some form of international legal personality distinct from that of their founding members? In other words, do they become international legal subjects in their own right with their own legal rights and duties? Or are they, rather, mere abstractions, something like ongoing diplomatic conferences at which the only real entities and participants, from the perspective of international law, are states?

Implicit in the foregoing questions is whether states, the primary subjects of international law, have the legal capacity to create new subjects of international law other than states.[203] Based on unambiguous state practice in the post-war period, there is no longer any doubt that states do indeed have such capacity and that they exercise it relative-

---

199 See Chapter 1.

200 See Shaw, above note 21 at 1162.

201 For an early discussion of the problem, see C.W. Jenks, "The International Legal Personality of International Organizations" (1945) 22 Brit. Y.B. Int'l L. 267.

202 For example, the United Nations is established by a multilateral treaty, the *UN Charter*, above note 9. Brownlie, above note 10 at 650, notes that while international organizations are usually established by treaty, nothing prevents states from achieving the same end by other means; for example, by way of a resolution at an international conference or by customary practice.

203 We have already seen that states participate, at least to some extent, in the "creation" of other states through the practice of recognition of states.

ly frequently. Thus, it is now generally accepted, including by states themselves, that they are no longer the sole subjects of international law but share the international legal stage, to some extent, with certain of their own creations, international organizations.[204]

While there is now no doubt that an international organization, constituted by the will of states, can become an international legal subject, what remains to be determined in each individual case is the precise character and extent of its international legal personality. While all states are considered juridically equal in international law, this need not necessarily be the case for secondary international legal subjects. Determining the precise attributes of secondary international legal personality frequently comes down to a functional inquiry. From the premise that an international organization can, theoretically, have international legal rights and obligations, the practical questions become to what extent it can enter into treaties with states or other international organizations; or whether it can bring an international claim against another international legal subject; or whether it is entitled to certain privileges or immunities, and so on. More fundamentally, what legal criteria are to be applied in answering these questions?

These questions are of such fundamental importance that they became the focus of one of the earliest advisory opinions sought from the International Court of Justice by the General Assembly of the United Nations.[205] The *Reparations Case*[206] arose in the wake of the killing of the UN Mediator in Palestine and a number of other UN personnel in 1948, shortly after the establishment of the state of Israel but before its admission to membership in the United Nations. The killings took place in Jerusalem, which at the relevant time was under Israeli control. The United Nations, considering that Israel was partially responsible for the deaths by failing to take adequate security measures to protect its envoys, thus sought to determine its legal capacity to press an international legal claim against Israel.[207] In particular, the General Assembly sought clarification as to whether it could press a claim in

---

204 See, for example, C.F. Amerasinghe, *Principles of the Institutional Law of International Organizations*, 2d ed. (Cambridge: Cambridge University Press, 2006) c. 3; Jenks, above note 201; P. Sands & P. Klein, eds., *Bowett's Law of International Institutions*, 5th ed. (London: Sweet & Maxwell, 2001) c. 15.

205 Pursuant to Article 96(1) of the *UN Charter*, above note 9: "The General Assembly or the Security Council may request the International Court of Justice to give an advisory opinion on any legal question."

206 *Reparations Case*, above note 4.

207 The law of state responsibility is described in Chapter 12. Note that there was no question of pursuing Israel for damages in the International Court of Justice, as the Court's non-advisory—that is, contentious—jurisdiction is strictly lim-

respect of its own damages as well as in respect of damages suffered by its representatives.

Given the circumstances, these questions implied several others. First was the issue of whether the United Nations was an international legal person capable of possessing legal rights and obligations, and more importantly, capable of pressing them at international law. Second was the issue of the extent or nature of such international legal personality. Was it as plenary as that of a state? If not, what were its limits and how would these be determined? Third and perhaps most interesting, was its international legal personality opposable only to members of the organization, that is, parties to the *Charter of the United Nations*? Or did the United Nations exist as a legal entity even for non-members of the organization, such as Israel?

In answering these questions the Court took a functional approach, examining the objects and purposes of the United Nations as described in Articles 1 and 2 of the *Charter*. It noted that, based on its *Charter*, the organization is a political body with important political tasks, such as the maintenance of peace and security; is equipped with permanent organs each with its own function; and has a detailed and intricate relationship, as an organization, *vis-à-vis* its members, suggesting a degree of detachment between the member states making up the organization and the organization itself. The Court also referred to a number of other side agreements in which members of the United Nations clearly contemplated that the organization would enjoy certain privileges and immunities akin to those generally enjoyed by states in international law.[208]

All of these factors led the Court to conclude that the states constituting the United Nations intended it to enjoy a "large measure" of international legal personality and a capacity to operate on the international plane.[209] The organization, wrote the Court, "could not carry out the intentions of its founders if it was devoid of international personality."[210] Thus, the organization was to be considered an international legal subject by virtue of the necessarily implied intent of its members. The Court was quick to caution, however, that the United Nations was not a state or a "superstate," and that it could not possess the full range of rights and obligations of a state as a primary subject of international law. Nevertheless, the Court concluded that, in order to be able to carry out the tasks assigned to it by the *Charter*, the organiza-

---

ited to claims between states: *Statute of the International Court of Justice*, 26 June 1945, Can. T.S. 1945 No. 7 (entered into force 24 October 1945), Article 34(1).

208 *Reparations Case*, above note 4 at 178–79.

209 *Ibid.* at 179.

210 *Ibid.*

tion required the legal capacity to bring a claim for its own injuries as well as to espouse claims for injuries sustained by its representatives while on UN business. The Court therefore derived such capacity, by necessary implication, from the terms of the *Charter*.[211]

While it has since become commonplace to consider the United Nations an international legal person with certain rights and obligations at international law, the Court's reasoning has far-reaching implications. First, the judgment confirms that the existence of legal personality in an international organization, and even its precise extent, is not to be gleaned from a narrow reading of its constitutive treaty. Rather, a purposive or functional approach is to be taken in order to understand the intent of the organization's founders. In other words, the extent of the legal personality of an international organization may be inferred from the treaty by which it is constituted in order to give effect to the underlying intentions of the parties to that treaty.[212] The somewhat surprising result is that an international organization can acquire an international legal personality that goes beyond that expressly provided for or agreed to by its member states. There is, however, a limit to this inferential approach: it is not permissible to infer legal capacities that are plainly inconsistent with the international organization's constitutive treaty.[213]

More surprising still is that the ruling in the *Reparations Case* expressly acknowledged that an international organization, brought into existence by agreement of states, can have an "objective" international legal personality—that is, an existence opposable against a state which is not a party to the treaty by which the organization is established:

> … [T]he Court's opinion is that fifty States, representing the vast majority of the members of the international community, had the power, in conformity with international law, to bring into being an entity possessing objective international personality, and not merely personality recognized by them alone, together with capacity to bring international claims.[214]

---

211 *Ibid.* at 179–84.

212 See also *Effect of Awards of Compensation Made by the UN Administrative Tribunal, Advisory Opinion*, [1954] I.C.J. Rep. 47 at 56–57; *Certain Expenses of the United Nations (Article 17, Paragraph 2, of the Charter), Advisory Opinion*, [1962] I.C.J. Rep. 151 at 168; *Legality of the Use by a State of Nuclear Weapons in Armed Conflict, Advisory Opinion*, [1996] I.C.J. Rep. 66 at para. 25 [*WHO Advisory Opinion*].

213 *WHO Advisory Opinion*, *ibid.* at paras. 21–27.

214 *Reparations Case*, above note 4 at 185.

This ruling was of significance because, it will be recalled, Israel was not yet a member of the United Nations and thus not bound by the *UN Charter*. The holding on this point is exceptional given that it is a general rule of treaty law that treaties create neither rights nor obligations for non-parties to them without their consent.[215] Yet, the Court was clear that the United Nations, a creature brought into being by a treaty between other states, had sufficient legal personality in international law to be able to bring a claim in damages against Israel.[216] The applicability of this part of the ruling beyond the special case of the United Nations, which stands in a somewhat unique position as an organization with near-universal membership and the broadest of mandates, is open to question.

In any case, the decision marked the first definitive pronouncement that an international organization can enjoy a certain degree of international legal personality and to that extent be considered an international legal subject.[217] This is not to say that all organizations or institutions established by treaty among states enjoy such personality. From the *Reparations Case* and subsequent state practice, authors are generally agreed that in order to enjoy a measure of legal personality, the following criteria must be present:

1) The organization must represent a permanent association of states and be equipped with permanent organs or institutions with international legal purposes or functions.
2) There must be a distinction, express or necessarily implied, between the legal powers and capacities of the organization or its organs on the one hand and those of its member states on the other.
3) The organization must have legal rights and duties that are exercisable in the international legal system (for example, treaty-making, immunities, et cetera) and not merely within the domestic legal system(s) of one or more of its member states.[218]

---

215 See Chapter 4.
216 Israel became a member of the United Nations in 1949 and in fact paid the amount claimed by the United Nations in 1950.
217 But see also *Jurisdiction of the European Commission of the Danube Between Galatz and Braila, Advisory Opinion* (1927), P.C.I.J., Ser. B. No. 14 at 64, where the Court held that an international institution's functions are to be derived from its constitutive instrument and must be consistent with it. The Court does not, however, discuss the legal personality of international institutions *per se*.
218 Brownlie, above note 10 at 649.

In any individual case, the foregoing criteria would be applied to the international organization under consideration, taking a functional approach to interpreting its constitutive treaty.[219]

Obviously, some organizations will be found to have little if any international legal personality of their own if the foregoing criteria are applied. An example of this might be the North Atlantic Treaty Organization (NATO), established pursuant to the *North Atlantic Treaty*[220] and having twenty-six members. While NATO could be said to satisfy the first and maybe to a limited extent the third criteria above, it has always operated exclusively on the basis of consensus decision-making, meaning that it cannot act contrary to the will of any of its members.[221] This clearly suggests that NATO, although an international organization, has little if any international legal personality of its own and thus is an unlikely candidate for international legal subject status.

Similarly, the British Commonwealth, although a permanent association of states with lawful objects, is not equipped with the sort of permanent organs and other institutional features and powers that would be required to constitute it a subject of international law.[222] By contrast, organizations such as the World Trade Organization[223] or the World Health Organization[224] definitely are equipped with organs with certain international legal rights and privileges, although their mandate is far narrower than that of the United Nations. Thus, it could be said that they are international legal subjects but that their international legal personality is far more limited than that of the United Nations.

In the end, whether an international organization is a subject of international law, and the extent of that status, will depend on a careful and contextual application of the foregoing criteria to the individual character and circumstances of the organization under consideration.

---

219 See J.E.S. Fawcett, "*Détournement de Pouvoir* by International Organizations" (1957) 33 Brit. Y.B. Int'l L. 311 at 313–14.

220 *North Atlantic Treaty*, 4 April 1949, [1949] Can. T.S. No. 7, 34 U.N.T.S. 243 (in force 24 August 1949).

221 NATO, *The NATO Handbook* (Brussels: NATO Office of Information and Press, 2001) at 152–55.

222 See J.E.S. Fawcett, *The British Commonwealth in International Law* (London: Stevens, 1963); Brownlie, above note 10 at 650; Shaw, above note 21 at 215.

223 See *Marrakesh Agreement Establishing the World Trade Organization*, 15 April 1994, 1867 U.N.T.S. 3 (in force 1 January 1995).

224 See *Constitution of the World Health Organization*, 22 July 1946, [1946] Can. T.S. No. 32, 14 U.N.T.S. 185 (in force 7 April 1948), as amended. See also *WHO Advisory Opinion*, above note 212 at paras. 21–27.

E. OTHER CANDIDATES

1) Individuals

The individual traditionally existed only as an object, rather than a subject, of international law. Individuals figured in international legal rules in various capacities,[225] but rarely if ever did international law actually create rights or obligations for those individuals.[226] Still less did international law clothe individuals with the standing or capacity to enter into international legal relations or to advance international legal claims. The individual at best lived a vicarious international legal existence, in the sense that his or her state of nationality could choose, in its discretion, to assert certain of his or her rights, claims, and interests on the international plane. However, the individual had essentially no international legal personality of his or her own at all.

Notwithstanding considerable developments in the nature of international legal subjects, this still largely remains the case. As a *general* rule, individuals still do not possess international legal rights nor do they owe international legal obligations. They still have no capacity to assert claims directly, as of right, on the international plane. On the international playing field, in short, individuals still have no *general* legal existence.

However, twentieth and twenty-first century innovations have introduced a number of discrete exceptions to these general rules. This has occurred in three principal areas. First, certain rules of conduct in times of armed conflict, in addition to protecting individuals (such as civilians, combatants, prisoners of war, the sick and wounded, and so on) are now generally considered to be directly binding upon individuals and not merely the states for which they may be acting.[227] This

---

225 For example, the law of diplomatic immunities provides that the person of a diplomatic envoy is inviolable (see further Chapter 9, Section C); rules of jurisdiction govern when and how a state may lawfully prosecute a foreign national (see further Chapter 8); and the law of diplomatic protection governs the assertion by a state of an international legal claim on behalf of an individual (see further Chapter 12).

226 Thus, taking the foregoing examples, the right of diplomatic immunity is actually held by the state sending the diplomatic envoy; the right of complaint in case of mistreatment or illegal prosecution of a foreign national belongs to the individual's state of nationality; and the law of diplomatic protection is, in fact, an affirmation of the individual's general lack of standing in international law.

227 See, generally, Y. Dinstein, *The Conduct of Hostilities under the Law of International Armed Conflict* (Cambridge: Cambridge University Press, 2004) c. 9; J-M. Henckaerts & L. Doswald-Beck, *Customary International Humanitarian Law,*

development has been closely tied to the development of a second body of international law that imposes obligations directly on individuals: international criminal law. International criminal law concerns not only violations by individuals of the laws of armed conflict but also other, usually large-scale, atrocities such as crimes against humanity and genocide, whether or not committed in times of conflict.[228] These rules and the consequences of their breach are most remarkable for the fact that they impose duties and consequences directly upon individuals and not only upon states. Thus, a military officer directing or carrying out a mass extermination of an ethnic minority, for example, may not only be held responsible under the domestic laws of his or her national state, but may also be held directly accountable as a matter of international criminal law.[229] In this sense, then, international law has imposed certain narrowly defined obligations and thus, arguably, a limited degree of international legal personality, directly upon individuals. The international legal system is still in the process of developing effective mechanisms for enforcing such obligations, although a major step forward in this regard has been the recent establishment of certain *ad hoc*[230] and hybrid international criminal tribunals[231] and, more permanently, the International Criminal Court.[232]

---

vol. 1 (Cambridge: Cambridge University Press, 2005) c. 43; Shaw, above note 21 at 1054–81.

228 See, for example, J.H. Currie, C. Forcese, & V. Oosterveld, *International Law: Doctrine, Practice, and Theory* (Toronto: Irwin Law, 2007) c. 15. See also A. Cassese, *International Criminal Law* (New York: Oxford University Press, 2003).

229 See, for example, Article 6 of the *Charter of the International Military Tribunal (Nuremberg)*, 8 August 1945, 82 U.N.T.S. 279.

230 In particular, the International Criminal Tribunals for the Former Yugoslavia and Rwanda. See *Statute of the International Criminal Tribunal for the Former Yugoslavia*, U.N.S.C. Res. 827 (1993), UN SCOR, 48th Sess., 3217th mtg, U.N. Doc. S/RES/827 (25 May 1993) (Annex) (as amended); *Statute of the International Criminal Tribunal for Rwanda*, U.N.S.C. Res. 955 (1994), UN SCOR, 49th Sess., 3453rd mtg., UN Doc. S/RES/955 (1994). For an overview of the mandates and accomplishments of these tribunals, see Currie *et al.*, above note 228, c. 15, Section B(5).

231 For example, the Special Court for Sierra Leone. See *Statute of the Special Court for Sierra Leone*, 16 January 2002, 2178 U.N.T.S. 137.

232 See *Rome Statute of the International Criminal Court*, 17 July 1998, 2187 U.N.T.S. 90 (in force 1 July 2002). For a review of the negotiating history of the *Rome Statute*, see also P. Kirsch & V. Oosterveld, "Negotiating an Institution for the 21st Century: Multilateral Diplomacy and the International Criminal Court" (2001) 46 McGill L.J. 1141; and Roy S. Lee, ed., *The International Criminal Court: The Making of the Rome Statute, Issues, Negotiations, Results* (Boston: Kluwer Law International, 1999).

The third major development has been the elaboration of a far-reaching body of international human rights law, beginning with the *Universal Declaration of Human Rights* in 1948.[233] In contrast to the first two developments noted above, which impose obligations on individuals, the aim of international human rights law is the recognition of certain basic rights and entitlements of individuals. These rights and entitlements may already have existed or been recognized in various domestic legal systems. What is new is their recognition or conferral as a matter of international law. In other words, such international legal rights are enjoyed directly by individuals, and produce corresponding obligations for states, *including the individual's state of nationality*. Theoretically at least, the individual thus becomes the holder of an international legal right that is valid against any and all states. In this sense, too, international law has thus conferred a limited degree of legal personality on the individual.

This latter development is, however, significantly undermined by the failure to confer general standing on individuals to bring claims for violations of these rights in an international forum with clear enforcement powers. This problem and the limited solutions to it to date will be examined in greater detail in a subsequent chapter,[234] but for now it suffices to note that while the imposition of obligations and the conferral of rights of an international legal character has in some sense made the individual a subject of international law for very limited purposes, the individual's capacities in international law remain tenuous at best.

2) Corporations

A corporation is an artificial legal person created pursuant to legal rules established for that purpose within a particular legal system. In international law, there are no rules providing for, and no body competent to oversee, the creation of such entities. Thus, corporations are strictly the creatures of domestic legal systems and as such draw their basic legal personality, including rights, obligations, and capacities, from the provisions of those legal systems.

The same is true of so-called multinational or transnational corporations, which today proliferate in an international legal system increasingly geared towards open global trade. Notwithstanding their "international" appearance, such corporations are merely a series of

---

233 *Universal Declaration of Human Rights*, U.N.G.A. Res. 217(III), UN GAOR, 3rd Sess., Supp. No. 13, UN Doc. A/810 (1948).

234 See Chapter 10.

linked artificial legal persons that have been constituted as such within the domestic legal systems of several states.

In other words, corporations as such do not exist as subjects of international law.[235] Insofar as they exist as objects of which international law takes some account, they are simply treated in much the same manner as individuals.[236] However, the development of the position of the individual as a subject of international law in the limited spheres reviewed above has not generally been mirrored in the case of corporations. While considerable activity has taken place in UN and other circles to create certain legal frameworks or codes of conduct related to multinational corporations, for the most part these have remained at the developmental stage and in any event have been formulated in terms of rights and obligations of states in relation to such entities, and not of the entities themselves.[237]

The foregoing discussion has focused on private, commercial corporations. However, many states have equipped themselves with corporate bodies for various economic and trade purposes. Thus, in Canada, the "Crown corporation" is a corporate legal entity created pursuant to legislation and usually controlled by government. Similar entities exist in other states and are particularly prominent in socialist states with centrally planned economies such as Cuba or China. When considering the international legal personality of this type of corporate entity, caution is required. Such entities do not acquire any standing or personality on the international stage by virtue of their corporate status; however, they may in fact constitute emanations, or at least agents,

---

235 See American Law Institute, *Restatement (Third) of the Foreign Relations Law of the United States* (St. Paul, MN: American Law Institute, 1987) at 126.

236 For example, rules governing the conferral of nationality, the espousal of claims, or the permissible jurisdictional reach of domestic legislation take account of corporations as objects, rather than subjects, of international law.

237 See, for example, Organisation for Economic Co-operation and Development, *OECD Guidelines for Multinational Enterprises*, revision 2000, (Paris: OECD Publications, 2000); Organisation for Economic Co-operation and Development, *OECD Principles of Corporate Governance* (Paris: OECD Publications, 2004); *United Nations Draft International Code of Conduct on Transnational Corporations*, U.N. Doc. E/C. 10/1984/S/5 (1984), (1984), 23 I.L.M. 626; International Labour Organization, *Tripartite Declaration of Principles Concerning Multinational Enterprises and Social Policy* (1977), 17 I.L.M. 422; World Bank, *Guidelines on the Treatment of Foreign Direct Investments* (1992), 31 I.L.M. 1366; and UN Sub-Commission on the Promotion and Protection of Human Rights (Sessional Working Group on the Working Methods and Activities of Transnational Corporations), *Draft Norms on Responsibilities for Transnational Corporations and Other Business Enterprises with Regard to Human Rights*, U.N. Doc. E/CN.4/Sub.2/2002/13 (August 2002).

of the state that has established them. They may therefore attract or be clothed with the international legal personality of their constituting state, and in this sense share the international legal rights and obligations of that state. However, it would be inaccurate to consider them free-standing international legal persons in their own right generally possessed of distinct legal rights and obligations in international law.

Similarly, a number of "multinational public enterprises" have been established by agreement between states. These generally contemplate some form of economic cooperation between the participating states and private or state corporate entities. Here again, any international legal personality attaching to such enterprises either depends on the international legal personality of the participating states or is akin to the international legal personality conferred by states on certain international organizations.[238]

It should also be remembered that the position of all commercial entities in international law has to some degree been influenced by framework trade agreements such as the North American Free Trade Agreement[239] and the General Agreement on Tariffs and Trade,[240] as well as the establishment of the World Trade Organization.[241] For a detailed treatment of that area of international law the reader is referred to a companion volume in this series.[242]

3) Non-Governmental Organizations (NGOs)

Non-governmental organizations are to be distinguished from intergovernmental organizations. As we have seen, intergovernmental or international organizations are associations of states potentially clothed with some degree of international legal personality. By contrast, non-governmental organizations ("NGOs") are civil society organizations or associations typically created to advance or represent some particular interest. By definition they tend not to have any particular affiliation

---

238 See, generally, Shaw, above note 21 at 223–24, discussing such entities as IN-TELSAT and Eurofima. See also P. Muchlinski, *Multinational Enterprises and the Law*, rev. ed. (Oxford: Blackwell, 1999).

239 *North American Free Trade Agreement Between the Government of Canada, the Government of Mexico and the Government of the United States*, 17 December 1992, Can. T.S. 1994 No. 2, 32 I.L.M. 289.

240 General Agreement on Tariffs and Trade, 1947, Can. T.S. 1948 No. 31.

241 *Marrakesh Agreement Establishing the World Trade Organization*, above note 223.

242 J.R. Johnson, *International Trade Law* (Concord, ON: Irwin Law, 1998). See also J-G. Castel et al., *The Canadian Law and Practice of International Trade with Particular Emphasis on Export and Import of Goods and Services* (Toronto: Emond Montgomery Publications, 1997).

with governments or states. Prominent examples of NGOs particularly active in the international field include the International Committee of the Red Cross, Amnesty International, Greenpeace, Human Rights Watch, and the International Olympic Committee.

Given their civil society status, NGOs in general have no international legal personality. As a general rule they have neither rights nor obligations under international law, but are rather governed by the rules of the domestic legal systems in which they are established. In terms of standing, the *UN Charter* in Article 71 provides that the UN Economic and Social Council may grant NGOs consultative status. Similar status is accorded less formally in other UN bodies or during international or diplomatic conferences. Such status permits NGOs to attend meetings and sometimes to present submissions or participate in discussions. However, such status carries no significant legal entitlements in international law, and does not even usually entail a right to vote.

That NGOs are not international legal subjects does not detract, however, from their very real contribution to international legal life and development. For example, the International Committee of the Red Cross is responsible for much of the pioneering work establishing basic norms of humanitarian conduct that now form the backbone of international humanitarian law.[243] States of course play the critical role in transforming ideas into internationally binding rules of law, but NGOs play an often overlooked and undervalued role in advancing an international justice agenda.

FURTHER READING

AMERASINGHE, C.F., *Principles of the Institutional Law of International Organizations*, 2d ed. (Cambridge: Cambridge University Press, 2005)

AUST, A., *Modern Treaty Law and Practice* (Cambridge: Cambridge University Press, 2000) c. 22

BALDWIN, T., "The Territorial State" in H. Gross & R. Harrison, eds., *Jurisprudence: Cambridge Essays* (Oxford: Clarendon Press, 1992) 207

---

243 On the exceptional degree of international legal personality conferred by states on the International Committee of the Red Cross, see further Shaw, above note 21 at 243 and 1078–79.

BROMS, B., "Subjects: Entitlement in the International System" in R. St. J. Macdonald & D.M. Johnston, eds., *The Structure and Process of International Law* (Boston: Kluwer, 1983) 383

CASSESE, A., *International Law in a Divided World* (Oxford: Oxford University Press, 1986) c. 4

CASSESE, A., *Self-Determination of Peoples: A Legal Reappraisal* (Cambridge: Cambridge University Press, 1995)

CRAWFORD, J., *The Creation of States in International Law*, 2d ed. (Oxford: Oxford University Press, 2006)

DUMBERRY P., *State Succession to International Responsibility* (Leiden: Martinus Nijhoff, 2007)

JAMES, A., *Sovereign Statehood: The Basis of International Society* (London: Allen & Unwin, 1986) c. 7–8

KNOP, K., *Diversity and Self-Determination in International Law* (Cambridge: Cambridge University Press, 2002)

MCWHINNEY, E., *Self-Determination of Peoples and Plural-Ethnic States in Contemporary International Law* (Leiden: Martinus Nijhoff, 2007)

O'CONNELL, D.P., *State Succession in Municipal Law and International Law*, 2 Vols., Cambridge Studies in International and Comparative Law Series No. 7 (Cambridge: Cambridge University Press, 1967)

SANDS, P. & KLEIN, P., eds., *Bowett's Law of International Institutions*, 5th ed. (London: Sweet & Maxwell, 2001)

SIMMA, B. *et al.*, eds., The Charter of the United Nations: A Commentary, 2d ed. (Oxford: Oxford University Press, 2002)

SUMMERS, J., *Peoples and International Law* (Leiden: Martinus Nijhoff, 2007)

TOMUSCHAT, C., ed., *Modern Law of Self-Determination*, Developments in International Law Series No. 16 (Boston: M. Nijhoff Publishers, 1993)

WHITE, N.D., *The Law of International Organisations* (Manchester: Manchester University Press, 1996)

CHAPTER 3

SOURCES OF INTERNATIONAL LAW

A. RELEVANCE OF "SOURCES"

The domestic lawyer or law student is rarely preoccupied with the sources of domestic law and even more rarely with its binding authority. Most domestic legal systems are sufficiently mature that the sources of the law are well established and grounded in an authoritative, albeit frequently complex, constitutional and institutional framework. In Canada, for example, it is a virtual article of faith that all binding legal rules find their source either in the enactments of constitutionally-sanctioned legislative bodies (Parliament and provincial legislatures) or their delegates (for example, federal or provincial cabinets and municipal authorities), or in the common law developed by the courts. In other words, in most domestic legal orders, it is a given that constitutionally competent institutions are assigned the task of promulgating and enforcing the law.

The situation is entirely different in the international legal system. As we have seen,[1] that system is typified by the absence of a formal constitutional structure, a lack of central organization, and only a tenuous institutional framework in which states participate on a purely voluntary basis. Hence, there is no central or constitutionally authorized legislature or law-making authority in international law. While

---

1   See Chapter 1.

the *Charter of the United Nations*[2] may have the outward appearance of an international constitution, it is at its root simply an international treaty, binding upon states who are parties to it in accordance with international treaty law.[3] Further, while the UN enjoys near-universal participation by the world's states[4] and certainly plays an important institutional role in providing a permanent forum for sustained international dialogue and diplomacy, it has no formal law-making powers of its own.[5] The powers of the UN General Assembly, for example, are limited to discussing and making recommendations on questions or matters coming within the scope of the *UN Charter*.[6] The International Court of Justice (ICJ), being the "principal judicial organ of the United Nations,"[7] only has jurisdiction to give advisory opinions to various UN organs and agencies and to decide cases submitted to it with the consent of the parties.[8] In any event, it has no power to create binding precedent as does a common law court.[9] Even the UN Security Council, which is given the power to make determinations and impose binding measures in matters of international peace and security, only has the authority to bind member states of the organization, that is, parties to the *UN Charter*.[10] In that sense, the Security Council is simply exercis-

---

2   *Charter of the United Nations*, 26 June 1945, Can. T.S. 1945 No. 7 (entered into force 24 October 1945) [*UN Charter*].

3   See Chapter 4.

4   At the time of writing 192 states were members of the United Nations.

5   But see O. Schachter, "United Nations Law" (1994) 88 A.J.I.L. 1. It is of course true that, in "providing a permanent forum for sustained international dialogue and diplomacy," the UN has multiplied the law-creating opportunities available to states, and in that sense fosters the growth of international law. The point made here, however, is that the UN and its organs are not formal sources of international law in their own right.

6   See, generally, *UN Charter*, above note 2, Chapter IV. Note, however, that the General Assembly has the power to control the budget of the UN (Article 17); to elect members to various UN bodies such as the Security Council (Article 23(1)), the Economic and Social Council (Article 61), the Trusteeship Council (Article 86(1)(c)), and the International Court of Justice (*Statute of the International Court of Justice*, below note 8, Article 4); and to admit, suspend, or expel members to or from the UN (Articles 4–6). It also enjoys certain other powers in respect of the administration of trust territories (Chapters XII–XIII).

7   *UN Charter*, above note 2, Article 92.

8   *Ibid.*, Article 96; *Statute of the International Court of Justice*, 26 June 1945, Can. T.S. 1945 No. 7 (entered into force 24 October 1945), Article 36 [*ICJ Statute*].

9   *Case Concerning East Timor (Portugal v. Australia)* [1995] I.C.J. Rep. 90 at 101, para. 26; *ICJ Statute, ibid.*, Article 59.

10 Note, however, that the *UN Charter* provides that the United Nations shall ensure that non-members comply with the principles of the organization insofar as necessary to maintain international peace and security: *UN Charter*, above

ing enforcement authority delegated to it by states in a treaty.[11] Further, in exercising these powers it is acting as a political or executive organ rather than as a judicial or law-making institution promulgating law with general normative effect.[12]

This perhaps remarkable fact—that there is no central law-making authority in our international legal system—is, in reality, hardly surprising at all. It is a natural result of the underlying structure of the international "community," which comprises, as we have seen, a

---

note 2, Article 2(6). On the debate this provision has generated in light of the general rule of treaty law that treaties do not create obligations for non-parties, see Chapter 4, Section G(4).

11 See, in particular, Articles 25, 39–42, 48–49, and 103 of the *UN Charter, ibid.*, which together constitute the core of the Security Council's binding and overriding authority to require states to take certain steps to maintain or restore international peace and security.

12 See *Case Concerning Armed Activities on the Territory of the Congo (Democratic Republic of the Congo v. Uganda), Provisional Measures, Order of 1 July 2000,* [2000] I.C.J. Rep. 111 at para. 36; *Case Concerning Military and Paramilitary Activities in and against Nicaragua (Nicaragua v. United States of America) Jurisdiction and Admissibility, Judgment,* [1984] I.C.J. Rep. 392 at para. 95; *Case Concerning Application of the Convention on the Prevention and Punishment of the Crime of Genocide (Bosnia and Herzegovina v. Yugoslavia (Serbia and Montenegro)), Provisional Measures, Order of 8 April 1993,* [1993] I.C.J. Rep. 3 at para. 33; *Case Concerning Questions of Interpretation and Application of the 1971 Montreal Convention Arising from the Aerial Incident at Lockerbie (Libyan Arab Jamahiriya v. United Kingdom), Provisional Measures, Order of 14 April 1992,* [1992] I.C.J Rep. 114 at para. 40. But note that the Security Council has, on occasion, exercised its power to establish free-standing judicial institutions, such as the International Criminal Tribunal for the Former Yugoslavia and the International Criminal Tribunal for Rwanda. On the Tribunal for the Former Yugoslavia, see *Report of the Secretary General Pursuant to Paragraph 2 of Security Council Resolution 808 (1993),* UN SCOR, 48th Year, UN Doc. S/25704, S/25704/Add.1, S/25704/Corr.1; SC Res. 827 (25 May 1993), UN SCOR, 48th Year, UN Doc. S/RES/827(1993); *Statute of the International Tribunal,* adopted by SC Res. 827, *ibid.*, Annex, UN Doc. 25704 (1993), as amended by SC Res. 1166 (13 May 1998), UN SCOR, 53rd Year, UN Doc. S/RES/1166(1998); as amended by SC Res. 1329 (30 November 2000), UN SCOR, 55th Year, UN Doc. S/RES/1329(2000). See also *Prosecutor v. Tadic* (1995), 35 I.L.M. 32 at paras. 28–35 (ICTY Appeals Chamber). On the Tribunal for Rwanda, see SC Res. 955 (8 November 1994), UN SCOR, 49th Year, UN Doc. S/RES/955(1994); *Statute of the International Tribunal for Rwanda,* adopted by SC Res. 955 (1994), UN SCOR, 49th Year, UN Doc. S/INF/50 (1994). It should also be noted that the Security Council has recently begun adopting binding resolutions requiring states to take legislative steps within their domestic legal systems to address, for example, issues of terrorist financing and proliferation of weapons of mass destruction: see, for example, UNSC Resolution 1373, 28 September, 2001, UN Doc. S/RES/1373 (2001); UNSC Resolution 1540, 28 April, 2004, UN Doc. S/RES/1540 (2004).

collection of independent, sovereign states which, by definition, are not subject to foreign authority. The originally rigid conception of the sovereignty of the nation-state has been somewhat relaxed, particularly in the twentieth and twenty-first centuries, but in the main the community of nations remains essentially that—a collection of nearly 200 independent nation-states that are largely not subject to external authority and that have so far resisted the establishment of any "world government" with law-making—much less law-enforcing—organs of its own.[13]

The dilemma for the international lawyer, then, is whether one can truly speak of international law at all. In the absence of some recognized law-making authority, whence does international law originate? What are its sources? While the principal and most widely accepted answers to these questions are the subject of this and the next two chapters, it should be noted that intense debate on these issues persists in scholarly and judicial opinion and, perhaps more significantly, in the practices and views of states themselves.

B. THE SEARCH FOR THE SOURCE OF BINDING OBLIGATION IN INTERNATIONAL LAW

As reviewed above,[14] it is generally accepted that our system of international law evolved not only in response to the emergence of the sovereign nation-state in the post-Peace of Westphalia period, but also under the influence of legal scholars who put forth various theories to explain how and why states are bound by a system of international law. International legal scholarship has undergone a number of transformations as theorists have sought to understand, describe, or in some cases prescribe the underlying source of binding obligation in international law. The main schools of thought that have dominated this evolution, natural law theories and positivism, in large measure mirror their analogues in domestic legal and political theory. However, the tension between natural law and positivist theories has been especially acute in international law, given the peculiar nature of international society and

---

13   The United Nations Security Council's powers to enforce maintenance of international peace and security pursuant to Chapter VII of the *Charter of the United Nations* is a notable but limited exception. See further Chapter 11.

14   See Chapter 1.

its inability to "constitutionalize" itself in a manner analogous to domestic societies.

The traditional approach to illustrating this tension is to describe various periods in international legal scholarship. This has the virtue of tracing the ebb and flow of the dominance of the underlying legal theories (natural and positive law) and of placing them in the context of the evolving international order itself. For present purposes, it will be useful to refer to three such periods: the "primitive" period, referring to scholarship pre-dating the Peace of Westphalia in 1648; the "classical" or "traditional" period, spanning approximately two and a half centuries between 1648 and the close of the First World War; and the so-called "modern" period, beginning with the establishment of the League of Nations in 1919.

1) The Primitives

Early international legal scholars such as Vitoria,[15] Gentili,[16] Suárez,[17] and Grotius[18] are now frequently referred to as the "primitives."[19] While each author differed to some extent in his precise conception of the international legal order, all drew upon then-prevailing natural law theories in order to devise a systematic explanation of the legal order governing sovereigns and other entities. A basic premise of the primitives' approach, building upon earlier conceptions of Canon and Roman law, was that all law could be deduced from some innate, pre-existing normative order that was not dependent for its authority on

---

15 Francisco de Vitoria (1480–1546), *De Indis et de Ivre Belli Relectiones* (*Reflections on the Indians and the Law of War*), 1557, ed. by E. Nys, trans. by J.P. Bate, Classics of International Law Series No. 7, J.B. Scott, ed. (Washington: Carnegie Institution, 1917). See also J.B. Scott, *The Spanish Origins of International Law: Francisco de Vitoria and His Law of Nations* (Oxford: Oxford University Press, 1934).

16 Alberico Gentili (1552–1608), *De Iure Belli Libri Tres* (*Three Books on the Law of War*), 1612, trans. by J.C. Rolfe, Classics of International Law Series No. 16, J.B. Scott, ed. (Oxford: Clarendon Press, 1933).

17 Francisco Suárez (1584–1617), *Selections from Three Works*, trans. by G.L. Williams, A. Brown, & J. Waldron, Classics of International Law Series No. 20, J. B. Scott, ed. (Oxford: Clarendon Press, 1944).

18 Hugo Grotius (1583–1645), *De Jure Belli ac Pacis Libri Tres* (*Three Books on the Law of War and Peace*), 1625, trans. by F. Kelsey, Classics of International Law Series No. 3, J. B. Scott, ed. (Oxford: Clarendon Press, 1925).

19 The term "primitives" is not used to cast aspersions on the quality of their scholarship but rather as an acknowledgment that their writings pre-dated the watershed events of 1648 which marked the crystallization of a new international order in Europe; see Chapter 1.

the will of its subjects. Law was not something to be created. Rather, it already existed and its content was pre-ordained by either God or the "nature" of the universe itself.

For the sixteenth century Catholics Vitoria and Suárez, the source of such "natural" normative authority was essentially theological or divine. In other words, all law and all legitimate authority was derived from God and Christian (specifically Catholic) doctrine. Law was simply a part of this divine order. Moreover, law was universal in scope; there was therefore little room in this conception for distinctions between domestic and international law, much less between international and natural law, or even morality. All proceeded in a seamless fashion from their faith in a supreme God and divine order.

Neither scholar addressed or even seemed to be aware of the difficulties potentially posed by a divine and presumably immutable normative order to which even "sovereigns" were subject. Such an issue could not in fact arise within their theoretical framework because they could not conceive of a form of sovereignty that did not originate in, and thus conform to, the divine order. In other words, purported exercises of sovereign authority that conflicted with the overarching natural order simply could not be sovereign or authoritative acts at all. Evidently, such an approach was an uneasy fit for a world inhabited by ever more powerful and factually sovereign monarchs.

By contrast, the Protestants Gentili and, especially, Grotius largely eschewed the role of divinity and theology in putting forth their own natural law theories. For Grotius, questions of divinity were thoroughly irrelevant to the existence of natural law. He even went so far as to assert, quite radically for the time, that the law of nature would exist even if there were no God.[20] Rather, he argued that human "reason" was the ultimate source of authority. Humanity was assumed to have the innate ability to discern, through the application of reason, the pre-existing law of nature that was inherent in the fabric of existence itself. Humanity was also assumed to have an innate tendency to follow the dictates of natural law so revealed. The law was "natural" in that it could be deduced by the simple application of reason to facts, often exemplified in the study of past societal practices. Grotius wrote, for example, that natural law could be deduced from, *inter alia*, the actions of individuals or states who had discovered the inherent "quality of moral baseness or moral necessity" of their actions. He made frequent reference, there-

---

20   He nevertheless clearly asserted his belief in God, while maintaining the irrelevance of such belief to the system he was describing.

fore, to the practices of the ancient Greeks or Romans as evidence of the natural domestic or international legal order.

While aspects of this approach (and particularly its reliance on empirical observations of how individuals or states behaved) might hint of positivism, in fact it was clearly not a positivist approach. Grotius did not invest past practice with any law-creating or binding authority *per se*. Rather, he merely viewed such practice as evidence of the application of human reason to various situations, and thus as a reliable guide to the content of the natural legal order itself.

Thus Grotius is generally credited with the radical secularization of natural law theories, particularly as they applied to the legal order governing the relations between sovereigns. It is partly for this reason, therefore, that he is often (controversially) dubbed the "founder" of modern international law. This characterization is occasionally questioned on the basis that, given his ultimate reliance on an inherent, immutable, and universal normative order, Grotius was no less of a "primitive" or proponent of natural law theories than his predecessors. On the other hand, his uncompromising secular approach, his empirical reliance on the practice of states as evidence of the content of the law if not of its legal authority, and the systematic comprehensiveness of his principal treatise on international law[21] all combined to differentiate Grotius from his fellow primitives. His work stands not so much as the progenitor of modern international law as it does as a harbinger of a dramatic shift in future thinking about international law. In this sense, at least, he can justifiably be viewed as standing, along with the participants in the negotiations that led to the Peace of Westphalia in 1648, on the very threshold of the era of the sovereign nation-state and hence of modern international law.

2) The Classical or Traditional Period

With the advent of a new political arrangement in Europe following the Peace of Westphalia and the emergence of independent, sovereign, and legally equal states, many of the "blind spots" of the primitives' natural law theories were exposed as untenable or at best unworkable. For example, even if one were to accept that there was such a thing as a universal divine or natural legal order to which sovereigns were subject, the difficulty that remained was how its dictates could be known authoritatively. Simply relying on the innate ability and desire of individuals or sovereigns to discern and observe the content of natural law

---

21   See above note 18.

was bound to be inadequate, as conflicting interpretations would (and did) inevitably result.

The potential for such conflicting and, presumably, equally authoritative interpretations of what was naturally right and wrong in any given situation was exacerbated on the international scene by the emergence of scores of newly sovereign states resulting from the effective dissolution of the Holy Roman Empire. Not surprisingly, along with the power to act independently came the desire to do so without regard for the courses chosen by other independent sovereigns. The ensuing conflicts were not easily reconciled with the idea of an objective, all-embracing system of law that proceeded naturally from humanity's assumed capacity and desire to know and favour the universal right over the universal wrong. As humanity's conclusions as to what was right and wrong, good and evil, lawful and unlawful increasingly diverged, faith in the existence of any such natural order was eroded. It became increasingly apparent that such disagreement was itself evidence of the lack of anything to be agreed upon — that is, the absence of any natural legal order, or at least of any such order that was objectively knowable and therefore relevant.

So-called "classical" or "traditional" international legal scholarship is thus typified by a repudiation of either the existence or the utility of any natural legal order. Classicists dismissed the primitives' reliance on either faith or reason, and in particular their assumption that humanity was in a sense "programmed" to know universal right from wrong. They attacked the primitives' claims of objective truth as being, in reality, thinly disguised subjective choice. Classicists adopted as their starting point, rather than a pre-established legal order, the basic proposition that states were essentially independent, sovereign, and thus free. From that premise they constructed a quasi-empirical approach to elucidating the law of nations by focusing on state behaviour. The law was whatever states willed it to be through their conduct. International law was therefore treated by classicists as a type of rudimentary behavioural science largely devoid of *a priori* claims of right or wrong, congruence or dissonance with the universe's intrinsic legal or moral order.

This is not to say that classical writers uniformly rejected natural law theory in its entirety. Many, and particularly early classical writers — the most pre-eminent and widely cited of whom was Emer de Vattel, a Swiss lawyer[22] — accepted that natural law existed but simply

---

22   E. de Vattel (1714–1767), *The Principles of Natural Law as Applied to the Conduct and to the Affairs of Nations and of Sovereigns*, 1758, trans. by C.G. Fenwick,

held that it was so abstract, unascertainable, or unenforceable as to be of no assistance in explaining, much less constraining, the relations of states. Its only practical significance was as a foundation upon which to erect a distinctly positivist legal edifice. In particular, the basic propositions that all states are equal, independent, and sovereign, or that their primary duties are to their own self-preservation and self-interest, were said to flow from the essential nature of the state and were, in that sense, natural law precepts. Everything after that, however, could only be explained or understood in terms of how such sovereign states *chose* to pursue their essential liberty or self-interest.

Thus, while the rise of classicism is rightly associated with the concomitant rise in positivism in both domestic and international political and legal theory,[23] it is also the case that not all natural law theory was rejected outright. It is true that the classicists' affinity for empirical studies of state practice and custom was essentially positivist in that it ascribed law-creating significance to such practice. In essence, such an approach was consistent with an extreme form of positivism, which asserted that law simply consisted of whatever was articulated as such or consented to by its subjects. However, natural law retained a vestigial role. It served as an explanation, whether expressly acknowledged by later classicists or not, for certain basic maxims — for example, the essential sovereignty and liberty of each state, or each state's duty of self-preservation and promotion — upon which positive law was to be constructed.

This period of international legal scholarship culminated, in the nineteenth and early twentieth centuries, in a heavily positivist conception of the source of binding obligation in international law. Virtually all of the numerous textbooks and treatises of the period started with the axiomatic proposition[24] that states, the sole subjects of international law, were also its sole authors. States were *a priori* free, and therefore only bound by law to which they had consented. Express consent was clearly preferred, but most scholars admitted that a state could be taken to have tacitly consented to certain norms by its behaviour and per-

---

Classics of International Law Series No. 4, ed. by J.B. Scott (Washington: Carnegie Institution, 1916).

23   For example, T. Hobbes, *Leviathan*, 1651, ed. by J.C.A. Gaskin (Oxford: Oxford University Press, 1996); J. Bentham, *Principles of International Law: Selections*, 1789, ed. by C.I.C. de Saint-Pierre (New York: Garland, 1974). See also G.W. Keeton & G. Schwarzenberger, *Jeremy Bentham and the Law: A Symposium* (London: Stevens, 1948; Westport: Greenwood Press, 1970).

24   By this time, the obvious natural law foundations for such an axiomatic starting point were virtually ignored by many or most authors.

haps even its acquiescence in norms promoted by other states. In short, *the* source of binding obligation in international law was considered to be, almost tautologically, the consent of its own subjects. The judicial *locus classicus* of this conception of the source of binding obligation in international law is the following dictum from the 1927 judgment of the Permanent Court of International Justice (predecessor to today's International Court of Justice) in *The SS Lotus* case:

> The rules of law binding upon States ... emanate from their own free will as expressed in conventions or by usages generally accepted as expressing principles of law.... Restrictions upon the independence of States cannot therefore be presumed.[25]

This view, which still holds considerable sway today, we will refer to as the "theory of consent."

Not all authors of the time were impressed with these developments. One nineteenth century legal philosopher, Austin, famously attacked the theory of consent as no basis for any system of law at all. Austin's view was based on an entirely different positivist conception of law: that true law could not exist in the absence of a sovereign who could both make and enforce it. As the international system and the theory of consent lacked any such hierarchical structure, Austin concluded it was not a legal but at best a "moral" or political system.[26] Most mainstream writers of the day rejected this characterization on at least two bases. First, it was said to follow from too narrow a premise as to potential law-making processes and conflicted to some degree with democratic theories then in vogue. Second, it accorded no significance to the fact that states themselves clearly subscribed to the "horizontal" legal system described by the theory of consent.[27]

Such was the theory's appeal to states that it is still the most prevalent theory advanced by them, and indeed by some scholars,[28] to ex-

---

25 *The Case of the SS Lotus (France v. Turkey)* (1927), P.C.I.J. (Ser. A) No. 10 at 18.

26 J. Austin, *The Province of Jurisprudence Determined, 1861–63*, 2d ed. (New York: Burt Franklin, 1970).

27 See, for example, Sir F. Pollock, *The League of Nations* (London: Stevens, 1920).

28 See, for example, H. Kelsen, *Pure Theory of Law*, trans. by M. Knight (Berkeley: University of California Press, 1967) at 323; H.L.A. Hart, *The Concept of Law*, 2d ed. (Oxford: Oxford University Press, 1994). Note that both Kelsen and Hart nevertheless characterized international law as a somewhat primitve form of law for reasons similar to those articulated by Austin for denying its existence as law at all—for example, its lack of centralized legislative or enforcement apparatus. See, for example, H. Kelsen, *General Theory of Law and State*, trans. by A. Wedberg (New York: Russell & Russell, 1973) at 328*ff*.; Hart, *The Concept of Law, ibid.* at 228–31.

plain the nature and underlying source of international law in the modern period.[29] This we will see when examining the most commonly accepted formal sources of international law below.[30]

Nevertheless, such an extreme theory of the underlying source of international legal obligation suffered from serious internal and external weaknesses. Internally, the theory was not whole. The theory of consent failed to explain *why* states would be bound by constraints to which they had consented. If a state's legal obligations were truly dependent upon its consent, why could it not at some future point simply withdraw its consent and thus change the content of its obligations at will? Answers to questions of this type, if given at all, were either question-begging or vague. For example, some positivists relied on Hegel's theory that a true sovereign had the ability to limit its own sovereignty but that only such limitations were valid. Thus a state could irrevocably fetter its freedom by consenting at one point in time to abide thenceforth by some undertaking or rule of international law.[31] This of course is not an answer to the question posed above at all, but merely a restatement of the axiom that prompts it. It simply repeats that states can be and therefore are bound by their consent. It also smacks of natural law, as it relies on a conception of the true, inherent, or "natural" meaning of sovereignty (namely, that it encompasses the power of auto-limitation). Others answered that it was in a state's self-interest to treat undertakings as binding so that it in turn could rely on other states' undertakings. This also is not a satisfactory explanation for why states *must* be bound by their undertakings; it is merely a factor to be weighed by a state in assessing its own self-interest.

The "external" flaws in the pure theory of consent were made evident in the types of state behaviour and interaction it promoted. In essence, the assumption of certain powerful entitlements of states (sovereignty, liberty, the pursuit of self-interest) and the reduction of international law to the status of a mere reflection of their will came close to a declaration of anarchy. While the *idea* of law was, significantly, not abandoned, its normative force was so evacuated of substantive content as to make it effectively incapable of constraining or prescribing international conduct. The results were ultimately catastrophic, as perhaps most clearly illustrated by the outrages of the First and Second World Wars.

---

29   See M. Koskenniemi, *From Apology to Utopia: The Structure of International Legal Argument* (Helsinki: Finnish Lawyers Publishing, 1989) at 106–9.

30   See Section C, below in this chapter.

31   See, generally, S. Avineri, *Hegel's Theory of the Modern State* (London: Cambridge University Press, 1972).

3) Modern International Legal Scholarship

International legal scholarship following the First World War was almost unanimously critical of the positivist excess that had preceded it. The unconditional theory of consent and its near-anarchic premises were generally condemned as having promoted a condition of virtual or practical lawlessness in international relations.[32] Such an unbridled form of positivism had appointed states as lawmakers, judges, and executioners in their own cause, and the result had been entirely subjective determinations of legality in their own, disastrously conflicting interests.

There thus emerged in the twentieth century an uneasy consensus among most theorists that if international law was to be considered relevant and binding, it would have to be based on something more normative than the simple will of states.[33] At the same time, a simple return to pure natural law theories, which were equally subject to charges of subjectivism or irrelevance, was unthinkable.

Twentieth and twenty-first century international legal scholarship is therefore typified by a series of attempts to combine elements of both schools of thought. Modern scholars tend to acknowledge the legal significance of both the practices and preferences of states, together with some constraining principles of justice (or at least law) that are somehow beyond the reach of states. They seek, in other words, to rely on elements of both the positivist and natural law schools of thought in order to neutralize the shortcomings and dangers of each.

They tend not to do so in a consistent manner, however. Positivist positions are advanced to address particular, mostly uncontroversial, matters while natural law theories are resorted to in more difficult cases, for example, where the law is not yet clear or where positivist arguments lead to untenable results (such as states' freedom to perpetrate human rights abuses against their own nationals). This pick-and-choose, neither-here-nor-there approach has been aptly dubbed "eclecticism" by some authors.[34]

The work of Brierly is a good illustration of an attempt to combine positivist and natural law elements into a complex explanation of international law's relevance and binding nature. Brierly accepts that both theories have a role to play. Natural law is useful and retained to the

---

32   See, for example, G. Schwarzenberger, *The Frontiers of International Law* (London: Stevens, 1962).

33   For example, J.L. Brierly, *The Law of Nations*, 6th ed. by H. Waldock (Oxford: Clarendon Press, 1963) at 49–56; H. Lauterpacht, *The Function of Law in the International Community* (Hamden: Archon Books, 1966) at 3–4.

34   See, for example, Koskenniemi, above note 29.

extent that it can suggest the purpose or general direction of the law, which can be particularly relevant where positive law is unavailable or undeveloped. Positive law will, on the other hand, prevail where it is well-developed and ascertainable. As to the ultimate question of why any of it, natural or positive, should be considered binding, Brierly opines that the question is beyond the reach of legal theory and is properly the domain of philosophy. He nevertheless states that:

> The ultimate explanation of the binding force of all law is that man, whether he is a single individual or whether he is associated with other men in a state, is constrained, in so far as he is a reasonable being, to believe that order and not chaos is the governing principle of the world in which he has to live.[35]

In some sense this is a resort to natural law, in that it suggests that humanity is trapped by its own inherent (and thus immutable) need for order. It is also somewhat positivist in that it is humanity's *belief* in the inescapability of such a need which, practically speaking, infuses law with its binding character.[36] The law is not externally imposed but *self*-imposed by humanity based on its *self*-perceived needs or interests.

It is important to note that while the eclectic approach to the basis of binding obligation in international law can be said to be a general characteristic of twentieth and twenty-first century scholarship, such scholarship has itself assumed an eclectic array of variants. These range from the last holdouts of overt positivism[37] to firm proponents of natural law as the basis of at least some distinctly twentieth century types of international law, most notably international human rights law.[38]

Beyond these two poles, however, international legal scholarship has in the twentieth and twenty-first centuries followed paths as diverse as those taken by its domestic counterparts. For example, some scholars, variously referred to as "realists" or "sceptics," have focused on power politics to marginalize the significance and particularly the binding force of most international law. While they do not reject the concept or possibility of binding international law outright, they claim to take the "realistic" view that, when considered in conjunction with political, economic, and social factors, international law is only rel-

---

35   Brierly, above note 33 at 56.
36   See Koskenniemi, above note 29 at 141.
37   See, for example, Kelsen, *Pure Theory of Law*, above note 28; Hart, above note 28.
38   See, for example, H. Lauterpacht, *International Law and Human Rights* (1950; repr. New York: Garland, 1973); J. Rawls, *A Theory of Justice*, rev. ed. (Cambridge, MA: Belknap Press, 1999); A. D'Amato, "Is International Law Part of Natural Law?" (1989) 9 Vera Lex 8.

evant in a relatively narrow set of areas. Even then it is only more or less binding depending on a host of contextual factors such as political, economic, or military power.[39]

A related (and much less sceptical) school posits that international law is not so much a set of rules as it is a comprehensive process of authoritative decision-making.[40] This school of thought, sometimes called "social process theory" or "behaviouralism," is extremely inclusive in that it considers policy, social values, institutional procedures, political authority, effectiveness, the identity of decision-makers, and so on in describing decision-making processes. However, unlike the sceptics, social process theorists do not use this wide array of phenomena to marginalize the role or significance of international law. Rather, all of these phenomena and the various decision-making processes to which they contribute are considered to be part of the substance of the law itself. In other words, social process theorists tend to minimize the distinction between law and policy. On this view, the question of binding force and its source is no longer particularly relevant; international law is simply present in social process itself. The generality of such a theory has raised questions as to its utility, but it reveals an eclectic combination of natural law and positivist approaches by its dual focus on policy and on what international actors do or decide.

Yet another strain of modern international legal scholarship adopts approaches reminiscent of the domestic field of critical legal studies. Critiquing, variously, the ascendancy of liberalism in domestic and international law-making, the indeterminacy of law, and traditional international law's disregard of the interests of the marginalized and dispossessed (including women, children, the poor, developing and formerly colonized states, *et cetera*), this body of work emphasizes the necessarily close nexus between law and society and the need for social justice perspectives in order to redress historical and ongoing inequi-

---

39 See, for example, H. Morgenthau, *Politics among Nations: The Struggle for Power and Peace*, 5th ed. (New York: Knopf, 1978). For an insightful analysis of this school of thought and its intellectual kinship with the realist school of international relations theory, see A-M. Slaughter, "International Law and International Relations Theory: A Dual Agenda" (1993) 87 A.J.I.L. 205.

40 See, for example, M.S. McDougal, ed., *Studies in World Public Order* (New Haven: Yale University Press, 1960); M.S. McDougal, H. Lasswell, & W.M. Reisman, "Theories About International Law: Prologue to a Configurative Jurisprudence" (1968) 8 Va. J.I.L. 188; M.S. McDougal & W.M. Reisman, *International Law in Contemporary Perspective: The Public Order of the World Community* (Mineola, NY: Foundation Press, 1981); R. Falk, *The Status of Law in International Society* (Princeton: Princeton University Press, 1970).

ties. Of course, the call for "justice" as something distinct from existing, positive law calls to mind concepts of natural rights and law.[41]

These are merely illustrative of the wide array of schools of thought that have flourished in the twentieth and twenty-first centuries to explain the fundamental relevance and binding force of international law, a full review of which would occupy (at least) the remainder of this book.

The eclectic approach has not been limited, however, to international legal scholars and theorists. Most twenty-first century international lawyers and judges are eclectics in that they borrow, for various purposes and in different contexts, elements of both consensual and natural law theories in constructing or evaluating international legal arguments. Indeed, as we shall see, the modern understanding of the sources of international law is itself complex, if nevertheless betraying a penchant for consent-based law-making mechanisms and thus, arguably, positivism.

Therefore, the most prevalent views as to the sources and binding force of international law exist in a state of tension. They are located somewhere between the theory of consent and the idea that there may be, after all, some aspect of the law that is not wholly dependent upon the whim of states. This, the most fundamental unresolved tension in modern international law, will be further illustrated in the discussion of sources throughout this book.

---

41   Examples of international legal scholarship that could be said to fall into the "critical legal studies" category include P. Allot, *Eunomia: New Order for a New World* (Oxford: Oxford University Press, 1990); P. Allot, *The Health of Nations: Society and Law Beyond the State* (Cambridge: Cambridge University Press, 2002); H. Charlesworth & C.M. Chinkin, *The Boundaries of International Law: A Feminist Analysis* (Manchester: Manchester University Press, 2000); T.M. Franck, *The Empowered Self: Law and Society in the Age of Individualism* (Oxford: Oxford University Press, 1999); D. Kennedy, *International Legal Structure* (Baden-Baden: Nomos Verlagsgesellschaft, 1987); B. Kingsbury, "Sovereignty and Inequality" (1998) 9 E.J.I.L. 599; K. Knop, *Diversity and Self-Determination in International Law* (Cambridge: Cambridge University Press, 2002); K. Knop, ed., *Gender and Human Rights* (Oxford: Oxford University Press, 2004); S.R. Marks, *The Riddle of All Constitutions: International Law, Democracy and the Critique of Ideology* (Oxford: Oxford University Press, 2000).

C. ARTICLE 38(1) OF THE *STATUTE OF THE INTERNATIONAL COURT OF JUSTICE*

1) Introduction

In a legal system clearly dominated by the sovereign authority of states, which are its principal subjects, the final word on the true sources of international law—that is, on the sources of rules to which states are willing to subject their sovereignty—naturally rests with states themselves.

By far the most widely-acknowledged statement of such sources is that crafted by states in 1945 when establishing the International Court of Justice, the principal judicial organ of the United Nations. The *Statute of the International Court of Justice*[42] sets out, in Article 38(1), the sources of law the Court is required to apply in resolving disputes submitted to it:

Article 38

1. The Court, whose function is to decide in accordance with international law such disputes as are submitted to it, shall apply:
    a. international conventions, whether general or particular, establishing rules *expressly recognized* by the contesting states;
    b. international custom, as evidence of a general practice *accepted* as law;
    c. the general principles of law *recognized* by civilized nations;
    d. subject to the provisions of Article 59, judicial decisions and the teachings of the most highly qualified publicists of the various nations, as subsidiary means for the determination of rules of law.

[Emphasis added]

While the language used in this provision is awkward and somewhat obscure, it is generally taken not only as a statement of the sources of law the Court is to apply, but also as an accurate description of the sources of international law generally.[43] This is evidenced by the fact that virtually all discussions of the sources of international law, whether by states, courts, or commentators, take as their starting point Article 38(1) of the *ICJ Statute*.

---

42 *ICJ Statute*, above note 8. The *ICJ Statute* forms "an integral part" of the *UN Charter*: *UN Charter*, above note 2, Article 92. All parties to the *UN Charter* are *ipso facto* parties to the *ICJ Statute*: *UN Charter*, ibid., Article 93(1).

43 Although, being simply a provision in a treaty, it is, strictly speaking, only truly binding on parties to the *Statute*.

There is an obvious distinction drawn between the sources listed in paragraphs (a), (b), and (c) (treaties, customary international law, and general principles of law) on the one hand, and those referred to in paragraph (d) (judgments, scholarly writings)[44] on the other. In particular, the words "as subsidiary means for the determination of rules of law" in paragraph (d) imply that judgments and the writings of scholars are not true sources of international law in themselves, but are, rather, merely means of determining the law's content. In other words, they are not law-creating sources, but merely law-finding sources. This distinction is frequently referred to as the difference between "formal" (law-creating) sources and "material" or "evidentiary" (law-finding) sources, and is borrowed from a similar distinction sometimes made in domestic law.

It should be noted, however, that applying such a distinction in international law remains controversial. In the absence of a constitutionally institutionalized international law-maker, it could be argued that *all* sources enumerated in Article 38(1) are material sources that are, at best, mere indicia of some true, underlying source of binding legal obligation in international relations.[45]

This argument is closely allied to criticisms of the apparent rigidity of the compartmentalization of sources in Article 38(1) and the possibility that this may, again, mask the underlying question of the ultimate source of binding obligation in international law. In other words, the structure of Article 38(1) might suggest that there is a finite and well-defined set of formal international legal sources, each having particular attributes and resulting from discrete processes, when in fact no such certainty exists. As to what *the* underlying source of binding obligation in international law might be, resort must be had to the theoretical models discussed above. Some would say, however, that the language used in paragraphs 38(1)(a) to (c) strongly supports the positivist theory of consent as the true source of binding obligation in international law, as that language refers ultimately to the consent of states in one form or another ("expressly recognized," "accepted," "recognized").[46]

Notwithstanding its convenience as a concise substitute for a clear "constitutional" definition of legal sources, Article 38(1) has also at-

---

44   The word "publicists" in the *ICJ Statute*, ibid., Article 38(1)(d), is an awkward reference to scholarly experts in international law rather than to press or publicity agents.

45   See, for example, I. Brownlie, *Principles of Public International Law*, 6th ed. (Oxford: Oxford University Press, 2003) at 1–2.

46   See emphasized language in Article 38(1), quoted above in text accompanying note 42. See also Brownlie, *ibid.* at 1.

tracted criticism on a number of other bases. It remains a point of contention, for example, as to whether the enumeration of sources in Article 38(1) is or was intended to be an exhaustive statement of all possible sources of international law. As we shall see below, the International Court of Justice itself has had occasion to refer to sources of binding legal obligation in international law that are not expressly enumerated in Article 38(1).[47] However, the language used in Article 38(1), particularly paragraphs (b) and (c), may be so broad as to be capable, on some readings, of encompassing all such other sources, making it a truly comprehensive restatement of the sources of international law.[48]

Another inadequacy of Article 38(1) is that it does not clearly specify the relationship, if any, between the various sources it enumerates.[49] Is there any significance to the order in which the various sources appear in the enumeration? Is the order suggestive of a "hierarchy" in the listed sources? Would certain sources prevail over others in the event of a conflict between their substantive content? For example, it is generally accepted in the Canadian legal system that a rule of the common law yields to inconsistent (but constitutionally sound) legislation. Are there similar rules applicable to the various sources of international law listed in Article 38(1)?

While there is evidence that early drafts of Article 38(1) included wording suggestive of such a hierarchy, this hardly answers the foregoing questions. The absence of such wording in the final version of Article 38(1) could suggest that the existence of such a hierarchy was rejected by the drafters or, conversely, that it was self-evident from the nature of the sources themselves and thus required no textual expression. This has not prevented some eminent international legal scholars, however, from concluding that Article 38 does indeed reveal a hierarchical order amongst the sources it catalogues, although even they caution that generalizations in this area can be misleading.[50]

In reality, the absence of any clear statement of the hierarchy of sources in Article 38(1) is probably best viewed as a testament to the uncertainty, or at least complexity, of the issue. For example, and as

---

47 See Section D, below in this chapter.

48 See M.N. Shaw, *International Law*, 5th ed. (Cambridge: Cambridge University Press, 2003) at 67.

49 Other than stating that the sources identified in paragraph (d) are "subsidiary means" for identifying the law. See above text accompanying note 44 for a discussion of the significance of this subordination.

50 See Brownlie, above note 45 at 5. Brownlie attaches particular significance to the fact that an early draft of Article 38 included the word "successively."

we shall see,[51] it is generally accepted that states may alter their mutual obligations flowing from customary international law by concluding a treaty having such effect. This would seem to indicate that customary rules are subordinate to treaty-based rules. However, this is true only as between parties to the treaty. The customary obligations remain, even for parties to the treaty, in their relations with non-parties to the treaty. Moreover, it is generally accepted that certain types of customary rules (such as *jus cogens* norms)[52] cannot be so displaced by treaty.[53]

Even more fundamentally, the very existence and enforceability of treaties (including those purporting to change customary international legal obligations as between treaty parties) rely ultimately for their effectiveness on a rule of customary international law, to the effect that all treaties must be performed by parties to them in good faith.[54] It could also be argued that the general rule that a customary norm can be displaced by treaty is itself a customary rule. Conversely, it is also generally accepted that consistent treaty practice can have an impact on the content of customary international law.[55] Yet, customary and treaty norms may retain a separate and parallel existence, even if such norms are identical in substantive content.[56] And so on. Such complex interactions of legal sources are reminiscent of modern international legal theory's eclecticism, that is, its uncertainty as to the true root—state consent, natural justice, or something else—of its binding force. The law of sources has only complex answers as to when (or why) express state consent (usually in the form of treaties) will or will not oust law formed through other processes (such as customary international law).

In short, the issue of how the various sources of international law interact with one another is either far too complex or unresolved to be codified in any concise manner in Article 38(1). The *ICJ Statute*'s silence

---

51   See Chapter 5, Section E.
52   A *jus cogens* norm is a "peremptory" or "non-derogable" rule of international law that is so fundamental to the international legal order that it cannot be set aside or suspended, even by the express consent of states. See further Chapter 4, Section I(2)(g) and Chapter 5, Section E(1).
53   Articles 53 and 64, *Vienna Convention on the Law of Treaties*, 23 May 1969, 1155 U.N.T.S. 331 (entered into force 27 January 1980) [*Vienna Convention*].
54   See further Chapter 4, Section G(1).
55   See, for example, *North Sea Continental Shelf Cases (Federal Republic of Germany v. Denmark; Federal Republic of Germany v. The Netherlands)*, [1969] I.C.J. Rep. 3 at paras. 61–73 [*North Sea Continental Shelf Cases*]; *Case Concerning Military and Paramilitary Activities in and against Nicaragua (Nicaragua v. United States of America)*, [1986] I.C.J. Rep. 14 at para. 181 [*Nicaragua*].
56   *North Sea Continental Shelf Cases*, *ibid.* at paras. 63 and 71; *Nicaragua*, *ibid.* at paras. 175–79.

on this point is therefore probably best viewed as an acknowledgment that the issue is neither simple nor entirely settled, and can be taken as an invitation to the Court, states, and scholars to continue to explore and define the precise nature of such relationships.

More generally, however, the practice of states, the reasoning of the International Court of Justice and other courts and tribunals, as well as the opinions of scholars, all clearly emphasize the central importance of treaties and custom (paragraphs 38(1)(a) and (b)) as the two principal sources of international law. Virtually all substantive international legal arguments are formulated in terms of these two sources, whatever their particular relationship to one another in a specific case. By contrast, "general principles" play only a secondary, but still significant role in shaping the content of international law. As mere "material" sources, judgments and scholarly writings as referred to in paragraph 38(1)(d) also play a secondary, if important, role. Finally, certain other sources not expressly referred to in Article 38(1) can have a fundamental impact on states' legal positions in ways that will be considered below.

2) Treaties: Article 38(1)(a)

Article 38(1)(a) refers to "international conventions, whether general or particular." The intent is to capture treaties (express agreements between states, or certain other subjects of international law, setting out their mutual legal rights and obligations) as a source of international law. The reference to "general or particular" treaties indicates that there is no distinction, in terms of binding force, between multilateral and bilateral treaties, or between treaties that establish general rules of law and treaties that provide for highly specific, contract-like performance obligations as between the parties.

Treaties are considered one of the two principal sources of international law and play a fundamental and ever-increasing role in international affairs. The twentieth century in particular witnessed explosive growth in the number of multilateral codification and law-making treaties, making them states' instruments of choice in developing or clarifying international law. The advantages offered by treaties as law-making devices include the speed and clarity with which the law may be created or advanced, as well as their influential effect on other international law-making processes such as customary international law. Their principal disadvantages include the fact that they bind only parties to them, and that they draw their binding force merely from the consent of parties to be bound rather than from actual performance or on-the-ground commitment to their principles.

Given their centrality in modern international law, treaties and the rules governing their formation, binding effects, and termination will be dealt with at greater length in the next chapter.

3) Customary International Law: Article 38(1)(b)

Article 38(1)(b) uses awkward language to describe customary international law, the other of the two major sources of international law. Unlike treaties, which depend for their binding force upon states' agreement (usually expressed through a formalized procedure), customary international law is said to arise simply from that sustained conduct of states which they themselves believe (for whatever reason) to be legally required. It is thus an "inductive" source of law, rooted in what states actually *do* and *believe* rather than what they expressly *agree* to do.

While its importance as a source of law predates the rise in multilateral treaty-making which characterized the mid- to late-twentieth century development of international law, it remains one of the most potent sources of international law today. This is due to its single most important feature: customary international law, unlike treaties, is with very few and narrow exceptions *universally* binding. It is thus a common basis for international legal relations among all states. Its principal weakness as a source of law, on the other hand, is that it is by definition *conservative*—being a source of law derived from patterns of state conduct, it is ill adapted to the need for rapid change in the law. Being *inductive*, moreover, it does not always produce precise or finely tuned rules to govern intricate situations, and its content at any point in time can be the subject of profound disagreement between states, lawyers, judges, and scholars.

Thus, it can be seen that customary international law and treaties have a complementary role to play as sources of international law, each largely offsetting the shortcomings of the other. Treaties articulate relatively clear and precise obligations and can be used to catalyze fundamental legal change over a short period of time. Customary international law, on the other hand, provides the universal legal substratum upon which the whole of the international legal system (including the law of treaties) rests, and comprises rules and principles by which all states are bound whether or not they expressly agree to them.

Given its fundamental importance to the international legal order, customary international law and its interaction with treaties will be the subject of Chapter 5 below.

4) General Principles of Law: Article 38(1)(c)

This is probably the least understood or agreed-upon source listed in Article 38(1) of the *ICJ Statute*. It has been said that there was no clear consensus even among the drafters of the *Statute* as to the provision's intent.[57] Questions raised about its meaning have included whether the reference to "general principles" may mean something other than mere "principles"; whether "principles" of law mean something other than "rules" of law; and whether "law" refers to international or domestic law.

The latter question is probably the most readily resolved. Most commentators today agree that the intent is to direct attention to domestic systems of law for inspiration in formulating international analogues, as necessary. Some socialist states and authors in the Soviet era, by contrast, insisted that the intended reference was to general principles of *international* law.[58] On that view, a general principle of law within the meaning of Article 38(1)(c) would only exist if it reflected generalized treaty or customary practice. This interpretation of course places the emphasis on the words "generally accepted by ... nations" and clearly seeks to bring Article 38(1)(c) closer to consent-based theories of international law in order to preserve the traditional role of sovereign states as gatekeepers in the international law-creating process. If such an interpretation were correct, however, it would be difficult to see the significance of naming this as an additional source in Article 38(1). The existence of a general principle of law would always require the prior existence of an international legal norm in either treaty or customary form (or both), thus rendering Article 38(1)(c) redundant. As a result, the predominant view is that "general principles of law" means general principles of *domestic* law rather than general principles of international law.[59]

---

57   Brownlie, above note 45 at 16. For further discussion of general principles, see D. Anzilotti, *Corso di diretto internazionale*, 3d ed. (Rome: Athenaeum, 1928) at 106–7; H. Lauterpacht, *Private Law Sources and Analogies of International Law* (London: Longmans, 1927); A.D. McNair, "The General Principles of Law Recognised by Civilized Nations" (1957) 33 B.Y.I.L. 1; G. Morelli, "Cours général de droit international public" (1956-I) 89 Rec. des Cours 437 at 470–71; Kelsen, above note 28 at 539–40; P. Guggenheim, *Traité de droit international public* (Genève: Librairie de l'Université, Georg et Cie, 1967) at 292; C. Rousseau, *Droit international public*, vol. 1 (Paris: Editions Sirey, 1970) at 371; B. Vitanyi, "Les Positions doctrinales concernant le sens de la notion de 'principes généraux de droit reconnus par les nations civilisées'" (1982) 86 R.G. D.I.P. 48.

58   See, for example, G.I. Tunkin, *Theory of International Law*, trans. by W.E. Butler (Cambridge: Harvard University Press, 1974) at 195.

59   See, for example, Brownlie, above note 45 at 16; Shaw, above note 48 at 94.

Perhaps the most striking (but also, as it turns out, the least significant) feature of paragraph 38(1)(c) is its atavistic reference to "civilized nations." Was this meant to suggest that only general principles of law recognized by a certain group of so-called "civilized nations" would be considered a source of international law? This would be a surprising intention, given that the United Nations, and hence the Court as its "principal judicial organ," are "based on the principle of the sovereign equality of all of its Members."[60] It would also be a significant derogation from the principle of consent, as it would suggest that at least some of the content of international law could be dictated by "civilized nations" on behalf of, presumably, "uncivilized" ones. This is to say nothing of the obvious difficulties that would be posed in seeking to distinguish the civilized from the uncivilized, or even in identifying factors relevant to such a distinction.

In fact, little if any exclusionary significance is generally attached to the phrase. One benign but strained interpretation of the phrase relies on a comparison with the language found in Article 9 of the *ICJ Statute*, which deals with factors to be considered by the General Assembly and Security Council when electing members of the Court:

Article 9

At every election, the electors shall bear in mind not only that the persons to be elected should individually possess the qualifications required, but also that in the body as a whole the representation of *the main forms of civilization and of the principal legal systems of the world* should be assured. [Emphasis added]

Taking inspiration from this language, it has been suggested that perhaps paragraph 38(1)(c) intends to refer to general principles of law present in all of the principal legal systems, or main forms of civilization, of the world.[61] This would of course transform a superficially exclusionary formulation into a powerfully inclusive one. However, such a dramatic shift in emphasis would be hard to justify on the basis of the simple reference to "civilized nations" in paragraph 38(1)(c). Such a strained interpretation would also be redundant given that the word "generally" in paragraph 38(1)(c) is widely interpreted as achieving the same effect, as we shall see.

A more probable explanation of this odd phrase is that it was simply copied in 1945 (as was most of Article 38(1)) from the *Statute of the*

---

60   *ICJ Statute*, above note 8, Article 1; *UN Charter*, above note 2, Article 2(1).
61   G. Schwarzenberger, *International Law*, 3d ed., vol. 1 (London: Stevens, 1957) at 44.

Permanent Court of International Justice,[62] the ICJ's immediate predecessor, which in turn was based on the same formulation appearing in a number of nineteenth century international arbitral clauses.[63] In other words, the reference to "civilized nations" is simply an anachronistic turn of phrase rooted in earlier but now obsolete legal distinctions between civilized and uncivilized states.[64] It is unlikely that it has any formal, juridical significance today.[65]

The remaining questions about paragraph 38(1)(c) have no definitive answers. In part, this is because international tribunals, and the International Court of Justice in particular, have rarely sought to define or explain the provision in any detail. While the International Court of Justice has frequently relied on general principles of law in the course of its judicial reasoning, the Court rarely makes this process explicit.[66]

The most frequently quoted exception to this is found in the Separate Opinion of Judge McNair in the *International Status of South-West Africa* case,[67] in which the Court was asked by the UN General Assembly to provide an advisory opinion on the international legal status of South-West Africa (now Namibia). South-West Africa had been in Germany's possession prior to and during the First World War, but was relinquished to the Allied Powers as part of the peace settlement that ended that war. The Allies, in keeping with the League of Nations arrangement that had been established after the war, entrusted the governance of a number of such relinquished, non-self-governing territories, including South-West Africa, to designated states under what was called the "mandates system." The essential idea behind the mandates system was that the administration of territories inhabited by peoples deemed incapable of governing themselves would be entrusted to more "advanced" states. However, the non-self-governing territories were not

---

62   See *Statute of the Permanent Court of International Justice*, 16 December 1920, as am. 14 September 1929, reprinted in (1930) 16 Trans. Grotius Soc. 131, Article 38. Also available online: http://fletcher.tufts.edu/multi/texts/historical/PCIJ-STATUTE.txt.

63   Brownlie, above note 45 at 15–16.

64   For an overview of this historical distinction and the role it played in the formulation of rules of international law, see the Separate Opinion of Judge Ammoun in *North Sea Continental Shelf Cases*, above note 55 at 132–35.

65   *Ibid.*

66   See, for example, *Chorzów Factory Case (Germany v. Poland)* (1928), P.C.I.J. (Ser. A), No. 17 at 29; *Case Concerning the Temple at Preah Vihear (Cambodia v. Thailand)*, [1962] I.C.J. Rep. 6 at 26; *Case Concerning Delimitation of the Maritime Boundary in the Gulf of Maine Area (Canada v. United States of America)*, [1984] I.C.J. Rep. 246 [*Gulf of Maine*] at paras. 129–48.

67   *International Status of South-West Africa, Advisory Opinion*, [1950] I.C.J. Rep. 128.

to be annexed, and the "mandatory" states were charged with "a sacred trust of civilization" to seek only the well-being and development of such territories.

In the case of South-West Africa, the appointed mandatory was the Union of South Africa, then part of the British Empire. Its mandate was subject to supervision by the Council of the League of Nations to ensure that the obligations of the mandate were fulfilled. The essential issue in the case, therefore, was the effect of the dissolution of the League of Nations on South-West Africa's status and on South Africa's role as mandatory. South Africa contended that its mandate had been conferred upon it by the League in a manner reminiscent of private contract law. As the League (one of the "contracting parties") no longer existed, the mandate itself—along with the legal restrictions it imposed on South Africa—must also have ceased to exist. Thus, the thrust of the South African argument was that it was free to deal with South-West Africa as it saw fit.

While the judgment of the Court rejected these arguments and held that the mandate had survived the dissolution of the League, only Judge McNair in his separate opinion referred explicitly to "general principles of law" in resolving the issue. After finding the available evidence as to the purpose of the mandates system inconclusive, he stated:

> What is the duty of an international tribunal when confronted with a new legal institution the object and terminology of which are reminiscent of the rules and institutions of private law? To what extent is it useful or necessary to examine what may at first sight appear to be relevant analogies in private law systems and draw help and inspiration from them? International law has recruited and continues to recruit many of its rules and institutions from private systems of law. Article 38(1)(c) of the *Statute* of the Court bears witness that this process is still active. ... The way in which international law borrows from this source is not by means of importing private law institutions "lock, stock and barrel," ready-made and fully equipped with a set of rules. ... In my opinion, the true view of the duty of international tribunals in this matter is to regard any features or terminology which are reminiscent of the rules and institutions of private law as an indication of policy and principles rather than as directly importing these rules and institutions.[68]

This at least suggests an answer to one of the questions posed at the beginning of this section. Judge McNair seems to say that Article

---

68   *Ibid.* at 148.

38(1)(c) does not authorize the wholesale transplantation of domestic *rules* of law into international law. Rather, "principles of law" in Article 38(1)(c) mean that the *policies* and *principles* underlying domestic rules of law, but not the rules of law themselves, may be borrowed for "help and inspiration."

The implications of this approach are then illustrated as Judge McNair canvasses domestic legal concepts that appear to be similar to the "mandate." He observes that the use of the term "sacred trust" in particular suggests an affinity between the mandates system and the concept of the "trust" developed in Anglo-American law. Judge McNair also refers to the French "*tutelle.*" He concludes, significantly, that "nearly every legal system possesses some institution whereby the property ... of those who are not *sui juris* ... can be entrusted to some responsible person as a trustee or *tuteur* or *curateur.*"[69] He then derives a number of principles "common to all these [domestic law] institutions" which he then "borrows" to flesh out the meaning of the mandate in international law.

This approach therefore implies that a particular meaning is to be given to the expression "*general* principles of law." These are to be determined by reference to a variety of domestic legal systems. If a sufficient number disclose rules or institutions with broadly similar underlying policies and principles, such underlying policies or principles can be considered sufficiently "general" to formulate a "general principle of law" within the meaning of Article 38(1)(c). This does not, however, require that the Court embark upon an exhaustively empirical comparative analysis of *all* domestic legal systems. Certainly Judge McNair did not do so in his judgment but was content, rather, to observe a general pattern discernible in the *major* legal systems then operative in the world.

This approach is consistent with the most prevalent interpretation of Article 38(1)(c). Most authors conclude that its intent is to permit international tribunals, when faced with certain "gaps" or ambiguities in international treaty or customary law, to fill such *lacunae* by analogy to legal principles generally found in the world's major domestic legal systems.[70] The required threshold of generality remains unclear. However,

---

69   *Ibid.* at 149. This conclusion, reached on the basis of only a limited review of the Anglo-American and French legal systems, may have been justifiable at the time, given that much of the non-European world was still subject to colonial control by states following the common law and civilist legal traditions. A wider-ranging inquiry addressing other major legal systems would likely now be required to support such a conclusion.

70   See, for example, J. Combacau & S. Sur, *Droit international public*, 5th ed. (Paris: Montchrestien, 2001) at 105; Shaw, above note 48 at 94; Brownlie, above note 45 at 16.

Judge McNair's reference to "nearly every legal system" is often taken as an indication that something approaching universality is necessary.

This latter point is of particular importance to a somewhat remarkable feature of Judge McNair's view of this source of international law. A strict adherent of the theory of consent might wonder why an international judge requires "inspiration" informed by domestic "policy and principles" in fulfilling the international judicial role. On a strict view of international law as emanating solely from the consent of states either by way of treaty or customary law, judges should not be seeking to fill any gaps that such law might reveal. It would be for states alone to do so (or not) in the exercise of their sovereign will. If this meant that judges were unable to render judgment in certain cases because international law on point was uncertain or non-existent, so be it.

Judge McNair's use of Article 38(1)(c) is clearly not consistent with such a narrow view and, in this sense, it illustrates, perhaps better than any of the formal sources listed in Article 38(1) of the *ICJ Statute*, that modern international law cannot be explained solely by reference to the theory of consent. However, the recognition that there is some scope for judicial "darning" through Article 38(1)(c) should not be understood as a general licence for international tribunals to create international law. That role is expressly forbidden by Article 59 of the *ICJ Statute*, which strips the Court's judgments of any binding precedential character.

Moreover, the scope for judicial creativity under paragraph 38(1)(c) has generally been interpreted narrowly by states and authors. In addition to the constraint of near-universality suggested in Judge McNair's opinion (which goes some way towards removing conflict with the theory of consent), most authors explain Article 38(1)(c) as playing a purely interstitial role. In particular, they stress that where treaty and customary law are not conducive to the elaboration of very detailed rules, international tribunals must of necessity be given some authority, not to legislate, but to fill in the fine details and thus give effect to the broader intent of states. They observe that the vast majority of "general principles" thus applied by the Court in its reasoning are confined either to detailed questions of procedure or to largely uncontroversial principles of private law.

These rationalizations go some way towards addressing the concerns of positivists. Nevertheless, it remains the case that paragraph 38(1)(c) cannot be wholly explained by reference to the theory of consent, thus illustrating the complex nature of the sources of international law.

5) Judicial Decisions and Scholarly Writings: Article 38(1)(d)

As noted above, the "sources" identified in Article 38(1)(d) were intended and are treated as merely material sources of international law. In other words, judgments and scholarly writings on international law may serve as an aid to understanding or even discovering the content of international law, but they do not in themselves "create" the law. This is implied in the closing words of paragraph 38(1)(d) ("as subsidiary means for the determination of rules of law"), which clearly suggest a purely evidentiary role for such sources.

With respect to judgments in particular, this point is emphasized by the opening words of paragraph 38(1)(d) ("subject to the provisions of Article 59"). Article 59 of the *ICJ Statute* provides as follows:

Article 59

> The decision of the Court has no binding force except between the parties and in respect of that particular case.

This is a clear repudiation of any concept in international law of *stare decisis* or binding precedent, doctrines that are familiar to lawyers schooled in the common law tradition. International tribunals are, quite simply, not common law courts and thus do not make generally applicable law in any formal sense. This is, of course, consistent with the theory that only states, by their consent, create international law.

This does not, however, detract from the enormous normative weight that judgments, particularly those of the International Court of Justice or its predecessor, the Permanent Court of International Justice, carry. The same can also be said of decisions of other international judicial or quasi-judicial bodies, such as the World Trade Organization's Appellate Body, the International Tribunal for the Law of the Sea, the ICTY and ICTR, or the International Criminal Court. The simple fact is that much of the content of international law, again due to the decentralized nature of the international legal system, is either ambiguous or arguable. In the absence of an international legislator, opportunities for authoritative and generally binding restatements of its content are virtually non-existent. Thus, notwithstanding international law's formal rejection of the notion of binding precedent, judgments of the ICJ and other international tribunals[71] tend to fill a very great void and

---

71 Although Article 38(1)(d) refers to "*judicial* decisions," the decisions of arbitral tribunals are also frequently referred to as authoritative restatements of the law. Arbitral tribunals are frequently convened under the auspices of the Permanent

help satisfy states' and international lawyers' need for legal certainty. Not only do they tend to be considered authoritative in their own right; they tend also to influence the behaviour and views of states and may in this way indirectly influence the shape and content of future international law.

For common law lawyers in the Anglo-Canadian tradition, such reliance on judgments as authoritative guides to the content of the law is a natural reflex grounded in their domestic legal training. For others, it is reasonable to assume that the ICJ, a body made up of fifteen of the most eminent international legal minds of the day, representing as they do "the main forms of civilization and ... the principal legal systems of the world,"[72] is likely to be the single most reliable authority on the law. Further, there is generally little reason to expect that the content of general international law will change radically from one case to the next, such that judgments of the ICJ are *de facto* (but never *de jure*) treated as "authority" in international legal arguments of all types.[73]

Occasionally the ICJ and other tribunals have been accused, usually but not exclusively by the losing party before them, of having departed from their role of simply applying existing international law and having, instead, developed (or, even more seriously, made up) the law they apply to cases before them.[74] Indeed, some of the judgments of the ICJ have come as a surprise to some observers, prompting the suggestion that, at least occasionally, the ICJ has acted as a judicial legislator. In fact, whether or not such a judgment has any lasting impact on the content of the law probably depends on how it is received and acted upon by states, thus preserving to some extent the theory of consent. In any event, the ICJ at least has generally been circumspect in its pronouncements and thus appears to command the respect and confidence

---

Court of International Arbitration, established by the *Convention for the Pacific Settlement of International Disputes*, 29 July 1899, reproduced in J.B. Scott, *The Hague Peace Conferences of 1899 and 1907*, vol. II (New York: Garland, 1972) at 80; and the *Convention for the Pacific Settlement of Disputes*, 18 October 1907, reproduced in *ibid.* at 308; also see P. Hamilton *et al.*, eds., *The Permanent Court of Arbitration: International Arbitration and Dispute Resolution: Summaries of Awards, Settlement Agreements and Reports* (The Hague: Kluwer Law International, 1999). Examples of widely cited, authoritative arbitral rulings include *The I'm Alone* (1935), 3 R.I.A.A. 1609; and *Island of Palmas Case (Netherlands v. United States of America)* (1928), 2 R.I.A.A. 829.

72   *ICJ Statute*, above note 8, Article 91.

73   For example, it is common to refer (as this book does) to certain judgments of the ICJ as "authority" for certain rules of international law.

74   See, for example, *Nicaragua*, above note 55.

of the majority of states, as evidenced by its wide membership[75] and, more recently, its extremely active docket.[76]

It should be noted that nothing in Article 38(1)(d) limits consideration, as a material source of law, to *international* judicial decisions. In this way the judgments of domestic courts and tribunals on international legal issues may be relied upon as guides to the content of international law, although given their unrepresentative character they usually carry less weight than do their international counterparts.[77] Further, altogether apart from their role as a material source under Article 38(1)(d), the judgments of domestic tribunals can be considered state practice, one of the constitutive elements of customary international law under Article 38(1)(b).[78]

As for scholarly writings (inelegantly captured in the phrase "the teachings of the most highly qualified publicists of the various nations"), these, too, technically play a purely material role as evidence of the content of the law.[79] However, the same institutional deficiencies that drive states and international lawyers to depend for authority on judgments of courts and tribunals also operate, albeit to a lesser extent, to elevate international legal scholarship to a somewhat exalted status.

---

75 All members of the UN are *ipso facto* parties to the *ICJ Statute*: *UN Charter*, above note 2, Article 93(1). At the time of writing, there were 192 members of the UN and, hence, 192 parties to the *ICJ Statute*. Note that states that are not UN members may nevertheless become parties to the *ICJ Statute*: *UN Charter*, *ibid.*, Article 93(2). This was the case, for example, with Nauru and Switzerland prior to their becoming members of the UN (in 1999 and 2002 respectively).

76 In the decade prior to the date of writing (1998–2007), thirty-eight cases were brought before the ICJ, as compared with ninety-eight in the preceding fifty years (1947–1997). At the time of writing, the ICJ has twelve cases pending on its docket.

77 This of course will vary with the international stature of the domestic court in question. For example, the judgment of the House of Lords in *R. v. Bow Street Stipendiary Magistrate and others, ex parte Pinochet Ugarte (No. 3)*, [1999] 2 All E.R. 97 is considered an important authority on the current status of sovereign immunities in international law as they apply to former heads of state (see Chapter 9), as is the judgment of the Supreme Court of Canada in *Reference Re Secession of Québec*, [1998] 2 S.C.R. 217, on the law of self-determination (see Chapter 2).

78 See further Chapter 5, Section B. This follows from the obvious fact that domestic tribunals are state organs and thus contribute to the overall pattern of that state's conduct or "practice." This does not mean that judgments of domestic tribunals alone can be constitutive of customary international law. However, such decisions contribute to the state's practice (and of course *opinio juris*) which, if consistent with the practice of a sufficient number of other states, can contribute to the process of formation of customary international law.

79 *R. v. Keyn* (1876), 2 Exch. 63 (C.C.R.) at 202–3, Cockburn C.J.

Thus most international legal arguments will be replete with authoritative references to the works of well-known international legal experts.

While the reputations and hence the credibility of such experts vary, at their best they can have a substantial impact on our understanding of the law by giving it coherent expression and, where possible, theoretical grounding. They may even propose and on occasion catalyze important developments in the law. This is not necessarily inconsistent with the theory of consent for, just as in the case of "creative" judgments of courts and tribunals, the practical relevance of any such attempt to influence the content of the law depends ultimately on whether states take it up either by way of treaty or customary practice.

D. OTHER SOURCES

1) Unilateral Declarations

Although not explicitly enumerated as a source of international law in Article 38(1) of the *ICJ Statute*, a state's unilateral declaration or undertaking may give rise to a legal obligation for that state. The essential ingredient for the creation of such an obligation is the state's intention that, in making the declaration or giving the undertaking, it should be bound thereby in accordance with its terms. Such intent, along with the somewhat ill-defined principle of good faith, combine to impose a binding legal obligation upon the state to honour its undertaking. This source of legal obligation is therefore closely tied to the premises underlying the binding effect of treaties, with the obvious difference that in the case of unilateral declarations, there is no reciprocal agreement with other "parties" to the undertaking. In other words, the obligation is created by a state acting alone and does not depend on the consent of others.

The existence of such a source of binding obligation in international law was identified by the International Court of Justice in the *Nuclear Tests*[80] cases between Australia and New Zealand on the one hand, and France on the other. In those cases, France had conducted, over the course of several years, a number of atmospheric nuclear tests in French Polynesia in the South Pacific. The principal firing site used for the tests was the Mururoa atoll, approximately 6,000 kilometres

---

80   *Nuclear Tests (Australia v. France)*, [1974] I.C.J. Rep. 253 [*Nuclear Tests*]; *Nuclear Tests Case (New Zealand v. France)*, [1974] I.C.J. Rep. 457. Subsequent references will be made to the [1974] I.C.J. Rep. 253 judgment.

east of the Australian mainland and 4,600 kilometres from New Zealand. Australia and New Zealand, fearing environmental damage due to radioactive fallout from the testing on their territories, protested and ultimately initiated proceedings against France in the ICJ seeking an end to the tests. France refused to recognize the jurisdiction of the ICJ and failed to participate in either case.

In June of 1973, the ICJ nevertheless ordered, as an interim measure, that France should avoid further testing pending the full hearing of the case. France, however, persisted with two further series of tests in 1973 and 1974. It was during the latter series of tests that the President, the Minister of Defence, and the Minister of Foreign Affairs of France made various declarations that the Court found to be cumulative evidence of France's "intention to cease the conduct of atmospheric nuclear tests following the conclusion of the 1974 series of tests."[81]

The true question in the case, however, was the legal significance of such a publicly stated future intention. On this crucial point the Court held, without citing authority, that:

> It is well recognized that declarations made by way of unilateral acts, concerning legal or factual situations, may have the effect of creating legal obligations.... When it is the intention of the State making the declaration that it should become bound according to its terms, that intention confers on the declaration the character of a legal undertaking, the State being henceforth legally required to follow a course of conduct consistent with the declaration. An undertaking of this kind, if given publicly, and with an intent to be bound, even though not made within the context of international negotiations, is binding. In these circumstances, nothing in the nature of a *quid pro quo* nor any subsequent acceptance of the declaration nor even any reply or reaction from other States, is required for the declaration to take effect....[82]

This somewhat surprising proposition of law, if left unqualified, would indeed be problematic. For example, the sole basis identified for finding a legal obligation is the subjective intention of the declaring state to be bound. This approach is clearly rooted in the positivist tradition of defining all legal obligations in international law solely in terms of the will of states. Further, no explicit reference is made by the Court in this passage to conditions that might attach to the *obligee*, such as reasonableness of expectation of performance, detrimental reliance, or

---

81 *Ibid.* at 266.
82 *Ibid.* at 267.

other such elements that would be required in most systems of domestic law to give binding effect to a so-called "unilateral," bare undertaking. In this sense, this source of legal obligation in international law would be, at least in theory, truly unilateral.

However, if taken to its unqualified extreme, it would also be utterly meaningless. For what would prevent a declaring state from subsequently declaring a diametrically opposite intention? Why would a subsequent declaration not have just as much binding legal force as an earlier one? Would not the latter statement alter the declaring state's legal obligations from that point forward, until such time as a further inconsistent unilateral declaration were made, thus leaving the declaring state free to change the content of its unilateral, self-imposed legal obligations at will? Could such a purely unilateral source of legal obligation truly be considered a source of "obligation" at all?

These questions go to the root of the dilemma of the true source of binding obligation that underlies all formal "sources" of international law. The Court's solution in the *Nuclear Tests* cases is found in a short passage added almost as an afterthought to the foregoing propositions. The Court, somewhat cryptically, stated the following:

> One of the basic principles governing the creation and performance of legal obligations, *whatever their source*, is the principle of good faith. Trust and confidence are inherent in international co-operation, in particular in an age when this co-operation in many fields is becoming increasingly essential. Just as the very rule of *pacta sunt servanda* in the law of treaties is based on good faith, so also is the binding character of an international obligation assumed by unilateral declaration. Thus interested States may take cognizance of unilateral declarations and place confidence in them, and are entitled to require that the obligation thus created be respected.[83] [Emphasis added]

This then is the Court's solution to the problem of perpetually shifting unilateral declarations. "Good faith" and the need for states to rely on one another's publicly stated intentions would appear to constrain a declaring state's ability to reverse unilaterally such intentions. In this there is, after all, some (albeit abstract) element of the "reasonable reliance" theories familiar in domestic law.[84] Thus, states giving unilateral undertakings with intent to be bound are not in fact free to withdraw them at will. One way of looking at this would be to think of a binding unilateral declaration as a sort of "gift" from one state to other states.

---

83   *Ibid.* at 268.
84   Although, apparently, not of *detrimental* reliance.

The gift is the giving state's to give until it is given; once given, however, it is no longer the giving state's to withdraw at will — rather it now belongs to all "interested states."

What remains unclear in the judgment, however, is the rigidity of the constraints imposed by the principle of good faith. Is a state that makes an unconditional binding declaration of intent forever estopped from reversing its intentions through future unilateral declarations (that is, can a state *never* demand the return of a gift, or never give a further gift that has the effect of destroying the first gift)? Or would a period of reasonable notice be required in order to accommodate other states' legitimate interests in relying on the original undertaking (that is, can a state require the return of a gift if it gives other states enough advance warning of its desire to do so)? Can a state avoid the effect of the good faith principle entirely by making all of its declarations expressly subject to any subsequent inconsistent declarations it might make?

The judgments in the *Nuclear Tests* cases also do not address the much more profound questions surrounding the source of the principle of good faith itself. *Why* are unilateral undertakings and the legal obligations they create governed by the "basic principle" of good faith? *How* does good faith become part of a unilaterally declaring state's legal obligations to other states? Is there a presumption that the declarant state, in giving its undertaking, impliedly includes a condition of good faith in its declaration?[85] Is good faith assumed to be "inherent" in international relations? Or is the principle of good faith something that is injected into the declaration by international law "from the outside", as it were? In other words, does good faith find its source *beyond* the intentions (actual, implied, or presumed) of the declarant state?

In short, both the judgments in the *Nuclear Tests* cases and the notion of unilateral declarations as a source of international legal obligation clearly illustrate the inadequacies of either positivist or natural law theories, when taken in isolation, in explaining the underlying source of binding obligation in international law. While clearly the intent of the declaring state is paramount in establishing such an obligation, it is ultimately necessary to have recourse to some external factor — "good faith" — to explain why such sovereign intent can be considered binding even over itself.

Two other aspects of the Court's discussion of unilateral declarations are worth noting. First, the Court observed that the *form* of a state's unilateral declaration is entirely irrelevant to its binding force.

---

85   If so, is such a presumption subject to rebuttal? Or even more fatally, is such a presumed intention itself subject to subsequent withdrawal?

An undertaking may be given orally or in writing, stated expressly, or implied in a state's actions. All that is important is that the state's intention to be bound be clear.[86] Second, the Court noted that, since binding unilateral declarations of intent limit, by their very nature, the freedom of action of the sovereign declaring state, a "restrictive interpretation is called for" in construing the state's words or actions.[87] In other words, the declaring state should normally be entitled to the benefit of any doubt as to its intention to be bound.[88]

In the result the Court found that the statements made by members of the French government, referred to above, amounted to legally binding undertakings that France was bound in international law to respect.[89] That finding effectively put an end to the cases, as Australia and New Zealand had essentially been seeking an order putting a halt to the testing. In the Court's view, France had already imposed that obligation on itself, thus obviating the need for any such order by the Court.[90]

Following nearly a decade of work, the International Law Commission (ILC)[91] has recently concluded a set of "Guiding Principles" on the topic of unilateral declarations which succinctly and fairly faithfully reflect the foregoing considerations. Due to their brevity they are quoted here in full:

Guiding Principles Applicable to Unilateral Declarations of States Capable of Creating Legal Obligations

1. Declarations publicly made and manifesting the will to be bound may have the effect of creating legal obligations. When the conditions for this are met, the binding character of such declarations is based on good faith; States concerned may then take them into consideration and rely on them; such States are entitled to require that such obligations be respected;

2. Any State possesses capacity to undertake legal obligations through unilateral declarations;

---

86 See *Nuclear Tests*, above note 80 at 267–68.

87 *Ibid.* at 267.

88 See also *Case Concerning the Frontier Dispute (Burkina Faso v. Republic of Mali)*, [1986] I.C.J. Rep. 554 at 573–74. In that case, the Court suggested that it would be reluctant to attribute binding legal effect to unilateral declarations in circumstances where the parties to a dispute could, had they intended to undertake legal obligations, readily have concluded a treaty.

89 *Nuclear Tests*, above note 80 at 269–70.

90 *Ibid.* at 271–72.

91 See further Section D(2), below in this chapter.

3. To determine the legal effects of such declarations, it is necessary to take account of their content, of all the factual circumstances in which they were made, and of the reactions to which they gave rise;

4. A unilateral declaration binds the State internationally only if it is made by an authority vested with the power to do so. By virtue of their functions, heads of State, heads of Government and ministers for foreign affairs are competent to formulate such declarations. Other persons representing the State in specified areas may be authorized to bind it, through their declarations, in areas falling within their competence;

5. Unilateral declarations may be formulated orally or in writing;

6. Unilateral declarations may be addressed to the international community as a whole, to one or several States or to other entities;

7. A unilateral declaration entails obligations for the formulating State only if it is stated in clear and specific terms. In the case of doubt as to the scope of the obligations resulting from such a declaration, such obligations must be interpreted in a restrictive manner. In interpreting the content of such obligations, weight shall be given first and foremost to the text of the declaration, together with the context and the circumstances in which it was formulated;

8. A unilateral declaration which is in conflict with a peremptory norm of general international law is void;

9. No obligation may result for other States from the unilateral declaration of a State. However, the other State or States concerned may incur obligations in relation to such a unilateral declaration to the extent that they clearly accepted such a declaration;

10. A unilateral declaration that has created legal obligations for the State making the declaration cannot be revoked arbitrarily. In assessing whether a revocation would be arbitrary, consideration should be given to:

(i)   any specific terms of the declaration relating to revocation;
(ii) the extent to which those to whom the obligations are owed have relied on such obligations;
(iii) the extent to which there has been a fundamental change in the circumstances.[92]

---

92   International Law Commission, "Guiding Principles Applicable to Unilateral Declarations of States Capable of Creating Legal Obligations," *Report of the*

As suggested above, these Guiding Principles by and large faithfully reflect the judgments of the ICJ on the topic, with perhaps one or two exceptions. One minor but logical innovation is Guiding Principle 8, which, by analogy with a fundamental rule of treaty law, provides for the invalidity of unilateral declarations that conflict with *jus cogens* norms.[93] Guiding Principle 9 is also analogous to the well-accepted rule of treaty law that states cannot, by entering into treaty relationships amongst themselves, create obligations for a non-party to the treaty without its consent.[94] It seems sensible that the same disability should exist for states acting unilaterally.

Guiding Principle 10 is an interestingly ambiguous attempt to broach, without definitively addressing, the issue of the revocability of unilateral declarations. Essentially, unilateral declarations cannot be revoked "arbitrarily", and the ILC furnishes a non-exhaustive enumeration of factors to be considered in determining whether any particular attempt at revocation is or is not arbitrary.[95] These factors harken to the terms of the declaration itself, the issue of reasonable reliance considered above, and—again by way of analogy to the law of treaties—the possibility that circumstances may have fundamentally changed since the declaration was made.[96]

The criterion of "arbitrariness" which is said to govern revocability is deduced by the ILC from the following assertion of the ICJ in the *Nuclear Tests* cases: "[T]he unilateral undertaking resulting from [the French] statements cannot be interpreted as having been made in implicit reliance on an arbitrary power of reconsideration."[97] This is interpreted by the ILC as prohibiting (only) arbitrary withdrawal or amendment of a unilateral declaration.[98] With respect, this is a considerable leap of logic. Observing that a unilateral declaration cannot be withdrawn arbitrarily because no "arbitrary power of reconsideration" accompanied the declaration in a particular case is quite a different (and more limited) proposition than suggesting that unilateral

---

International Law Commission on the Work of its Fifty-eighth Session (2006), UN Doc. A/61/10, c. IX at 369–81, para. 176.

93   See above note 52.

94   See further Chapter 4, Section G(4).

95   See Commentary to Guiding Principle 10 in *Report of the International Law Commission on the Work of its Fifty-eigth Session*, above note 92 at 380: "The Commission has drawn up an open-ended list of criteria to be taken into consideration when determining whether or not a withdrawal is arbitrary."

96   See further Chapter 4, Section J(2)(d).

97   *Nuclear Tests*, above note 80 at para. 51.

98   See Commentary to Guiding Principle 10 in *Report of the International Law Commission on the Work of its Fifty-eigth Session,* above note 92 at 380.

declarations may only ever be withdrawn non-arbitrarily. Assuming a unilateral declaration *is* accompanied by an arbitrary power of reconsideration, on what basis could it be said that the declarant state cannot subsequently withdraw the declaration at will? Neither good faith nor reasonable reliance would be jeopardized, as all interested states would be aware from the outset that the declarant state reserved the right to arbitrarily reverse its position.

Guiding Principle 10 in fact implicitly acknowledges this (albeit in a somewhat ambiguous manner) by providing that, in determining whether a purported revocation is arbitrary (and thus impermissible), "consideration should be given to any specific terms of the declaration relating to revocation." While this fails to resolve the potentially circular situation where the "specific terms of the declaration relating to revocation" include a power of arbitrary revocation, it at least has the virtue of underlining the importance of the terms of the declaration itself. This, then, is a return to the all-important caveat accompanying the ICJ's seminal recognition, in the *Nuclear Tests* cases, of the potentially binding character of unilateral declarations: "When it is the intention of the State making the declaration that it should become bound *according to its terms*, that intention confers on the declaration the character of a legal undertaking...."[99] Ultimately, it is the terms of the declaration and the circumstances surrounding its making that will determine *both* the extent of the legal obligations to which it gives rise *and* its revocability.

2) "Soft" Law

The institutional developments that were the hallmark of the latter half of the twentieth century, most notably the establishment of the UN and its various organs and agencies, have fostered an unprecedented intensity of international discourse between states. From relatively straightforward beginnings, the United Nations system now embraces virtually every aspect of human endeavour, and has prompted the growth of related regional or activity-specific systems. Moreover, the growth of a global public consciousness, catalyzed in part by the proliferation of mass media, accessible telecommunications technologies, and the widespread diffusion of electronic information, has in turn generated enormous civil society interest in the shape and direction of international policy-making. The result has been an essentially new international culture of multilateral diplomacy involving both state

---

99 *Nuclear Tests* cases, above note 80 at 267 [emphasis added].

and non-state actors which has produced overwhelming amounts of documentation, statements, communiqués, studies, declarations, resolutions, codes of conduct, draft conventions, and the like. The question that arises for the international lawyer when faced with such massive quantities of material is whether the material or the processes that lead to its production have any law-making significance and, if so, precisely what that significance is.

This question has prompted many commentators to draw a distinction between *lex lata* ("hard law") and *lex ferenda* ("soft law"). Proponents of this classification would include in the category of *lex lata* only the products of the traditional, formal sources of international law reviewed above (namely, treaties, customary international law, general principles of law, and perhaps unilateral declarations). Only such *lex lata* would be considered truly binding international law. However, rather than consign the rest of diplomatic and non-governmental activity and materials to complete legal irrelevance (which would be a difficult position to defend), much of it is instead relegated to the status of *potential* legal relevance. The euphemism used to capture this category of potential law-in-the-making is *lex ferenda*, or soft law.

The precise criteria for and significance of *lex ferenda* are open to question. The category is reminiscent of the distinction drawn between formal and material sources, and some authors accommodate the concept of soft law in just that way—they consider it to be a reservoir of *evidence* of state practice, *opinio juris*, or general principles, rather than a formal source of law in itself. This evidence can then be called upon to support an argument that some new norm is emerging or has emerged and should therefore be recognized as *lex lata* or hard law in accordance with the requirements of the formal sources of law reviewed above.

The materials most commonly said to constitute *lex ferenda* include draft multilateral law-making treaties,[100] which can have an influence on state patterns of behaviour prior to their coming into force, as well as on non-states parties afterward; UN General Assembly resolutions which, as we have seen, generally have no formal binding force of their own[101] but which frequently purport to be "declaratory" of international law;[102] various "codes of conduct" prepared by UN organs or agen-

---

100 See Chapter 4, Section A.

101 *UN Charter*, above note 2, c. IV.

102 Perhaps the best known example of such a UN General Assembly "Declaration" is the so-called "Friendly Relations Declaration," which sets out a number of principles that restate basic rights and obligations of states at international law: *Declaration on Principles of International Law Concerning Friendly Relations and*

cies with a view to bringing uniformity to state conduct in areas of international concern;[103] official communiqués, reports, declarations, or accords emerging from major international conferences, which can at least state broad agreements of principle where the participants have otherwise been unable to agree on legally binding obligations enshrined in a convention;[104] and, arguably, studies, reports, recommendations, statements of principles, manifestos, and the like emanating from the work of non-governmental organizations, academic institutions, think-tanks, and other civil society groups.[105]

Particularly significant as *lex ferenda* is the work of the International Law Commission (ILC), an international commission of jurists estab-

---

Co-operation Among States in Accordance with the Charter of the United Nations, GA Res. 2625 (XXV), UN GAOR, 25th Sess., Supp. No. 28, UN Doc. A/8028 (1971) [*Friendly Relations Declaration*]. See also G. Arangio-Ruiz, *The United Nations Declaration on Friendly Relations and the System of the Sources of International Law* (Germantown: Sijthoff & Noordhoff, 1979).

103 See, for example, the Model Law on Electronic Commerce of the United Nations Commission on International Trade Law (UNCITRAL): *Model Law on Electronic Commerce of the United Nations Commission on International Trade Law*, GA Res. 51/ 162, UN GAOR, 51st Sess., Supp. No. 49, Annex, UN Doc. A/51/162 (1996), as amended by the *Report of the United Nations Commission on International Trade Law on the Work of its Thirty-First Session 1–12 June 1998*, UN Doc. A/53/17, paras. 201–21 and endorsed by the UN General Assembly in Resolution 51/162 (1996). UNCITRAL states that the "purpose of the Model Law is to offer national legislators a set of internationally acceptable rules as to how a number of … legal obstacles [to the use of electronic messages in trade] may be removed, and how a more secure legal environment may be created for what has become known as 'electronic commerce.'"

104 A good example of this would be the twenty-six Principles of the *Declaration of the United Nations Conference on the Human Environment* (the "Stockholm Declaration"), which purport to enunciate rights and responsibilities of states with respect to the global environment: *Report of the United Nations Conference on the Human Environment*, UN Doc. A/Conf.48/14/Rev 1, c. 1 (New York: United Nations, 1972). A second highly significant example would be the non-binding *Helsinki Accords* signed by thirty-five states from Eastern and Western Europe as well as North America at the Conference on Security and Cooperation in Europe in 1975: (1975), 14 I.L.M. 1292. The *Accords* set out ten basic principles regarding peaceful relations between the participating states as well as human rights issues at a time when the Cold War prevented the adoption of a formally binding set of agreements.

105 See, for example, Princeton Project on Universal Jurisdiction, "Princeton Principles on Universal Jurisdiction" (Princeton: Program in Law and Public Affairs, Princeton University, 2001), online: http://lapa.princeton.edu/hosted-docs/unive_jur.pdf; Urban Morgan Institute *et al.*, "The Siracusa Principles on the Limitation and Derogation Provisions in the International Covenant on Civil and Political Rights" (1985) 7 Hum. Rts. Q. 3.

lished in 1947 by the UN General Assembly[106] pursuant to its mandate to encourage "the progressive development of international law and its codification."[107] The ILC thus has a dual mandate which includes not only the codification of existing (customary) international law but also the preparation of draft conventions in areas where the law is unclear or undeveloped.[108] This double role tends to introduce uncertainty as to whether any particular ILC draft or part thereof is meant to be merely declaratory or, rather, "progressive development."[109] To the extent a draft set of articles is the latter, it can often, notwithstanding its non-binding nature, influence the posture and behaviour of states and thus, ultimately, the content of international law. In this sense ILC drafts, while not binding in themselves, play a "soft law" role in shaping future legal developments.

In all of this, the most widely accepted view is that *lex ferenda* or soft law is not truly law at all but rather a category of potentially significant legal developments or materials. To the extent such developments or materials ultimately achieve legally binding status, they only do so through one or more of the formal law-creating processes described above. The misleading term "soft law" may suggest otherwise and therefore may have the unfortunate effect of confusing a discussion of the true sources of international law. The concept nevertheless serves the useful role of acknowledging the potential law-influencing significance of certain international transactions while preserving a relatively rigorous definition of the truly binding sources of international law.

---

106 *Establishment of an International Law Commission*, GA Res. 174(II), UN GAOR, 2nd Sess., UN Doc. A/RES/174(II) (1947).

107 *UN Charter*, above note 2, Article 13(1).

108 *Statute of the International Law Commission*, Annex, GA Res. 174(II), above note 106, Articles 1(1) and 15.

109 An example of the ILC's recent work that combines codification and progressive development is its set of Draft Articles on State Responsibility in "Report of the International Law Commission on the Work of its Forty-Eighth Session" (UN Doc. A/51/10) in *Yearbook of the International Law Commission 1996*, vol. II (New York: United Nations, 1996) 58. See further Chapter 12.

FURTHER READING

BOYLE, A., & CHINKIN, C., *The Making of International Law* (Oxford: Oxford University Press, 2007)

BRIERLY, J.L., *The Basis of Obligation in International Law, and Other Papers*, H. Lauterpacht & C.H.M. Waldock., eds. (Oxford: Clarendon Press, 1958)

BROWNLIE, I., *Principles of Public International Law*, 6th ed. (Oxford: Oxford University Press, 2003) c. 1

CHARLESWORTH, H. & CHINKIN, C., *The Boundaries of International Law: A Feminist Analysis* (Manchester: Manchester University Press, 2000)

CHARLESWORTH, H., CHINKIN, C., & WRIGHT, S., "Feminist Approaches to International Law" (1991) 85 A.J.I.L. 613

CHINKIN, C.M., "The Challenge of Soft Law: Development and Change in International Law" (1989) 38 Int'l Comp. L.Q. 850

FRANCK, T.M., *The Power of Legitimacy among Nations* (Oxford: Oxford University Press, 1990)

HART, H.L.A., *The Concept of Law*, 2d ed. (Oxford: Oxford University Press, 1994) c. 10

HENKIN, L., *International Law: Politics and Values* (Dordrecht: M. Nijhoff, 1995)

JENKS, C.W., *Law, Freedom and Welfare* (London: Stevens, 1963) c. 5

JOHNSTON, D.M., "World Constitutionalism in the Theory of International Law" in R. St. J. Macdonald & D.M. Johnston, eds., *Towards World Constitutionalism: Issues in the Legal Ordering of the World Community* (Leiden: Martinus Nijhoff, 2005)

KENNEDY, D., "Primitive Legal Scholarship" (1986) 27 Harv. Int'l L.J. 1

KOSKENNIEMI, M., *From Apology to Utopia: The Structure of International Legal Argument* (Helsinki: Finnish Lawyers' Publishing Company, 1989) c. 2

KOSKENNIEMI, M., *The Gentle Civilizer of Nations: The Rise and Fall of International Law 1870–1960* (Cambridge: Cambridge University Press, 2002)

KOSKENNIEMI, M., "Theory: Implications for the Practitioner" in *Theory and International Law: An Introduction* (London: British Institute of International and Comparative Law, 1991) 1

LAUTERPACHT, H., *Private Law Sources and Analogies of International Law* (London: Longmans, 1927)

MARKS, S., *The Riddle of All Constitutions: International Law, Democracy and the Critique of Ideology* (Oxford: Oxford University Press, 2000)

MCDOUGAL, M.S., LASSWELL, H.D., & REISMAN, W.M., "Theories about International Law: Prologue to a Configurative Jurisprudence" (1968) 8 Va. J. Int'l L. 191

MORGAN, E., *The Aesthetics of International Law* (Toronto: University of Toronto Press, 2007)

SCHACHTER, O., "United Nations Law" (1994) 88 A.J.I.L. 1

SHAW, M.N., *International Law*, 5th ed. (Cambridge: Cambridge University Press, 2003) c. 2–3

TOMUSCHAT, C., "Obligations Arising for States Without or Against Their Will" (1993) 241 Rec. des Cours 195

TOMUSCHAT, C., & THOUVENIN, J.M., *The Fundamental Rules of the International Legal Order: Jus Cogens and Obligations Erga Omnes* (Leiden: Martinus Nijhoff, 2006)

WEIL, P., "Towards Relative Normativity in International Law?" (1983) 77 A.J.I.L. 413

ZEMANEK, K., "The Legal Foundations of the International System" (1997) 266 Rec. des Cours 9

CHAPTER 4

THE LAW OF TREATIES

A. NATURE AND IMPORTANCE OF TREATIES

As described above,[1] treaties are express and usually formalized agreements between states or other subjects of international law—they set out the parties' mutual legal rights and obligations, and are governed by international law. They may take the form of reciprocal undertakings between as few as two states ("bilateral" treaties), or more generalized agreements adhered to by several or even, on occasion, most states in the world ("multilateral" treaties). Their subject matter ranges from very specific undertaking-and-performance agreements between states—akin to domestic law contracts and therefore sometimes called "treaty-contracts"—to broad codifications or restatements of certain substantive areas of international law, designed to govern the ongoing conduct of all the parties to them in the relevant subject-area (sometimes called "law-making" or "codification" treaties).

Treaties are thus supple legal tools in the hands of states, permitting them to enter into individual relationships with other states on very specific issues or projects, or to establish widely applicable norms intended to govern legal relationships with as many other states as will expressly agree to their terms. Indeed, in the twentieth and twenty-first centuries states have even made use of treaties to reshape and redefine the structure of the international legal system itself. For example, the

---

1 See Chapter 3, Section C(2).

United Nations (UN), with its enormous institutional apparatus (including the International Court of Justice), is merely the product of one of the most successful and widely ratified multilateral treaties of all time, the Charter of the United Nations and its annexed Statute of the International Court of Justice.[2]

Thanks largely to such institutional innovations, treaties have had pride of place in developing and clarifying international law in the past century. Previously, customary international law was clearly the primary source of generally applicable international norms, early treaty practice being largely bilateral and situation-specific in nature. This began to change in the late nineteenth and early twentieth centuries with the elaboration of broader-based treaty regimes, mostly concerned with the conduct of war and humanitarian law.[3] The last half of the twentieth century, however, witnessed explosive growth in the number of multilateral codification or law-making treaties in virtually all areas of the law.

As suggested above, this phenomenal growth can be attributed partly to the establishment of international institutions such as the United Nations and its agencies, which have provided permanent fora for the negotiation of such broad-based agreements.[4] Of particular importance to this process has been the work of the International Law Commission (ILC), a panel of experts established by the General Assembly of the United Nations in 1947 in partial fulfilment of its mandate to "encourage the progressive development of international law and its codification."[5] The ILC has been at the forefront of the "codification" movement, steadily producing draft texts in a variety of fields, texts that have served as the starting point for state negotiations leading to the conclusion of some of the most successful multilateral treaties.[6]

The rise in the relative importance of treaties as a source of generally applicable international law can also in part be attributed to the

---

2   *Charter of the United Nations*, 26 June 1945, Can. T.S. 1945 No. 7 (entered into force 24 October 1945) [*UN Charter*]; *Statute of the International Court of Justice*, 26 June 1945, Can. T.S. 1945 No. 7 (entered into force 24 October 1945) [*ICJ Statute*].

3   For example, *Convention for the Pacific Settlement of International Disputes (Hague I)*, 29 July 1899, reproduced in J.B. Scott, *The Hague Peace Conferences of 1899 and 1907*, vol. II (New York: Garland, 1972) at 80; and *Convention Respecting the Laws and Customs of War on Land (Hague IV)*, 18 October 1907, reproduced in *ibid.* at 368.

4   See O. Schachter, "United Nations Law" (1994) 88 A.J.I.L. 1 at 1–2.

5   *UN Charter*, above note 2, Article 13(1). See also Chapter 3, Section D(2).

6   For a more thorough overview of the mandate, procedure, and work of the ILC, see the International Law Commission's homepage, online: www.un.org/law/ilc/.

peculiar advantages offered by treaties as law-making devices. These include the speed and clarity with which the law may be codified, created, or advanced, which has been important in accommodating the dramatically increased intensity and breadth of international discourse since the Second World War.

Given their requirement of express consent, moreover, treaties dovetail neatly with positivist notions of the source of binding obligation in international law. They represent the ultimate embodiment of the theory of consent and thus of the sovereignty of states.[7] As such, states may feel they are "taking charge" of their own legal obligations by participating in multilateral treaty negotiations, thus providing yet more momentum to the multilateral treaty juggernaut.

Numerous terms have been coined to refer to treaties in one form or another, the most common of which include "conventions," "charters," "covenants," "protocols," "pacts," "acts," "statutes," or, simply, "agreements." While various factors will influence states in their choice of title for any particular treaty, the term used has no legal significance in itself. All treaties, whatever their designation, and as long as they represent the express will of the parties to be bound by their terms in accordance with international law, are equally binding upon the parties.

B. THE *VIENNA CONVENTION ON THE LAW OF TREATIES*

It is one of the ironies of international law that the legal rules governing the formation, legal effects, and dissolution of treaties have for the most part evolved as a matter of customary international law.[8] Through the centuries states have, by their conduct and attitude, confirmed that an express agreement between them must be honoured in good faith. They

---

7   See Chapter 3. Even this most positivist of formal international legal sources has a natural law seam running through it, however. Although states are only bound by treaties to which they expressly consent, once that consent is unconditionally given it cannot unilaterally be withdrawn. The fundamental rule that treaties *must* be performed in good faith (see Section G(1), below in this chapter) is a clear derogation from the theory of consent: see above Chapter 3, Section C(2).

8   The role of domestic law is of course also important in the treaty formation process, but this chapter focuses on the *international* legal rules governing treaties. The significance of domestic constitutional orders on treaty formation and implementation will be discussed in Sections G(1) and I(2)(a), below in this chapter, as well as in Chapter 6.

have further confirmed that such an agreement is subject to a number of binding rules external to the agreement itself. These external rules—rules about rules, as it were—make up the "law of treaties."

Given that treaties are one of the two principal sources of international law and that, once formed, they must be honoured, it is obvious that any set of rules governing how treaties come into existence, how they are applied, and so on will be of fundamental importance. It is especially important that such rules be clear and precise, given that treaties are increasingly resorted to in order to define or establish broad-based international legal obligations.

In this light, one of the most important and successful "codification and progressive development" projects ever undertaken by the ILC was the preparation of a draft text of a treaty about treaties. While at first blush it might seem odd (not to mention circular) to conclude a treaty setting out the law of treaties,[9] the ILC nevertheless considered such a project "to be extremely desirable in order that the law of treaties may be placed upon the widest and most secure foundations."[10] The UN General Assembly concurred.[11] The text of a draft multilateral treaty was thus prepared by the ILC over the course of eighteen years and then submitted for further direct negotiations between states at the United Nations Conference on the Law of Treaties held in Vienna in 1968 and 1969.

The resulting *Vienna Convention on the Law of Treaties* (*Vienna Convention*) was adopted in 1969[12] and, having attained a sufficient number of ratifications, came into force in 1980.[13] Currently, the *Vienna Convention* has 108 parties and 45 signatories.[14] Moreover, most of its substantive provisions are widely considered either to reflect the pre-existing customary international law of treaties or to have become customary

---

9   An issue of which the ILC was acutely aware: see, for example, "Summary Records of the Eleventh Session" (UN Doc. A/CN.4/SER.A/1959) in *Yearbook of the International Law Commission 1959*, vol. 1 (New York: United Nations, 1959) at 93.

10   "Report of the International Law Commission on the Work of its Fourteenth Session" (UN Doc. A/5209) in *Yearbook of the International Law Commission 1962*, vol. II (New York: United Nations, 1962) at para. 17.

11   *International Conference of Plenipotentiaries on the Law of Treaties*, GA Res. 2166(XXI), UN GAOR, 21st Sess., Supp. No. 16, UN Doc. A/RES/2166(XXI).

12   *Vienna Convention on the Law of Treaties*, 23 May 1969, 1155 U.N.T.S. 331 [*Vienna Convention*].

13   27 January 1980.

14   As of 30 December 2007. As will be seen below, a party to a treaty has formally expressed its consent to be bound by it. A signatory, in contrast, has merely expressed its agreement with the text of the treaty and a future intent to become bound by it. Thus, a party is presently bound to perform a treaty in force whereas a signatory is not—though a signatory does have certain negative obligations vis-à-vis the treaty, as will be seen in Section F(2), below in this chapter.

international law since it came into force.[15] The significance of this is that even non-parties to the *Vienna Convention* can be considered bound by the content of most of its provisions.[16] Given the fundamental importance of its subject-matter to the modern international legal order, some have likened the *Vienna Convention* to a quasi-constitutional international legal document, second in importance only to the *UN Charter.*[17]

As intended by the ILC and the UN General Assembly, therefore, the *Vienna Convention* has become a convenient reference point for most of the law of treaties.[18] In keeping with the usual practice in this area of the law, the *Vienna Convention* will therefore be referred to throughout this chapter as authority for various propositions of law even though such propositions may have identical or very similar analogues in the customary international law of treaties.

C. DEFINITION AND ESSENTIAL ELEMENTS OF INTERNATIONAL TREATIES

1) Defining Treaties

The *Vienna Convention* defines a treaty for its own purposes as:

> an international agreement concluded between States in written form and governed by international law, whether embodied in a single in-

---

15   See, for example, *Legal Consequences for States of the Continued Presence of South Africa in Namibia (South West Africa), Advisory Opinion,* [1971] I.C.J. Rep. 3 at 47 [*South West Africa Case*]; *Fisheries Jurisdiction Case (United Kingdom v. Iceland) (Jurisdiction of the Court),* [1973] I.C.J. Rep. 3 at 18; *Case Concerning the Gabčíkovo-Nagymaros Project (Hungary v. Slovakia),* [1997] I.C.J. Rep. 7 [*Gabčíkovo-Nagymaros Case*] at 38 and 62; P. Reuter, *Introduction to the Law of Treaties,* 2d ed., trans. by J. Mico & P. Haggenmacher (London: Kegan Paul International, 1995) at 15; A. Aust, *Modern Treaty Law and Practice* (Cambridge: Cambridge University Press, 2000) at 10–11; I. Brownlie, *Principles of Public International Law,* 6th ed. (Oxford: Oxford University Press, 2003) at 580. For discussion of the process by which treaty norms may become customary international law, see further Chapter 5, Section E(2).

16   Although not, technically, directly by the *Vienna Convention* itself.

17   J.A. Beesley & C.B. Bourne, eds., "Canadian Practice in International Law in 1970 As Reflected Mainly in Public Correspondence and Statements of the Department of Foreign Affairs" (1971) 9 Can. Y.B. Int'l L. 276 at 300.

18   See M.N. Shaw, *International Law,* 5th ed. (Cambridge: Cambridge University Press, 2003) at 811. It should be noted, however, that the *Vienna Convention* does not deal directly with such issues as general state responsibility or liability for breach of treaty terms (see further on this topic Chapter 12), or the law of treaties in times of war or hostilities, a topic currently being considered by the ILC.

strument or in two or more related instruments and whatever its particular designation.[19]

While this definition is in many ways a useful guide to the essential elements of treaties, it is narrower in several respects than it need be. For reasons peculiar to the process by which the *Vienna Convention* was drafted, its specific terms exclude certain agreements which are nevertheless considered full-fledged treaties as a matter of customary international law.[20] The *Vienna Convention* makes this clear in stating that its specific focus on certain types of treaties is without prejudice to the legal force of, or application of the general law of treaties to, other types of treaties.[21] Thus caution is in order in relying exclusively on the definition of "treaty" furnished by the *Vienna Convention*.

With this in mind, a general working definition of an international treaty would include four principal elements. Adapting slightly the *Vienna Convention*'s definition in order to reflect customary international law on the subject, an international treaty could therefore be defined as:

(a) an international agreement
(b) between subjects of international law
(c) formed with intent to create binding legal obligations, and
(d) governed by international law.

2) Four Essential Treaty Elements

a) International Agreement

The first element, the requirement of an international agreement, flows from the basic premise that treaties are essentially participatory sources of international law. In other words, treaties "make" international law through the process of agreement between international legal subjects. Further, such international law is only applicable as between the subjects so agreeing. This can be contrasted with customary international law, which is produced through the unilateral, albeit cumulative, acts and attitudes of states, and which is, moreover, of presumptive universal application.[22] Further, the "agreement" requirement appropriately underscores that a treaty requires a minimum of two parties.

---

19   *Vienna Convention*, above note 12, Article 2(1)(a).
20   For example, oral treaties.
21   *Vienna Convention*, above note 12, Article 3.
22   See further Chapter 5, Section A. Also distinguishable from binding agreements giving rise to legal obligations are unilateral declarations (see Chapter 3, Section D(1)) and other potential sources of obligation such as (in appropriate

b) Between International Legal Subjects

The second requirement is that the agreement be between international legal subjects. By far the most common participants in treaties are states;[23] indeed, until the twentieth century it was a well-received view that *only* states could conclude treaties. This is due to the very nature of international legal subjects, one of the attributes of which is the capacity to enter into legal relations with other international legal subjects.[24] Treaties are the principal such relations. Thus, corporations, individuals, and non-governmental organizations are generally ineligible to enter into treaty relations.[25] While such entities might well enter into agreements with states, such agreements would not be governed by the international law of treaties but rather (if at all) by the domestic law of one or more states.[26]

The *Vienna Convention*'s focus on treaties between states, but not between states and other international legal subjects such as international organizations, tells only part of the story. The recognition of permanent international organizations as potential subjects of international law[27] and the necessities surrounding their dealings with states have given rise to their frequent participation in treaties.[28] In fact, a companion convention dealing with the application of the law of treaties to conventions between states and international organizations, or simply between international organizations, has now been concluded.[29] Its provisions

---

circumstances) acquiescence, estoppel, preclusion, and the like (see Chapter 7, Section B(2)(a)(ii)).

23   Article 6 of the *Vienna Convention*, above note 12, confirms that "[e]very state possesses capacity to conclude treaties."

24   See Chapter 2, Section B(2)(d).

25   See Aust, above note 15 at 15–16. But see Reuter, above note 15 at 32–33. On the lack of international legal personality of corporations, individuals, and nongovernmental organizations, see above Chapter 2, Section E.

26   See, for example, *Anglo-Iranian Oil Co. Case (United Kingdom v. Iran) (Jurisdiction)*, [1952] I.C.J. Rep. 93 at 112 [*Anglo-Iranian Oil*].

27   On the international legal subject status of international organizations, see Chapter 2, Section D.

28   See, for example, *Convention on the Privileges and Immunities of the United Nations*, 13 February 1946, 1 U.N.T.S. 15, corrigendum in 90 U.N.T.S. 327 (entered into force 17 September 1946); or the *Agreement Between the United Nations and Sierra Leone on the Establishment of a Special Court for Sierra Leone*, 16 January 2002, appendix to the Report of the Secretary-General on the Establishment of a Special Court for Sierra Leone, 4 October 2000, U.N. Doc. S/2000/915.

29   *Vienna Convention on the Law of Treaties between States and International Organizations or between International Organizations*, 21 March 1986, (1986) 25 I.L.M. 543. Not yet in force, the Convention has attracted thirty-nine signatories and forty parties (as of 30 December 2007).

largely mirror, with minor adaptations, the substantive law of treaties applicable between states.[30]

As seen above, the precise bounds of who or what might enjoy international legal personality, and for what purposes, has become more fluid in the past century. Accordingly, the general rule here is best expressed by observing that only international legal subjects may be parties to treaties. If it is determined that a party to an agreement does not possess the international legal personality necessary to conclude binding treaties, it will follow logically that the agreement under consideration is not in fact a treaty.

As they are by far the most common participants in treaties, "states" will be used throughout this chapter for convenience when referring to parties to treaties.

c)   Intent to be Bound

The third element of a treaty, that it be concluded with an intent to create binding legal obligations, is crucial. States frequently enter into agreements, reach understandings, and even sign accords without any intent or expectation that such acts will produce legally binding obligations at international law. Given that there is no prescribed form for a binding international treaty,[31] the only way a treaty can be distinguished from such a non-binding agreement is to search for the parties' mutual intent on the matter.[32] The ascertainment of such intent, in the absence of reliable formal indicators familiar in some domestic legal systems,[33] is often a difficult and uncertain process that relies upon all available evidence, circumstantial and otherwise, to shed light on the parties' motivations.[34] In other words, formality in the creation of an international agreement alone is not sufficient to make that agreement a binding treaty, just as informality is not in itself determinative of the parties' intent to conclude a non-binding agreement or no agreement at all.

---

30   See P.K. Menon, *The Law of Treaties Between States and International Organizations* (Lewiston, NY: Edwin Mellen Press, 1992).

31   See Section C(3), below in this chapter.

32   S. Rosenne, *Developments in the Law of Treaties, 1945–86* (Cambridge: Cambridge University Press, 1989) at 86; Shaw, above note 18 at 812–14; Brownlie, above note 15 at 581.

33   For example, the payment of consideration to evidence the binding character of a common law contract.

34   Brownlie, above note 15 at 581. See, for an illustration of the complexities of making such determinations, the *Aegean Sea Continental Shelf Case*, [1978] I.C.J. Rep. 3 at 39.

An example of a formally concluded multilateral agreement which is nevertheless not considered to have binding legal force as a treaty is the *Helsinki Final Act* (sometimes also called the "*Helsinki Accord*") signed by 35 states from Europe and North America at the Conference on Security and Cooperation in Europe in 1975.[35] The *Final Act* set out ten basic principles bearing on peaceful relations between the participating states and on human rights issues. The terms of the *Final Act* made it clear, however, that the parties did not intend it to be a legally binding agreement and it would thus be inaccurate to characterize it as a treaty.[36] The clear evidence of the parties' intent on the matter is conclusive.

Saying that treaty-making does not require observation of any particular formalities is not to say that such formalities are always irrelevant to the ascertainment of intent to enter into binding treaty relations. In ascertaining the intentions of the parties, particularly where one has to rely on their conduct rather than on their express statements, it is important to understand such conduct in its context. Part of that context will normally be circumstantial evidence of the usual meaning attributed (or not) to certain acts. Thus, the ordinary practice of the parties is a key circumstance against which purported evidence of the parties' intent to become bound by an agreement is to be evaluated.[37] For example, in the *North Sea Continental Shelf Cases*,[38] Denmark and the Netherlands contended that Germany, while not formally a party to the 1958 Geneva *Convention on the Continental Shelf*,[39] had nevertheless become bound by its rules through various acts and statements. The Court reacted strongly to this submission:

> As regards these contentions, it is clear that only a very definite, very consistent course of conduct on the part of a state … could justify the Court in upholding them; and … if there had been a real intention to manifest acceptance or recognition of the applicability of the conventional regime — then it must be asked why it was that the Federal Republic [of Germany] did not take the obvious step of giving expression to this readiness by simply ratifying the Convention. In

35 *Conference on Security and Co-operation in Europe: Final Act (1 August, 1975)* (1975), 14 I.L.M. 1292.

36 *Ibid.*, Preamble.

37 Reuter, above note 15 at 59.

38 *North Sea Continental Shelf Cases (Federal Republic of Germany v. Denmark; Federal Republic of Germany v. The Netherlands)*, [1969] I.C.J. Rep. 3 [*North Sea Continental Shelf Cases*].

39 *Convention on the Continental Shelf*, 29 April 1958, 499 U.N.T.S. 311 (entered into force 10 June 1964).

principle, when a number of States, including the one whose conduct
is invoked, and those invoking it, have drawn up a convention specifically providing for a particular method by which the intention
to become bound by the regime of the convention is to be manifested—namely by the carrying out of certain prescribed formalities
(ratification, accession), it is not lightly to be presumed that a State
which has not carried out these formalities, though at all times fully
able and entitled to do so, has nevertheless somehow become bound
in another way....[40]

Thus, departure from the usual formalities may very well be taken as
evidence of a lack of intent to be bound by a treaty.

Questions of form will be examined in greater detail below,[41] but
for the time being the important point is that whether or not a treaty
exists depends above all on the mutual intent of the parties to enter
into binding treaty relations, and only secondarily—as an evidential
matter—on the form in which that intent is expressed.

d)   Governed by International Law

The fourth and final element of a treaty, also of overriding importance, is that it be governed by international law. This means that the
parties must intend that the agreement itself should be subject to the
law of treaties with respect to such matters as its validity, application,
interpretation, and enforceability. It also entails subjection of the treaty
relationship to the general law of state responsibility should there be a
failure by any party to fulfil its obligations under the treaty.[42]

This requirement therefore distinguishes treaties from domestic
law contracts, which are governed by the law of one or more domestic
jurisdictions. States are free to enter into such domestic law contracts,[43]
whether with other subjects of international law (including states) or
with persons having no such status, such as corporations or individuals. The important point, however, is that "the mere participation of
states or other international legal subjects in such an agreement (even
if they are the only parties) will not in itself make it a treaty."[44] Rather,
whether the agreement is an international treaty governed by inter-

---

40   *North Sea Continental Shelf Cases*, above note 38 at para. 38.

41   Section C(3), below in this chapter.

42   Article 73 provides that the *Vienna Convention*, above note 12, is without preju-
     dice to issues of state responsibility; see also the *Rainbow Warrior Arbitration
     (New Zealand v. France)* (1990), 82 I.L.R. 499. For further discussion of state
     responsibility for internationally wrongful acts, see Chapter 12.

43   Frequently referred to as "concession contracts."

44   *Anglo-Iranian Oil*, above note 26 at 112.

national law or a concession contract governed by some system of domestic law depends on the parties' mutual intent on this issue.

3) Questions of Form

The scope of the *Vienna Convention* is confined to written treaties. Oral treaties are nevertheless permissible at customary international law and are governed by the same substantive rules.[45] In fact, as seen above,[46] the general law of treaties imposes virtually no restrictions of form whatsoever on treaties, as evidenced even by the *Vienna Convention*'s permissive reference to all manner of agreements "whether embodied in a single instrument or in two or more related instruments and whatever [their] particular designation."[47] This flexibility of form extends even to the terminology used to describe such agreements; terms such as "treaty," "convention," "agreement," or "protocol" are all interchangeable in international law.[48]

The extent of this flexibility is well illustrated in the decision of the International Court of Justice in the *Aegean Sea Continental Shelf Case*.[49] In that case, Greece contended that a joint communiqué issued directly to the press by the Prime Ministers of Greece and Turkey immediately following a meeting between them constituted a binding agreement to submit, either jointly or unilaterally, their maritime boundary dispute to the International Court of Justice. The communiqué bore neither signatures nor initials. The relevant text of the communiqué was as follows:

> They [the two Prime Ministers] decided that those problems [between the two countries] should be resolved peacefully by means of negotiations and as regards the continental shelf of the Aegean Sea by the International Court at The Hague.

The Court observed that no rule of international law precluded a joint communiqué from constituting a binding international treaty. Whether it does depends not on its form, but "on the nature of the act or transaction to which [it] gives expression." The Court added:

---

45 See, for example, *Legal Status of Eastern Greenland (Denmark v. Norway)* (1933), P.C.I.J. Rep. Ser. A/B No. 53 at 71; Reuter, above note 15 at 30; Brownlie, above note 15 at 582.
46 Section C(2)(c), above in this chapter.
47 *Vienna Convention*, above note 12, Article 2(1)(a).
48 Reuter, above note 15 at 29.
49 *Aegean Sea Continental Shelf Case*, above note 34.

> [I]n determining what was indeed the nature of the act or transaction embodied in the Brussels Communiqué, the Court must have regard above all to its actual terms and to the particular circumstances in which it was drawn up.[50]

The Court noted that the actual terms of the communiqué contemplated ongoing discussions and meetings of experts on the issue of the Aegean Sea continental shelf. This did not appear consistent, in the Court's view, with an immediate and unqualified commitment to submit the dispute to the Court, as urged by Greece. The Court also found that negotiations prior to the date of the communiqué revealed that Turkey was at most willing to consider a joint submission of the dispute to the Court by way of special agreement. "When read in that context," the Court held, "the terms of the communiqué do not appear to the Court to evidence any change in the position of the Turkish Government …."[51] This suggests that where the terms and even the nature of the document are vague, the prior positions of the parties can shed light on the document's intent.

The Court also examined the subsequent conduct of the parties; it found that the Turkish position remained consistent. The Court added that it was "significant" that, in the negotiations between the parties subsequent to the joint communiqué, there had been no suggestion by Greece that the basis of the Court's jurisdiction had already been resolved by the communiqué itself. Further, in the course of those negotiations, Greece itself expressly acknowledged that a special agreement was necessary in order to submit the issue to the Court. In other words, Greece's subsequent conduct did not suggest that it itself considered the communiqué to constitute a binding agreement.[52]

The Court therefore concluded that the communiqué "was not intended to … constitute an immediate commitment" on the part of both parties to seize the Court of jurisdiction.[53]

Thus, whether a particular document constitutes a treaty depends upon the "nature of the act or transaction to which it gives expression." That nature is determined by the terms of the document itself, as well as the positions of the parties in prior and subsequent negotiations. The ultimate test appears to be whether the document, its terms, and the behaviour of the parties both prior and subsequent to issuing the document, together evidence an intent by the parties to commit to its terms.

---

50   *Ibid.* at 39.
51   *Ibid.* at 43.
52   *Ibid.* at 44.
53   *Ibid.*

Another, more recent decision of the International Court of Justice illustrates the potentially far-reaching effects of an apparently informal arrangement between states. In the *Case Concerning Maritime Delimitation and Territorial Questions* between Qatar and Bahrain,[54] the minutes of a meeting held between state representatives and an exchange of letters between governments were each held to be sufficient evidence of the parties' intent to be bound by the contents of the minutes and the letters respectively. Each was thus held to constitute a treaty enforceable at international law.[55]

In that case, both states had agreed in 1976 to third-party mediation of their dispute by the King of Saudi Arabia. No progress was made until 1987, when the Saudi King proposed a settlement by way of letters in identical terms to each party. The heads of state of both parties accepted the proposed settlement by way of return letters. A key proposal thus adopted was that "[a]ll the disputed matters shall be referred to the International Court of Justice, at The Hague, for a final ruling binding upon both parties, who shall have to execute its terms."

These events were followed by two years of unsuccessful negotiations on a mutually acceptable formulation of the issues to be submitted to the Court. The matter was again discussed at a meeting in 1990, at which time Qatar accepted a proposed Bahraini formulation of the issues to be submitted to the Court. Following the meeting, the Foreign Ministers of Bahrain, Qatar, and Saudi Arabia signed minutes recording that they had reaffirmed their prior agreement, would continue to negotiate for a defined period and, failing agreement, "the parties may submit the matter to the International Court of Justice in accordance with the Bahraini formula, which has been accepted by Qatar."

The parties agreed that the exchange of letters of 1987 constituted an international agreement with binding force. Bahrain, however, maintained that the minutes of the 1990 meeting were no more than a simple record of negotiations, not an international agreement seizing the Court of jurisdiction of the issues as described in the "Bahraini formula."

The Court reaffirmed that questions of form do not govern whether a binding agreement has or has not come into existence. Rather, it recalled its *dicta* in the *Aegean Sea Continental Shelf Case* to the effect that the "actual terms" and "particular circumstances" in which the document was drawn up prevailed. Here, the Court emphasized that the

---

54   *Case Concerning Maritime Delimitation and Territorial Questions between Qatar and Bahrain (Jurisdiction and Admissibility)*, [1994] I.C.J. Rep. 112 [*Qatar v. Bahrain*].
55   *Ibid.* at 120–22.

minutes referred to what had been "agreed" by the parties; that they included "a reaffirmation of obligations previously entered into"; and that they did "not merely give an account of discussions and summarize points of agreement and disagreement," but "enumerate[d] the commitments to which the Parties have consented." Thus, the Court concluded, the minutes "create[d] rights and obligations in international law for the Parties. They constitute[d] an international agreement."[56]

The Court further rejected Bahrain's objection that its representative had no intention to enter into a legally binding obligation upon signing the minutes (and indeed that he could not have intended to do so given domestic Bahraini law limiting his powers). The Court found the subjective intentions of the individual representatives irrelevant:

> The two Ministers signed a text recording commitments accepted by their Governments, some of which were to be given immediate application. Having signed such a text, the Foreign Minister of Bahrain is not in a position subsequently to say that he intended to subscribe only to a "statement recording a political understanding," and not to an international agreement.[57]

The case may therefore stand for the proposition that the individual intentions of the persons signing the minutes or issuing statements may not be relevant to the existence of a binding agreement, depending on the circumstances. Where such circumstances include agreement by the states themselves as to their mutual rights and obligations, such agreement ("commitments accepted by their Governments") prevails over the individual intentions of the state representatives. An alternative interpretation may be that, while intent to enter into binding legal obligations is the key, such intention is to be gleaned from objective, outward manifestations and behaviours rather than from subjective, unexpressed motivations.

The cases thus clearly support the proposition that requirements of form do not govern the formation of treaties. This approach has the advantage of giving states maximum flexibility in concluding binding agreements. It is also sensible in that it privileges issues of substance over form, relying upon the actual intent of the parties, however it may be manifested, rather than on any conclusive presumptions based on the existence or absence of formalities.

As discovered by Bahrain in its dispute with Qatar, however, it also exacts a price insofar as it introduces an element of uncertainty and

---

56   *Ibid.* at 121.
57   *Ibid.* at 122.

unpredictability as to the full legal significance of a state's interactions with other states. Circumspection is required in one's behaviour *vis-à-vis* other states in order to avoid the creation of unexpected treaty relations with them.

For these reasons, states are hesitant to interpret the absence of any conduct at all as evidence of an intent to be bound. While the form in which such intent is manifested may vary widely, it nevertheless remains the case that such intent must, in fact, be manifested in *some* way. Thus, purely passive conduct is likely not to furnish the requisite evidence of intent to be bound by a proposed treaty.[58]

D. TREATY-MAKING

1) Formalities Subject to Will of Parties

As with questions of form, the formalities of treaty-making are highly variable and depend ultimately on the will of the intended parties to the treaty.[59] Thus, treaty law prescribes no set procedure in order to bring a treaty into force. A treaty may be concluded by the simple expedient of an exchange of diplomatic notes between governments (often the practice in the case of bilateral agreements), or through much more formal machinery, particularly for a multilateral treaty concluded during the course of a diplomatic conference. In each case, the parties themselves set the formal procedures to be followed in negotiating and concluding the treaty. Of course, a number of formalities may be required by the parties' domestic legal or constitutional systems before the treaty will be considered to have domestic legal effect. However, these have no direct effect upon the *international* legal validity of the treaty or of the procedures adopted to bring it into force on the international plane.

There are nevertheless certain habitual formalities—the presentation of full powers during negotiations, adoption of a text, authentication of a text, formal expression of consent to be bound—that tend to be followed by states, particularly when participating in the elaboration of a multilateral treaty. As we will see below, Articles 7 through 17 of the *Vienna Convention* describe these formalities of treaty-making in generic terms, but it is important to remember that these are default

---

58   Reuter, above note 15 at 30–31.

59   "Form" relates to the means by which a treaty is manifested (written, oral, express, tacit, etc.), whereas "formalities" relate to the procedures by which the treaty is concluded and brought into force.

provisions and that their applicability is subject to the overriding will of the states involved in the treaty-making process.

2) Full Powers

Historically, state representatives purporting to negotiate on behalf of and bind their sovereign, government, or state were required to present "full powers," meaning documents or other proof attesting to such authority.[60] In modern practice, however, such formalities are often dispensed with, particularly in the case of high-ranking or readily recognized state officials. Indeed, an expression of consent to be bound by certain state officials, such as a minister of foreign affairs, will usually suffice to bind the state without further formality.[61]

Thus, Article 7(1) of the *Vienna Convention* provides that full powers need not be produced during a treaty negotiation if circumstances show that such is not required by other participating states. Article 7(2) also provides that heads of state or government, foreign ministers, and in some cases diplomatic envoys need not produce full powers. Article 8 further provides that a state may subsequently confirm the acts of its representative if the latter's authority is in doubt.

3) Adoption

Once the terms of a treaty have been successfully negotiated, a final text is adopted. In the case of a multilateral treaty, adoption has little legal significance of its own other than to signal the close of negotiations on the text. In particular, adoption of the text of a multilateral treaty does not, in itself, signal the parties' consent to be bound by its terms, nor does it bring it into force for any of them.

On the other hand, particularly in cases of bilateral treaties, the stages of adoption, authentication, and final expression of consent to be bound may be collapsed into a single procedure, such as the exchange of signed letters of agreement. Whether or not a single procedure has such compound significance will depend on the intent of the parties. Assuming it does, the importance of adoption is eclipsed by the more fundamental significance of the parties' expression of consent to be bound.

---

60   Article 2(1)(c) of the *Vienna Convention*, above note 12, defines such documents as "emanating from the competent authority of a State designating a person or persons to represent the State for negotiating, adopting or authenticating the text of a treaty, for expressing the consent of the State to be bound by a treaty, or for accomplishing any other act with respect to a treaty."

61   See, for example, *Qatar v. Bahrain*, above note 54 at 122.

The text of a multilateral treaty is usually adopted by a vote of the states participating in the negotiations. Historically, such votes required unanimity before the text could be considered adopted. This is still frequently the case where the treaty, while multilateral, is drawn up by a relatively discrete number of states to govern their own particular relations. However, more modern practice in the case of general multilateral treaties, often negotiated at universal diplomatic conferences convened under UN auspices, is to consider a treaty text adopted if it secures the support of two-thirds of the conference delegates. On some occasions, the UN General Assembly or other international organizations themselves have directly adopted the text of a multilateral treaty either by simple majority vote or by consensus.[62] These procedures have also sometimes been used by states negotiating the text of a multilateral treaty outside of the UN context.[63]

All of this again illustrates that the method, requirements, and legal significance of adoption are fully dependent upon the will of the parties participating in the treaty-negotiation process. The parties are free to determine the voting requirements as they see fit. Article 9(1) of the *Vienna Convention* reflects this flexibility to a large extent in providing that adoption of the text of a treaty presumptively requires the consent of all participating states. In the case of adoption of the text of a treaty at an international conference, however, Article 9(2) requires the consent of only two-thirds of participating states, unless the same majority agrees to a different threshold.

4) Authentication

Closely related to adoption of the final text of a treaty is its authentication. Authentication is simply a procedure by which the negotiating parties signal their agreement that a given text is definitive and correct and that it corresponds to the treaty as adopted. It does not, in itself,

---

62   This of course does not give the treaty's terms any legal force. Only the subsequent expression of consent to be bound, given by individual states, combined with the coming into force of the treaty, can have this effect.

63   For example, during the "Ottawa Process" that led to the adoption of the *Convention on the Prohibition of the Use, Stockpiling, Production and Transfer of Anti-Personnel Mines and on Their Destruction*, 3 December 1997, 2056 U.N.T.S. 211 (entered into force 1 March 1999) [*Landmines Convention*], the negotiating conference participants merely adopted the text of the treaty by consensus: see D. Chatsis, "The Ottawa Process" in *Lessons from the Past, Blueprints for the Future* (Proceedings of the XXVIth Annual Conference of the Canadian Council on International Law, 16–18 October 1997, Ottawa, Canada) 6 at 9.

signal final consent to be bound by the terms of the treaty, nor does it bring it into force.

A treaty text may be authenticated by any method agreed upon by the parties. The traditional method is by signature of the authenticated text, although initialling is also common. Again, the flexibility of the law of treaties on such questions of form is faithfully reflected in Article 10 of the *Vienna Convention,* which defers to agreement of the parties on this issue.

5) Consent to Binding Effect

By far the most significant stage in treaty-making is the parties' expression of their consent to be bound by the treaty. This is the ultimate act by which the state (or other international legal person) fetters its freedom of action and becomes bound as a matter of international law to perform the treaty's obligations in good faith once it comes into force.[64] In the case of multilateral treaties, this act normally does not coincide with earlier, less significant acts such as adoption and authentication, but usually requires some further, unequivocal step that clearly signals the parties' intent to assume the legal obligations described in the treaty.

Again, however, state practice evidences a surprising degree of variation in how states manifest their consent to be bound by a treaty. Among the most common methods are signature, ratification, and accession, as noted in Article 11 of the *Vienna Convention.*[65]

a)   Signature as Consent to be Bound

The first of these, signature, presents difficulties because signature is also commonly used as a method of authenticating the text of a treaty which, as we have seen, has a vastly different legal significance. States also frequently sign treaties subject to subsequent ratification, meaning that it is not their intent that the act of signature should itself signify consent to be bound. The possibility therefore arises that signature of a treaty can send the wrong message; namely, an expression of consent to be bound rather than authentication of the text. This potential situation is addressed in Article 12(1) of the *Vienna Convention,* which

---

64   On the delayed entry into force of certain treaties, see Section F, below in this chapter.

65   Other less significant methods referred to in Article 11 (some of which seem merely to be semantic equivalents) are: the exchange of instruments constituting a treaty, acceptance, approval, and "any other means if so agreed." See also *Vienna Convention,* above note 12, Articles 13 and 14(2). In short, virtually any act that can fairly be construed as an expression of consent to be bound will do.

provides that signature is only evidence of intent to be bound if the parties have agreed or the treaty itself provides that it is to have that effect. Alternatively, the signing state's conduct at the time of signature may indicate that it intended it to have such effect.[66]

A state which has signed a treaty subject to ratification or some other subsequent act expressing consent to be bound is referred to as a "signatory," whereas a state which has expressed its consent to be bound, whether by signature or any other means, is referred to as a "party" to the treaty.

b) Ratification

Ratification refers to any number of procedures whereby a party which has participated in the negotiation, adoption, and authentication of the text of the treaty formally and finally expresses its consent to be bound by the treaty. This step often occurs after a hiatus during which the state takes any steps necessary under its domestic law to permit it either to give such final consent or to perform the treaty's obligations once undertaken. Whether or not consent to be bound may or must be expressed by way of ratification will depend on the intentions of the negotiating parties themselves.[67] Ratification is often effected by exchanging or depositing an "instrument of ratification" (usually a formal written declaration of final consent to the treaty's terms) with the other parties (or with a "depositary" designated by the parties). Alternatively, ratification may take place simply by notifying the other parties of one's consent to be bound.[68] Again, the precise modalities of ratification are established by the parties themselves.

c) Accession

Accession is very similar to ratification except that it is the process by which a state which did not participate in the adoption or authentication of the treaty nevertheless indicates its consent to be bound by its terms. As a general rule of treaty law, treaties are not open to such unilateral, after-the-fact accession by non-participating states. This flows from the essentially contractual nature of treaties and the reciprocity of relations they entail. However, many, if not most, multilateral lawmaking or codification treaties often expressly provide that they are indeed open to accession by other states, either before or after the treaty comes into force. This more liberal approach is in keeping with the aim

---

66 See also Article 12(2), which provides that initialling a treaty can be considered a signature expressing consent to be bound in certain circumstances.

67 *Vienna Convention*, above note 12, Article 14(1).

68 *Ibid.*, Article 16.

of most such treaties, which is to secure as close to universal participation as possible.

Article 15 of the *Vienna Convention* thus provides that third party states may accede to a treaty if the treaty so provides, or if it can be established that the negotiating parties were or have subsequently agreed that after-the-fact accession is permitted. The precise modalities are, again, usually provided for in the treaty itself, and largely mirror their analogues in the case of ratification.[69]

E. RESERVATIONS AND OBJECTIONS TO RESERVATIONS

1) The Dilemma of Reservations

With the rise of multilateral treaty-making as one of the principal ways in which modern international law is developed, there has arisen also the difficulty of securing universal or even widespread agreement on all of a treaty's terms. The fact that multilateral treaties are now frequently adopted either by two-thirds or even simple majority votes is not an answer to this problem. As we have seen above, adoption does not usually, in itself, bind the parties to the treaty or bring it into force.[70] A state that is dissatisfied with any particular provision that has been adopted as part of a treaty may simply opt not to ratify or accede to it. Thus, adoption of a treaty text by a simple or even two-thirds majority of negotiating parties can be a hollow victory if significant numbers of states choose in the end not to ratify or accede to the treaty and thus fail to become parties.

Treaty regimes seeking to attract universal or near-universal adherence can widen their appeal in a number of ways. One approach is to water down the terms of the treaty to the extent necessary to secure broad-based support. This avenue is of course not particularly desirable as it has the potential to undermine the ultimate utility of the treaty regime. Another course is to permit states to express their consent to be bound by certain provisions of the treaty, but not others. This possibility is contemplated in Article 17 of the *Vienna Convention*, but only where the terms of the treaty so permit or the other parties

---

69   *Ibid.*

70   Although it may arguably have legal significance as evidence either of state practice or *opinio juris* supporting the existence of corresponding customary international law: see further Chapter 5, Section E(2).

agree to such "partial" consent. Still another, closely related, approach is to permit a state to become a party to the treaty generally, while at the same time either excluding or modifying the effect on it of certain of the treaty's provisions. This latter device, widely used in modern multilateral treaty practice, is known as a "reservation."

A "reservation" is defined in Article 2(d) of the *Vienna Convention* as follows:

> "[R]eservation" means a unilateral statement, however phrased or named, made by a State, when signing, ratifying, accepting, approving or acceding to a treaty, whereby it purports to exclude or to modify the legal effect of certain provisions of the treaty in their application to that State.

Reservations have the advantage of encouraging wide ratification of multilateral treaties, but they exact a price in return. When a state ratifies or accedes to a treaty subject to one or more reservations, it effectively creates an asymmetry in the treaty relationships between the parties. Assume for example that states A and B ratify a treaty without reservation. State C, however, ratifies subject to a reservation excluding, say, the application to it of Articles 20 and 21 of the treaty. The result is that, while all parties are bound by the same treaty, A's treaty relationship with B is governed by a set of provisions (which includes Articles 20 and 21) that differs from that governing A's treaty relationship with C (which excludes Articles 20 and 21).

This asymmetry of relationships under the same treaty is potentially problematic in at least two ways. First, it undermines the basic notion of mutuality of obligation which underlies the very idea of a treaty. It is difficult to claim that all parties to the treaty are *ad idem* as to their mutual rights and obligations if some of them have unilaterally modified the terms of the agreement for themselves. The second, and arguably much more serious, potential difficulty is that some reservations might essentially "gut" the treaty of its overall significance. This could occur if, say, the reservation purported to oust the operation of the central obligations imposed by the treaty but left the treaty's benefits to the reserving party intact.

These concerns had a significant impact on historic treaty practice with respect to reservations. Until the late nineteenth century, treaty law barely admitted the possibility of making reservations. Under the so-called "classical theory" of treaties, the basic rule was essentially contractual, such that only states accepting exactly the same mutual rights and obligations as all other parties were considered parties to a treaty. If a state purported to reserve one of the treaty's provisions, that state would only be considered to be in treaty relations with the other parties if they *all* accepted the reservation.[71] Later, during the League of Nations period, the rules were relaxed somewhat to admit the possibility of treaty relations between a reserving party and those other parties that did not object to the reservation, notwithstanding that not *all* parties accepted the reservation.[72] Subsequent state practice has been more flexible still, as we will now see.

2) The *Reservations to the Genocide Convention Case*

Modern treaty law on the issue of reservations was partially clarified by the International Court of Justice in the *Reservations to the Genocide Convention Case*.[73] In that case, the UN General Assembly requested an Advisory Opinion from the Court on certain questions relating to the use of reservations. Controversy had arisen as to whether states should be permitted to lodge reservations and, if so, under what conditions, while ratifying or acceding to the *Genocide Convention*.[74] In the wake of the atrocities of the Second World War, one of the primary purposes of the *Genocide Convention* was to enshrine universal condemnation of acts of genocide. The prospect that certain states might reserve some provisions of such an elemental treaty was therefore repugnant to many.

Thus, two of the three questions put to the Court were:[75]

I.   Can the reserving State be regarded as being a party to the Convention while still maintaining its reservation if the reservation is objected to by one or more of the parties to the Convention but not by others?

II. If the answer to Question I is in the affirmative, what is the effect of the reservation as between the reserving State and:
     (a) The parties which object to the reservation?
     (b) Those which accept it?[76]

71   See Brownlie, above note 15 at 584.

72   *Ibid.*

73   *Reservations to the Convention on the Prevention and Punishment of the Crime of Genocide, Advisory Opinion*, [1951] I.C.J. Rep. 15 [the *Reservations Case*].

74   *Convention on the Prevention and Punishment of the Crime of Genocide*, 9 December 1948, 78 U.N.T.S. 277 (entered into force 12 January 1951) [*Genocide Convention*].

75   The third question concerned the significance of objections to reservations raised by non-parties to the treaty. Essentially, such objections are legally insignificant until the objector becomes a party to the treaty.

76   *Reservations Case*, above note 73 at 16.

In answering these questions, the Court noted the competing principles at stake. On the one hand, the theory of consent required that states not be bound by reservations to which they had not agreed.[77] In other words, states should not be forced into treaty relations with other states which unilaterally altered the applicable terms of the treaty when ratifying or acceding to it, most particularly where the reservations would have the effect of undermining the purposes of the treaty. On the other hand, the Court noted that widespread ratification, which was one of the principal objectives of treaties such as the *Genocide Convention*, would be virtually impossible to achieve in the absence of some system of reservations.[78] Accordingly:

> The object and purpose of the Convention thus limit both the freedom of making reservations and that of objecting to them. It follows that *it is the compatibility of a reservation with the object and purpose of the Convention that must furnish the criterion* for the attitude of a State in making the reservation on accession as well as for the appraisal by a State in objecting to the reservation.[79] [Emphasis added]

The Court also emphasized that the permissibility or otherwise of any particular reservation would depend on its compatibility with the terms of the treaty itself. Thus, the answers given by the Court to the questions posed were:

I. [A] state which has made and maintained a reservation which has been objected to by one or more of the parties to the Convention but not by others, can be regarded as being a party to the Convention if the reservation is compatible with the object and purpose of the Convention; otherwise, that State cannot be regarded as being a party to the Convention.

II. (a) [I]f a party to the Convention objects to a reservation which it considers to be incompatible with the object and purpose of the Convention, it can in fact consider that the reserving State is not a party to the Convention;

(b) [I]f, on the other hand, a party accepts the reservation as being compatible with the object and purpose of the Convention, it can in fact consider that the reserving State is a party to the Convention.[80]

---

77   *Ibid*. at 21.
78   *Ibid*. at 23–24.
79   *Ibid*. at 24.
80   *Ibid*. at 29–30.

This compromise position facilitates widespread adherence to a multilateral treaty by permitting reservations (as long as they are compatible with the treaty's "object and purpose"), while at the same time allowing individual parties to object to reservations they consider repugnant to the treaty's object and purpose (and thus preclude treaty relationships between themselves and the reserving state). While the Court was careful to confine its answers to the specific case of the *Genocide Convention*, its reasoning—at least with respect to the requirement that reservations be compatible with the object and purpose of a treaty—has since been applied to multilateral treaty reservations in general.[81]

3) Reservations and the *Vienna Convention*

Given the controversial nature of reservations, the *Vienna Convention*'s provisions on the topic are somewhat more detailed than the discrete rulings of the Court in the *Reservations Case*. They also go a little further in relaxing the contract-like rigidity of treaties.

The starting point in the *Vienna Convention* is that reservations are permissible unless prohibited by the treaty or incompatible with the treaty's object and purpose.[82] Reservations not expressly objected to by other parties are deemed to have been accepted by them in most circumstances.[83] In these cases, the accepted reservation *mutually* modifies, as between the reserving and accepting states, the provisions of the treaty to which the reservation relates.[84] In this way, the reservation has reciprocal effect: the accepting party can take advantage of the reserving party's reservation vis-à-vis the reserving party to the same extent as can the reserving party vis-à-vis the accepting party. On the other hand, the accepting party's treaty relations with other (non-reserving) parties to the treaty remain unaffected by the reservation or its acceptance.[85] The net result is a "bilateralization" of the

---

81   In 1952, the UN General Assembly requested that the Secretary-General conform his practice to the Court's Advisory Opinion in the *Reservations Case* and that he continue to act as depositary of instruments, including reservations and objections to reservations. Rather than take a position on their legal effects, he was requested to communicate the deposit of such instruments to all states concerned so that they might draw their own conclusions as to validity in accordance with the Court's opinion in the *Reservations Case*, above note 73: see UNGA Resolution 598(VI), 12 January 1952.

82   *Vienna Convention*, above note 12, Article 19.

83   *Ibid.*, Article 20.

84   *Ibid.*, Article 21(1).

85   *Ibid.*, Article 21(2).

parties' treaty relations. In order to understand any two parties' mutual rights and obligations under a multilateral treaty where several parties may have formulated reservations or acceptances (or, for that matter, objections), it is necessary to take those reservations, acceptances, and objections into account in a bilateral, reciprocal sense.

It should be noted that the *Vienna Convention*'s rules on objections to reservations depart significantly from the ruling in the *Reservations Case*. Perhaps most notable is that nothing in the *Vienna Convention* limits the grounds upon which a party may object to a reservation to incompatibility with the treaty's object and purpose. This is a failure to codify that part of the Court's judgment in the *Reservations Case* where it held that "[t]he object and purpose of the Convention thus limit both the freedom of making reservations *and that of objecting to them*."[86] This failure appears to have been a deliberate rejection of the Court's view of the limited grounds upon which objections to reservations, as distinct from reservations themselves, may be formulated. The view that prevailed in the drafting of the *Vienna Convention* on this point was that, while it is sensible to limit the scope of unilateral reservations to treaties, there is no corresponding rationale for constraining the ability of states parties to object to reservations which they find unpalatable, for whatever reason. In fact, the basic notion that states should not be forced into treaty relations to which they do not freely consent supports the view that states should be free to object to reservations whether or not such reservations are consistent with the object and purpose of the treaty. Moreover, the practice of states on this matter clearly shows that they do not consider their right to object to be confined in the manner suggested by the *Reservations Case*.[87]

This position also seems consistent with the remainder of the *Vienna Convention*'s rules applicable to objections to reservations. According to those rules, even an express objection to a reservation does not necessarily preclude the entry into force of the treaty as between the objecting and reserving state.[88] Rather, unless the objecting state ex-

---

86 *Reservations Case*, above note 73 at 24 [emphasis added].

87 For a succinct overview of the considerations that led to rejection, in the *Vienna Convention*, of the *Reservations Case*'s limitations on the freedom of states to formulate objections, see Alain Pellet, Special Rapporteur, "Eleventh Report on Reservations to Treaties", International Law Commission, Fifty-eighth Session (2006), U.N. Doc. A/CN.4/574 (10 August 2006) at paras. 60–86. Pellet summarizes the legal position implicit in the *Vienna Convention* thus: "States and international organizations are free to object for any reason whatsoever and that reason may or may not have to do with the non-validity of the reservation": *ibid.* at para. 63.

88 *Vienna Convention*, above note 12, Article 20(4)(b).

pressly indicates that it objects to the entire treaty coming into force between it and the reserving state, an objection to a reservation merely ousts the application as between the two states of the provisions to which the reservation and objection relate, while allowing the remainder of the treaty to come into force between them.[89] It is difficult to see the utility or desirability of such an outcome if objections to reservations were necessarily premised on the incompatibility of the latter with the object and purpose of the treaty.

On the other hand, even the Court in the *Reservations Case* seemed to contemplate situations where, notwithstanding objections by some parties (presumably on the basis of incompatibility of the reservation with the treaty's object and purpose), a reserving state could be considered a party to the treaty on the basis that its reservation *was* compatible with the treaty's object and purpose.[90] What this seeming logical inconsistency underscores is a central shortcoming of the "object and purpose" compatibility criterion, whether applied to reservations or objections: in the absence of provisions to the contrary, the determination of compatibility with the object and purpose of a treaty is a subjective matter left to each party to the treaty. Thus, some parties may consider a reservation to be compatible with the treaty's object and purpose, whereas others may not. In the absence of some authoritative, third-party adjudication of the issue, a reservation may at once be permissible and impermissible — the object and purpose of a treaty being in the eye of the beholder. The result, notwithstanding the *Vienna Convention*'s veneer of objective criteria, is a highly subjective and uncoordinated system of treaty reservations and objections thereto.[91]

The difficulties posed by this state of affairs are especially acute in the case of multilateral human rights treaties. Unlike most other treaties, which concern reciprocal rights and obligations of states, the primary beneficiaries of human rights treaties are individuals. As a result, states

---

89   *Ibid.*, Article 21(3). Thus, an objection to a reservation also has reciprocal effect: neither party can rely on the reserved elements of the provision at all. In the result, the principal difference between accepting and objecting to a reservation is that the former allows the treaty to come into force between the reserving and accepting states subject to mutual *modification* of the reserved provision to the extent of the reservation; whereas the latter (presumptively) allows the treaty to come into force between the reserving and objecting states subject to mutual *non-applicability* of the reserved provision to the extent of the reservation.

90   See the Court's answer to the first question posed to it in the *Reservations Case*, above note 73 at 29.

91   Recall the UN General Assembly's 1952 instruction to the Secretary-General to leave it to each state to formulate its own views as to the compatibility of a reservation or objection with a treaty's object and purpose: above note 81.

parties to human rights treaties tend to have fewer direct incentives to object to reservations that are incompatible with their object and purpose. Recognizing this fact, and reacting to the large number of reservations formulated by certain states upon becoming parties to fundamental human rights treaties such as the *International Covenant on Civil and Political Rights (ICCPR)*,[92] the UN Human Rights Committee[93] has famously but controversially taken the view that reservations to certain provisions of the *ICCPR* are impermissible *per se*.[94] Even more controversially, it has opined that the determination of whether any particular reservation to the *ICCPR* is compatible with its object and purpose should be made by the Committee, rather than by states parties as contemplated in the *Vienna Convention*.[95] Further still, following the lead of the European Court of Human Rights,[96] the Committee has taken the view that incompatibility of a reservation with a provision of a human rights treaty does not result in non-applicability of the provision or the treaty to the reserving state; rather, it considers that the reservation is to be severed, leaving the full, unreserved provisions of the treaty applicable to the purportedly reserving state.[97] A number of states,[98] and even the ILC,[99] have objected to

---

92 *International Covenant on Civil and Political Rights*, 16 December 1966, 999 U.N.T.S. 171 (entered into force 23 March 1976; Article 41 entered into force 28 March 1979) [*ICCPR*].

93 The body established under the *ICCPR* to monitor compliance by states with its obligations.

94 UN Human Rights Committee, *General Comment 24(52): General comment on issues relating to reservations made upon ratification or accession to the Covenant or the Optional Protocols thereto, or in relation to declarations under article 41 of the Covenant*, UN Doc. CCPR/C/21/Rev.1/Add.6 (1994) at para. 8: "... [P]rovisions in the [*ICCPR*] that represent customary international law (and *a fortiori* when they have the character of peremptory norms) may not be the subject of reservations...."

95 *Ibid.* at para. 18: "It necessarily falls to the Committee to determine whether a specific reservation is compatible with the object and purpose of the [*ICCPR*]. This is in part because, as indicated above, it is an inappropriate task for States parties in relation to human rights treaties, and in part because it is a task that the Committee cannot avoid in the performance of its functions...."

96 See *Belilos v. Switzerland* (1988), E.C.H.R. Ser. A, No. 132 at para. 60; *Weber v. Switzerland* (1990), E.C.H.R. Ser. A, No. 177 at paras. 38–40. See also *Loizidou v. Turkey (Preliminary Objections)* (1995), E.C.H.R. Ser. A, No. 310 at paras. 90–98.

97 *General Comment 24(52)*, above note 94 at para. 17.

98 Most notably the United States, the United Kingdom, and France: see (1995) 16 Hum. Rts L.J. 422*ff*.

99 See *Report of the International Law Commission on the Work of its Forty-ninth Session*, UN GAOR, 52nd Sess., Supp. No. 10, UN Doc. A/52/10, (1997) c. V, "Reservations to Treaties" at paras. 124, 127, and 129–57.

most of these positions,[100] but the point is that the current framework (or lack thereof) for implementing the "object and purpose" compatibility criterion—whether in the context of human rights or other treaties—is deeply deficient.

This deficiency may explain why many modern multilateral treaties forestall controversy by either clearly spelling out their object and purpose, or expressly specifying which if any of their provisions may be reserved.[101] A good example of this practice is the Ottawa *Landmines Convention*, which expressly provides that no reservation to its provisions whatsoever is permitted.[102] To similar effect is the *Rome Statute of the International Criminal Court*.[103] Short of such absolute prohibitions on reservations, however, the problems associated with subjective determinations of their validity persist.

Acutely aware of some of these difficulties, the ILC has been preparing, since 1994, a set of "draft guidelines" which, rather than proposing reform of the reservations scheme of the *Vienna Convention*, is intended to "be of assistance for the [reservations] practice of states and international organizations."[104] While these draft guidelines (also dubbed a "Guide to Practice" by the ILC) remain a work in progress, to date they concern themselves primarily with definitional and procedural issues, such as formalities of communication of reservations, acceptances and objections.[105] On issues of substance, such as the determination of validity of reservations, the draft guidelines provisionally adopted to date remain faithful to the provisions of the *Vienna*

---

100 See, generally, C.J. Redgwell, "Reservations to Treaties and Human Rights Committee General Comment No. 24(52)" (1997) 46 I.C.L.Q. 390; and S. Marks, "*Reservations* Unhinged: The *Belilos* Case Before the European Court of Human Rights" (1990) 39 I.C.L.Q. 300.

101 A practice that had been recommended to states by the UN General Assembly in 1952: see UNGA Resolution 598(VI), 12 January 1952.

102 *Landmines Convention*, above note 63, Article 19. Such a blanket prohibition has moreover not impeded the widespread and rapid ratification of the Convention. Opened for signature in Ottawa in December 1997, the Convention came into force on 1 March 1999 and, as of 30 December 2007, has 155 parties.

103 Article 120 of the *Rome Statute of the International Criminal Court*, July 17, 1998, 2187 U.N.T.S. 90 (entered into force 1 July 2002). As of 30 December 2007, the *Rome Statute* had 105 parties.

104 See *Report of the International Law Commission on the Work of its Fifty-Ninth Session*, UN GAOR, 62nd Sess., Supp. No. 10, UN Doc. A/62/10 (2007) c. IV, "Reservations to Treaties" at para. 37. The *Report* summarizes developments on the draft guidelines to date and sets out the text of those draft guidelines that have already been provisionally adopted by the ILC.

105 For the text of the draft guidelines provisionally adopted by the ILC to date, see *ibid.*, sections C.1 & C.2, paras. 153–54

Convention, apparently in deference to the wishes expressed on this issue by states when consulted by the ILC.[106] It therefore appears unlikely that the draft guidelines, even once complete, will significantly improve the current lack of coordination of the *Vienna Convention*'s reservations regime.

F. ENTRY INTO FORCE OF TREATIES

1) Coming into Force

Treaties come into force in accordance with the intentions of the parties, either as expressed in the treaty itself or as otherwise manifested. Ratification or accession by a party does not always mean the treaty immediately has legal effect for that (or any other) party. Frequently, the coming into force of a treaty is deferred until some triggering event or date specified in the treaty text itself. The most common event in the case of multilateral treaties is the achievement of a threshold number of ratifications or accessions. Alternatively, a fixed date or, on occasion, a specified lapse of time following the achievement of a threshold number of ratifications or accessions determines the coming into force date of a treaty.

It is of course circular to have the text of a treaty determine the date of the treaty's own coming into force. The *Vienna Convention* addresses this logical impossibility by providing that provisions regulating a treaty's coming into force (as well as "other matters arising necessarily before the entry into force of the treaty") "apply" from the time of the adoption of its text.[107] This is theoretically possible if the negotiating parties to the treaty are assumed to have intended such provisions to have immediate effect pending the formal coming into force of the substance of the treaty.[108]

In the event the treaty contains no "triggering" provisions, and in the absence of any agreement on the issue among the negotiating states, the treaty is deemed to come into force once *all* negotiating states have expressed their consent to be bound.[109]

---

106 *Ibid.,* section A, para. 37.
107 *Vienna Convention,* above note 12, Article 24(4).
108 See also *ibid.,* Article 25 for the provisional application of other treaty provisions upon the consent of the negotiating states.
109 *Ibid.,* Article 24(2).

In the case of a party ratifying or acceding after the treaty has come into force, such party is immediately bound unless the instrument of ratification or accession, or the treaty, provide otherwise.[110]

2) Obligations Pending Entry Into Force

A question that frequently arises is whether a signatory that has not yet expressed its consent to be bound has any obligations under the treaty. A related question is whether a party that has expressed its intent to be bound has any obligations under the treaty pending its entry into force. From a policy perspective the answers to these questions are important, as holding that obligations arise before expression of consent to be bound or prior to the treaty's coming into force has the potential to obliterate the legal significance of both events.

It appears that no positive obligations of performance of the treaty's terms arise in either of these situations.[111] On the other hand, there is a general good faith obligation in such situations "to refrain from acts that would defeat the object and purpose" of the treaty.[112] While there is some ambiguity as to the precise extent of such an obligation or the consequences of its breach, it appears to be principally negative in nature. That is, it is aimed at prohibiting acts that would frustrate or impede either the coming into force of the treaty or its future performance (by parties) once it comes into force.[113] It should be noted that there is some uncertainty as to the existence of a rule analogous to Article 18 of the *Vienna Convention* in customary international law.[114]

3) Registration

One formality following the entry into force of a treaty that is of considerable significance to its enforceability is its registration with, and subsequent publication by, the Secretariat of the United Nations. The obligation to register is set out both in the *Vienna Convention*[115] and the *Charter of the United Nations*,[116] and is said to be necessary to avoid se-

---

110 *Ibid.*, Article 24(3).
111 Subject, of course, to a contrary intention of the parties: see *ibid.*, Article 25.
112 *Ibid.*, Article 18.
113 *Case Concerning Certain German Interests in Polish Upper Silesia (Merits)*, P.C.I.J. (Ser. A) No. 7 at 30; A. McNair, *The Law of Treaties*, rev. ed. (Oxford: Clarendon Press, 1961) at 199 and 204.
114 See Aust, above note 15 at 94.
115 *Vienna Convention*, above note 12, Article 80(1).
116 *UN Charter*, above note 2, Article 102(1).

cret treaties which might undermine international stability and order.[117] An alternative view is that such central registration is important merely as a matter of the "smooth administration of international relations."[118]

The penalty for failing to register a treaty with the UN Secretariat is the inability of any of its parties to rely upon it before any UN organ, including the International Court of Justice.[119] However, the Court has been at pains to observe that this provision does not undermine the essential validity of the treaty nor does it relieve the parties of their obligations under the treaty.[120]

G. BINDING FORCE AND APPLICATION OF TREATIES

1) *Pacta Sunt Servanda*

The doctrine of *pacta sunt servanda* expresses one of the most basic tenets of international law, to the effect that legal undertakings by international legal subjects must be performed in good faith. In a legal system that depends largely upon freely given consent as the basis of legal obligation, it is axiomatic that fundamental legal consequences will follow upon such free expressions of consent. *Pacta sunt servanda* articulates the most elemental of such consequences in asserting that unconditional consent, even though unilaterally given, cannot unilaterally be withdrawn.

In the specific context of treaties, *pacta sunt servanda* simply means that, once an international legal subject has expressed its consent to be bound by a treaty and the treaty has come into force, the treaty is bind-

---

117 See Brownlie, above note 15 at 588; Rosenne, above note 32 at 89; Shaw, above note 18 at 832. The requirement of mandatory registration and publication can be traced to Article 18 of the *Covenant of the League of Nations*, which was a response to the perception that a web of secret treaties had helped precipitate the First World War: *Covenant of the League of Nations Adopted by the Peace Conference at Plenary Session, April 28, 1919* (1919) 13 A.J.I.L. Supp. 128. Indeed, American president Woodrow Wilson had insisted, in his "Fourteen Points" concerning the peace negotiations following the First World War, that "there shall be no private international understandings of any kind but diplomacy shall proceed always frankly and in the public view": see Point 1 of "Woodrow Wilson's Fourteen Points," reproduced in M. MacMillan, *Paris 1919: Six Months That Changed the World* (New York: Random House, 2002) at 495–96 (Appendix).

118 See Rosenne, *ibid.* at 398–99; McNair, above note 113 at 185–86.

119 *UN Charter*, above note 2, Article 102(2).

120 See, for example, *Qatar v. Bahrain*, above note 54 at 122.

ing on that subject and must be performed by it in good faith. In other words, even a sovereign state cannot invoke its sovereignty to renege on its treaty obligations. Thus, Article 26 of the *Vienna Convention* sets out the most essential precept of treaty law:

> ### Pacta Sunt Servanda
>
> Every treaty in force is binding upon the parties to it and must be performed by them in good faith.

While enshrined as a matter of treaty law in the *Vienna Convention*, the *pacta sunt servanda* principle is (again, somewhat ironically) first and foremost a rule of customary international law. In fact, it is so well established and so essential to the whole architecture of the international legal order that it could be considered a pre-eminent example of a rule of *jus cogens*, or a customary rule from which no derogation is permissible.[121]

On its face, such an uncompromising rule is a serious derogation from the principle of consent and the sovereignty of states. If one of the attributes of sovereignty is the competence to create or modify binding obligations through the expression of consent, why should such competence come to an end once consent has been expressed at a particular point in time? In other words, how can a true sovereign fetter its own sovereignty to the point of relinquishing its ability to withdraw consent or even express a contrary or conflicting intention at some future point in time?

At least two answers to these questions can be suggested, the one theoretical and the other practical. Theoretically speaking, there would be no conflict between the principle of consent and *pacta sunt servanda* if consent were viewed as being given with foreknowledge that, once given, it is irrevocable. In other words, a sovereign state consents not only to the content of a treaty but also to its future binding effect.

More practically speaking, however, a treaty could only ever be considered a source of binding rules if the parties to it are in fact bound, that is, not free to release themselves from their obligations at will. In other words, displacing the seemingly rigid *pacta sunt servanda* principle would reduce international treaties to an ever-changing, never truly

---

121 But see J. Crawford, *The Creation of States in International Law*, 2d ed. (Oxford: Oxford University Press, 2006) at 100, where the author limits peremptory norms to substantive, as opposed to "structural," rules, and excludes the *pacta sunt servanda* principle from the former. This view appears to turn on an exclusive distinction being drawn between *impermissibility* and *logical impossibility* of derogation: however, it is not clear to this author why a rule may not be nonderogable on either or both grounds.

binding set of contingent "obligations" that could hardly be considered a source of international law in any practical sense at all.

In any event, the seeming rigidity of the *pacta sunt servanda* principle must be understood in light of the fact that it is always open to states to provide, in their treaty, that the treaty will either come to an end, or that one or more of the parties may either terminate, suspend, or withdraw from it, at a certain future time or upon the occurrence of a certain event. Similarly, nothing prevents the parties to a treaty from subsequently agreeing in another treaty either to amend, terminate, or release one or more of the parties to the former treaty. Further, as we shall see below, certain occurrences can also give rise to a legal termination or suspension of treaty obligations by operation of law, regardless of whether the parties have so provided in the treaty itself or subsequently agreed to such effect.

Thus, *pacta sunt servanda* really means that a valid treaty in force continues to bind the parties to it and must be performed by them in good faith until it is either terminated or suspended in accordance with the treaty's own terms, pursuant to the consent of the parties to it, or by operation of the law of treaties.

That a treaty must be performed in good faith usually entails executive or legislative action by each party to the treaty within its own domestic legal or constitutional system in order either to ensure that the party is able to perform the obligations assumed under the treaty or to give the treaty domestic legal effect.[122] It is this threshold obligation of performance—domestic legal steps enabling further performance or execution of the treaty—that can frequently give rise to difficulties. For example, a duly authorized representative of a state may express the state's consent to be bound by a treaty, but due to changes in government, policy, or domestic law, some essential element of the state's domestic legal order either refuses or is unable to proceed with performance of the treaty. The question that arises is whether such domestic legal impediments have any effect on the state's legal obligation to perform the treaty in good faith.

The answer to this question will obviously depend on one's legal frame of reference. A state's government will presumably be required to adhere to the dictates of its own domestic legal order, including but not necessarily limited to the requirements of its constitution. However, when viewed from the perspective of international treaty law and of the principle of *pacta sunt servanda*, such domestic legal impediments

---

122 See Chapter 6 for a description of the requirements imposed in this regard by Canadian constitutional law.

to implementation or performance provide no escape from the basic international legal obligation of good faith performance.[123] In other words, a failure to perform a binding treaty obligation, even due to a domestic constitutional obstacle, will constitute an international legal wrong potentially giving rise to an international claim for reparations by other parties to the treaty.

This basic and necessary corollary of the *pacta sunt servanda* principle has been codified in unconditional terms in Article 27 of the *Vienna Convention*:

Internal Law and Observance of Treaties

A party may not invoke the provisions of its internal law as justification for its failure to perform a treaty. This rule is without prejudice to Article 46.[124]

The necessity of such a rule can be readily understood by considering the likely results of its non-existence. If a state could invoke provisions of its internal law in justification of its failure to perform a treaty, this would be an open invitation to abuse. A state wishing to subtract itself from a treaty obligation could do so unilaterally merely by engineering, through its own domestic legal order (one over which it has sovereign control), a conflict with the treaty's requirements. If the objective of treaty law is to provide a stable basis upon which states can build reliable relationships of mutual obligation, subjecting these obligations to such a transparent avoidance mechanism would quickly undermine the entire treaty system. No state could rely upon any other state's expression of consent to be bound because it would always be subject to the overriding effect of that other state's evolving internal legal system. It would be the practical equivalent of allowing a state to withdraw from its treaty obligations at will.

---

123 *Treatment of Polish Nationals and Other Persons of Polish Origin or Speech in the Danzig Territory, Advisory Opinion* (1932), P.C.I.J. (Ser. A/B) No. 44 at 24.

124 The operation and significance of Articles 27 and 46 should not be conflated. Article 27 provides that a treaty, *once validly concluded and in force*, must be performed in good faith notwithstanding a conflict with a party's domestic legal system. Article 46, by contrast, provides that a state may not assert that its consent to be bound by the treaty was expressed in violation of its domestic law as a means of invalidating that consent, unless the violation was fundamental and manifest. In other words, Article 27 expresses the supremacy of treaty law over domestic law in matters of *treaty performance*, whereas Article 46 expresses the supremacy of treaty law over domestic law (with a narrowly defined exception) in matters of *valid treaty-making*.

Thus, the law of treaties asserts that domestic law cannot dictate the existence or extent of international legal obligations undertaken in good faith by way of treaty. This is not the same thing as saying that states must violate their internal law in order to perform any conflicting treaty obligations they may have. International law rarely dictates how a state must behave within its domestic legal order. Rather, treaty law provides that a conflicting domestic legal rule provides no justification for a failure to perform treaty obligations, meaning that if a state chooses to respect its domestic law by breaching its treaty obligations, it will be internationally responsible to other parties to the treaty for its breach.[125]

2) Temporal and Territorial Application

Given that states are sovereign entities, it is entirely possible for them to consent to be bound by a treaty which provides for its own retroactive effect. However, it is a general principle of law that agreements are presumed to apply prospectively and not to affect past relations or obligations.[126] Thus, if it is the intention of the parties to a treaty that it should have retroactive effect, it is incumbent upon them to make that intention plain. Without a clear indication of such intention in the treaty or in the circumstances of its conclusion, a treaty only affects the relations of the parties from the date of its entry into force.[127]

Similarly, unless a contrary intention appears from the terms of a treaty or from the circumstances surrounding its conclusion, its terms are presumed to apply to the entire territory of each of the parties to it.[128] This is of particular importance in the case of federal states which are parties to treaties. In such cases and again absent any clear indications to the contrary, the treaty will apply to and bind the entire federal state — as a single international legal subject — and not merely some of its constituent federal units.

As for the possible extraterritorial scope of a treaty's obligations — that is, its legal effect beyond the national territory of the parties to the treaty — this may raise issues relating to impermissible exercises of extraterritorial jurisdiction. Whether this is the case or not will depend on the extent to which such purported extraterritorial

---

125 See Section J, below in this chapter, and see further Chapter 12.
126 See Reuter, above note 15 at 100.
127 *Vienna Convention*, above note 12, Article 28.
128 *Ibid.*, Article 29.

scope interferes with the sovereign independence of non-parties to the treaty within their own legitimate spheres of jurisdiction.[129]

3) Successive Treaties

As a general rule, nothing prevents parties to one treaty from concluding a subsequent treaty dealing with similar or the same subject matter as the original treaty.[130] Indeed, as we have seen, it is through the recognition of this freedom that the principle of consent is reconciled with the principle of *pacta sunt servanda*.[131]

The effect of the conclusion of such a subsequent treaty depends upon:

1) the identity of the parties to it in relation to the identity of the parties to the original treaty;
2) the degree of overlap between the two treaties;
3) the compatibility or incompatibility of the overlapping provisions of the two treaties; and of course
4) any express or implied terms of the treaties addressing the potential for such overlap.

The clearest case is that of a subsequent treaty, between precisely the same set of parties, which expressly supplants or amends the terms of the prior treaty.[132] Equally clear is the situation where the subsequent treaty, again between the same set of parties, expressly provides that it is subject to or not incompatible with the prior treaty. In each case it is the express terms of the subsequent treaty that prevail—in the former case, to displace the terms of the original treaty to the extent expressly provided; in the latter case, to preserve them.[133]

However, many treaties address similar subject-matter as prior treaties without expressly specifying the effect of such overlap; and rarely are the parties to the subsequent treaty exactly the same as those to the original. It is in these cases that rules are required to clarify the legal effects of successive, incompatible treaties.

---

129 See further Chapter 8.
130 *Vienna Convention*, above note 12, Article 30.
131 See Section G(1), above in this chapter.
132 Article 39 of the *Vienna Convention*, above note 12, provides that a treaty may be amended by agreement between the parties to it. Similarly, Article 54 of the *Vienna Convention* provides that a treaty may be terminated by consent of all the parties.
133 *Ibid.*, Articles 30(2) & (3).

Again, the governing principle here is that the later treaty governs the earlier, but only with respect to relations between parties to the later treaty. Thus, if a subsequent treaty is silent as to the effect of any incompatibility between its provisions and those of a prior treaty, the subsequent treaty, as between the parties to it, impliedly abrogates any incompatible terms of the prior treaty.[134] However, non-parties to the subsequent treaty continue to be governed by the terms of the prior treaty. Similarly, as between one party to the prior treaty which has consented to be bound by the later treaty, and another party to the prior treaty which has not, the prior treaty's terms will continue to govern.[135]

A common illustration of the sometimes complicated relationship between successive treaties governing the same subject matter between similar but not identical sets of parties is the interplay between the four 1958 *Geneva Conventions* on various aspects of the law of the sea,[136] and the 1982 *United Nations Convention on the Law of the Sea*.[137] Many but not all states parties to the latter are parties to some or all of the former. As we shall see further below,[138] the subject matter of the latter is also in many cases similar but not identical to that of the former. Understanding the mutual legal obligations of any two states in this context therefore requires careful consideration of their mutual membership in any of the relevant treaty regimes and of the degree of incompatibility between those regimes, in accordance with the rules set out in Article 30 of the *Vienna Convention*.

In considering the legal effects of successive treaties between overlapping but not identical sets of parties, it may be helpful to bear certain terminological distinctions in mind. It is only where all the parties to a treaty subsequently agree to bring it to an end that all of its provisions cease to have effect; it is then said that the treaty has been *terminated*.[139] Where all or, where permitted by the treaty, some of the parties to a treaty subsequently agree to change its terms for all parties, the treaty

---

134 *Ibid.*, Article 30(3).

135 *Ibid.*, Article 30(4).

136 *Convention on the Territorial Sea and the Contiguous Zone*, 29 April 1958, 516 U.N.T.S. 205 (entered into force 10 September 1964); *Convention on the High Seas*, 29 April 1958, 450 U.N.T.S. 11 (entered into force 30 September 1962); *Convention on Fishing and Conservation of the Living Resources of the High Seas*, 29 April 1958, 559 U.N.T.S. 285 (entered into force 20 March 1966); *Convention on the Continental Shelf*, above note 39.

137 *United Nations Convention on the Law of the Sea*, 10 December 1982, 1833 U.N.T.S. 3 (entered into force 16 November 1994).

138 See Chapter 7, Section C.

139 *Vienna Convention*, above note 12, Article 54.

is said to be *amended*.[140] Where only some parties to a multilateral treaty subsequently agree to change its terms as between themselves alone, it is said that the treaty has been *modified* as between those parties.[141] In the latter case, much the same limitations are imposed on the ability of certain parties to mutually modify the terms of a multilateral treaty as are imposed on parties purporting to accede to or ratify a multilateral treaty subject to reservations.

4) Treaties and Non-Parties

Given their essentially consensual nature, it is a fundamental principle that treaties create neither rights nor obligations for non-parties. If it were otherwise, the entire apparatus for the giving and ascertainment of consent to be bound by treaty obligations would be largely superfluous. The principle of the sovereign equality of states would also be jeopardized as some states, by concluding treaties, could affect the legal positions of others without their consent. The *Vienna Convention* thus consecrates as a "general rule" the proposition that treaties do not apply to non-parties.[142]

There remains some controversy over possible exceptions to this general principle.[143] For example, the situation where the substance of a treaty's provisions enter the corpus of customary international law is sometimes characterized as an exception to the non-party rule. Of course, it is nothing of the kind as the legal obligation for the non-party flows from the customary status of the rule and not the existence of the treaty between other states.[144] The special case of Article 2(6) of the *UN Charter*, which appears to impose a duty on states members to ensure that non-members respect the principles of the UN insofar as necessary to maintain international peace and security, is also sometimes cited as an example of a treaty provision that imposes duties of compliance on non-parties.[145] However, again, any such effect is more likely the result

---

140 *Ibid.*, Article 40.
141 *Ibid.*, Article 41.
142 *Ibid.*, Article 34.
143 See, generally, Brownlie, above note 15 at 599–600; Reuter, above note 15 at 121–29.
144 See *Vienna Convention*, above note 12, Article 38, which foresees such a possibility. See further Chapter 5, Section E(2).
145 See, for example, H. Kelsen, *The Law of the United Nations: A Critical Analysis of its Fundamental Problems* (New York: F.A. Praeger, 1951) at 106–10.

of the passage of the UN principles into the body of universally applicable customary international law.[146]

There is some authority, however, for the proposition that treaties may create enforceable rights, if not obligations, for non-parties. In the *Free Zones Case*,[147] the issue was a term of the *Treaty of Versailles* of 1919, to which France was a party but Switzerland was not. Article 435 of the *Treaty* provided that both states were to settle the status of certain "free zones" on their common border. When negotiations between the two states failed, France unilaterally abrogated the status of the free zones. One issue put before the Permanent Court of International Justice was whether the *Treaty of Versailles* could impose an obligation on Switzerland to concur in such abrogation. The Court confirmed that such could only be the case if Switzerland, a non-party to the *Treaty*, had accepted such an obligation. However, the Court went on to suggest that the same was not necessarily true in the case of the conferral of rights by treaty on a non-party:

> It cannot be lightly presumed that stipulations favourable to a third State have been adopted with the object of creating an actual right in its favour. There is however nothing to prevent the will of sovereign States from having this object and this effect. The question of the existence of a right acquired under an instrument drawn between other States is therefore one to be decided in each particular case: it must be ascertained whether the States which have stipulated in favour of a third State meant to create for that State an actual right which the latter has accepted as such.[148]

This statement seems to suggest, albeit ambiguously, that an enforceable right can be created unilaterally by parties to a treaty in favour of a non-party.[149] Such a proposition should not seem too startling given that international law has come to recognize that unilateral undertakings by states can give rise to obligations enforceable by recipients of such undertakings.[150] The difficulty, however, is whether such a result is a treaty right or obligation properly so-called.

As seen above, the *Vienna Convention* has adopted the conventional view that the creation of rights and obligations for non-parties requires,

---

146 Brownlie, above note 15 at 599.
147 *Case of the Free Zones of Upper Savoy and the District of Gex (France v. Switzerland)* (1932), P.C.I.J. (Ser. A/B) No. 46 [*Free Zones Case*].
148 *Ibid.* at 147–48.
149 The use of the expression "as such" seems to suggest that the right accepted already exists "as such"; see Brownlie, above note 15 at 600.
150 See Chapter 3, Section D(1).

at least on some level, their consent. Some practical accommodation of the view that the unilateral imposition of obligations is a substantially different matter than the unilateral conferral of benefits has been provided, however. Thus, the imposition of obligations on a non-party requires its express consent, whereas consent to the conferral of rights is presumed unless the contrary is established.[151] Thereafter, revocability of unilaterally conferred rights depends on the intent of the conferring states,[152] whereas obligations, once accepted, may only be altered by consent of the parties and the non-party.[153]

H. INTERPRETATION OF TREATIES

1) General Principles: The "Ordinary Meaning" Rule and its Qualifications

This important area is the subject of considerable uncertainty and inconsistency in the practice of international and domestic tribunals called upon to interpret treaties. Based on an early review of the jurisprudence of the International Court of Justice, Fitzmaurice noted at least three dominant schools of thought on the correct approach to treaty interpretation:

1) the "intentions of the parties" approach, which seeks out the original intent of the parties by reference to any evidence of such intent, whether textual or extrinsic;
2) the "textual" or "ordinary meaning" approach, which focuses on the words used in the treaty itself and gives them their usual and natural interpretation; and
3) the "teleological" or "aims and objects" approach, which attempts to give effect to the court's understanding of the overall or general purpose of the treaty by interpreting its various provisions in conformity with that understanding.[154]

All have shortcomings, involve varying degrees of circular reasoning, and overlap to some extent. It appears, moreover, that international tribunals resort from time to time to all of these approaches, either singly

---

151 *Vienna Convention*, above note 12, Articles 35 & 36.
152 *Ibid.*, Article 37(2).
153 *Ibid.*, Article 37(1).
154 G. Fitzmaurice, "The Law and Procedure of the International Court of Justice: Treaty Interpretation and Certain Other Treaty Points" (1951) 28 Brit. Y.B. Int'l L. 1 at 1–2.

or in combination, with little sustained discussion of the appropriateness of doing so.

Notwithstanding this variable practice, the International Law Commission formed the opinion that the textual or ordinary meaning approach is predominant.[155] However, the uncertainty of the topic probably explains why the Commission chose to limit its treatment in the *Vienna Convention* to a statement of very general guiding principles contained in only three articles.[156]

Thus, Article 31, the "general rule of interpretation," refers in the first instance to the "ordinary meaning to be given to the terms of the treaty." This is a clear reference to the textual approach which privileges, above all else, the natural meaning of the words used in the treaty itself.[157] However, that rule is immediately qualified by the requirement that the terms be interpreted "in good faith," "in their context," and in light of the treaty's "object and purpose."[158] The latter qualification is obviously reminiscent of the teleological approach described by Fitzmaurice, whereas "context" is defined to include such extrinsic materials as corollary agreements concluded between the same set of parties or other instruments made in connection with the conclusion of the treaty.[159] The reference to context, and arguably the requirement of good faith, therefore appear to point in the direction of the original intentions of the parties.

In addition, subsequent agreements or practices of the parties related to the treaty may be referred to as a guide to its interpretation.[160] This is justifiable in that a treaty ultimately derives its legal force from the consent of the parties to it. They are therefore presumably in the best position to determine, by express agreement or common conduct, the meaning of their own treaty obligations. The same cannot be said,

---

155 "Report of the International Law Commission on the Second Part of its Seventeenth Session (Monaco, 3–28 January 1966) and on its Eighteenth Session" (UN Doc. A/6309/Rev.1) in *Yearbook of the International Law Commission 1966*, vol. II (New York: United Nations, 1966) at 220 [ILC Report (1966)].

156 *Vienna Convention*, above note 12, Articles 31–33. The latter Article deals with issues of priority should a conflict arise between versions of a treaty that has been authenticated in two or more languages. Subject to contrary agreement between the parties, all official language versions rate equally and are to be reconciled.

157 However, if it is established that the parties intended to attribute a special meaning to a term, that meaning should prevail: *ibid.*, Article 31(4).

158 *Ibid.*, Article 31(1).

159 *Ibid.*, Article 31(2).

160 *Ibid.*, Article 31(3).

however, of the unilateral practice of only some parties to the treaty that is not concurred in by the others.[161]

Finally, resort may be had in cases of ambiguity or absurdity to other extrinsic materials such as the preparatory work of the treaty (often referred to by international lawyers as the *travaux préparatoires*).[162] Such preparatory work might include drafts, comments of governments, and other evidence relating to the process of treaty-making. Resort to such inconclusive material is generally resisted, however, unless made necessary by the obscurity of the text finally adopted in the treaty.[163]

It can thus be seen that the textual or ordinary meaning approach to treaty interpretation is merely a point of departure and that, in fact, elements of all three approaches described by Fitzmaurice are present in the *Vienna Convention*'s rules of treaty interpretation. While the result may seem untidy at best and unprincipled at worst, it nevertheless reflects the fundamental lack of clarity in this evolving area of treaty law.[164]

2) The Intertemporal Rule

One particular problem of treaty interpretation that frequently arises is whether and how a treaty's meaning may evolve over time. This is an important issue as treaties are, depending on their terms and surrounding circumstances, of potentially indefinite duration. Present rights and obligations of states are frequently affected by treaties concluded in the relatively distant past. It is in this context that the doctrine of intertemporal law plays an important role in treaty interpretation.

The doctrine of intertemporal law provides that a legal right or obligation (whether or not set out in a treaty) must be appreciated in light of the law applicable at the time it arose, and not of the law applicable at the time when a dispute in respect of such right or obligation arises.[165] The doctrine is broadly applicable to any situation where the determination of current rights or obligations depends on a legal

---

161 See, for example, the case of *Jesse Lewis (United States) v. Great Britain (David J. Adams)* (1921), 6 R.I.A.A. 85.

162 *Vienna Convention*, above note 12, Article 32.

163 This explains the description of this provision in the *Vienna Convention* as a "supplementary means of interpretation."

164 See, for example, the *Interpretation of Peace Treaties with Bulgaria, Hungary and Romania (Second Phase), Advisory Opinion*, [1950] I.C.J. Rep. 221, where the Court, while nominally applying the ordinary meaning rule, also refers to the general practice of states and the overall purpose of the treaty when read as a whole in interpreting it.

165 See, for example, G. Schwarzenberger, *International Law*, vol. 1, 3d ed. (London: Stevens & Sons, 1957) at 23; J.H.W. Verzijl, *International Law in Historical Perspec-*

assessment of past events or circumstances.[166] In the context of treaty law, such past events or circumstances include, of course, the entry into force of a treaty between the parties at a time when its terms may have borne a different legal meaning than today. The basic rationale of the rule has been explained thus:

> ... [I]t is not permissible to import into the legal evaluation of a pre-viously existing situation, or of an old treaty, doctrines of modern law that did not exist or were not accepted at the time, and only resulted from the subsequent development or evolution of inter-national law.[167]

The *locus classicus* of the doctrine is generally considered to be the explanation for its application in the award of Judge Huber in the *Island of Palmas Case*.[168] The issue in that case was whether the Netherlands had established and maintained sovereignty over the Island of Palmas, to the exclusion of Spain, up to the date (1898) when Spain had pur-ported to alienate the island by treaty to the United States. In assessing the argument that Spain had discovered, and thereby established its sovereignty over, the island in the early sixteenth century, Judge Huber applied the following rule:

> [A] juridical fact must be appreciated in the light of the law contem-porary with it, and not of the law in force at the time when a dispute in regard to it arises or falls to be settled. The effect of discovery by Spain [of the Island of Palmas] is therefore to be determined by the rules of international law in force in the first half of the sixteenth century....[169]

Judge Huber was not specifically considering the application of the intertemporal rule to treaty interpretation; however, the International Court of Justice has widely endorsed the doctrine he expounded in the *Island of Palmas* case in a variety of contexts. For example, the Inter-national Court of Justice applied the doctrine in the treaty context in

---

tive, Modern International Law Series No. 12, vol. 8 (Leiden: A.W. Sijthoff, 1976) at 296; Brownlie, above note 15 at 124–25; and Shaw, above note 18 at 429–30.

166 G. Fitzmaurice, "The Law and Procedure of the International Court of Justice, 1951–54: General Principles and Sources of Law" (1953) 30 Brit. Y.B. Int'l L. 1 at 5–8.

167 *Ibid.* at 5 (footnote omitted from quotation).

168 *Island of Palmas Case (Netherlands v. United States of America)* (1928), 2 R.I.A.A. 829. See also the *Decision of the Permanent Court of Arbitration in the matter of the Maritime Boundary Dispute between Norway and Sweden (Grisbadarna Case)* (1909), (1910) 4 A.J.I.L. 226 at 231–32.

169 *Island of Palmas Case, ibid.* at 845.

the *Case Concerning Rights of Nationals of the United States of America in Morocco*.[170] There the Court had to assess the significance of a number of treaties concluded between the United States and Morocco. It did so in light of the intertemporal rule as follows:

> The Treaty of 1836 replaced an earlier treaty between the United States and Morocco which was concluded in 1787. The two treaties were substantially identical in terms and Articles 20 and 21 are the same in both. Accordingly, in construing the provisions of Article 20 … it is necessary to take into account the meaning of the word "dispute" at the times when the two treaties were concluded. For this purpose it is possible to look at the way in which the word "dispute" or its French counterpart was used in the different treaties concluded by Morocco. … It is clear that in these instances the word was used to cover both civil and criminal disputes. … It is also necessary to take into account that, at the times of these two treaties, the clear-cut distinction between civil and criminal matters had not yet been developed in Morocco.[171]

An important qualification to the doctrine's application in the treaty context is set out in the Court's judgment in the *Aegean Sea Continental Shelf Case*.[172] As seen above, that case concerned a dispute between Greece and Turkey as to the maritime boundary dividing their respective continental shelves. The Court's jurisdiction was said by Greece to be founded in part upon the *1928 General Act for Pacific Settlement of International Disputes*, to which both Greece and Turkey were parties.

Turkey objected to the Court's jurisdiction in part on the basis that Greece, in acceding to the *General Act*, had formulated a reservation excluding "disputes relating to the territorial status of Greece." Turkey sought to rely upon this reservation, whereas Greece urged a restrictive reading of the reservation due to the "historical context in which that expression was incorporated into the reservation."[173] In particular Greece urged that, since the concept of the continental shelf had yet not emerged in international law at the time of the formulation of the reservation, the reservation's reference to "territorial status" could not be read to include disputes relating to the status of the continental shelf. The Court rejected this argument on the following basis:

---

170   *Case Concerning Rights of Nationals of the United States of America in Morocco (France v. United States of America)*, [1952] I.C.J. Rep. 176 [*US Nationals in Morocco Case*].
171   *Ibid.* at 189.
172   *Aegean Sea Continental Shelf Case*, above note 34.
173   *Ibid.* at 28–29.

Once it is established that the expression "the territorial status of Greece" was used in Greece's instrument of accession as a generic term denoting any matters comprised within the concept of territorial status under general international law, the presumption necessarily arises that its meaning was intended to follow the evolution of the law and to correspond with the meaning attached to the expression by the law in force at any given time. This presumption ... is even more compelling when it is recalled that the *1928 Act* was a convention for the pacific settlement of disputes designed to be of the most general kind and of continuing duration, for it hardly seems conceivable that in such a convention terms like "domestic jurisdiction" and "territorial status" were intended to have a fixed content regardless of the subsequent evolution of international law.[174]

Accordingly, the Court concluded that the intent of parties (including Greece) to the *General Act* was that it should have *continuing* effect and that its terms should therefore receive a *continuing* interpretation in the light of *evolving* international law. Greece's argument that "territorial status" could not have referred to the concept of the continental shelf in 1928 was thus rejected as irrelevant.

This "continuing" aspect of the intertemporal rule simply flows from the fact that most treaties, at least those of a norm-creating character, continue to "speak" during their lifetime. Thus, the Court held in the *South West Africa Case*, for example, that the operation of the mandates and trust systems established under the *Covenant of the League of Nations* and under the *UN Charter* had to be interpreted and applied in the light of current developments in the general international legal framework, within which those instruments continued to operate.[175]

Finally, note that the intertemporal doctrine also has implications for the very process of treaty formation itself, as illustrated in the Court's judgment in the *Case Concerning Right of Passage over Indian Territory*.[176] In that case Portugal relied on a late eighteenth century treaty concluded between it and local Indian rulers in which the latter had conferred on Portugal sovereignty over certain enclaves as well as a right of passage to and from such enclaves. India objected to reliance on this treaty in part because it had not been validly concluded. The Court rejected this argument thus:

---

174 *Ibid.* at 32.
175 *South West Africa Case*, above note 15 at 31.
176 *Case Concerning Right of Passage over Indian Territory (Portugal v. India) (Merits),* [1960] I.C.J. Rep. 6 [*Right of Passage Case*].

The Court does not consider it necessary to deal with these and other objections raised by India to the form of the Treaty and the procedure by means of which agreement upon its terms was reached. It is sufficient to state that the validity of a treaty concluded as long ago as the last quarter of the eighteenth century, in the conditions then prevailing in the Indian Peninsula, should not be judged upon the basis of practices and procedures which have since developed only gradually....[177]

Thus, the validity of the conclusion of a treaty, and not only its interpretation, is to be judged not by reference to current treaty law but rather the legal circumstances prevailing at the time of that conclusion.

I. INVALIDITY OF TREATIES

1) Introduction

There may be instances in which all of the prescribed procedures and formalities for bringing a treaty into force have been complied with, and yet there remains some fundamental legal flaw that goes to the very root of the treaty's validity. As treaties are based on consent freely given by states in the exercise of their sovereign will, the most serious such flaws are those that in some way taint the validity of that consent. Thus, customary international law and the *Vienna Convention* provide for a number of bases of "invalidity of treaties."[178]

Given their fundamental effects, to be reviewed below, the recognition of bases of invalidity could potentially undermine the entire treaty system. This would particularly be so if it were open to states to invoke too readily a basis of invalidity in order to evade treaty obligations duly undertaken. The reliability of treaty engagements would always be open to question and the *pacta sunt servanda* principle thus seriously jeopardized. It is for this reason that the recognized bases of invalidity of treaties are quite narrow in scope and subject to strict application. Furthermore, it is generally considered that the bases of invalidity enumerated in the *Vienna Convention* are exhaustive — there

---

177 *Ibid.* at 37.
178 *Vienna Convention*, above note 12, Articles 46–53. As for the customary status of these rules, it has been observed that there is very little state practice in this area. However, the rules set out in Articles 46–53 are merely elementary extensions or corollaries of fundamental international legal principles, such as the requirement of consent, that have a solid basis in customary international law: see Reuter, above note 15 at 173.

are no other circumstances in which a state may assert that its apparent consent to be bound should be set aside.[179]

2) Bases of Invalidity

a) Domestic Legal Competence to Conclude Treaties

The first basis of invalidity is particularly narrow because it relies upon provisions of domestic law of the apparently consenting state to invalidate that consent. This comes perilously close to conflicting with the basic principle that domestic law provides no excuse for failing to perform a treaty obligation,[180] but in fact the two issues are quite distinct. The obligation to perform treaty obligations notwithstanding domestic legal impediments, codified in Article 27 of the *Vienna Convention*, relies upon the existence of a valid treaty in force for, and thus binding upon, the parties. Successful invocation of a domestic legal impediment to the validity of a state's expression of consent to be bound, however, goes to the very act of creation of a valid and enforceable treaty obligation. Technically, therefore, there is no conflict between a treaty obligation and a domestic legal obligation because the former has not truly come into existence.

Nevertheless, the general antipathy in international law towards subordinating international to domestic legal obligations, and the very real policy concerns underlying that antipathy,[181] have resulted in very little scope for invalidating a treaty on this basis. In fact, Article 46 of the *Vienna Convention* states as the general rule that a state may *not* rely upon the fact that its consent to be bound by a treaty was expressed in violation of its domestic law, except in specific circumstances.

There are essentially two such circumstances. The first is where the domestic rule violated by the expression of consent was "manifest" and of "fundamental importance." A "manifest" violation of domestic law is defined as one that would be "objectively evident" to other states in the normal course of events.[182] The chief difficulty with this definition lies in its indeterminacy. Moreover, what constitutes a domestic rule of "fundamental importance" remains undefined. The obvious intent is at least to exclude invocation by a state of technical breaches of its domestic law in order to escape treaty obligations. It also seems to be generally recognized that violations of a constitutional order would be fundamental although it is open to question whether all such violations

179 *Vienna Convention*, above note 12, Article 42(1).
180 *Ibid.*, Article 27; and see Section G(1), above in this chapter.
181 See, generally, *ibid.*
182 *Vienna Convention*, above note 12, Article 46(2).

would be plainly obvious to other states. An example of a fundamental violation that would presumably be manifest would be an attempt by a Canadian province, or clearer still, a Canadian municipality, to conclude a treaty with a foreign state.[183]

However, it remains unclear just how "manifest" or "fundamental" a rule must be in order to qualify as an exception to the general rule that domestic law is irrelevant to the validity of treaty formation. In these circumstances it is probably necessary to refer for guidance to the underlying policy of the rule and its exceptions. In addition to the maintenance of stability in treaty relations, there is a clear need for predictability and reasonable reliance between states when concluding treaties. Thus, if a state reasonably appears to express its consent to be bound in the normal way, other states ought to be able to rely on that appearance in good faith. The good faith requirement means, however, that if such other states knew or ought to have known, because of its notorious character, of some domestic legal impediment to the state's capacity to express its consent, their reliance is no longer reasonable. The International Law Commission, in preparing what has since become Article 46 of the *Vienna Convention*, took the view that such a principled approach, accommodating the legitimate and reasonable interests of all parties, was supported in state practice and the decisions of international tribunals.[184]

The second exception, narrower still, concerns restrictions on a state representative's authority to express consent on behalf of the state. In general, a failure by the state representative to observe such restrictions is not a basis for vitiating that consent.[185] For example, if a state representative is only authorized to ratify a treaty subject to the formulation of a reservation, but the treaty is ratified by the representative unconditionally, that ratification and the treaty will be valid. This flows from elementary principles of agency and the full powers of the state representative. However, if the restriction on the representative's authority was previously notified to the other negotiating parties, his or her failure to observe it can then be invoked by the state to invalidate its consent. Again it will be seen that this approach seeks to preserve the stability of treaties to the fullest extent possible while recognizing

---

183 This would violate the basic constitutional position in Canada that only the federal government has the power to conclude treaties on behalf of Canada: see below Chapter 6, Section C(3)(c)(i).

184 ILC Report (1966), above note 155 at 240–42.

185 *Vienna Convention*, above note 12, Article 47.

that no unfairness would result to other states by holding them to a situation of which they had actual knowledge.[186]

b) Mistake of Fact

Error is probably the most widely accepted basis for invalidating a state's consent to be bound by a treaty.[187] It is generally recognized in customary international law and is now expressly stated in Article 48 of the *Vienna Convention*. In particular, a state's mistaken belief in a fact or situation at the time of the conclusion of a treaty will invalidate its expression of consent to be bound by that treaty, but only where that fact or situation was an essential basis of its consent.[188]

The basis of this rule is simply the requirement of genuine consent in treaty law. If a state's consent to the terms of a treaty was premised on a non-existent state of affairs, there has in fact been no true consent at all. The difficulty, of course, is in establishing the "essential" connection between the mistaken belief and the expression of consent, and this may be an area open to potential abuse. However, a certain rigidity is introduced to the rule in providing that a state cannot invoke its error if it contributed to it or if the state ought in the circumstances to have recognized its mistake.[189] Thus, permissible errors are errors of fact, not of law. Moreover, states will be held to an objective standard in relying upon their mistakes of fact, thereby reducing the likelihood of undue exploitation of the rule.

c) Fraud

Closely related to error but involving the added element of deceit by another state is the case of fraud. Article 49 of the *Vienna Convention* provides that where a state has been induced to enter into a treaty by the fraudulent conduct of another negotiating party, that state can invalidate its consent to be bound by the treaty. If the fraud relates to an essential fact, there will be almost complete overlap with the concept of error. It may thus be wondered whether there is any need for a separate basis of invalidity in the case of fraud.

---

186 ILC Report (1966), above note 155 at 243.

187 See Reuter, above note 15 at 176. See also Brownlie, above note 15 at 590.

188 *Vienna Convention*, above note 12, Article 48(1).

189 *Ibid.*, Article 48(2). For example, a state cannot escape its mistaken recognition of another state's sovereignty over territory if its mistake is attributable to its own poorly drawn map: see *Case Concerning the Temple of Preah Vihear (Cambodia v. Thailand) (Merits)*, [1962] I.C.J. Rep. 6 at 57–58, Separate Opinion of Fitzmaurice J.

It has been noted, however, that the act of fraud itself furnishes virtually conclusive proof that the misrepresented fact is an "essential basis" of the defrauded state's consent, thus easing the injured state's burden of proof in this regard.[190] Otherwise, the defrauding state would have had little to gain from its deceit. Further, the act of fraud may itself be an internationally wrongful act that will entail consequences beyond the validity of the treaty.[191] This may in part explain why there are few if any precedents disclosing fraud in the treaty-making context.[192]

d) Bribery

Bribery or "corruption" of a state representative is also recognized in the *Vienna Convention* as a basis for invalidating a state's consent to be bound by a treaty, as long as there is a causal relationship between the act of corruption and the representative's act of expressing consent.[193] There was considerable debate in the International Law Commission as to whether this possibility was already adequately covered by other provisions, such as those addressing fraud. In the end it was considered prudent to address this rather particular form of deceit in a separate article.[194]

Some authors consider this to have been justified due to the underlying differences between a direct act of fraud and the surreptitious corruption of a state representative's loyalty: a corrupted representative ceases to be a representative at all in any real sense.[195] Any expression of consent given by such a "representative" ought, therefore, to be subject to withdrawal by the state on whose behalf it was purportedly given.

Article 50 stipulates that, to give rise to invalidity, the act of corruption can either be "directly or indirectly" that of another negotiating state. It is thus contemplated that acts of persons not officially connected to the offending state, but acting at its behest or in circumstances otherwise rendering it internationally responsible for such acts,[196] will suffice.

e) Coercion of State Representatives

Beyond acts of bribery or corruption, blackmail and other personal threats made against a state representative obviously call into question

---

190 See Reuter, above note 15 at 177.
191 See further Chapter 12.
192 See Brownlie, above note 15 at 590; Reuter, above note 15 at 177; ILC Report (1966), above note 155 at 244–45.
193 *Vienna Convention*, above note 12, Article 50.
194 ILC Report (1966), above note 155 at 245.
195 See, for example, Reuter, above note 15 at 178.
196 See further Chapter 12, Section A(4)(b).

his or her ability to give true expression to the will of the represented state. In effect, where a representative's expression of consent to a treaty is brought about by threats made against his or her person, family, property, or reputation, no true representation exists at all.[197] Accordingly, an expression of consent to be bound procured by threats against a representative has no legal effect in binding a state to a treaty.[198]

Such acts of coercion are generally considered serious violations of international law. Given the agency relationship between state representatives and the states they represent, coercion is in many respects tantamount to threats directed at the represented state itself. This explains in part why the terms of Article 51 of the *Vienna Convention* are at once more permissive and severe than in the case of fraud (Article 49) and corruption (Article 50). They are more permissive in that there is no express requirement that the act of coercion be attributable to another negotiating party. Further, coercion leads to the automatic invalidity of the expression of consent to be bound, without the need for the offended state to invoke such invalidity. Thus, coercion of a state representative, regardless of its author, automatically vitiates expressions of consent to be bound given by that representative.[199]

f) Coercion of State

A still more serious basis of invalidity recognized in the *Vienna Convention* is direct coercion of the state itself. Article 52 provides that a treaty brought about by the threat or use of force contrary to the *UN Charter* is void. This is a relatively straightforward proposition, as consent procured by an illegal threat or use of force can hardly be considered a free expression of a state's sovereign will. Note however that not all force, but only that contrary to the provisions of the *UN Charter*, automatically voids treaties thus brought about.[200]

It should be noted that, during the negotiation of the *Vienna Convention*, several states pushed for an expanded notion of coercion that would have included economic and political coercion in addition to armed coercion. As such a rule would likely have jeopardized virtually every treaty in existence and made the negotiation of future treaties

---

197 See, generally, Reuter, above note 15 at 179–80.

198 *Vienna Convention*, above note 12, Article 51.

199 See, generally, Reuter, above note 15 at 179–80.

200 For example, the *UN Charter* permits the use of force in self-defence: see *UN Charter*, above note 2, Article 51. It also permits the threat or use of force as a collective measure of enforcement sanctioned by the UN Security Council pursuant to its Chapter VII powers: see further Chapter 11. Thus, not all peace treaties procured by the threat or use of armed force are necessarily invalid.

a very delicate if not impossible matter, this initiative was rejected.[201] While economic or political coercion may, if sufficiently serious, violate important principles of international law and lead to state responsibility,[202] it therefore appears that only coercion involving the illegal threat or use of armed force, within the meaning of the *UN Charter*, will give rise to the invalidity of a treaty.[203]

The relative seriousness with which such acts of state coercion are viewed by the international community is reflected in the finality of the provisions of Article 52. In contrast to all prior bases of invalidity, which invalidate the offended state's consent to be bound, Article 52 automatically voids the treaty itself, in its entirety. What is at stake, therefore, is not merely the participation of the wronged party in a multilateral treaty, but the very existence of the treaty itself for all parties.

g) Conflict with *Jus Cogens*

Finally, the *Vienna Convention* provides that a treaty is void if at the time of its conclusion it conflicts with a "peremptory norm of general international law."[204] Such norms, also known in international law as *jus cogens*, generally take the form of rules of customary international

---

201 Although the Vienna Conference adopted a declaration condemning the "threat or use of pressure in any form, whether military, political or economic … in violation of the principles of the sovereign equality of States and freedom of consent": "Declaration on the Prohibition of the Threat or Use of Economic or Political Coercion in Concluding a Treaty," in *UN Conference on the Law of Treaties*, UN CLTOR, 1968-1969, UN Doc. A/CONF.39/1/Add.2 (1971). The difficulty with this condemnation, of course, is its ambiguity: its meaning turns critically on the degree of pressure or coercion required to violate the sovereign equality of another state or its freedom of consent, and states tend to take different views on that issue. In any event, note the significance of the adoption of this principle in a declaration rather than in the text of the *Vienna Convention* itself.

202 See, for example, "Declaration of Principles of International Law Concerning Friendly Relations and Co-operation Among States in Accordance with the *Charter of the United Nations*," UNGA Res. 2625, 25 U.N. GOAR Supp. (No. 28) at 121, U.N. Doc. A/8028 (1970) [*Friendly Relations Declaration*]. While not binding on states *per se*, the *Friendly Relations Declaration* restates fundamental principles of customary international law, including the prohibition on intervention by states in the domestic affairs of other states. In particular: "No State may use or encourage the use of economic, political or any other type of measures to coerce another State in order to obtain from it the subordination of the exercise of its sovereign rights and to secure from it advantages of any kind."

203 See, generally, Brownlie, above note 15 at 590–91; Reuter, above note 15 at 180–84.

204 *Vienna Convention*, above note 12, Article 53.

law.[205] Their distinguishing and defining feature is that they are universally recognized as so fundamental to the fabric of the international legal system that states may not, even by mutual consent, modify or derogate from their application.[206] They thus represent a body of "higher law" binding upon all states notwithstanding agreements to the contrary.[207] By definition, therefore, a treaty that purports to oust the application of a peremptory norm must be void.

There has been considerable controversy in the international community concerning the existence, character, and effects of peremptory norms or *jus cogens*. These difficulties clearly stem from the apparent incompatibility of the concept with the theory of consent.[208] Such criticisms overlook the fact that peremptory norms are generally considered to emanate from a general or universal consensus among states as to their peremptory and fundamental character. In any event, the debate has shifted in recent years from the existence of such peremptory norms to their extent and content.[209] Widely recognized examples of rules of *jus cogens* include the principle of *pacta sunt servanda*; the general prohibition on the unilateral use of force by states; the prohibition of international criminal acts such as genocide or of violations of fundamental human rights such as torture; and the illegality of colonial domination or alien subjugation.[210]

---

205 Although, strictly speaking, nothing prevents a treaty provision from acquiring the status, or codifying a rule, of *jus cogens*.

206 Article 53 sets forth one of the first succinct and widely endorsed definitions of the concept: "... a peremptory norm of general international law is a norm accepted and recognized by the international community of states as a whole as a norm from which no derogation is permitted and which can be modified only by a subsequent norm of general international law having the same character."

207 See, generally, G.M. Danilenko, *Law-Making in the International Community* (Dordrecht: Martinus Nijhoff, 1993) c. 8; J. Sztucki, *Jus Cogens and the Vienna Convention on the Law of Treaties: A Critical Appraisal* (Wien: Springer-Verlag, 1974); G.A. Christenson, "The World Court and *Jus Cogens*" (1987) 81 A.J.I.L. 93.

208 See further Chapter 3, Section B(2), and Chapter 5, Section E.

209 See, generally, J.G. Starke & I.A. Shearer, *Starke's International Law*, 11th ed. (London: Butterworths,1994) at 49. For example, the International Court of Justice recognized the general prohibition of the use of force by states as a principle of *jus cogens* in its judgment in *Case Concerning Military and Paramilitary Activities in and against Nicaragua (Nicaragua v. United States of America)*, [1986] I.C.J. Rep. 14 at 100 [*Nicaragua*].

210 See, generally, International Law Commission, "Commentaries to the Draft Articles on Responsibility of States for Internationally Wrongful Acts" in *Report of the International Law Commission on the Work of its Fifty-Third Session*, U.N. Doc. A/56/10 (2001) at 283–84.

Again, given the fundamental impermissibility of treaties that conflict with norms of *jus cogens,* their invalidity is general and not confined to the expression of any particular state's expression of consent to be bound. Thus a treaty containing a provision that is inconsistent with a peremptory norm will automatically be void in its entirety.

3) Consequences of Invalidity

A treaty or an expression of consent to be bound that is invalid pursuant to the bases reviewed above is generally considered void from the beginning.[211] Articles 46 to 53 of the *Vienna Convention* all relate to situations which in one way or another vitiate the validity of a state's (or in the case of Article 53, all states') consent to be bound by the treaty, and thus undermine the very basis for treaty relations from the outset.

However, there is an important distinction between the less serious bases of invalidity (Articles 46 through 50), on the one hand, and the cases of coercion and conflict with peremptory norms (Articles 51 through 53) on the other. In the former category, the establishment of a basis of invalidity places the aggrieved state in a position either to invalidate or to affirm its consent to be bound by the treaty. Any obligations involved are thus said to be voidable, rather than void. In other words, the expression of consent remains valid and effective until some positive step is taken by the aggrieved state to exercise its option to invalidate that consent. A failure to do so within a reasonable period of becoming aware of the basis of invalidity may be construed as an implied election to affirm, and thus as a waiver of the right to invalidate, the state's consent.[212] If the right to void one's expression of consent is exercised in a timely manner, however, consent is thereby voided *ab initio.* By contrast, the latter category of cases results in invalidity of either the treaty (Articles 52 and 53) or the aggrieved state's consent to be bound (Article 51) *automatically,* by operation of law. Any obligations involved are simply deemed to be void, again *ab initio.*

Whether a treaty or expression of consent to be bound is voided or void, the parties are to be returned as far as possible to the position they occupied prior to the purported conclusion of the treaty or expression of consent.[213] This is without prejudice to any potential legal

---

211 *Vienna Convention,* above note 12, Article 69.
212 *Ibid.,* Article 45.
213 *Ibid.,* Article 69(2).

ramifications for a state guilty of wrongdoing and thus responsible for the invalidity of the treaty or expression of consent to be bound.[214]

A further distinction exists between invalidity pursuant to Articles 46 through 50 on the one hand and Articles 51 through 53 on the other. As a general rule, invalidity operates with respect to the whole treaty.[215] If, however, the basis of invalidity relates only to certain clauses, those clauses may in certain circumstances be severed from the treaty, leaving the rest of it in force for the aggrieved party. This is only possible where those clauses can be separated from the remainder of the treaty in their application; were not an essential basis of the other parties' participation in the treaty; and the result would not otherwise be unjust.[216] However, in the case of invalidity under Articles 51 through 53, such severance is not permissible and the entire treaty is affected.[217] In the cases of fraud and corruption, which may be considered of intermediate seriousness, the aggrieved state has the option of voiding the treaty in whole or in part (or not at all),[218] as long as the foregoing conditions of severability are respected.[219]

J. TERMINATION AND SUSPENSION OF TREATY OBLIGATIONS

1) Introduction

It is implicit in the *pacta sunt servanda* principle that a validly constituted treaty is presumed to continue in force until it is either validly terminated or suspended. In the former case the obligation is brought to an end in its entirety,[220] whereas in the latter, performance is merely held in abeyance for a period without affecting the continued existence of the underlying treaty obligations themselves.[221]

As with the bases of invalidity reviewed above (which concern the validity of the creation rather than the termination of treaty obligations), the grounds for terminating or suspending treaty obligations

---

214 *Ibid.*, Article 69(3), with particular reference to acts of fraud, corruption, and coercion (Articles 49–52). See further Chapter 12.

215 *Vienna Convention*, above note 12, Article 44(2).

216 *Ibid.*, Article 44(3).

217 *Ibid.*, Article 44(5).

218 See above text accompanying note 212.

219 *Vienna Convention*, above note 12, Article 44(4).

220 *Ibid.*, Article 70.

221 *Ibid.*, Article 72.

are subject to strict constraints. In either case, the same policy concern for destabilizing the treaty system and undermining the reliability of treaty relations informs this strictness of approach. However, in cases of termination and suspension, the competing concern to give effect only to genuine expressions of consent is absent, given the starting assumption that the treaty to be terminated or suspended is valid. Thus, if anything, the scope for termination or suspension of treaty obligations is even more tightly circumscribed than it is for invalidation.

Nevertheless, respect for the sovereign will of states is never far from the core of treaty law. As we shall see, therefore, there are *some* circumstances in which states may avoid treaty obligations of indefinite duration while still respecting the principle of *pacta sunt servanda*. However, Article 42 of the *Vienna Convention* confirms that a treaty may only be terminated or suspended in accordance with its own terms or by application of one of the bases specifically set out in the *Vienna Convention*.[222]

A terminological issue should be addressed before examining the permissible bases for terminating or suspending treaties. The *Vienna Convention* uses the terms "denunciation" and "withdrawal" in connection with the termination of a treaty.[223] These concepts are relevant in those cases where the termination of a treaty obligation depends on an act of repudiation by the terminating party. In the case of a bilateral treaty, such an act is referred to as "denunciation" and will, if effective, bring about not only the end of the denouncing party's treaty obligations but also the treaty itself. In the case of a multilateral treaty, by contrast, the act of repudiation by a party is designated a "withdrawal." If effective, this terminates the withdrawing party's treaty obligations but potentially leaves the treaty itself intact for the remaining parties.

---

222 Note, however, that Article 73 provides that the *Vienna Convention*, above note 12, is without prejudice to the operation of other rules of law that may have an impact on a treaty, including the rules of state succession, state responsibility, or war. For example, we have seen that successor states do not as a general rule inherit the treaty obligations of a predecessor, which may bring about the termination of the treaty depending on the number of other parties to it and its subject matter: see further Chapter 2, Section B(5)(b). The outbreak of war does not necessarily lead to a termination of treaty obligations but in practice states may suspend performance until hostilities cease: see Brownlie, above note 15 at 593. Similarly, the severance of diplomatic relations between states does not entail termination or suspension of a mutual treaty unless the maintenance of such relations is indispensable to its performance: *Vienna Convention*, above note 12, Article 63.

223 See, for example, *Vienna Convention*, ibid., Articles 42(2), 54, and 56.

2) Bases for Suspension and Termination

a) Consent of the Parties

In keeping with the theory of consent, it is perfectly possible to terminate or suspend the operation of a treaty with the consent of all the parties. This may occur in a number of ways.

One of the most common devices is to provide expressly, in the treaty itself, for the circumstances under which either a party may withdraw or the treaty may be terminated or suspended.[224] This is, in effect, consent given before the fact of withdrawal, termination, or suspension. Such *a priori* consent can also be inferred from the circumstances surrounding the conclusion of the treaty or the subject matter of the treaty itself.[225] There is however a presumption against such an implied term that must be rebutted by the party purporting to denounce or withdraw from the treaty.[226] In the case of an implied term permitting denunciation or withdrawal, moreover, the *Vienna Convention* provides that twelve months' notice must be given of a party's intent to exercise such an option.[227] This provision echoes notice periods commonly included in express treaty provisions permitting denunciation or withdrawal.

The other common device for securing the consent of all parties, of course, is the conclusion of a subsequent treaty providing for termination, withdrawal from, or suspension of the original treaty.[228] This can occur at any time following the conclusion of the original treaty. While unanimous participation by the original parties is generally required, two or more parties to a multilateral treaty may suspend its operation as between themselves, but only as long as the rights of the other parties are not thereby prejudiced.[229]

As we have already seen, moreover, a subsequent treaty between (at least) the same parties that does not expressly provide for termination or suspension of the prior one may nevertheless implicitly do so.[230] Whether it has this effect or not will depend on the extent to which the subsequent treaty deals with the same subject matter, and either its terms or the circumstances disclose such an implied intent by the parties.

---

224 *Ibid.*, Articles 54(a) and 57(a).
225 *Ibid.*, Article 56(1).
226 See Shaw, above note 18 at 851.
227 *Vienna Convention*, above note 12, Article 56(2).
228 *Ibid.*, Articles 54(b) and 57(b).
229 *Ibid.*, Article 58.
230 *Ibid.*, Article 59; and see Section G(3), above in this chapter.

b) Material Breach

A material breach of a treaty occurs where one or more parties either repudiate it (other than on one of the bases of invalidity, withdrawal, or renunciation recognized in the *Vienna Convention*), or violate one of its essential provisions.[231] It has long been recognized that one response available to an aggrieved party when faced with a material breach by another party is either termination or suspension of performance of the treaty.[232] Such a self-help remedy aims to encourage respect for treaty obligations but also recognizes the reciprocal interests of a party faced with substantial non-performance by another. It is of course a purely optional response to a material breach, and therefore leaves the aggrieved party with the choice either to invoke the breach and terminate or suspend the treaty, or to affirm the treaty and demand performance. In neither case are further potential legal consequences for the offending party, including those foreseen in the treaty itself,[233] precluded.[234]

The difficulty with unilateral termination or suspension for material breach is that, notwithstanding its intended deterrent effect, its results can ultimately be destructive of the treaty relationship. This is obviously a more serious concern in the case of multilateral than bilateral treaties. Thus in the case of material breach of a bilateral treaty, the *Vienna Convention* merely provides that the treaty may be either terminated or suspended by the aggrieved party, either in whole or in part.[235] In the case of a multilateral treaty, however, the *Vienna Convention's* provisions are quite complex. In general, the possibilities envisaged are that:

1) all other parties to the treaty may, by unanimous agreement, *terminate or suspend* the treaty in whole or in part, either vis-à-vis the breaching party or altogether;[236]
2) a party specially affected by the breach may *suspend* the treaty between itself and the breaching state;[237] or
3) if the breach radically alters the obligations of every party to the treaty, any one of them may *suspend* the treaty in whole or in part with respect to itself.[238]

---

231 *Vienna Convention*, above note 12, Article 60(3).
232 See *Gabčíkovo-Nagymaros Case*, above note 15 at 65; *South West Africa Case*, above note 15 at 94–96.
233 *Vienna Convention*, above note 12, Article 60(4).
234 *Ibid.*, Article 73; and see further Chapter 12.
235 *Vienna Convention*, above note 12, Article 60(1).
236 *Ibid.*, Article 60(2)(a).
237 *Ibid.*, Article 60(2)(b).
238 *Ibid.*, Article 60(2)(c).

All of these provisions are subject, however, to the special importance attached to humanitarian treaties. In short, it is not permissible
for one state, aggrieved by another state's breach of a humanitarian
treaty, to jeopardize such humanitarian interests yet further by terminating or suspending such a treaty.[239]

c) Supervening Impossibility of Performance

If performance of treaty obligations is made impossible by some occurrence following its conclusion, this may furnish a ground for withdrawal from, terminating, or suspending the operation of the treaty.
However, the conditions in which this rule may be invoked are extremely narrow. The impossibility likely must be physical, as indicated
by the *Vienna Convention*'s requirement that it result from the "disappearance or destruction of an object indispensable for the execution
of the treaty."[240] Typical situations where the rule is invoked are the
disappearance of a geographical feature such as a river or an island, or
some installation necessary to the performance of the agreement.[241] If
the impossibility is permanent, termination is warranted; otherwise,
only suspension during the period of impossibility is permissible.[242]

The International Court of Justice has commented on the stringency of the requirement of impossibility in the *Case Concerning the
Gabčíkovo-Nagymaros Project*,[243] the facts of which have been described
above.[244] Hungary argued, *inter alia*, that the "object" referred to in
Article 61 of the *Vienna Convention* could include a legal regime, a relationship of a particular type, or perhaps even a more abstract concept such as the financial viability of a project. On the facts, Hungary
argued that the essential "object" of the treaty between itself and Slovakia[245] was "an economic joint investment which was consistent with
environmental protection and which was operated by the two contracting parties jointly," and that this had "disappeared."[246]

The Court noted, however, that at the time the *Vienna Convention*
was adopted, a proposal to expand the concept of impossibility to include such situations as impossibility to make payments because of
serious financial difficulties was rejected. While the Court did not find

---

239 *Ibid.*, Article 60(5).
240 *Ibid.*, Article 61.
241 See Brownlie, above note 15 at 594; Shaw, above note 18 at 855.
242 *Vienna Convention*, above note 12, Article 61(1).
243 *Gabčíkovo-Nagymaros Case*, above note 15.
244 See Chapter 2, Section B(5)(b).
245 As successor to Czechoslovakia.
246 *Gabčíkovo-Nagymaros Case,* above note 15 at 63–64.

it necessary in the end to resolve the precise extent of the concept of "object," as Hungary had brought about its own "impossibility" in any event, it is clear that the Court found the very expansive reading of the term urged by Hungary to be objectionable.[247]

Of course, if the party seeking to invoke impossibility has created the situation of impossibility by breaching the treaty or another obligation, this ground of termination or suspension will be unavailable.[248]

d) Fundamental Change of Circumstances

A more controversial basis for terminating or suspending treaty obligations is a so-called fundamental change of circumstances.[249] What is contemplated here is something other than physical impossibility, but the required seriousness of the obstacles presented by the fundamental change appears to be no less stringent. The essential features of a qualifying fundamental change are that it relate to an "essential basis" of the party's consent to the treaty and that it be so fundamental in effect as to radically transform the obligations still to be performed.[250] In other words, the situation must have changed so dramatically from that which existed at the time the treaty was concluded that the nature of the obligations are radically different from those initially contemplated.

Given the inherent fluidity of such notions as "essential basis" and "radically transformed," and the concomitant danger they pose to the stability of treaties, treaty law is particularly hostile to this ground of termination. The presumptive position in Article 62 of the *Vienna Convention* is therefore that a fundamental change of circumstances may *not* be invoked as a ground of termination or suspension unless the two foregoing elements are established. Further, a fundamental change may not be invoked if the possibility of such a change was foreseen at the time the treaty was concluded. For example, if a treaty provides for its own dispute resolution mechanism, this may evidence foresight of potential changes to the positions of the parties which would, in consequence, not qualify as grounds for termination under Article 62.[251]

The International Court of Justice in the *Case Concerning the Gabčíkovo-Nagymaros Project*[252] also had occasion to comment on the

---

247 *Ibid.*
248 *Vienna Convention*, above note 12, Article 61(2).
249 Often referred to as the *rebus sic stantibus* doctrine.
250 *Vienna Convention*, above note 12, Article 62(1).
251 See, for example, *Fisheries Jurisdiction Case*, above note 15 at paras. 35–43 and Separate Opinion of Fitzmaurice J. at para. 17. See also *Gabčíkovo-Nagymaros Case*, above note 15 at 64.
252 *Gabčíkovo-Nagymaros Case*, ibid.

stringent requirements of Article 62. Hungary had argued that various changes in the economic, environmental, and political viability of its joint undertaking with Slovakia amounted cumulatively to a fundamental change of circumstances that warranted termination of the treaty. The Court rejected these submissions, noting that the possibility of such changes was neither unforeseen by the parties at the time they concluded their agreement nor of such a fundamental character as to radically transform the nature of that treaty. The Court captured the rarity with which Article 62 may be validly invoked thus:

> The negative and conditional wording of Article 62 of the Vienna Convention on the Law of Treaties is a clear indication moreover that the stability of treaty relations requires that the plea of fundamental change of circumstances be applied only in exceptional cases.[253]

Finally, note that, in the interests of the stability of international borders and the maintenance of international peace and security, a fundamental change of circumstances may not be invoked to terminate or withdraw from a treaty that establishes such a boundary.[254]

e) Conflict with New Norm of *Jus Cogens*

Just as a treaty incompatible with a pre-existing norm of *jus cogens* is by definition invalid *ab initio*,[255] so too is a treaty inconsistent with a new norm of *jus cogens* automatically terminated, by operation of law, from the moment of emergence of that new *jus cogens* norm. This follows from the very nature of a norm of *jus cogens*, which is not subject to derogation by any rule of international law other than one having the same *jus cogens* character.

3) Consequences of Suspension or Termination

Unlike a situation of invalidity, the suspension or termination of treaty obligations presupposes that there are valid treaty obligations to be suspended or terminated in the first place. There is thus no basis for denying the legal effects of those treaty relations prior to the moment of suspension or termination. Article 70 of the *Vienna Convention* therefore takes the logical position that, absent agreement between the parties to the contrary, the termination of treaty relations releases parties from further performance of the treaty but does not otherwise affect

---

253 *Ibid.* at 64–65.
254 *Vienna Convention*, above note 12, Article 62(2)(a).
255 See Section 1(2)(g), above in this chapter.

the positions of the parties resulting from prior performance of the treaty.[256] In effect this means there is no obligation for any party to return any other party to the position it occupied prior to the coming into force of the treaty.

In the case of suspension, the release from the obligation of further performance is, naturally, limited to the period of suspension, during which time the parties are to refrain from acts that would inhibit resumption of the operation of the treaty.[257]

FURTHER READING

AUST, A., *Modern Treaty Law and Practice* (Cambridge: Cambridge University Press, 2000)

BOWETT, D.W., "Reservations to Non-Restricted Multilateral Treaties" (1976–77) 67 Brit. Y.B. Int'l L. 88

GARDINER, R. *Treaty Interpretation* (Oxford: Oxford University Press, 2007)

GOTLIEB, A.E., *Canadian Treaty-Making* (Toronto: Butterworths, 1968)

HORN, F., *Reservations and Interpretative Declarations to Multilateral Treaties* (New York: Elsevier Science, 1988)

MCNAIR, A., *The Law of Treaties* (Oxford: Clarendon Press, 1961)

MENON, P.K., *The Law of Treaties Between States and International Organizations* (Lewiston, N.Y.: Edwin Mellen Press, 1992)

REUTER, P., *Introduction to the Law of Treaties*, 2d ed., trans. by J. Mico & P. Haggenmacher (London: Kegan Paul International, 1995)

ROSENNE, S., *Developments in the Law of Treaties 1945–86* (Cambridge: Cambridge University Press, 1989)

ROSENNE, S., *The Law of Treaties: A Guide to the Legislative History of the Vienna Convention* (Leyden: Sijthoff, 1970)

SINCLAIR, SIR I., *The Vienna Convention on the Law of Treaties*, 2d ed. (Manchester: Manchester University Press, 1984)

---

256 Assuming, of course, that those positions do not themselves conflict with a newly-emerged *jus cogens* norm: *Vienna Convention*, above note 12, Article 71(2)(b).

257 *Ibid.*, Article 72.

CHAPTER 5

CUSTOMARY INTERNATIONAL LAW

A. NATURE OF CUSTOMARY INTERNATIONAL LAW

Recalling the largely anarchic state of the international legal system and the resulting conundrum of how to "make" (or, for natural lawyers, how to "discover") international law, one potential solution is to borrow a page from domestic legal systems which sometimes treat certain habitual or customary societal practices as evidence of a form of law. For example, the modern common law system could be considered such a form of customary law in that it represents the cumulative and generally consistent practice of a certain set of actors (namely, courts) over time.[1] Moreover, such consistent practice is self-conscious in that the relevant actors subjectively believe (for whatever reason) that their consistent practice is required as a matter of law (usually expressed as the rule of *stare decisis*). That is, common law judges would not explain their pattern of deciding like cases alike as a random or merely practical phenomenon, but would rather consider their consistent practice to be legally required.[2]

---

1   On the similarity between customary legal systems and the common law tradition, see J.L. Brierly, *The Law of Nations: An Introduction to the International Law of Peace*, 6th ed. by H. Waldock (Oxford: Clarendon Press, 1963) at 70.

2   Caution is in order so as not to take this illustrative analogy too far. The reference to common law as a type of customary law is not meant to suggest that

The apparent circularity of such a customary system of law (conduct is legally required because it is regularly engaged in and *believed* to be legally required) is in fact well suited to an international society composed of sovereign entities. The theory requires no legislator but rather derives the law from the consistent actions and subjective convictions or perceptions of its own subjects.

Superficially such a source of law would also appear to be consonant with the positivist theory of consent, particularly if consistent practice and subjective belief are considered law-creating rather than simply law-evidencing. That is, states that consistently engage in certain conduct which they subjectively believe to be legally required can be considered to consent, in some sense, to the resultant rules of customary international law. In fact, as we shall see, the consistency of customary international law with the theory of consent depends crucially on what is meant by "consent" and on certain other factors, such as the meaning given to "consistently," or the number of subjects which must be found to "believe." However, the idea of customary international law can also be argued to be consistent with natural law theories, particularly if practice and subjective belief are considered law-evidencing rather than law-creating. More fundamentally, natural law theories might furnish an explanation for *why* states would believe certain practices are legally obligatory, whereas positivism might not. Thus, customary international law mirrors the modern eclecticism of international legal theory.[3]

In any case, the idea that binding rules of international law can be derived from the behaviour and beliefs of states has long been accepted by international legal theorists[4] as well as by states themselves. Some twentieth and twenty-first century theorists have questioned the continued importance of custom as a source of international law given the proliferation of multilateral codification or law-making treaties, which occupy much of the "territory" formerly covered only by custom. Some have wondered if this tendency to codify is a natural result (and indicator) of international law's evolution from its primitive customary origins to a more deliberate, thought-out system. Notwithstanding these musings, customary international law continues today to be widely accepted, along with treaties, as one of the two principal sources of international

---

customary international law is a form of international common law. As we have seen (Chapter 3, Section C(5)), there is no concept of binding judicial precedent in international law. In customary international law, as we shall see, it is not the consistent practice of judges that is legally significant, but rather the consistent practice of states.

3   See Chapter 3, Section B(3).
4   See Chapter 3, Sections B(1) & (2).

law. Article 38(1)(b) of the *Statute of the International Court of Justice* gives modern expression to this acceptance by identifying "international custom, as evidence of a general practice accepted as law" as a source of international law upon which the International Court of Justice is to rely.

It would be difficult to overstate the profoundly important role played by the concept of customary international law in the international legal system. In contrast to treaty law, customary international law is, with rare exceptions to be noted below,[5] universally binding on all states. It thus constitutes the substratum of common legal rights and obligations of the entire community of states, upon which their more particularized legal relationships (usually in the form of treaties) are built. What is more, customary international law is an enormously powerful normative concept in that it can have the effect, under certain circumstances, of binding states which have not actually consented to its content at all. It thus challenges positivist interpretations of the theory of consent. At the same time, it receives universal endorsement as a valid and binding source of international law.

The other striking implication of such a source of law is that it is forever evolving under the influence of the actions of its own subjects. In other words, the legal significance of a state's behaviour is not limited to its consistency or inconsistency with the law. Its significance can extend, in the right circumstances, to influencing the content of the law itself. This can, of course, pose problems for the application of the law in particular instances. If the content of customary international law is by definition dynamic, how can its content be determined or applied with any precision at any given point in time? Should a state's behaviour which is not in conformity with past state practice be condemned as contrary to customary international law, or should it rather be considered evidence of a new customary rule? The requirements for the formation and determination of customary international law reviewed below provide partial answers to these and similar questions, but the fundamental paradox persists—a system of law which governs the behaviour of its subjects while itself being subject to modification by such behaviour.

B. ELEMENTS OF CUSTOMARY INTERNATIONAL LAW

Even viewing the expression "international custom" in paragraph 38(1)(b) as a convenient short form for the more accurate expression

---

5   See Sections C & D, below in this chapter.

"customary international law," commentators have noted that paragraph 38(1)(b) is poorly drafted in that it reverses the relationship between customary international law and "general practice."[6] Customary international law does not provide evidence of a general practice accepted as law. Precisely the opposite is true: a general practice accepted as law is evidence of a rule of customary international law.

Notwithstanding its awkward drafting, paragraph 38(1)(b) accurately conveys the generally accepted view[7] that two elements must in all cases be present before a rule of customary international law can be said to exist. The first of these, state practice, is also variously referred to as the "objective" or "material" element of customary international law. Its emphasis is obviously on the actual behaviour of states. Such behaviour, however, must be general and uniform. These threshold requirements of generality and uniformity of behaviour will be examined in greater detail below. The second element, most commonly referred to as *opinio juris sive necessitatis*[8] (or *opinio juris* for short), captures the idea that a state's behaviour is only legally significant if it is accompanied by that state's belief in its legally obligatory character. The importance of and challenges posed by the requirement of *opinio juris*, sometimes also called the "subjective" or "psychological" element of customary international law, will also be described below.

1) State Practice

As noted above, customary international law is primarily manifested behaviourally and thus one of the international lawyer's principal preoccupations in determining its content is ascertaining what states actually do. The mere acknowledgement by states of the existence of a particular rule is insufficient to ground the conclusion that the rule exists in customary international law. In all cases it is necessary that such acknowledgment be "confirmed by practice."[9]

---

6   See, for example, G. Schwarzenberger, *International Law*, vol. 1, 3d ed. (London: Stevens & Sons, 1957) at 39.

7   Although it should be noted that a few respected voices have held that only the first element, state practice, is truly necessary: see, for example, P. Guggenheim, *Traité de droit international public*, vol. 1, 2d ed. (Genève: Georg, 1967) at 103–5; H. Kelsen, *Principles of International Law*, 2d ed. by R.W. Tucker (New York: Holt, Rinehart & Winston, 1966) at 450–51. For more recent questioning of the value of the *opinio juris* requirement, see J. Goldsmith & E. Posner, "A Theory of Customary International Law" (1999) 66 U. Chicago L. Rev. 1113 at 1118.

8   Latin for "opinion that an act is necessary by rule of law."

9   *Case Concerning Military and Paramilitary Activities in and against Nicaragua (Nicaragua v. United States of America)*, [1986] I.C.J. Rep. 14 at 98 [*Nicaragua*].

Not all state practice is legally significant, however. Only generally consistent *patterns* of state conduct have the potential to shape customary international law. This focus on trends in state behaviour, rather than isolated acts, is best understood by considering the dual requirements of (a) generality and (b) uniformity of state practice which are implicit in paragraph 38(1)(b)'s perfunctory reference to "general practice."

a) Generality of State Practice

The requirement of generality of practice refers to the number or distribution of states that must be found to follow the relevant practice before it can be said to be a candidate for customary international law status. Strikingly, state practice need not be universal to satisfy the generality requirement, even though customary international law is, in general, universally binding.[10] This means that, as long as a sufficient number of states adhere to a given practice (and the other requirements of customary international law are met), a corresponding rule of international law can be said to exist that binds all states, not merely those engaging in the practice.

This is a clear derogation from the principle of consent and is one of the principal distinctions between customary international law and other, purely consensual sources of international law such as treaties. The requirement of mere generality but not universality is sometimes said to permit certain states to influence the content of customary international law for all by engaging unilaterally in certain practices. If true, this would also be a violation of the fundamental principle of the sovereign equality of states, which logically implies that no state can dictate the law to another.

The answers most frequently put forward to address these criticisms, and to reconcile the non-universality of practice requirement with the universally binding effect of custom, rely heavily on notions of necessity and tacit consent or acquiescence. First, necessity dictates that if state practice is ever to be a source of legal obligation, universality of practice cannot be a requirement. If it were, the moment one state departed from a previously universal practice, any rule of customary international law premised on that practice would cease to exist. Therefore no legal consequence (such as a finding of illegality) could flow from a state's departure from a previously universal practice. Quite simply, rules of law requiring universal adherence for their existence would be completely irrelevant. Further, such rules would be either few and far between or exceedingly short-lived, as there is virtually no uni-

---

10   *Ibid.*

versally consistent practice among states in any field. Thus, something less than universality of state practice is required if one is to derive meaningful law from that practice.

Second, states which do not overtly participate in or even take a position with respect to the relevant state practice (whether due to their approval of it, lack of interest in the matter, or lack of opportunity to participate) are presumed to accede to it. Their inaction is treated as a form of tacit consent, tantamount to behaviour consistent with the practice in question.[11] In this way, it can be said that it is not so much the unilateral behaviour of some states as the sufficiently general acquiescence of others that creates obligations binding on all.[12]

Further, while universality is not required in the sense of unanimous participation by all states, evidence that state practice is at least representative of the "main forms of civilization and of the principal legal systems of the world"[13] is preferred.[14] In this way, the specific charge of imperialism is avoided in that no significant bloc of states can claim to have been excluded from the law-making process.

Of course, the most compelling answer to the charge of "unilateralism," or some states effectively "legislating" for others, would be to require a sufficiently large number of participating (or at least acquiescing) states before the generality threshold could be said to be satisfied. Unfortunately, neither the judgments of the International Court of Justice, scholarly opinion, nor even the positions of states themselves disclose any agreement on how widespread a practice must be before it can be qualified as "general." The Court has variously used such terms as "general," "widespread," or "settled" to describe the required threshold. The following excerpt from the judgment of the Court in the *Nicaragua* case is illustrative of the Court's vagueness on this issue: "In order to deduce the existence of customary rules, the Court deems it sufficient that the conduct of States should, *in general*, be consistent with such rules...."[15] [Emphasis added.]

---

11   See, for example, *Fisheries Case (United Kingdom v. Norway)*, [1951] I.C.J. Rep. 116 at 138–39 [*Fisheries Case*].

12   M.S. McDougal, "The Hydrogen Bomb Tests and the International Law of the Sea" (1955) 49 A.J.I.L. 356 at 358.

13   Article 9, *Statute of the International Court of Justice*, 26 June 1945, Can. T.S. 1945 No. 7 (entered into force 24 October 1945) [*ICJ Statute*].

14   See M.H. Mendelson, "The Formation of Customary International Law" (1998) 272 Rec. des Cours 155 at 226. The representativity requirement was explicitly set out in the *North Sea Continental Shelf Cases (Federal Republic of Germany v. Denmark; Federal Republic of Germany v. The Netherlands)*, [1969] I.C.J. Rep. 3 at 42 [*North Sea Continental Shelf Cases*].

15   *Nicaragua*, above note 9 at 98.

Individual judges have on occasion been somewhat more forthcoming while still using equivocal language. For example:

> [T]o become binding, a rule or principle of international law need not pass the test of universal acceptance. ... Not all States have ... an opportunity or possibility of applying a given rule. The evidence should be sought in the behaviour of a *great number* of States, *possibly the majority* of States, in any case the *great majority of the interested* States.[16] [Emphasis added]

Others have been forthright in admitting the uncertainty of the requirement:

> The repetition, the number of examples of State practice ... required for the generation of customary law cannot be mathematically and uniformly decided. Each fact requires to be evaluated relatively according to the different occasions and circumstances. ... [W]hat is important in the matter at issue is not the number or figure of ... examples of ... State practice, but the meaning which they would imply in the particular circumstances.[17]

In other words, generality of state practice does not denote a threshold number of states that would be required in all cases. Its meaning is flexible. For example, on an issue of interest to all states, such as diplomatic immunities or the use of force, "general practice" would presumably require the representative participation or acquiescence of a great proportion of all states. By contrast, in a specialized area of interest only to certain states, such as sovereignty over the Arctic, "general practice" might require the participation of the preponderance of far northern states even though this would only constitute a very small fraction of the total number of states in the world.

Thus, what constitutes sufficiently general practice will vary from case to case. In the end, it may be more useful to turn the issue on its head and ask whether there is significant *dissenting* practice among states. If so, it is probably safe to say that state practice has not achieved the level of generality required to ground a universally binding rule of customary international law.

b) Uniformity of State Practice
As distinct from "generality" of practice, which focuses on the distribution of such practice, "uniformity" refers to the consistency or

---

16   *North Sea Continental Shelf Cases*, above note 14 at 229, Lachs J. (dissenting).
17   *Ibid.* at 175–76, Tanaka J. (dissenting).

homogeneity of that practice among practising states. In other words, it examines whether those states adopting the relevant practice remain constant in their adherence to it or whether they drift into and out of such conformity.

The rigour with which this requirement is applied parallels that of "generality." To be considered sufficiently "uniform," state practice need not be perfectly consistent at all times. Only substantial uniformity is required. For example, the International Court of Justice, in considering the customary international legal status of the prohibition of the unilateral use of force, has stated that:

> It is not to be expected that in the practice of States the application of the rules in question should have been perfect, in the sense that States should have refrained, with complete consistency, from the use of force or from intervention in each other's internal affairs. The Court does not consider that, for a rule to be established as customary, the corresponding practice must be in absolutely rigorous conformity with the rule. ... [T]he Court deems it sufficient ... that instances of State conduct inconsistent with a given rule should generally have been treated as breaches of that rule, not as indications of the recognition of a new rule.[18]

It can be seen that this flexible approach results at least in part from the same necessity as does the non-universality of practice requirement. If complete uniformity of practice were required, any state departing from the uniform practice even once would not only be breaking the law but simultaneously "unmaking" it. While such a result might appear to be required by the theory of consent, in fact it would be quite antithetical to it. It would mean that even one isolated action of even one state could radically transform the content of customary international law for all states. Once again, such a system of law would quite rapidly become irrelevant.

Unfortunately, while only substantial uniformity appears to be required, there is no more certainty as to when that threshold is reached than there is when it comes to the number of states required to satisfy the generality requirement. This will vary with the circumstances surrounding the uniform practice as well as deviations from it. In particular and as suggested in the above-quoted passage, the legal significance of non-conforming behaviour probably depends on the attitude of the non-conforming state as well as of other states with respect to that behaviour. Is it asserted or accepted as legal conduct? Is it justified by resorting to

---

18 *Nicaragua*, above note 9 at 98.

some exception to an otherwise generally recognized rule? Is it generally condemned as illegal? These questions of course cross over into the *opinio juris* element of custom, to be discussed more fully below.[19]

Customary international law therefore relies on the overall behaviour of states rather than the idiosyncratic or occasionally inconsistent acts of a few. In general, it focuses on the predominating pattern of state conduct and treats isolated deviations therefrom as breaches of the law rather than as evidence of new law. Of course, this is not to say that customary international law is static. If the predominating pattern of conduct were to shift to a new general and uniform practice, customary international law would evolve in a corresponding fashion. In any event, what constitutes "predominating" and "isolated" conduct will vary from case to case, depending on the circumstances.

c) Duration of State Practice

Semantically, the term "custom" seems to imply a long-standing practice, rooted perhaps in the mists of time or even dating from "time immemorial." While a long-established pattern of behaviour may provide very good evidence of a general and uniform practice accepted as law, the question is whether international law requires any minimum duration before a given practice can be considered "customary." The general view appears to be that there is no such minimum requirement.

The International Court of Justice addressed this issue in the *North Sea Continental Shelf Cases*.[20] These cases involved a dispute between the Federal Republic of Germany on the one hand, and Denmark and the Netherlands on the other, as to how to establish the maritime boundaries between their respective, adjacent continental shelves. The parties sought clarification from the Court as to the "principles and rules of international law" governing such a maritime delimitation. This was an area of the law where state practice had evolved significantly in the post-war period, particularly under the influence of a multilateral treaty dealing with the continental shelf.[21] Indeed, the whole legal concept of the continental shelf was itself relatively new, having been unilaterally proposed by the United States in 1945.[22] As Germany was not a party to the relevant treaty, one of the main questions for the Court in these

---

19   See Section B(2), below in this chapter. See also *Nicaragua*, *ibid.* at 108–9.

20   *North Sea Continental Shelf Cases*, above note 14.

21   *Convention on the Continental Shelf*, 29 April 1958, 499 U.N.T.S. 311 (entered into force 10 June 1964). The interaction of treaties and customary international law is discussed in Section E, below in this chapter.

22   *The Truman Proclamation on the Continental Shelf*, 10 Fed. Reg. 12303 (1945). This development is described in greater detail in Chapter 7, Section C(2)(f).

highly dynamic circumstances was the content of customary international law on the point. On the duration issue the Court stated:

> As regards the time element, ... [a]lthough the passage of only a *short period of time is not necessarily*, or of itself, *a bar to the formation of a new rule of customary international law* on the basis of what was originally a purely conventional rule, an indispensable requirement would be that within the period in question, short though it might be, State practice, including that of States whose interests are specially affected, should have been both *extensive and virtually uniform* in the sense of the provision invoked....[23] [Emphasis added]

Thus, while the sustained duration of state practice is not critical, time is not wholly irrelevant to the formation of a new rule of customary international law. Notice the more exacting language used to describe the required practice ("extensive," rather than "general"; "virtually uniform," not merely "uniform") in cases where the elapsed time is relatively short. In other words, the shorter the duration under consideration, the more evidence of generality and uniformity of practice will be required in order to formulate a convincing argument that a new rule of customary international law has emerged. This relationship might be crudely represented in the following graphical form, where generality ("G") and uniformity ("U") of state practice are on the vertical scale, and time ("T") on the horizontal scale:

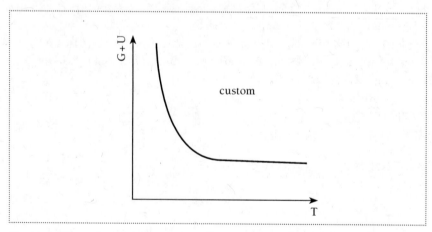

Figure 1: Customary requirements of generality and uniformity of state practice as a function of time

---

23   *North Sea Continental Shelf Cases*, above note 14 at 43.

Of course, saying that no minimum duration is required to form a new rule of customary international law has a common sense limit. Given the general lack of coordination in international affairs, it will be rare that evidence of state practice sufficient to satisfy the exacting standards mentioned above will be generated in anything less than a few years. Patterns of conduct may emerge relatively quickly in the right circumstances but any pattern requires at least enough time to be perceived as such. By the same token and at the other end of the time scale, even very lengthy periods of time will not reduce the rigour of the generality and uniformity requirements below the general thresholds discussed above.

2) *Opinio Juris*

The *opinio juris* element is said to be critical in order to distinguish between those practices of states that result merely from political expediency, diplomacy, convenience, domestic policy, or habit—that is, those practices that neither create nor evidence legal obligations—and those that flow from legal obligation. Sometimes the term "usage" is invoked to denote the former category.[24]

While some authors have questioned the necessity of this further "psychological" element for the formation of a customary rule,[25] the great majority of judicial, scholarly, and state opinion supports it.[26] The requirement is implicit in paragraph 38(1)(b) of the *Statute* of the Court when it refers to general practice "accepted as law." Its central importance has also been clearly emphasized by the International Court of Justice in a number of cases. The following excerpt from the Court's judgment in the *Nicaragua* case is illustrative:

> In considering the instances of the conduct above described, the Court has to emphasize that, as was observed in the *North Sea Continental Shelf Cases*, for a new customary rule to be formed, not only must the acts concerned "amount to a settled practice," but they must be accompanied by the *opinio juris sive necessitatis*. Either the States taking such action or other States in a position to react to it, must have behaved so that their conduct is

---

24 See I. Brownlie, *Principles of Public International Law*, 6th ed. (Oxford: Oxford University Press, 2003) at 8.

25 See above note 7.

26 See, for example, Brownlie, above note 24 at 8–10; Schwarzenberger, above note 6 at 40; M.N. Shaw, *International Law*, 5th ed. (Cambridge: Cambridge University Press, 2003) at 80–84; A. Cassese, *International Law*, 2d ed. (Oxford: Oxford University Press, 2005) at 157–60.

> "evidence of a belief that this practice is rendered obligatory by the existence of a rule of law requiring it. The need for such a belief, i.e. the existence of a subjective element, is implicit in the very notion of the *opinio juris sive necessitatis*." (*I.C.J. Reports 1969*, p.44, para.77.)[27]

Therefore, mere practice, even if general and uniform, is not sufficient in itself to constitute customary international law. Such practice, to be legally significant, must be accompanied by a conviction that it is legally required. For example, in the *Nicaragua* case itself, the Court rejected the submission that past American interventions in the affairs of other states could in themselves form the basis of a new customary norm "legalizing" such interventions against Nicaragua:

> The significance for the Court of cases of State conduct prima facie inconsistent with the principle of non-intervention lies in the *nature of the ground offered as justification* ... [T]he Court finds that States have not justified their conduct by reference to a new right of intervention or a new exception to the principle of its prohibition. The United States authorities have on some occasions clearly stated their grounds for intervening in the affairs of a foreign State for reasons connected with, for example, the domestic policies of that country, its ideology, the level of its armaments, or the direction of its foreign policy. But these were statements of international policy, and not an *assertion of rules of existing international law.*[28] [Emphasis added]

This passage underlines that a sense of *legal* justification, not simply justification on political, security, or other grounds, is required to satisfy the *opinio juris* requirement. It also emphasizes the critical importance of proof of *opinio juris* in establishing a new rule of customary international law.

Of course, as with all inquiries into motive, adducing satisfactory proof of the requisite subjective or psychological conviction of legality is the principal difficulty with the *opinio juris* requirement. Given that a state is by definition a corporate entity, with no single directing mind, how can its subjective convictions be determined? Further, as motivations are usually complex, consisting for example at once of self-interest, practicality, and a belief in legal requirement, need all of these be sorted out and if so, how?

The preferred approach of the Court, particularly in cases where the very existence of customary international rules is hotly contested, is to

---

27   *Nicaragua*, above note 9 at 108–9.
28   *Ibid.* at 109.

rely on the express views of states themselves. The Court has clearly stated that it has no "authority to ascribe to States legal views which they do not themselves advance."[29] The Court will search for evidence of how states have explained their own motives when acting in certain ways. The danger that a state might misrepresent the true *animus* behind its actions is somewhat attenuated by looking for evidence of the state's views expressed at the time of the practice in question, not its views on the matter once a dispute has arisen and is before the Court. To the extent opportunity for misrepresentation of true motives exists even at the time the practice is being engaged in, this is simply one of the unavoidable risks associated with a source of law premised on the behaviour and convictions of its own subjects. If states are sovereign and bound by rules of law to which they have expressly or tacitly consented, presumably their contemporaneous views on the legal significance of their actions are not to be lightly second-guessed.

In any event, there is usually no shortage of express assertions by states to rely upon. Given their potential for influencing the content of customary international law, states usually equip themselves with the instruments necessary to disseminate their views as to the legal significance of their own and other states' actions. State officials are forever taking positions on legal matters before the UN and related organs, during diplomatic conferences, or in direct communications with their opposite numbers in other states in response to various events of international significance. As a result, evidence of *opinio juris* can be gleaned from diplomatic correspondence, government press statements, conference communiqués, summit reports, ministerial statements, speeches before UN bodies such as the General Assembly or Security Council, comments made by governments to the International Law Commission, government statements made in national legislatures, submissions made to national or international tribunals, recitals contained in treaties, and so on. Frequently resort is had to sources comprising the *lex ferenda*,[30] most notably UN General Assembly Declarations, as evidence of general *opinio juris* on particular matters.[31]

On occasion the Court has taken a more subtle approach to determining the *opinio juris* of states on certain issues. Rather than relying exclusively on states' express positions as to the legal character of their practice, the Court has looked for quasi-objective evidence of states' views. For example, in the *North Sea Continental Shelf Cases*,[32] one of

---

29   *Ibid.*
30   See Chapter 3, Section D(2).
31   See, for an example of such reliance, *Nicaragua*, above note 9 at 106–8.
32   *North Sea Continental Shelf Cases*, above note 14.

the contentions put forward by Denmark and the Netherlands was that a certain multilateral treaty provision concerning maritime boundary delimitation had "crystallized" a nascent rule of customary international law.[33] That is, they contended that the adoption of the treaty provision by a number of states was itself evidence of state practice and *opinio juris* supporting the existence, in customary international law, of the delimitation rule contained in the provision.[34] However, the Court observed that the treaty permitted unilateral reservations to be made to the relevant provision by acceding states. This, it held, was inconsistent with:

> general or customary law rules and obligations which, by their very nature, must have equal force for all members of the international community, and cannot therefore be the subject of any right of unilateral exclusion exercisable at will by any one of them in its own favour.[35]

The *opinio juris* apparently evidenced by the inclusion of the treaty provision was therefore belied by states' ability to exclude its operation by way of reservation; that is, to deny its legal force unilaterally. The ability to reserve the provision was taken by the Court as an implicit rejection of its legally binding character at customary international law.

Aside from this more objective approach, several commentators have observed that, particularly in cases where the content of the rules of customary international law is not especially contentious, the Court has on occasion merely inferred the necessary *opinio juris* from extensive state practice itself, or from general agreement on the issue in the authorities or prior judgments.[36] This presumptive approach should not be taken, however, as a signal that the burden of proof on the *opinio juris* element is reversed, or that it merges with proof of state practice.

---

33   The treaty in question was the *Convention on the Continental Shelf*, above note 21, the pertinent provision being Article 6, which provided that the boundary between continental shelves was to be fixed using the equidistance principle or other equitable principles.

34   *North Sea Continental Shelf Cases*, above note 14 at 38.

35   *Ibid.* at 38–39.

36   See, for example, Schwarzenberger, above note 6 at 40; Brownlie, above note 24 at 8–9; Guggenheim, above note 7 at 103–5. An example of this approach, cited by Brownlie, is the judgment in the *Case Concerning Delimitation of the Maritime Boundary in the Gulf of Maine Area (Canada v. The United States of America)*, [1984] I.C.J. Rep. 246 at 293–94 [*Gulf of Maine*], where the Court noted the extent to which it had contributed to customary law in the field of maritime boundary delimitation through its pronouncements in past cases dealing with the continental shelf.

Rather, it would simply appear to be a matter of judicial economy in cases where, due to the previously well-established nature of a customary rule, little would be gained by an exhaustive inquiry into the motivations underlying state practice.

Indeed, in cases of doubt, states seeking to rely upon a rule of customary international law that may in any way be contentious are well-advised to put their best foot forward in establishing both elements—state practice and *opinio juris*. In fact, the Permanent Court of International Justice, the predecessor of the International Court of Justice, expressly rejected the notion that *opinio juris* may be inferred from simple state practice. In *The SS Lotus* case,[37] France contended against Turkey that there was a rule of customary international law that forbade Turkey from prosecuting a French national for criminal acts occurring outside Turkish territory. As evidence of the existence of such a legal prohibition, France pointed to the extreme rarity of such prosecutions. The Court responded:

> Even if the rarity of the judicial decisions to be found ... were sufficient to prove ... the circumstance alleged ..., it would merely show that States had often, in practice, abstained from instituting criminal proceedings, and not that they recognized themselves as being obliged to do so; for only if such abstention were based on their being conscious of having a duty to abstain would it be possible to speak of an international custom. *The alleged fact does not allow one to infer that States have been conscious of having such a duty....*[38] [Emphasis added]

This dictum has been quoted with express approval by the International Court of Justice,[39] clearly affirming the importance of explicit proof of *opinio juris* in all but the very clearest of cases.

C. PERSISTENT OBJECTORS

One of the most remarkable features of customary international law noted above is its universally binding nature, notwithstanding that the state practice required to establish a given customary rule need not itself be universal. As discussed,[40] this is difficult to reconcile with the theory of consent, or the positivist view that states are bound by the

---

37   *The Case of the SS Lotus (France v. Turkey)* (1927), P.C.I.J. (Ser. A) No. 10.
38   *Ibid.* at 28.
39   *North Sea Continental Shelf Cases*, above note 14 at 44.
40   See Chapter 3, Section C(3).

law because they have created it with the intent that it should bind them.

A somewhat grudging exception to customary international law's universality, which goes some way towards dulling its incompatibility with the theory of consent, is the rule of the so-called "persistent objector." This rule acknowledges that in certain tightly circumscribed situations, a state may escape the binding force of a rule of customary international law to which it objects. The conditions that must be satisfied before a state may avail itself of this loophole are as follows:[41]

1) The state must have objected to the rule of customary international law in the course of its formation, that is, from the very beginning. If objection comes late, after state practice and *opinio juris* have begun to coalesce around the existence of a rule, the objecting state will be caught by the rule.

2) The state must, from the rule's inception, consistently maintain its objection without exception. Even a single lapse will be fatal to the state's claim of persistent objector status.

3) The state's consistently maintained objection must be express. Mere silence or inaction will be construed as acquiescence in, not objection to, the rule, and the state will accordingly be bound.

It can be seen that these requirements will tend to minimize instances where states may successfully claim persistent objector status. For example, the requirement of objection *ab initio* means that states that come into existence[42] or that acquire certain relevant interests[43] after the formation of a customary rule will nevertheless be bound.[44] Similarly, the requirement of consistent objection without exception will tend, over time, to bring objecting states irrevocably "into the fold" if and when their resolve wavers. Further, a state's objection will not be presumed but must be strictly proven by the objecting state. Thus, while the persistent objector rule notionally supports the theory of consent, the foregoing strict conditions clearly signal customary inter-

---

41   See M. Akehurst, "Custom as a Source of International Law" (1974–75) 47 Brit. Y.B. Int'l L. 1 at 24.

42   For example, through secession or independence from another state.

43   For example, a landlocked state that acquires coastline (say, by way of union with another state) after the customary law of the sea is well settled.

44   See Akehurst, above note 41 at 27–28. However, some authors take a dissenting view: see, generally, C. Tomuschat, "Obligations Arising for States Without or Against Their Will" (1993-IV) 241 Rec. des Cours 195 at 305–6 for a review of such dissenting views.

national law's bias against the validity of such objections to its universally binding character.

While there is some debate among authors as to the validity[45] of the persistent objector doctrine, the majority of opinion supports its existence, albeit subject to the strict conditions outlined above.[46] Moreover, states and the International Court of Justice itself appear to recognize its soundness. An example of such recognition is the *Fisheries Case* between the United Kingdom and Norway.[47] That case raised the issue of how baselines were to be established for purposes of measuring the seaward extent of Norway's territorial sea.[48] Norway contended that in establishing its coastal baselines, it was entitled to depart from the actual coastline and draw straight lines across the mouths of bays along its deeply indented coast. The United Kingdom contended, *inter alia*, that customary international law only permitted such an approach where the mouth of the bay was less than ten nautical miles in width. The Court rejected this latter proposition, finding insufficient generality and uniformity of state practice to evidence such a rule. The Court then added:

> In any event the ten-mile rule would appear to be inapplicable as against Norway inasmuch as she has always opposed any attempt to apply it to the Norwegian coast.[49]

The Court has similarly endorsed the persistent objector doctrine, although not always in the clearest of terms, in other cases.[50]

D. REGIONAL, SPECIAL, OR LOCAL CUSTOMARY INTERNATIONAL LAW

In a similar vein, customary international law recognizes that, on occasion, groups of states (as opposed to individual objectors) may adopt a certain pattern of practice that departs from a more general (or universal) rule of customary international law. They may even, over time,

---

45 Or, one surmises, the desirability.

46 For a useful list of authors both endorsing and rejecting the doctrine, see Tomuschat, above note 44 at 285, n. 214, and generally at 284–90.

47 *Fisheries Case*, above note 11.

48 See Chapter 7, Section C(2)(a).

49 *Fisheries Case*, above note 11 at 131. Both parties appear also to have agreed that such historic opposition to the rule, if found, would exempt Norway from the rule's application: see *ibid.* at 130–31.

50 *Asylum Case (Colombia v. Peru)*, [1950] I.C.J. Rep. 266 at 277–78; *North Sea Continental Shelf Cases*, above note 14 at 26–27.

come to regard this distinctive practice as legally obligatory as between themselves. This phenomenon is recognized as having a law-making or law-modifying character as between the relevant states, and is thus dubbed "regional," "special," or "local" customary international law. It is akin to the conclusion of a treaty where the parties exclude or modify the operation *inter se* of general customary international law in the subject-area covered by the treaty. However, in the case of regional or local custom, agreement is of course not express as in a treaty but rather tacit and based on a pattern of reciprocal conduct accompanied by a sense of mutual legal obligation.

The recognition of such local or special customary law flows, as in the case of the persistent objector, from the theory of consent. If the will of states (as inferred from their practice) is the true source of their binding legal obligations, there is little basis for denying the law-making effect of their reciprocal practice in arenas smaller than the global community of nations. However, just as with the persistent objector, local custom is a threat to the universality of general customary international law and is therefore subject to exacting requirements for its recognition and enforcement.

In particular, the elements of local custom must be proven strictly by the state seeking to rely upon it. This is because the local or regional rule will usually be in conflict with a general rule of customary international law which, as we have seen, is presumed to be universally binding. In other words, regional customary rules frequently take on the appearance of exceptions to more generally applicable rules and, as with most exceptions, require rigorous proof.

As for the elements of local customary law, these are the same as for customary international law—that is, state practice and *opinio juris*. The difference is in the rigour with which each of these elements must be established. In particular, generality of state practice by definition loses much of its significance when considering the existence of a local custom. The number of states participating in the regional custom could be very few. Far more determinative will be the mutual participation in the practice of both the claimant state and the specific state against which the local rule is said to be applicable. In this sense, "local universality" rather than generality is required. For example, even if a regional customary rule were established among, say, South American states, and was generally adhered to by those states, it could not be invoked against a South American state that had not clearly committed, through practice and *opinio juris*, to the regional rule.

These peculiarities of local customary law are well illustrated in the *Right of Passage over Indian Territory* case between Portugal and India.[51] That case concerned certain landlocked enclaves held by Portugal within the territory of India. Portugal claimed that it had enjoyed, for at least a century, a right of free passage over Indian territory between these enclaves and Daman, a Portuguese coastal territory also on the Indian peninsula. In 1954, however, civil unrest resulted in the overthrow of Portuguese authority in one of the enclaves and thereafter the Indian government suspended Portuguese passage to and from the enclaves as a security measure. Portugal claimed that this suspension effectively denied it the ability to exercise its sovereignty over its territories.

Among the issues to be resolved by the Court were:

1) whether a local or regional rule of customary international law could arise between only two states;
2) whether such a rule was established here; and
3) the effect of such a local customary rule in the face of general customary international law, which holds that the territorial sovereign has virtually unfettered authority to refuse access to or use of its territory by any other state.

On the first issue, the Court reasoned that:

> It is difficult to see why the number of States between which a local custom may be established on the basis of long practice must necessarily be larger than two. The Court sees no reason why long continued practice between two States accepted by them as regulating their relations should not form the basis of mutual rights and obligations between the two States.[52]

On the remaining issues, after reviewing the largely uncontested evidence that Portugal had in fact enjoyed, for over a century, essentially free civilian access over Indian territory to, from, and between the enclaves, the Court held that:

> [T]here existed during the British and post-British periods a constant and uniform practice allowing free passage between Daman and the enclaves. This practice having continued over a period extending beyond a century and a quarter unaffected by the change of regime ... when India became independent, the Court is ... satisfied that that

---

51 *Case Concerning Right of Passage over Indian Territory (Portugal v. India)*, [1960] I.C.J. Rep. 6.
52 *Ibid.* at 39.

practice was accepted as law by the Parties and has given rise to a right and a correlative obligation.

...

Where ... the Court finds a practice clearly established between two States which was accepted by the Parties as governing the relations between them, the Court must attribute decisive effect to that practice for the purpose of determining their specific rights and obligations. *Such a particular practice must prevail over any general rules.*[53] [Emphasis added]

In the result, although the Court concluded that a local customary rule gave Portugal the right of civilian (although not military) passage over Indian territory between its enclaves, it held that the Indian actions had not been inconsistent with such a right.

The *Right of Passage* case established that local customary international law could arise between as few as two states. It did not expressly deal with the importance of individual state participation in a broader, regional customary practice. In fact, the Court had already dealt with this concern in the earlier *Asylum Case* between Colombia and Peru.[54] That case involved a Peruvian dissident and fugitive who sought and was granted asylum as a political refugee in the Colombian embassy in Lima, Peru. In the ensuing dispute between the two states, Colombia claimed that it had a unilateral right to grant such asylum (and thus interfere with Peru's territorial jurisdiction over its own nationals) pursuant to a regional custom among Latin American states permitting such interference. The Court characterized the requirements for such a regional customary rule thus:

The Party which relies on a custom of this kind must prove that this custom is established *in such a manner that it has become binding on the other Party.* The Colombian Government must prove that the rule invoked by it is in accordance with a constant and uniform usage practised *by the States in question* and that this usage is the expression of a right appertaining to the State granting asylum and a duty *incumbent on the territorial State.*[55] [Emphasis added]

After concluding that it could not find sufficient uniformity of Latin American state practice to support the existence of the purported regional rule, the Court went on to add:

---

53   *Ibid.* at 40 and 44.
54   *Asylum Case,* above note 50.
55   *Ibid.* at 276.

[E]ven if it could be supposed that such a custom existed between certain Latin-American States only, it could not be invoked against Peru which, far from having by its attitude adhered to it, has, on the contrary, repudiated it by refraining from ratifying the Montevideo Conventions of 1933 and 1939, which were the first to include a rule concerning the qualification of the offence in matters of diplomatic asylum.[56]

It is therefore essential not only to establish the existence of a regional customary rule by adducing sufficient evidence of regional state practice and *opinio juris*, but also to show that the state against which the rule is to be applied has directly and actively participated in the relevant practice and *opinio juris*.[57] Notice too that no persistent and express objection would have been required to exempt Peru from the regional custom, had it been found to exist. Rather, Peru's inaction would have been sufficient to remove it from the operation of the rule. This is in sharp contrast to general customary international law, where inaction can be taken as acquiescence in the formation of a universal customary rule. The difference in approach can again be understood by remembering that regional customary rules are usually exceptions to universal customary international law. Silence or inaction by any particular state, therefore, is more readily construed as acquiescence in the universally applicable rule than in the exceptional, regional one.

E. INTERACTION OF CUSTOM AND TREATIES

One of the most perplexing issues in the study of the sources of international law is the relationship between customary international law and treaty law. Both are formal sources of international law, as we have seen, and yet their coexistence poses theoretical and methodological problems. These range from fundamental questions — such as whether treaties and custom are not really formal sources of law at all but simply material sources that provide evidence of some deeper law-creating process[58] — to practical ones, such as whether adherence to a treaty can furnish evidence of state practice and *opinio juris* and thus of corresponding customary international law.[59]

---

56   *Ibid.* at 277–78.
57   See also *Case Concerning Rights of Nationals of the United States of America in Morocco (France v. United States of America),* [1952] I.C.J. Rep. 176 at 200.
58   See Brownlie, above note 24 at 3–4.
59   See above, text accompanying notes 32–35.

While the literature tackling these issues is vast and a comprehensive review is beyond the scope of this chapter, some of the more basic propositions can be reviewed.

1) Precedence in Cases of Conflict

Consider first the question of whether a treaty or customary rule should prevail in the case of a conflict between their provisions. Assuming that all relevant parties to the transaction or dispute are also parties to the treaty, the general answer to this question is that the treaty provision prevails. This is because the affected parties have mutually agreed, in the treaty, to modify their legal relationship as it may have existed under customary international law, albeit only to the extent provided for in the treaty. For example, customary international law provides that a state's jurisdiction over its own territory is essentially absolute. However, if two states by treaty agree that one of them may build a pipeline across the other's territory, the host state's customarily unfettered territorial jurisdiction is altered vis-à-vis the visiting state such that it cannot (legally) block the project unilaterally after a few months' work.[60]

This seemingly simple proposition — that treaty rules trump incompatible customary rules as between parties to the treaty — is subject to exceptions and caveats, however. First, as seen above,[61] there exists a class of customary rules that are *non-derogable* — that is, that cannot be displaced by treaty. These rules, known as *jus cogens*, are considered so fundamental to the international legal order that treaties purporting to alter or displace them are simply void.[62] An apposite example of such a peremptory norm of international law would be the *pacta sunt servanda* principle, which as we have seen provides that states must perform their treaty undertakings in good faith.[63] An agreement by states to set aside this rule by way of treaty would be not only unthinkable, but nonsensical.

Second, treaties are rarely completely unambiguous as to their meaning. It is accordingly generally recognized that one of the most reliable guides to their interpretation is the meaning given to them by states parties themselves. This can be gleaned from the consist-

---

60   Barring of course any special circumstances that would permit it to escape its treaty obligations. See Chapter 4, Section J.

61   See above Chapter 4, Section I(2)(g).

62   Article 53, *Vienna Convention on the Law of Treaties*, 23 May 1969, 1155 U.N.T.S. 331 (entered into force 27 January 1980) [*Vienna Convention*].

63   See above Chapter 4, Section G(1).

ent practice of such parties when applying a treaty's provisions.[64] In this way, subsequent general and uniform practice among parties to the treaty, accompanied by the requisite *opinio juris*—in other words, custom—can affect the legally enforceable content of the treaty's provisions. It is even theoretically possible that subsequent state practice and *opinio juris*, if sufficiently general and uniform, could effectively bring an end to a treaty or at least to the binding force of some of its provisions.[65] Thus, customary international law does not always yield to treaty rules; depending on the circumstances, it may carry the day.

Finally, although a treaty provision can displace the *applicability* of a customary rule as between the parties to the treaty, it would be inaccurate to say that the treaty provision subsumes or destroys the customary norm, even as between the parties to the treaty, as discussed more fully below.[66]

2) Treaties as a Source of Customary International Law

The interaction of custom and treaties goes beyond the question of precedence in cases of conflict. The more subtle issue is whether they can also have an innovative effect on one another. We have already seen that state practice may modify the meaning and content of treaty obligations in a number of ways. Can treaties have a similar effect on custom?

The simple answer to this question is "yes," although this masks complicated issues as to *how* treaties may influence customary international law. A common approach to sorting out these intricacies is to focus specifically on multilateral treaties[67] and to refer to three princi-

---

64   *Vienna Convention*, above note 62, Article 31(3)(b) points to, as part of the context that can assist in interpreting a treaty provision, "any subsequent practice in the application of the treaty which establishes the agreement of the parties regarding its interpretation."

65   Article 54(b) of the *Vienna Convention, ibid.*, obliquely suggests this possibility in providing that the "termination of a treaty … may take place … at any time by consent of all the parties," assuming consistent practice and *opinio juris* among all parties can furnish the required "consent." Similarly, Article 64 provides that "[i]f a new peremptory norm of general international law emerges, any existing treaty which is in conflict with that norm becomes void and terminates," illustrating that subsequent customary developments (in this example, having the character of *jus cogens*) can override treaty rules.

66   See Section E(3), below in this chapter.

67   As distinct from bilateral treaties. The focus on multilateral treaties clearly stems from their broader-based adherence and thus significance as evidence of general state practice. There is no reason in principle, however, to conclude that several bilateral treaties adopting the same approach to a given area of international relations could not similarly provide significant evidence of state prac-

pal types of relationship between such treaties and customary international law.[68] First, the *declaratory* or *codification* treaty purports to reduce well-settled rules of customary international law to treaty form. These treaties will tend to attract wide participation given that they merely reflect existing law and have the benefit of expressing it in a readily ascertainable form. Their significance as a source of customary international law is thus merely evidentiary, except insofar as the express reduction of customary rules to conventional form may have the effect of petrifying state practice and thus stifling or retarding further evolution of the corresponding rules of customary law.

Second, the *crystallizing* treaty contains provisions consistent with state practice and *opinio juris* which are already advanced but which have not, prior to the treaty's entry into force, reached the critical mass required to provide firm evidence of a customary rule. The widespread ratification of the treaty in such circumstances is itself said to constitute state practice and *opinio juris* in support of the corresponding customary rule. Therefore the crystallizing treaty, if successful, provides the necessary "final push" to bring into existence a rule of customary international law where it might otherwise have failed or been delayed. The significance of this process, of course, is that all states, even those which do not become parties to the treaty, become bound by the substance of the rule if not by the treaty itself.

Third, the *law-making* treaty ventures into new territory and establishes new rules not previously reflected in the customary practice of states. If ratification of the treaty is sufficiently widespread, it may generate a new pattern of general and uniform state practice which, if accompanied by *opinio juris*, can have the effect of creating a new, corresponding, customary international norm. As with the crystallizing treaty, the significance of this phenomenon is again that non-parties to the treaty nevertheless become bound by the content of the rule as it emerges in universal customary international law.

Of course, multilateral treaties, particularly those that seek to deal comprehensively with a given area of the law, frequently combine elements of all three categories described above. That is, some of their provisions will be merely declaratory, others will reflect emerging state

---

tice: see, for example, Brownlie, above note 24 at 14. The difficulty, however, is in deducing convincing evidence of *opinio juris* from discrete bilateral agreements: see, for example, the unfavourable comments of the International Court of Justice on such reliance on bilateral agreements in the *North Sea Continental Shelf Cases*, above note 14 at 43–44.

68　See, generally, R.R. Baxter, "Multilateral Treaties as Evidence of Customary International Law" (1965–66) 41 Brit. Y.B. Int'l L. 275.

practice, and still others will represent complete departures from prior custom.[69] The process of drawing customary international law inferences from treaty practice becomes still more complicated, as states will either adhere to, reserve certain provisions of, or reject outright a treaty for a variety of reasons related to its individual provisions (whether declaratory, crystallizing, or law-making).

One of the leading judgments of the International Court of Justice on these issues is the *North Sea Continental Shelf Cases*.[70] Readers will recall that, in that case, Denmark and the Netherlands claimed that Article 6 of the 1958 Geneva *Convention on the Continental Shelf* had either crystallized an emerging norm of customary international law[71] or had generated a new one.[72] The importance of this argument lay in the fact that Germany was not a party to the Convention, whereas Denmark and the Netherlands were and wished to rely upon its favourable maritime delimitation rules, contained in Article 6, as against Germany.

With respect to the first contention, namely, that Article 6 had crystallized an emergent norm of customary international law, the Court rejected the argument outright while implicitly acknowledging that in different circumstances, such a process was possible:

> [T]he principle of equidistance, as it now figures in Article 6 of the Convention, was proposed by the [International Law] Commission with considerable hesitation, somewhat on an experimental basis, at most *de lege ferenda*, and not at all *de lege lata* or as an emerging rule of customary international law. This is clearly not the sort of foundation on which Article 6 of the Convention could be said to have reflected or crystallized such a rule.[73]

As for the second submission, that Article 6 had catalyzed sufficient state practice to bring a new customary international rule into existence, the Court again recognized that such a process was possible, but only under certain circumstances:

> There is no doubt that this process is a perfectly possible one and does from time to time occur: it constitutes indeed one of the recognized methods by which new rules of customary international law

---

69   A good example of a treaty combining all three elements is the *United Nations Convention on the Law of the Sea*, 10 December 1982, 1833 U.N.T.S. 3 (entered into force 16 November 1994) [*UNCLOS*]; see Chapter 7, Section C(1)(c).
70   *North Sea Continental Shelf Cases*, above note 14.
71   *Ibid.* at 37–38.
72   *Ibid.* at 41–43.
73   *Ibid.* at 38.

may be formed. At the same time *this result is not lightly to be regarded as having been attained.*[74] [Emphasis added]

The Court's admonition in the last sentence is worthy of note. It is understandable given that the process being considered (namely, "treating [the] Article as a norm-creating provision which has ... become binding even for countries which have never, and do not, become parties to the Convention"[75]) sits uneasily with the theory of consent. If not treated rigorously, such a process has the potential to destroy the distinction between parties and non-parties to treaties.[76] Even more fundamentally, it could call into question the bedrock principle of the sovereign equality of states—effectively allowing some states to legislate for others by adopting multilateral treaty regimes which ultimately, by catalyzing new rules of customary international law, become binding for all. Therefore, strict guidelines governing the customary impact of law-making treaties are in order.

The first such requirement articulated by the Court is that the provision under consideration be of a "fundamentally norm-creating character such as could be regarded as forming the basis of a general rule of law."[77] In other words, if a treaty provision is to be treated as a rule of customary international law, it must have the normative characteristics of such a rule. Such characteristics might include a degree of generality, so as to be relevant to a significant cross-section of states in a variety of circumstances. Similarly, the universal applicability of the rule would presumably be required in keeping with this general feature of customary international law. For example, the equidistance principle in Article 6 of the Convention is only articulated as a fallback position should the parties fail to reach agreement on the delimitation of their respective continental shelves on some other basis. Article 6 also makes vague references to "special circumstances" that can oust the operation of the equidistance principle. Thus the rule contended for by Denmark and the Netherlands was merely contingent and not in fact an obligatory rule of general application. The Court further noted, as discussed above,[78] that the Convention permitted parties to reserve Article 6 unilaterally, further undermining its "fundamentally norm-creating character."

---

74   *Ibid.* at 41.
75   *Ibid.*
76   See Chapter 4, Section G(4).
77   *North Sea Continental Shelf Cases*, above note 14 at 42.
78   See discussion above, in text accompanying notes 32–35.

The other significant limitation relied upon by the Court to deny customary status to the Article 6 equidistance principle is more difficult to understand or justify. The Court suggested that in considering state conduct generated by the adoption of a law-making treaty provision, only the practice and *opinio juris* of non-parties to the treaty was relevant:

> [O]ver half the States concerned … were or shortly became parties to the Geneva Convention, and were therefore presumably, so far as they were concerned, acting actually or potentially in the application of the Convention. *From their action no inference could legitimately be drawn as to the existence of a rule of customary international law* in favour of the equidistance principle.[79] [Emphasis added]

This surprising dictum appears to treat the practice and *opinio juris* of parties to the treaty as irrelevant to the subsequent formation of a customary international rule. It implies that *opinio juris* requires a belief that a certain practice is obligatory not only as a matter of law, but specifically as a matter of customary and not treaty law. It also gives rise to a paradox, sometimes called the "Baxter paradox" after the scholar who first pointed it out.[80] Baxter observed that, if taken at face value, the Court's statement means that the more parties a multilateral treaty attracts (and thus the more universal the practice in accordance with the treaty's terms), the less likely are its provisions to become customary international law. If the practice and *opinio juris* of only non-parties count in establishing a subsequent customary rule, near-universal ratification of the treaty would presumably reduce the pool of potentially relevant practice to well below the "generality" threshold. At the extreme, in the case of one hundred percent participation in the treaty, no corresponding customary rule could be formed notwithstanding perfectly uniform state practice.[81] This, to put it mildly, seems counter-intuitive. It also does not advance the theory of consent, which as we have seen is likely the underlying concern driving the Court to formulate strict conditions on the custom-making potential of treaties in the first place.

It is possible to read the Court's statement more narrowly so as to avoid the paradox, however. It may be that the Court did not intend to state as a general rule that the practice of parties to a treaty could never

---

79   *North Sea Continental Shelf Cases*, above note 14 at 43.
80   R.R. Baxter, "Treaties and Custom" (1970) 129 Rec. des Cours 25 at 64.
81   Of course, the existence of a customary rule in such circumstances would be of little significance in any event, as all states would be bound by the treaty directly.

be relevant in establishing subsequent custom based on the treaty's provisions. Rather, it may merely have meant that in the absence of evidence that such states regarded their practice as required by anything other than the treaty, the Court could not draw such an inference from their mere observance of the treaty's provisions. This is suggested by the Court's use of the term "presumably," its subsequent refusal to infer *opinio juris* from state practice alone, and its overall dissatisfaction with the relatively small number of instances of state practice advanced by Denmark and the Netherlands in support of their claim.[82] On this reading, therefore, as long as there is sufficient evidence of treaty adherents' belief in the independently obligatory character of their actions, their practice can be relevant in establishing an independent rule of customary international law and the Baxter paradox is thus resolved.[83]

This latter interpretation is moreover consistent with the Court's later treatment of similar issues in the *Nicaragua* case.[84] There, one of the principal issues was the degree of overlap between the *UN Charter*'s prohibition on the unilateral use of force[85] and corresponding customary international law on the matter. The Court observed:

> [T]he Charter gave expression in this field to principles already present in customary international law, and *that law has in the subsequent four decades developed under the influence of the Charter, to such an extent that a number of rules contained in the Charter have acquired a status independent of it.*[86] [Emphasis added]

These statements would not be particularly startling but for the earlier statements by the Court in the *North Sea Continental Shelf*

---

82   *North Sea Continental Shelf Cases*, above note 14 at 44. Such a reading is also more readily reconciled with an earlier, apparently inconsistent statement by the Court at 42: "With respect to the other elements usually regarded as necessary before a conventional rule can be considered to have become a general rule of international law, it might be that, even without the passage of any considerable period of time, *a very widespread and representative participation in the convention might suffice of itself* ..." [emphasis added].

83   See also F.A. Mann, "British Treaties for the Promotion and Protection of Investments" (1981) 52 Brit. Y.B. Int'l L. 241 at 249. The author observes that where treaties "express a duty which customary international law imposes *or is widely believed to impose*, they give very strong support to the existence of such a duty *and preclude the Contracting States from denying its existence*" [emphasis added].

84   *Nicaragua*, above note 9.

85   Article 2(4), *Charter of the United Nations*, 26 June 1945, Can. T.S. 1945 No. 7 (entered into force 24 October 1945).

86   *Nicaragua*, above note 9 at 96–97.

Cases,[87] combined with the near-universal participation of states in the *UN Charter* since its adoption in 1945. If the Court's earlier statements intended to exclude the practice of treaty parties when considering customary law developments consequent upon that treaty, it is hard to see how customary law on the use of force could have "developed under the influence of the *Charter*." It is harder still to understand how *Charter* rules could "have acquired [customary] status." In each case, there could be virtually no non-member state practice or *opinio juris* to support such a conclusion.

It can therefore be inferred that the less paradoxical reading of the Court's statements in the *North Sea Continental Shelf Cases* is correct, and that the practice of parties (as well as, of course, non-parties) to a treaty is *potentially* relevant to the formation of subsequent custom if sufficient evidence of the appropriate *opinio juris*[88] is adduced. In the *Nicaragua* case, the Court in fact went on to review evidence of just such *opinio juris* before concluding that the *UN Charter*'s prohibition on the use of force had indeed acquired a counterpart in customary international law.[89] Moreover, the Court has in several other cases relied upon multilateral treaties as evidence of state practice and *opinio juris* tending to establish the existence of parallel customary rules,[90] such that this can now be considered a well-established approach.

3) The Parallel Existence of Custom and Treaty

A question closely related to that of precedence in cases of conflict between treaty and customary norms is whether very similar or identical treaty and customary rules can coexist. This is an important question, because if they can, it might be wondered how treaty rules can ever effectively modify legal obligations between parties. For example, assume states A and B conclude a treaty that modifies, slightly, their mutual customary legal rights and obligations in a given area. If the customary rules continue to exist in some sense, even in the presence of similar but incompatible treaty rules, can A invoke the customary rule against B, thus defeating the purpose of the treaty?

The *Nicaragua* case raised issues very close to these.[91] One of Nicaragua's principal claims was that the United States had violated

---

87   See *North Sea Continental Shelf Cases*, above note 14.

88   See above, text accompanying notes 32–35.

89   *Nicaragua*, above note 9 at 98–102.

90   See, for example, *Gulf of Maine*, above note 36 at 294; *Case Concerning the Continental Shelf (Libyan Arab Jamahiriya v. Malta)*, [1985] I.C.J. Rep. 13 at 30.

91   See *Nicaragua*, above note 9.

international law prohibiting the use of force against Nicaragua's territorial integrity and political independence. The parties agreed that this prohibition existed both in customary international law and treaty law (viz. Article 2(4) of the *UN Charter*). The United States further maintained that the content of each source was identical on this issue. Thus, contended the United States, the *Charter* had "subsumed" and "supervened" the corresponding customary rules so that the dispute could only be resolved by reference to the *Charter*'s provisions and not customary law.

The importance of this argument was that the United States had formulated a reservation to its submission to the jurisdiction of the Court so as to exclude all "disputes arising under a multilateral treaty, unless ... all parties to the treaty affected by the decision are also parties to the case before the Court."[92] The United States therefore argued that the Court had no jurisdiction over the dispute because it arose exclusively under multilateral treaties including, *inter alia*, the *UN Charter*, and not all affected parties to those treaties were before the Court. Nicaragua countered that the dispute also arose under parallel customary international rules such that the American reservation did not deprive the Court of jurisdiction.

The Court rejected the American reasoning first by disagreeing that the content of custom and the *Charter* was identical on the use of force. It went on to hold that:

> [E]ven if the customary norm and the treaty norm were to have exactly the same content, this would not be a reason for the Court to hold that the incorporation of the customary norm into treaty-law must deprive the customary norm of its applicability as distinct from that of the treaty norm. The existence of identical rules in international treaty law and customary law has been clearly recognized by the Court in the *North Sea Continental Shelf Cases*. ... [T]here are *no grounds for holding that when customary international law is comprised of rules identical to those of treaty law, the latter "supervenes" the former, so that the customary international law has no further existence of its own.*[93][Emphasis added]

The Court justified this conclusion by pointing out that a treaty provision might be unenforceable due to procedural features of the treaty which would have no relevance to the customary rule.[94] Simi-

---

92   *Ibid.* at 31.
93   *Ibid.* at 94–95.
94   This was in fact the case here, due to the reservation to the jurisdiction of the Court invoked by the United States.

larly, a treaty obligation, even though identical to a customary norm, might receive a different interpretation in a different venue than its customary analogue.[95] In other words, the Court concluded that treaty and customary norms, even if identical, might receive different *applications* and thus must be treated as having a parallel existence and applicability. A procedural bar to the application of one source did not, therefore, prevent the court from applying the other:

> It will therefore be clear that customary international law continues to exist and to apply, separately from international treaty law, even where the two categories of law have an identical content.[96]

While it is easy to accept that a customary norm continues to exist notwithstanding an identical treaty rule, it is not so evident how it can *apply* as between two parties who have expressly agreed that their relations (including disputes) on the topic should be governed by the terms of the treaty.[97] If states are free to modify their mutual customary legal obligations (if not the existence of customary rules) by treaty, how can this be reconciled with the continued applicability of the customary rules to their relations?

This was the thrust of a secondary argument put forward by the United States. Essentially it argued that if the Court adjudicated the dispute on the basis of customary rules on the use of force, it would in fact be ignoring the express agreement between the parties as to how such disputes were to be resolved.[98] The Court largely side-stepped this compelling argument. It observed that, while not identical, the substantive content of custom and the *Charter* on the use of force was so similar that a ruling of the Court based on the former would not depart significantly from the parties' mutual *Charter* undertakings on the same topic. Of course, this ignored entirely the American submission, which was based on a crucial *procedural* difference between the relevant customary and treaty regimes.

A stronger rebuttal of the American argument might have been that, while the US submission to the jurisdiction of the Court stipulated that the Court had no jurisdiction over disputes arising under multilateral treaties in these circumstances, it did not also *expressly*

---

95   *Nicaragua*, above note 9 at 95.
96   *Ibid.* at 96.
97   The answer to this apparent conundrum may be that, where two parties have not expressly agreed that their relations should be *exclusively* governed by the terms of the treaty, there is no reason why their relations should not continue to be governed by customary international law as well.
98   *Nicaragua*, above note 9 at 96.

provide that the Court had no jurisdiction over disputes arising under parallel customary international law. The American position apparently considered this exclusion of jurisdiction to flow implicitly from the act of entering into treaty commitments that mirrored customary international law; whereas the Court's conclusion (if not its reasoning) appeared to turn on a requirement that such ouster of customary international law's continued applicability, as between parties to a treaty, be explicit. In light of the Court's opaque reasoning, however, the question that remains is whether, had the *Charter* included a provision expressly ousting the applicability of customary rules regulating the use of force, the Court would nevertheless have applied customary rules to resolve the dispute? If so, would this not mean that inconsistent custom in fact trumps treaties?

While these questions of applicability remain unresolved,[99] it is clear that treaty and custom, whether identical or divergent in content, retain a separate and parallel existence even as they influence one another in the ways discussed above.

FURTHER READING

AKEHURST, M., "Custom as a Source of International Law" (1974–75) 47 Brit. Y.B. Int'l L. 1

BAXTER, R.R., "Multilateral Treaties as Evidence of Customary International Law" (1965–66) 41 Brit. Y.B. Int'l L. 275

BAXTER, R.R., "Treaties and Custom" (1970-I) 129 Rec. des Cours 25

BYERS, M., *Custom, Power and the Power of Rules* (Cambridge: Cambridge University Press, 1999)

CHARNEY, J.I., "The Persistent Objector Rule and the Development of Customary International Law" (1985) 56 Brit. Y.B. Int'l L. 1

D'AMATO, A., *The Concept of Custom in International Law* (Ithaca, NY: Cornell University Press, 1971)

---

99 For academic criticism of the judgment on this issue and others, see A. D'Amato, "Trashing Customary International Law" (1987) 81 A.J.I.L. 101; M.H. Mendelson, "The *Nicaragua Case* and Customary International Law" (1989) 26 Coexistence 85 at 90–91; R.F. Turner, "Peace and the World Court: A Comment on the *Paramilitary Activities Case*" (1987) 20 Vand. J.Transnat'l L. 53; R. St. J. Macdonald, "The *Nicaragua Case*: New Answers to Old Questions?" (1986) 24 Can. Y.B. Int'l L. 127.

D'AMATO, A., "Trashing Customary International Law" (1987) 81 A.J.I.L. 101

DANILENKO, G.M., "International *Jus Cogens*: Issues of Law-Making" (1991) 2 Eur. J. Int'l L. 42

DANILENKO, G.M., "The Theory of International Customary Law" (1988) 31 Germ. Y.B. Int'l L. 9

GOLDSMITH, J. & POSNER, E., "A Theory of Customary International Law" (1999) 66 U. Chicago L. Rev. 1113

LOSCHIN, L., "The Persistent Objector and Customary Human Rights Law: A Proposed Analytical Framework" (1996) 2 U.C. Davis. J. Int'l L. & Pol'y 147

MENDELSON, M.H., "The Formation of Customary International Law" (1998) 272 Rec. des Cours 155

SCHACHTER, O., "Entangled Treaties and Custom" in Y. Dinstein & M. Tabory, eds., *International Law at a Time of Perplexity: Essays in Honour of Shabtai Rosenne* (Dordrecht: M. Nijhoff, 1989) 717

WALDEN, R.M., "Customary International Law: A Jurisprudential Analysis" (1978) 13 Isr. L. Rev. 86

WEIL, P., "Towards Relative Normativity in International Law?" (1983) 77 A.J.I.L. 413

CHAPTER 6

RECEPTION OF INTERNATIONAL LAW IN DOMESTIC LAW

A. THE INTERNATIONAL/NATIONAL LAW INTERFACE

Having reviewed the origins, nature, subjects, and sources of international law, it is now appropriate to consider the international legal system's interaction with national, or domestic, legal systems. What is the connection, if any, between international and domestic law? Does international law, which is primarily concerned with regulating the conduct of states, have domestic legal effect *within* states? Does it create rights and obligations for sub-national actors such as individuals, corporations, and government organs? If so, how and why?

To inquire into the effects of one legal system on or in another is, of course, to ask a legal question. Its answer will depend on rules that determine, as a matter of law, how one legal system treats another. Given that a single subject or situation will potentially be governed by more than one system of law, most, if not all, legal systems have developed such rules to address these situations of potential overlap and conflict. These rules often dictate which system of law will apply or "trump" in particular circumstances, although sometimes such rules will avoid the conflict by variously aligning the two legal systems for the purposes of resolving a particular problem.

Given that each legal system may be expected to develop its own set of rules for regulating its interaction with other legal systems, it is evident that one cannot determine, in the abstract, the way in which legal systems will interact. Rather, the answer to the question "how will legal systems A and B interact?" will depend on whether one is asking the question from within the framework of legal system A — complete with its rules governing interactions with other legal systems — or from within the framework of legal system B — again, with its own set of rules governing interactions with other legal systems. Each legal system may develop incompatible rules for resolving which system of law applies in what circumstances, giving rise to the potential for yet further conflict. The point, however, is that how two or more legal systems will interact will vary depending on which legal system's rules for resolving this issue are applied; that is, on one's legal frame of reference.

Transposing this to the relationship between international and domestic legal systems, the nature of that relationship will thus depend on whether one is considering the issue from the perspective of international or domestic law. For example, we have already seen a number of instances where an international legal rule is deemed by international law to prevail over a conflicting rule of domestic law.[1] This does not, however, prejudge the answer that might be given to the same question by the relevant domestic legal system. Considering the issue from that perspective, it might well be that international law would be considered subordinate to the dictates of the domestic legal system.

Moreover, while there is only one international legal system, there are nearly two hundred national legal systems (not to mention those operating within federal units which make up federal states) and thus the nature of the interaction between international and domestic law will potentially vary with each such national or domestic legal system. While one domestic system might, as above, deem a conflicting rule of international law to be subordinate to the domestic legal rule, another might yield entirely to the international rule. It all depends on the rules of interaction adopted by each domestic legal system.

---

1   For example, the rule of treaty law providing that domestic legal impediments are no excuse for failing to perform a binding treaty obligation: see Article 27 of the *Vienna Convention on the Law of Treaties*, 23 May 1969, 1155 U.N.T.S. 331 (entered into force 27 January 1980) [*Vienna Convention*] and discussion in Chapter 4, Section G(1). Of course, it will not always be the case that international law deems its rules to override conflicting domestic norms. There are instances in which even international law subordinates itself to the dictates of domestic legal systems. For example, the legal personality of political or territorial units such as provinces within federal states depends, in the international legal system, upon whether and to what extent these units are entitled under the domestic constitution to conduct their own foreign affairs.

It would of course be a monumental task to try to describe the rules governing the relationship between every domestic legal system and international law. However, it is possible to describe here two broad theoretical models that have been advanced to explain, or argue for, the appropriate relationship between international and domestic legal systems. We will see that, in the present practice of states, elements of both theoretical models are present. We will then turn to consider in some detail, by way of illustration, the particular rules developed by the Canadian legal system to govern its own relationship with international law. It bears repeating, however, that those rules are peculiar to the Canadian legal system and do not necessarily apply to the relationship between other domestic legal systems and international law.

B. PRINCIPAL THEORETICAL MODELS— DUALISM VS. MONISM

While there are many ways of theorizing about the interaction between international and domestic legal systems, the two main theoretical models developed by international lawyers are known as "dualism" and "monism."[2]

The first of these, dualism, was championed by such international legal philosophers as Hegel.[3] As its moniker suggests, this model focuses on the peculiar nature of the international legal system and draws a rigid distinction between it and domestic legal systems. In its purest form, dualism emphasizes that international and domestic law govern distinct subjects, regulate discrete subject matter, and emanate from different sources. Dualism posits that international and domestic legal systems exist in complete legal isolation from one another. Neither is superior to the other such that, in the event of a conflict between the

---

2   For a concise overview of the monist-dualist debate among international lawyers generally, see G. Fitzmaurice, "The General Principles of International Law: Considered from the Standpoint of the Rule of Law" (1957-II) 92 Rec. des Cours 5 at 68–85.

3   G.W.F. Hegel, *Natural Law: The Scientific Ways of Treating Law, its Place in Moral Philosophy, and its Relation to the Positive Sciences of Law*, trans. by T.M. Knox (Philadelphia: University of Philadelphia Press, 1975); see also L. Oppenheim, *International Law: A Treatise*, vol. I, 8th ed. by H. Lauterpacht (London: Longmans, 1955) at 37–39; K. Strupp, "Règles générales du droit de la paix" (1934-I) 47 Rec. des Cours 263 at 389–418.

two legal orders,[4] the resolution of the conflict depends solely upon which legal system happens to govern the forum in which the conflict is being considered. Dualism, in other words, treats international and domestic law as operating in completely different spheres.[5]

In its somewhat less rigid formulations, dualism would admit that rules from one legal system, usually international law, might indeed make their way into the other, but only through a process known as "transformation." That is, the receiving legal system would have to transform the outside (international) rule into one of its own domestic rules. In this way, while the rules of one legal system would technically still never have any direct legal effect on the other, they might be espoused by the latter as its own and in this sense might play some indirect role in shaping its content.

The second of these theoretical models, monism, has been advocated by such international legal scholars as Kelsen and Lauterpacht.[6] In sharp contrast to dualists, monists argue that there either is or should be no essential dichotomy between international and domestic legal systems. Rather, monists tend to view law as an organic whole governing a continuum of subjects and subject matter. On this view, the fact that international law primarily governs state relations rather than individuals or corporations does not entail a fundamental bifurcation between it and domestic law any more than the basic differences between various fields of domestic law (such as corporate, administrative, or criminal law) entail their classification as separate and distinct legal systems.

International and domestic law are thus considered by monists to be part of one and the same continuous legal system. In this way, international legal rules should automatically have direct legal effect within a domestic legal system and form part and parcel of the "law of the land," as it were. Most versions of monism, moreover, posit that in the event of a conflict between a rule of international law and one of domestic law,[7] the international legal rule should take precedence, even within a domestic forum. The long-term and somewhat idealistic effect

---

4   An unlikely event given the rigidly distinct spheres of operation of the legal systems that are assumed in this model.

5   For a recent statement of a rigid dualist position in the Canadian context, see S. Beaulac, "National Application of International Law: The Statutory Interpretation Perspective" (2003) 41 Can. Y.B. Int'l L. 225, especially at 229–41.

6   H. Kelsen, *Pure Theory of Law*, trans. by M. Knight (Berkeley: University of California Press, 1967); H. Lauterpacht, *The Function of Law in the International Community* (Hamden: Archon Books, 1966). See also J.G. Starke, "Monism and Dualism in the Theory of International Law" (1936) 17 Brit. Y.B. Int'l L. 66.

7   An event that would not be so rare, given that both legal systems would operate simultaneously in the domestic sphere.

of the operation of this form of monism would be to bring about the gradual harmonization of all domestic legal systems with international law, and hence with one another.[8]

These two theoretical models clearly sit at opposite extremes of the continuum of possible relationships between international and domestic law, and, as such, leave much to be desired in terms of describing the current reality of such relationships. However, as with any good theoretical model, they are useful in that they allow us at once to recognize certain features of the currently prevailing rapport between the international and domestic legal spheres, and to highlight certain legal implications of those features.

So to what extent do dualist and monist models accurately describe the interaction of international and domestic legal systems? Again, this depends upon one's legal frame of reference. Viewing the matter from the perspective of the international lawyer, it is probably fair to say that there are signs of a gradual evolution, far from complete, from a predominantly dualist position to one in which growing integration or at least overlap between the reach of international and domestic legal systems is becoming evident.

The still prevailing ascendancy of dualism is apparent, however, when one considers the extent to which international and domestic law continue to govern quite distinct classes of subjects and subject matter. International law is still overwhelmingly concerned with regulating the conduct of and interactions *between* states, while domestic law is still primarily focused on governing activities taking place *within* states. This of course is evolving, such that international law now addresses a number of economic, environmental, and human rights matters that, until relatively recently, were the sole preserve of domestic legal orders. Even in these new areas, however, international law generally (though not invariably) addresses the rights and obligations of the *state* in relation to these matters rather than attempting to create directly enforceable legal rights and obligations for sub-state actors. Thus, for most practical purposes, the subjects of international law remain overwhelmingly distinct from those of domestic legal systems.[9]

Moreover, and as we shall see exemplified in at least part of the Canadian legal system's attitude toward international law, many domestic legal systems maintain a rigidly dualist stance in order to insulate and preserve their own domestic sovereignty. In fact, this is

---

8   See J.H. Currie, "International Treaties and Conventions as Agents of Convergence and Multijuralism in Domestic Legal Systems" in A. Breton *et al.*, eds., *Emergence and Evolution of Multijuralism* (forthcoming) (copy on file with author).

9   See further Chapter 2.

a product of both domestic and international law. Traditional international law, as we have seen, is constructed around the premise of the sovereign independence of states, a basic tenet of which is that "matters which are essentially within the domestic jurisdiction of any state"[10] are of no legitimate concern to the international community or international law. Domestic legal systems have tended to reinforce this notion in order to enhance their own independence. Further, traditional international law, which after all was fashioned by states themselves, developed a predominantly "hands-off" or *laissez-faire* approach when it came to legal issues habitually governed by domestic law. Dualism thus captures the traditional isolationism, still evident in international affairs, of the international and domestic legal systems.

As suggested above, however, more recent countervailing influences are tending toward a more monistic integration of international and domestic law. For example, international criminal law has recently been developing quite rapidly in such a way as to impose criminal sanctions directly on individuals for certain international criminal acts, notwithstanding the fact that criminal law has traditionally been viewed as a matter quintessentially within the domestic jurisdiction of sovereign states.[11] Similarly, the development of international human rights law over the past sixty years or so has radically redefined the nature of the relationship between states and individuals by substantially narrowing the class of civil, political, economic, social, and cultural rights that can be said to remain within the exclusive domestic jurisdiction of states.[12] These are prime examples of modern international law's tendency to intrude into subject areas hitherto considered the sole preserve of domestic legal systems.

Further but perhaps less dramatically, the relatively recent proliferation of multilateral "law-making" treaties has had the effect of harmonizing domestic laws as states parties to these treaties implement them domestically. This phenomenon illustrates the process by which international law may in time modify the content of domestic law.[13] Conversely, we have seen that domestic laws and domestic judicial decisions are elements of state practice which may, if combined with the

---

10   To borrow the language used in Article 2(7) of the *Charter of the United Nations*, 26 June 1945, Can. T.S. 1945 No. 7 (entered into force 24 October 1945) [*UN Charter*].

11   See, for example, J.H. Currie, C. Forcese, & V. Oosterveld, *International Law: Doctrine, Practice, and Theory* (Toronto: Irwin Law, 2007) c. 15. See also A. Cassese, *International Criminal Law* (New York: Oxford University Press, 2003).

12   See further Chapter 10.

13   See Currie, above note 8.

requisite *opinio juris*, influence the content of customary international law.[14]

It will be seen from the foregoing that the current interaction between international and domestic legal systems is in a state of flux and in fact has both dualist and monist tendencies. To the extent that international law continues to develop and extend its substantive scope, it is likely that dualism alone will provide an ever-less satisfactory model to describe its relation to domestic law. However, it is important to bear in mind that in its present state of development, the international legal system remains, at least notionally and in many ways formally and practically, quite distinct in its application and effects from national systems.

In any case and as suggested above, the precise extent to which the interface between international and domestic legal systems is accurately described in dualist or monist terms will depend crucially on each domestic legal system's chosen approach to the "reception" of international law. By way of illustration, therefore, we turn now to consider the Canadian legal system and the manner in which it takes cognizance of, or receives, international law. Of course, the way in which any domestic legal system interacts with international law is a matter to be determined by reference to the applicable legal rules of that domestic legal system, and so the reader is again cautioned that prudence must be exercised in generalizing the Canadian approach to other domestic legal contexts.[15]

C. CANADIAN APPROACHES TO THE RECEPTION OF INTERNATIONAL LAW

1) Transformationist vs. Adoptionist Models of Reception

The extent to which international law is received in the domestic Canadian legal system is a question of domestic constitutional law. Given

---

14 See J. Brunnée & S.J. Toope, "A Hesitant Embrace: The Application of International Law by Canadian Courts" (2002) 40 Can. Y.B. Int'l L. 3 at 8, 16, & 57, n. 216. For example, the customary international law of state immunity has evolved considerably in the light of state practice and *opinio juris* as expressed through the decisions of domestic tribunals: see further Chapter 9, Section B.

15 For concise comparative overviews of the reception of international law by various domestic legal systems, see A. Cassese, *International Law*, 2d ed. (Oxford: Oxford University Press, 2005) c. 12, and M.N. Shaw, *International Law*, 5th ed. (Cambridge: Cambridge University Press, 2003) at 143–62.

Canada's legal and constitutional heritage,[16] the approach taken is similar in many respects to that taken in British constitutional law. In that system, international law is treated according to one of two different models of reception, depending on the nature of the international legal rule being received. These models of reception are, in many respects, analogous to their international theoretical counterparts, dualism and monism.

The first of these, the "transformationist" model, is distinctly dualist in nature. According to the transformationist model, a rule of international law cannot have effect domestically unless it has been "transformed" into a domestic legal rule by one of the domestic system's law-making processes.[17] As we shall see below, this is usually interpreted in Canada as a requirement for legislation transforming or implementing the international legal rule domestically, although there would appear to be no reason in principle why the same could not be achieved, at least in the common law provinces of Canada, by binding judicial pronouncement.[18]

In other words, under the transformationist model the international legal rule has no direct effect at all in the domestic legal system. Rather, the latter system creates a new legal rule of its own which mirrors the international legal rule, and it is that new, domestic, "transformed" legal rule which has effect. Such an approach is said to be dualist be-

---

16   It will be recalled that the preamble to the *Constitution Act, 1867* provides in part that Canada shall have "a Constitution similar in principle to that of the United Kingdom": *Constitution Act, 1867* (U.K.), 30 & 31 Vict., c. 3, reprinted in R.S.C. 1985, App. II, No. 5.

17   See *The Parlement Belge*, [1878–89] 4 P.D. 129; *Chung Chi Cheung v. The King*, [1939] A.C. 160 at 167–68 (P.C.), Lord Atkin. This rule is also sometimes attributed to the decision in *R. v. Keyn (The Franconia Case)* (1876), 2 Exch. 63 at 202–3 (C.C.R.), Cockburn C.J. It should be noted, however, that the majority disposed of the case on the basis that the existence of the alleged rule of international law could not be proven. In fact, six judges (forming a majority of the court) maintained, contrary to Cockburn C.J., that an international rule proven to exist applies automatically: Coleridge J. at 154. As such, some scholars have read the views of Cockburn C.J. in this respect as *obiter dicta*: see, for example, C. Vanek, "Is International Law Part of the Law of Canada?" (1949–50) 8 U.T.L.J. 251 at 261–62. See also I. Brownlie, *Principles of Public International Law*, 6th ed. (Oxford: Oxford University Press, 2003) at 42–43.

18   See Brunnée & Toope, above note 14 at 27–28, arguing for a flexible approach to the means by which domestic transformation may occur. See also A.L.C. de Mestral & E. Fox-Decent, "Implementation and Reception: The Congeniality of Canada's Legal Order to International Law" in O.E. Fitzgerald, ed., *The Globalized Rule of Law: Relationships between International and Domestic Law* (Toronto: Irwin Law, 2006) 31 at 42–56.

cause it preserves the receiving legal system's ability to accept, reject, or modify the effect of the international legal rule in the domestic legal system as it sees fit. It preserves domestic control over the content of domestic law.

By contrast, the "adoptionist" or "incorporationist"[19] model assumes that international legal rules are automatically part of the domestic legal order and form part of the fabric of legal rules that have direct legal effect for sub-national actors, such as individuals and corporations. This is so without any necessary intervention or transformation of international legal rules by domestic law-making processes. Such an approach is monist in that changes to international law automatically and *ipso jure* entail modifications to domestic law—indeed, in this view, international law *is* domestic law.

As suggested above, it is necessary to understand the operation of both models because it appears that the Canadian legal system espouses and applies both. There is no express provision in Canada's various constitutional documents dictating the nature of the relationship between international and domestic law, and so the rules have been elaborated by the Courts (both British and Canadian) in accordance with prevailing constitutional principles. Pursuant to this jurisprudential development, the model of reception to be applied in any given case depends on the nature or source of the international legal rule under consideration. In particular, it is generally said that when it comes to customary international law, Canada takes an adoptionist stance, whereas in the case of treaty law, Canada takes a distinctly transformationist approach.

However, these seemingly straightforward propositions in fact mask a considerable amount of uncertainty in the precise relationship between international and Canadian law. The reasons for the distinct approaches to customary and treaty law, as well as for the continuing uncertainty in the application and implications of both the adoptionist and transformationist models in Canada, will be discussed below.

2) Canadian Reception of Customary International Law

In the United Kingdom, it is well-settled that in the case of customary international law, the adoptionist or incorporationist model of recep-

---

19   The term "incorporationist" is more common in English practice whereas "adoptionist" tends to be used in Canadian practice. On the vagaries of the terminology used in this area of the law, see G. van Ert, *Using International Law in Canadian Courts* (The Hague: Kluwer Law International, 2002) at 49–51.

tion prevails.[20] The situation has until very recently been less clear in Canadian law, largely because the courts have tended not to address the issue squarely and expressly. Rather, Canadian courts for many years appeared to have adopted this position implicitly, giving rise to the cautious conclusion that "there is room for the view that the law on the relationship of customary international law to domestic law in Canada is the same as it is in England."[21] Other commentators, writing more recently, have been more sanguine.[22] As we shall see below, recent case law tends to bear out the latter view, although the matter is still not clear of all doubt.

The leading early case here, usually cited as probable—albeit ambiguous—support for the adoptionist approach to customary international law in Canada, is the *Foreign Legations Reference*.[23] In that case, the Supreme Court of Canada was asked to give an advisory opinion on whether the Ontario *Assessment Act*[24] applied to property owned by foreign states in the national capital region. A positive answer to this question would make property owned by foreign states subject to municipal property taxation by the City of Ottawa and the Village of Rockcliffe Park. Section 4 of the Act did not expressly address this issue but simply provided that "All real property in Ontario ... shall be liable to taxation." The potential difficulty was that customary international law grants certain sovereign and diplomatic immunities to foreign states, exempting them from local taxation by a receiving or host state.[25] Im-

---

20 See, for example, *Trendtex Trading Corp. v. Central Bank of Nigeria*, [1977] Q.B. 529 (Eng. C.A.). In that judgment (at 533), Lord Denning traces the origins of this rule to the early eighteenth century and provides a succinct overview of the relevant precedents. See also *Buvot v. Barbuit* (1737), 25 E.R. 777 (Ch.); *Heathfield v. Chilton* (1767), 4 Burrow 2015, Lord Mansfield; S. Fatima, *Using International Law in Domestic Courts* (Oxford: Hart, 2005) at 403–36. A similar position is taken in the United States: see, for example, *The Paquette Habana*, 175 U.S. 677 at 700 (1900).

21 R. St. J. Macdonald, "The Relationship between International Law and Domestic Law in Canada" in R. St. J. Macdonald, G.L. Morris, & D.M. Johnston, eds., *Canadian Perspectives on International Law and Organization* (Toronto: University of Toronto Press, 1974) 88 at 111 [*Canadian Perspectives*]. See also Brunnée & Toope, above note 14 at 42–51, reviewing the ambiguous and sometimes conflicting Canadian case law and tentatively concluding (at 44) that "the best view appears to be that customary law can operate directly within the Canadian legal system."

22 See, for example, van Ert, above note 19 at 150.

23 *Reference Re Powers of Ottawa (City) and Rockcliffe Park*, [1943] S.C.R. 208 [*Foreign Legations Case*].

24 *Assessment Act*, R.S.O. 1937, c. 272; now R.S.O. 1990, c. A.31.

25 See further Chapter 9, Section C.

plicit in the question referred to the Court, therefore, was the issue of the relationship between domestic law and potentially conflicting customary international law.

In his judgment, Chief Justice Duff appeared to adopt as his starting point the proposition that, in keeping with the older British authorities, customary international law was presumptively part of the common law of Canada. The Chief Justice nevertheless conceded that the legislative branch retained the power, as with any common law rule, to override any such customary international law forming part of Canadian common law. However, Chief Justice Duff maintained that legislation must expressly provide for such effect.[26] In this case, the general language of the *Act* was deemed by Chief Justice Duff not to evince the requisite legislative will to override the customary international rules relating to state immunities from local taxation.

It will be seen that this approach preserves at once the basic adoptionist presumption that customary international law has automatic, direct, legal effect in Canada via the common law as well as the principle of legislative supremacy by permitting legislatures to oust, through clear language, the customary/common law rule should they deem it appropriate to do so.

Unfortunately, although Justice Taschereau concurred in a separate opinion with the Chief Justice, the other judges in the case were not so explicit in their support of an adoptionist approach to customary international law. Justice Rinfret appears merely to have assumed, without actually saying so, that the customary international law of state immunities described by Chief Justice Duff applied, so as to render the enforcement of provincial legislation against foreign states legally impossible. Justice Kerwin seems to have assumed that the terms of the *Act* could be applied to the property of foreign states without creating any conflict with customary international law; and, on the relationship between international and domestic law, merely observed enigmatically that "these questions ... must be decided under those rules of international law that have become part of the domestic law of this country."[27] Justice Hudson, in a somewhat confusing judgment, appears to have held that the extent of immunities enjoyed by foreign states depended upon the degree to which these had been transformed into domestic law by the appropriate legislative branch.

---

26 The Chief Justice relied in this regard on the judgment of the United States Supreme Court in *Schooner Exchange v. McFaddon* (1812), 7 Cranch. 116 at 146; see *Foreign Legations Case*, above note 23 at 231. See also *The Paquette Habana*, above note 20.

27 *Foreign Legations Case*, *ibid*. at 238.

From this mix of opinions, one discerns a predominating preference for the adoptionist stance as articulated and qualified by Chief Justice Duff. Unfortunately, that view did not unambiguously command a clear majority of the opinions in the case. Nevertheless, the overall tendency in the cases following the *Foreign Legations Case* was implicitly to endorse the position articulated by Chief Justice Duff.

Cases that could be cited in this regard include the advisory opinion given by the Supreme Court of Canada in *Re Newfoundland Continental Shelf*.[28] In that case one of the principal issues was whether customary international law relating to the status of the continental shelf[29] had progressed sufficiently by 1949, the date of Newfoundland's entry into Confederation, to have vested Newfoundland with sovereign rights over the continental shelf off its coasts. While the Court did not expressly address the nature of the relationship between customary international law on this issue and the domestic legal and constitutional questions before it, the careful review of customary international law carried out by the Court would appear to be an implicit acknowledgment of its direct legal relevance in Canadian law.

Similarly, in the *Québec Secession Reference*,[30] the Supreme Court considered at length the customary international law of self-determination of peoples[31] in determining the legality of a potential unilateral declaration of independence by the National Assembly of Québec. It addressed objections to its jurisdiction to consider international law in this context by stating:

> In addressing this issue, the Court does not purport to act as an arbiter between sovereign states or more generally within the international community. The Court is engaged in rendering an advisory opinion on certain legal aspects of the continued existence of the Canadian federation. *International law has been invoked as a consideration and it must therefore be addressed.*[32] [Emphasis added]

While a somewhat cryptic and cursory statement on a complex and critical issue, this could be read as an endorsement of the direct legal effect or relevance of customary international law in construing the common law constitution of Canada.[33]

---

28 *Re Newfoundland Continental Shelf*, [1984] 1 S.C.R. 86.
29 See further Chapter 7, Section C.
30 *Reference re Secession of Québec*, [1998] 2 S.C.R. 217 [*Québec Secession Reference*].
31 See further Chapter 2, Section C.
32 *Québec Secession Reference*, above note 30 at 276.
33 But see S.J. Toope, "Case Comment on the *Québec Secession Reference*" (1999) 93 A.J.I.L. 519 at 523–25, referring to the Court's "complete disregard for customary

There are many similar examples of such implicit adoption of customary international law in Canadian common law.[34]

More recently, a number of Canadian courts have been more explicit in their support for the adoptionist approach to customary international law. For example, in litigation arising from the 1995 boarding and arrest by Canadian officials of the Spanish fishing trawler *Estai* in international waters (during the so-called "turbot war"), the Federal Court (Trial Division) considered "well settled" the proposition that "accepted principles of customary international law are recognized and are applied in Canadian courts, as part of the domestic law unless, of course, they are in conflict with domestic law."[35] Similarly, in address-

---

law"; and Brunnée & Toope, above note 14 at 45, arguing that the Court "failed completely to engage with the customary law on self-determination," suggesting that "a dualist position may implicitly have been adopted." This seems an overly pessimistic view. While the Court did fail to advert to customary international law as such, it did indicate, at para. 114, that "the principle [of self-determination] has acquired a status beyond 'convention' and is considered a general principle of international law." Moreover, the Court did, in fact, refer to several elements of non-conventional state practice and *opinio juris* (admittedly, without labelling them as such), suggesting that, at least in substance, it was applying customary international law. Certainly the Court failed to take account of some recent, mainly European, state practice in this area, but that speaks to the quality of the Court's analysis of customary international law rather than to rejection of its applicability. Finally, while the reference to international law as a "consideration" to be "addressed"—rather than a formal source of law to be applied—is regrettably ambiguous, it is unclear on what basis one would raise such ambiguity to the level of an implicit rejection of the domestic relevance of customary international law. If anything, the Court's subsequent exclusive reliance on international legal sources to dispose of the issue seems to imply the opposite.

34 See, for example, *Saint John v. Fraser-Brace Overseas Corp.*, [1958] S.C.R. 263 at 268–69, Rand J. (again dealing with the effect of the customary international law of state immunities from municipal taxation); *Pushpanathan v. Canada*, [1998] 1 S.C.R. 982 at 1029–35 (referring to the customary international legal meaning attributed to the words "contrary to the principles of the United Nations" in interpreting legislation implementing treaty obligations relating to refugee status). See also *The Ship "North" v. The King* (1906), 37 S.C.R. 385 at 394, Davies J.; *Reference as to Whether Members of the Military or Naval Forces of the United States of America Are Exempt from Criminal Proceedings in Canadian Criminal Courts*, [1943] S.C.R. 483 at 502, Kerwin J.; *114957 Canada Ltée (Spraytech, Société d'arrosage) v. Hudson (Ville)*, [2001] 2 S.C.R. 241 at paras. 30–32 [*Spraytech*]; *Suresh v. Canada (Minister of Citizenship and Immigration)*, [2002] 1 S.C.R. 3 at paras. 61–65; *Schreiber v. Canada (Attorney General)*, [2002] 3 S.C.R. 269 at paras. 48–50, per LeBel J. [*Schreiber*]. But see *Gouvernement de la République démocratique du Congo v. Venne*, [1971] S.C.R. 997.

35 *Jose Pereira E Hijos S.A. v. Canada (Attorney General)*, [1997] 2 F.C. 84 at para. 20 (T.D.).

ing a lawsuit brought by an Iranian expatriate against Iran for alleged torture, the Ontario Court of Appeal accepted that "customary rules of international law are directly incorporated into Canadian domestic law unless explicitly ousted by contrary legislation."[36]

Given these clear, unequivocal statements, it might have been best had the matter rested there. However, a majority in the Supreme Court of Canada has recently revisited the issue in considering whether the *Canadian Charter of Rights and Freedoms*[37] applies to extraterritorial searches and seizures by Canadian police officers.[38] After reviewing the somewhat ambivalent adoptionist stance taken by the Canadian courts to date, LeBel J., writing for five members of the Court, concluded:

> Despite the Court's silence in some recent cases, the doctrine of adoption has never been rejected in Canada. Indeed, there is a long line of cases in which the Court has either formally accepted it or at least applied it. In my view, following the common law tradition, it appears that the doctrine of adoption operates in Canada such that prohibitive rules of customary international law should be incorporated into domestic law in the absence of conflicting legislation. *The automatic incorporation of such rules is justified on the basis that international custom, as the law of nations, is also the law of Canada unless, in a valid exercise of its sovereignty, Canada declares that its law is to the contrary.* Parliamentary sovereignty dictates that a legislature may violate international law, but that it must do so expressly. Absent an express derogation, the courts may look to prohibitive rules of customary international law to aid in the interpretation of Canadian law and the development of the common law.[39] [Emphasis added]

While at first blush the sentence emphasized in the above passage may seem to put the question of the direct domestic effect of customary international law beyond doubt, there are a number of reasons for lingering doubt. Most prominently, that sentence does not stand alone. It is arguably inconsistent with the immediately preceding statement

---

36 *Bouzari v. Islamic Republic of Iran* (2004), 71 O.R. (3d) 675 at para. 65 (C.A.), leave to appeal to S.C.C. refused, [2005] 1 S.C.R. vi. See also *Mack v. Canada (Attorney General)* (2002), 60 O.R. (3d) 737 at para. 32 (C.A.), leave to appeal to S.C.C. refused, [2003] 1 S.C.R. xiii.

37 Part I of the *Constitution Act, 1982*, being Schedule B to the *Canada Act 1982* (UK), 1982, c. 11 [*Charter*].

38 *R. v. Hape*, 2007 SCC 26. The accused had been convicted of money laundering based in part on evidence gathered abroad by Canadian police officers working cooperatively with local police.

39 *Ibid.* at para. 39.

that "prohibitive rules of customary international law should be incorporated into domestic law in the absence of conflicting legislation."
If custom "is also the law of Canada" by "automatic incorporation,"
what does it mean to say that it "*should be* incorporated" [emphasis
added]?[40] This odd phrasing might suggest that incorporation is not in
fact automatic but rather something that "should be" brought about,
presumably by a court. This might have been a distinction without a
difference had LeBel J. indicated that incorporation was something that
"shall be" or "must be" brought about, but the use of the significantly
less imperative "should be" seems to imply that a rule of customary
international law cannot safely be assumed to be part of Canadian law
until a Canadian court says so.[41]

Moreover, this unwelcome element of uncertainty is many times
magnified in the last sentence of the above passage, according to which
the courts "*may* look to prohibitive rules of customary international
law *to aid in the interpretation of Canadian law and the development of
the common law*" [emphasis added]. Taken at face value, this suggests
a vastly different rule: rather than a directly applicable source of domestic law, customary international law is reduced to the dual role of
merely optional interpretive aid and source of inspiration for potential
changes to the common law. Anything *less* like automatic, direct domestic effect is hard to imagine.[42] Another, more benign, possibility is
that this was merely an ill-considered attempt to paraphrase the "automatic incorporation" rule, although the patently different meaning of
the words used makes this somewhat implausible. We are therefore left
with substantially inconsistent statements of the rule—one providing
for direct, binding effect, and another implying the very opposite.

Finally with respect to wording, LeBel J.'s apparent limitation of
automatic incorporation to "prohibitive" rules of customary international law is puzzling. This qualification does not figure prominently in the authorities cited by LeBel J., nor is its meaning explained.
Is its use meant to suggest that the automatic incorporation doctrine
(whatever its correct interpretation) does not apply to *permissive* rules

---

40   The French version of the judgment does not assist, as it uses "devraient être
     incorporées" rather than "doivent être incorporées."
41   See also *Hape*, above note 38 at para. 46, where LeBel J. finds that "the [custom-
     ary international legal] principles of non-intervention and territorial sovereign-
     ty *may be* adopted into the common law of Canada in the absence of conflicting
     legislation" [emphasis added].
42   For similar concerns arising from *Spraytech*, above note 34 at paras. 30–32, see
     Brunnée & Toope, above note 14 at 47–48.

of customary international law? If not, why not? Unfortunately, no reasons are provided for this apparent distinction.

While it may be that some or all of these textual ambiguities are unintended and that the Court meant simply to endorse an unqualified adoptionist approach to customary international law, absolute clarity on this point is essential. What is at stake is nothing less than the content of Canadian law. Moreover, in the absence of any provision in Canadian constitutional documents addressing the domestic effect of customary international law, the issue is entirely governed by judicial pronouncement. It is therefore to be regretted that the majority's choice of words in *Hape* failed to put Canada's adoptionist approach to customary international law beyond all doubt.

A more formal reason for doubting that *Hape* ends uncertainty as to Canada's approach to customary international law is that the majority's discussion of the issue was arguably *obiter dicta*. The central issue in the case was the correct interpretation of the *Charter*'s ambiguous applicability provision, section 32(1). As we shall see below, the Canadian courts have developed a somewhat flexible presumption of conformity with Canada's international legal obligations (whether customary or treaty-based) in interpreting the *Charter*,[43] a presumption that was in fact applied by LeBel J. to resolve the ambiguity in section 32(1) and support his conclusion that "extraterritorial application of the *Charter* is impossible."[44] However, the operation of this presumption of conformity does not depend on the domestic reception of Canada's international legal obligations, whether by common law adoption or legislative transformation.[45] In other words, the status of customary international law in Canadian domestic law was not, strictly speaking, germane to interpretation of section 32(1) of the *Charter* or the outcome of the case. In that sense, LeBel J.'s statements on the adoption

---

43   See further Section C(3)(d)(iv), below in this chapter.

44   See *Hape*, above note 38 at paras. 55–56 and 85. LeBel J. relied in part on the customary international legal principles of territorial sovereignty and non-intervention in reaching this conclusion on the interpretation of s. 32(1) of the *Charter*.

45   It would be somewhat surprising if it did, given that Canada's Constitution, including the *Charter*, controls the interpretation and application of legislation and (somewhat less directly) common law rules—not the other way around: see *Constitution Act, 1982*, above note 37, s. 52(1); P.W. Hogg, *Constitutional Law of Canada*, 5th ed. Supp. (looseleaf) (Scarborough, ON: Thomson Carswell, 2007) at §§12.2(a)–(b) and 37.2(g); *RWDSU v. Dolphin Delivery*, [1986] 2 S.C.R. 573 at 603; *Dagenais v. Canadian Broadcasting Corporation*, [1994] 3 S.C.R. 835 at 878; *Hill v. Church of Scientology*, [1995] 2 S.C.R. 1130 at paras. 95–98.

of customary international law in Canada, whatever their correct interpretation, are likely not formally binding.[46]

To summarize, it can—still only cautiously—be concluded that,
unless a statute or binding rule of precedent[47] is expressly and irreconcilably to the contrary effect, a rule of customary international law will
probably be deemed, *ipso jure,* to form part of the common law of Canada and to have direct domestic legal effect as such. As a logical corollary, existing statute and common law that does not expressly override
inconsistent rules of customary international law will generally be interpreted by the courts in such a way as to conform to the latter.[48] In
this way, it is probable that customary international law is readily received in Canadian domestic law via the common law while preserving
the domestic legal system's ultimate ability, primarily through its legislative branch, to control the content of domestic law through express
override of a customary rule.

Of course, the implication of this ultimate power is that the legislative branch may, if it so chooses, violate or override customary
international law. This flows from the basic constitutional principle
of legislative supremacy which, although subject to constitutional im-

---

46   It should, however, be noted that another, far more revolutionary, interpretation
of the majority's judgment in *Hape* is possible. In particular, the judgment could
be read as holding that the customary international legal principles of territorial sovereignty and non-intervention have direct effect in Canada not only
as common law rules but also as part of Canada's common law constitution:
see *Hape,* above note 38 at paras. 68–69, where LeBel J. asserts—*semble* on the
basis of customary international law alone—that Canadian law *cannot* be enforced in another state's territory without the other state's consent; and at para.
94, where he holds that a "criminal investigation in the territory of another
state *cannot* be a matter within the authority of Parliament or the provincial
legislatures, *because they have no jurisdiction to authorize enforcement abroad*"
[emphasis added]. While these are, as we shall see in Chapter 8, generally correct statements of *international* law, they would appear to be inconsistent with
the fundamental Canadian constitutional principle of parliamentary supremacy
(which includes Parliament's power to violate international law) recognized
elsewhere by LeBel J: see *ibid.* at paras. 39, 53, and 68. It is therefore submitted
that the less radical reading of the judgment proposed in the text above—one
that does not attribute direct common law *constitutional* effect to customary
international law—is to be preferred.

47   See *Chung Chi Cheung,* above note 17 at 169.

48   See R. Sullivan, *Sullivan and Driedger on the Construction of Statutes,* 4th ed.
(Markham, ON: Butterworths, 2002) at 422; P-A. Côté, *The Interpretation of
Legislation in Canada,* 3d ed. (Scarborough, ON: Carswell, 2000) at 367–68;
Hape, above note 38 at paras. 53–54; *Jose Pereira E Hijos S.A.,* above note 35 at
para. 20.

peratives, is not subject to any requirement of compliance with international law, whether of a customary or conventional nature.[49]

3) Canadian Reception of International Treaty Law

a) General Rule: Treaty Law Must Be Transformed

In contrast to the presumptive adoptionist stance seemingly taken by the Canadian legal system with respect to customary international law, treaty law is given a distinctly transformationist treatment. That is, international treaties (even those that have been signed and ratified by Canada and therefore bind it internationally) have no formal, direct legal effect of their own within the Canadian legal system. To have such effect, they generally must be transformed or implemented through a domestic law-making process. For example, a treaty cannot as a general rule be invoked as a source of law in a Canadian court unless it has been transformed or implemented into Canadian law, usually by legislation.[50]

The reason for this markedly dualist position has little if anything to do with the nature of international law in general or of treaty law in particular. Rather, it flows, almost by historical accident, from a domestic constitutional concern to preserve the fundamental separation of powers between the executive and legislative branches of government. To understand this, it is necessary to recall briefly the evolution of this separation of powers in Anglo-Canadian constitutional history.

b) Constitutional Separation of Treaty-Making and Treaty-Implementing Powers

Historically, the sovereign held broad discretionary powers of governance, sometimes called the royal prerogative, comprising all three of what we today conceive of as the judicial, legislative, and executive

---

49   See *Hape, ibid.* at paras. 39, 53, and 68; R. St. J. Macdonald, above note 21 at 119. But see G.V. La Forest, "May the Provinces Legislate in Violation of International Law?" (1961) 39 Can. Bar Rev. 78, where the provincial authority to legislate in violation of customary international law, although not treaties, is doubted; and Vanek, above note 17 at 266, where it is argued that neither Parliament nor the provincial legislatures may enact legislation violating international law.

50   *A.-G. Canada v. A.-G. Ontario,* [1937] A.C. 326 (J.C.P.C.) [*Labour Conventions Case*]; *Capital Cities Communications v. Canadian Radio-Television Commission,* [1978] 2 S.C.R. 141 at 173; *Francis v. The Queen,* [1956] S.C.R. 618 at 621. For the position taken in the United Kingdom, see *Maclaine Watson v. Department of Trade and Industry,* [1989] 3 All E.R. 523 at 531 (H.L.), Lord Oliver; *R. v. Secretary of State for the Home Department, ex parte Ahmed and Patel,* [1999] Imm. A.R. 22 at 36 (C.A.). See also Fatima, above note 20 at 269–382.

branches of government. Much of the constitutional history of Great Britain, however, has concerned various attempts to curb this broad power and subject it either to the will of Parliament or to the review jurisdiction of the courts, thus bringing about a constitutional separation of powers. By the end of the fifteenth century, for example, the sovereign's direct participation in the judicial process had all but disappeared.[51] By the early seventeenth century, moreover, the courts had held that only Parliament could enact domestic legislation, putting an end to royal proclamations with domestic legislative effect.[52] Similarly, the *Bill of Rights* of 1688 brought an end to the sovereign's powers of suspension or dispensation of laws enacted by Parliament.[53]

In short, the royal prerogative was at an early stage limited to largely executive powers. Moreover, many of those executive powers were further eroded by the courts or by legislation, such that today the royal prerogative can be thought of as a residual source of executive power—now exercised, in Canada, by either the federal or provincial cabinets.

For our purposes, the continuing importance of the royal prerogative, as the "residue of discretionary or arbitrary authority, which at any given time is legally left in the hands of the Crown,"[54] is that it includes the constitutional power to conduct foreign affairs. More specifically, the power to negotiate and ratify treaties, as one of the key aspects of the conduct of foreign affairs, has remained an exclusively executive function in the Anglo-Canadian constitutional tradition.[55] This means that no legislative concurrence is necessary before an internationally binding treaty obligation may be entered into on behalf of Canada by the executive branch.[56]

---

51   *Reference re Remuneration of Judges of the Provincial Court of Prince Edward Island*, [1997] 3 S.C.R. 3 at 176, La Forest J., dissenting on another point, citing W.R. Lederman, "The Independence of the Judiciary" (1956) 34 Can. Bar Rev. 769 and 1139, and Sir William Blackstone, *Commentaries on the Laws of England*, 4th ed., Book 1 (Dublin: Exshaw, 1771) at 267. The formal end of the sovereign's power to judge criminal or civil cases was announced by the courts in *Prohibitions del Roy* (1607), 12 Co. Rep. 64, 77 E.R. 1342.

52   *Proclamations* (1611), 12 Co. Rep. 74, 77 E.R. 1352; and see, generally, Hogg, above note 45 at §1.9. Note that the sovereign nevertheless retained the power to issue proclamations in effect enacting laws for British colonies and overseas possessions: *ibid.*

53   See Hogg, *ibid.*

54   A.V. Dicey, *Introduction to the Study of the Law of the Constitution*, 10th ed. (London: Macmillan, 1964) at 424.

55   See Hogg, above note 45 at §11.2.

56   A.E. Gotlieb, *Canadian Treaty-Making* (Toronto: Butterworths, 1968) at 14; Hogg, *ibid.* at §11.3(c). Note that since the prerogative power is subject to legislative curtailment, it would be open to Parliament to legislate a role for itself in the

It is this peculiarity of Anglo-Canadian constitutional law—the fact that the executive branch has the sole power to conclude internationally binding treaties but has no power to change or enact domestic law—that drives the need for transformation of treaty obligations before they can have domestic legal effect. From the domestic legal perspective, therefore, treaty practice has two distinct elements or stages, treaty-making and treaty implementation, each of which falls under the jurisdiction of distinct branches of government—respectively, the executive and the law-making branches.

The executive branch is thus competent to conclude treaties that bind Canada, as a matter of international law, on the international plane. From the domestic legal perspective, however, such treaties do not in themselves modify the content of or have direct effect within Canadian law. If it were otherwise this would circumvent the basic constitutional principle that the executive branch cannot make domestic law. Any domestic legal effect is thus contingent on domestic law-making activity (usually assumed to be legislative) that "transforms" the relevant treaty rule into a rule of domestic law that may be invoked before Canadian courts by Canadian legal persons.

This separation of treaty-making and treaty-implementation powers means, of course, that there is no (domestic) legal or constitutional obligation on the domestic law-maker to transform or implement a treaty entered into by the executive branch. If there were, this would again obviously short-circuit the separation of powers by forcing the legislative branch to follow the lead of the executive branch.

The result is that Canada may find itself bound, as a matter of international law, by treaty obligations duly concluded by the executive branch but not implemented by the competent domestic law-making

---

treaty-making process. Private members' bills to this effect have been introduced in the past, but have not been enacted: see, for example, Bill C-315, *An Act to provide for the conduct of public hearings and approval by the House of Commons before the ratification of important treaties*, 1st Sess., 37th Parl., 2001, cls. 3(1)–(3). On 25 January 2008, however, the Government of Canada announced that it would table treaties, to which it intends to bind Canada, in the House of Commons twenty-one days before doing so. The purpose of this procedure is to give members of the House the opportunity to "review and discuss" proposed treaties, although the executive "will maintain the legal authority to decide whether to ratify the treaty": see "Canada Announces Policy to Table International Treaties in House of Commons," DFAIT News Release No. 20 (25 January 2008). For a review of the policy issues involved, see J. Harrington, "Scrutiny and Approval: The Role for Westminster-Style Parliaments in Treaty-Making" (2006) 55 I.C.L.Q. 121; and J. Harrington, "Redressing the Democratic Deficit in Treaty Law-Making: (Re-)Establishing a Role for Parliament" (2005) 50 McGill L.J. 465.

authorities. Should such a treaty be one that requires changes to the domestic legal order for its performance,[57] the result is that Canada will be in breach of its international legal obligations to other states parties and may well be found internationally responsible to those states for any resulting prejudice.[58] This possibility makes close coordination and cooperation between branches of government essential if international responsibility for breach of treaty obligations is to be avoided.[59] As we shall see next, however, such cooperation and coordination is made still more complicated by Canada's federal nature.

c)   Treaty-Making and Treaty Implementation in a Federal State

As suggested above, there is a discontinuity in Canada between the constitutional power to enter into international treaties, which rests in the hands of the executive, and the power to implement such treaty obligations domestically, which rests in the hands of domestic law-makers, typically legislatures. However, the potentially difficult situation to which this discontinuity can give rise, described above, is even more complicated in Canada due to its federal structure. The questions that arise include: (1) which incarnations of the executive branch are competent to conclude international treaties—the federal executive,

---

57   Not every treaty requires changes to domestic law for its performance. If a treaty does not, for example if it may be performed by previously authorized executive action, or if existing domestic law is sufficient to give effect to the treaty's requirements, no action is required on the part of domestic law-makers in order to perform the treaty: see H.M. Kindred, "The Use and Abuse of International Legal Sources by Canadian Courts" in Fitzgerald, above note 18, 5 at 10–17. For an example of a treaty that requires no legislative action for its performance, see also the agreement between Canada and the United States for the purposes of extending NORAD: *Agreement between the Government of Canada and the Government of the United States of America on the North American Aerospace Defense Command*, 28 April 2006 (in force 12 May 2006).

58   Recall that domestic legal impediments to treaty performance are no excuse for a failure to perform binding treaty obligations: see *Vienna Convention*, above note 1, Article 1; and see further Chapter 4, Section G(1).

59   Although in our system of responsible government the executive is generally controlled by the legislative branch, this does not wholly eliminate the potential for conflict between these branches, particularly in a minority government situation. Moreover, it is not uncommon for the composition of Parliament or the legislatures to change after a treaty has been concluded but before it has been implemented domestically. In practice, these difficulties tend to be avoided either by delaying treaty ratification until implementing legislation is in place, or by seeking an expression of legislative support for the treaty scheme prior to expressing Canada's consent to be bound by it: see Hogg, above note 45 at §11.3(c); A-M. Jacomy-Millette, *L'introduction et l'application des traités internationaux au Canada* (Paris: Librairie générale de droit et de jurisprudence, 1971) at 114.

the provincial executives, or both? and (2) regardless of the answer to the first question, which legislature(s) is (are) competent to implement treaty obligations domestically?

i) Concentration of Treaty-Making Power in Federal Executive

In modern Canadian constitutional practice it is generally accepted that the federal executive has the sole constitutional authority to represent Canada internationally, and in particular has the sole authority to conclude and ratify treaty obligations on behalf of Canada or any of its constituent federal units.[60] This position has been contested on occasion by some provinces and continues to be a point of contention particularly with respect to the province of Québec,[61] but in fact it represents the daily reality of Canadian treaty practice.[62]

The starting point for the argument that treaty-making power lies exclusively with the federal executive is that the *Constitution Act, 1867*[63] is silent on the issue.[64] The obvious implication is that, at Confederation, the power to conduct international affairs and to conclude treaties was retained by the Imperial executive and did not devolve to the Queen's representatives in Canada, the Governor General at the federal level and the Lieutenant-Governors at the provincial level.[65] Indeed, until approximately 1926, treaties were negotiated and concluded on

---

60   Hon. P. Martin, Secretary of State for External Affairs, *Federalism and International Relations* (Ottawa: Queen's Printer, 1968) at 11–33; G.L. Morris, "The Treaty-Making Power: A Canadian Dilemma" (1967) 45 Can. Bar Rev. 478 at 484.

61   See, for example, C. Emanuelli, *Droit international public: contribution à l'étude du droit international selon une perspective canadienne*, 2d ed. (Montréal: Wilson & Lafleur, 2004) at 92; J-Y. Morin, "La personnalité internationale du Québec" (1984) 1 R.Q.D.I. 163; J-Y. Morin, "Le Québec et le pouvoir de conclure des accords internationaux" (1966) 1 Études Jur. Can. 136; *An Act Respecting the Ministère des Relations Internationales*, R.S.Q., c. M-25.1, ss. 19–22.4.

62   Hogg, above note 45 at §§11.2 and 11.6; Gotlieb, above note 56 at 4–6.

63   Above note 16.

64   The federal power of performance of so-called "Empire Treaties" set out in s. 132 of the *Constitution Act, 1867, ibid.*, has no direct relevance to the broader issue of the power to conclude international treaties. But see *Thomson v. Thomson*, [1994] 3 S.C.R. 551 at para. 112, L'Heureux-Dubé J. (McLachlin J. concurring), stating without explanation that "[f]ederal treaty-making power is found in s. 132 of the *Constitution Act, 1867*...." This is likely a mere judicial slip as s. 132 is clearly limited to the federal power to *perform* treaties entered into by the United Kingdom Government on behalf of Canada as part of the British Empire; a now-spent practice. See also *Labour Conventions Case*, above note 50 at para. 10 (J.C.P.C.), Lord Atkin, stating that given "that it was not contemplated in 1867 that the Dominion would possess treaty-making powers, it is impossible to strain the section [s. 132] so as to cover the uncontemplated event."

65   Hogg, above note 45 at §11.2.

behalf of Canada by the Imperial Government, albeit with increasing participation and consultation as Canada gradually assumed the various trappings of statehood.

During the Imperial Conference of 1926, however, the Dominions, including Canada, gained the power to establish direct foreign relations and in particular to negotiate and conclude directly their own treaties, although some treaties still required formal ratification by the United Kingdom Government.[66] This *de facto* passing of the prerogative power to conduct foreign affairs and conclude treaties was subsequently formalized in the Letters Patent of 1947, by which all of the prerogative powers in respect of Canada were delegated to the Governor General.[67] These, in turn, are of course exercised, as a matter of constitutional convention, on the advice of the federal cabinet.[68]

The conclusion reached, that treaty-making power now rests exclusively with the federal executive, received early and express endorsement by the Supreme Court of Canada in the *Labour Conventions Reference*.[69] That opinion has not since been reconsidered by the Supreme Court.[70]

The provinces nevertheless retain the ability to enter into various reciprocal arrangements with foreign jurisdictions,[71] although these do not amount to treaties at international law unless they have been negotiated and ratified at the provinces' behest by the federal government. In fact, the federal and provincial governments cooperate in a number of ways in order to accommodate provincial interests in the treaty-making process. In return, the federal government often gains provincial legislative cooperation in the treaty-implementation process, to which we now turn.

---

66   *Ibid.* at §11.5(a). See also I.C. Rand, "Some Aspects of Canadian Constitutionalism" (1960) 38 Can. Bar Rev. 135 at 138.

67   *Letters Patent Constituting the Office of Governor General of Canada*, R.S.C. 1985, App. II, No. 31.

68   Hogg, above note 45 at §11.2.

69   *Reference re The Weekly Rest in Industrial Undertakings Act, The Minimum Wages Act, and The Limitation of Hours of Work Act*, [1936] S.C.R. 461 at 488–89 [*Labour Conventions Reference*], Duff C.J. (writing for himself and Justices Kerwin and Davis). On appeal, the opinion of the Supreme Court concerning the treaty-implementation power of Parliament was reversed by the Privy Council: *Labour Conventions Case*, above note 50. However, the holding of the case with respect to the treaty-making power still stands.

70   See also *Thomson*, above note 64 at paras. 112–13, where L'Heureux-Dubé J. (McLachlin J. concurring) refers to the "exclusive" federal treaty-making jurisdiction.

71   For example, with respect to the enforcement of judgments; see *Ontario (Attorney General) v. Scott*, [1956] S.C.R. 137. Other examples are described in Gotlieb, above note 56 at 25. See also Hogg, above note 45 at §11.6.

ii)   Constitutional Division of Treaty-Implementation Power: The Labour
Conventions Case

As we have seen above, while the treaty-making power rests with the
executive, the power to make any changes to domestic law that may be
necessary to perform or implement a treaty resides with the law-making branch. However, it does not necessarily follow from the concentration of treaty-making power in the federal executive that legislative
competence to implement or transform treaties is concentrated solely
in Parliament, to the exclusion of the provincial legislatures.

Again, the *Constitution Act, 1867* does not expressly resolve this
issue. While Parliament does enjoy exclusive authority to implement
so-called Empire treaties,[72] this power does not catch the vast majority
of treaties binding on Canada, which have been negotiated by Canada
on its own behalf since it acquired the right to do so in the early twentieth century.[73] That leaves only the constitutional division of legislative
powers set out in sections 91 and 92 of the *Constitution Act, 1867*, but
these do not specifically address the locus of the legislative power to
implement treaties concluded by the federal government.

The matter was resolved in 1937 in a decision of the Privy Council that has since been much debated and criticized. The issue in the
so-called *Labour Conventions Case* was the authority of the Canadian
Parliament to enact three statutes implementing conventions adopted
by the International Labour Organization in 1919, 1921, and 1928, and
ratified by the Canadian government in 1935.[74] The conventions obligated states parties to respect certain minimum labour standards designed to protect the welfare of workers in member states. Ontario,
New Brunswick and British Columbia challenged the federal legislation, contending that it was *ultra vires* Parliament and trespassed upon
provincial areas of jurisdiction under section 92 of the *Constitution Act,
1867*.

The Supreme Court divided evenly on this issue,[75] but on appeal
to the Privy Council, Lord Atkin found that the legislation was indeed

---

72   *Constitution Act, 1867*, above note 16 at s. 132.

73   See text above, accompanying notes 63–70.

74   *Hours of Work (Industry) Convention*, 28 November 1919, ILO C001, 1st Sess.
(entered into force 13 June 1921); *Weekly Rest (Industry) Convention*, 17 November 1921, ILO C014, 3rd Sess. (entered into force 19 June 1923); *Minimum
Wage-Fixing Machinery Convention*, 16 June 1928, ILO C026, 11th Sess. (entered
into force 28 May 1947).

75   The Court comprised only six members, with three judges finding in favour of
(Duff C.J., Davis, and Kerwin JJ.) and three against (Rinfret, Cannon, and Crocket
JJ.) the *vires* of the legislation: *Labour Conventions Reference*, above note 69.

ultra vires Parliament. In doing so, he set out his now-famous "water-tight compartments" metaphor,[76] the gist of which maintained that, in the absence of any applicable express treaty-implementation power in the *Constitution Act, 1867*,[77] that power implicitly but rigidly followed the distribution of legislative powers set out in sections 91 and 92. Further:

> For the purposes of sections 91 and 92 (that is, the distribution of legislative powers between the Dominion and the Provinces) there is no such thing as treaty legislation as such. The distribution is based on classes of subjects; and as a treaty deals with a particular class of subjects so will the legislative power of performing it be ascertained. No one can doubt that this distribution is one of the most essential conditions, probably the most essential condition, in the inter-provincial compact to which the British North America Act gives effect.[78]

In other words, "treaty implementation" is not in itself a discrete jurisdictional category for purposes of the section 91–92 classification. Rather, it is the correspondence between the underlying subject matter of any given treaty—or more precisely, the subject matter of any legislation that might be required to implement the treaty—and one or more of the enumerated categories in sections 91 or 92 that will determine which legislative body is competent to enact the implementing legislation.

The result is of course problematic. The consequence of the ruling is that, while the treaty-making power is concentrated in the hands of the federal government, jurisdiction to implement treaties will sometimes rest in the federal Parliament, sometimes in the provincial legislatures, and perhaps even, on occasion, in both, depending on the range of subject matter in the treaty. The resulting asymmetry between the treaty-making and treaty-implementing powers potentially multiplies the number of situations in which Canada may find itself in breach of its international treaty obligations because one or more legislatures refuse to follow suit.

---

76   Above note 50 at para. 15, Lord Atkin.
77   Then the *British North America Act, 1867.* For the Privy Council, Lord Atkin dismissed the applicability of s. 132, the Empire treaties provision, holding that it conferred no implementing power with respect of treaties between Canada and foreign states, as distinct from treaties between the British Empire and foreign states: *Labour Conventions Case*, above note 50 at para. 10.
78   *Labour Conventions Case, ibid.* at para. 12.

The decision of the Privy Council in the *Labour Conventions Case* has frequently been criticized on these and other grounds,[79] and members of the Supreme Court have even on occasion, in *obiter dicta*, suggested that it ought to be reconsidered.[80] Much of this criticism is premised on the notion that the federal executive's capacity to conclude treaties binding Canada internationally ought to be matched by full federal legislative competence to implement those treaty obligations. This would certainly be desirable if the only goal were to minimize the instances where Canada might find itself in default of its treaty obligations *vis-à-vis* other states due to a lack of legislative cooperation by the provinces. It would also be somewhat defensible on the theory that Canada's foreign affairs, including most if not all treaty obligations undertaken by it, affect Canada as a whole in one way or another, and should be the subject of federal legislative control.[81]

However, the consequences of overruling the *Labour Conventions Case* on this point would likely be devastating to federalism as we know it. In particular, the current balance of legislative power between Parliament and the provincial legislatures would likely be drastically altered if Parliament acquired exclusive legislative jurisdiction to implement Canada's treaty commitments. This is so because those treaty commitments have grown enormously both in number and in scope.[82] Many of today's treaties deal with matters clearly coming within the classes of subjects in respect of which the provinces now enjoy exclusive legislative competence under section 92.[83] There is also the possibility that many more treaties of this nature might be concluded by the federal government if by doing so it could thereby confer jurisdiction upon Parliament over areas otherwise beyond its reach. In other words, a reversal of the *Labour Conventions Case* would pose a very real threat to provin-

---

79   See, for example, Hogg, above note 45 at §11.5(c); Symposium in (1937) 15 Can. Bar Rev. 393*ff.*; Lord Wright, "Rt. Hon. Sir Lyman Poore Duff, G.C.M.G. 1865–1955" (1955) 10 Can. Bar Rev. 1123 at 1126–27.

80   See, for example, *MacDonald and Railquip Enterprises Ltd. v. Vapor Canada Ltd.*, [1977] 2 S.C.R. 134 at 169, Laskin C.J.; *Francis v. The Queen*, above note 50 at 621, Kerwin C.J.

81   For a variation on this argument, see W.R. Lederman, *Continuing Canadian Constitutional Dilemmas* (Toronto: Butterworths, 1981) c. 19. For the rather different approach, based in part on these considerations, taken to the locus of the treaty-implementation power in the Australian constitution, see *Commonwealth of Australia v. State of Tasmania* (1983), 46 A.L.R. 625 (H.C.A.).

82   See Kindred, above note 57 at 9.

83   For example, the implementation of the *Convention on Protection of Children and Co-operation in Respect of Intercountry Adoption* by way of the Ontario *Intercountry Adoption Act, 1998*, S.O. 1998, c. 29.

cial spheres of jurisdiction and risk undermining the whole structure of federalism erected by sections 91 and 92 of the *Constitution Act, 1867*.[84]

In fact, many of the concerns that have fuelled criticism of the outcome in the *Labour Conventions Case* can be, and to a large extent have been, addressed by various mechanisms available to the federal government when undertaking treaty commitments on behalf of Canada. The most obvious of these include arrangements for consultation and cooperation with provinces prior to the conclusion of treaties, which can minimize those situations where a provincial legislature subsequently refuses to cooperate in the implementation process. Of course, cooperation of this nature cannot always be assured or sustained, and other solutions may be required.

One such solution available to the federal government is to negotiate, as part of the treaty text, a so-called "federal state clause."[85] A typical such clause commits a ratifying federal state to performance only of those treaty obligations that come within federal or central implementing jurisdiction, along with a "best efforts" undertaking to secure provincial or other sub-national adherence as well. Such clauses may not be popular with other states given that they introduce a lack of reciprocity into the treaty relationship.[86]

In the absence of agreement on such a clause, the federal government may also choose to ratify a treaty subject to a reservation in respect of treaty obligations falling within provincial spheres of implementing jurisdiction. This also is not a perfect solution as it introduces strains into the treaty relationship with other states, which may perceive the reservation as either incompatible with the objects and purposes of the treaty or with their own national interests.[87]

---

84   For further discussion of this subject see G.L. Morris, "Canadian Federalism and International Law" in *Canadian Perspectives*, above note 21 at 55; A. Dufour, "Fédéralisme canadien et droit international" in *Canadian Perspectives, ibid.* at 72; R. Howse, "The Labour Conventions Doctrine in an Era of Global Interdependence: Rethinking the Constitutional Dimensions of Canada's External Economic Relations" (1990) 16 Can. Bus. L.J. 160; A.L.C. de Mestral, "The Implementation of Canada's International Economic Obligations" (1986) Queen's L.J., *International Law: Critical Choices for Canada 1985–2000* (Special Issue) 192.

85   See, for example, Article 11 of the *Convention on the Recovery Abroad of Maintenance*, 10 June 1956, 268 U.N.T.S. 32 (entered into force 25 May 1957); and see, generally, H.A. Leal, "Federal State Clauses and the Conventions of the Hague Conference on Private International Law" (1984) 8 Dal. L.J. 257.

86   See H.M. Kindred & P.M. Saunders, eds., *International Law Chiefly as Interpreted and Applied in Canada*, 7th ed. (Toronto: Emond Montgomery, 2006) at 210.

87   *Ibid.* For further discussion of the strains introduced into treaty relationships by reservations, and of permissible reservations, see Chapter 4, Section E.

While these mechanisms may ease some of the concerns arising from the lack of a federal implementing power corresponding to the federal treaty-making power, as suggested, they have shortcomings. This perhaps explains why the Supreme Court of Canada, while not reversing the *Labour Conventions Case*, nevertheless appears to have demonstrated an occasional willingness to construe Parliament's section 91 powers generously when considering the *vires* of federal legislation implementing some of Canada's international treaty obligations.

The most obvious candidate for an expansive reading in such circumstances would be the "national concern" aspect of the federal "peace, order and good government" power. For example, in the *Crown Zellerbach* case,[88] the issue was the constitutionality of federal legislation regulating marine pollution.[89] As the legislation at issue went beyond the terms and requirements of the corresponding treaty to which Canada was a party, the federal government chose not to defend it on the basis that it implemented treaty obligations of national concern. Justice LeDain for the majority, however, viewed the terms of the treaty as evidence that marine pollution had a "predominantly extra-provincial as well as international character" that was "clearly a matter of concern to Canada as a whole" and was thus within the national concern doctrine of the peace, order, and good government power.[90]

There are other candidates in section 91 for such generous treatment, including the general trade and commerce power.[91] It remains to be seen just how far the courts will be willing to go in accommodating the perceived need for federal legislative competence to implement an ever-widening array of treaty obligations while still respecting the "watertight compartments" theory of the *Labour Conventions Case*.

Summarizing our examination of the relationship between treaties and Canadian law so far, we have seen that, as a general rule, treaties must be transformed or implemented before having formal, domestic legal effect. Whereas treaty-making is a function of the federal executive branch, treaty implementation comes within the purview of the law-

---

88   *R. v. Crown Zellerbach Canada Ltd.*, [1988] 1 S.C.R. 401.

89   *Ocean Dumping Control Act*, R.S.C. 1985, c. O-2.

90   *Crown Zellerbach*, above note 88 at 436.

91   See, for example, *General Motors of Canada Ltd. v. City National Leasing*, [1989] 1 S.C.R. 641, where it was held that intrusive federal trade legislation may be found *intra vires* where the legislation is part of a general regulatory scheme, continuously monitored by an agency; where the legislation is concerned with trade generally rather than with a particular industry; where the provinces are constitutionally incapable of enacting legislation of such a nature; and where a failure to include one or more provinces would jeopardize the successful operation of the scheme elsewhere in Canada.

making branch. Finally, the subject-matter of the treaty, in conjunction with sections 91 and 92 of the *Constitution Act, 1867,* will determine whether the legislative implementation role is to be played by the federal Parliament or the provincial legislatures. The apparent clarity of this summary of the rules belies, however, considerable complexity when it comes to their practical application. Nowhere has this been more evident than in the constantly evolving domestic legal significance attached by Canadian courts to treaties, both implemented and unimplemented. It is to this evolving judicial practice that we now turn.

d) Canadian Courts and Treaties: From Rigidity to Complexity

i) Traditional Judicial Approach to Treaties

Applied rigidly, a transformationist approach to treaty law would mean that Canadian courts need take no account of a treaty in the absence of domestic law clearly implementing it. Indeed, it could be argued that the requirement of transformation means that even an implemented treaty need never be considered by a Canadian court because the court is governed only by the implementing legislation and not the underlying treaty. However, the cases disclose no such clear-cut and rigid approach by the courts, raising continuing doubts as to the precise relationship between treaty and domestic law in Canada. The requirement of transformation is all well and good as a theory preserving certain constitutional imperatives, but its true significance must be evaluated in light of its actual application by the courts. Unfortunately, in its present state of development, the case law appears to be tending towards greater, not less, uncertainty with respect to the correct application of the theory of transformation.

In keeping with the basic proposition that treaties do not in themselves have direct legal force within the Canadian legal system, Canadian courts historically refused to give any effect at all to unimplemented treaties. An oft-cited example of this rigid approach is the case of *Francis v. The Queen.*[92] Francis was an Indian, within the meaning of the *Indian Act,*[93] residing on the St. Regis Indian Reserve in the Province of Québec. He had refused to pay customs duties and sales tax on several household appliances purchased in the United States. The Crown seized the appliances and Francis paid the duties and taxes to secure their release. He thereafter applied for the return of the monies and a declaration that he was exempt from the duty requirements under Canadian law due to Article III of the *Treaty of Amity, Commerce and Navi-*

---

92   *Francis,* above note 50.
93   *Indian Act,* R.S.C. 1985, c. I-5.

gation (Jay Treaty) of 1794 between the United Kingdom and the United States, which exempted Indians from such duties or levies. In rejecting this claim, Chief Justice Kerwin observed that the *Jay Treaty* had not been implemented in Canadian legislation, and therefore held that:

> ... in Canada such rights and privileges as are here advanced by subjects of a contracting party to a treaty are enforceable by the Courts only where the treaty has been implemented or sanctioned by legislation.[94]

To similar effect was the majority judgment in *Capital Cities Communications*.[95] In that case, American television broadcasters challenged a Canadian Radio-Television Commission (CRTC) decision permitting the deletion of commercial advertisements from signals originating in the United States. The advertisements were substituted with local public service announcements before transmission to cable subscribers in Canada. The challenge was based in part on an apparent conflict between the CRTC decision and the terms of the *Inter-American Radio Communications Convention*, to which Canada was a party.[96] Chief Justice Laskin for the majority in the Supreme Court of Canada dismissed the broadcasters' argument, rehearsing the fundamental rule that:

> There would be no domestic, internal consequences unless they arose from implementing legislation giving the Convention a legal effect within Canada.[97]

In finding that no Canadian legislation had implemented the Convention, Chief Justice Laskin adopted what the dissenting judges[98] clearly considered a narrow reading of the existing legislative framework governing telecommunications. Further, the Chief Justice rejected the argument that, in the absence of express implementing legislation, the existing statutory framework could and should be read so as to conform to the terms of the Convention:

---

94 *Francis*, above note 50 at 621. See also the judgment of Rand J. to the same effect.

95 *Capital Cities Communications*, above note 50.

96 *Inter-American Radio Communications Convention*, 13 December 1937, 7 Int'l Leg. No. 503 (entered into force 1 July 1938).

97 *Capital Cities Communications*, above note 50 at 173. Pigeon J. (writing for the dissenting minority) referred to Chief Justice Laskin's position as "an oversimplification": *ibid.* at 188.

98 In dissent, Pigeon J. (writing for Beetz and de Grandpré JJ.) argued that the CRTC could not issue authorizations to Canadian providers in a manner that violated Canadian treaty obligations; indeed, the broadcasters were entitled to the protection of certain legal interests in Canada by virtue of the Convention: *ibid.* at 189.

I do not find any ambiguity that would require resort to the Convention, which is, in any event, nowhere mentioned in the *Broadcasting Act*; and certainly the Convention *per se* cannot prevail against the express stipulations of the Act.[99]

This inflexible attitude towards treaties, particularly where their terms appear to be in conflict with domestic legislation,[100] has increasingly softened, however. This has occurred, as we shall now see, through the courts' adoption of a series of interpretive presumptions and devices that seek to avoid finding conflicts between treaties and domestic law—whether in the nature of implementing legislation or not.

ii) Reconciling Treaty Obligations and Domestic Implementing Legislation

One issue that arises in considering the requirement of transformation is how the courts should interpret legislation purportedly implementing a treaty. As suggested above, a rigid application of the theory of transformation would suggest that a domestic court is only ever bound by the domestic implementing legislation (the "transformed," and hence domestically effective, treaty obligation), and never by the treaty itself. One difficulty with such an approach is that the terms, or even the meaning of the terms, of the treaty might be modified in the process of transformation, such that the domestic legislation does not correspond exactly to the international treaty obligation. Should courts ignore this fact and simply apply the domestic legislation?

The answer to this question might be expected to vary depending on the precise relationship between the treaty and the implementing legislation. For example, a treaty may be implemented through legislation that essentially repeats or paraphrases, in the body of the legislation, the terms of the treaty.[101] Another device is simply to enact the provisions of the treaty itself, either selectively or in their entirety, by incorporating them by reference into the implementing legislation.[102]

---

99 *Capital Cities Communications*, above note 50 at 173.

100 See also, for example, *R. v. Canada Labour Relations Board* (1964), 44 D.L.R. (2d) 440 at 453–56 (Man. Q.B.), Smith J.

101 For example, the definition of "Convention Refugee" in s. 2 of the *Immigration Act*, R.S.C. 1985, c. I-2, echoes the phrasing of the *Convention Relating to the Status of Refugees*, 28 July 1951, 189 U.N.T.S. 137 (entered into force 22 April 1954), as amended by the *Protocol Relating to the Status of Refugees*, 31 January 1967, 606 U.N.T.S. 267 (entered into force 4 October 1967). The relationship between the Act and the Convention is considered in the *Baker* case, below note 139.

102 An example of the selective approach to implementation by reference is the *Foreign Missions and International Organizations Act*, S.C. 1991, c. 41, s. 3 which

In such a case, the body of the legislation usually contains only references to the provisions of the treaty being implemented, and the text of those provisions may be appended to the legislation as a Schedule.[103]

In fact, the jurisprudence does not appear to distinguish between these modes of implementation in considering what domestic weight if any should be accorded to the treaty's terms. Rather, in a series of recent decisions,[104] the Supreme Court of Canada appears to have adopted the view that, regardless of the mechanism of implementation, implementing legislation is where possible to be reconciled with the corresponding treaty obligations.

For example, in the *National Corn Growers* case,[105] the Canadian Import Tribunal had referred to the General Agreement on Tariffs and Trade (GATT), to which Canada is a party, in interpreting section 42 of the *Special Import Measures Act*.[106] It was common ground that section 42 was intended to implement Canada's treaty obligations. However, given a potential inconsistency between those obligations and section 42, the question arose as to whether the domestic tribunal was bound to apply the domestic legislation as enacted or whether it could resort to the underlying treaty to assist in its understanding of the legislation.

The majority in the Supreme Court left no doubt that it considered the latter approach to be the correct one:

> In interpreting legislation which has been enacted with a view towards implementing international obligations, as is the case here, it is reasonable for a tribunal to examine the domestic law in the context of the relevant agreement to clarify any uncertainty. Indeed *where the text of the domestic law lends itself to it, one should also strive*

---

implements various provisions of the *Vienna Convention on Diplomatic Relations*, 18 April 1961, 500 U.N.T.S. 95 (entered into force 24 April 1964) and the *Vienna Convention on Consular Relations*, 24 April 1963, 596 U.N.T.S. 261 (entered into force 19 March 1967).

103 For a discussion of these and other implementation techniques, see J. M. Keyes & R. Sullivan, "A Legislative Perspective on the Interaction of International and Domestic Law" in Fitzgerald, above note 18, 277 at 311–18. See also Sullivan, above note 48 at 430–35; Beaulac, above note 5 at 241–48.

104 *National Corn Growers Assn. v. Canada (Import Tribunal)*, [1990] 2 S.C.R. 1324 [*National Corn Growers*]; *Canada (A.G.) v. Ward*, [1993] 2 S.C.R. 689; *Thomson v. Thomson*, above note 64; *Pushpanathan*, above note 34; *GreCon Dimter inc. v. J.R. Normand inc.*, [2005] 2 S.C.R. 401 [*GreCon Dimter*].

105 *National Corn Growers*, ibid.

106 *General Agreement on Tariffs and Trade*, 30 October 1947, 55 U.N.T.S. 187 (applied provisionally as from 1 January 1948); *Special Import Measures Act*, R.S.C. 1985, c. S-15.

to expound an interpretation which is consonant with the relevant international obligations.[107] [Emphasis added]

The majority went further still in holding that resort to the treaty text is not limited to situations where the domestic legislation is ambiguous on its face, as was suggested by Laskin C.J. in *Capital Cities Communications*.[108] Rather, it is permissible to refer to the treaty text at the outset of the inquiry in order to *reveal* an ambiguity in the domestic legislation.[109]

More recently, in *GreCon Dimter inc. v. J.R. Normand inc.*,[110] the Supreme Court was faced with the task of determining which of two inconsistent provisions of the *Civil Code of Québec*[111] should prevail in determining whether the Québec courts had jurisdiction over an action in warranty brought by a Québec importer against a German manufacturer. Noting that Canada (and thus Québec) is a party to the *Convention on the Recognition and Enforcement of Foreign Arbitral Awards*[112] and that the "legislature has incorporated the principles of the *New York Convention* … into Quebec law by enacting the substance of the Convention,"[113] LeBel J. found that the "*New York Convention* is therefore a formal source for interpreting the domestic law provisions."[114] That

---

107 *National Corn Growers*, above note 104 at 1371, Gonthier J. (for the majority).

108 *Capital Cities Communications*, above note 50 at 173.

109 *National Corn Growers*, above note 104 at 1371.

110 *GreCon Dimter*, above note 104.

111 S.Q. 1991, c. 64, arts. 3139 and 3148(2).

112 10 June 1958, 330 U.N.T.S. 3, [1986] Can. T.S. No. 43 [*New York Convention*]; see *GreCon Dimter*, above note 104 at para. 40.

113 *GreCon Dimter*, *ibid.* at para. 41. This is an interesting finding in itself, given the somewhat indirect evidence that the relevant provisions of the *Québec Civil Code* were intended to implement the *New York Convention*. In particular, the Court noted that the *Civil Code*'s rules governing international arbitration agreements were based on those of the *UNCITRAL Model Law on International Commercial Arbitration*, 21 June 1985, U.N. Doc. A/40/17 (1985), Ann. I. As these "closely follow the provisions of the *New York Convention*," the Court concluded that the *Civil Code* implemented "the substance" of the *New York Convention*. This seems to signal that the Court, in determining whether or not a given treaty has been legislatively implemented, will look to the substance of domestic legislation rather than more formal indicators of legislative intent to implement. For further discussion of the increasingly flexible approach taken by Canadian courts in determining whether or not a treaty has been implemented, see Brunnée & Toope, above note 14 at 22–31; Kindred, above note 57 at 10–17; de Mestral & Fox-Decent, above note 18 at 42–56. But see Beaulac, above note 5 at 245–48.

114 *GreCon Dimter*, *ibid.* at para. 41. See also *Dell Computer Corp. v. Union des consommateurs*, 2007 SCC 34 at paras. 38–41, 44–47, and 73–75, DesChamps J.; and at para. 175, Bastarache and LeBel JJ. dissenting.

finding is essentially consistent with the above ruling in *National Corn Growers*. However, LeBel J. went further still in characterizing the role of the relevant treaty provisions in interpreting domestic law:

> The interpretation of the provisions in issue, and the resolution of the conflict between them, *must necessarily* be harmonized with the international commitments of Canada and Quebec.[115] [Emphasis added]

National Corn Growers articulated a rebuttable presumption of conformity of implementing legislation with international treaty obligations, one that courts "should ... strive" to apply "where the text of the domestic law lends itself to it."[116] The above sentence from *GreCon Dimter*, by contrast, appears to make such conformity mandatory and to give the treaty controlling effect. LeBel J. ties this rule to the "presumption that the legislature is deemed not to intend to legislate in a manner that cannot be reconciled with the state's international obligations,"[117] but does not explain why such a "presumption" entails a restatement of the *National Corn Growers* rule in such unqualified, compulsory terms. Given the brevity of the Court's discussion of the issue, clarification of whether this reformulation of the rule is meant to be of general application or rather confined to the facts of *GreCon Dimter* will have to await future cases.[118]

Whatever its precise ambit, the principle that a domestic court should have recourse to treaties in interpreting domestic implementing legislation signals a marked departure from the strict rule of transformation described above and introduces a monist vein into the Canadian legal system's posture towards treaties. It does so by allowing a treaty to have at least indirect domestic effect through the interpretive device of reconciliation of domestic implementing legislation with the corresponding treaty. The result is in some sense to place the onus on a legislature purporting to implement a treaty to indicate explicitly and clearly any departures from the treaty's provisions it intends to enact in the domestic law.[119] While this technically preserves legisla-

---

115 *GreCon Dimter, ibid.* at para. 39.

116 *National Corn Growers,* above note 104 at 1371.

117 *GreCon Dimter,* above note 104 at 39, citing Côté, above note 48 at 367.

118 While both the majority and dissenting judgments in the subsequent *Dell Computer* case relied on *GreCon Dimter*'s conclusion that the *New York Convention* was a formal source for the interpretation of domestic law, neither addressed the seemingly mandatory rule enunciated by LeBel J. in *GreCon Dimter*: see *Dell Computer,* above note 114 at paras. 38–41, 44–47, and 73–75, DesChamps J.; and at para. 175, Bastarache and LeBel JJ. dissenting.

119 This statement assumes that the Court in *GreCon Dimter* did not intend, by holding without qualification that domestic implementing legislation "must

tive supremacy, a failure to express such statutory intent clearly will often mean that the treaty itself will govern the domestic legal effect of the implementing legislation. The parallels between this effect and the presumption that customary international law is part of the common law until a legislature clearly and irreconcilably says otherwise are striking.

A direct effect of allowing reference to a treaty as a means of interpreting implementing legislation has been to raise the issue of how the treaty, in turn, is to be interpreted. Should the courts apply traditional domestic rules of statutory construction in order to understand the terms of a treaty, or should international legal rules of treaty interpretation be preferred? The two bodies of law, while similar insofar as their primary rules of construction are concerned, differ considerably in the extent to which they permit reference to extrinsic materials for purposes of interpreting the primary text (statute or treaty).[120]

Here too the Supreme Court of Canada has chosen to take an outward looking approach that favours the primacy of treaty law over domestic law. For example, in the *Pushpanathan* case,[121] the issue was the meaning to be given to the expression "acts contrary to the purposes and principles of the United Nations," which appears in Article 1F(c) of the *Convention Relating to the Status of Refugees*.[122] That provision is implemented in Canada by means of incorporation by reference in the *Immigration Act*.[123] In addressing the meaning to be given to the terms of Article 1F(c) thus enacted as part of a Canadian statute, Bastarache J. for the majority held:

> Since the purpose of the Act incorporating Article 1F(c) is to implement the underlying Convention, *the Court must adopt an interpretation consistent with Canada's obligations under the Convention*. The wording of the Convention and *the rules of treaty interpretation will therefore be applied* to determine the meaning of Article 1F(c) in domestic law....[124] [Emphasis added]

---

necessarily be harmonized" with treaty obligations, to remove the legislature's power to enact implementing legislation that *cannot* be so reconciled. It may simply be that, as there was no evidence in that case of a legislative intent to depart from the treaty's provisions, there was no need to add a qualification in that regard.

120 See, generally, Sullivan, above note 48 at 433. See also Beaulac, above note 5 at 249–60.

121 *Pushpanathan*, above note 34.

122 *Convention Relating to the Status of Refugees*, above note 101.

123 *Immigration Act*, above note 101, s. 2(1).

124 *Pushpanathan*, above note 34 at 1019–20.

Thus, the Court affirmed that as a general rule courts will be required to interpret implementing legislation so as to conform not only with treaty terms, but with treaty obligations. As treaty obligations are international legal obligations they can only be fully understood from an international legal perspective. It is to the rules of international legal interpretation that a domestic court must turn.

In *Pushpanathan*, Justice Bastarache went on to apply the rules of treaty interpretation set out in Articles 31 and 32 of the *Vienna Convention on the Law of Treaties*[125] while commenting that those rules contemplate the use of various extrinsic sources, including the treaty's *travaux préparatoires*, to aid in its interpretation.[126] At first blush, the application of Articles 31 and 32 of the *Vienna Convention* by a domestic Canadian court may seem anomalous, given that the *Vienna Convention* itself has not been directly implemented by domestic legislation.[127] However, when it is remembered that the majority of the provisions (including Articles 31 and 32) of the *Vienna Convention* are also found in customary international law, and that customary international law presumptively forms part of the common law of Canada, reference to those rules of interpretation is in fact perfectly understandable.

By way of summary, it can be seen that, while treaties may have to be implemented to have domestic legal effect, courts will read domestic implementing legislation so as to conform with the corresponding treaty wherever possible. This will be so whether or not the implementing legislation discloses any ambiguity on its face, but not if the implementing legislation is irreconcilably in conflict with the treaty — in such a case, the domestic legislation will prevail. Further, the courts will apply rules of international treaty interpretation, as codified in Articles 31 and 32 of the *Vienna Convention*, in construing the terms of a treaty, which will in turn have an impact on interpretation of the implementing legislation.

Thus, the courts have introduced a substantial qualification to the strict theory of transformation, one potentially permitting considerable infiltration of international treaty rules into domestic law. One answer to any potential concerns to which this might give rise is to recall that these developments have occurred in cases where the legislature has, at

---

125 *Vienna Convention*, above note 1.

126 *Pushpanathan*, above note 34 at 1021–22. See Chapter 4, Section H.

127 Legislation implementing particular treaty regimes does, however, on occasion direct the domestic courts to have regard to the international meaning of the implemented treaty's terms in construing the implementing legislation: see, for example, *International Commercial Arbitration Act*, R.S.O. 1990, c. I.9, s. 13.

least arguably,[128] made the decision to implement a treaty. In this sense, the courts have not done away at all with the need for transformation by implementation but have merely eased the passage of treaty law into Canadian law. Recall too that if a legislature is unhappy with the domestic effect that has been given by a court to a treaty through application of the above rules, it retains the legislative power, within constitutional bounds, to overrule that effect by enacting sufficiently express legislation to the contrary.[129]

However, other recent judicial developments have gone further, suggesting that the domestic legal effects of treaties are not limited to those that have been implemented by legislation after all.

iii) Reconciling Unimplemented Treaty Obligations and Domestic Law

One of the earliest attempts by the Canadian courts to reconcile un-implemented treaty obligations and domestic legislation (rather than flatly refusing to give any consideration at all to the former) was in the *Arrow River* case.[130] Pursuant to Ontario legislation,[131] the Arrow River Company had constructed a system for moving timber down the Arrow River and its tributaries, including the Pigeon River, which runs along the border between Canada and the United States. The legislation also permitted the Arrow River Company to charge a toll for use of its system. The Pigeon Timber Co. objected to this arrangement on the basis that the *Webster-Ashburton Treaty* of 1842, between the United Kingdom and the United States, provided that all bordering "water communications" would remain free and open to use by the nationals of both countries.

In the Ontario Court of Appeal, Riddell J.A. held that, although the *Treaty* had not been implemented, there was a presumption that legislation was intended not to conflict with binding international agreements. Thus, if the legislation could be construed in such a manner as to avoid a conflict with a treaty obligation binding upon Canada, even if unimplemented, it was incumbent upon the courts to do so.[132] Riddell J.A. accordingly read down the Ontario legislation so as to make it inapplicable to bordering rivers such as the Pigeon River, thus construing away any conflict between the treaty and the domestic legislation.

---

128 See discussion, above note 113.
129 See Kindred, above note 57 at 8–9.
130 *Arrow River & Tributaries Slide & Boom Co. Ltd. v. Pigeon Timber Co. Ltd.*, [1932] S.C.R. 495 [*Arrow River*].
131 *Lakes and Rivers Improvements Act*, R.S.O. 1927, c. 43 [now R.S.O. 1990, c. L.3].
132 *Re Arrow River and Tributaries Slide and Boom Co. Ltd.* (1931), 2 D.L.R. 216 at 217 (Ont. C.A.).

The Supreme Court of Canada allowed the appeal on the basis that the legislation could not be so narrowly construed. As a result the legislation was held to grant the right to the Arrow River Company to charge tolls on the Pigeon River notwithstanding the *Treaty*. What is interesting, however, is that all of the judges who wrote opinions in the judgment went to considerable lengths to show that, while the domestic legislation prevailed, there was in fact no conflict between the legislation and the *Treaty*. In other words, all of the judgments read down the treaty (as opposed to the legislation, as had been done by Riddell J.A.) in such a way as to avoid any conflict between its terms and the domestic legislation.[133]

The question that remained unanswered by the case was whether there was any general duty on the courts to interpret domestic law and unimplemented treaties in such a manner as to avoid, where possible, any conflict between the two. Such a rule would come very close to the presumptive adoptionist stance taken by the Canadian courts with respect to customary international law, and thus represent a very substantial departure from the orthodox understanding of the requirement of transformation espoused by the majority in *Capital Cities Communications*.

In the years following *Arrow River* there were contradictory *dicta* in the case law on this issue.[134] More recently, however, the Supreme Court of Canada has indeed clearly adopted a presumption that domestic legislation should where possible be interpreted in such a manner as to comply with Canada's binding international legal obligations, even if unimplemented.[135] The twin bases for this presumption are, first, that

---

133 *Arrow River*, above note 130 at 497–98, Anglin C.J.C.; 500–2, Smith J.; and 506–9, Lamont J.

134 See, for example, *Daniels v. White and The Queen*, [1968] S.C.R. 517 at 541, Pigeon J., referring to a "rule of construction that Parliament is not presumed to legislate in breach of a treaty or in any manner inconsistent with the comity of nations and the established rules of international law"; and *National Corn Growers Assn. v. Canada (Import Tribunal)*, [1989] 2 F.C. 517 (C.A.), aff'd *National Corn Growers*, above note 104 at 528, Iacobucci C.J., relying upon the English authority of *Salomon v. Commissioners of Customs and Excise*, [1966] 3 All E.R. 871 (C.A.) in support of such a presumption; but see *contra* the minority judgment of Wilson J. on appeal to the S.C.C. in *National Corn Growers*, *ibid.* at 1349 ("I do not think that it is this Court's role ... to look beyond the Tribunal's statute to determine whether the Tribunal's interpretation of that statute is consistent with Canada's international obligations"); and the holdings in *Francis v. The Queen*, above note 50 and *Capital Cities Communications*, above note 50, which are plainly inconsistent with the existence of such a presumption.

135 See, for example, *Zingre v. The Queen*, [1981] 2 S.C.R. 392 at 409–10, Dickson J.; *Ordon Estate v. Grail*, [1998] 3 S.C.R. 437 at para. 137, Iacobucci & Major JJ.; *Schreiber*, above note 34 at para. 50; *Canadian Foundation for Children, Youth and*

Canada's binding international legal obligations form part of the legal context in which legislatures act and, second, that legislatures should be taken not to intend to violate binding international law unless they make such intention clear.[136] Accordingly, where more than one interpretation of domestic law is possible, the interpretation that accords with Canada's international legal obligations will be preferred.[137] Of course, the presumption is rebuttable where the terms of the domestic rule cannot, through interpretive ingenuity, be reconciled with the international legal obligation.[138]

It should be noted, however, that strains of uncertainty have been injected into this relatively straightforward presumption of conformity. These strains can be traced to the decision of the Supreme Court of Canada in *Baker*.[139] Ms. Baker, a Jamaican citizen, had come to Canada in 1981. Although she had had four children in Canada, she had not acquired permanent resident status. When in 1992 she was ordered deported, Ms. Baker applied for permanent resident status on humanitarian and compassionate grounds pursuant to section 114(2) of the *Immigration Act*.[140] Her application was denied. Ms. Baker applied for judicial review of this decision, arguing that the ministerial discretion under section 114(2) had been improperly exercised in that the best interests of her children had not been considered as a primary factor in assessing her application. The legislation did not in terms require any such consideration but Ms. Baker maintained that such a requirement should be read in due to Canada's treaty commitments under the

---

the *Law v. Canada (Attorney General)*, [2004] 1 S.C.R. 76 at para. 31, McLachlin C.J.; *Hape*, above note 38 at paras. 53–54. See also Sullivan, above note 48 at 421–22; Brunnée & Toope, above note 14 at 25–26 and 32; van Ert, above note 19 at 99–136; and G. van Ert, "What is Reception Law?" in Fitzgerald, above note 18, 85 at 89 (characterizing this presumption as a "basic doctrine of reception law"). But see Beaulac, above note 5 at 256–60, arguing that this presumption has been displaced in favour of a rule that merely considers international law a contextual interpretive element, to be given more or less weight by courts depending on its source and degree of legislative implementation in domestic law.

136 See Sullivan, above note 48 at 422. But see van Ert, "What is Reception Law?," *ibid.* at 89, suggesting that application of the presumption "tends more to resemble a rule of judicial policy to the effect that the court will not, by its decisions, bring the state into violation of international law."

137 Sullivan, *ibid.* at 422.

138 See Sullivan, *ibid.* at 429; Côté, above note 48 at 367–68; *Hape*, above note 38 at para. 53.

139 *Baker v. Canada (Minister of Citizenship and Immigration)*, [1999] 2 S.C.R. 817 [*Baker*].

140 *Immigration Act*, above note 101, s. 114(2).

Convention on the Rights of the Child.[141] Article 3(1) of the Convention requires states parties to consider the best interests of children when decisions are made that affect their future, but it was not implemented in Canadian legislation.

Justice L'Heureux-Dubé, writing for the majority of five, acknowledged the general rule that unimplemented treaties are not part of Canadian law, citing *Francis v. The Queen*[142] and *Capital Cities Communications.*[143] She nevertheless held that "the values reflected in international human rights law may help inform the contextual approach to statutory interpretation and judicial review."[144] Having reviewed the provisions of the Convention and other international law sources, Justice L'Heureux-Dubé thus concluded that the best interests of children must be considered under section 114(2) as an important factor.[145]

While the *outcome* of this judgment appears consistent with the presumption of conformity described above, the effect of L'Heureux-Dubé J.'s *reasoning* left the status of that presumption in a state of some uncertainty. In particular, Justice L'Heureux-Dubé did not elaborate on what she meant by "values reflected by international human rights law," as distinct from "international human rights law" *per se*. Was the distinction meant to suggest that the content of the Convention could also be found in customary international law and thus in common law principles directly applicable in construing the ministerial discretion?[146]

---

141 *Convention on the Rights of the Child*, 20 November 1989, 1577 U.N.T.S. 3 (entered into force 2 September 1990).

142 *Francis*, above note 50.

143 *Capital Cities Communications*, above note 50.

144 *Baker*, above note 139 at 861.

145 In a judgment concurring in the result, Iacobucci J. (writing for himself and Cory J.) voiced strong concern for the effects of such an approach on the rule of transformation: "I do not share my colleague's confidence that the Court's precedent in *Capital Cities* … survives intact following the adoption of a principle of law which permits reference to an unincorporated convention during the process of statutory interpretation. Instead, the result will be that the appellant is able to achieve indirectly what cannot be achieved directly, namely, to give force and effect within the domestic legal system to international obligations undertaken by the executive alone that have yet to be subject to the democratic will of Parliament": *ibid.* at 866, Iacobucci J. This seems an odd objection given that Iacobucci J. had, the year before, endorsed the rule that "a court must presume that legislation is intended to comply with Canada's obligations under international instruments": see *Ordon Estate v. Grail*, above note 135 at para. 137, Iacobucci & Major JJ.

146 See W.A. Schabas, "Twenty-Five Years of Public International Law at the Supreme Court of Canada" (2000) 79 Can. Bar Rev. 174 at 182; Brunnée & Toope, above note 14 at 45.

If not, was it meant to signal that the presumption of conformity only operated with respect to the "values," rather than the rules, reflected in Canada's binding international legal obligations?[147] Further, describing such values "as an aid in interpreting domestic law" that "may help inform ... statutory interpretation," falls well short of relying on a presumption of conformity that places an obligation on courts to construe domestic legislation in accordance with international human rights law wherever possible. Was this language intended to signal abandonment of the presumption of conformity in favour of a much weaker approach in which Canada's international legal obligations are merely one of many optional sources of contextual guidance available to courts in interpreting domestic law?[148] If so, would this not simply lump Canada's binding international legal obligations in with non-binding sources, such as unratified treaties and even "soft law" instruments,[149] as part of an amorphous reservoir of optional and merely "informative" sources of inspiration for judicial interpretation?

While there were some signs in the subsequent case law that *Baker* had indeed weakened the presumption of conformity,[150] more recent decisions appear to signal a return to the pre-*Baker* position.[151] Most recently, a majority of the Supreme Court in *Hape* has reiterated the "well-established principle of statutory interpretation that legislation will be presumed to conform to international law.... The presumption applies equally to customary international law and treaty obligations."[152]

For the time being, therefore, the rigid *Capital Cities Communications* relegation of Canada's unimplemented treaty obligations to domestic legal irrelevance has been very substantially revised. In its stead, the presumption of conformity, while not conferring direct domestic effect on unimplemented treaties, nevertheless clothes them with substantial *indirect* effect: wherever possible, domestic legislation will be interpreted so as to comply with them. Again, as with the rules applicable to the interpretation of domestic implementing legislation, the parallels

---

147 For the argument that this was indeed the implication, see Brunnée & Toope, *ibid.* at 37–38.

148 See Beaulac, above note 5 at 259, answering this query in the affirmative. See also Brunnée & Toope, *ibid.* at 38–39, 41–42, and 45–46, fearing that this may have been the effect of the judgment even if not intended.

149 See Chapter 3, Section D(2).

150 See, for example, *Spraytech*, above note 34 at paras. 30–32. See also Brunnée & Toope, above note 14 at 46–50.

151 See, for example, *Canadian Foundation for Children*, above note 135 at para. 31, McLachlin C.J.: "Statutes should be construed to comply with Canada's international obligations."

152 *Hape*, above note 38 at paras. 53 and 54.

between the effects of this presumption and the rule that customary international law is deemed part of the common law until a legislature clearly and irreconcilably says otherwise are striking. It nevertheless remains to be seen whether Canadian courts will remain steadfast in their application, and understanding, of this presumption.

iv) Reconciling Unimplemented Treaty Obligations and the Charter

In a related but much less certain development, Canadian courts have also had to consider the relevance of Canada's unimplemented treaty obligations, particularly in the human rights area, when construing the fundamental guarantees set out in the *Canadian Charter of Rights and Freedoms*.[153] The starting point here is the relatively early indication by the Supreme Court of Canada in *Slaight Communications*[154] that, even though the *Charter* is not expressly stated to be in implementation of Canada's binding human rights obligations:

> ... the *Charter* should generally be presumed to provide protection at least as great as that afforded by similar provisions in international human rights documents which Canada has ratified.[155]

In other words, human rights treaties to which Canada is a party should be taken to express the minimum content of corresponding rights guaranteed in the *Charter*. This approach to interpretation may be justifiable in the *Charter* context given the fact that much of the inspiration for its provisions was drawn from Canada's international human rights treaty commitments.[156]

Note, however, the qualifications attached to the presumption: it is only to operate "generally" and is characterized as an aid to interpretation. Subsequent decisions of the Supreme Court have tended to focus on these qualifications, such that Canada's human rights treaty

---

153 Above note 37.

154 *Slaight Communications Inc. v. Davidson*, [1989] 1 S.C.R. 1038 [*Slaight*].

155 *Ibid.* at 1056–57, Dickson C.J. recalling his earlier comment in *Reference re Public Service Employee Relations Act (Alta.)*, [1987] 1 S.C.R. 313 at 349 (dissenting on another point).

156 See W. Tarnopolsky, "A Comparison Between the *Canadian Charter of Rights and Freedoms* and the *International Covenant on Civil and Political Rights*" (1982–83) 8 Queen's L.J. 211; Hogg, above note 45 at §33.8(c). But see the cautionary note sounded with respect to such a "minimum content" presumption by I. Weiser, "Effect in Domestic Law of International Human Rights Treaties Ratified without Implementing Legislation" in Canadian Council on International Law, *The Impact of International Law on the Practice of Law in Canada: Proceedings of the 27th Annual Conference of the Canadian Council on International Law, Ottawa, October 15-17, 1998* (The Hague: Kluwer Law International, 1999) 132 at 138–39.

obligations have generally been taken merely to "inform" *Charter* interpretation rather than positively guide it.[157] Moreover, the international sources that can be relied upon to "inform" *Charter* interpretation
in this way have been expanded to include "declarations, covenants,
conventions, judicial and quasi-judicial decisions of international tribunals [and] customary norms."[158] While reference to these various
sources—some internationally binding on Canada, others not—may
indeed be informative, treating them all as equally persuasive tends
to undermine the particular relevance of Canada's binding treaty and
customary international law commitments.[159]

The idea that the *Charter's* content should not be interpreted less generously than Canada's international human rights obligations has also
been weakened. *Suresh* in particular signalled a retreat from that presumption. There the Court accepted that deportation to torture is categorically
prohibited by the *International Covenant on Civil and Political Rights*[160] and
the *Convention Against Torture*,[161] to both of which Canada is a party.[162]
Yet it also found that "in exceptional circumstances, deportation to face
torture might be justified, either as a consequence of the balancing process mandated by s. 7 of the *Charter* or under s. 1."[163] This either signals

---

157 See, for example, *Slaight Communications*, above note 154 at 1056–57; *R. v.
   Keegstra*, [1990] 3 S.C.R. 697 at 750, Dickson C.J. and at 837, McLachlin J.,
   dissenting; *United States v. Burns*, [2001] 1 S.C.R. 283 at paras. 79–81 [*Burns*];
   Suresh, above note 34 at paras. 46 and 60; and, *semble*, *Canadian Foundation for
   Children*, above note 135 at paras. 9–10; *Health Services and Support—Facilities
   Subsector Bargaining Assn. v. British Columbia*, 2007 SCC 27 at paras. 20, 69,
   and 78 [*Health Services*]. See also discussion of this evolution in the case law in
   Brunnée & Toope, above note 14 at 33–35.

158 *Burns*, *ibid*. at para. 80, adopting the enumeration of sources by Dickson C.J.
   (dissenting) in *Public Service Employee Relations Act Reference*, above note 155 at
   348. See also *Suresh*, *ibid*. at para. 46, seemingly according the same interpretive
   weight to *jus cogens* norms as to other rules of international law, notwithstanding their "peremptory" character in international law. For comment, see Brunnée & Toope, *ibid*. at 49–50.

159 See Brunnée & Toope, *ibid*. at 35 and 51–55 and Beaulac, above note 5 at 264–67,
   arguing for a differential approach by Canadian courts to (unimplemented) binding and non-binding sources of international law. For a recent example apparently
   relying on customary international law to construe *Charter* rights, see *Charkaoui
   v. Canada (Minister of Citizenship and Immigration)*, 2007 SCC 9 at para. 90.

160 *International Covenant on Civil and Political Rights*, 16 December 1966, 999
   U.N.T.S. 171, (entered into force 23 March 1976; Article 41 entered into force 28
   March 1979) [*ICCPR*].

161 *Convention Against Torture and Other Cruel, Inhuman or Degrading Treatment or
   Punishment*, 10 December 1984, 1465 U.N.T.S. 85 (entered into force 26 June 1987).

162 *Suresh*, above note 34 at paras. 66–75.

163 *Ibid*. at para. 78.

abandonment of the minimum content presumption, or underscores the significance of Chief Justice Dickson's use of the qualification "generally" in first setting it out.[164] More recently, however, in the collective bargaining/freedom of association context, the Court has reiterated the minimum content presumption *without* such a qualification.[165] Yet in another judgment released the day before, a majority of the Court relied upon Canada's customary international legal obligations—significantly, not of a human rights character—to *restrict* the potential scope of application of the *Charter* and, hence, of the protections it extends.[166]

In light of such contradictory signals, precisely whether and when the human rights protections afforded by the *Charter* will be bolstered or undermined by Canada's international legal obligations remains difficult to predict.

v) Conclusions

By way of summary, while the courts have clung, at least formally, to the requirement of transformation before a treaty can have direct legal effect in Canada, such a position masks a complex relationship between domestic law and treaties.

In the case of an implemented treaty, there is a clear presumption that the implementing legislation should be read if possible so as to

---

164 *Public Service Employee Relations Act Reference*, above note 155.

165 *Health Services*, above note 157 at para. 70: "… [T]he *Charter* should be presumed to provide at least as great a level of protection as is found in the international human rights documents that Canada has ratified." See also *ibid.* at para. 79: "… s. 2(d) of the *Charter* should be interpreted as recognizing at least the same level of protection [as international conventions to which Canada is a party]." Note, however, the somewhat non-committal language used by the Court in describing Canada's international legal obligations as an "interpretive tool" that "can assist" courts in interpreting the *Charter*: *ibid.* at para. 69.

166 *Hape*, above note 38 at para. 56, LeBel J., writing for the majority: "In interpreting the scope of application of the *Charter*, the courts should seek to ensure compliance with Canada's binding obligations under international law where the express words are capable of supporting such a construction." The majority relied in part on the customary international legal principles of territorial sovereignty and non-intervention in reaching its conclusion that "extraterritorial application of the *Charter* is impossible": *ibid.* at paras. 55–56 and 85. See also *Canada (Attorney General) v. JTI-Macdonald Corp.*, 2007 SCC 30 at paras. 10 and 66–67, *semble* relying on Canada's treaty obligations to bolster the government's s. 1 justification of a *prima facie* infringement of s. 2(b) *Charter* rights. Of course, these cases illustrate that allowing interpretation of the *Charter* to be influenced by Canada's international legal obligations can be a double-edged sword. On the dangers of allowing international law to act as a limit on the protections afforded by the *Charter*, see *R. v. Cook*, [1998] 2 S.C.R. 597 at para. 148, Bastarache J.

conform to the treaty obligations it purportedly implements. Recent case law also seems to have embraced, with periodic hesitations, a similar presumption of conformity of all statute law with Canada's binding treaty obligations, whether implemented or not. In all such cases, however, should there be a clear and unavoidable conflict between domestic law and a treaty, the courts will give precedence to the former.

By way of contrast, the effect of Canada's treaty obligations on interpretation of the *Charter* is more difficult to state. While there is nominal support in the case law for the proposition that *Charter* guarantees should be read no less generously than their counterparts in international human rights treaties to which Canada is a party, this rule has not been consistently applied in practice, even by the Supreme Court. Moreover, Canada's international legal obligations outside the human rights context have on occasion been relied upon to curtail the scope of the *Charter*'s protections. This, when added to the vague and arguably contradictory language used to describe the role of Canada's international obligations in construing the *Charter* ("protection at least as great,"[167] "informative,"[168] an "interpretive tool" that "can assist,"[169] etc.) suggests that the precise relationship between Canada's treaty obligations and the *Charter* remains to be fully worked out by the courts.

Other areas requiring clarification include the standards by which courts will determine whether treaties have been implemented; what role non-binding sources (such as treaties which Canada has signed but not ratified, treaties which Canada has neither signed nor ratified, or "soft law" instruments) should play in interpreting domestic law; and whether these various categories of non-binding sources should be treated differently from one another or Canada's binding international legal obligations.

All of these are issues that await further judicial development as Canada continues to define the porosity of the membrane that currently separates international from domestic law.

---

167 *Slaight*, above note 154 at 1056–57.
168 *Suresh*, above note 34 at para. 46: "The inquiry into the principles of fundamental justice is informed not only by Canadian experience and jurisprudence, but also by international law...."
169 *Health Services*, above note 157 at para. 69.

FURTHER READING

BAYEFSKY, A., *International Human Rights Law: Use in* Canadian Charter of Rights and Freedoms *Litigation* (Toronto: Butterworths, 1992)

BEAULAC, S., "National Application of International Law: The Statutory Interpretation Perspective" (2003) 41 Can. Y.B. Int'l L. 225

BRUNNÉE, J. & TOOPE, S.J., "A Hesitant Embrace: The Application of International Law by Canadian Courts" (2002) 40 Can. Y.B. Int'l L. 3

FALK, R., *The Role of Domestic Courts in the International Legal Order* (Syracuse: Syracuse University Press, 1964)

FATIMA, S., *Using International Law in Domestic Courts* (Oxford: Hart Publishing, 2005)

FITZGERALD, O.E., ed., *The Globalized Rule of Law: Relationships between International and Domestic Law* (Toronto: Irwin Law, 2006)

GOTLIEB, A. E., *Canadian Treaty-Making* (Toronto: Butterworths, 1968)

HARRINGTON, J., "Scrutiny and Approval: The Role for Westminster-Style Parliaments in Treaty-Making" (2006) 55 I.C.L.Q. 121

KNOP, K., "Here and There: International Law in Domestic Courts" (2000) 32 N.Y.U.J. Int'l L. & Pol. 50

KRATOCHWIL, F.V., "The Role of Domestic Courts as Agencies of the International Legal Order" in R. Falk, F. Kratochwil, & S.H. Mendlovitz, eds., *International Law: A Contemporary Perspective* (Boulder: Westview, 1985) 236

LA FOREST, G.V., "May the Provinces Legislate in Violation of International Law?" (1961) 39 Can. Bar Rev. 78

MACDONALD, R. ST. J., "The Relationship between International Law and Domestic Law in Canada" in R. St.J. Macdonald, G.L. Morris, & D.M. Johnston, eds., *Canadian Perspectives on International Law and Organization* (Toronto: University of Toronto Press, 1974) 88

MACDONALD, R. ST. J., "International Treaty Law and the Domestic Law of Canada" (1975) 2 Dal. L.J. 307

SCHABAS, W.A. & BEAULAC, S., *International Human Rights and Canadian Law: Legal Commitment, Implementation and the Charter*, 3rd ed. (Toronto: Thomson Carswell, 2007)

SPERDUTI, G., "Dualism and Monism: A Confrontation to Be Overcome" (1977) 3 Ital. Y.B. Int'l L. 31

TOOPE, S.J., "Inside and Out: The Stories of International Law and Domestic Law" (2001) 50 U.N.B.L.J. 11

VAN ERT, G., *Using International Law in Canadian Courts* (The Hague: Kluwer Law International, 2002)

VAN ERT, G., "Using Treaties in Canadian Courts" (2000) 38 Can. Y.B. Int'l L. 3

VANEK, C., "Is International Law a Part of the Law of Canada?" (1949–50) 8 U.T.L.J. 251

CHAPTER 7

STATES AND TERRITORY

A. INTRODUCTION

We turn now to a more detailed consideration of the relationship between states and territory. As we have already seen,[1] the link between
a state and defined territory is crucial to its existence as a person in
international law.[2] Indeed, the very notion of statehood is so deeply
rooted in the requirement of territory that the existence of a state without some minimal territory over which it enjoys sovereignty is virtually unthinkable in the Westphalian system of international law. This
continues to be the case even in the UN era. The *UN Charter* itself is
founded upon the sovereign equality of all of its members and the obligation of those members to respect one another's territorial integrity.[3]
The massive decolonization process in the second half of the twentieth
century, resulting in the establishment of scores of newly independent

---

1   See Chapter 2, Section B(2)(b).
2   J. Crawford, *The Creation of States in International Law*, 2d ed. (Oxford: Clar-
    endon Press, 2006) at 46 and 48; M.N. Shaw, *International Law*, 5th ed. (Cam-
    bridge: Cambridge University Press, 2003) at 409–10.
3   *Charter of the United Nations*, 26 June 1945, Can. T.S. 1945 No. 7 (entered into
    force 24 October 1945) [*UN Charter*], Articles 2(1), (4), and (7); *Declaration on
    Principles of International Law Concerning Friendly Relations and Co-operation
    among States in Accordance with the Charter of the United Nations*, GA Res. 2625
    (XXV), UN GAOR, 25th Sess., Supp. No. 28, UN Doc. A/8028 (1971) [*Friendly
    Relations Declaration*].

but territorially defined states, also bears witness to the continuing centrality in modern international law of the essentially territorial conception of the state.

As we have also seen, the exclusive ability of a state to regulate activities occurring in its territory, subject only to the strictures of international law, is the ultimate hallmark of a state's independence and, hence, of its sovereign status in international law.[4] Thus, exclusive possession of territory is not only required of a state as a matter of legal definition, it is also one of the principal methods by which a state exhibits its sovereignty and evidences its existence as a primary subject of international law.

With so much at stake, therefore, it is not surprising that the lawful extent of state territory, and the means by which it may lawfully be acquired, have been among the principal preoccupations of international law throughout its history. This chapter will therefore focus on the principal legal doctrines that have been developed in international law to address both of these issues. As we will see, the principles of sovereign equality and territorial integrity not only define the importance of territory to states; they also serve, in a world inhabited by multiple sovereigns, to limit the means by which the extent of any one state's territory may be increased at the expense of another's.

Beyond the basic issues of the extent and acquisition of state territory, however, international law has also had to grapple with the nature of the legal relationship between states and "territory" in the broader sense of the term. Aside from the relationship of sovereignty that exists between a state and its own territory in the strict sense, international law also regulates the jurisdictional competence of states over certain areas beyond their borders. For example, coastal states enjoy particular jurisdictional rights over portions of the sea, seabed, and airspace off their coasts, but not generally over the "high seas" or other elements of the "global commons," in respect of which the community of all states enjoys certain rights. Moreover, the extension of human activity to outer space and the various "celestial bodies" of our solar system has also required the development of new legal regimes governing the permissible jurisdictional reach of states in such areas.

An overall assessment of these various developments reveals that international law has developed roughly four broad types of relationship between states and territory in the larger sense, as follows:

1) *Sovereign State Territory*: This includes land territory (together with any islands), inland rivers and lakes and, in the case of coastal states,

---

4   See Chapter 2, Section B(2)(d).

internal coastal waters and a thin band of coastal waters known as the "territorial sea,"[5] all of which come under the full range of jurisdictional competencies recognized by international law as accruing to the territorial sovereign. Essentially these areas are subject to the exclusive and plenary sovereign jurisdiction of a single state, subject only to limitations imposed by international law.

2) *Res Communis*: Areas subject to the legal regime of the *res communis* are not part of, nor may they be incorporated into, the sovereign territory of any state. Being thus, by definition, beyond appropriation by states, they are essentially open areas available for unilateral use and exploitation by all states, subject again to certain limits imposed by international law. Because of their existence outside of the sovereign territory of any state, these expanses of territory are frequently referred to as the "global commons." The limitation implied by this expression is somewhat misleading, however, in that the regime includes not only the high seas but also, as we shall see, certain portions of outer space.[6]

3) *Res Nullius*: Territory constituting a *res nullius* is similar to a *res communis* in that it is not currently under the sovereignty of any state. However, the legal regime of the *res nullius* differs dramatically from that of the *res communis* in that the former is subject to potential appropriation by states and incorporation into their sovereign territory, whereas the latter, by definition, is not. The concept of the *res nullius* is largely of historical interest given that most land territory on the planet has by now been made the subject of claims of sovereignty by one state or another.[7] Further, the concept has not been extended to outer space or the celestial bodies of our solar system.[8] The concept remains potentially significant, however, in evaluating the current legal effects of past acts of occupation that are sought to be justified on this basis,[9] and possibly in the case where a state abandons territory in such a way that it reverts to the status of a *res nullius*.

4) *Common Heritage of Humankind*: This is a relatively new legal regime propounded mainly by newly independent and developing

---

5   See further Section C(2)(b), below in this chapter. One would have to include archipelagic waters to this enumeration in the case of an archipelagic state: see further Section C(2)(c), below in this chapter.

6   See further Section E, below in this chapter.

7   There is, however, one sector of the Antarctic which has not yet been claimed: see further Section D(3), below in this chapter.

8   See further Section E, below in this chapter.

9   See, for example, *Western Sahara, Advisory Opinion*, [1975] I.C.J. Rep. 12.

states in the second half of the twentieth century. The concept has emerged mainly in multilateral treaty regimes relating to the law of the sea and, arguably, the legal status of the Earth's Moon and other celestial bodies in our solar system. In essence, it is said to apply to areas which otherwise bear the essential characteristics of a *res communis*—that is, areas not subject to appropriation by states as part of their sovereign territory—but with the additional feature that their resources are not open to unilateral use or exploitation by states for their own benefit. Rather, the proceeds of economic exploitation of an area designated as the common heritage of humankind[10] are reserved for the community of nations as a whole. This regime, still of uncertain scope and controversial application, will be explored more fully in examining the legal regimes applicable to the deep seabed, the Moon, and other celestial bodies.[11]

The application and legal significance of each of the foregoing regimes will be illustrated in the sections that follow in examining the various ways in which, through international law, states have carved up and defined their jurisdictional reach over virtually every component of our planet, as well as areas beyond.

B. STATE TERRITORY

1) Elements and Extent

As suggested above, a state's sovereign territory extends beyond its land mass. It encompasses, in addition to the mainland and any islands over which it enjoys sovereign title, all inland waterways, including rivers, canals, and lakes. In addition, the territory of a coastal state—that is, a state having a sea coast—extends to coastal waters (known as "internal waters") lying landward of any straight baselines established by the state for purposes of measuring the seaward extent of its maritime zones, as well as a thin belt of sea known as the "territorial sea" lying immediately beyond such baselines.[12] In the case of an archipelagic state—that is, a state composed entirely of islands—sovereign territory also includes the archipelagic waters lying between its constituent

---

10   Note that most international instruments use the expression "common heritage of mankind." The more inclusive expression "common heritage of humankind" is to be preferred and will be used throughout this book.

11   See further Sections C(2)(g) and E, below in this chapter.

12   See further Section C(2)(b), below in this chapter.

islands.[13] In other words, a coastal or archipelagic state's sovereign territory extends, in international law, to all areas lying within the outer limits of its territorial sea, whereas the outer limits of a landlocked state's territory will coincide with its land boundaries.[14] With the exception of very limited rights of passage in favour of other states imposed by the law of the sea,[15] the sovereignty of a state over its inland waterways as well as, where applicable, its internal or archipelagic waters and territorial sea, is as plenary as that over its land territory. As we have seen above, that sovereignty encompasses the full range of jurisdictional competencies recognized by international law as accruing exclusively to the territorial sovereign and subject only to limitations imposed by international law itself.

There is also a three-dimensional aspect to territorial sovereignty, in keeping with what some authors refer to as the principle of appurtenance.[16] That principle merely reflects a general presumption that the legal regime applicable to the surface of territory also applies to whatever lies directly above or below. If a particular surface comes within the sovereign territory of a state, so too does the subsoil or subsurface below it (to a depth limited only by physical realities), as does the air column above it.[17] Similarly, if the legal regime applicable to a particular surface is one other than state sovereignty (for example, the regime of the high seas), the principle of appurtenance dictates that that same legal regime applies, at least *prima facie*, to the subsurface below and the air column above it.[18]

While traditionally no limit was imposed by international law upon the upward extent of a state's sovereign airspace, the realities of modern space flight, and in particular the deployment of artificial Earth satellites, have led to the universal recognition by states of outer space as an area not susceptible to incorporation within state territory. The difficulty

---

13 See further Section C(2)(c), below in this chapter.

14 Or, in some cases, any boundaries falling within bordering lakes and rivers.

15 Such as the right of "innocent passage" and the right of transit through international straits: see further Section C(2)(b), below in this chapter.

16 See, for example, I. Brownlie, *Principles of Public International Law*, 6th ed. (Oxford: Oxford University Press, 2003) at 117–18.

17 See, for example, *Convention on the Territorial Sea and the Contiguous Zone*, 29 April 1958, 516 U.N.T.S. 205 (entered into force 10 September 1964) [*GCTS 1958*], Article 2 and *United Nations Convention on the Law of the Sea*, 10 December 1982, 1833 U.N.T.S. 3 (entered into force 16 November 1994) [*UNCLOS 1982*], Article 2(2), both of which provide that a state's sovereignty over its territorial sea "extends to the air space over the territorial sea as well as to its bed and subsoil."

18 See further Section C(2)(g), below in this chapter.

has been, however, to reach consensus on the altitude at which outer space begins and state sovereignty over airspace superjacent to state territory accordingly ends. While no resolution of this issue can yet be said to have emerged as a matter of customary international law, proposals range between 50 and 100 miles above sea level, corresponding variously to the highest altitude at which aircraft can fly, the lowest viable orbital trajectory for Earth satellites, the height at which the concentration of certain atmospheric gases drops below certain levels, and so on.[19]

Again, the sovereignty enjoyed by states over the air column above and the subsoil or subsurface below their surface territory is as plenary as that enjoyed with respect to the surface itself. This means that states are free to control access to such areas, as well as regulate all activities occurring in them, subject of course to any applicable rules of international law generally limiting states' sovereignty.[20] Given the potential threat to territorial security posed by modern aviation technology, states have been particularly concerned to safeguard their sovereignty over airspace, including their right to exclude all foreign intrusion.[21] The requirements of modern civil aviation have led to the elaboration of multilateral treaty regimes by which states grant various rights of access to their airspace for civil purposes only.[22] Nevertheless, such regimes are consent-based and as such confirm the sovereign status in customary international law of airspace superjacent to state territory.[23]

2) The Establishment of Sovereignty over Territory

a) General Principles

i) Importance and Relativity of Territorial Sovereignty

Disputes between states regarding sovereignty over territory are surprisingly common, even in modern international affairs. Consider for

---

19   See Shaw, above note 2 at 480. See further Section E, below in this chapter.
20   For example, the general principle that a state may not use or knowingly permit the use of its territory in a manner harmful to the interests of other states: see further Chapter 8, Section D.
21   See Shaw, above note 2 at 463–64.
22   See, for example, (Chicago) Convention on International Civil Aviation, 7 December 1944, 15 U.N.T.S. 295 (entered into force 4 April 1947). The International Civil Aviation Organization (ICAO) is a specialized agency of the UN that develops and promotes common rules for international air transport. The ICAO Council adopts standards and recommendations that are transformed into national legislation by states parties.
23   See Military and Paramilitary Activities in and against Nicaragua (Nicaragua v. United States of America), [1986] I.C.J. Rep. 14 at paras. 91 and 251.

example the disputes between Iraq and Kuwait over the whole of the latter's territory; the United Kingdom and Argentina over the Falkland (or Malvinas) Islands; the United Kingdom and Spain with respect to Gibraltar; India, China, and Pakistan over Kashmir; Russia and Japan over the islands of Etorofu, Kunashiri, and Shikotan; Equatorial Guinea and Cameroon over an island at the mouth of the Ntem River; Niger and Libya with respect to the Tommo region; Canada and the United States with respect to Machias Seal Island, North Rock, and portions of the Gulf of Maine; Canada and Denmark over Hans Island in the Kennedy Straits; Israel and several of its neighbours over the West Bank and the Golan Heights; and so on.[24]

In order to minimize resort to the use of force to resolve such disputes, a number of legal doctrines have emerged to assist in ascertaining which state enjoys "title" to a given territory. In the absence of any centralized institution with the authority to grant states sovereignty over territory, however, the establishment of sovereign title relies primarily on the conduct of states in relation to such territory over time. In resolving disputes over territory, the focus of international law is thus generally to weigh the relative merits of competing states' claims to territory based on such conduct rather than to make any absolute or *in rem* determinations as to sovereign title.[25]

Typically, therefore, arbitral or other international tribunals resolve territorial disputes by examining various bases of sovereign title advanced by the parties. In some instances these arguments relate to the means by which sovereign title to the disputed territory was originally acquired, whereas in others the ongoing conduct of the parties in relation to the territory—typically conduct in the nature of displays of sovereign authority—will be the principal focus of inquiry. The most common of these modes of acquisition or bases of title will be examined in turn below, but it is important to note that they should not be considered in rigid isolation from one another.[26] Rather, each represents one or more aspects of the relationship expected in international law between a state and its territory, and all play a potential role in solidifying one claim over another. In practice, therefore, states generally

---

24 An instructive list of hundreds of current territorial disputes can be found in Central Intelligence Agency, *The World Factbook 2007* (Washington: CIA Office of Public Affairs, 2007), "Field Listing – Disputes – International," online: www.cia.gov/library/publications/the-world-factbook/index.html.

25 See Shaw, above note 2 at 412–13; Brownlie, above note 16 at 154–55.

26 See Brownlie, *ibid.* at 126–27.

rely upon a combination of such arguments in order to prevail in the contest for the best relative claim to territorial title.[27]

ii)   *The Role of Recognition, Acquiescence, and Estoppel*

Often, it will not only be the conduct of a claimant in support of its own claim, but also conduct which appears inferentially to support a rival's claim, that is important in resolving territorial disputes. In particular, recognition of or acquiescence in a rival claim may prove fatal to one's own, as such acquiescence or recognition is generally inconsistent with one's own claim of sovereignty. Recognition acts as a form of express consent to the rival claim and is often determinative of any subsequent dispute.[28] More subtly, silence or passivity in the face of a clear assertion by another state of sovereignty over territory may subsequently be construed as acquiescence in that claim.[29] If maintained for a sufficient period and accompanied by detrimental reliance, such acquiescence may in turn give rise to an estoppel against the assertion of a contrary claim.[30]

This possibility was illustrated in the *Temple Case*.[31] That case involved a dispute between Thailand and Cambodia as to sovereignty over the precincts of an ancient temple situated along their common border. That border had been established by treaty in 1904, which provided that the boundary was to follow the watershed between the two countries. Maps erroneously showing the temple on the Cambodian side of the watershed (and hence boundary) were prepared in 1907 and shared with Thailand, which did not protest the course of the boundary thus depicted. In addition, the International Court of Justice attributed particular importance to the 1930 visit of a Thai prince to the temple. During that visit, the prince was received by the French authorities with the French flag flying over the temple.[32] This, the Court held, constituted a clear affirmation of title on the part of the French that "demanded a reaction"; but "Thailand did nothing."[33] The Court moreover observed that the language used by the prince in correspondence after

---

27   Shaw, above note 2 at 413.

28   See Brownlie, above note 16 at 151; Shaw, *ibid.* at 437–38.

29   See I.C. MacGibbon, "The Scope of Acquiescence in International Law" (1954) 31 Brit. Y.B. Int'l L. 143 at 143; H. Thirlway, "The Law and Procedure of the International Court of Justice, 1960–1989" (1989) 60 Brit. Y.B. Int'l L. 1 at 45–46.

30   See D.W. Bowett, "Estoppel Before International Tribunals and its Relation to Acquiescence" (1957) 33 Brit. Y.B. Int'l L. 176 at 176–77.

31   *Case Concerning the Temple of Preah Vihear (Cambodia v. Thailand)*, [1962] I.C.J. Rep. 6 [*Temple Case*].

32   Cambodia at the time was under French "protection," meaning in part that France conducted Cambodia's foreign affairs on its behalf.

33   *Temple Case*, above note 31 at 30.

the fact seemed to admit that the French had acted as host country. Taken on its own, this incident was characterized by the Court as:

> ... a tacit recognition by Siam [Thailand] of the sovereignty of Cambodia ... over Preah Vihear, through a failure to react in any way, on an occasion that called for a reaction in order to affirm or preserve title in the face of an obvious rival claim. What seems clear is that either Siam did not in fact believe she had any title—and this would be wholly consistent with her attitude all along, and thereafter, to the Annex I map and line—or else she decided not to assert it, which again means that she accepted the French claim, or accepted the frontier at Preah Vihear as it was drawn on the map.[34]

The Court accordingly concluded that Thailand had either recognized or acquiesced in Cambodia's claim to sovereignty over the temple and was thus estopped, fifty years after her initial acceptance of the boundary as depicted on the relevant maps, from reversing its position.[35] The case is thus a vivid illustration of the potential importance of recognition, acquiescence, and estoppel in determining issues of sovereignty over territory.

iii) Geographical Presumptions and the Extent of Sovereign Title

Aside from the challenge of establishing the existence of title in favour of any one state, states and international tribunals often also rely on a number of "geographical presumptions" in order to establish its extent. In other words, doubts may arise as to the precise extent of the territory over which sovereignty is established through one or more of the bases described below. For example, does the establishment of title over the mainland extend to nearby offshore islands? Or does the establishment of sovereignty over a portion of an island extend to the rest of the island also?[36] In order to address such questions, a number of presumptions based on geographic "realities" are often pressed into service in the reasoning of states and tribunals. For example, the so-called principles of "geographic unity," "contiguity," "continuity," and "appurtenance" are frequently invoked to justify the conclusion that sovereignty over certain territory extends also to attached, contiguous, or nearby territory. These principles are merely working presumptions, however, and do not operate as principles of law requiring a particu-

---

34 *Ibid.* at 31.
35 *Ibid.* at 32.
36 See, for example, *Legal Status of Eastern Greenland (Denmark v. Norway)* (1933), P.C.I.J. Rep. (Ser. A/B) No. 53.

lar outcome.[37] For example, they yield to any countervailing, stronger claims of sovereignty, established on one or more of the bases of title described below, in respect of the relevant contiguous or appurtenant territory. In short, these principles are aids to reasoning which may serve to dispose of territory ancillary to a principal claim, but usually only where title to such ancillary territory is not a primary focus of the territorial dispute.[38]

iv) The Role of the Doctrine of Intertemporal Law

As resolution of territorial disputes tends to require extensive analysis of past acts and transactions in relation to the disputed territory, the doctrine of intertemporal law often plays a prominent role in such cases. As the doctrine has already been introduced,[39] only its main elements will be recalled here. Essentially, the intertemporal rule provides that the legal significance of past transactions is to be evaluated according to the law that was applicable at the time. Applied in the context of claims to sovereignty over territory, this essentially means that the relevance of past acts relating to territory—say, conquest or discovery—must not be judged by current international law, but rather by the law prevailing at the time of the act.[40]

While this has prompted some commentators to condemn the intertemporal doctrine as a device for legitimating past acts of territorial acquisition that today would be considered unlawful,[41] in practice it is rarely determinative of modern sovereignty disputes. This is because modern international law tends to focus on ongoing exercises of (lawful) sovereign authority over territory, rather than discrete past acts in relation to that territory, in determining present-day sovereignty.[42] This is, of course, merely a manifestation of the intertemporal doctrine itself: if transactions are to be judged according to the law in force at the time of their occurrence, and the maintenance of sovereignty over territory is an ongoing phenomenon rather than a point-in-time event, the resolution of a sovereignty dispute will generally have regard not

---

37 See Shaw, above note 2 at 435; *Territorial and Maritime Dispute between Nicaragua and Honduras in the Caribbean Sea (Nicaragua v. Honduras)* (8 October 2007) (I.C.J.) at para. 161 [*Nicaragua v. Honduras*].

38 See, generally, Brownlie, above note 16 at 142–43.

39 See Chapter 4, Section H(2).

40 *Island of Palmas (Miangas) Case (Netherlands v. United States of America)* (1928), 2 R.I.A.A. 829 at 845 (P.C.A.) [*Island of Palmas*].

41 See, for example, J. Castellino & S. Allen, *Title to Territory in International Law* (Burlington, VT: Ashgate, 2003) at 3.

42 See further Section B(2)(b)(i), below in this chapter.

only to past international law governing the acquisition of title to territory but also to modern international law governing its continuance.[43] For example, a nineteenth century act of conquest or colonization may, pursuant to the intertemporal doctrine, have to be considered lawful in light of nineteenth century international law; but that does not prevent application of twenty-first century principles of self-determination to declare an ongoing regime of alien subjugation or colonial domination internationally unlawful.[44]

Accordingly, the intertemporal rule—far from giving uncritical, controlling effect to obsolete rules of international law in determining current sovereignty disputes— is a subtle doctrine requiring careful application and appreciation.[45] Some of its subtleties will be illustrated in the following discussion of bases of acquisition of sovereignty over territory.

b) Bases of Acquisition of Sovereignty Over Territory

i) Occupation

As the international legal rules relating to sovereignty over territory tend to legitimate existing situations of fact rather than require hypothetical outcomes,[46] by far the most satisfactory and widely recognized basis for a claim of sovereignty over territory is effective occupation. Very much analogous to the domestic common law concept of possession, effective occupation does not depend on a discrete event or act as the legal basis of title, but rather relies on a demonstrated pattern of ongoing conduct in relation to the territory in question.

In essence, the doctrine of effective occupation as a basis of sovereign title requires an effective and continuous display of state authority over territory, coupled with a demonstrated intent by the state to establish and maintain its sovereignty over that territory. Traditionally, it has also been considered that the doctrine of effective occupation may only be invoked in respect of territory which was, originally, a *res nullius*—that is, territory not yet subject to the sovereignty of any state but susceptible to such subjection.[47] Some authors, however, take the view that the principle of effective occupation can operate in a variety of cir-

---

43 *Island of Palmas*, above note 40 at 845.
44 See further Chapter 2, Section C.
45 Shaw, above note 2 at 430; Brownlie, above note 16 at 124–25.
46 See Shaw, above note 2 at 410. The modern rules relating to the illegality of conquest and annexation as a basis of title may be an exception here: see further Section B(2)(b)(ii), below in this chapter.
47 See, for example, *Legal Status of Eastern Greenland*, above note 36 at 44*ff.* and 63*ff.*; *Western Sahara*, above note 9 at para. 79; Shaw, above note 2 at 424–25;

cumstances to ground current claims of sovereignty notwithstanding the status of the territory in question at the time such effective occupation commenced.[48] In any event, the key in all cases is whether the state has in fact, as at the "critical date,"[49] managed effectively to assert its sovereignty over the relevant territory in a sustained manner.[50]

An essential ingredient of a claim to sovereignty based on effective occupation is that displays of authority over the relevant territory be "*à titre de souverain*" — that is, sovereign in nature.[51] In other words, such displays must either be unambiguously governmental in nature, authorized by the state, or subsequently ratified by it as such.[52] Nevertheless, what constitutes a sufficient display of state authority or sovereign intent for purposes of establishing title based on effective occupation will vary from case to case.[53] Relevant state activities may take such obvious forms as the official establishment and maintenance of settlements or industry, but may also extend to other less direct manifestations of sovereign authority such as the enactment of legislation or the conclusion of treaties that apply to the territory in question.[54] The required intensity of any such activity is also variable, depending upon the surrounding circumstances. For example, in the case of remote or uninhabited areas where there is little or no competing activity by

---

and H. Kindred & P. Saunders, eds., *International Law Chiefly as Interpreted and Applied in Canada*, 7th ed. (Toronto: Emond Montgomery, 2006) at 433.

48   See, for example, Brownlie, above note 16 at 134.

49   The "critical date" in a territorial dispute is the date at which the valid exercise of sovereignty by a state over territory is determinative of the dispute. This will often be the date at which the dispute initially emerges between the parties, but it may also be another date, for example, the date of conclusion of a treaty pursuant to which one of the disputing states purports either to alienate or acquire disputed territory: see, for example, discussion of the *Island of Palmas* case below in the text accompanying notes 57–64. See also Brownlie, above note 16 at 125–26; Shaw, above note 2 at 431–32; L.F.E. Goldie, "The Critical Date" (1963) 12 I.C.L.Q. 1251.

50   In conformity, of course, with any international legal constraints existing at the critical date that are relevant to the means by which such effective control is exercised. For example, effective occupation as a basis of sovereign title following the Second World War would have to be carried out in a manner consistent with the provisions of the *UN Charter* regulating the use of force by states.

51   See Brownlie, above note 16 at 133; Shaw, above note 2 at 434.

52   See *Sovereignty over Pulau Litigan and Pulau Sipadan (Indonesia/Malaysia)*, [2002] I.C.J. Rep. 625 at para. 140; *Case Concerning Kasikili/Sedudu Island (Botswana/Namibia)*, [1999] I.C.J. Rep. 1045 at paras. 98–99 [*Kasikili/Sedudu Island*].

53   See *Rann of Kutch Arbitration (India v. Pakistan)* (1968) 7 I.L.M. 633 at 673–75.

54   See, for example, *Legal Status of Eastern Greenland*, above note 36 at 47–54; *The Minquiers and Ecrehos Case (France/United Kingdom)*, [1953] I.C.J. Rep. 47 at 65–70; *Nicaragua v. Honduras*, above note 37 at paras. 176–208.

other states, very little will be required.[55] In contrast, if the territory in question is subject to regular human activity or competing claims by other states, much more will be required to establish that exercises of authority over the territory are indeed "effective."[56]

This variable content of the requirements for title based on effective occupation is well illustrated in the *Island of Palmas Case*,[57] considered the *locus classicus* in the field. In the *Island of Palmas*, the issue was a dispute between the United States and the Netherlands over Palmas, a small island near the Philippines. The United States had acquired sovereignty over the Philippines from Spain in 1898 pursuant to a treaty of cession between the two states following the Spanish-American War.[58] Assuming that Palmas had been part of that grant, an American general visited the island in 1906 only to discover elements of a Dutch administration in residence. Subsequent investigation revealed that the Netherlands considered Palmas to be part of its territory in the Dutch East Indies, and as a result both states referred the question of sovereignty over Palmas to arbitration.

Judge Huber, the sole arbitrator, approached the issue by reasoning that Spain could not have transferred to the United States more territory than it in fact had,[59] and the real question was therefore the status of the island as at the critical date — that is, the date of the purported transfer in 1898. Judge Huber examined the history of both Spain's and the Netherlands' relationship with the island. While the evidence suggested that Spain had initially "discovered" and established a European settlement on the island in the early seventeenth century, it also showed that Spain had not maintained a presence on the island from the mid-seventeenth century onward. In contrast, there was evidence that the Netherlands had displayed varying degrees of interest in and activity on the island in a more or less continuous fashion in the period 1700–1906. Moreover, neither Spain nor any other state had protested the Netherlands' right to do so during that period.

---

55 See, for example, the *Clipperton Island Case (France v. Mexico)* (1931), 2 R.I.A.A. 1105, translated in (1932) 26 A.J.I.L. 390; *Minquiers and Ecrehos*, ibid. at 65–70.

56 See, for example, *Legal Status of Eastern Greenland*, above note 36 at 46.

57 *Island of Palmas*, above note 40.

58 *Treaty of Peace between the United States and Spain (Treaty of Paris)*, 10 December 1898, US Congress, 55th Cong., 3rd Sess., Senate Doc. No. 62, Part 1 (Washington: Government Printing Office, 1899) 511.

59 An application of the general principle of law known as *nemo dat qui non habet*, meaning essentially that one cannot give what one does not have: see B.A. Garner, ed., *Black's Law Dictionary*, 7th ed. (St. Paul, MN: West Group, 1999), s.v. "*nemo dat qui non habet*" at 1660.

Judge Huber went on to articulate the general principle of effect-ive occupation, observing that "the continuous and peaceful display of territorial sovereignty ... is as good as a title."[60] Concerning the sparse exercises of Dutch sovereignty over the island, particularly in earlier years, Judge Huber remarked:

> The acts of indirect or direct display of Netherlands sovereignty at Palmas (or Miangas), especially in the 18th and early 19th centuries are not numerous, and there are considerable gaps in the evidence of continuous display. But apart from the consideration that the mani-festations of sovereignty over a small and distant island, inhabited only by natives, cannot be expected to be frequent, it is not neces-sary that the display of sovereignty should go back to a very far dis-tant period. It may suffice that such display existed in 1898, and had already existed as continuous and peaceful before that date long enough to enable any Power who might have considered herself as possessing sovereignty over the island, or having a claim to sover-eignty, to have, according to local conditions, a reasonable possibility for ascertaining the existence of a state of things contrary to her real or alleged rights.[61]

Thus, while displays of sovereign authority should be sustained, no particular minimum period is mandated by international law, and the intensity of such displays may in fact be quite thin as long as circum-stances warrant the drawing of conclusions on such a basis. This is, of course, merely an illustration that what counts in this area of inter-national law are the relative merits of competing claims of sovereignty rather than any established, objective threshold for the establishment of sovereignty in the abstract.[62]

The case also illustrates the limited significance of past events, such as the Spanish "discovery" of Palmas, or its brief exercise of sovereign

---

60   *Island of Palmas*, above note 40 at 839.

61   *Ibid.* at 867. The dismissive reference to habitation "only by natives," and the reliance by the United States on the supposed Spanish "discovery" of the island, are instructive of the earlier view taken in international law that territory inhabited by human communities not organized along the lines of European societies was for all intents and purposes not subject to any sovereignty and was thus *res nullius*. Such territory was therefore considered open to occupation and acquisition by states constituted on a Westphalian, European model. This view has since given way to a far more rigorous understanding of the *res nullius* con-cept, which excludes territory "inhabited by tribes or peoples having a social and political organization": see *Western Sahara*, above note 9 at 39.

62   Shaw, above note 2 at 432–33; *Nicaragua v. Honduras*, above note 37 at paras. 173–75.

authority over the island. Judge Huber was dismissive of the legal significance of such acts where they are not followed by sustained displays of state activity. In particular he held that the claim of the Netherlands, which was based on the "peaceful and continuous display of state authority over the island," would "prevail over a title of acquisition of sovereignty not followed by actual display of state authority."[63] While discovery or other acts may serve as initial elements of the pattern of state exercises of authority required to establish sovereignty by effective occupation, they are in themselves merely inchoate bases of title which "cannot prevail over a definite title founded on continuous and peaceful display of sovereignty."[64] It will therefore be seen that effective occupation is among the most potent of the various bases of acquisition of sovereign title to territory.

ii) Conquest and Annexation

Until the early part of the twentieth century and possibly as late as the Second World War, military conquest followed by annexation was generally recognized as a legal means of acquiring sovereign title to territory. However, various developments, including the establishment of the League of Nations in 1919,[65] the adoption in 1928 of the *General Treaty for the Renunciation of War*,[66] the Nuremberg judgments imposing criminal sanctions for the "waging of aggressive war,"[67] and, ultimately, the adoption of the general prohibition on the use of force in Article 2(4) of the *UN Charter*, all played a role in displacing annexation following conquest as a valid root of title.[68] Thus, it is generally

---

63 *Island of Palmas*, above note 40 at 867.

64 *Ibid.* at 869. See also Brownlie, above note 16 at 139–40; S.P. Sharma, *Territorial Acquisition, Disputes and International Law* (The Hague: Martinus Nijhoff, 1997) at 40.

65 *Covenant of the League of Nations Adopted by the Peace Conference at Plenary Session*, April 28, 1919 (1919) 13 A.J.I.L. Supp. 128.

66 *General Treaty for Renunciation of War as an Instrument of National Policy*, 27 August 1928, 94 L.N.T.S. 57 (entered into force 24 July 1929). Also known as the Pact of Paris or the Kellogg-Briand Pact, the *General Act* bound the parties to it to renounce war as an instrument of national policy and international relations. It is still in force but has effectively been superseded by the provisions of the *UN Charter*, above note 3.

67 *Trial of the Major War Criminals before the International Military Tribunal*, Nuremberg, 14 November 1945–1 October 1946, Official Documents (1947); *Affirmation of the Principles of International Law Recognized by the Charter of the Nürnberg Tribunal*, in GA Res. 95(I), UN GAOR, 1st Sess., UN Doc. A/64/Add.1 (1946).

68 On this evolution of international law regulating the use of force, see further Chapter 11, Section B.

acknowledged that no sovereignty may be established by a state over foreign territory by military means.[69] For example, Iraq's invasion of Kuwait in 1990 was generally condemned as an illegal act of aggression contrary to Article 2(4) of the *UN Charter*.[70] Far from recognizing the attempted Iraqi annexation of Kuwait following this very effective act of conquest, therefore, the international community forcibly ejected Iraq from Kuwaiti territory through the collective security mechanisms of the *UN Charter*.[71]

Conquest followed by annexation as a method of acquiring sovereign title to territory nevertheless remains relevant in modern international law due to the operation of the intertemporal rule. As seen above, the legal significance and effects of past events are generally to be judged, in international law, within the legal context that prevailed at the time of such events.[72] While sovereignty may no longer be acquired through conquest and annexation, a valid root of title may still be traced to acts of conquest occurring prior to the early twentieth century, at a time when such a mode of acquisition was legally permissible. Of course, whether or not sovereignty thus originally established continues to be lawful today depends on whether modern principles of self-determination are being respected.[73]

The clear basis of title historically acquired by conquest was the effective and actual exercise of control, and hence sovereignty, over the conquered territory. However, even prior to twentieth century developments, mere *de facto* control of territory by means of military conquest was not sufficient in itself to establish sovereignty over such territory. As in the case of effective occupation,[74] the conquering state also had to display an intent to establish its sovereignty over the territory in question, an element analogous to the *animus possedendi* requirement for the establishment of possessory title to real property at common law. For

---

69   See, for example, the *Friendly Relations Declaration*, above note 3. See also Shaw, above note 2 at 422–24; Brownlie, above note 16 at 160.

70   SC Res. 660(1990), UN SCOR, 45th Year, UN Doc. S/RES/660(1990) (2 August 1990) (determining a breach of international peace and security); and SC Res. 662 (1990), UN SCOR, 45th Year, U.N. doc. S/RES/662(1990) (2 August 1990) (declaring that the purported Iraqi annexation of Kuwait "under any form and whatever pretext has no legal validity and is considered null and void").

71   See, *inter alia*, SC Res. 678(1990), UN SCOR, 45th Year, UN Doc. S/RES/678(1990) (29 November 1990) (authorizing collective measures).

72   See further Chapter 4, Section H(2), especially the discussion of Judge Huber's articulation of the intertemporal rule in the *Island of Palmas* case, above note 40; and Section B(2)(a)(iv), above in this chapter.

73   See further Chapter 2, Section C.

74   See further Section B(2)(b)(i), above in this chapter.

example, no sovereignty over Germany was transferred to the Allies at the conclusion of the Second World War, as they evinced no intent to fold German territory into their own. Rather, a shared management regime was established pending reinstatement of a German government which could assume, eventually, the full exercise of sovereignty over German territory in accordance with international law.[75] Thus, the act of annexation, as a manifestation of the conquering state's intent to assume sovereignty over the conquered territory, was necessary in order to consummate the transfer of sovereignty by conquest.[76]

Of course, to constitute a continuing basis for sovereignty over territory today, any initial act of conquest and annexation must also have been followed by continuing, effective and lawful occupation since that time. In short, conquest, even if valid in itself pursuant to the doctrine of intertemporal law, will generally be but one element in a chain of bases of title establishing current sovereignty over territory.

iii) Prescription

This basis of title is closely related to that of effective occupation, in that both require essentially the same displays of continuous and effective authority over territory, accompanied by intent to establish and maintain sovereignty. The distinction between the two bases, however, relates to the original status of the territory subject to occupation. Whereas, as we have seen, effective occupation traditionally applies only to territory not formerly subject to existing claims of sovereignty,[77] acquisition by prescription implies that a prior sovereign is being displaced by the sustained acts of another state that are inconsistent with the maintenance of the former's sovereignty. Depending on one's understanding of the facts, the *Island of Palmas* case could be considered one of prescription rather than effective occupation in the traditional sense, in that the sustained activities of the Netherlands following the Spanish "discovery" effectively displaced any initial claim of sovereignty that Spain may have had over Palmas.

---

75 See the *(Berlin) Declaration Regarding the Defeat of Germany and the Assumption of Supreme Authority by Allied Powers*, 5 June 1945, 3 Bevans 1207. Although the Berlin Declaration was never revoked, it was effectively superseded by the *Treaty on the Final Settlement with Respect to Germany*, 12 September 1990, which terminated the supervisory role of the Allies over Germany: reproduced in (1990) 29 I.L.M. 1187. In 1990, unification was accomplished by the accession of the German Democratic Republic (GDR) to the Federal Republic of Germany (FRG) by way of an FRG statute: 1990 Gesetzblatt der DDR, Teil I at 995.

76 L. Oppenheim, *International Law*, 8th ed. by H. Lauterpacht, vol. 1 (London: Longmans, Green, 1955) at 566; Shaw, above note 2 at 423.

77 See Section B(2)(b)(i), above in this chapter.

Prescription is in reality merely a particular manifestation of the potent principle of effective occupation, applied to situations where no clear original *res nullius* can be established. Practically, claiming prescription rather than effective occupation demands an increased intensity of the activity required of the claimant state, given that displacement of a prior sovereign is involved rather than mere occupation of previously unclaimed territory. This is so due, again, to the overarching importance of the relative strengths of the competing claims. In other words, the existence of a prior claim is one circumstance affecting (usually by increasing) the nature and concentration of state activity that will be required before a rival may establish its sovereignty over the same territory on the basis of continuous and effective displays of state authority. Arguably, therefore, there is no particular significance to be attached to the designation of prescription as an independent basis for the acquisition of sovereign title to territory. Rather, it might be viewed as merely a particularization of the effective occupation principle with heightened evidentiary requirements due to the unique circumstance of the existence of prior, competing claims.[78]

It should also be noted that, while acquisitive prescription contemplates the usurpation of one state's sovereignty by another, such usurpation must be peaceful.[79] Resort to forceful displacement comes under the separate rubric of conquest and is subject, in modern international law, to important limitations.[80] Thus, what is contemplated in the case of acquisition of title by prescription is peaceful conduct which nevertheless evidences an intent to exercise sovereignty over territory subject to another state's prior claim. Examples might include the passage of laws or the conclusion of treaties applicable to the territory, but might also include on the ground activity that does not result in any physical conflict. The prior claimant may, by inattention or lack of interest, either acquiesce in such rival displays of authority[81] or evince less compelling intent and ability to exercise overall and effective sovereignty. In the latter case, the relative strength and effectiveness of the competing exercises of sovereign jurisdiction will ultimately determine the issue of sovereignty.[82]

---

78   See Brownlie, above note 16 at 147; Shaw, above note 2 at 426–27.
79   See, for example, *Island of Palmas*, above note 40 at 839, where Judge Huber refers to the requirement of a "continuous and peaceful display of territorial sovereignty."
80   See further Section B(2)(b)(ii), above in this chapter.
81   On acquiescence, see further Section B(2)(a)(ii), above in this chapter.
82   See, generally, Brownlie, above note 16 at 145–50; Shaw, above note 2 at 426–29; Sharma, above note 64 at 107–10. See also the requirements of prescription

iv) Cession, Renunciation, and Abandonment

Sovereignty encompasses the power to alienate elements of one's territory by agreement. Cession simply refers to the transfer of sovereignty over territory pursuant to agreement between the ceding and acquiring states. Usually such agreement is expressed in the form of a treaty of cession.[83] However, the treaty or agreement does not in itself effect the transfer of sovereignty. Such transfer must be evidenced by actual relinquishment of authority over the relevant territory in accordance with the agreement. In other words, a transfer of sovereignty over territory by cession must occur in fact as well as in law.

Familiar examples of cession include the transfer by Russia of Alaska to the United States in 1867,[84] the sale of Louisiana by France to the United States in 1803,[85] or the many territorial adjustments included in the various peace treaties that followed the First and Second World Wars.[86]

Closely related to cession is renunciation, a process by which one state renounces its sovereignty over territory in favour of another. The distinction between cession and renunciation is that the former depends on agreement between the ceding and the acquiring states, whereas the latter depends on the unilateral act of the renouncing state.[87] Examples would include cases of decolonization where no agreement of cession was concluded between the predecessor colonial power and the successor newly independent state,[88] or a pattern of unilateral behaviour implicitly renouncing sovereignty.[89] To be effective, however, renuncia-

---

agreed to by the parties in *Kasikili/Sedudu Island*, above note 52 at paras. 94 and 96. Note, however, that the Court took no position on these agreed elements: *ibid.* at para. 97.

83   For example, in the *Island of Palmas* case, above note 40, Spain had ceded the Philippines to the United States by treaty of cession in 1898; see *Treaty of Paris*, above note 58.

84   *Treaty Concerning the Cession of the Russian Possessions in North America by his Majesty the Emperor of all the Russias to the United States of America*, 30 March 1867, 1 Malloy 357. Under Article VI, the United States agreed to pay Russia US$7,200,000 in consideration for the territory.

85   *Treaty between the United States of America and the French Republic (Louisiana Purchase Treaty)*, 30 April 1803, 2 Miller No. 11.

86   See, for example, the peace treaties with Italy, Bulgaria, Hungary, Romania, and Finland: A.C. Leiss & R. Dennett, eds., *European Peace Treaties after World War II* (Boston: World Peace Foundation, 1954).

87   Brownlie, above note 16 at 131.

88   For example, Mali and Burkina Faso: see *Case Concerning the Frontier Dispute (Burkina Faso v. Mali)*, [1986] I.C.J. Rep. 554.

89   See, for example, the *Rann of Kutch Arbitration*, above note 53 at 667–73, 685–88. See also *Land and Maritime Boundary between Cameroon and Nigeria*

tion must be followed by an actual assumption of sovereignty by the successor state.

Abandonment differs from cession and renunciation in that it does not entail a withdrawal of sovereignty in favour of another state but rather a withdrawal of sovereignty leaving a void or, more accurately, a *res nullius*. It is, accordingly, not a basis of acquisition of sovereignty at all, although it may pave the way for subsequent claims of sovereignty by other states based on effective occupation. However, given that questions of sovereignty over territory turn on the relative strengths of competing claims, there is in effect a general presumption in international law against abandonment. In other words, once a state has exercised sovereignty over territory, its mere failure to continue active displays of such sovereignty will not generally be construed as abandonment, particularly in the absence of any rival claims by other states to the same territory. In the absence of competing claims, such earlier displays of state authority constitute a *prima facie* basis for continuing sovereignty unless the state has clearly and unequivocally abandoned any such claim.[90]

This effective presumption against abandonment, and hence against the re-emergence of a *res nullius*, was illustrated in the *Eastern Greenland Case*.[91] That case involved a dispute between Norway and Denmark over the eastern portions of Greenland. The evidence established that Denmark had at an early date claimed sovereignty over the whole of Greenland and had engaged in various state activities over most of the island. Over time, however, Denmark had abandoned its settlements on Greenland's east coast. According to Norway, this evidenced abandonment by Denmark of its sovereignty over the eastern portions of the island, which Norway argued, had thus become a *res nullius* susceptible to its own subsequent assertions of sovereignty. While Norway's claims to sovereignty failed on a number of other bases as well, the Court in particular rejected the contention of abandonment, citing the lack of any unequivocal or definite evidence of such intent.[92] Thus, the mere failure to engage in positive displays of sovereignty, in the absence of any competing claims, will not in general defeat continuing sovereignty unless a clear intent to abandon is manifested.[93]

(*Cameroon v. Nigeria; Equatorial Guinea Intervening*), [2002] I.C.J. Rep. 303 at paras. 203–9 [*Cameroon v. Nigeria*].

90   See the arbitral award in the *Clipperton Island Case*, above note 55 at 394.

91   *Legal Status of Eastern Greenland*, above note 36.

92   "As regards voluntary abandonment, there is nothing to show any definite renunciation on the part of the Kings of Norway or Denmark": *ibid.* at 47. See also *Cameroon v. Nigeria*, above note 89 at paras. 223–24.

93   See Brownlie, above note 16 at 138, n. 123.

v)   Accretion and Erosion

Accretion and erosion refer to natural processes that have the effect of gradually adding to or decreasing the extent of territory already under the sovereignty of a state. Typically such changes are attributable to the action over time of water flows, particularly rivers, or to geological processes such as volcanic activity. In general, accretion and erosion cause little difficulty in the ascertainment of sovereignty over territory, the assumption being that any increase in territory simply accrues to the state already enjoying sovereignty over the appurtenant territory. New land territory created through the growth of river deltas or the dropping of sea levels is simply folded into the appurtenant state's existing sovereign territory by operation of law. Such extensions of territory do not therefore generally require formal acts of occupation, as the exercise of sovereign authority over the overall territory is presumed to extend to these new formations.[94] Obviously, states also bear the risk of any loss of territory through erosion or other natural processes.

The effects of accretion and erosion are to be distinguished from those of "avulsion," a process by which the course of a river suddenly shifts to a considerable degree, for example as a result of heavy storms. If such a river marks a boundary between two states, its sudden shift will, as a general rule, not affect the course of the original boundary.[95] If, on the other hand, the change in the course of the river is gradual, amounting to accretion and/or erosion, the boundary will in general shift along with it.[96]

While accretion and erosion are a basis for the gradual acquisition or loss of sovereign territory through natural processes, it should be noted that a number of states have engaged in various reclamation projects which have largely the same results.[97] The legal basis for the acquisition of sovereignty over territory created by such artificial processes, however, likely rests on effective occupation, through displays of state authority over the newly created territory.

---

94   See Brownlie, *ibid.* at 144–45; Shaw, above note 2 at 419–20.

95   See *Land, Island and Maritime Frontier Dispute (El Salvador/ Honduras; Nicaragua intervening)*, [1992] I.C.J. Rep. 351 at para. 308.

96   *Ibid.* See also *Chamizal Arbitration (United States of America v. Mexico)*, (1911) 5 A.J.I.L. 782 applying the same distinction in the light of relevant treaty provisions.

97   For example, the Hong Kong International Airport at Chek Lap Kok was constructed upon 900 hectares of reclaimed marine area.

C. OCEANS

1) Introduction: The Law of the Sea

a) General Scope of the Law of the Sea

Notwithstanding its well-established and complex nature, the law of the sea, a vast and ancient area of international law, is perhaps most remarkable for its constant and at times rapid evolution. This propensity for detailed rules and constant change is likely due to the relative "density" of state practice in relation to the seas: oceans have always played enormously important socio-economic, transport, and strategic roles, and states have made heavy use of them accordingly. More recently they have become not only the object of dramatically increased economic activity but also the focus of heightened environmental concern. Some of the more important aspects of the modern law of the sea therefore address such issues as fisheries management and protection of the marine environment.[98] Another important area, as coastal states have made ever-increasing jurisdictional claims to coastal waters, has been the delimitation of maritime boundaries between states with adjacent or opposing coastlines.[99]

As this chapter concerns the relationship between states and territory, however, we will focus on a subject which, while having its roots in the very origins of the law of the sea, has undergone radical change since the mid-twentieth century. This subject concerns the nature of the legal relationship between states and various maritime zones lying off the coasts of coastal states.

b) Coastal State Rights vs. Freedom of the High Seas

Coastal state claims have been made against the backdrop of the most basic rule of the law of the sea, the rule that the Earth's oceans—or, in the language of the law of the sea, the "high seas"—constitute a

---

98 See S.B. Kaye, *International Fisheries Management* (The Hague: Kluwer Law International, 2000); J.W. Kindt, *Marine Pollution and the Law of the Sea* (Buffalo: W.S. Hein, 1986); D. Brubaker, *Marine Pollution and International Law* (London: Belhaven Press, 1993); E.J. Molenaar, *Coastal State Jurisdiction Over Vessel-Source Pollution* (The Hague: Kluwer, 1998); L.S. Johnson, *Coastal State Regulation of International Shipping* (Dobbs Ferry, NY: Oceana, 2004).

99 See J.I. Charney & L.M. Alexander, eds., *International Maritime Boundaries*, vols. 1–3 (Dordrecht: M. Nijhoff, 1993, 1998); J.I. Charney & R.W. Smith, eds., *International Maritime Boundaries*, vol. 4 (The Hague: M. Nijhoff, 2002); D.A. Colson & R.W. Smith, eds., *International Maritime Boundaries*, vol. 5 (Leiden: M. Nijhoff, 2005); D.M. Johnston & P.M. Saunders, *Ocean Boundary Making: Regional Issues and Developments* (London: Croom Helm, 1988).

res communis. Notwithstanding early attempts by some states to claim sovereignty over the high seas,[100] it rapidly became a core principle of the law of the sea, mainly under pressure from other major maritime powers,[101] that the high seas could not be appropriated by any state as part of its territory. Rather, the high seas were to be freely available for use — whether for navigation, fishing, or otherwise — by all states, whether coastal or not.[102]

However, it was early conceded that, for security and economic reasons, coastal states retained a form of exclusive jurisdiction approaching sovereignty over a thin "belt" of the sea lying immediately off their coasts. This in time came to be known as the territorial sea, a concept that as we shall see underwent further development in the twentieth century.

The early law of the sea therefore developed along the lines of an essential dichotomy between a narrow coastal band of waters subject to coastal state sovereignty or jurisdiction, and the much vaster oceans beyond that were subject to the sovereignty of no state but were open to enjoyment by all. These two regimes have frequently been in tension with one another as coastal states have sought over time to extend their jurisdictional reach seaward, while other states, particularly the great sea-going powers, have sought to preserve the freedom of the high seas over as great a proportion of the oceans as possible.

Modern developments in the law of the sea relating to maritime zones have largely been shaped by this dual jurisdictional regime and the tension it reflects. Thus, the twentieth century witnessed various innovations in the types and extent of coastal jurisdiction asserted by coastal states, innovations usually designed to impair as little as possible the inherent *res communis* nature of the high seas. The result has been the emergence of a variety of maritime zones, some of which in fact overlap with the high seas regime while nevertheless granting certain functional, jurisdictional preferences to coastal states to the waters off their coasts. These maritime zones and the nature of the jurisdictional rights they confer on coastal states will be the focus of section 2 below.

---

100 Principally Spain and Portugal, with the support of the Catholic Church in the form of the Papal Bulls of 1493 and 1506.
101 For example, the United Kingdom, Russia, the Netherlands, France and, later, the United States of America.
102 See, generally, Brownlie, above note 16 at 224–27; Shaw, above note 2 at 542–45.

c) Sources of the Law of the Sea

While the law of the sea has largely developed as a matter of customary international law, the twentieth century saw two massive codification efforts aimed at rationalizing and modernizing that law. In part, these codification exercises were also driven by the fear of some, mostly seafaring, states that the principle of the freedom of the high seas was under threat, particularly from somewhat extravagant claims of jurisdiction or even sovereignty that were increasingly being asserted by some developing and newly independent states. In 1958, four separate multilateral law-making conventions were thus concluded, each dealing with various aspects of the law of the sea: the *Geneva Convention on the Territorial Sea and Contiguous Zone (GCTS 1958)*;[103] the *Geneva Convention on the Continental Shelf (GCCS 1958)*;[104] the *Geneva Convention on the High Seas (GCHS 1958)*;[105] and the *Geneva Convention on Fishing and Conservation of the Living Resources of the High Seas (GCFC 1958)*.[106] These conventions remain in force and have a significant, although far from universal, number of parties to them.[107]

To some extent, however, the 1958 *Geneva Conventions* have been overtaken by a comprehensive new convention governing virtually all aspects of the law of the sea, which was negotiated over the course of a decade-long diplomatic conference beginning in 1973. The effort to conclude the 1982 *United Nations Convention on the Law of the Sea ("UNCLOS 1982")*[108] was in part the result of continuing change in the international law of the sea which made many of the provisions of the 1958 *Conventions* obsolete almost as soon as they came into force. *UNCLOS 1982* was also intended to secure much wider ratification than had been achieved with the 1958 *Conventions*, thus making it a truly law-making treaty. Notwithstanding the massive effort that went into its negotiation, however, ratifications of *UNCLOS 1982* were insufficient to bring it into force until late 1994. In part, this was due to its controversial provisions relating to the deep seabed, which caused many developed states to withhold their support.[109] That impasse was broken with the

---

103 *GCTS 1958*, above note 17.

104 *Convention on the Continental Shelf*, 29 April 1958, 499 U.N.T.S. 311 (entered into force 10 June 1964).

105 *Convention on the High Seas*, 29 April 1958, 450 U.N.T.S. 11 (entered into force 30 September 1962).

106 *Convention on Fishing and Conservation of the Living Resources of the High Seas*, 29 April 1958, 559 U.N.T.S. 285 (entered into force 20 March 1966).

107 *GCTS 1958*: fifty-two parties; *GCCS 1958*: fifty-eight parties; *GCHS 1958*: sixty-three parties; *GCFC 1958*: thirty-eight parties.

108 *UNCLOS 1982*, above note 17.

109 See further Section C(2)(h), below in this chapter.

negotiation of a side agreement designed to mitigate some of the more controversial aspects of *UNCLOS 1982*'s deep seabed provisions, such that *UNCLOS 1982* now enjoys quite broad ratification.[110] However, important reservations remain as to the customary status, and thus the universal applicability, of some of its provisions, particularly due to the failure of the United States to sign or ratify it.

The result is a patchwork quilt of sources of the law of the sea—custom, the 1958 *Conventions*, *UNCLOS 1982*, and a number of other specialized treaties—any or all of which may be relevant, depending on the parties to a dispute and whether or not they have ratified one or more of the relevant conventions. In any given situation, therefore, it is necessary to take careful account of the treaty relationships of the various parties in order to ascertain if one or more of the conventional regimes, or the more generally applicable rules of customary international law, govern their relations. Moreover, it is far from easy to state the current content of customary international law in many areas of the law of the sea where the conventions have sought to progressively develop that law. To the extent that it is possible to do so, or where trends are apparent, however, the following section will comment upon the customary status of such conventional rules. In any case, reference will be made to various sources throughout the following in order to highlight their points of distinction.

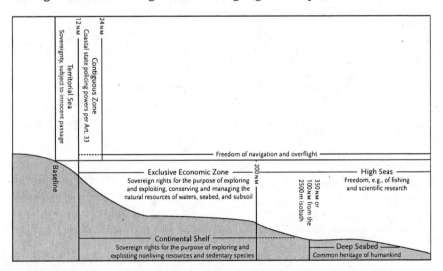

Figure 1: Maritime Zones as Defined in *UNCLOS 1982*

Source: J.H. Currie, C. Forcese & V. Oosterveld, *International Law: Doctrine, Practice, and Theory* (Toronto: Irwin Law, 2007) at 357.

---

110 155 parties at the time of writing.

2) Maritime Zones

a) Establishing Baselines

Once it is established that all coastal states enjoy sovereign rights over a strip of the seas lying off their coasts, as well as more limited jurisdictional rights (not amounting to sovereignty) over certain marine areas lying further out to sea, it becomes necessary to settle upon a method for delimiting the permissible extent or breadth of such marine zones. This is particularly important because the recognition of coastal state rights to certain maritime zones adjacent to their coasts necessarily affects the rights and interests of other states with respect to such zones. States therefore need to know with certainty and precision where a coastal state's various maritime zones begin and end. For this purpose it is necessary that rules for defining the appropriate point of departure for the seaward measurement of a coastal state's maritime zones (a process known as establishing the coastal state's baselines) be generally recognized (see Figure 1, above).

The default method for the establishment of such baselines, recognized in customary international law and treaty law, is to trace the low-water mark along the coast,[111] including the coast of any islands lying off the mainland.[112] This approach has long been adopted in state practice and appropriately reflects the underlying theory of coastal state maritime zones—that coastal states' rights over such zones flow from the zones' adjacency or appurtenance to the states' land territory.[113]

The apparent simplicity of adopting the low-water mark as the point of departure for the seaward measurement of a coastal state's maritime zones disappears, however, in cases where the coastline is highly irregular, deeply indented by fjords or narrow bays, or fringed with numerous small islands. All of these features make the use of baselines following the low-water mark practically unfeasible. The issue that therefore arises is whether and under what circumstances a coastal state may depart from the normal, low-water mark method of establish-

---

111 See *Fisheries Case* (*United Kingdom v. Norway*), [1951] I.C.J. Rep. 116 at 128 [*Anglo-Norwegian Fisheries*]; *GCTS 1958*, above note 17, Article 3; *UNCLOS 1982*, above note 17, Article 5. For purposes of establishing the low-water mark, the coastal state may rely upon large-scale charts officially recognized by it: *ibid.*

112 See *GCTS 1958*, *ibid.*, Article 10; *UNCLOS 1982*, *ibid.*, Article 121. Both provisions define an island as a natural land formation that is above water at high tide. By contrast, "low-tide elevations"—rocks and other land formations that are above water at low tide but submerged at high tide—only generate baselines if they are within the territorial sea as measured from the mainland or an island: see *GCTS 1958*, *ibid.*, Article 11; *UNCLOS 1982*, *ibid.*, Article 13.

113 *Anglo-Norwegian Fisheries*, above note 111 at 128.

ing baselines and adopt, rather, a system of "straight" baselines enclosing irregular features along its coasts.

That issue came to the fore in the landmark *Anglo-Norwegian Fisheries* case, a case that illustrates the significance of choosing one method of establishing baselines over the other. The dispute between the
parties arose due to increased British fishing in the waters off Norway's
coasts, which Norway contended jeopardized the economic well-being of several of its coastal communities that were highly dependent
upon fishing for their livelihood. As a result, in a 1935 decree Norway
established a four-mile wide territorial sea along its coasts in which foreign fishing activities were prohibited. More controversially, however,
the seaward extent of that four-mile zone was measured from a series
of straight baselines enclosing Norway's coastal archipelago and spanning the mouths of a number of deeply indented fjords and bays along
its highly irregular coast. The Norwegian system made use of forty-
eight fixed points along its coast which it then connected by straight
baselines. Eighteen of these lines were greater than 15 nautical miles
in length, and one measured approximately 44 nautical miles in length.
The effect of this method of establishing baselines was to extend considerably the outer limits of the territorial sea, in which no foreign fishing was permitted, beyond that which would have resulted from the
use of a strict low-water mark method. The United Kingdom thus challenged the Norwegian approach to establishing its coastal baselines.

While the outcome of the case ultimately turned on the effects of
the United Kingdom's acquiescence in the system of straight baselines
adopted by Norway, the reasoning of the International Court of Justice
left no doubt that it considered the Norwegian approach to be sound in
international law. In particular, the Court noted that the unique geographical nature of Norway's coast made the low-water mark method practically unworkable. Moreover, the Court viewed the fringe of
islands constituting Norway's coastal archipelago and the deeply indented nature of its mainland coast as evidence of a fragmented coastline that should be viewed as a whole in determining the outer limits of
Norway's coast.[114] Given such a "geographical reality," the Court found
that state practice supported use of a geometric abstraction in the form
of straight baselines enclosing the outer points of Norway's archipelago
and broken coastline.[115]

Having lost on the basic contention that the straight baseline method was either not permissible in international law or not appropriate

---

114 *Ibid.* at 127.
115 *Ibid.* at 128–30.

in this case, the United Kingdom further urged that in any event, the maximum permissible length of any such straight baseline could not exceed 10 nautical miles. This was an important point, as a longer straight baseline encloses more coastal waters within the coastal state's internal waters and, concomitantly, pushes out the outer limits of marine zones that are measured seaward from that baseline. For example, if the maximum permissible length for a straight baseline is 10 nautical miles, as contended by the United Kingdom in the *Anglo-Norwegian Fisheries* case, it would not be possible to close off the mouth of even a deeply indented fjord that measured 15 nautical miles across using such a straight baseline. Rather, it would at most be permissible to use a series of ten-mile straight baselines connecting various points along the shoreline within the fjord. The result would be to enclose dramatically less water within such straight baselines than if the entire fjord could be so enclosed with the use of a single line across its mouth.

In any case, the International Court of Justice rejected the United Kingdom's contention, holding that there was insufficient state practice or *opinio juris* to support such an arbitrary upper limit to the permissible length of straight baselines. Rather, it found that, given the close relationship of appurtenance between a coastal state's land territory and its maritime zones, the baselines from which such zones are measured should not depart appreciably from the "general direction" of the coast.[116] Rather than recognizing an arbitrary upper limit to the permissible length of straight baselines, therefore, the Court held that customary international law merely imposes an indirect limit by requiring that baselines should in general reflect the overall contours of the coast.

Thus, while affirming that tracing the low-water mark was the normal, default approach required by international law for the establishment of baselines, the *Anglo-Norwegian Fisheries* case also legitimized the use of straight baselines in certain cases. In particular, such cases are limited to coastal states with fragmented or deeply indented coastlines, or coastlines fringed by small islands or rocks.[117] In such instances, and in the absence of any particular limit on the permissible length of straight baselines, the coastal state is generally recognized as being in the best position to choose how and where precisely to use such straight baselines.[118] Relevant factors include any close relationship between waters and adjacent land formations that suggests that

---

116 *Ibid.* at 133.

117 See *Case Concerning Maritime Delimitation and Territorial Questions between Qatar and Bahrain (Qatar v. Bahrain), Merits,* [2001] I.C.J. Rep. 40 at para. 212.

118 *Anglo-Norwegian Fisheries,* above note 111 at 130–32.

such waters "are sufficiently closely linked to the land domain to be subject to the regime of internal waters,"[119] as well as "certain economic interests peculiar to a region, the reality and importance of which are clearly evidenced by long usage."[120] In general, however, these rules are subject to the proviso that the coastal state's choice of straight baselines must reflect the "general direction" of the coast.

While many commentators were initially critical of the judgment in the *Anglo-Norwegian Fisheries* case on the basis that it probably represented considerable judicial development of previously accepted customary rules, the principles it laid down have since become firmly entrenched in customary international law and in the relevant treaty regimes.[121] In addition to the default low-water mark method, many coastal states, including Canada,[122] today make use of the straight baseline method along irregular portions of their coasts.[123] Further, there are several instances where states have used straight baselines measuring between 30 and 50 nautical miles or even longer.[124]

b)   Internal Waters and the Territorial Sea

i)   Distinction and Sovereign Status
Once baselines have been established using either the default method of tracing the low-water mark along the coast or, where justifiable, the method of straight baselines, it is possible to distinguish between a coastal state's internal waters and its territorial sea (see Figure 2). Essentially, a state's internal waters are all those marine waters located on

---

119 *Ibid.* at 133.

120 *Ibid.*

121 See *GCTS 1958*, above note 17, Article 4; and *UNCLOS 1982*, above note 17, Article 7, which reproduce almost exactly the *dicta* of the Court on the permissible use of straight baselines. See also *UNCLOS 1982*, Articles 5–6, 9–10, and 14.

122 See the *Oceans Act*, S.C. 1996, c. 31, s. 5. Canada has made extensive use of straight baselines to enclose various rugged portions of its coasts, particularly along the Nova Scotia and Newfoundland and Labrador coasts as well as the coasts of Vancouver Island and the Queen Charlotte Islands. Some were declared as early as 1967: see, for example, the *Proclamation Declaring the Harbour of Fortune, in the Province of Newfoundland, to be a Public Harbour and Defining its Limits*, 11 March 1967, C. Gaz. 1967.I.10. See further the *Territorial Sea Geographical Coordinates Order*, C.R.C., c. 1550. Canada has also enclosed the Arctic archipelago to its north by a system of straight baselines in part on the basis that it constitutes a fringe of islands analogous to Norway's coastal archipelago: see the *Territorial Sea Geographical Coordinates (Area 7) Order*, below note 260. See further Section D(2), below in this chapter; and D. Pharand, "Remarks—Legal Regimes of the Arctic" (1988) 82 Proc. Am. Soc. Int'l L. 328 at 330–31.

123 See Brownlie, above note 16 at 179, n. 38.

124 See Kindred & Saunders, above note 47 at 927.

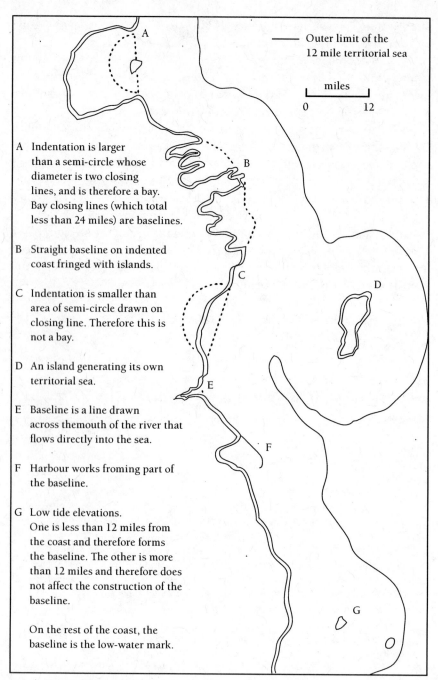

A Indentation is larger than a semi-circle whose diameter is two closing lines, and is therefore a bay. Bay closing lines (which total less than 24 miles) are baselines.

B Straight baseline on indented coast fringed with islands.

C Indentation is smaller than area of semi-circle drawn on closing line. Therefore this is not a bay.

D An island generating its own territorial sea.

E Baseline is a line drawn across the mouth of the river that flows directly into the sea.

F Harbour works froming part of the baseline.

G Low tide elevations. One is less than 12 miles from the coast and therefore forms the baseline. The other is more than 12 miles and therefore does not affect the construction of the baseline.

On the rest of the coast, the baseline is the low-water mark.

Figure 2: The Construction of Baselines

Source: R.R. Churchill & A.V. Lowe, *The Law of the Sea*, 3d ed. (Manchester: Manchester University Press, 1999).

the landward side of its baselines,[125] whereas the territorial sea extends seaward from those same baselines.[126]

As we shall see, the principal legal significance of this distinction is that certain rights of passage in favour of foreign states apply in the latter but not the former. This in turn imposes certain very limited restrictions on a coastal state's exercise of sovereignty over its territorial sea that do not exist in respect of its internal waters. A coastal state's sovereign jurisdiction over its internal waters is as plenary as over its land territory.[127] It is nevertheless widely accepted that a coastal state's sovereign territory extends to the outer limits of its territorial sea, and not merely to the outer limits of its internal waters.[128]

ii) Bays

Internal waters typically comprise river mouths,[129] harbours,[130] the waters lying between fringes of islands enclosed by straight baselines, and other marine waters lying behind straight baselines.[131] A distinct practice, aside from the usual rules relating to the drawing of straight baselines reviewed above, has arisen with respect to enclosing coastal bays within a state's internal waters by drawing straight baselines across their mouths.

A bay for this purpose is generally defined as more than a mere curvature of the coast, being rather a sufficiently pronounced indentation that the waters within it have the appearance of being landlocked. The *GCTS 1958* and *UNCLOS 1982* give this idea geometric expression by requiring in essence that the depth of the indentation be greater than the width of its mouth.[132] While no general consensus has emerged in

---

125 See *GCTS 1958*, above note 17, Article 5(1); *UNCLOS 1982*, above note 17, Article 8(1).

126 See *GCTS 1958*, ibid., Article 6; *UNCLOS 1982*, ibid., Article 4.

127 R.Y. Jennings & A.D. Watts, eds., *Oppenheim's International Law*, 9th ed., vol. 1 (London: Longmans, 1992) at 572. However, some states recognize that a vessel entering a foreign port under distress is immune from the application of local law. Canadian courts have recognized the existence of such immunity in customary international law: see, for example, *Cashin v. The King*, [1935] 4 D.L.R. 547 at 551–52 (Ex. Ct.); *The Queen City v. The King*, [1931] S.C.R. 387. Similarly, it is generally acknowledged that foreign military vessels in internal waters enjoy immunity from coastal state jurisdiction: see Shaw, above note 2 at 494–95.

128 See *GCTS 1958*, above note 17, Article 1; *UNCLOS 1982*, above note 17, Article 2.

129 See *GCTS 1958*, ibid., Article 13; *UNCLOS 1982*, ibid., Article 9.

130 See *GCTS 1958*, ibid., Article 8; *UNCLOS 1982*, ibid., Article 11.

131 See *GCTS 1958*, ibid., Article 5(1); *UNCLOS 1982*, ibid., Article 8(1).

132 More accurately, the area of the purported bay must be at least as large as that of a semi-circle of a diameter equal to the width of the bay's mouth: see *GCTS*

customary international law with respect to the maximum permissible length for straight baselines used to enclose a fragmented or deeply indented coastline, states have generally agreed, in both *GCTS 1958* and *UNCLOS 1982*, that the maximum permissible length of a baseline used to enclose a bay is 24 nautical miles.[133] If the mouth of the bay is wider than 24 nautical miles, such that it may not be entirely enclosed with a straight baseline across its mouth, the coastal state may nevertheless use a 24-nautical mile straight baseline within the bay in order to enclose as much of the bay as possible.[134]

Moreover, many states claim sovereignty over bays as internal waters on the basis of historic use and occupation and enclose them with straight baselines drawn across their mouths, regardless of their size or the length of the straight baselines required to do so. Canada has made a number of such claims, for example with respect to Hudson's Bay, Hudson Strait, and Ungava Bay.[135] While the legal basis for claiming such large expanses as part of a state's internal waters is somewhat unclear, it would appear to rest on a combination of continuous and effective occupation coupled with acquiescence in or recognition of the claim by other states.[136] The rules applicable to bays under both the *GCTS 1958* and *UNCLOS 1982* are without prejudice to such claims based on historic title.[137]

iii) Breadth of the Territorial Sea

As seen above, the principal purpose of drawing baselines is to use them as a point of departure for measuring the seaward extent of the coastal state's territorial sea and, hence, the outer limits of its sovereign territory. This begs the question of the maximum permissible breadth

---

    1958, *ibid.*, Article 7; *UNCLOS 1982*, *ibid.*, Article 10.

133 See *GCTS 1958*, *ibid.*, Article 7(4); *UNCLOS 1982*, *ibid.*, Article 10(4). There is some controversy as to whether this is a departure from earlier customary practice which favoured a ten-nautical-mile rule (see Brownlie, above note 16 at 182) or whether state practice disclosed no such rule (see Shaw, above note 2 at 499).

134 See *GCTS 1958*, *ibid.*, Article 7(5); *UNCLOS 1982*, *ibid.*, Article 10(5).

135 See *Oceans Act*, above note 122, s. 5(3); *Territorial Sea Geographical Coordinates (Area 7) Order*, below note 260. While Canada also claims, for example, the Gulf of St. Lawrence, the Bay of Fundy, and Queen Charlotte Sound (including Hecate Strait and the Dixon Entrance) as historic waters, it has not formally enclosed them with straight baselines (unless the broad language of s. 5(3) of the *Oceans Act* can be considered to have had this effect). To date it has instead relied on "fisheries closing lines" drawn across their mouths: see *Fishing Zones of Canada (Zones 1, 2 and 3) Order*, C.R.C., c. 1547.

136 See Brownlie, above note 16 at 157–58; Shaw, above note 2 at 499–501.

137 See *GCTS 1958*, above note 17, Article 7(6); *UNCLOS 1982*, above note 17, Article 10(6).

of a coastal state's territorial sea measured in this way. In early practice this breadth varied, from the maximum range of cannon-fire from shore to the range of unaided vision on a fair day. By the early nineteenth century, however, the cannon-shot rule had crystallized into a broadly recognized (and more precise) limit of 3 nautical miles measured from the state's baselines.[138]

General practice recognizing a customary three-mile limit for the territorial sea remained prevalent until the twentieth century, when a number of states began asserting jurisdictional rights, usually amounting to something less than full sovereignty, over ever-wider bands of their coastal seas. This led to several expansionist claims, frequently by newly independent states, of territorial seas of up to 200 nautical miles in breadth. These developments generated considerable concern over the potential threat they represented to the freedom of the high seas, and in large measure such concern catalyzed the codification exercises that led to the 1958 and 1982 conventions on the law of the sea.

Given the controversy generated by this rapidly evolving state practice, the issue of the maximum breadth of the territorial sea was not resolved in the *GCTS 1958*. However, broad consensus was achieved in the negotiations leading to the adoption, in *UNCLOS 1982*, of a twelve-mile limit for the territorial sea as measured from the baselines.[139] The great preponderance of state practice, as reflected in coastal state claims to their territorial sea, now reflects this rule, even though a very small number of (mainly developing) states still clings to claimed territorial seas of up to 200 nautical miles in breadth.[140] Aside from the potential position of such states as persistent objectors, it can be said that customary international law now recognizes 12 nautical miles as the maximum permissible breadth for a state's territorial sea.

iv) Legal Regime of the Territorial Sea: The Right of Innocent Passage
As seen above, a state's sovereign territory extends to the outer limits of its territorial sea. Practically speaking, this means that a coastal state is presumed to enjoy full and exclusive jurisdictional rights over all

---

138 See, generally, Brownlie, above note 16 at 174–75 and 180–81.
139 See *UNCLOS 1982*, above note 17, Article 3.
140 See Annex II ("Summary of National Claims to Maritime Zones") in *Report of the Secretary General on Oceans and the Law of the Sea*, U.N. Doc. A/56/58 (9 March 2001) at 118–24. An updated "Table of Claims to Maritime Jurisdiction" (current, at the time of writing, to 24 October 2007), prepared by the Division of Ocean Affairs and the Law of the Sea of the UN Office of Legal Affairs, is available online: www.un.org/Depts/los/LEGISLATIONANDTREATIES/PDF-FILES/table_summary_of_claims.pdf.

activities within its territorial sea, subject only to such limitations on the exercise of that sovereignty as may be prescribed by international law. Thus, as a general starting point, a coastal state may regulate (or refuse) access to and activities within its territorial sea in much the same way as in the case of its land territory and internal waters. However, unlike the case of land territory and internal waters, this starting presumption is subject to certain qualifications only applicable to the territorial sea.

These qualifications are mainly designed to reconcile the extension of a coastal state's sovereignty to the limits of its territorial sea with the competing interests, mainly navigational, of other states. Customary international law thus recognizes a right of peaceful or innocent passage by foreign vessels, without prior authorization, through the territorial sea. Passage essentially refers to direct transit through the territorial sea, but includes passage through the territorial sea in order to reach or depart from the coastal state's port facilities, as well as temporary layovers that are incidental to passage through the territorial sea in accordance with standard navigational practices.

This customary right of innocent passage has largely been codified in the *GCTS 1958* and *UNCLOS 1982*,[141] although the conventions have added certainty to the requirements of innocence of passage. Essentially, innocent passage means passage that is not prejudicial to the peace, good order, or security of the coastal state.[142] The *GCTS 1958* adds an explicit requirement that foreign vessels obey coastal state laws prohibiting fishing,[143] and *UNCLOS 1982* lists a number of activities that are deemed not innocent, including most military manoeuvres, smuggling, wilful pollution, fishing, marine research, and any other activity not directly related to mere passage through the territorial sea.[144] While there is some controversy as to whether foreign warships enjoy a right of innocent passage as a matter of customary international law,[145] both the *GCTS 1958* and *UNCLOS 1982* appear to extend the same right of innocent passage without prior coastal state authorization to both foreign military and merchant vessels.[146]

---

141 See *GCTS 1958*, above note 17, Article 14; *UNCLOS 1982*, above note 17, Articles 17–18.

142 See *GCTS 1958*, *ibid.*, Article 14(4); *UNCLOS 1982*, *ibid.*, Article 19(1).

143 See *GCTS 1958*, *ibid.*, Article 14(5).

144 See *UNCLOS 1982*, above note 17, Article 19.

145 See, for example, Brownlie, above note 16 at 188.

146 Note, for example, that the provisions of both conventions relating to the basic right of innocent passage appear under headings indicating "rules applicable to all ships," as distinct from subsequent rules designated as applicable to

The coastal state remains free to pass laws and regulations applicable to the territorial sea, including laws regulating the exercise by foreign states of their right of innocent passage.[147] Coastal states also remain free to stop passage which is not innocent, and may even suspend (although not permanently) the right of innocent passage, on a non-discriminatory basis with respect to the vessels of all foreign states, if such suspension is essential to its security.[148] Otherwise, however, no charges may be levied for innocent passage nor may any other measures be taken by the coastal state to hamper or impair the enjoyment by foreign states of their right of innocent passage.[149]

In order to forestall any unnecessary interference with the enjoyment of the right of innocent passage, moreover, custom as well as the 1958 and 1982 conventions restrict the coastal state's criminal and civil jurisdiction over ships exercising their right to pass through the territorial sea.[150] First, as a matter of customary international law, foreign warships and non-commercial government vessels generally enjoy absolute immunity from coastal state jurisdiction of any kind over persons or events occurring aboard such vessels. In such cases, the coastal state may at most require the departure of the foreign vessel and pursue an international claim against the relevant foreign state.[151]

Second, in the case of foreign commercial vessels, the exercise of coastal state criminal jurisdiction over acts committed in the course of passage is limited, rather than prohibited, to acts that affect the interests of the coastal state or in respect of which coastal state assistance has been requested by the master of the vessel. Such jurisdiction is not so limited, however, with respect to vessels passing through the ter-

---

"merchant ships," "warships," et cetera. See. G. Fitzmaurice, "Some Results of the Geneva Conference on the Law of the Sea" (1959) 8 I.C.L.Q. 73 at 98–99 and 102–3; D.P. O'Connell, *The International Law of the Sea* (Oxford: Clarendon Press, 1982) at 290–91. But see Brownlie, above note 16 at 188–89, arguing that neither the *GCTS 1958* nor *UNCLOS 1982* resolve the issue.

147 See *GCTS 1958*, above note 17, Articles 14(5) and 17; *UNCLOS 1982*, above note 17, Articles 21–22.

148 See *GCTS 1958*, ibid., Article 16; *UNCLOS 1982*, ibid., Article 25.

149 See *GCTS 1958*, ibid., Articles 17–18; *UNCLOS 1982*, ibid., Articles 24 and 26.

150 For the general rules relating to states' criminal and civil jurisdiction over events and persons within their territory, see further Chapter 8. As the territorial sea comes within a state's sovereign territory, these rules govern the coastal state's criminal and civil jurisdiction over persons and events within its territorial sea, except to the extent specific limitations are placed on that jurisdiction by the provisions of the relevant convention or a rule of customary international law.

151 See also *GCTS 1958*, above note 17, Article 23; *UNCLOS 1982*, above note 17, Articles 30–32. See also Shaw, above note 2 at 512.

ritorial sea after leaving the internal waters of the coastal state. On the other hand, a coastal state generally has no criminal jurisdiction over a foreign vessel merely transiting through the territorial sea without entering internal waters with respect to acts committed abroad.[152]

Third, again with respect to commercial vessels in passage, the coastal state's civil jurisdiction is more restrictive still. The coastal state may not divert or stop a commercial vessel in passage for purposes of exercising civil jurisdiction over a person aboard that vessel (the service of process, for example, or the levying of execution), and may not arrest or levy execution against a vessel in passage in connection with civil proceedings, except with respect to obligations incurred by the vessel in the course or for the purpose of such passage. On the other hand, the coastal state has jurisdiction to arrest or levy execution against a commercial vessel it finds lying in its territorial sea or that is passing through its territorial sea after leaving the coastal state's internal waters.[153]

v)   International Straits and the Right of Transit Passage

Closely related to the regime of innocent passage through the territorial sea is the specialized right of passage enjoyed by states through international straits. International straits are narrow sea passages, bordered by opposing coastlines, which join larger sea zones, usually the high seas. As such they are frequently used by states to navigate between those larger sea zones. In general, straits pose no jurisdictional difficulties, except when the strait is so narrow that, for example, the territorial sea of one coastal state extends to and meets the territorial sea of the facing coastal state. The number of such situations has, of course, multiplied with the extension of the maximum permissible breadth of the territorial sea from 3 to 12 nautical miles.

While the general right of innocent passage through the territorial sea will operate in most instances to permit continued transit by foreign vessels through even such a narrow strait, such passage may be stopped, as we have seen, if it is not innocent and may even be suspended entirely in the interests of the coastal state's security. Furthermore, some straits may pass through a state's internal waters, in which there is no general right of innocent passage as there is through the territorial sea.[154] The potential impediments to navigation through international

---

152 See *GCTS 1958, ibid.*, Article 19; *UNCLOS 1982, ibid.*, Article 27.
153 See *GCTS 1958, ibid.*, Article 20; *UNCLOS 1982, ibid.*, Article 28.
154 For example, the United States claims that the Northwest Passage, which passes through Canada's Arctic archipelago and which Canada considers to be within its internal waters, constitutes an international strait. For a discussion of the

straits has therefore led to the elaboration of an even more robust intrusion into coastal state sovereignty over those parts of its internal waters or territorial sea that form part of an international strait.

The customary international legal regime applicable to international straits was explained by the International Court of Justice in the 1949 *Corfu Channel Case*.[155] That case arose from British warships transiting through the Corfu Channel, an international strait between the Greek island of Corfu and the Albanian mainland, but lying principally in Albanian territorial waters. The strait had long been used by the United Kingdom and other states in order to pass from one area of the Mediterranean to another, notwithstanding the availability of other routes and notwithstanding long-standing Albanian claims that it had the right to control transit through the Channel. At the time of the relevant passage, Albania was in a state of war with Greece, and considerable tension already existed between Albania and the United Kingdom over the latter's insistence on its right of passage through the strait.

During one such transit through the Channel, British warships struck and were seriously damaged by a minefield in Albanian territorial waters. The origins of the minefield were uncertain and there was no clear evidence that it had been laid by Albania. The British Navy subsequently returned and swept the Channel for mines. It then instituted proceedings against Albania in the International Court of Justice seeking compensation for the damage caused to it and to its nationals (there had been forty-four deaths as a result of the explosion of the mines). Albania responded by claiming a violation of its sovereignty both through the initial act of passage and the subsequent minesweeping operations carried out by the British Navy in its territorial waters.

Rather than hold Albania directly accountable for the presence of the minefield and consequent damages, the Court awarded compensation to the United Kingdom for the Albanian government's failure to exercise sufficient diligence in ensuring that its territory was not used in such a way as to cause prejudice to another state.[156] On the sovereignty issue, moreover, the Court affirmed a legal regime for international straits that derogated from Albanian sovereignty over its territorial sea. In particular, the Court held that foreign vessels, including warships, enjoy a right of innocent passage through international straits without prior authorization. The major distinction from the general right of innocent passage through the territorial sea, however, is that the right

---

legal issues, see D.M. McRae, "Arctic Sovereignty? What is at Stake?" (2007) 64:1 Behind the Headlines 1 at 7–17.

155 *Corfu Channel Case (Merits) (United Kingdom v. Albania)*, [1949] I.C.J. Rep. 4.

156 *Ibid.* at 22–23.

of innocent passage through international straits cannot be suspended by the coastal state, even for security reasons. The coastal state does nevertheless retain the ability to regulate the exercise of the right of innocent passage, as long as such regulation does not amount to an effective suspension of the right or a requirement of prior authorization.[157] Moreover, any particular passage that is not innocent may be stopped or prevented. For example, the Court held that the minesweeping operations conducted by the British Navy did not constitute innocent passage and were, therefore, a violation of Albania's sovereignty over its territorial sea.[158]

In addition, the Court rejected Albania's contention that the right of innocent passage through international straits only exists where there is no alternative route other than the international strait in question. All that is required, held the Court, is that the strait be in a "geographic situation ... connecting two parts of the high seas and ... used for international navigation."[159]

The essence of these rules, which represent a considerable incursion into a coastal state's sovereignty, was thereafter incorporated into the *GCTS 1958*.[160] However, in exchange for the expansion of territorial seas from 3 to 12 nautical miles, several states sought and obtained an even more robust regime for international straits in *UNCLOS 1982*. Rather than a mere right of innocent passage that may not be suspended, the *UNCLOS 1982* regime provides for a right of "transit passage."[161] While there is no express condition of innocence attached to such right of transit passage, the right is limited to continuous and expeditious transit through the international strait. States availing themselves of the right are also bound to confine their activities to such expeditious transit and, in particular, not to interfere with the sovereignty or territorial integrity of the coastal state.[162] However, those obligations are not matched by any general powers of enforcement by the coastal state, which, in particular, is forbidden from preventing, stopping, or suspending the right of transit passage.[163] Rather, the coastal state is limit-

---

157 *Ibid.* at 29. For example, the coastal state may designate sea lanes or promulgate regulations aimed at ensuring navigational safety, but cannot require transiting vessels to undergo a burdensome administrative or regulatory process that would effectively frustrate the right of innocent passage.
158 *Ibid.* at 32–35.
159 *Ibid.* at 28.
160 See *GCTS 1958*, above note 17, Article 16.
161 See *UNCLOS 1982*, above note 17, Article 38.
162 *Ibid.*, Article 39.
163 *Ibid.*, Articles 38 and 44.

ed to other remedies, such as bringing a claim in state responsibility,[164] in the event of a breach of duties attaching to the exercise of the right of transit passage.

It is the removal of the right to stop or prevent non-innocent passage (or, more accurately, passage which does not comply with the requirements of continuous and expeditious transit) that distinguishes the *UNCLOS 1982* regime from the earlier *GCTS 1958* and *Corfu Channel* regime of innocent passage through international straits.[165] Some states have asserted that the *UNCLOS 1982* regime has superseded the prior regime as a matter of customary international law, a position that has gained weight with the wide ratification and consequent coming into force of *UNCLOS 1982*, but which remains debatable in the light of ambiguous state practice.[166] Whether or not customary international law comes to reflect the *UNCLOS 1982* right of transit passage through international straits will depend, therefore, on whether states in fact consistently implement it in practice.

c) Archipelagic Waters

UNCLOS 1982 establishes a special regime for "archipelagic states;" that is, states constituted wholly of islands.[167] An example of such a state would be the Solomon Islands. Essentially, this special regime permits the archipelagic state to draw straight baselines connecting the outermost points of the outermost islands constituting its land territory, subject to certain limits as to the permissible length of such baselines.[168] These baselines then serve, as with other baselines, as the starting point for measuring the seaward extent of the archipelagic state's maritime zones, such as its territorial sea, contiguous zone, and so on.[169]

However, the inter-island waters enclosed by these baselines, or "archipelagic waters," are not considered internal waters, although they do come under the sovereignty of the archipelagic state.[170] The essen-

---

164 See further Chapter 12.

165 See, generally, S.N. Nandan & D.H. Anderson, "Straits Used for International Navigation : A Commentary on Part III of the *UN Convention on the Law of the Sea 1982*" (1989) 60 Brit.Y.B. Int'l L. 159 at 169.

166 R.R. Churchill & A.V. Lowe, *The Law of the Sea*, 3d ed. (Manchester: Manchester University Press, 1999) at 113; Shaw, above note 2 at 514.

167 *UNCLOS 1982*, above note 17, Articles 46–54.

168 *Ibid.*, Article 47.

169 *Ibid.*, Article 48.

170 *Ibid.*, Article 49. Note, however, that an archipelagic state may, within its archipelagic waters, delimit internal waters by drawing closing lines across the mouths of rivers, bays and ports: *ibid.*, Article 50.

tial distinction between internal and archipelagic waters is that the latter are subject to rights of innocent passage[171] and of "archipelagic sea lanes passage,"[172] whereas the former are not. The right of archipelagic sea lanes passage is similar to the right of transit passage in the case of international straits, although in the case of the former, the archipelagic state may designate the sea lanes to be used for that purpose.

d) The Contiguous Zone

We now leave the realm of the coastal state's sovereign jurisdiction, which as we have seen ends at the outer limit of its territorial sea, and focus on a number of maritime zones that have been superimposed on the general, underlying *res communis* regime of the high seas that traditionally commences where the coastal state's territorial sea ends.[173] As such we are leaving those areas where the coastal state is presumed to enjoy plenary sovereign jurisdiction, subject to explicit derogations therefrom, to areas where the starting presumption is precisely the opposite— where the coastal state enjoys no special jurisdictional rights or privileges other than those specifically provided for by a positive rule of international law.

Customary international law has long recognized one such set of special rights in providing that coastal states are entitled to exercise limited forms of jurisdiction over a narrow band of sea just beyond, or contiguous to, their territorial sea. The purpose of recognizing such a "contiguous zone" is to permit coastal states to take steps necessary, in a narrow band of the high seas immediately outside their sovereign territory, to protect themselves from certain activities that would be prejudicial to them or their territory (including their territorial sea). Such a zone must be claimed by the coastal state, and many states, including Canada, have done so.[174]

The key issues are the permissible breadth of contiguous zones and the forms of jurisdiction that may be exercised in such zones once they are declared. On the first of these questions, no clear customary limit was generally recognized until the matter was addressed in the multilateral conventional regimes. The *GCTS 1958* provides that the maximum seaward extent for a contiguous zone is 12 nautical miles,

---

171 *Ibid.*, Article 52.

172 *Ibid.*, Article 53.

173 Although technically, as we shall see below, *UNCLOS 1982* has legally defined the "high seas" as commencing at the outer limit of a coastal state's exclusive economic zone, where such is claimed: see further Section C(2)(e), below in this chapter.

174 See, for example, the *Oceans Act*, above note 122, ss.10–12.

as measured from the coastal state's baselines.[175] Given that at the time
of its conclusion custom generally prescribed a maximum breadth for
the territorial sea of 3 nautical miles, this essentially meant that states
were permitted to declare a contiguous zone 9 nautical miles in width.
Given the extension of the territorial sea to 12 nautical miles in *UN-
CLOS 1982*, the maximum seaward extent for contiguous zones was
also extended to 24 nautical miles from the coastal state's baselines,
yielding a maximum contiguous zone of 12 nautical miles in width.[176]

On the second issue, the jurisdiction of the coastal state over its
contiguous zone is generally limited to measures designed either to
prevent or punish violations of its customs, fiscal, immigration, and
"sanitary" laws.[177] This is typically accomplished by policing the contiguous zone in order to deny entry into the territorial sea by vessels
suspected of various smuggling activities (including so-called "human
smuggling"), or vessels which would pose a threat to the pollution or
other sanitary standards established by the coastal state if such vessels
were admitted to territorial or internal waters. Conversely, the coastal
state is competent in the contiguous zone to arrest or take other enforcement measures against vessels that have already committed such
acts in the territory (including the territorial sea) of the coastal state
and have already departed the territorial sea. While the contiguous
zone thus represents an extension of a coastal state's enforcement jurisdiction beyond its territorial limits,[178] that extension is limited both
spatially, to a narrow band of the high seas, and substantively, to a very
restrictive range of offences.

e)   Fisheries Zones and the Exclusive Economic Zone

Beyond the needs of protection, addressed in part by the contiguous
zone, coastal states have also been driven by economic factors to claim
at least limited forms of preferential economic jurisdiction over the
waters extending beyond their relatively narrow territorial seas. This
has particularly been the case in the twentieth and twenty-first centuries as states' capacity to exploit the economic resources of the seas has
been considerably extended, through technological and scientific innovation, beyond the relatively shallow waters of most territorial seas.
Legal developments here have been overshadowed, however, by the interests of most maritime powers in maintaining a regime of free naviga-

---

175 *GCTS 1958*, above note 17, Article 24(2).
176 *UNCLOS 1982*, above note 17, Article 33(2).
177 See *GCTS 1958*, above note 17, Article 24(1); *UNCLOS 1982*, *ibid.*, Article 33(1).
178 On the general territorial limitation of a state's enforcement jurisdiction, see,
     generally, Chapter 8, Section B.

tion on the high seas, and thus in resisting undue extensions of coastal state sovereignty over ever-wider tracts of coastal seas. The focus has therefore been on recognizing preferential economic rights for coastal states while, at the same time, preserving the essential freedoms of the high seas in areas beyond the territorial sea.

Among the earlier developments here were the numerous proclamations by coastal states, beginning at about the close of the Second World War, of fisheries zones. Essentially such proclamations amounted to claims of either exclusive or preferential rights over all fisheries activities in the relevant coastal zone. Foreign states were restricted to fishing either in their own waters, on the high seas beyond claimed fisheries zones, or in coastal waters where no exclusive fisheries zone had yet been claimed (but beyond any territorial seas, of course). So widespread was the practice of claiming such zones that, by 1978, seventy-four coastal states (including Canada,[179] the United States, the Soviet Union, Japan, and most European Community members) had claimed fisheries zones extending 200 nautical miles from their baselines, while a further ten states had claimed less extensive zones.[180]

This widespread practice clearly established the legality of the fisheries zone in customary international law, a development recognized in 1974 by the International Court of Justice in the *Fisheries Jurisdiction Case*.[181] Such a zone must be claimed, however, and it is likely that its current outward permissible limit is 200 nautical miles as measured from the coastal state's baselines, in accordance with the overwhelming preponderance of state practice in this regard.[182]

While the fisheries zone likely retains its customary status today, its rapid development has since been somewhat overtaken by the inclusion, in *UNCLOS 1982*, of a more generally applicable regime of exclu-

---

179 See now *Oceans Act*, above note 122, s. 16.
180 See, generally, Brownlie, above note 16 at 197–99; Shaw, above note 2 at 517–18.
181 *Fisheries Jurisdiction Case (United Kingdom v. Iceland) (Merits)*, [1974] I.C.J. Rep. 3. The ICJ accepted that customary international law permitted the declaration of an exclusive fisheries zone of up to twelve nautical miles from the coastal state's baselines (recall that customary international law at this time likely limited the width of the territorial sea to three nautical miles from baselines). In addition, a further but less well defined "preferential" fisheries zone was recognized as permissible by the Court: see *ibid.* at paras. 52–62.
182 Such a limit appears to have been implicitly accepted by the ICJ in the *Case Concerning Maritime Delimitation in the Area between Greenland and Jan Mayen (Denmark v. Norway)*, [1993] I.C.J Rep. 38 at 59–62. For Canada's claims to fisheries zones, see *Oceans Act*, above note 122, s. 16; *Fishing Zones of Canada (Zones 1, 2 and 3) Order*, above note 135; *Fishing Zones of Canada (Zones 4 and 5) Order*, C.R.C., c. 1548; *Fishing Zones of Canada (Zone 6) Order*, C.R.C., c. 1549.

sive economic rights in favour of coastal states, the "exclusive economic zone" (EEZ).[183] In essence, the concept of the EEZ permits a coastal state to make an all-encompassing claim to exclusive rights of exploitation of all economic (living or non-living) resources in the waters, on the seabed, and in the subsoil of a coastal zone extending, at most, 200 nautical miles from the state's baselines.[184]

The EEZ resembles an exclusive fisheries zone, but encompasses all economic resources in the zone, as well as all economic activities that might be pursued in the zone, such as the generation of power.[185] The coastal state also enjoys jurisdiction over marine scientific research, protection and preservation of the marine environment, and the establishment of artificial islands or installations in the EEZ.[186] However, as a corollary to the sweeping economic rights granted to coastal states in their EEZ, coastal states also bear responsibility for the management and conservation of living resources in the EEZ and have a duty not to over-exploit them.[187] They are further required to promote the "optimal" exploitation of the living resources of the EEZ by granting other states access to such resources to the extent that the coastal state does not have the capacity to exploit such resources itself to sustainable levels.[188]

The general character of the legal regime applicable to the EEZ is also novel. Unlike contiguous or fisheries zones, which are superimposed on the high seas regime, *UNCLOS 1982* defines the EEZ as a *sui generis* zone which comes neither within the regime of the sovereign territory of the coastal state nor within the *res communis* regime of the high seas.[189] Thus, a coastal state enjoys "sovereign rights" to the economic resources of the EEZ without, however, enjoying sovereignty over the zone itself.[190] The concept of sovereign rights is not well-developed in international law, but likely strengthens the exclusivity of the coastal state's rights over the resources of its EEZ. The distinction between the EEZ and the high seas contemplated in *UNCLOS 1982* is largely formal, as most of the freedoms otherwise enjoyed by other

---

183 *UNCLOS 1982*, above note 17, Articles 55–75.
184 Technically, the EEZ begins at the outer limit of the territorial sea: see *ibid.*, Article 55.
185 See *ibid.*, Article 56.
186 *Ibid.*
187 See *ibid.*, Article 61.
188 See *ibid.*, Article 62.
189 See *ibid.*, Articles 55, 58, and 86–87.
190 See *ibid.*, Article 56(1)(a).

states in the high seas,[191] other than those specifically assigned to the coastal state, continue to be enjoyed by other states in the EEZ.[192] While foreign vessels may not fish or drill for oil in a coastal state's EEZ without leave of that coastal state, they are free to navigate within the EEZ in such a way that does not interfere with the coastal state's enjoyment of its economic rights in the zone.

Since the conclusion of *UNCLOS 1982*, approximately 125 states have claimed EEZs, including Canada.[193] In some cases such claims coincide with claims to fisheries zones, and there is in principle no reason why the two claims cannot co-exist.[194] The customary status of the EEZ is now widely recognized[195] and can only be solidified as state practice continues to be guided by implementation of the now widely-ratified *UNCLOS 1982*.

f)   The Continental Shelf

The seabed lying off the shores of most coastal states is relatively shallow for some distance until it drops off to the deep seabed. It is thus known as the "continental shelf." Its configuration suggests that it is a natural prolongation of the coastal state's land territory; which, from a geological perspective, it is. Coinciding with the rise in coastal states' interest in the economic resources of the waters off their coasts was a growing awareness of the economic potential of petroleum, natural gas, and other mineral resource deposits in the subsoil of most continental shelves. The combination of these factors gave rise, mainly in the second half of the twentieth century, to the rapid recognition of exclusive coastal state rights to the resources of the continental shelves extending seaward from their shores.

The decisive catalyst for these developments was the 1945 proclamation by the United States, known as the "*Truman Proclamation*," in which it laid claim to the "natural resources of the subsoil and seabed of the continental shelf" appurtenant to its coasts.[196] That initial claim extended to a point where the shelf reached a depth of 100 fathoms, or

---

191 See *ibid.*, Article 87.

192 See *ibid.*, Articles 58, 86.

193 See Table of Claims to Maritime Jurisdiction, above note 140.

194 For example, Canada has maintained its claim to fisheries zones while also claiming an exclusive economic zone: see *Oceans Act*, above note 122, ss. 13–16.

195 See, for example, *Continental Shelf Case (Tunisia v. Libya) (Merits)*, [1982] I.C.J. Rep. 18 at 38, 47–49, and 79; *Gulf of Maine (Merits)*, [1984] I.C.J. Rep. 246 at 294–95; *Case Concerning the Continental Shelf (Libya v. Malta)*, [1985] I.C.J. Rep. 13 at 32–34.

196 *The Truman Proclamation*, 28 September 1945, 10 Fed. Reg. 12303.

approximately 200 metres. The key to the later development of the concept was the proclamation's focus on claiming jurisdiction and control over the natural resources of the shelf, rather than asserting sovereignty over the shelf itself. Further, the American claim was made expressly without prejudice to the legal status of the waters above the shelf, particularly those portions that constituted the high seas. In this way, the extension of American coastal state rights over the natural resources of its continental shelves did not seek to enlarge its territory, and therefore did not represent a further encroachment upon the all-important freedom of navigation associated with the high seas.

The *Truman Proclamation* triggered a number of similar claims by other states, although early practice was highly variable in terms of the legal regime claimed for the continental shelf, with some states making claims amounting to full sovereignty.[197] The potential threat to freedom of the high seas led directly to the negotiation of the 1958 *Geneva Convention on the Continental Shelf*,[198] in which the legal regime advocated in the *Truman Proclamation* ultimately prevailed. That model either already reflected, or rapidly became accepted as, customary international law on the topic, and this is still largely the case today.[199] Moreover, the essence of that legal regime has been incorporated into the provisions of *UNCLOS 1982* addressing the continental shelf.[200]

Thus, the essential elements of a coastal state's entitlements to its continental shelf are that:

1) the coastal state has sovereign rights for purposes of exploring and exploiting the natural resources of the continental shelf;[201]

2) such rights arise by operation of law, meaning that they need not be claimed, and therefore may not be the subject of appropriation by other states if the coastal state fails to make a claim or to exploit the resources;[202]

3) the existence of such rights does not otherwise affect the legal status of the waters or the airspace superjacent to the continental shelf, whether as high seas or the EEZ as the case may be;[203] and,

---

197 See Brownlie, above note 16 at 206–7.

198 Above note 104.

199 See, for example, *North Sea Continental Shelf Cases* (*Federal Republic of Germany v. Denmark; Federal Republic of Germany v. The Netherlands*), [1969] I.C.J. Rep. 3 at 39.

200 See *UNCLOS 1982*, above note 17, Articles 76–85.

201 See *GCCS 1958*, above note 104, Article 2(1); *UNCLOS 1982*, above note 17, Article 77(1).

202 See *GCCS 1958*, ibid., Article 2(2), (3); *UNCLOS 1982*, ibid., Articles 77(2) & (3).

203 See *GCCS 1958*, ibid., Article 3; see also *UNCLOS 1982*, ibid., Article 78(1). Thus, coastal states must enjoy their continental shelf rights with due regard for the

4) the natural resources over which the coastal state enjoys sovereign rights include all mineral and other non-living resources of the seabed or subsoil, as well as any sedentary living resources living on the seabed or in the subsoil.[204]

While very broadly cast, the continental shelf regime, in its most economically significant manifestation, grants coastal states the exclusive right to explore for and exploit oil and natural gas deposits lying in the subsoil of their continental shelves, but not to expand their territory so as to encompass such deposits.

There is less consistency, however, with respect to the permissible seaward extent of the coastal state's continental shelf. It is generally agreed that the inner limit of the continental shelf coincides with the outer limit of the territorial sea.[205] However, the GCCS 1958 defines the outer limit of the continental shelf by reference to a dual "depth-exploitability" criterion.[206] In particular, the continental shelf is said to extend to the point where it reaches a depth of 200 metres or the point at which the depth of the shelf permits exploitation of its resources. The difficulty with such a definition is that, while it may have posed little concern at the time of its adoption, given prevailing technological and economic constraints on deep-sea exploration and exploitation, it establishes no fixed, outer limit to the continental shelf as ever deeper exploration and exploitation become viable. Some authors have argued, based on the *travaux préparatoires* leading to the final text of the *GCCS 1958*, that the underlying intent was always to limit the legal definition of the continental shelf to, at most, its outward geological limit.[207] That interpretation has the advantage that it corresponds with the preponderance of state practice, in which continental shelf claims do not in general exceed the geological limits of the actual shelf.[208]

For greater certainty and consistency, however, in *UNCLOS 1982* states agreed to a new method for determining the extent of the continental shelf, one that depends in part on distance from the coastal state's baselines and in part on the geological nature of the continental shelf as a seaward extension of the continental land mass, rather than on the depth of the shelf or its exploitability. Thus, *UNCLOS 1982* defines the

---

competing rights of other states to use the superjacent waters for navigation or (in the absence of an exclusive fisheries zone or an EEZ) fishing activities: see *GCCS 1958, ibid.*, Article 5; see also *UNCLOS 1982, ibid.*, Article 78(2).

204 See *GCCS 1958, ibid.*, Article 2(4); see also *UNCLOS 1982, ibid.*, Article 77(4).
205 See *GCCS 1958, ibid.*, Article 1; see also *UNCLOS 1982, ibid.*, Article 76(1).
206 See *GCCS 1958, ibid.*, Article 1.
207 See, for example, Brownlie, above note 16 at 211.
208 See, for example, *North Sea Continental Shelf Cases*, above note 199.

continental shelf as the natural prolongation of the coastal state's land territory to a distance of at least 200 nautical miles from the coastal state's baselines.[209] This is so even if the geological continental shelf does not extend to such a distance. Broader continental shelves may be claimed by coastal states if the geological shelf extends beyond the 200-nautical-mile limit. Whether it does depends on a number of complex criteria specified in the convention.[210] However, there is a general maximum limit on such extended continental shelf claims of 350 nautical miles from the coastal state's baselines, or 100 nautical miles from the 2,500 metre isobath, whichever is further.[211] In order to prevent abuse, continental shelf claims extending beyond 200 nautical miles are subject to final and binding review by a Commission on the Limits of the Continental Shelf, established under Annex II to *UNCLOS 1982*.[212] Further, revenues derived from exploitation of non-living resources of the continental shelf beyond 200 nautical miles are subject to a sharing regime in accordance with a similar regime established under *UNCLOS 1982* with respect to the deep seabed.[213]

The rapid adoption in state practice of this alternative method of delineating the outer reaches of the continental shelf after the conclusion of *UNCLOS 1982* led to early recognition by the International Court of Justice of its customary status.[214] It is likely that, with the wide

---

209 See *UNCLOS 1982*, above note 17, Article 76(1).

210 See *ibid.*, Article 76(4). It has been estimated that up to fifty-four states may be able to claim continental shelves extending beyond 200 nautical miles: see P. Cook & C. Carleton, *Continental Shelf Limits: The Scientific and Legal Interface* (Oxford: Oxford University Press, 2000) at 3.

211 See *UNCLOS 1982*, *ibid.*, Article 76(5). An isobath is a contour line of constant depth on the seabed.

212 See *ibid.*, Article 76(8). At the time of writing, Canada is in the process of preparing its application to the Commission, claiming extended continental shelves—amounting to an area of some 1,750,000 square kilometres—off its Atlantic and Arctic coasts: see Government of Canada News Release, "Canada's New Government Moves Forward to Establish Limits of Our Continental Shelf" (20 July 2006), online: www.dfo-mpo.gc.ca/media/newsrel/2006/hq-ac26_e.htm. Meanwhile, on 2 August 2007, a Russian submersible deposited a capsule containing a Russian flag on the seabed near the North Pole, symbolically reasserting its claim to an extensive Arctic continental shelf notwithstanding earlier rejection of such a claim by the Commission: see CBC News Online, "Russia Plants Flag Staking Claim to Arctic Region" (2 August 2007), online: www.cbc.ca/world/story/2007/08/02/russia-arctic.html.

213 See *UNCLOS 1982*, *ibid.*, Article 82; and see further Section C(2)(h), below in this chapter.

214 See *Libya v. Malta*, above note 195 at paras. 34 and 39.

ratification and consequent coming into force of *UNCLOS 1982*, that customary status is now beyond doubt.

g) The High Seas

Beyond the territorial sea or, where applicable, the EEZ, lies the *res communis* of the high seas, not subject to appropriation by any state,[215] but open to use and exploitation by all. The wide ranging freedoms enjoyed by all states on the high seas are deeply entrenched in customary international law and are largely the result of the influence of the great maritime powers whose interests, military and economic, are best served by such a liberal regime. More recently, these broad freedoms have been given concrete expression in the *GCHS 1958*[216] *and UNCLOS 1982*,[217] and include:

1) freedom of navigation;
2) freedom of overflight;
3) freedom to lay submarine cables and pipelines;
4) freedom to construct artificial islands and other installations;
5) freedom of fishing; and
6) freedom of scientific research.

This list is not comprehensive but illustrative of the basic principle that all states, whether coastal or non-coastal,[218] are entitled to make use of the high seas for their own purposes. Given that they are to be enjoyed by all states, these freedoms are of course subject to the general limitation that the enjoyment of such rights and freedoms should not unreasonably interfere with similar enjoyment by other states.[219] They are further subject to any particularized rights enjoyed by coastal states in their respective contiguous fisheries or exclusive economic zones,[220] or in their continental shelf. In addition to the sea surface, the high seas

---

215 See *UNCLOS 1982*, above note 17, Article 89.
216 See *GCHS 1958*, above note 105, Article 2.
217 See *UNCLOS 1982*, above note 17, Article 87.
218 See *GCHS 1958*, above note 105, Articles 2 & 3; *UNCLOS 1982*, ibid., Article 87(2).
219 See *GCHS 1958*, ibid., Article 2; *UNCLOS 1982*, ibid., Article 87(2). This general obligation is given further substance in *UNCLOS 1982* in the form of certain obligations relating to the conservation of high seas fisheries (Articles 116-20) and environmental protection more generally (Part XII). Practically speaking, however, enforcement of such limits on abuse of the high seas has proven highly problematic, and states have had largely to resort to various multilateral treaty regimes to attempt to control such activities as ocean dumping, whaling, nuclear testing, over-fishing, and so on.
220 Although the high seas are technically defined, in *UNCLOS 1982*, as excluding the exclusive economic zone: see above note 189 and accompanying text.

are traditionally conceived of as encompassing the air column above the surface as well as the water column, seabed, and subsoil below it. However, *UNCLOS 1982* has established a particular regime in respect of the deep seabed that places further constraints on the traditional freedoms enjoyed by states with respect to that component of the high seas.[221]

The principal difficulty with asserting such a liberal regime is the maintenance of order on the high seas. In other words, mechanisms are required to ensure that the concept of freedom of the high seas does not lead to a state of lawlessness. This is achieved in international law through the imposition of a general state obligation to maintain certain standards of law and order on the high seas. Aside from imposing a direct duty on states to respect such standards, this also requires states to cooperate in enforcing respect for such standards by non-state actors.

Practically, this is accomplished by requiring that all vessels on the high seas have a "nationality." Ships are deemed, in international law, to have the nationality of the state whose flag they fly or of the state in which they are registered.[222] States are free to fix the conditions under which they will grant their nationality to ships, although there is a general requirement, as with nationality more generally, of a genuine link between the state and the ship.[223] The "flag state" then bears responsibility for ensuring that ships sailing under its flag, and persons aboard such vessels, respect the general laws of the sea. For such purposes, the flag state is clothed with criminal and civil jurisdiction over ships flying its flag while on the high seas.[224]

Moreover, in order to prevent jurisdictional conflicts between states, the enforcement jurisdiction of the flag state is generally considered exclusive. This means that only the flag state may exercise its enforcement jurisdiction over a vessel and persons aboard it while on the high seas. This rule is particularly rigid in the case of warships and other non-commercial government vessels, which enjoy absolute immunity from interference by foreign vessels while on the high seas.[225]

---

221 See further Section C(2)(h), below in this chapter.

222 See *GCHS 1958*, above note 105, Article 5, *UNCLOS 1982*, above note 17, Article 91.

223 *UNCLOS 1982*, ibid., Article 91(1). See also *Convention on Conditions for the Registration of Ships*, 7 February 1986, U.N. Doc. TD/RS/CONF/19/Add.1 (not yet in force); *M/V Saiga (No. 2) (Saint Vincent and the Grenadines v. Guinea) (Admissibility and Merits)*, (1999) 120 I.L.R. 143 at 175–79 (I.T.L.O.S.).

224 See *GCHS 1958*, above note 105, Articles 10–13 and 27–28; *UNCLOS 1982*, above note 17, Articles 94, 97, 99, 108–9, and 113–14.

225 See *GCHS 1958*, ibid., Articles 8–9; *UNCLOS 1982*, ibid., Articles 95–96.

However, in the case of merchant vessels, the general rule of exclusive flag-state jurisdiction is subject to exceptions, particularly where the vessel is suspected of piracy, in which case the vessel or persons aboard it are liable to seizure or arrest by government vessels of any state.[226] The government vessels of any state also have a right to approach foreign vessels on the high seas for purposes of verifying their nationality, and may also board them on grounds of suspicion of piracy, slave trading,[227] illicit broadcasting,[228] or statelessness.[229] In addition, the government vessels of a coastal state have a limited right to board, arrest, or seize a foreign vessel on the high seas following continuous "hot pursuit" of that vessel, undertaken within one of the coastal state's coastal zones in respect of a violation of the coastal state's laws.[230] Stateless vessels found on the high seas—that is, vessels not sailing under the flag of a state which has duly authorized the use of its flag, not registered in any state, or sailing under the flags of more than one state[231]—are essentially without protection from boarding or seizure by the vessels of any state.[232]

h) The Deep Seabed
In principle, and as a matter of well-established customary international law, the regime of the high seas—that of a *res communis* with broad concomitant freedoms of individual use and exploitation by all states—extends to the seabed and subsoil below the waters of the high seas. In the 1960s, however, that well-established rule was put under strain with the discovery of large deposits of rare metals such as manganese, nickel, copper, and cobalt on the deep seabed. Such deposits, largely concentrated on the ocean floors of the Pacific and Indian Oceans, frequently take the form of polymetallic nodules, raising the prospect of their eventual exploitation through deep seabed mining. In the years following these discoveries, it appeared that a number of interests considered the exploitation of such deposits potentially viable. For the most part, however, the necessary technology for such exploita-

---

226 See *GCHS 1958, ibid.*, Articles 14–21; *UNCLOS 1982, ibid.*, Articles 101–7.

227 See *GCHS 1958, ibid.*, Articles 13 and 22; *UNCLOS 1982, ibid.*, Articles 99 and 110.

228 See *UNCLOS 1982, ibid.*, Article 109.

229 See *GCHS 1958*, above note 105, Article 22; *UNCLOS 1982, ibid.*, Article 110.

230 See *GCHS 1958, ibid.*, Article 23; *UNCLOS 1982, ibid.*, Article 111. The right is limited in that it does not permit the coastal state to sink or destroy the foreign vessel if apprehension proves impossible: see *SS "I'm Alone"* (1933), 3 R.I.A.A. 1609, 29 A.J.I.L. 326.

231 See *GCHS 1958, ibid.*, Article 6; *UNCLOS 1982, ibid.*, Article 92.

232 See, generally, Brownlie, above note 16 at 237; Shaw, above note 2 at 547.

tion was and continues to be concentrated in the hands of developed states or of private actors within them.

These developments prompted calls, mainly, but not exclusively, from developing and newly independent states for the establishment of a legal regime that would forestall the unilateral exploitation of these resources, and the wealth they potentially represent, by technologically advanced states. Under the high seas regime, such unilateral exploitation would be perfectly legal. However, the plight of developing states and the search for means of reducing the gap between the developed and the developing world placed the preservation of the riches of the deep seabed firmly on the international legal agenda.

In 1969, the General Assembly adopted a resolution calling for a moratorium on exploitation of the resources of the deep seabed until a new legal regime applicable to such exploitation could be established.[233] Although the resolution was not widely supported by developed states,[234] a subsequent General Assembly resolution containing a declaration of principles applicable to the deep seabed was adopted without dissent.[235] That resolution declared the resources of the deep seabed and subsoil, beyond the limits of state territory, to be the "common heritage of mankind." The declaration contained little more by way of detail other than a general indication that exploitation of the resources of the deep seabed was to be "carried out for the benefit of mankind as a whole," in accordance with a legal regime to be established.

The elaboration of such a legal regime was taken up in the course of the negotiations leading to *UNCLOS 1982*, resulting in the adoption of Part XI of that convention governing activities in the "Area."[236] Part XI confirms that the Area and its resources are the "common heritage

---

233 *Question of the Reservation Exclusively for Peaceful Purposes of the Sea-bed and the Ocean Floor, and the Subsoil Thereof, Underlying the High Seas beyond the Limits of Present National Jurisdiction, and the use of their Resources in the Interest of Mankind*, GA Res. 2574 (XXIV), UN GAOR, 24th Sess., Supp. No. 30, UN Doc. A/ 7630 (1969).

234 See, for example, the "Statement" by J.R. Stevenson, Legal Advisor to the United States Department of State, reported at (1970) 9 I.L.M. 831. States voting against the resolution were: Australia, Austria, Belgium, Bulgaria, Byelorussia, Canada, Czechoslovakia, Denmark, France, Ghana, Hungary, Iceland, Ireland, Italy, Japan, Luxembourg, Malta, Mongolia, Netherlands, New Zealand, Norway, Poland, Portugal, South Africa, Ukraine, USSR, United Kingdom, and the United States of America.

235 *Declaration of Principles Governing the Sea-Bed and the Ocean Floor, and the Subsoil Thereof, beyond the Limits of National Jurisdiction*, GA Res. 2749 (XXV), UN GAOR, 25th Sess., Supp. No. 28, UN Doc. A/8028 (1970).

236 The "Area" is defined in Article 1 of *UNCLOS 1982*, above note 17, as "the sea-bed and ocean floor and subsoil thereof, beyond the limits of national jurisdiction."

of mankind."[237] Essentially this entails the establishment of an institutional framework,[238] the organs of which are to enjoy the exclusive right to regulate and carry out exploitation of the resources of the Area. The proceeds of such exploitation are, after the institutional and financial requirements for administration of the regime are provided for, to be distributed equitably among all states, with some preference given to developing states and to states contributing directly to the costs and technological requirements of exploitation.[239] As a corollary, states are forbidden from engaging in unilateral exploitation of the resources of the Area.[240]

In other words, Part XI of *UNCLOS 1982* contemplates an internationalized regime for the deep seabed, under the rubric of the "common heritage of mankind," that departs quite radically from the customary high seas regime otherwise applicable. However, the application of that regime is limited to activities related to the Area's economic resources, leaving intact any remaining elements of the high seas regime otherwise applicable to the Area.[241]

Nevertheless, these provisions proved highly controversial and were the main reason for which *UNCLOS 1982* failed for many years to attract a sufficient number of ratifications, particularly by developed states, to be brought into force. This period was characterized by an ongoing debate between developing states on the one hand and developed states on the other. The former asserted that the common heritage concept, as it applied to the deep seabed, had acquired the status of customary international law and was binding upon developed states regardless of their ratification or the coming into force of *UNCLOS 1982*. Developed states generally rejected such claims, and some went so far as to sanction or establish various schemes with a view to further exploring the economic viability of unilateral exploitation of the resources of the Area.[242]

---

237 See *UNCLOS 1982*, ibid., Article 136.
238 The principal organ of which is the International Seabed Authority, an intergovernmental organization established pursuant to *UNCLOS 1982*, ibid., Articles 156–91.
239 *Ibid.*, Article 140.
240 *Ibid.*, Article 137.
241 *Ibid.*, Article 135.
242 See, for example, the *US Deep Seabed Hard Mineral Resources Act*, 30 U.S.C., §§ 1401–3, 1411–28, 1441–44, 1461–71, reported at (1980) 19 I.L.M. 1003; and the UK *Deep Sea Mining (Temporary Provisions) Act*, 1981, c. 53. France, the Federal Republic of Germany, Italy, and Japan established similar schemes. See also "Claim of Exclusive Mining Rights by Deepsea Ventures Inc." reproduced in (1975) 14 I.L.M. 51.

Ultimately, diplomatic intervention by the Secretary General of the United Nations resulted in resolution of the impasse through the negotiation, in 1994, of a protocol to *UNCLOS 1982* relating to the implementation of Part XI.[243] Essentially, that protocol sought to address several of the key concerns of developed states while preserving the core of the common heritage concept as it would apply to the Area. In particular, the *UNCLOS Part XI Agreement*:

1) provides for a reduced bureaucracy to oversee activities in the Area;
2) minimizes the direct participation of the International Seabed Authority in the actual exploration and exploitation of deep seabed resources, requiring instead that such activities be contracted out to joint ventures and private sector actors;
3) subjects, by various means, the activities in the Area to market disciplines; and,
4) greatly reduces the technology transfer obligations originally imposed by Part XI on developed states in favour of developing states.

In short, therefore, the exploration and exploitation scheme foreseen in Part XI is largely commercialized by virtue of the *UNCLOS Part XI Agreement*. However, the essence of the common heritage concept remains untouched, meaning that states parties may not unilaterally exploit the resources of the Area, and that the proceeds of any exploitation conducted under the provisions of Part XI, as amended by the *UNCLOS Part XI Agreement*, are to be equitably shared by all states.

Many states adopted and subsequently ratified the *UNCLOS Part XI Agreement*, which in turn paved the way for dramatically increased ratification and the coming into force of *UNCLOS 1982* in 1994.[244] The International Seabed Authority has therefore been established and has undertaken various preparatory and licensing activities necessary for the eventual exploitation of the resources of the Area.[245] As such activities unfold, as the number of ratifications of *UNCLOS 1982* continues to grow, and as states align their practices with the obligations of Part XI and the *UNCLOS Part XI Agreement*, it is probable that the traditional customary regime applicable to the deep seabed will evolve along the lines of the regime established in Part XI and the *UNCLOS Part XI*

---

243 *Agreement Relating to the Implementation of Part XI of the United Nations Convention on the Law of the Sea of 10 December 1982*, 28 July 1994, UN Doc. A/ RES.48/263 (entered into force definitively 28 July 1996) [*UNCLOS Part XI Agreement*].
244 The *UNCLOS Part XI Agreement* has, at the time of writing, 131 parties.
245 See *Report of the Secretary-General of the International Seabed Authority under Article 166, Paragraph 4, of the United Nations Convention on the Law of the Sea*, ISBA OR, 13th Sess., Doc. ISBA/13/A/2 (2007).

Agreement.[246] However, the United States in particular has failed either to sign or ratify *UNCLOS 1982*, thereby apparently reserving its position with respect to the status of the deep seabed. While such resistance may not have the effect of forestalling the development of general customary international law in this area, it may nevertheless be the basis for a claim of persistent objection, thus potentially exempting a very important economic actor from the internationalized regime that appears to be emerging with respect to the deep seabed.[247]

D. POLAR REGIONS

1) Introduction

There is no reason, in principle, why general rules of international law defining the relationships between states and territory or maritime areas should not apply equally in polar regions, and indeed they largely do.[248] However, certain peculiarities of these regions have given rise to particularized regimes that must be reconciled with general rules. These peculiarities flow in large part from the generally inhospitable climate of polar regions, which results in sparse human habitation or other occupation, only sporadic economic or other human activity, and the presence of unique geographical features such as permanent or semi-permanent ice formations.

Moreover, while the climate is severe in both the Arctic and Antarctic, there are many differences between the two polar regions. The most significant of these, for purposes of evaluating potential state claims of sovereignty or jurisdiction in these areas, are that (1) the Arctic is essentially an ocean covered by a permanent ice-cap, whereas Antarctica is a continental land mass, albeit also under a permanent ice-cap; and (2) the Arctic is ringed by (and in many areas extends onto) contiguous land masses clearly coming under the sovereignty of a limited number of circumpolar states, whereas Antarctica is surrounded by high seas and has only relatively remote territorial neighbours. These essential differences have translated into distinct legal regimes for each polar region.[249]

---

246 See Churchill & Lowe, above note 166 at 226–28.
247 See Brownlie, above note 16 at 244.
248 *Ibid.* at 143.
249 See, generally, D. Pharand, "The Legal Status of the Arctic Regions" (1979-II) 163 Rec. des Cours 49.

2) The Arctic

In the case of the Arctic, the relative scarcity of human activity raises the issue of the appropriate basis upon which states may make claims of sovereignty, while its peculiar geography raises the question of which of its geographical features are susceptible to any such claims at all.

On the first of these questions, some states and authors have advanced the so-called "sector theory" as a basis for claiming sovereignty over Arctic regions.[250] The sector theory would in essence operate in favour of states having land territory falling within, or at least along the outer perimeter of, the Arctic.[251] Application of the theory generally involves drawing longitudinal lines northward, from the western- and eastern-most points of such territory, to the pole. The effect is to enclose a sector, or pie-shaped wedge, of the Arctic, which is then used as a basis for asserting sovereignty over various geographical features falling within that sector. For example, Canada's application of the sector theory could result in a claim over all northward territory within the sector bounded by lines of longitude running through the western- and eastern-most points (approximately 141°W and 60°W respectively) of Canada's territory lying along the Arctic Circle.

State practice has remained ambivalent with respect to the validity of the sector theory as a basis for claiming title over territory, however. The former Soviet Union made it the explicit basis of its claim over the Arctic regions to its north as early as 1926.[252] By contrast, Canada has not explicitly or formally invoked the sector theory as such, but has asserted claims over the Arctic regions to its north that are consistent with it. Indeed, a Canadian senator is credited with the first articulation of the Arctic sector theory during parliamentary debates in 1907, and Canadian politicians have from time to time referred to it in advan-

---

250 See a review of such claims in the Canadian context by McRae, above note 154 at 2–3.

251 The Arctic can be defined in a number of ways, including all areas north of the Arctic Circle, the tree line, or the 10°C surface air isotherm for July, the warmest month of the year: see Pharand, above note 249 at 59. See also I.L. Head, "Canadian Claims to Territorial Sovereignty in the Arctic Regions" (1963) 9 McGill L.J. 200 at 202–3. The Arctic Circle corresponds roughly to latitude 66°30' N (marking the latitude above which the sun either does not rise or set for at least one day each year, due to the Earth's inclination): see Encyclopaedia Britannica, "Arctic Circle," online: www.britannica.com.

252 Decree of the Presidium of the Central Executive Committee of the Union of Soviet Socialist Republics, "Territorial Rights of the Soviet Union in the Arctic," 15 April 1926, (1926) 124 State Papers, Part II, 1064–65.

cing arguments concerning Canada's foreign policy over the Arctic.[253] In general, however, Canada has preferred to rely primarily on historic title and effective occupation of the territory to its north as the mainstay of its claim to sovereignty in the Arctic.[254]

Other states eligible to apply the sector theory, such as the United States, Denmark, and Norway, have avoided doing so but have also not expressly challenged its validity or Russia's explicit and Canada's implicit reliance upon it. This leaves its customary status as an effective basis of title somewhat unclear. The notional underpinning of the sector theory is clearly the presumed geographical relationship of contiguity between the claiming state and the sector in question, assuming of course there is no intervening foreign state territory interrupting such a claim of contiguity.[255] However, as we have seen, contiguity is not generally considered a sufficient basis of title over territory in itself, but rather acts as a starting presumption in the light of which other considerations, such as effective occupation, are evaluated. As such, it is unlikely to form a sufficient basis of title in the absence of any supporting exercises of state activity or jurisdiction in or over the relevant sector. This will especially be so in the face of any competing, on-the-ground activity in the same sector by other states. Conversely, recognition of or acquiescence in a state's claim over a particular Arctic sector can act to consolidate title quite independently of any legal effects flowing from the sector theory itself.[256]

While these factors tend to undermine the customary status of the sector theory as a free-standing basis of title in Arctic regions, the ambivalence of state practice and *opinio juris* in this area can likely also be traced to the highly variable types of claims the theory has been used to support. For example, early Soviet claims based on the sector theory extended to all land, ice, and waters in the sector between their territory and the Pole. This extreme position is no longer viable (or asserted) given developments in the law of the sea and the realization that the Arctic ice cap is simply a frozen area of the high seas.[257] As such, claims of sovereignty in the Arctic, whether or not based on the sector theory, are principally confined to land territory (including islands),

---

253 See Head, above note 251 at 202–5, 206–10; McRae, above note 154 at 2–3.
254 See, generally, McRae, *ibid.*
255 See Head, above note 251 at 205.
256 See Brownlie, above note 16 at 143–44.
257 However, note that on 2 August 2007, a Russian submersible deposited a capsule containing a Russian flag on the seabed at the North Pole, symbolically asserting a claim to an extensive Arctic continental shelf reaching that far: see "Russia Plants Flag Staking Claim to Arctic Region," above note 212.

internal waters, and the territorial sea. In keeping with generally applicable rules relating to the extent of coastal state sovereignty, such claims are relatively uncontroversial.[258] The usual law of the sea rules relating to maritime zones then apply with respect to the definition of limited, functional jurisdiction over adjacent maritime areas. Remaining unresolved issues include the status of ice shelves, which might be treated as extending the land mass (and hence baselines) seaward, and floating ice islands.[259]

Canada's claims in the Arctic were consolidated in 1986 with the promulgation of a system of straight baselines enclosing its Arctic archipelago, a move that has been controversial as it treats the waters between the islands of the archipelago as part of Canada's internal waters, and therefore subject to its full sovereignty.[260] The United States in particular has been critical of this stance on the basis of its own assertion that the Northwest Passage, which traverses the archipelago, is an international strait and hence subject to a right of transit passage. Indeed the promulgation of the internal waters regime by Canada was in response to repeated transiting of the Northwest Passage by American vessels, notwithstanding Canadian protests. The regime of archipelagic waters set out in *UNCLOS 1982* does not resolve the issue, as it concerns only states composed entirely of islands or archipelagos, and thus the dispute remains outstanding.[261] However, Canada, while maintaining its position, has since concluded (in 1988) an agreement with the United States on cooperation in the Arctic.[262] In that agreement, the United States agrees, albeit without prejudice to its legal position, to obtain Canada's consent prior to transiting the Northwest Passage.[263]

---

258 For a review of state practice in the Arctic, see Pharand, above note 249 at 62–66.

259 See D. Pharand, "The Legal Regime of the Arctic: Some Outstanding Issues" (1984) 39 Int'l. J. 742.

260 *Territorial Sea Geographical Co-ordinates (Area 7) Order*, S.O.R./85-872 (1986), promulgated pursuant to the *Territorial Sea and Fishing Zones Act*, R.S.C. 1985, c. T-8, s. 5(1), since superseded by the *Oceans Act*, above note 122.

261 See *UNCLOS 1982*, above note 17, Articles 46–54.

262 *Agreement on Arctic Cooperation*, United States and Canada, 31 January 1988, (1989) 28 I.L.M. 142 (entered into force 11 January 1988). For commentary, see M. Leir, "Canadian Practice in International Law at the Department of Foreign Affairs in 2000-2001: Canada's Sovereignty in Changing Arctic Waters" (2001) 39 Can. Y.B. Int'l L. 485 at 487–89.

263 For an overview of the dispute between Canada and the United States over the status of the Northwest Passage and the waters of the Arctic archipelago, see H.S. Fairley & J.H. Currie, "Projecting Beyond the Boundaries: A Canadian Perspective on the Double-Edged Sword of Extraterritorial Acts" in M.K. Young & Y. Iwasawa, eds., *Trilateral Perspectives on International Legal Issues: Relevance*

3) The Antarctic

As suggested above, the evolution of the legal regime of the Antarctic has differed from that of the Arctic, due principally to its divergent geographical realities. In particular, most of the Antarctic ice cap sits above a continental land mass.[264] *A priori,* therefore, until subjected to legally effective claims of sovereignty or some other legal regime, Antarctica constitutes a *res nullius* subject to appropriation by states, rather than, as in the case of much of the Arctic, the *res communis* of the high seas.

In fact, several states have asserted various sector-like claims to the Antarctic land mass. Argentina, Australia, Chile, France, New Zealand, Norway, and the United Kingdom have all made claims to various pie-shaped slices of Antarctica, in some cases overlapping.[265] These claims are asserted on a variety of legal bases, including extended applications of the principles of contiguity and effective occupation. However, several states which have not yet asserted claims, including Japan, Russia, and the United States, have rejected the validity of existing claims, thus preserving their legal positions with respect to potential claims of their own in the future. No claim has yet been made in respect of a sizeable sector covering Marie Byrd Land, which therefore clearly remains a *res nullius.*

The potential for acrimonious territorial disputes in the Antarctic was forestalled early on, however, by the conclusion of the *Antarctic Treaty* of 1959.[266] The overall purpose of the treaty was to place all outstanding territorial claims in abeyance in order to permit a cooperative international approach to carrying out scientific research and conservation of the Antarctic environment. To that end the treaty reserves all areas south of the 60th parallel[267] for peaceful, scientific research purposes and thereby establishes the only demilitarized zone on Earth.[268] From an initial twelve signatories in 1959, membership in the treaty

---

of Domestic Law and Policy (Irvington, NY: Transnational Publishers, 1996) 119 at 135–40.

264 See Pharand (1979), above note 249 at 114.

265 The United Kingdom claim overlaps with both those of Argentina and Chile, which in turn overlap with one another: see Kindred & Saunders *et al.,* above note 47 at 464.

266 *The Antarctic Treaty,* 1 December 1959, reproduced in (1960) 54 A.J.I.L. 476 (entered into force 23 June 1961).

267 *Ibid.,* Article VI. The defined area includes all ice shelves, but leaves intact the legal status of, and hence the rights and obligations of states with respect to, the high seas south of the 60th parallel.

268 *Ibid.,* Article I.

has grown to include forty-six states, all of which are thereby entitled to participate in peaceful research and conservation activities. Subject to review after thirty years, the treaty was affirmed unchanged by the parties in 1991.[269] It has further been supplemented by a number of corollary agreements, mainly of an environmental character, including the *Convention for the Conservation of Antarctic Seals*,[270] the *Convention on the Conservation of Antarctic Marine Living Resources*,[271] and the *Protocol on Environmental Protection to the Antarctic Treaty* (with six Annexes).[272]

While the treaty of course only creates binding legal obligations for the parties to it, in fact it appears that non-parties have acquiesced in its terms such that it in effect defines a unique and broadly recognized international legal regime for the Antarctic.[273] While the possibility of adapting that regime to mesh with the common heritage of humankind concept has occasionally been debated,[274] that is not currently the basis of the treaty. Rather, the treaty appears to preserve the *res nullius* character of the continent.[275] It is important to note, moreover, that the treaty does not set aside various state claims to sovereignty in the Antarctic. Rather, it merely places them in abeyance and forbids the assertion of new claims while the treaty remains in force. It therefore acts as a general reservation of rights in favour of all parties subscribing to

---

269 See "Declaration by Contracting Parties in the Thirtieth Anniversary Year of the Entry into Force of the Antarctic Treaty" in *Final Report of the Sixteenth Antarctic Treaty Consultative Meeting*, Bonn, 7–18 October 1991, Part III, at 133–39.

270 *Convention for the Conservation of Antarctic Seals*, 1 June 1972, reproduced in (1972) 11 I.L.M. 251 (entered into force 11 March 1978).

271 *Convention on the Conservation of Antarctic Marine Living Resources*, 20 May 1980, reproduced in (1980) 19 I.L.M. 837 (entered into force 7 April 1982).

272 *Protocol on Environmental Protection to the Antarctic Treaty*, 4 October 1991, reproduced in (1991) 30 I.L.M. 1455 (entered into force 14 January 1998) [*Madrid Protocol*]. The six Annexes relate to environmental impact assessment (Annex I), conservation of Antarctic fauna and flora (Annex II), waste disposal and waste management (Annex III), prevention of marine pollution (Annex IV), management of protected areas (Annex V), and liability for environmental emergencies (Annex VI). All can be viewed online: www.ats.aq/. The *Madrid Protocol* essentially marks abandonment of the earlier *Convention on the Regulation of Antarctic Mineral Resource Activities*, 2 June 1988, reproduced in (1988) 27 I.L.M. 860 (not in force).

273 See Brownlie, above note 16 at 254–55; Shaw, above note 2 at 457. See also D.R. Rothwell, *The Polar Regions and the Development of International Law* (Cambridge: Cambridge University Press, 1996) at 154.

274 See, for example, D. Pharand, "L'Arctique et l'Antarctique: patrimoine commun de l'humanité?" (1982) 7 Ann. Air & Sp. L. 415.

275 See Brownlie, above note 16 at 255.

its terms. It remains to be seen whether the unique, cooperative regime established by the treaty can survive, and for how long, if and when economically exploitable resources are discovered in the area.

E. OUTER SPACE AND CELESTIAL BODIES

1) Early Developments

So far we have considered the various legal regimes—whether in the nature of sovereignty or more limited, functional jurisdiction—that have emerged in international law to govern the relationships between states and the various elements of our planet. With the advent of space exploration in the 1950s, however, came the inevitable questions of the legal status of outer space and the various celestial bodies that make up our solar system, and the legal regime (if any) that should apply to such hitherto unexplored "territory."

A logically prior issue, however, was whether international law, originally conceived as a system of law regulating relations between (obviously earthbound) states, had any application at all in outer space and therefore whether it was amenable to settling these questions. As there is no logical reason for restricting the reach of international law to the Earth, and given that space exploration has been primarily a state-sponsored activity, it is not particularly surprising that the UN General Assembly took the view, at a very early stage, that "[i]nternational law, including the *Charter of the United Nations*, applies to outer space and celestial bodies."[276]

The General Assembly had already, in 1959, established the Committee on the Peaceful Uses of Outer Space (COPUOS) with the mandate of "review[ing], as appropriate, the area of international co-operation and study[ing] practical and feasible means for giving effect to programmes in the peaceful uses of outer space which would appropriately be undertaken under United Nations auspices."[277] There was an element of urgency to these and subsequent developments given that the "space race," a new phase of the Cold War, was already well underway between the Soviet Union and the United States. It was also clear that these and other states would soon develop the means at least to visit nearby celestial bodies. If international law did indeed apply to such

---

276 *International Co-operation in the Peaceful Uses of Outer Space*, GA Res. 1721 (XVI), UN GAOR, 16th Sess., Supp. No. 17, UN Doc. A/5100 (1961).
277 COPUOS has both a legal as well as a scientific and technical subcommittee.

bodies, this raised the spectre that they were susceptible to claims of territorial appropriation by states on the basis that each such body constituted a *res nullius*.[278]

In order to forestall such developments, the General Assembly adopted a further resolution in 1963, setting out a declaration of legal principles applicable to the exploration and use of outer space by states.[279] The key element of the resolution was the principle that neither outer space nor celestial bodies were subject to national appropriation by states. The resolution was adopted unanimously and reflected general acceptance, and hence the early customary status, of this fundamental rule.[280]

2) The Treaty Framework

Through the efforts of COPUOS, relatively rapid progress was made thereafter towards the elaboration of a framework treaty regime that would solidify and expand upon the basic legal principles set out in the 1963 resolution. In 1967, the *Treaty on Principles Governing the Activities of States in the Exploration and Use of Outer Space, Including the Moon and Other Celestial Bodies* (the *Outer Space Treaty*) was concluded and brought into force.[281] At the time of writing the *Outer Space Treaty* has been ratified by ninety-nine states and in any event is now widely considered to be reflective of universally binding customary international law on the topic.[282]

The basic legal regime established by the *Outer Space Treaty* is in part similar to that of a *res communis*, such as the high seas. In particular, Article II confirms the already widely recognized and accepted principle that outer space and celestial bodies are not subject to appropriation by states as part of their territory. This principle is no doubt responsible for the fact that, for example, the Moon and Mars are not part of American, and Venus is not part of Russian, territory, notwithstanding the considerable exploratory activities carried out by each state on each such body respectively.

---

278 See Brownlie, above note 16 at 256, n. 38.
279 *Declaration of Legal Principles Governing the Activities of States in the Exploration and Use of Outer Space*, GA Res. 1962(XVIII), UN GAOR, 18th Sess., Supp. No. 15, UN Doc. A/5515 (1963).
280 See Brownlie, above note 16 at 256.
281 *Treaty on Principles Governing the Activities of States in the Exploration and Use of Outer Space, Including the Moon and Other Celestial Bodies*, 27 January 1967, 610 U.N.T.S. 205 (entered into force 10 October 1967) [*Outer Space Treaty*].
282 See Brownlie, above note 16 at 256; Shaw, above note 2 at 481.

Article III of the *Outer Space Treaty* affirms that, in order to promote international peace and security, states are subject to international law in general, and the *UN Charter* in particular, in carrying out space exploration and other activities. Article IV goes further in this vein, however, by establishing a partial regime of demilitarization in outer space. This is accomplished by banning the placement of nuclear weapons or other weapons of mass destruction in orbit, on celestial bodies, or elsewhere in outer space. However, the deployment of other military hardware, such as spy satellites or other weaponry, is not prohibited. Nevertheless, the Moon and other celestial bodies are reserved for peaceful purposes only, meaning that no military installations, testing, or research are permitted on such bodies. Peaceful research and exploration is, however, permitted and, indeed, encouraged,[283] and states parties agree to disseminate the results of such research and exploration.[284]

Subsequent articles address various matters of practical concern. Article V imposes a general duty of assistance to astronauts of other states parties, an obligation that has been considerably enlarged upon in the subsequent *Rescue Agreement*.[285] Articles VI and VII govern the responsibility of states for national space exploration activities and in particular their liability for damage caused to other states by their space objects, a matter again taken up in greater detail in the subsequent *Liability Convention*.[286] Article VIII establishes the basic jurisdictional regime over objects and persons in outer space or on celestial bodies by requiring that each state maintain a registry of its spacecraft. Jurisdiction is extended to spacecraft and their personnel on the basis of the state of registry of the spacecraft, in a manner analogous to the extension of state jurisdiction over vessels on the high seas on the basis of nationality. This system is further developed, and a central United

---

283 *Outer Space Treaty*, above note 281, Article I.
284 *Ibid.*, Article XI.
285 *Agreement on the Rescue of Astronauts, the Return of Astronauts and the Return of Objects Launched into Outer Space*, 22 April 1968, 672 U.N.T.S. 119 (entered into force 3 December 1968), currently ninety states parties.
286 *Convention on International Liability for Damage Caused by Space Objects*, 29 March 1972, 961 U.N.T.S 187 (entered into force 1 September 1972), currently eighty-six states parties. The *Liability Convention* essentially establishes a regime of absolute liability for such damage, and was the basis for Canada's claim against the Soviet Union for the cleanup costs associated with the re-entry and deposit, on Canadian territory, of fragments of the Soviet Cosmos 954 satellite: see, generally, *Cosmos 954 Claim (Canada v. USSR)*, (1979) 18 I.L.M. 899.

Nations register of space objects is established, in the subsequent *Registration Convention*.[287]

Returning to the overall character of the legal regime established by the *Outer Space Treaty*, Article I, which essentially establishes a system of free and equal access to outer space and celestial bodies by all states for peaceful purposes, uses some puzzling language. In particular, Article I provides that space exploration and use is to be "carried out for the benefit and in the interests of all countries ... and shall be the province of all mankind." This formulation has shades of the common heritage of humankind concept, and might therefore be read as a departure from a pure *res communis* regime in which all states are free to exploit the resources of the common amenity for their own benefit. In other words, some of the language used in Article I suggests that any exploitation of the resources of outer space may have to be carried out for the benefit of all states, much as contemplated by Part XI of *UNCLOS 1982* in respect of the deep seabed, rather than unilaterally. However, Article I goes on to stipulate that outer space and celestial bodies "shall be free for exploration and use by all States," language seeming to affirm the *res communis* character of outer space.

This imprecise language, and the incompatible legal regimes it potentially establishes, in fact masks a long-simmering debate between developed states, which to date have been in the exclusive position to carry out space exploration activities, and developing states, which have not. Demands by the latter for a more robust internationalized regime, at least with respect to the Moon and other celestial bodies within the solar system—the only likely candidates for economic exploitation in the foreseeable future—culminated in the adoption in 1979 by the General Assembly of the "*Moon Treaty*."[288]

Much of the *Moon Treaty* reaffirms the basic legal framework set out in the *Outer Space Treaty*, but its most significant departure is that it purports explicitly to establish the Moon and other celestial bodies of our solar system as the "common heritage of mankind."[289] Essentially this would mean that, not only are such celestial bodies not amenable to national appropriation in the sense of incorporation into national territory, but no property rights may be acquired by states or persons in

---

287 *Convention on Registration of Objects Launched into Outer Space*, 12 November 1974, 1023 U.N.T.S. 15 (entered into force 15 September 1976), currently fifty-one states parties.

288 *Agreement Governing the Activities of States on the Moon and Other Celestial Bodies*, 5 December 1979, 1363 U.N.T.S. 3 (entered into force 11 July 1984), currently thirteen states parties.

289 *Ibid.*, Article 11(1).

their natural resources either.[290] Rather, as with the common heritage concept enshrined in Part XI of *UNCLOS 1982*, any exploitation of natural resources is to be carried out for the equitable benefit of all states, but with special consideration to the economic needs of developing states, pursuant to a regime to be established when such exploitation becomes feasible.[291] To date, this conception of the legal regime applicable to the Moon and other celestial bodies has met with considerable resistance, with the result that the *Moon Treaty*, although in force since 1984, has an extremely small number of parties, virtually none of which engage in space exploration.[292] As such it cannot be considered reflective of customary international law. Indeed, this general reluctance of states to subscribe to the common heritage concept as it would apply to the Moon and other celestial bodies appears to clarify that the regime established in the *Outer Space Treaty*, and therefore in customary international law, is indeed more akin to that of a *res communis* than to the common heritage concept.

3) Other Developments

Whereas the *Outer Space Treaty* and related treaties establish a broad conceptual framework defining the relationship of states to outer space and celestial bodies, that framework remains sparse and many issues relating to the permissible uses of outer space and celestial bodies remain unresolved. In this respect the ongoing activities of COPUOS are important in giving further direction to the development of international law in this area. The work of COPUOS has focused on various uses of outer space such as remote sensing,[293] direct television broadcasting by

---

290 *Ibid.*, Article 11(3).

291 *Ibid.*, Article 11(5), (7).

292 See C.Q. Christol, "Current Developments: The *Moon Treaty* Enters into Force" (1985) 79 A.J.I.L. 163.

293 See the *Draft Principles Relating to Remote Sensing of the Earth from Space,* in *Report of the Committee on the Peaceful Uses of Outer Space,* UN GAOR, 41st Sess., Supp. No. 20, Annex II, UN Doc. A/41/20 (1986). The Draft Principles were subsequently adopted by the UN General Assembly in *Principles Relating to Remote Sensing of the Earth from Outer Space,* GA Res. 41/65, 41st Sess., Supp. No. 53, UN Doc. A/41/53 (1987).

satellites,[294] the allocation of orbital slots for geostationary satellites,[295] the use of nuclear power sources in outer space,[296] and so on.

Other matters requiring further attention include development of the demilitarization regime set out in the *Outer Space Treaty* to address innovations in the technology of warfare; the elaboration of rules, beyond the basic provisions of Article VI of the *Outer Space Treaty*, governing the growth in private sector activity in space; the institution of a system for controlling the hazards posed by ever-increasing volumes of space debris in Earth's orbit; reaching agreement on the upper limits of states' sovereign airspace and, by implication, the lower boundaries of outer space subject to the regime of the *Outer Space Treaty*;[297] increasing opportunities for developing states to participate in such space-based research and exploration activities as the establishment and operation of the International Space Station;[298] and, ultimately, resolution of the stalemate between developed and developing states over the application of the common heritage concept to the Moon and other celestial bodies of our solar system.

In part, the international legal agenda on some of these issues has been advanced by the periodic convening, under UN auspices, of international conferences on the exploration and peaceful uses of out-

---

294 See the *Principles Governing the Use by States of Artificial Earth Satellites for International Direct Television Broadcasting*, GA Res. 37/92, UN GAOR, 37th Sess., Supp. No. 51, UN Doc. A/RES/37/92 (1983).

295 The topic was placed on the COPUOS agenda in December 1977 by resolution of the UN General Assembly, although no concrete resolution of the debate between equatorial and other states on this topic has yet been achieved: *International Co-operation in the Peaceful Uses of Outer Space*, GA Res. 32/196, UN GAOR, 32nd Sess., Supp. No. 45, UN Doc. A/RES/32/196 (1977).

296 See the Committee on the Peaceful Uses of Outer Space, *Principles Relevant to the Use of Nuclear Power Sources in Outer Space*, 31st Sess., UN Doc. A/AC.105/L.198 (1992).

297 The *Outer Space Treaty* does not address this issue, and it has proven sufficiently contentious among states that no clear consensus has yet emerged. See, for example, the latest report by COPUOS to the UN General Assembly on this issue: *Report of the Committee on the Peaceful Uses of Outer Space*, UN GAOR, Sixty-Second Session, U.N. Doc. A/62/20 (2007), c. II.D.3, "Matters relating to the definition and delimitation of outer space and the character and utilization of the geostationary orbit," at paras. 191–200.

298 See the *Agreement Concerning Cooperation on the Civil International Space Station*, 28 January 1998, reproduced as a schedule to the *Canadian Civil International Space Station Agreement Implementation Act*, S.C. 1999, c. 35. The Agreement establishes a cooperative regime between the United States, Russia, Canada, Japan, and the nine member states of the European Space Agency for the construction, operation, and use of the International Space Station.

er space. To date three such conferences have been held.[299] The latest such conference, UNISPACE III, formulated a plan of action aimed at fostering the participation of developing states in space exploration and further exploring legal aspects of space debris, the use of nuclear power sources in space, ownership and access to the resources of celestial bodies, and intellectual property rights for space-related technologies.[300] COPUOS reports annually to the UN General Assembly on implementation of this plan of action.[301] These and other initiatives will be of crucial importance in further refining the international legal regime applicable in this area of constant growth and innovation.

FURTHER READING

BASLAR, K., *The Concept of the Common Heritage of Mankind in International Law* (Boston: Kluwer Law International, 1998)

BÖCKSTIEGEL, K.H. & BENKÖ, M., *Space Law: Basic Legal Documents*, 3 vols. (Boston: Martinus Nijhoff, 1990–)

BROWNLIE, I., *Principles of Public International Law*, 6th ed. (Oxford: Oxford University Press, 2003) cc. 6–12

CASTELLINO, J. & ALLEN, S., *Title to Territory in International Law* (Burlington, VT: Ashgate, 2003)

CHURCHILL, R.R., & LOWE, A.V., *The Law of the Sea*, 3d ed. (Manchester: Manchester University Press, 1999)

COOK, P. & CARLETON, C., *Continental Shelf Limits: The Scientific and Legal Interface* (Oxford: Oxford University Press, 2000)

CRAWFORD, J., *The Creation of States in International Law*, 2d ed. (Oxford: Oxford University Press, 2006)

---

299 Such conferences, dubbed "UNISPACE" conferences, were held in 1968 (UNISPACE I), 1982 (UNISPACE II) and 1999 (UNISPACE III).

300 See the *Vienna Declaration on Space and Human Development*, in the *Report of the Third United Nations Conference on the Exploration and Peaceful Uses of Outer Space, Vienna, 19-30 July 1999*, UN Doc. A/CONF.184/6 (1999).

301 These reports can be found on the website maintained by the United Nations Office for Outer Space Affairs, online: www.unoosa.org/oosa/en/Reports/gadocs/coprepidx.html. See, for example, the latest report available at the time of writing: *Report of the Committee on the Peaceful Uses of Outer Space*, above note 297, c. II.B, "Implementation of the Recommendations of the Third United Nations Conference on the Exploration and Peaceful Uses of Outer Space" at paras. 46–66.

FAWCETT, J.E.S., *Outer Space: New Challenges to Law and Policy* (Oxford: Clarendon Press, 1984)

JENNINGS, R., *The Acquisition of Territory in International Law* (Manchester: Manchester University Press, 1963)

JOHNSTON, D.M., *Canada and the New International Law of the Sea* (Toronto: University of Toronto Press, 1985)

LALONDE, S., *Determining Boundaries in a Conflicted World: The Role of Uti Possidetis* (Montreal: McGill-Queen's University Press, 2002)

MORELL, J.B., *The Law of the Sea: An Historical Analysis of the 1982 Treaty and its Rejection by the United States* (Jefferson, NC: McFarland, 1992)

PHARAND, D., *Canada's Arctic Waters in International Law* (Cambridge: Cambridge University Press, 1988)

REYNOLDS, G.H., & MERGES, R.P., *Outer Space: Problems of Law and Policy* (Boulder, CO: Westview Press, 1989)

ROTHWELL, D.R., *The Polar Regions and the Development of International Law* (Cambridge: Cambridge University Press, 1996)

SAHURIE, E.J., *The International Law of Antarctica* (Boston: Kluwer Law International, 1992)

SHARMA, S.P., *Territorial Acquisition, Disputes and International Law* (Boston: Kluwer Law International, 1997)

CHAPTER 8

STATE JURISDICTION

A. INTRODUCTION

The exercise of jurisdiction over persons, conduct, property, and resources is one of the more important manifestations of a state's sovereignty. Such jurisdiction is commonly exercised through a variety of acts, including those of a legislative, judicial, administrative, executive, and enforcement nature. All such powers are implied in the notion of sovereignty. They are the means by which the state displays and exerts its sovereign will within its own particular sphere of influence or jurisdictional domain.

The difficulty for the international lawyer, here as elsewhere, is that the international community is made up of many sovereign states, each with its own jurisdictional domain and set of jurisdictional competencies. Moreover, as we have seen, each sovereign is under a legal obligation not to interfere in the exercise of another state's sovereignty. Such a system would pose few problems if the world were truly made up of totally insular states between which there were no exchanges whatsoever. However, the institution of the sovereign state has not had this effect and, indeed, international contact and cross-border flows of people, communications, trade, and so on continue to grow at an ever-increasing pace.

The resulting potential for overlap between the interests of different states, and hence for conflict between competing exercises of state jurisdiction, requires that there be rules delineating the permissible jurisdictional reach of each state. In other words, it is necessary to define where one state's legitimate jurisdictional domain leaves off and where that of another state takes effect. To address this need, generally applicable rules governing the allowable bases and extent of state jurisdiction have emerged in customary international law. These have been supplemented either by special treaty or customary regimes providing for particular jurisdictional rules that apply in specific locations or legal contexts, such as jurisdiction on the high seas or aboard air or space craft. Some of these have been reviewed above.[1] The focus of this chapter, however, is on the general rules regulating the nature and extent of the jurisdictional reach of states more broadly.

As we shall see, the customary rules governing jurisdiction do not always provide for absolute and exclusive jurisdictional rights in favour of one state only. Rather, this area of the law proceeds on a relative basis, that is, by contrasting the strength of one state's jurisdictional claim over a given event or person with that of another.[2] The approach is therefore similar to that taken by international law in evaluating any given state's claim of sovereignty over territory: the relative merits of the competing claims govern the outcome in any particular case, rather than any abstract and absolute finding of jurisdiction.

Some texts approach this topic by drawing a distinction between "criminal" jurisdiction on the one hand and "civil" jurisdiction on the other.[3] It is true that jurisdictional conflicts in the criminal context tend both to be more frequent and to provoke stronger reactions from states. This is probably due to a perception by most states that the exercise of penal jurisdiction and the maintenance of a system of public order are intimately connected to the core of the jurisdictional competence implied in state sovereignty. Given the frequency and intensity of disputes in this area, therefore, considerable case law and literature focus on jurisdiction in criminal cases.

However, altogether aside from the practical difficulty of clearly distinguishing between "criminal" and "civil" exercises of jurisdiction,[4]

---

1   See, for example, Chapter 7, Sections C(2)(g) and E(2).

2   See I. Brownlie, *Principles of Public International Law*, 6th ed. (Oxford: Oxford University Press, 2003) at 297–98.

3   See, for example, M.N. Shaw, *International Law*, 5th ed. (Cambridge: Cambridge University Press, 2003) at 578–97; Brownlie, *ibid.* at 298–305; H. Kindred & P. Saunders, eds., *International Law Chiefly as Interpreted and Applied in Canada*, 7th ed. (Toronto: Emond Montgomery, 2006) at 548–50.

4   For example, is a contempt order made in a civil proceeding civil or criminal in nature? And how does one classify various administrative or regulatory proceedings which may affect civil entitlements but may also carry penal or quasi-penal consequences, such as fines?

there is little clear distinction in principle between the jurisdictional rules that apply in either of these or indeed other substantive contexts.[5] This is not to say that the legal systems of individual states treat issues of jurisdictional conflict in the civil and criminal contexts in the same fashion. However, such differences of treatment are a matter of private, not public, international law. The point here is that, from the perspective of public international law, the basic customary rules governing when a state may exercise jurisdiction over any given event or person do not vary significantly according to whether the jurisdiction to be exercised is classified as civil or criminal in nature.[6]

A much more useful distinction, as it reflects a substantial difference of approach in the applicable rules, is that between "prescriptive" and "enforcement" jurisdiction. In essence, prescriptive jurisdiction concerns a state's power to regulate or prescribe conduct, usually through the passage of laws or regulations and the interpretation of such rules by domestic courts or tribunals. It is, in other words, the power to make rules governing people, property, and transactions. By contrast, enforcement jurisdiction concerns the power to take action consequent upon those rules, usually by way of executive or administrative action, and includes all measures of constraint aimed at securing compliance with such rules. It includes, for example, powers of arrest, the service of process, the conduct of investigations, the seizure of evidence, prosecution, and other coercive judicial procedures. For example, if Canada passes a law regulating activities that may cause pollution in the Arctic, that is an exercise of its prescriptive jurisdiction.[7] If Canada chooses to patrol or prevent passage through the Arctic, or to arrest, charge, and prosecute persons or vessels pursuant to the legislation so passed, such acts would be exercises of Canada's enforcement jurisdiction.

Within most domestic legal systems there is a close symmetry between the extent of the state's prescriptive and enforcement jurisdiction. For example, rarely will jurisdiction exist to enact domestic

---

5   See Brownlie, above note 2 at 298 and 308; but see M. Akehurst, "Jurisdiction in International Law" (1972–73) 46 Brit. Y.B. Int'l L. 145 at 177 and Kindred & Saunders, above note 3 at 548–49, suggesting that international law prescribes no limiting jurisdictional rules in the case of civil transactions. The latter position seems difficult to reconcile with state practice related to foreign anti-trust measures (see further Section C(2)(c), below in this chapter), unless one chooses to classify anti-trust legislation as criminal rather than civil in nature.

6   There are, of course, special rules that apply to particular types of transactions, but for present purposes our focus is on generally applicable jurisdictional rules. In any case, such special rules do not generally correspond to any classification based on the civil or criminal designation of the transaction.

7   See the *Arctic Waters Pollution Prevention Act*, R.S.C. 1985, c. A-12.

legislation without the concomitant jurisdiction to enforce that legislation, even though separate governmental organs may exercise distinct jurisdictional competencies. However, as we shall see, no such symmetry exists in international law: the legitimate scope of a state's prescriptive jurisdiction may differ radically from the permissible extent of its enforcement jurisdiction, depending on the circumstances. Given that the permissible reach of enforcement jurisdiction is more restricted and easier to state, we will begin with an examination of those rules before turning to the more permissive approach taken in public international law to issues of prescriptive jurisdiction.

B. ENFORCEMENT JURISDICTION

1) Territorial Basis of Enforcement Jurisdiction

States being in essence territorially-defined entities, the starting point for their enforcement jurisdiction is naturally territorial. In other words, it is a starting presumption in international law that, within its borders, a state is sovereign and free to exercise plenary enforcement jurisdiction with respect to persons and property situated within those borders.[8] The necessary corollary of this presumption, which is based on territorial sovereignty, is that the enforcement jurisdiction of a state is in fact *limited* to its territory absent some special rule of international law or other basis permitting the exercise of such jurisdiction abroad.[9] Otherwise, a state exercising enforcement jurisdiction in the territory of another state would necessarily be violating the exclusive jurisdiction of that state over all enforcement measures within its territory.

The classic statement of the essentially territorial basis of a state's enforcement jurisdiction is found in the judgment of the Permanent Court of International Justice in *The SS Lotus* case:[10]

---

8   Of course, within any bounds set by international law itself, such as those relating to respect for human rights or the treatment of aliens: see further Chapter 10, and Section D, below in this chapter. Jurisdictional immunities must also be respected: see further Chapter 9.

9   For example, enforcement jurisdiction on the high seas with respect to vessels flying the state's flag (see Chapter 7, Section C) or enforcement jurisdiction on foreign territory with the consent of the territorial sovereign. See, generally, Brownlie, above note 2 at 306; R. Jennings & A. Watts, eds., *Oppenheim's International Law*, 9th ed., vol. 1 (London: Longmans, 1992) at 463.

10   *The Case of the SS "Lotus" (France v. Turkey)* (1927), P.C.I.J. (Ser. A) No. 10 at 18–19 [*The SS Lotus*].

Now the first and foremost restriction imposed by international law upon a State is that—failing the existence of a permissive rule to the contrary—it may not exercise its power in any form in the territory of another State. In this sense jurisdiction is certainly territorial; it cannot be exercised by a State outside its territory except by virtue of a permissive rule derived from international custom or from a convention.

This strict territorial limitation of enforcement jurisdiction means that a state is legally powerless to take any measures of enforcement in the territory of another state. For example, it would be a violation of Canada's sovereignty and an improper extension of the United States' enforcement jurisdiction if American undercover police officers were to conduct an investigation or apprehend a suspect in Canadian territory without the consent of the Canadian government. This would be so even if the investigation related to a crime committed in the United States by an American national. Regardless of the connections between the enforcing state and the object of enforcement, enforcement jurisdiction ultimately comes down to whether or not the latter happens to be within the territory of the enforcing state.

2) Obtaining Custody: Illegal Means vs. Extradition

There are two principal avenues available to a state wishing to exercise enforcement jurisdiction against persons or property not present in its territory. The first option is to abduct the suspect or seize the property and forcibly return him, her, or it to the territory of the enforcing state, where further enforcement measures may be taken, usually in the local courts. A variation on this approach is to lure the suspect back into the enforcing state's territory, and hence its territorial enforcement jurisdiction, by various fraudulent means.

Once the object of enforcement is in the enforcing state's territory, the international legal jurisdictional barrier to enforcement no longer exists. This is apparently so even if the means by which the presence in the enforcing state's territory was obtained is illegal, as in the case of abduction. In other words, the practice of states and customary international law governing enforcement jurisdiction generally appear to take no account of the reasons for or means by which the presence of the person or property in the enforcing state's territory is secured.[11]

---

11   For example, the chief administrator of the "final solution" in Nazi Germany, Adolf Eichmann, was abducted from Argentina in 1960 by Israeli agents to face trial in Israel for crimes related to his role in the Holocaust. Although initial protests by Argentina over the abduction led to a determination by the UN

Once the suspect or property is present in the territory, by whatever means, enforcement jurisdiction is established.[12]

Of course, there will usually be other consequences flowing from the illegal acts by which custody is obtained or other enforcement measures that are taken in foreign territory. In particular, abduction, seizure, and other measures of enforcement in another state's territory are violations of that state's sovereignty, and may give rise to state responsibility.[13] In fact, such actions in themselves constitute an internationally illegal exercise of the abducting or seizing state's enforcement jurisdiction, as they constitute enforcement actions occurring at least partially in foreign territory. On this basis too, then, such illegal acts may give rise to a claim against the wrongdoing state in state responsibility.

The second and far preferable option, in that it avoids the possibility of international conflict or illegality, is to secure custody or possession of the person or property through cooperation with the territorial state. In criminal matters the most common cooperative arrangement is extradition, whereby the state in whose territory the suspect is located exercises its territorial enforcement jurisdiction to apprehend and surrender that suspect to the state wishing to obtain custody and, hence, enforcement jurisdiction. The process is purely consensual, meaning that there is no general obligation to extradite in customary international law. The right (not the duty) to extradite is simply a manifesta-

---

Security Council that the act constituted a violation of Argentina's sovereignty, Eichmann was ultimately convicted and sentenced to death by the District Court of Jerusalem: see *Attorney-General of the Government of Israel v. Eichmann*, (1961), 36 I.L.R. 5 (Dist. Ct. Jerusalem), aff'd (1962), 36 I.L.R. 277 (S. Ct.). In another example, in 1981, Sydney Jaffe, a Canadian national wanted pursuant to an arrest warrant in Florida, was abducted from Canada and incarcerated in Florida over Canadian protests at this violation of its sovereignty (and the United States' failure to request extradition, despite the existence of a bilateral extradition treaty): see M.N. Leich, "Contemporary Practice of the United States Relating to International Law" (1984) 78 A.J.I.L. 200 at 207–9. See also *Ker v. Illinois*, 119 U.S. 436, 7 S. Ct. 225 (1886); *United States v. Alvarez-Machain*, 504 U.S. 655, 112 S. Ct. 2188 (1992); *Prosecutor v. Nikolic* (5 June 2003), ICTY Case No. IT-94-2-AR73 at paras. 24 and 26 (Appeals Chamber).

12 There may, however, be certain domestic legal impediments to the exercise of jurisdiction, in particular due process or constitutional constraints. As a matter of international law, however, the illegality of apprehension does not in itself impair the legality of subsequent enforcement jurisdiction within the territory.

13 See further Chapter 12; see also the UN Secretary-General's "Ruling Pertaining to the Differences Between France and New Zealand Arising from the Rainbow Warrior Affair" (1987) 81 A.J.I.L. 325 and the subsequent arbitral award in the *Rainbow Warrior Arbitration (New Zealand v. France)* (1990), 82 I.L.R. 499.

338 PUBLIC INTERNATIONAL LAW

tion of the territorial state's sovereign enforcement jurisdiction over all persons within its territory.[14]

Extradition may be arranged on an *ad hoc* basis between states in individual cases. More commonly, states tend to conclude bilateral extradition treaties providing for reciprocal rights and obligations in the extradition process.[15] In this way, states essentially "barter" their respective enforcement jurisdiction in a bid effectively to expand their jurisdictional reach through international cooperation. Common terms of such bilateral extradition treaties[16] include double-criminality requirements,[17] undertakings by the requesting state to prosecute only such offences as may be included in the extradition request, the ability of the extraditing state to seek and receive assurances from the requesting state prior to extradition,[18] and various human rights guarantees.[19] Occasionally, bilateral extradition treaties will include an obligation on the territorial state to prosecute the requested suspect if extradition is refused. Such provisions are, however, more common in multilateral conventions aimed at the suppression of international crimes, and are

---

14   Again, subject to any overriding obligations to respect basic human rights norms: see further Chapter 10. States may have obligations of extradition pursuant to multilateral treaty regimes, particularly those establishing legal mechanisms for the suppression of international criminal activity. Some regimes contain human rights protections for the person subject to extradition; for example, Article 3(1) of the *Torture Convention* prohibits parties from "[extraditing] a person to another State where there are substantial grounds for believing that he would be in danger of being subjected to torture": *Convention against Torture and Other Cruel, Inhuman or Degrading Treatment or Punishment,* 10 December 1984, 1465 U.N.T.S. 85 (entered into force 26 June 1987) [*Torture Convention*], Article 3(1).

15   For example, *Extradition Treaty between Canada and the United States of America,* 3 December 1971, as amended by exchange of notes, 28 June and 9 July 1974, 1976 Can. T.S. No. 3, (entered into force 22 March 1976); amended 11 January 1988, 1991 Can. T.S. No. 37 (in force 26 November 1991); amended 12 January 2001, 2003 Can. T.S. No. 11 (in force 30 April 2003).

16   See, for example, the *Model Treaty on Extradition* adopted by the General Assembly of the United Nations, UNGA Res. 45/116, U.N. Doc. A/RES/45/116 (1990).

17   That is, the requirement that the transaction for which extradition is sought is an offence under the law of both the requesting and the territorial states.

18   For example, guarantees that certain punishments will not be imposed upon conviction. Canada has often invoked its right under the Canada-United States extradition treaty, above note 15, to seek assurances that the persons requested will not face the death penalty. In 2001, the Supreme Court of Canada ruled that seeking such assurances is constitutionally required in all but exceptional cases: see *United States of America v. Burns,* [2001] 1 S.C.R. 283.

19   For example, provisions stipulating that no extradition will be sought or granted for political offences.

designed to eliminate safe havens for such international criminals.[20] In either case, the existence of the obligation either to extradite or prosecute can be traced to the consent of the territorial state to the relevant extradition regime, and hence to its sovereignty over enforcement matters within its own borders.

C. PRESCRIPTIVE JURISDICTION

1) Introduction

The classic enunciation of international law's approach to prescriptive jurisdiction is also found in the decision of the Permanent Court of International Justice in *The SS Lotus*.[21] However, in contrast to the strictly territorial extent of enforcement jurisdiction recognized there, the approach of the Court to prescriptive jurisdiction was quite liberal.

The case arose from a collision on the high seas between French and Turkish steamers. The Turkish vessel was so heavily damaged that it sank, killing eight Turkish crew members and passengers. The French steamer, although also seriously damaged, managed to put into the nearby Turkish port of Constantinople, where one of its officers was arrested and charged by Turkish authorities with involuntary manslaughter. The officer was ultimately tried and convicted of various offences under Turkish law in a Turkish court.

France brought a claim in the Permanent Court of International Justice in which it objected to the Turkish proceedings on the basis that only the flag state has jurisdiction over events aboard vessels on the high seas.[22] As seen above, the Court adopted a narrow view of the scope of a state's enforcement jurisdiction. However, Turkey had not exceeded such enforcement jurisdiction, as all enforcement measures had oc-

---

20 The "extradite or prosecute" obligation found in multilateral conventions dealing with international offences generally binds the state party with territorial enforcement jurisdiction, "if it does not extradite [the offender], to submit the case to its competent authorities for the purpose of prosecution": *Torture Convention*, above note 14, Article 7(1); see also for example *Convention for the Suppression of Unlawful Acts against the Safety of Civil Aviation*, 23 September 1971, 974 U.N.T.S. 178 (entered into force 26 January 1973), Article 7; *International Convention for the Suppression of Terrorist Bombings*, 15 December 1997, 2149 U.N.T.S. 256 (entered into force 23 May 2001), Article 8(1) [*Terrorist Bombings Convention*]; *International Convention for the Suppression of Acts of Nuclear Terrorism*, 14 September 2005, U.N. Doc. A/RES/59/290 (entered into force 7 July 2007), Article 9(4).

21 *The SS Lotus,* above note 10.

22 See Chapter 7, Section C(2)(g).

curred after the French vessel had voluntarily entered Turkish territory. The real core of the dispute, therefore, was whether Turkey was able to extend the reach of its penal laws, that is, its prescriptive jurisdiction, to events occurring outside Turkish territory, on the high seas.

The Court ultimately resolved this issue by resorting to the now obsolete fiction that the Turkish vessel was a notional extension of Turkish territory while on the high seas, and therefore that the criminal acts at issue had been committed at least partially on Turkish "territory."[23] Therefore, prescriptive jurisdiction was established.[24] Of more general significance, however, is the general view of the law of prescriptive jurisdiction taken by the Court:

> Far from laying down a general prohibition to the effect that States may not extend the application of their laws and the jurisdiction of their courts to persons, property and acts outside their territory, [international law] leaves them in this respect a wide measure of discretion which is only limited in certain cases by prohibitive rules; as regards other cases, every State remains free to adopt the principles which it regards as best and most suitable.[25]

This passage suggests that states have a very broad discretion to extend their prescriptive jurisdiction to virtually any person or event, whether or not within its territory. While the Court did add that a state "should not overstep the limits which international law places upon its jurisdiction,"[26] it did not articulate any generally applicable limits. Thus, in the Court's view, the starting premise, when it comes to the extent of states' prescriptive jurisdiction, is essentially permissive.

This is, of course, not to say that prescriptive jurisdiction is limitless in international law. First, it remains the case that states are under a general obligation not to interfere in one another's domestic affairs,

---

23   Above note 10 at 23. The fiction that a vessel flying a state's flag is an extension of that state's territory has since been rejected in international law. Rather, jurisdiction over vessels on the high seas is now based on the nationality (that is, state of registration) of the vessel: see further Chapter 7, Section C(2)(g).

24   See further Section C(2), below in this chapter. The Court was evenly divided (6-6) on the outcome and the decision was only carried by the casting vote of the President of the Court. The discrete ruling as it applied to jurisdiction over vessels on the high seas proved highly controversial and was subsequently overruled in both Article 11 of the 1958 *Geneva Convention on the High Seas*, 29 April 1958, 450 U.N.T.S. 11 (entered into force 30 September 1962) [*GCHS*]; and Article 97 of the 1982 *United Nations Convention on the Law of the Sea*, 10 December 1982, 1833 U.N.T.S. 3 (entered into force 16 November 1994) [*UNCLOS*].

25   *The SS Lotus*, above note 10 at 19.

26   *Ibid.*

which necessarily implies a general obligation not to seek to regulate such foreign domestic affairs.[27] Second, states do not in general assert unlimited prescriptive jurisdiction, but rather confine such assertions to a limited and generally recognized set of jurisdictional "principles," to be reviewed below. States purporting to extend their prescriptive jurisdictional reach beyond such recognized principles generally meet with resistance or protest by other states. Third, and as a result, scholars have not generally supported the virtually unfettered discretionary approach to prescriptive jurisdiction seemingly advocated by the Court in *The SS Lotus*. Rather, as we shall see further below, the idea has gradually taken hold in international law that, before a state may extend its prescriptive jurisdiction to a person or event, it must have some genuine link to that person or event.[28]

Subject to these qualifications, the essence of the foregoing passage from *The SS Lotus* has set the tone for the general development of the law relating to prescriptive jurisdiction. There is no strict limitation, as in the case of enforcement jurisdiction, of a state's prescriptive jurisdiction to persons and events within its own territory. Rather, a state is, as a general matter, *prima facie* free to legislate or regulate with respect to persons or events beyond its territory, as long as doing so does not interfere with the jurisdictional rights of states that may have a closer connection to those persons or events.[29]

Prescriptive jurisdictional conflicts, therefore, generally come down to the relative strengths of competing states' connections to the subject matter of the prescriptive measures. The following principles or bases of prescriptive jurisdiction can thus be regarded as a more or less hierarchical catalogue of connecting factors justifying the exercise of prescriptive jurisdiction in any given case.

2) The Territorial Principle

a) Generally
In keeping again with the territorial basis of statehood, by far the soundest basis of prescriptive jurisdiction is that the subject matter of regulation is within the prescribing state's territory. The "territorial principle" of prescriptive jurisdiction is a natural corollary of the

---

27   See Shaw, above note 3 at 574–76.
28   See Brownlie, above note 2 at 297 and 309.
29   For a summary of the Canadian position in this regard, see C. Swords, "Canadian Practice in International Law at the Department of Foreign Affairs in 2001–2002: Jurisdiction and Territorial Sovereignty, Extraterritorial Evidence Gathering" (2002) 40 Can. Y.B. Int'l L. 469 at 494–95.

fundamental rule that a state has sovereign jurisdiction over all matters occurring within its borders. It is further justified by a presumed genuine interest of the territorial state in all matters occurring within its territory. Thus, it is universally recognized that states enjoy full prescriptive jurisdiction over persons and events within their territory.[30]

b) "Subjective" and "Objective" Territorial Principles

The basic territorial principle is easily stated but, in fact, it has a number of variants that account for events or transactions that cannot be said to occur in only one place. The somewhat facile but classic example is that of a firearm being discharged from the territory of one state into the territory of another. More sophisticated (and likely) examples include international drug trafficking, trans-border fraud schemes, smuggling, the electronic dissemination of hatred or obscene materials, or transnational terrorism. All such cases share the possibility that various aspects of the offending activity may occur, at least on some characterizations of the facts, in the territories of more than one state.

The territorial principle in fact operates so as to grant each such territorial state prescriptive jurisdiction.[31] For example, the so-called "subjective" territorial principle provides a jurisdictional basis for the state in which activity originates to regulate such activity. Conversely, the "objective" territorial principle also permits a state in which activity is consummated to regulate the activity.[32]

Obviously, this generous application of the principle of territoriality, to permit the exercise of prescriptive jurisdiction whenever an element of the relevant transaction has a territorial link to the state, gives rise to the potential for jurisdictional overlap. There is nothing impermissible about this *per se* in international law: more than one state may well have a legitimate interest in regulating a particular activity. Any conflicts generated tend to be resolved by the practical realities of the much more restrictive enforcement jurisdiction enjoyed by states: while the laws of more than one state may be broken by any particular activity, it is the state with enforcement jurisdiction (the state in whose

---

30   Brownlie, above note 2 at 299; Shaw, above note 3 at 579; A. Cassese, *International Law*, 2d ed. (Oxford: Oxford University Press, 2005) at 49.

31   See, for example, *Treacy v. Director of Public Prosecutions*, [1971] A.C. 537 (H.L.); *Libman v. The Queen*, [1985] 2 S.C.R. 178.

32   The objective territorial principle was ultimately the basis upon which the Court in *The SS Lotus*, above note 10 at 25, justified Turkey's extension of the application of its penal laws to events occurring outside its territory but having an impact on the Turkish vessel, a notional extension of its territory.

territory the actor is located) that will, as a practical matter, be in a position to enforce its laws.[33]

c)   The "Effects Doctrine"

The territorial principle, including its application to events occurring only partially in any one state's territory, is largely uncontroversial in international law. However, the American courts in the twentieth century developed a variation of the objective territorial principle, the so-called "effects doctrine," which has proven particularly antagonistic to other states and a serious source of contention in the international law of prescriptive jurisdiction.

The effects doctrine can be traced to the 1945 decision of the United States Court of Appeals for the Second Circuit in *Alcoa*,[34] where the Court found that American antitrust legislation could be applied to alleged anticompetitive conduct occurring entirely outside the United States. As such, the case stands for the sweeping proposition that:

> Any state may impose liabilities, even upon persons not within its allegiance, for conduct outside the state's borders that has consequences within its borders which the state reprehends, and such liabilities other states will ordinarily recognize.

This extremely broad interpretation of the objective territorial principle was subsequently applied by several American courts in antitrust cases to reach conduct occurring wholly in foreign states but alleged to have anticompetitive effects in the American marketplace.[35] Typically such cases resulted in remedies being granted against American parents or subsidiaries of offending foreign corporate actors, although at times American courts would order relief which was subsequently sought to be enforced in foreign courts.[36] Foreign courts tended to be uncooperative in this regard and several states, including Canada, objected strenuously to these applications of American law to conduct occurring wholly in the territory of other states. This opposition was all

---

33   Shaw, above note 3 at 580–81.

34   *United States v. Aluminium Company of America*, 148 F. 2d 416 (2d Cir. 1945).

35   For example, *United States v. National Lead Co.*, 63 F. Supp. 513 (S.D.N.Y. 1945), aff'd 332 U.S. 319 (1947); *United States v. General Electric Co.*, 82 F. Supp. 753 (D.N.J. 1949), final decree 115 F. Supp. 835 (1953).

36   For example, *Central Canada Potash Co. v. Government of Saskatchewan*, [1979] 1 S.C.R. 42; *In re Uranium Antitrust Litigation*, 480 F. Supp. 1138 (N.D. Ill. 1979), 617 F. 2d 1248 (7th Cir. 1980); *In re Westinghouse Electric Corp. and Duquesne Light Co.* (1977), 16 O.R. (2d) 273 (H.C.J.); *Rio Tinto Zinc Corp. v. Westinghouse Electric Corp.*, [1978] 2 W.L.R. 81 (H.L.); *Burmah Oil Co. Ltd. v. Bank of England*, [1979] 3 All E.R. 700 (H.L.); *Gulf Oil Corp. v. Gulf Canada Ltd.*, [1980] 2 S.C.R. 39.

the stronger in that, in most cases, the targeted conduct was completely legal under the laws of the territorial state. Thus, American enforcement measures, designed to secure compliance with American law and judicial rulings in this area, had the effect of modifying or curbing conduct deemed acceptable under the law of the state in which it was occurring.

Many states responded to what they considered to be unacceptable American legislative and judicial intrusions into the domestic regulation of their own marketplaces by enacting "blocking" statutes. These enactments sought in various ways to compel corporations within their borders to observe local law and ignore any conflicting American law or judicial order.[37]

In the face of this hostile international response, some American courts experimented with various ways of muting the unbridled effects doctrine. For example, it was acknowledged that "at some point the interests of the United States are too weak and the foreign harmony incentive for restraint too strong to justify an extraterritorial assertion of jurisdiction."[38] The answer, according to the Ninth Circuit Court of Appeals, was to recognize a doctrine of international comity that would require consideration of various factors before assuming jurisdiction over extraterritorial acts, including:

> [1] the degree of conflict with foreign law or policy; [2] the nationality or allegiance of the parties and the locations or principal places of business of corporations; [3] the extent to which enforcement by either state can be expected to achieve compliance; [4] the relative significance of effects on the United States as compared with those elsewhere; [5] the extent to which there is explicit purpose to harm or affect American commerce; [6] the foreseeability of such effect; and [7] the relative importance to the violations charged of conduct within the United States as compared with conduct abroad.[39] [Semicolons and numbering added]

---

37 For example, Canada's *Foreign Extraterritorial Measures Act*, R.S.C. 1985, c. F-29. See further W.C. Graham, "The *Foreign Extraterritorial Measures Act*" (1986) 11 Can. Bus. L.J. 410.

38 *Timberlane Lumber Co. v. Bank of America Nat. Trust and Sav. Ass'n.*, 549 F. 2d 597 at 609 (9th Cir. 1976). See also *Mannington Mills Inc. v. Congoleum Corp.*, 595 F. 2d 1287 (3rd Cir. 1979).

39 *Timberlane, ibid.* at 614. Comity is a term frequently used to describe the consideration due, arguably as a matter of good neighbourliness rather than of legal obligation, to a fellow sovereign state: see Jennings & Watts, above note 9 at 50–51.

In some cases, the application of this approach, which became known as the "rule of reason," would result in American courts declining to extend the reach of American law to foreign acts. On the other hand, in situations where the American interest in regulating such conduct was found to outweigh that of the territorial state, jurisdiction would be assumed. While the United States Supreme Court seemed to signal, in 1991, an affinity for this "rule of reason" approach,[40] it since appears to have rejected any decisive role for considerations of comity and affirmed the intrusive *Alcoa* approach to defining the reach of American antitrust laws.[41]

The legality of the American effects doctrine, and even of the more moderate rule of reason, as more and less radical variants of the objective territorial principle, remains a contentious point in international law. Given the generally hostile reaction by other states to the former, it is unlikely that it constitutes a valid basis in customary international law for the assertion of prescriptive jurisdiction over wholly extraterritorial acts. Moreover, given the United States Supreme Court's failure to endorse the latter, its status is more uncertain still.

3) The Nationality Principle

A connection of nationality between a state and a person is also generally recognized, in the practice of states and, hence, in customary international law, as a valid basis for extending that state's prescriptive jurisdiction to that person.[42] This is so regardless of the location of the person at the time of the relevant activity. The nationality principle is thus one of the most widely recognized bases upon which states may legitimately exercise prescriptive jurisdiction over conduct occurring outside their territory. For example, France would be justified in enacting legislation generally governing the activities of French nationals abroad.

---

40   See *Equal Employment Opportunity Commission v. Arabian American Oil Company (ARAMCO)*, 499 U.S. 24, 111 S.Ct. 1227 (1991).

41   See *Hartford Fire Insurance Co. v. California*, 113 S. Ct. 2891 (1993). The majority in the United States Supreme Court refused to accede to forceful arguments put forward by Canada and the United Kingdom in support of mitigating the effects doctrine and giving increased weight to considerations of international comity: see J.H. Currie, "Extraterritoriality, Antitrust Law and the US Supreme Court's Decision in *Hartford Fire Insurance Company v. California*" (1994) 1 Can. Int'l Lawyer 25.

42   J.G. Starke & I.A. Shearer, *Starke's International Law*, 11th ed. (London: Butterworths, 1994) at 210.

States are generally free to determine the basis upon which they confer their nationality on individuals,[43] subject to the general requirement of a "genuine and effective link" between the individual and the state.[44] Most commonly, states accord nationality to individuals based either on birth within the state's territory (*jus soli*), on the nationality of one or both of the individual's parents (*jus sanguinis*), or on various criteria relating to the process of naturalization. In the case of corporate entities, the general presumption in international law is that the state in which the entity is incorporated or has its registered head office is the state of the corporation's "nationality," although other factors may lead to different conclusions.[45]

Of course, recognition of extraterritorial prescriptive jurisdiction based on a link of nationality will once again give rise to potential overlapping prescriptive jurisdiction between the national state and the state in whose territory the activity occurs. Such overlap is in itself unproblematic, in that any conflict is usually resolved by virtue of the fact that the state in whose territory the actor happens to be at the time of the exercise of enforcement jurisdiction has the upper hand. Moreover, the nationality principle is a useful doctrine in cases where either the relevant activity has no clear territorial link to any particular state, or the territorial state displays no interest in prosecuting the person or activity; or where, in cases of serious crimes, it is preferable to assert several prescriptive jurisdictional bases rather than risk having the actor escape the reach of the national laws of any state.

4) Other Potential Bases of Prescriptive Jurisdiction

a) General
The territorial and nationality principles account for the vast majority of state practice in the area of prescriptive jurisdiction. Most states that have a domestic legal system based on the common law favour the territorial principle as the presumptive basis for the application of their domestic legislation, whereas those following the civil law tradition

---

43   *Nationality Decrees Issued in Tunis and Morocco, Advisory Opinion,* (1923) P.C.I.J. (Ser. B) No. 4 at 24; *Hague Convention on Certain Questions Relating to the Conflict of Nationality Laws,* 12 April 1930, 179 L.N.T.S. 89 (in force 1 July 1937).

44   See, generally, *Nottebohm Case (Second Phase) (Liechtenstein v. Guatemala),* [1955] I.C.J. Rep. 4. See also *Flegenheimer Case (Case No. 182)* (1958), 14 R.I.A.A. 327 at 377 (United States-Italian Conciliation Commission).

45   See *Barcelona Traction, Light and Power Company, Ltd. (Second Phase),* [1970] I.C.J. Rep. 3 at para. 70.

favour the extension of their laws to their nationals, even if abroad.[46] This concentration of state practice has led some to conclude that only the territorial and nationality principles are legitimate bases for the exercise of prescriptive jurisdiction.[47] This view is likely too narrow in that it fails to take account of the overall permissive stance taken by international law in the field of prescriptive jurisdiction, as seen above in *The SS Lotus*.[48] It also fails to take account of the occasional assertion of prescriptive jurisdiction on other bases. Such alternative bases, albeit often controversial and far less general in scope, are asserted frequently enough to serve as reminders that the permissible bases of prescriptive jurisdiction are not rigidly confined to either the territorial or nationality principles. Perhaps reflecting this practice, and the uncertainties it generates as to the precise limits of each state's jurisdictional reach, the International Law Commission has recently added the topic "Extraterritorial Jurisdiction" to its long-term programme of work.[49]

b) The Passive Personality Principle

This principle is occasionally invoked to found prescriptive jurisdiction over acts committed abroad by non-nationals but which have injurious effects on the prescribing state's nationals. It is the converse of the nationality principle in that it focuses on a link of nationality between the state and victims, rather than the state and perpetrators.

This principle was the basis of the Turkish claim to prescriptive jurisdiction in *The SS Lotus* case, given that the acts of the French officer of the watch had led to the deaths of eight Turkish nationals. France objected that no such basis of jurisdiction was recognized in international law. The majority of the Court failed either to endorse or reject the passive personality principle, preferring, as seen above, to found

---

46 Canada, following a predominantly common law approach, adopts a presumption of territorial application of national laws, subject to certain exceptions based on the nationality of the perpetrator in the case of serious crimes: see, for example, *Criminal Code of Canada*, R.S.C. 1985, c. C-46, s. 6(2) (general principle of territoriality of criminal law); s. 7(3)(c) (extending jurisdiction in respect of certain offences committed abroad against internationally protected persons by Canadian citizens); and s. 46(3) (extending jurisdiction to acts of treason by Canadian citizens while abroad).

47 See, for example, the submissions of the Commission of the European Communities in *A. Ahlström Oy v. Commission (In re Wood Pulp Cartel)* (1988), 96 I.L.R. 148 at 169 (E.C.J.).

48 *The SS Lotus,* above note 10.

49 See "Report of the International Law Commission on the Work of its Fifty-Eighth Session", UN GAOR, 61st Session, Supplement No. 10 (A/61/10) (2006) at para. 257.

Turkish jurisdiction on the objective territorial principle. Writing in dissent, however, Judge Moore strongly criticized the passive personality principle as an unjustified intrusion into the domestic affairs of foreign states. In effect, he held, the passive personality principle:

> ... means that the citizen of one country, when he visits another country, takes with him for his "protection" the law of his own country and subjects those with whom he comes into contact to the operation of that law. In this way an inhabitant of a great commercial city, in which foreigners congregate, may in the course of an hour unconsciously fall under the operation of a number of foreign criminal codes.[50]

In other words, the principle is problematic in that it would permit the extension of one state's laws to foreigners acting wholly within their own state but coming into contact with visiting nationals of the first state. This strikes deeply into the domestic jurisdiction of states over acts of their own nationals occurring within their own territories. It is also inconsistent with the general rule that foreign nationals are under a general obligation to respect the domestic law of the states they visit. Given these difficulties, the passive personality principle is not widely invoked and usually meets with strong condemnation by states when it is.[51]

Certain exceptions to this generally hostile attitude to the passive personality principle are nevertheless established in certain multilateral conventions. These tend to relate to serious international criminal activity, such as hostage-taking and attacks against internationally protected persons such as diplomats.[52] This exceptional reliance on the

---

50 *The SS Lotus*, above note 10 at 92.
51 See Shaw, above note 3 at 590.
52 For example, *Convention on Prevention and Punishment of Crimes Against Internationally Protected Persons, Including Diplomatic Agents*, 13 December 1973, 1035 U.N.T.S. 167 (in force 20 February 1977), Article 3(1)(c) [*Internationally Protected Persons Convention*]; *International Convention Against the Taking of Hostages*, 17 December 1979, 1316 U.N.T.S. 205 (in force 3 June 1983), Article 5(1)(d) [*Hostages Convention*]; *Torture Convention*, above note 14, Article 5(1)(c); *Terrorist Bombings Convention*, above note 20, Article 6(2). Canada's *Criminal Code*, above note 46, contains limited provisions extending jurisdiction to certain extraterritorial acts on the basis of the passive personality principle in keeping with such treaty obligations: see, for example, s. 7(3)(d) (extending jurisdiction to acts committed abroad against Canadian diplomats or other internationally protected persons representing Canada); s. 7(3.1)(e) (extending jurisdiction to hostage-taking of Canadian citizens abroad even by non-nationals of Canada); s. 7(3.7)(d) (extending jurisdiction over acts of torture committed abroad against Canadian citizens); ss. 7(3.72)(e),7(3.73)(g), and 7(3.75)(a)

passive personality principle reflects a policy choice to multiply the bases of jurisdiction available to states in combating such activity lest perpetrators escape liability for their acts. In general, however, such invocations of the passive personality principle rely for their legality on the existence of an underlying treaty regime. In other words, it is unlikely that customary international law recognizes the passive personality principle as a *generally* valid basis for the extraterritorial extension of states' prescriptive jurisdiction.

c) The Protective Principle

The protective principle is similar to the passive personality principle in that it focuses on acts committed abroad by foreign nationals that have a detrimental effect on the state purporting to exercise jurisdiction. Because the principle entails an even greater extension of the state's extraterritorial jurisdiction to foreign acts that do not even cause direct injury to the state's nationals, its rare invocation has generally been confined to serious acts that strike at the state's security or territorial integrity. Thus, it is generally advanced as a justification for criminalizing such foreign acts as espionage or counterfeiting.[53] However, state practice is uneven beyond these core aspects of the state's security interests and many states, including Canada, are hostile to the principle as a general basis of prescriptive jurisdiction in the absence of other connecting factors between the prescribing state and the actors or acts in question.[54]

d) The Universal Principle

Essentially, the universal principle provides that the domestic penal laws of any state can be applied as a basis for the prosecution of certain acts, regardless of the location of the offence or the nationality of the offender or victim. In other words, any state having enforcement jurisdiction (through presence of the offender in its territory) would be in a position to prosecute the individual pursuant to its domestic

---

(extending passive personality jurisdiction in respect of various terrorism-related offences committed against Canadian citizens). See also *Crimes Against Humanity and War Crimes Act*, S.C. 2000, c. 24, s. 8(a)(iii) [*CAHWCA*], extending jurisdiction in respect of war crimes, crimes against humanity and genocide committed against Canadian citizens.

53   See Shaw, above note 3 at 592; Brownlie, above note 2 at 302; Starke & Shearer, above note 42 at 211–12.

54   But note that the Canadian *Criminal Code*, above note 46, invokes the protective principle where this is called for or permitted by various multilateral treaty regimes dealing with serious transnational crimes: see, for example, ss. 7(3.1) and 7(3.71)–(3.75).

law. In this way, the chances that such acts will go unpunished are minimized.

Some states have asserted such jurisdiction with respect to certain acts committed abroad by non-nationals, regardless of any direct effects on their nationals or security.[55] In general, such assertions have been confined to only the most serious criminal acts, which by their nature are considered to jeopardize the international public order itself. On this basis, all states may be considered to have an interest and a role to play in the suppression of such acts.

The clearest cases to which universal jurisdiction applies as a matter of both treaty and customary international law are piracy[56] and war crimes.[57] Other candidates, in respect of which there remain varying degrees of controversy (at least with respect to the availability of universal jurisdiction as a matter of customary international law) include

---

55 For example, in 1993 and 1999, Belgium enacted legislation asserting jurisdiction over certain serious international crimes regardless of the place of their commission, the nationality of their perpetrators or victims, or even the presence of the accused in Belgium: see *Loi du 16 juin 1993 relative à la répression des infractions graves aux Conventions internationales de Genève du 12 août 1949 et aux Protocoles I et II du 8 juin 1977*, Moniteur Belge (5 August 1993) at 17751, as amended by *Loi du 10 février 1999 relative à la répression de violations graves du droit international humanitaire*, Moniteur Belge (23 March 1999) at 9286. On 1 August 2003, in the face of strong opposition to this assertion of jurisdiction by various states (particularly the United States: see S. Murphy, "U.S. Reaction to Universal Jurisdiction Law" (2003) 97 A.J.I.L. 984 at 984–87) and an unfavourable outcome in the *Case Concerning the Arrest Warrant of 11 April 2000 (Democratic Republic of the Congo v. Belgium)*, [2002] I.C.J. Rep. 3 [*DRC v. Belgium*], the legislation was significantly amended to limit its reach to cases where Belgian interests were engaged or where jurisdiction was provided for by treaty: see *Loi du 1er août 2003 relative aux violations graves du droit international humanitaire*, Moniteur Belge (7 August 2003) at 40506.

56 See *UNCLOS*, above note 24, Article 105; *GCHS*, above note 24, Article 19; *In re Piracy Jure Gentium*, [1934] A.C. 586 (J.C.P.C.); *DRC v. Belgium*, ibid., Separate Opinion of President Guillaume at para. 5.

57 See J.-M. Henckaerts & L. Doswald-Beck, *Customary International Humanitarian Law*, Volume I: Rules (Cambridge: Cambridge University Press. 2005) at 604–7 (Rule 157); *Geneva Convention for the Amelioration of the Condition of the Wounded and Sick in Armed Forces in the Field*, 12 August 1949, 75 U.N.T.S. 31, Article 49; *Geneva Convention for the Amelioration of the Condition of Wounded, Sick and Shipwrecked Members of Armed Forces at Sea*, 12 August 1949, 75 U.N.T.S. 85, Article 50; *Geneva Convention Relative to the Treatment of Prisoners of War*, 12 August 1949, 75 U.N.T.S. 135, Article 129; *Geneva Convention Relative to the Protection of Civilian Persons in Time of War*, 12 August 1949, 75 U.N.T.S. 287, Article 146; and, *semble*, *DRC v. Belgium*, ibid., Joint Separate Opinion of Judges Higgins, Kooijmans, and Buergenthal at para. 51.

genocide,[58] crimes against humanity,[59] torture, slavery, terrorism, international drug trafficking, and similar offences.[60] The customary availability of universal jurisdiction with respect to these acts is complicated by the fact that most are outlawed by multilateral treaty regimes that call for the exercise of jurisdiction by states parties on a wide number of bases, including mere (after-the-fact) presence of the suspect in the territory of a state party.[61] There is a somewhat semantic debate as to whether such an exercise of prescriptive jurisdiction, on no other basis than presence of the accused on one's territory after commission of the criminal act, amounts to "universal jurisdiction properly so-called"[62] or is rather some other form of "quasi-universal jurisdiction."[63] Requiring the presence of the accused in one's territory is, of course, merely to reiterate the requirement of enforcement jurisdiction. The purported distinction between universal and quasi-universal prescriptive jurisdiction therefore does not appear to be particularly meaningful or useful. In any case, however it is designated, the trend established by treaty practice appears to be a multiplication of the categories of serious criminal acts that states are willing to subject to their domestic prescriptive jurisdiction in the absence of any connecting factors other than the mere presence of the accused in their territory.[64] Given the potential for

---

58   See *Eichmann*, above note 11 at para. 19.

59   See *DRC v. Belgium*, above note 55, Joint Separate Opinion of Judges Higgins, Kooijmans and Buergenthal at paras. 52 and 65; see also Jennings & Watts, above note 9 at 998.

60   See S. Macedo, ed., *The Princeton Principles on Universal Jurisdiction* (Princeton: Program in Law and Public Affairs, Princeton University, 2001), Principle 2, for an enumeration of crimes potentially amenable to universal jurisdiction.

61   Typically, failure to exercise such jurisdiction gives rise to a concomitant duty to extradite the accused to another state party willing to do so: see, for example, *Internationally Protected Persons Convention*, above note 52, Article 3(2); *Hostages Convention*, above note 52, Article 5(2); *Torture Convention*, above note 14, Article 5(2); *Terrorist Bombings Convention*, above note 20, Article 6(4).

62   See *DRC v. Belgium*, above note 55, Joint Separate Opinion of Judges Higgins, Kooijmans and Buergenthal at para. 45.

63   See Shaw, above note 3 at 597–98.

64   See *DRC v. Belgium*, above note 55, Joint Separate Opinion of Judges Higgins, Kooijmans and Buergenthal at paras 46–52. This trend has also been encouraged by ratification and implementation by states of the *Rome Statute of the International Criminal Court*, 17 July 1998, 2187 U.N.T.S. 90, entered into force 1 July 2002 [*Rome Statute*]. The *Rome Statute* encourages states parties to prosecute perpetrators of genocide, crimes against humanity and war crimes, failing which it requires states parties to surrender suspected perpetrators of such crimes to the Court for prosecution: *ibid.*, Article 86. In implementation of the *Rome Statute*, Canada has enacted legislation extending jurisdiction over genocide, war crimes, and crimes against humanity simply on the basis that "after

jurisdictional conflicts that it entails, however, the availability of universal jurisdiction is likely to remain confined to only the most serious international crimes.[65]

5) Synthesis of Principles: The Requirement of a Genuine and Effective Link

It will be apparent that all of the foregoing principles or bases of prescriptive jurisdiction concern, in one way or another, various factors justifying any given state's interest in extending the reach of its domestic law to persons or events. The territorial principle reflects a general consensus among states that each of them has a genuine interest in regulating events occurring within its own territory. Similarly, the nationality principle recognizes the importance to many states of maintaining a jurisdictional link to persons bearing their nationality. In contrast, states' reticence with respect to the more liberal passive personality, protective, and universal principles reflects the more tenuous links between states and persons acting in circumstances where such principles would apply. It also shows that states, in practice, take a considerably more restrained approach to questions of prescriptive jurisdiction than the virtually unrestricted approach propounded by the Court in *The SS Lotus* case.[66]

This has led some commentators and courts to suggest that, when viewed as a whole, state practice discloses a deeper principle in which all of the foregoing jurisdictional principles are rooted: that of the requirement of a genuine and effective link justifying the extension of a state's prescriptive jurisdiction to any particular person or transaction.[67] In other words, each of the bases of jurisdiction reviewed above would simply be a manifestation of a general requirement of a real connection between the state purporting to exercise prescriptive jurisdiction and the actor or event. Such an approach would in particular be consistent

---

the time the offence is alleged to have been committed, the person is present in Canada": see *CAHWCA*, above note 52, s. 8(b). Canada also extends jurisdiction to a number of other acts on either a universal or quasi-universal basis: see, for example, *Criminal Code*, above note 46, ss. 7(2) (hijacking), 7(3.1)(f) (hostage-taking), 7(3.7)(e) (torture by government officials), 7(3.71)(d) (offences against internationally protected persons), 7(3.72)(d) and 7(3.73)(d) (terrorism offences), and 74(2) (piracy).

65   See *DRC v. Belgium*, above note 55, Joint Separate Opinion of Judges Higgins, Kooijmans and Buergenthal at para. 60.

66   *Ibid.*, Separate Opinion of President Guillaume at paras. 15–16.

67   See, for example, Brownlie, above note 2 at 297 and 309.

with the fact that few, if any, states base all exercises of prescriptive jurisdiction solely on one of the above principles. Rather, various principles are applied depending on the circumstances and the nature of the state's interest in the matter. For example, the Canadian *Criminal Code* itself resorts to each of the above principles of jurisdiction in various circumstances, albeit placing emphasis on the territorial principle.

A good illustration of the theoretical approach requiring a genuine and effective link as a basis for prescriptive jurisdiction is the decision of the Supreme Court of Canada in *Libman*.[68] That case involved an international fraud ring in which individuals in Canada fraudulently solicited investments by Americans in supposed gold mining operations in Costa Rica. American investors made payments to offices located in Costa Rica and Panama, where Libman and his associates collected the proceeds. When Libman was charged in Canada with fraud, he argued that no fraud could be complete until the American investors had been deprived of their funds, which occurred either in the United States, Costa Rica, or Panama, but in any event not in Canada. Thus, Libman argued that the Canadian *Criminal Code* provisions relating to fraud did not extend to him or his acts.

In rejecting this argument, Justice La Forest for the Court noted that, while Canadian law has traditionally confined itself to acts occurring within Canadian territory, this has never been exclusively the case, as we have seen above. In deciding in any particular case whether Canadian criminal law applies to a particular transaction, Justice La Forest held that:

> ... we must, in my view, take into account all relevant facts that take place in Canada that may legitimately give this country an interest in prosecuting the offence. One must then consider whether there is anything in those facts that offends international comity.
>
> ...
>
> As it is put by modern academics, it is sufficient that there be a "real and substantial link" between an offence and this country, a test well known in public and private international law....[69]

Justice La Forest found it unnecessary to describe in any detail what might constitute a real and substantial link, contenting himself with observing that in this case, the fact that elements of the fraudulent activity occurred in Canada and that the fruits of the scheme were

---

68 *Libman v. The Queen*, above note 31.

69 *Ibid.* at 211 and 213. See also *R. v. Hape*, 2007 SCC 26 at para. 62, LeBel J. writing for the majority.

ultimately brought to Canada were more than sufficient to ground a Canadian interest in prosecuting the offence under its criminal laws.[70] Moreover, it was found that comity in this case did not require the Court to decline jurisdiction in favour of another, perhaps more intimately connected, jurisdiction. On the contrary, comity, in the sense of consideration for the interests of other states,[71] seemed to dictate that it was incumbent on Canada to do whatever it could to suppress international fraud and thus protect the interests of other affected states.[72]

The requirement of a genuine and effective link between the state and the person or transaction provides a flexible basis, while at the same time providing outer limits, for the exercise of prescriptive jurisdiction. In this way the practice of states in adhering to one or more of the above principles of jurisdiction is reconciled with the *prima facie* permissive approach to jurisdiction articulated by the Court in *The SS Lotus.*[73]

D. CONCOMITANT JURISDICTIONAL RESPONSIBILITIES: TREATMENT OF ALIENS

1) Introduction

Our discussion so far has focused on the jurisdictional powers, rights, and privileges that states enjoy by virtue of their sovereignty. However, these privileges come with certain corresponding responsibilities or duties in international law. Some of the most important of these responsibilities spring from the general duty of states not to injure the interests of other states and, in particular, not to allow their territory to be used so as to cause such injury.[74] An important and practical manifestation of this general obligation is the duty owed by all states to extend basic standards of treatment and protection to visiting foreign nationals or "aliens." This obligation acts as a fetter on what would otherwise be the host state's full freedom, in the exercise of its sovereignty, to regulate

---

70   *Libman v. The Queen*, above note 31 at 213. Indeed, these connecting factors might give rise to jurisdiction based either on the subjective or objective territorial principles, or both.

71   See Jennings & Watts, above note 9 at 50–51.

72   *Libman v. The Queen*, above note 31 at 214.

73   *The SS Lotus*, above note 10.

74   See *Corfu Channel Case (Merits) (United Kingdom v. Albania)*, [1949] I.C.J. 4 at 22.

conduct and affairs within its own borders as it sees fit.[75] It is a constraint on a state's territorial jurisdiction. Such derogation can be understood in that it relates to the treatment of foreign nationals and, hence, does not strictly concern the domestic affairs of the host state alone.

Once it is recognized that visiting foreign nationals, although under a general obligation to respect local law, are nevertheless owed certain basic standards of treatment by the host state, the obvious question that arises is how the required standard of treatment is defined. International law has developed two approaches to this issue, as we shall now see.

2) National Treatment vs. International Minimum Standard

The traditional but now controversial approach to defining the required conduct of states towards aliens is known as the national treatment standard. In applying the national treatment standard, the host state would only be obligated to extend treatment to foreign nationals that is no less generous than that extended to its own nationals.[76] Such an approach has a superficial attraction in that it appears to be consistent with principles of non-discrimination on the basis of nationality and perhaps even the formal equality of states. However, the national treatment standard also raises the possibility that unacceptable treatment of foreign nationals would be justified on the basis that the host state's own nationals are treated just as badly or perhaps worse. Such a consequence would be inconsistent with universally applicable international human rights norms which require that all states accord certain basic rights and standards of treatment to individuals of any (or no) nationality.

The competing approach is that of requiring a minimum international standard of treatment regardless of how poorly a state treats its own nationals.[77] Such an approach has the benefit of setting uniform minimum expectations for visiting foreigners. It is also consistent with the parallel emergence in the twentieth century of international human rights norms which, as observed above, provide for certain minimum protections for individuals regardless of their nationality or of the state in which they find themselves.

---

75   International law, of course, also imposes other limits on how a state may treat individuals, whether or not its own nationals: see further Chapter 10.

76   See R.B. Lillich, "Duties of States Regarding the Civil Rights of Aliens" (1978-III) 161 Rec. des Cours 329 at 349.

77   See *Encyclopaedia of Public International Law*, cons. lib. ed., vol. 3 (Amsterdam: North Holland Publishing, 1997) at 408–9, "minimum standard".

In general, developed states have favoured the latter, minimum international standard, approach. In large measure, this is because these states have effectively set the international minimum standard to match the minimum expectations of their own domestic legal systems. In addition, a minimum standard tends to provide better protection for the interests of their nationals who may hold property or investments abroad. In contrast, several developing states continue to advocate the national treatment standard as the correct approach to defining the basic level of treatment due to foreign nationals. In part, this position is justified by developing states' desire to assert more complete control over economic activities occurring within their own borders, but it also reflects a deeper resistance to the universalization of what are frequently perceived as Western, liberal-democratic standards of conduct. The imposition of such standards of conduct on all states with respect to matters occurring within their own territories is seen as reminiscent of the period when Europe defined the content of international law, which was subsequently proclaimed universally applicable.[78]

3) A Low International Minimum Standard: The *Neer* Formulation

While the question of the required standard for the treatment of aliens continues to be contentious in international law, the majority of scholarly opinion and arbitral awards in the twentieth and twenty-first centuries have favoured the idea of an international minimum standard.[79] This is not surprising given the widespread endorsement of international human rights norms in international law. It can also be explained on the basis that, while customary international law appears to be tending towards an international minimum standard in this area, in fact the standard is not particularly stringent. In this way, the interests of developed and developing states are at least partially reconciled.

---

78   R.B. Lillich, *The Human Rights of Aliens in Contemporary International Law* (Manchester: Manchester University Press, 1984) at 14–15.

79   See, for example, Brownlie, above note 2 at 502–3 (albeit suggesting, at 504, that there may be exceptions to its applicability); Shaw, above note 3 at 734; J. Brierly, *The Law of Nations: An Introduction to the Law of Peace*, 6th ed. (Oxford: Clarendon Press, 1963) at 279; American Law Institute, *Restatement of the Law (Third): Foreign Relations Law of the United States* (St. Paul, MN: American Law Institute, 1987) at §711 [*Restatement*]; *Case Concerning Certain German Interests in Polish Upper Silesia* (1926), P.C.I.J., Ser. A, No. 7 at 21–22; *Garcia Claim (United States of America v. United Mexican States)* (1926), 4 R.I.A.A. 119; *Roberts Claim (United States of America v. United Mexican States)* (1926), 4 R.I.A.A. 77.

It can probably be said that customary international law requires that states, in dealing with foreign nationals, must observe the standard described by the United States-Mexico Claims Commission in the *Neer* claim.[80] In that case, an American national was killed by unknown persons while working in Mexico. The United States brought a claim against Mexico on the basis that the latter had not adequately investigated the occurrence in order to find the perpetrators. In rejecting the claim, the Claims Commission stated what has since come to be regarded as the touchstone for the permissible treatment of foreign nationals:

> Without attempting to announce a precise formula, it is in the opinion of the Commission possible ... to hold (first) that the propriety of governmental acts should be put to the test of international standards, and (second) that the treatment of an alien, in order to constitute an international delinquency, should amount to an outrage, to bad faith, to wilful neglect of duty, or to an insufficiency of governmental action so far short of international standards that every reasonable and impartial man would readily recognize its insufficiency. Whether the insufficiency proceeds from deficient execution of an intelligent law or from the fact that the laws of the country do not empower the authorities to measure up to international standards is immaterial.[81]

The required minimum standard of treatment is thus quite low, essentially only requiring avoidance of "outrage[ous]" or "bad faith" conduct. Moreover, the imposition of such a standard is, in practice, confined to a relatively discrete set of situations or subject areas, with the result again that the potential intrusiveness of such a standard into a state's territorial sovereignty is generally quite modest.[82]

---

80   *L.F.H. Neer and P. Neer Claim (United States of America v. United Mexican States)* (1926), 4 R.I.A.A. 60 [*Neer*]. But see the decision of the Arbitral Tribunal established under Chapter 11 of the *North American Free Trade Agreement* (17 December 1992, (1994) Can. T.S. No. 2 [*NAFTA*]) in *Mondev International v. United States*, (2002), ARB(AF)/99/2, holding that *NAFTA* Article 1105, which guarantees "fair and equitable treatment and full protection and security" to foreign investors, reflects the modern standard of minimum treatment for foreign investors under customary international law. Such a standard, if generalized to other treatment of aliens' situations, would be considerably more exacting than the "outrage" or "bad faith" standard articulated in the *Neer* claim.

81   *Neer, ibid.* at 61–62.

82   See, generally, *Declaration on the Rights of Individuals Who Are Not Citizens of the Country in Which They Live*, UNGA Res. 144(XL), UN GAOR, 40th Sess., Supp. No. 53 (1985).

Among the situations where minimum standards are applied to the treatment of foreign nationals is their expulsion from a state's territory. While a state is generally free to refuse admission to aliens or to impose virtually any conditions on their admission into its territory,[83] once admitted, a foreign national may only be expelled in a manner that is procedurally fair and non-discriminatory, and that provides him with a reasonable opportunity to secure his personal or property interests in the territory of the expelling state.[84]

Another area in which the international minimum standard is frequently invoked is in cases of personal injury suffered by a foreign national. For example, a state may apply its enforcement jurisdiction to detain a foreign national within its territory who violates local law, but the state is then accountable for that foreign national's safety and well-being while in detention.[85] This is in fact a particularization of the more general rule that personal injury caused to foreign nationals by unlawful, cruel, or harsh treatment by the state itself, or through the wilful or bad faith failure of the state to control the conduct of private persons, will constitute a violation of the minimum standard for the treatment of aliens.

Similarly, the acts of any branch of a state's government—legislative, executive, or judicial—that deprive foreign nationals of the minimum protections of civil or criminal justice will also fall below the required international minimum standard.[86] Examples include situations where the state fails to maintain an effective system of civil justice or bars access of foreign nationals to the same, or where the local criminal justice system fails to respect basic procedural guarantees required by international human rights law. What is required here is not a sophisticated judicial system or compliance with an elaborate set of procedural protections. Rather, in keeping with the low threshold of the *Neer* formulation, what is prohibited are such outrageous and manifest injustices as egregious delay, biased decision-making, show trials, and other perversions of justice.[87]

---

83   Short of conditions that would violate international human rights norms or other international legal obligations of the admitting state.

84   See, for example, *Rankin v. Iran* (1987), 17 Iran-U.S. C.T.R. 135. Note that the International Law Commission has recently added the topic "Expulsion of Aliens" to its long-term programme of work in order to further clarify this area of the law.

85   See, for example, *Quintanilla Claim (United States of America v. United Mexican States)* (1926), 4 R.I.A.A. 101.

86   See, for example, the *B.E. Chattin Claim (United States of America v. United Mexican States)* (1927), 4 R.I.A.A. 282.

87   See, generally, Brownlie, above note 2 at 506–8.

Perhaps the most frequently litigated area relating to the treatment of aliens is that of expropriation of their property. The traditional, nineteenth-century view on expropriation of the property of foreign nationals was that all such acts were wrongful and required full compensation. Such a rule tended to protect the interests of wealthy states, the nationals of which frequently held property or investments abroad.

This view of the law changed quite dramatically in the twentieth century. First, a number of Latin American states adopted the practice of including, in concession contracts with foreign investors, a so-called "Calvo clause."[88] By this clause, foreign investors generally agreed not to seek the protection of their national states but to submit to local law and jurisdiction with respect to all matters or disputes arising under the contract. In this way, it was sought to legitimize expropriations by legalizing them domestically.

Further pressure was placed on the traditional rule that all expropriations of foreign property or investments were unlawful with the emergence, first, of socialist states and then of newly independent states. These states advocated greater sovereign rights over their own natural resources and other property within their boundaries, even if held by foreign nationals, and thus asserted their right to expropriate foreign-owned property in their own national, economic interests.[89]

The effect of this new but widespread state practice was to remove the stigma of international illegality from the act of expropriation itself, as long as certain criteria are respected.[90] In particular, the expropriation must be for a public purpose and carried out according to due process of law. Further, it must be carried out on a non-discriminatory basis (in the sense of not singling out foreign property-holders from a particular state only). Most importantly, however, expropriation must be followed

---

88   So named after the Argentinian diplomat and lawyer who pioneered its use as a means of restricting the rights of aliens to a national treatment standard: see R.B. Lillich, "The Current Status of the Law of State Responsibility for Injuries to Aliens" in R.B. Lillich, ed., *International Law of State Responsibility for Injuries to Aliens* (Charlottesville: University Press of Virginia, 1983) 1 at 4.

89   Such assertions were most prominently made in a number of UN General Assembly Declarations, adoption of which was assured by the numerically superior developing and socialist states: see, for example, *Resolution on Permanent Sovereignty Over Natural Resources*, GA Res. 1803 (XVII), UN GAOR, 17th Sess., Supp. No. 17, UN Doc. A/S217 (1962) at 17 [*Permanent Sovereignty Resolution*]; *Charter of Economic Rights and Duties of States*, GA Res. 3281 (XXIX), UN GAOR, 29th Sess., Supp. No. 31, UN Doc. A/9631 (1974) at 50.

90   See, for example, *Amoco International Finance Corp. v. Iran* (1987), 15 Iran-U.S. C.T.R. 189 at paras. 113–16 [*Amoco*].

by compensation.[91] Assuming all of these requirements are met, the expropriation will be considered legal in international law. If they are not, the expropriation will constitute a violation of the minimum standard of treatment owed by the state to the foreign national and may give rise to a claim in state responsibility by that foreign national's state.[92] While this view of the law is now generally accepted by states, important differences continue to persist, mainly between developed and developing states, as to the appropriate measure of compensation due upon expropriation.[93]

4) Consular Protection of Nationals Abroad

As a corollary of the above substantive rules relating to the treatment by states of foreign nationals, international law has developed a number of preventative or remedial mechanisms by which the legal interests of such nationals may be protected. The two principal such mechanisms are consular and diplomatic protection. The latter of these, diplomatic protection, is a doctrine of international law permitting the state of nationality of an injured person (individual or corporate) to "espouse" that person's claim and to seek redress for the injury from the injuring state at the international level. Given its close connection to the rules of state responsibility, we will examine the doctrine of diplomatic protection at greater length below, in Chapter 12.[94]

Consular protection, by contrast, is primarily concerned with preventing, rather than remedying, mistreatment of one's nationals while abroad. Pursuant to the widely ratified *Vienna Convention on Consular Relations*,[95] this is chiefly accomplished by guaranteeing freedom of communication between a state's consular officials and its nationals

---

91   See Starke & Shearer, above note 42 at 272.

92   See *Case Concerning the Factory at Chorzow (Germany v. Poland)* (1928), P.C.I.J. Ser. A, No. 17 at 47. See further Chapter 12.

93   See, for example, *Amoco*, above note 90 at para. 117. See also the *Permanent Sovereignty Resolution*, above note 89; *Charter of Economic Rights and Duties of States*, above note 89; *World Bank Guidelines on the Treatment of Foreign Direct Investment* (1992), 31 I.L.M. 1363 at 1382; *NAFTA*, above note 80, Article 1110; *Restatement*, above note 79 at §712; *Texaco Overseas Petroleum Company and California Asiatic Oil Company (TOPCO) v. Libyan Arab Republic* (1977), 53 I.L.R. 389; *Kuwait v. American Independent Oil Company (AMINOIL)* (1982), 66 I.L.R. 518; *Libyan American Oil Company (LIAMCO) v. Libyan Arab Republic* (1977), 62 I.L.R. 140; *AMCO Asia Corp. v. Indonesia* (1985), 89 I.L.R. 405 at 504; *Metalclad Corporation v. United Mexican States* (2000), 119 I.L.R. 615 at 641–42.

94   See Chapter 12, Section B(2).

95   *Vienna Convention on Consular Relations*, 24 April 1963, 596 U.N.T.S. 261 (in force 19 March 1967) [VCCR]. At the time of writing, the VCCR has 171 states parties.

abroad.[96] In this way, the latter may request assistance of the former to ensure that their rights and interests are respected while in another state. The most important manifestation of this right of communication arises when an individual is detained or imprisoned by a foreign state. In such a case, the detained individual must be informed without delay of her right to communicate with the local consular authorities of her state of nationality.[97] The duty to inform the individual of this right arises as soon as the detaining state's officials learn or suspect that the detained individual is a foreign national.[98] Moreover, if the detained individual requests it, the detaining state must advise the detainee's state of nationality of the detention.[99] Thereafter, consular officials may visit or communicate with the detained person as well as arrange for appropriate legal representation, unless the detained person expressly refuses such assistance.[100] In this sense, consular protection is mutually discretionary as between the protecting state and its nationals: the former is not obliged as a matter of international law to provide such protection, while the latter are not obliged to accept it. Assuming both are willing, however, the "host" state is subject to the mandatory obligation to permit the exercise of such protection in the ways described above.

FURTHER READING

AKEHURST, M., "Jurisdiction in International Law" (1972–73) 46 Brit. Y.B. Int'l L. 145

BOWETT, D.W., "Jurisdiction: Changing Problems of Authority over Activities and Resources" (1982) 53 Brit. Y.B. Int'l L. 1

BROWNLIE, I., *Principles of Public International Law*, 6th ed. (Oxford: Oxford University Press, 2003) cc. 15 and 24

CASTEL, J-G., *Extraterritoriality in International Trade, Canada and United States of America Practices Compared* (Toronto: Butterworths, 1988)

---

96 *Ibid.*, Article 36(1)(a).
97 *Ibid.*, Article 36(1)(b).
98 See *Case Concerning Avena and Other Mexican Nationals (Mexico v. United States of America)*, [2004] I.C.J. No. 128 at para. 63. See also *LaGrand Case (Germany v. United States of America)*, [2001] I.C.J. Rep. 466.
99 VCCR, above note 97, Article 36(1)(b).
100 *Ibid.*, Article 36(1)(c).

DAWSON, F.G. & HEAD, I.L., *International Law, National Tribunals and the Rights of Aliens* (Syracuse, NY: Syracuse University Press, 1971)

LA FOREST, A.W., *La Forest's Extradition to and from Canada*, 3d ed. (Aurora, ON: Canada Law Book, 1991)

LILLICH, R.B., *The Human Rights of Aliens in Contemporary International Law* (Manchester: Manchester University Press, 1984)

MACEDO, S., ed., *The Princeton Principles on Universal Jurisdiction* (Princeton: Program in Law and Public Affairs, Princeton University, 2001)

MANN, F.A., "The Doctrine of Jurisdiction in International Law" (1964-I) 111 Rec. des Cours 1

MANN, F.A., "The Doctrine of Jurisdiction in International Law Revisited After Twenty Years" (1984-III) 186 Rec. des Cours 9

MEESSEN, K.M., ed., *Extraterritorial Jurisdiction in Theory and Practice* (Boston: Kluwer Law International, 1996)

MORGAN, E., *International Law and the Canadian Courts: Sovereign Immunity, Criminal Jurisdiction, Aliens' Rights and Taxation Powers* (Agincourt, ON: Carswell, 1990)

REISMAN, M., ed., *Jurisdiction in International Law* (Aldershot: Ashgate, 1999)

REYDAMS, L., *Universal Jurisdiction: International and Municipal Legal Perspectives* (Oxford: Oxford University Press, 2003)

SHAW, M.N., *International Law*, 5th ed. (Cambridge: Cambridge University Press, 2003) c. 12

SHEARER, I.A., *Extradition in International Law* (Dobbs Ferry: Oceana, 1971)

SORNARAJAH, M., *The International Law on Foreign Investment*, 2d ed. (Cambridge: Cambridge University Press, 2004)

WILLIAMS, S.A. & CASTEL, J-G., *Canadian Criminal Law: International and Transnational Aspects* (Toronto: Butterworths, 1981)

ZANOTTI, I., *Extradition in Multilateral Treaties and Conventions* (Leiden: Martinus Nijhoff, 2006)

CHAPTER 9

JURISDICTIONAL IMMUNITIES

A. INTRODUCTION

As seen in the preceding chapter, the essentially permissive approach taken in international law to questions of prescriptive jurisdiction en- counters limits when one state's exercise of such jurisdiction trespasses upon the jurisdictional domain of another. This is a consequence of the existence in international law of multiple sovereigns, each with a legal duty to respect one another's sovereignty. As we have seen, one general manifestation of this duty is the broad jurisdictional limit imposed on states not to intervene in one another's domestic affairs. International law has, however, developed other, more specific, "blocking" rules that prohibit certain exercises of jurisdiction by states, even within their own territory, when the effect of such an exercise of jurisdiction would be inconsistent with the sovereign equality of other states. Such rules, because they have the effect of ousting jurisdiction in circumstances in which it would otherwise exist (for example, on the basis of the ter- ritorial principle, or one of the other principles reviewed in Chapter 8 above) are known as "jurisdictional immunities."

The two most important categories of jurisdictional immunity are state immunity, on the one hand, and diplomatic and consular im- munities, on the other. While both categories spring from a common underlying concern to preserve respect for the sovereign equality of states, we shall see that each is distinct in its historical development, functional objectives, and scope.

B. STATE IMMUNITY

1) Nature, Basis, and Scope of State Immunity

a) Nature of State Immunity

State immunity is a narrowly focused but potent immunity in that it protects states from one another's enforcement jurisdiction. It is usually applied to forestall or halt domestic judicial proceedings against a foreign state. In other words, state immunity, a long-established and universally recognized doctrine of customary international law, essentially blocks a state's courts from exercising jurisdiction over foreign states. This immunity extends to all phases of the judicial process, including interlocutory or interim preservation orders as well as post-trial execution measures and appeals. It encompasses civil and criminal proceedings alike.

However, it is important to distinguish the domestic judicial process of applying and enforcing domestic law from international judicial or quasi-judicial proceedings. State immunity is only relevant in the former context. In other words, the immunity operates with respect to the judicial process of courts of another state, not of international tribunals.[1]

Historically, an immunity from domestic enforcement (including adjudicative) jurisdiction attached to the person of a visiting foreign sovereign, as that sovereign was considered the embodiment of the foreign state.[2] For this reason state immunity is still sometimes referred to as "sovereign immunity." So strong was the attachment of the immunity to the person of the foreign sovereign that there remained some doubt in international law until the mid-nineteenth century as to whether the same immunity attached to heads of state of republics.[3] With the evolution of the conception of the state as a legal and political entity separate from the person of the monarch, however, sovereign immunity evolved

---

1   See *Case Concerning the Arrest Warrant of 11 April 2000 (Democratic Republic of the Congo v. Belgium)*, [2002] I.C.J. Rep. 3 at para. 61 [*DRC v. Belgium*]; *Prosecutor v. Taylor, Decision on Immunity* (31 May 2004) SCSL-2003-61, 3014-3039 at paras. 49–54 (S.C.S.L. App. Ch.), online: www.sc-sl.org/Documents/SCSL-03-01-I-059.pdf [*Prosecutor v. Taylor*].

2   See J-M. Arbour & G. Parent, *Droit international public*, 5e éd. (Cowansville, QC: Yvon Blais, 2006) at 332; M.N. Shaw, *International Law*, 5th ed. (Cambridge: Cambridge University Press, 2003) at 621–22.

3   See, for example, *United States of America v. Wagner* (1867), L.R. 2 Ch. App. 582. See also J.G. Starke & I.A. Shearer, *Starke's International Law*, 11th ed. (London: Butterworths, 1994) at 192.

to become a general immunity enjoyed not only by monarchs, but also by the state more generally in its various manifestations.[4]

It is important to note that state immunity does not imply an absence of jurisdiction *per se*. Rather, state immunity applies as a procedural bar to the exercise of jurisdiction that otherwise, substantively, exists. As has been observed by the International Court of Justice (ICJ), "jurisdiction does not imply absence of immunity, while absence of immunity does not imply jurisdiction."[5] The significance of this feature of state immunity will be apparent when we consider the ability of a state to waive its immunity from the jurisdiction of foreign courts.

b) Basis for State Immunity

The classic enunciation of both the doctrine of state immunity and its underlying rationales is generally acknowledged to be that of the United States' Supreme Court in the early nineteenth century case of *The Schooner Exchange* v. *McFadden*:

> This full and absolute territorial jurisdiction being alike the attribute of every sovereign, and being incapable of conferring extraterritorial power, would not seem to contemplate foreign sovereigns nor their sovereign rights as its objects. One sovereign being in no respect amenable to another; and being bound by obligations of the highest character not to degrade the dignity of his nation, by placing himself or its sovereign rights within the jurisdiction of another, can be supposed to enter a foreign territory only under an express license, or in the confidence that the immunities belonging to his independent sovereign station, though not expressly stipulated, are reserved by implication, and will be extended to him.
>
> This perfect equality and absolute independence of sovereigns, and this common interest impelling them to mutual intercourse, and an interchange of good offices with each other, have given rise to a class of cases in which every sovereign is understood to waive the exercise of a part of that complete exclusive territorial jurisdiction, which has been stated to be the attribute of every nation.[6]

A number of bases for the doctrine of state immunity emerge from this statement. The most widely acknowledged is somewhat formal: the requirement of state immunity is said to flow as a necessary corollary of the principle of the sovereign equality of states. If all states are equal in

---

4   See, generally, I. Brownlie, *Principles of Public International Law*, 6th ed. (Oxford: Oxford University Press, 2003) at 322.

5   *DRC v. Belgium*, above note 1 at para. 59.

6   *The Schooner Exchange v. McFadden*, 11 U.S. 114 at 136 (1812).

international law, so the theory goes, no one state should be able to subject another to the process of its courts. Viewed from a slightly different angle, subjection to foreign judicial or other enforcement processes could be considered inconsistent with the dignity of sovereign states.

A more informal and functional justification is that the immunity evidences restraint and consideration and therefore fosters friendly relations between states. It may also serve to facilitate contact between states in that a state may generally assume it will not be subject to foreign judicial proceedings by virtue merely of entering the territory of, or engaging in a transaction in, a foreign state.

Yet another explanation is based on the idea that when foreign states or their representatives are permitted by a host state to enter into or engage in transactions within its territory, one of the implied terms of that permission is an immunity from the process of the local courts. Theoretically, this rationalization is attractive in that it preserves the notional sovereignty of the territorial sovereign, including its enforcement jurisdiction over activities occurring within its territory. In other words, the foreign state's immunity is considered a right granted to it by consent of the territorial sovereign, rather than an *a priori* limitation on the latter's territorial sovereignty. There is, however, a fictional element to such a rationale in that it implies that a host state could withhold, if it so chose, the extension of immunity to the foreign state. This is inconsistent with the generally accepted view that states enjoy immunity from foreign judicial process as of right, and that host states are obliged as a matter of customary international law[7] to extend such immunity.[8]

c) *Ratione Personae* and *Ratione Materiae* Immunities Distinguished

Returning briefly to the origins of state immunity as a personal entitlement of a foreign sovereign, its evolution into an immunity enjoyed by the state and its various organs and representatives is sometimes said to have given rise to two aspects of the immunity: immunity *ratione personae* and immunity *ratione materiae*. Immunity *ratione personae* attaches to the persons of key representatives of the foreign state—in particular, the head of state or government, the foreign minister, and, perhaps, other senior members of the government—but only while

---

7   And treaty law, in the case of a party to the *United Nations Convention on the Jurisdictional Immunities of States and Their Property*, 2 December 2004, UNGA Res. 59/38, U.N. Doc. A/RES/59/38 (2004), Annex (not yet in force) [*Jurisdictional Immunities Convention*] — once it comes into force.

8   For further discussion of the bases for state immunity, see H. Fox, *The Law of State Immunity* (Oxford: Oxford University Press, 2002) at 28.

such persons hold office. In other words, these high-ranking state representatives are, as long as they remain in office, personally immune from the jurisdiction of foreign courts, regardless of the nature of their acts or the subject matter of the judicial proceedings. Once out of office, however, these key state representatives no longer enjoy immunity from the process of foreign courts in their personal capacity. The underlying rationale for *ratione personae* immunity is the overriding need to preserve each state's independence and capacity to govern itself. This is accomplished by ensuring that its key governmental representatives are unimpeded in the performance of their functions by foreign judicial or other enforcement proceedings.

In contrast, immunity *ratione materiae* attaches to official acts of the foreign state rather than to the person(s) representing it. In determining whether such immunity arises, the focus becomes the nature of the relevant act or transaction rather than the identity of the actor.[9] If the act or transaction is an official act of a foreign state, *ratione materiae* immunity will attach to the act or transaction in such a way as to shield the foreign state from local judicial jurisdiction in respect of that act or transaction.[10] This will be so even if the act or transaction is carried out on behalf of the state by a low-ranking representative or *ad hoc* agent who would not normally be entitled to immunity *ratione personae*.[11]

It can be readily seen that the circumstances in which *ratione personae* and *ratione materiae* immunity arise will not always coincide. For example, it may be that no *ratione personae* immunity arises in a given case because the actor in question either was not or is no longer a senior member of a foreign government, but *ratione materiae* immunity arises because of the subject matter of the relevant transaction. Similarly, acts of a visiting foreign head of state may not attract *ratione materiae* immunity if the acts are of a purely private nature (for example, those committed while the foreign head of state is vacationing abroad), and yet will attract *ratione personae* immunity solely due to the official position held personally by the actor.

The relevance of the distinction between immunity *ratione personae* and *ratione materiae* was recently highlighted by the British House of

---

9   Although the identity of the actor may, of course, shed light on whether the act or transaction is an official act of the foreign state. On the range of actors whose acts may be covered by state immunity see further Section B(2)(d), below in this chapter.

10   Subject to certain limits on the scope of *ratione materiae* immunity, to be reviewed below.

11   See further Section B(2)(d), below in this chapter.

Lords in the well-known *Pinochet* case.[12] In that case, a Spanish prosecutor alleged that Augusto Pinochet had committed or ordered acts of torture, hostage-taking, and other illegal acts during his tenure as head of state of Chile between 1973 and 1990. In 1998, Spain therefore requested that Pinochet be extradited from the United Kingdom, where he was undergoing medical treatment, in order to face these charges in a Spanish court. Pinochet was arrested by the British authorities and the question ultimately posed to the House of Lords was whether the British courts could subject Pinochet to the extradition proceedings.

Several of the Law Lords noted the significance of the distinction between immunity *ratione personae* and *ratione materiae* in addressing this question. At the time of the proceedings, Pinochet was no longer Chile's head of state, but was merely a Chilean senator with no direct participation or role in Chile's government. As such, he did not enjoy immunity *ratione personae* because, although head of state at the time of the alleged illegal acts, he no longer held the post at the time of the proposed extradition proceedings. The issue therefore came down to whether the alleged acts themselves could be characterized as official acts on behalf of the state of Chile and thus attract immunity *ratione materiae*. In the end, it was found by a majority in the House of Lords that immunity *ratione materiae* did not attach to some of the alleged acts of torture because Chile had waived immunity in respect of those acts by ratifying the *Torture Convention*.[13]

---

12   *Ex parte Pinochet Ugarte (No. 3)*, [1999] 2 All E.R 97 (H.L.) [*Pinochet*]. In 1998, Pinochet had brought an application to have the warrants issued against him quashed before the Divisional Court. The application was successful on the Court's reasoning that the former head of state was entitled to state immunity in respect of the alleged acts: [1998] All E.R. 509. The Crown successfully appealed to the House of Lords, a majority of which ruled that Senator Pinochet was not entitled to immunity for international crimes: [1998] 4 All E.R. 897. However, that judgment was set aside due to the improper constitution of the panel based on a reasonable apprehension of bias: [1999] 1 All E.R. 577. The case was thus heard again, leading to the final House of Lords decision referred to here.

13   *United Nations Convention against Torture and Other Cruel, Inhuman or Degrading Treatment or Punishment*, 10 December 1984, 1465 U.N.T.S. 85 (entered into force 26 June 1987) [*Torture Convention*]. See Section B(1)(e), below in this chapter, for further discussion of the decision of the House of Lords in *Pinochet*, above note 12. Notwithstanding the ruling by the House of Lords that Pinochet was not entitled to immunity from the jurisdiction of the British courts in respect of some of the alleged acts, Pinochet was released on grounds of ill health by UK Home Secretary Jack Straw. Upon his return to Chile, the Chilean courts denied Pinochet domestic immunity as a Senator and he was charged with various offences arising from his alleged human rights violations and placed

The distinction between immunity *ratione personae* and *ratione materiae* was also central to the judgment of the ICJ in *DRC v. Belgium*.[14] In that case, a Belgian investigating judge had issued an arrest warrant *in absentia* against the incumbent foreign minister of the Democratic Republic of the Congo (DRC) on charges of war crimes and crimes against humanity.[15] The DRC, considering that this action violated the immunity traditionally enjoyed by foreign ministers in office, applied to the ICJ for an order that the arrest warrant be rescinded as well as other relief.

After affirming the existence of *ratione personae* immunity from both criminal and civil jurisdiction for heads of state, heads of government, and foreign ministers in office,[16] the ICJ enlarged upon the scope of, and rationale for, such immunity in the following terms:

> 53. In customary international law, the immunities accorded to Ministers for Foreign Affairs are not granted for their personal benefit, but to ensure the effective performance of their functions on behalf of their respective States …. He or she is in charge of his or her Government's diplomatic activities and generally acts as its representative in international negotiations and intergovernmental meetings…. In the performance of these functions, he or she is frequently required to travel internationally, and thus must be in a position freely to do so whenever the need should arise ….

> 54. The Court accordingly concludes that the functions of a Minister for Foreign Affairs are such that, throughout the duration of his or her office, he or she when abroad enjoys full immunity from criminal jurisdiction and inviolability. That immunity and that inviolability protect the individual concerned against any act of authority of another State which would hinder him or her in the performance of his or her duties.

> 55. In this respect, no distinction can be drawn between acts performed by a Minister for Foreign Affairs in an "official" capacity, and those claimed to have been performed in a "private capacity," or, for that matter, between acts performed before the person concerned assumed office as Minister for Foreign Affairs and acts committed

---

under house arrest. Amid delays caused in part by recurring health problems, Pinochet died on 8 December 2006, before he could be brought to trial.

14   *DRC v. Belgium*, above note 1.

15   For a description of the Belgian legislation that purported to extend Belgian jurisdiction to such acts on the basis of universal jurisdiction, see Chapter 8, Section C(4)(d), note 55.

16   *DRC v. Belgium*, above note 1 at para. 51.

during the period of office. Thus, if a Minister for Foreign Affairs is arrested in another State on a criminal charge, he or she is clearly thereby prevented from exercising the functions of his or her office. The consequences of such impediment to the exercise of those official functions are equally serious, regardless of whether the Minister for Foreign Affairs was, at the time of arrest, present in the territory of the arresting State on an "official" visit or a "private" visit, regardless of whether the arrest relates to acts allegedly performed before the person became the Minister for Foreign Affairs or to acts performed while in office, and regardless of whether the arrest relates to alleged acts performed in an "official" capacity or a "private" capacity ....[17]

It will thus be seen that immunity *ratione personae* is, at least for those few state representatives that enjoy it, an enormously potent shield against foreign exercises of jurisdiction.[18] However, its protections are fleeting, surviving only for so long as the representative holds office. Once out of office (and for lower-ranking state representatives not entitled to immunity *ratione personae* in any event), immunity *ratione materiae* offers more modest protection in respect of acts performed in an official capacity on behalf of a state. Appreciating the full scope of this more modest form of state immunity therefore requires consideration of what constitutes an official act on behalf of a state, an issue to which we will return below.

d) Absolute vs. Restrictive State Immunity and the Work of the International Law Commission

As indicated above, the international law of state immunity has evolved primarily as a matter of customary international law.[19] Given its importance, however, the International Law Commission had the topic on its agenda between 1977 and 1991, when it adopted the "Draft Articles on Jurisdictional Immunities of States and Their Property."[20] The Draft

---

17   *Ibid.* at paras. 53–55.

18   It should be noted that the International Law Commission has recently added the topic "Immunity of State Officials from Foreign Criminal Jurisdiction" to its long-term programme of work, suggesting that it considers this area of the law to be in need of clarification: see "Report of the International Law Commission on the Work of its Fifty-Eighth Session", UN GAOR, 61st Session, Supplement No. 10 (A/61/10) (2006) at para. 257.

19   An important qualification to this general statement is the *European Convention on State Immunity*, 16 May 1972, E.T.S. No. 072 (entered into force 11 June 1976). See now also the *Jurisdictional Immunities Convention*, above note 7.

20   The Draft Articles are reproduced in "Report of the International Law Commission on the Work of its Forty-Third Session" (UN Doc. A/46/10) in *Yearbook*

Articles were subsequently the subject of discussion and debate in the UN General Assembly and further consideration by the International Law Commission,[21] and ultimately formed the basis of a multilateral convention on state immunity adopted by the General Assembly in 2004.[22] The *Jurisdictional Immunities Convention*[23] is not yet in force, but it is early in the signature and ratification process and the debates preceding its adoption by the General Assembly suggest that it is viewed by most states as broadly consistent with extant customary international law on the topic.[24]

One of the principal objectives of thus codifying the principles of state immunity was to clarify some of the considerable uncertainties surrounding the topic resulting from certain twentieth century developments. One of these developments was the increasing propensity of the modern state to participate in the marketplace as a significant economic actor. This was particularly (although by no means exclusively) the case with socialist states with centrally planned economies.

---

of the International Law Commission 1991, vol. II, Part 2 (New York: United Nations, 1991) [ILC Report (1991)].

21 In response to the 1991 report by the International Law Commission, the General Assembly created a Working Group to consider the Draft Articles: see *Report of the Working Group on the Convention on Jurisdictional Immunities of States and their Property*, UN GAOR, 47th Sess., UN Doc. A/C.6/47/L.10 (1992); *Report of the Working Group on the Convention on Jurisdictional Immunities of States and their Property*, UN GAOR, 48th Sess., UN Doc. A/C.6/48/L.4 (1993). Acting upon the Commission's recommendation in its 1991 report, the General Assembly in 1994 decided that an international conference should be convened to consider the Draft Articles and to conclude a convention: *Convention on Jurisdictional Immunities of States and their Property*, GA Res.49/61, UN GAOR, 49th Sess., UN Doc. A/RES/49/ 61 (1994). However, the Working Group's work continued and no definitive arrangements for the convening of such a conference were concluded. In light of this ongoing discussion, the Commission also created a Working Group to consider the views of states: see *Report of the Working Group on the Convention on Jurisdictional Immunities of States and their Property*, Annex to "Report of the International Law Commission on the Work of its Fifty-First Session" (UN Doc. A/54/10 and Corr.1 & 2) in *Yearbook of the International Law Commission 1999* (New York: United Nations, 1999) [ILC Report (1999)].

22 See UNGA Res. 59/38, U.N. Doc. A/RES/59/38 (2004).

23 *Jurisdictional Immunities Convention*, above note 7.

24 See *AIG Capital Partners Inc. v. Republic of Kazakhstan*, [2006] 1 All E.R. 284 at para. 80 (Q.B.); *Jones v. Ministry of Interior Al-Mamlaka Al-Arabiya AS Saudiya (the Kingdom of Saudi Arabia)*, [2006] UKHL 26 at paras. 26 (Lord Bingham) and 47 (Lord Hoffmann) [*Jones v. Saudi Arabia*]. At the time of writing the *Jurisdictional Immunities Convention*, above note 7, has twenty-eight signatories and four parties. Thirty parties are required to bring it into force: *ibid.*, Article 30(1).

When states as commercial actors engage in transnational business dealings—that is, commercial transactions with one or more foreign elements—the difficulty posed is whether such states should enjoy greater privileges or immunities than any other commercial actor in the international marketplace. For example, a food wholesaler in Canada might contract with a privately owned Russian supplier for the delivery of certain food products. If the Russian supplier breaks the contract, the Canadian wholesaler may, depending on the terms of the contract, have recourse to the Canadian courts for a remedy. However, if the other party to the contract is not a private entity but, rather, the Russian government, ought the doctrine of state immunity apply to deprive the Canadian wholesaler of the same remedial option?

Under the strict or "absolute" theory of state immunity that clearly prevailed in customary international law until well into the twentieth century,[25] the answer to the foregoing question would be "yes." The fact that the relevant party to the contract is a foreign state would alone, under the absolute theory of state immunity, be sufficient to oust the jurisdiction of the local courts, regardless of the fact that the foreign state happened to be acting as a commercial rather than a sovereign actor in the transaction.

Such an approach has many potential results. First, it places foreign governments at an unfair advantage in international economic dealings, as they can escape enforcement measures in foreign courts and walk away from their contractual undertakings with relative impunity. Second, this introduces uncertainty into the marketplace and undermines the rule of law necessary for stable economic relations. Third, and as a further consequence, this uncertainty may make commercial actors unwilling to enter into private legal dealings with foreign governments out of concern that they will be without a local remedy if the foreign government chooses not to honour its contractual commitments. In short, the overall effect could be a "chilling" of the global marketplace.

In order to address some of these concerns, several Western states began, in the twentieth century, to advocate a "restrictive" form of immunity. Under the restrictive theory, states would continue to enjoy their traditional immunity from the jurisdiction of foreign domestic courts in most areas, but certain transactions, particularly those of a commercial or "private" character, would no longer attract *ratione materiae* immunity. The distinction that emerged was between acts *jure imperii* (acts that are essentially sovereign or governmental in nature)

---

25   See Shaw, above note 2 at 625. See also *The Parlement Belge* (1880), L.R. 5 P.D. 197 at 214–15 (Eng. C.A.).

and acts *jure gestionis* (acts that are essentially commercial or "private" in nature). By drawing such a distinction and denying immunity to the latter category, the essential *raison d'être* of state immunity would largely be preserved while accommodating the competing need to ensure that states that choose to enter the marketplace as economic actors do so on a relatively even playing field.

Of course, many difficulties are posed by the restrictive theory of state immunity. First and foremost is the reluctance of some states to forego the full extent of the immunity they previously enjoyed at customary international law.[26] In part, this is because the effects of a restrictive form of state immunity are not felt evenly by all states. For example, a state with a centrally planned economy is more likely to be frequently involved in international business transactions than a state with a market economy, and will find itself disproportionately affected by the partial retrenchment of its traditional immunities in the sphere of international economic transactions. Many developing states in particular have found themselves in this situation, as many of them find it necessary both to be actively involved in developing their economies and to be reliant on foreign goods, services, and investment to this end.

Another principal challenge posed by the restrictive theory of state immunity is the need to clearly define the line between transactions that will or will not attract immunity. How does one distinguish a "commercial" transaction involving a state, to which restrictive state immunity would not apply, from "sovereign" state activity, to which it would? Should there be other categories of acts, to which immunity does not extend, beyond commercial and "private" transactions?[27] Further, how does one define those state agencies or representatives whose acts will be considered commercial as opposed to those that will not? For example, should transactions entered into by a state's central bank be considered commercial and thus not protected by state immunity, or are they, rather, sovereign acts which should not be subject to scrutiny in the courts of another sovereign?[28]

---

26   See Fox, above note 8 at 258–59.

27   See Section B(1)(e), below in this chapter; see also M. Copithorne, "'If Commerce, Why Not Torture?' An Examination of Further Limiting State Immunity with Torture as a Case Study" in O.E. Fitzgerald, ed., *The Globalized Rule of Law: Relationships between International and Domestic Law* (Toronto: Irwin Law, 2006) 603; J. Cooper-Hill, *The Law of Sovereign Immunity and Terrorism* (Dobbs Ferry, NY: Oceana, 2006).

28   See, for example, *Trendtex Trading Corp. Ltd. v. Central Bank of Nigeria*, [1977] 1 Q.B. 529 at 560 (Eng. C.A.), where Lord Denning M.R., in *obiter dicta*, concluded that the Nigerian Central Bank was not a department of the state of Nigeria,

Notwithstanding these difficulties, the tide definitely began to turn in the late twentieth century as states increasingly adopted one form or another of the restrictive theory of state immunity and began subjecting foreign states to the jurisdiction of their courts in certain situations. Beginning in Europe, but rapidly spreading to many other jurisdictions either by judicial or legislative development, restrictive immunity has largely displaced the absolute theory in respect of commercial transactions and a limited number of other defined categories of state activity.[29] The collapse of the Soviet Union in 1991 and the intensification of global trade have further weakened the absolute theory of state immunity to the point where it can cautiously be stated that the restrictive theory, at least as a concept, has emerged as the new customary international legal norm. While much state practice remains variable in terms of the precise scope of the restrictive theory, in general the idea that immunity is no longer absolute in commercial matters and other "private" transactions has been widely accepted.[30] The consensus adoption by the UN General Assembly in 2004 of the *Jurisdictional Immunities Convention*, which espouses a restrictive approach to state immunities, appears to confirm this. As it is anticipated that the *Jurisdictional Immunities Convention* will in time be widely ratified and implemented, thus bringing greater uniformity to state practice, Section 2 below will therefore describe the international law of restrictive state immunity in greater detail with reference to the Convention.

Before doing so, however, it is necessary to refer to the latest challenge to the traditional, absolute theory of state immunity: the call to further restrict state immunity in proceedings arising from gross violations of human rights or humanitarian law.

e) State Immunity and Gross Violations of Human Rights and Humanitarian Law

We have already noted a number of recent cases that have considered the availability of state immunity in domestic legal proceedings against foreign state officials resulting from gross violations of international

---

based on an examination of its functions and the degree of control exercised over its activities by the Nigerian government.

29   See, for example, the *European Convention on State Immunity*, above note 19; the UK *State Immunity Act, 1978* (U.K.), 1978, c. 33; and the US *Foreign Sovereign Immunities Act of 1976*, 28 U.S.C. §§ 1602–11. See now also the *Jurisdictional Immunities Convention*, above note 7, Articles 10–16 and 19(c).

30   See, generally, ILC Report (1999), above note 21. See also Shaw, above note 2 at 628–31; Brownlie, above note 4 at 323–25.

human rights or humanitarian law.[31] These cases can be seen as a natural outgrowth of the relatively recent establishment of various international criminal tribunals, before which individual perpetrators of serious international crimes are brought to account, regardless of their rank or official position as state representatives.[32] As we have already seen, the doctrine of state immunity does not act as a bar to the exercise of such jurisdiction given that such tribunals are international, rather than domestic, in character. As such, subjection of even a head of state to the jurisdiction of these tribunals entails no violation of the fundamental principle of the sovereign equality of states. In short, such proceedings do not involve one state standing in judgment of another; rather, they involve condemnation, by the international community, of internationally criminal conduct.[33]

While the growth in the number of such international criminal accountability mechanisms might be expected to have forestalled national judicial proceedings arising out of gross human rights and humanitarian violations (with all the complex state immunity issues they raise), this has not been the case. There are at least four reasons for this. First, the jurisdiction of international criminal tribunals is limited in various ways.[34] Second, by their very nature, international criminal tribunals tend to focus on criminal accountability by individual perpetrators, rather than responsibility of the state on behalf of which

---

31   See *Pinochet*, above note 12; *DRC v. Belgium*, above note 1.

32   For example, the International Criminal Court, the International Criminal Tribunals for the Former Yugoslavia and Rwanda, and the Special Court for Sierra Leone, amongst others, all have jurisdiction to try individuals, including the most highly-placed state representatives and even heads of state, for serious international crimes: see *Rome Statute of the International Criminal Court*, 17 July 1998, 2187 U.N.T.S. 90, entered into force 1 July 2002, Article 27 [*Rome Statute*]; *Statute of the International Criminal Tribunal for the Former Yugoslavia*, 25 May 1993, UNSC Res. 827, U.N. Doc. S/RES/827 (1993) (as amended), Annex, Article 7; *Statute of the International Criminal Tribunal for Rwanda*, 8 November 1994, UNSC Res. 955, U.N. Doc. S/RES/955 (1994), Annex, Article 6; *Statute of the Special Court for Sierra Leone*, 16 January 2002, 2178 U.N.T.S. 137, Article 6. See also *Prosecutor v. Taylor*, above note 1 at paras. 50–53.

33   See further the text accompanying note 1, above in this chapter.

34   For example, their subject-matter jurisdiction tends to be limited to only the most serious international crimes (such as genocide, crimes against humanity, and war crimes) and they therefore provide no accountability for gross breaches of human rights or humanitarian law that do not meet the strict definitions given to these crimes in international criminal law. Similarly, the jurisdiction of international criminal tribunals tends to be limited to events occurring during certain periods or conflicts or in certain geographical areas.

they may have acted, or civil remedies for their victims.[35] Third, the fact that the restrictive theory of state immunity has not engendered a general collapse of international relations has led many academics, civil society groups and even some states to ask why, in this era of heightened concern for human rights, states and their representatives should be subject to foreign proceedings related to their commercial, but not their international criminal, activities.[36] Fourth, the subjection of even heads of state to international criminal proceedings has apparently kindled the view that they should be amenable to proceedings in domestic courts as well.

The result has been a surge in attempts, both by state prosecutors and individuals or groups in civil proceedings, to prosecute or sue foreign states or their representatives in domestic courts for gross violations of international human rights or humanitarian law. To date, however, the success of such attempts has been extremely limited, suggesting that a further restriction of state immunity for such acts has not yet come about as a matter of customary international law.[37]

Consider for example the *Pinochet* case.[38] As we have seen, a majority of the Law Lords in that case denied Pinochet's claim of state immunity. On its face, this is an instance of state practice denying state immunity in criminal proceedings arising from one of the more heinous violations of international human rights — torture. Yet a careful reading of the seven speeches given in the case discloses a much more restrained precedent. In particular, while the speeches of some of the Law Lords[39] include *dicta* suggesting in various ways that torture should not, in principle, be considered an official act of a state that can attract *ratione materiae* immunity, the House of Lords nevertheless limited its denial of immunity to the period following the coming into force, as between Chile and the

---

35   A notable but limited exception here is the *Rome Statute* of the International Criminal Court, which provides for the establishment of a victims' compensation fund: see *Rome Statute*, above note 32, Article 75; *Establishment of a Fund for the Benefit of Victims of Crimes Within the Jurisdiction of the Court, and of the Families of Such Victims*, ICC-ASP/1/Res. 6 (9 September 2002), Official Records, Assembly of States Parties to the Rome Statute of the International Criminal Court, First Session, New York, 3–10 September 2002 at 340.

36   See, for example, Copithorne, above note 27.

37   See Fox, above note 8 at 260, describing a purported restriction on state immunity for "[a]cts contrary to international law and in particular violations of certain fundamental human rights" as "[c]ontroversial and unsupported by general State practice."

38   *Pinochet*, above note 12.

39   *Ibid.*, Lords Hope (at 152), Hutton (at 166), Millett (at 179) and, *semble*, Phillips (at 190).

United Kingdom, of the *Torture Convention*. This strongly suggests (and the majority of the Law Lords made this explicit[40]) that the basis for refusing to grant Pinochet immunity was Chile's *treaty* commitments vis-à-vis the United Kingdom, rather than a customary international legal rule precluding state immunity for such acts generally or in principle. Thus, notwithstanding objection by three Law Lords to use of the expression "waiver" to describe the effect of Chile's ratification of the *Torture Convention*,[41] in the end the outcome of the case turned crucially on Chile's ratification of the Convention and its concomitant acceptance of foreign assertions of jurisdiction over torture committed by Chilean officials. Thus, if anything, *Pinochet* appears to *affirm* state immunity, even in criminal proceedings arising from foreign acts of torture, except to the extent that such immunity has been relinquished by the state otherwise entitled to its protection.

Consider also the judgment of the ICJ in *DRC* v. *Belgium*.[42] We have already seen that in that case the ICJ affirmed the general applicability

---

40   See *ibid.*, Lord Browne-Wilkinson at 115 ("... Senator Pinochet ... was not
     acting in any capacity which gives rise to immunity *ratione materiae* because
     ... Chile had agreed with the other parties to the *Torture Convention* that all
     signatory states should have jurisdiction to try official torture ...."); Lord Hope
     at 152 ("... once the machinery which [the *Torture Convention*] provides was put
     in place to enable jurisdiction over such crimes to be exercised in the courts of
     a foreign state, it was no longer open to any state which was a signatory to the
     convention to invoke the immunity *ratione materiae* in the event of allegation of
     systematic or widespread torture committed after that date ...."); Lord Hutton
     at 165 ("... having regard to the provisions of the *Torture Convention*, I do not
     consider that Senator Pinochet or Chile can claim that the commission of acts
     of torture after 29 September 1988 were functions of the head of state ....");
     Lord Saville at 169 ("...so far as the allegations of official torture against Senator
     Pinochet are concerned, there is now by this agreement [the *Torture Conven-
     tion*] an exception or qualification to the general rule of immunity *ratione
     materiae*...."); Lord Phillips at 190 ("The [*Torture*] Convention is ... incompatible
     with the applicability of immunity *ratione materiae* ...."); Lord Millett at 179
     ("... the Republic of Chile was a party to the *Torture Convention*, and must be
     taken to have assented to the imposition of an obligation on foreign national
     courts to take and exercise criminal jurisdiction in respect of the official use of
     torture"). Note that the seventh Law Lord, Lord Goff, would have found Pino-
     chet entitled to state immunity given the *Torture Convention*'s failure to remove
     it expressly: *ibid.* at 123–30. See also *Jones v. Saudi Arabia*, above note 24 at para.
     19, per Lord Bingham: "The *Torture Convention* was the mainspring of the deci-
     sion [in *Pinochet*] ...."; and at para. 71, Lord Hoffmann: "The Torture Conven-
     tion ... was held in *Pinochet (No. 3)* ... by necessary implication, to remove the
     immunity from criminal prosecution which would ordinarily attach to acts
     performed by individuals in a public capacity."
41   *Ibid.*, Lords Hope (at 152), Hutton (at 166), and Millett (at 179).
42   *DRC v. Belgium*, above note 1.

of *ratione personae* immunity to high-ranking foreign state representatives. In doing so the ICJ addressed Belgium's argument that, whatever its rationale, such immunity could not, as a matter of principle, shield a foreign minister from prosecution for serious international crimes such as war crimes or crimes against humanity. The ICJ concluded that it was "unable to deduce from [state] practice that there exists under customary international law any form of exception to the rule according immunity from criminal jurisdiction and inviolability to incumbent Ministers for Foreign Affairs, where they are suspected of having committed war crimes or crimes against humanity."[43] The Belgian arrest warrant was thus illegal. The ICJ was careful to observe, however, that this did not mean that foreign ministers or other high-ranking state representatives could never be made to answer in foreign courts for serious international crimes. This would be possible, for example, once they left office, assuming that jurisdictional requirements were met[44] and that such acts did not amount to official acts attracting immunity *ratione materiae*.[45] Thus, the case affirms immunity *ratione personae* for high-ranking state representatives, even if they are accused of serious violations of human rights or humanitarian law; although it does leave open the question of whether immunity *ratione materiae* may be available for such violations.

DRC v. *Belgium* highlights a particular problem with seeking redress for another state's gross violations of human rights or humanitarian law by means of domestic *criminal* proceedings. Because such proceedings by their nature target individuals, they tend, at least in prosecutions of very high-ranking foreign state representatives, to run afoul of the apparently absolute *ratione personae* immunity enjoyed by such representatives. A strategy increasingly being pursued, therefore,

---

43   *Ibid.* at para. 58. It is important to note that in reaching this conclusion, the ICJ distinguished state practice which clearly subjects state representatives, even those in very high office, to the jurisdiction of *international* criminal tribunals. State immunity has no application in that context as subjection to international legal process involves neither subjection of one state's representatives to the judicial process of another state nor violation of the principle of the sovereign equality of states. See further the text accompanying note 1, above in this chapter.

44   See Chapter 8.

45   *DRC v. Belgium*, above note 1 at para. 61. The Court also observed that high-ranking state representatives accused of perpetrating serious international crimes could also be made answerable in a number of other circumstances: for example, their own state might either waive its immunity or seek to prosecute them domestically (as in the case of *Pinochet*: see above note 12); or they might be indicted by an international criminal tribunal, such as the International Criminal Court: see *Rome Statute*, above note 32, Article 27.

is to seek domestic *civil* redress for such violations.[46] Such actions have the virtue that they can be framed against the foreign state itself or its agencies, rather than individuals, with the result that the state immunity issues tend to be focused on the *ratione materiae* rather than *ratione personae* aspects of the doctrine. However, as we shall see, such actions have met with even less success than their criminal counterparts.

For example, in *Bouzari v. Iran*,[47] Bouzari sought civil relief against Iran in the Canadian courts for acts of torture committed against him by Iranian agents in Iran. The Ontario Court of Appeal, relying on expert evidence as to current state practice, concluded that "there is no principle of customary international law which provides an exception from state immunity where an act of torture has been committed outside the forum, even for acts contrary to *jus cogens*."[48] Moreover, the Court of Appeal distinguished *Pinochet* on the basis that it denied state immunity in criminal, rather than civil, proceedings. If anything, reasoned the Court, the claim to state immunity is *stronger* in civil than in criminal proceedings because, in the latter, "sanction[s] can be imposed on the individual without subjecting one state to the jurisdiction of another."[49] Thus, pursuing civil remedies in order to evade the potency of *ratione personae* immunity runs headlong into the concern that civil proceedings against a foreign state itself will be perceived as a direct challenge to the sovereign equality of states. State practice does not currently appear to countenance such a challenge, at least outside the recognized categories of commercial and private law transactions inherent in the restrictive theory of state immunity.

This point was also recently affirmed by the House of Lords in *Jones v. Saudi Arabia*,[50] a case raising issues very similar to those in *Bouzari*. Jones and others brought civil claims in the United Kingdom against Saudi Arabia and a number of Saudi police officers and other officials for alleged acts of torture. Relying on certain *dicta* in *Pinochet*, the claimants argued that their claims were not barred by state immunity given that torture, being categorically outlawed in international law, cannot be an official or governmental act that would attract immunity *ratione materiae*. As in *Bouzari*, however, the House of Lords distin-

---

46 See, generally, the essays collected in C.M. Scott, ed., *Torture as Tort: Comparative Perspectives on the Development of Transnational Human Rights Litigation* (Oxford: Hart Publishing, 2001).

47 *Bouzari v. Islamic Republic of Iran* (2004), 71 O.R. (3d) 675 (C.A.), leave to appeal to S.C.C. refused (2005), [2004] S.C.C.A. No. 410 [*Bouzari v. Iran*].

48 *Ibid.* at para. 88, quoting the decision of the motions judge below.

49 *Ibid.* at para. 91.

50 *Jones v. Saudi Arabia*, above note 24.

guished *Pinochet* on the basis that it concerned only state immunity in criminal proceedings.[51] Further, the House of Lords found that neither state practice nor *opinio juris* currently support the existence of an exception to state immunity in civil proceedings arising from torture.[52] Indeed, Lord Bingham noted that this issue had been considered by the International Law Commission in formulating the Draft Articles that ultimately became the *Jurisdictional Immunities Convention*. That the Draft Articles and Convention ultimately omitted any restriction of state immunities in cases of torture or other serious violations of human rights or humanitarian law was thus taken as evidence that such restriction did not currently exist in international law.[53]

Similar conclusions have generally been reached by other national and international courts considering the question.[54] However, while accepting that this is the current state of international law, most courts and commentators generally express the view that the development of a further restriction on state immunity in cases of gross violations of human rights or humanitarian law would be desirable, or at least consistent with the importance attached to these areas of international law. While it can therefore be anticipated that attempts to displace state immunity in such cases will continue, it remains to be seen whether state practice, either legislative or judicial, will eventually yield in the face of this pressure.

For the time being, though, it seems that the restrictions on the modern law of state immunity remain limited to those concerning commercial and other private law transactions of states. The precise extent of these restrictions will be explored further in the next section.

---

51 *Ibid.* at paras. 19, 49, and 71.
52 *Ibid.* at paras 18 and 85.
53 *Ibid.* at para. 26. For commentary see H. Fox, "In Defence of State Immunity: Why the UN Convention on State Immunity is Important" (2006) 55 I.C.L.Q. 399; E. Denza, "The 2005 UN Convention on State Immunity in Perspective" (2006) 55 I.C.L.Q. 395; R. Gardiner, "UN Convention on State Immunity: Form and Function" (2006) 55 I.C.L.Q. 407; K. Hall, "UN Convention on State Immunity: The Need for a Human Rights Protocol" (2006) 55 I.C.L.Q. 411; L. McGregor, "State Immunity and *Jus Cogens*" (2006) 55 I.C.L.Q. 437.
54 See, for example, *Al-Adsani v. United Kingdom* (2001), 34 E.H.R.R. 273 at paras. 61–66 (E.C.H.R.); *Al-Adsani v. Government of Kuwait (No. 2)* (1996), 107 I.L.R. 536 (Eng. C.A.); *Kalegoropoulou v. Greece and Germany* (12 December 2002), Application No. 50021/00 (E.C.H.R.); *Siderman de Blake v. Republic of Argentina*, 965 F.2d 699 at 718 (9th Cir. 1992); *Greek Citizens v. Federal Republic of Germany (The Distomo Massacre Case)* (2003) 42 I.L.M. 1030 at 1033 (S.C. Germany). But see *Ferrini v. Federal Republic of Germany* (2004), 87 Riv. dir. Int. 539 (Ital. Ct. Cass.); *In re Estate of Ferdinand Marcos*, 25 F.3d 1467 at 1470–71 (9th Cir. 1994); and, *semble, Filartiga v. Pena-Irala*, 630 F.2d 876 (2d Cir. 1980).

2) General Principles of State Immunity: The *Jurisdictional Immunities Convention*

a) Basic Presumption of and Duty to Respect Immunity

The overall scheme adopted in the *Jurisdictional Immunities Convention* is a general presumption of immunity in favour of the foreign state, subject to a number of exceptions. The *Convention* is clearly predicated on the restrictive theory of state immunity described above. Thus, Article 5 provides as a starting point that states enjoy immunity from the jurisdiction of the courts of other states. This general immunity extends to state property situated in foreign territory, in keeping with well-established customary international law. Article 6 complements Article 5 by recognizing a duty on states to respect the immunity of other states and to take the necessary steps to ensure that their domestic courts do so as well.

The exceptions to the general rule of immunity may roughly be categorized as (1) exceptions flowing from the consent, express or implied, of the state that would otherwise enjoy immunity; and (2) exceptions based on the subject matter of the transaction or proceedings.

b) Exceptions Based on Consent: Express or Implied Waiver

It is well recognized in customary international law that a state may waive its immunity and submit to the jurisdiction of a foreign court. There is no inconsistency here with the principle of the sovereign equality of states, as subjection to foreign jurisdiction in such cases flows notionally from an exercise of the state's own sovereign will. Indeed, a choice by a state to waive its immunity and subject itself to the jurisdiction of a foreign court may, in fact, enhance the dignity of the submitting state in that it thereby demonstrates its willingness to respect the law of the local sovereign and to honour resulting legal obligations.

The capacity of states to waive their immunity and submit to the jurisdiction of local courts underscores a fundamental feature of state immunity: namely, that the immunity is from the process of application or enforcement of the local law rather than from the substance of the law itself.[55] Again, notionally, states retain a duty to respect local law when operating within the prescriptive jurisdictional reach of a foreign state, all the while enjoying a general immunity from enforcement of that law. When a state waives its immunity, therefore, no issue

---

55 See *DRC v. Belgium,* above note 1 at para. 59; and see further the text accompanying note 5, above in this chapter.

generally arises as to the applicability *per se* of domestic law to the foreign state.[56]

The capacity of a state to waive its immunity also highlights the fact that, while the immunity may *prima facie* apply to the acts of various state agencies or representatives and provide protection to those agencies or representatives, the immunity remains ultimately that of the state itself. Thus, if the state chooses to waive its immunity, its representative loses the benefit of such immunity and therefore becomes subject to local enforcement jurisdiction.[57] For example, had Chile expressly waived at the outset any immunity it might have enjoyed in respect of Senator Pinochet, the British courts would not have been required to agonize over their ability to subject him to extradition proceedings. Any protection enjoyed by Pinochet as a result of Chile's state immunity would have dissolved once that immunity had been waived by the state of Chile itself.[58]

The clearest case of waiver is where a state expressly renounces its immunity. Article 7 of the *Jurisdictional Immunities Convention* contemplates that an express waiver may take a number of forms, including a declaration in a treaty, in a private law contract, or directly before the foreign court, although in reality there are no limitations on the form in which waiver of immunity may be expressed. However, merely designating foreign law as the proper law of a transaction will not be interpreted as waiver of immunity from the jurisdiction of a foreign court, given that, as seen above, the two matters are conceptually distinct.[59] Further, consent to jurisdiction over the merits does not entail consent to jurisdiction to enforce a judgment or take other measures of constraint in connection with a judgment on the merits.[60]

---

56   Although it may, of course, do so in the absence of any connecting factors between the forum state and the conduct of the foreign state that is the subject-matter of the proceedings: see further Chapter 8.

57   See *DRC v. Belgium*, above note 1 at para. 61.

58   Indeed, it is probable that the basis upon which the majority in the House of Lords concluded that Pinochet did not enjoy immunity in respect of certain allegations brought against him was that Chile had implicitly waived its immunity by becoming a party to the *Torture Convention*, which extends quasi-universal jurisdiction to states parties for acts of torture. This interpretation is consistent with the majority's limitation of Chile's loss of immunity to acts occurring after Chile and the United Kingdom had become parties to the *Torture Convention*. See further the text accompanying notes 12–13 and 38–41, above in this chapter.

59   *Jurisdictional Immunities Convention*, above note 7, Article 7(2).

60   *Ibid.*, Article 20.

Waiver may also be implied by a state's conduct. The fact that state immunity does not prevent a state from availing itself, if it so chooses, of domestic foreign courts to obtain redress for various injuries it may have sustained, gives rise to the most common form of such implied waiver: the corollary of a state invoking its right to sue in a foreign court is its relinquishment of immunity from that foreign court's jurisdiction in the same or a related matter.[61] Similarly, where the state intervenes or takes steps in a proceeding that has already been initiated, it impliedly waives its immunity from that court's jurisdiction unless it does so merely for purposes of invoking immunity or for asserting a right or interest in property that is at issue in the proceeding.[62] However, neither the mere appearance of a state representative as a witness in a proceeding, nor the failure of a state to enter an appearance in a proceeding at all, imply waiver of the state's immunity.[63]

Waiver of immunity may, of course, also be implied by conduct other than that contemplated in the *Jurisdictional Immunities Convention*, and it is unlikely that customary international law places any constraints on the forms that an implied waiver may take. However, given the nature of the interests at stake, such an implication must generally be clear and unambiguous.[64]

c)   Subject-Matter Exceptions

Aside from situations of waiver, the *Jurisdictional Immunities Convention* adopts a restrictive theory of immunity in prescribing certain categories of transactions to which, because of their subject matter, no state immunity attaches. The first and most important of these are commercial transactions, following the predominant trend in state practice in the late twentieth and early twenty-first centuries.

The basic rule is that no immunity attaches with respect to commercial transactions involving a foreign state.[65] However, this rule does not apply if both parties to the transaction are states, as their relations should be resolved on a state-to-state basis in an appropriate

---

61   "Related matters" refer to counterclaims and other claims arising out of the same legal relationship or factual transaction: *ibid.*, Article 9.

62   *Ibid.*, Article 8.

63   *Ibid.*, Articles 8(3)–(4).

64   See Brownlie, above note 4 at 335–36; Shaw, above note 2 at 659–60; Starke & Shearer, above note 3 at 195.

65   *Jurisdictional Immunities Convention*, above note 7, Article 10(1). An extension of the commercial transactions exception is found in Article 16, which provides that admiralty actions involving state-owned or operated vessels do not attract immunity unless the vessel was at the relevant times in use for "governmental, non-commercial purposes."

international forum rather than in the domestic courts of one or the other.[66]

Of course, the exception to immunity in respect of commercial transactions also does not apply if the parties to the transaction have expressly agreed otherwise.[67]

The real difficulty with the commercial transaction exception to immunity, however, is how to define which acts of states qualify as commercial. The difficulty can be illustrated by reference to the case of *I Congreso del Partido*, decided by the British House of Lords in 1981.[68] The case arose out of a contract for delivery of sugar, by a state-owned Cuban enterprise in a state-owned Cuban vessel, to Chile. At the time of delivery, the Chilean government was overthrown in a military coup led by Augusto Pinochet. The Cuban government, in protest, ordered the delivery stopped and converted the sugar cargo to its own use. The vessel thereafter put into a British port, where it was arrested in connection with an action for damages brought by the owners of the sugar against Cuba in the British courts. Given that the United Kingdom had in 1978 enacted a new *State Immunity Act*[69] implementing a restrictive form of state immunity, the issue that arose was whether the act of the Cuban government was commercial in nature or rather was an act of foreign policy emanating from its sovereign will.

State practice suggests that the principal approaches for resolving such issues are, on the one hand, to examine the nature of the transaction itself and, on the other, to scrutinize the purpose of the state's involvement in the transaction.[70] In the first of these approaches, a commercial transaction would be recognized simply by virtue of the nature of its subject matter—in this sense, the "nature of the transaction" criterion has an air of objectivity about it. In general, the "nature of the transaction" test would also tend to be more restrictive. For example, the fundamentally commercial nature of a contract for the supply of goods does not differ depending on whether one of the parties to it is a foreign government or intends to use the goods for sovereign purposes. In the second approach, by contrast, an examination of the motivation of the state would be required in order to determine whether its purpose was to act as a mere commercial entity in the transaction, or whether it was to advance some governmental or sovereign objective,

---

66   *Ibid.*, Article 10(2)(a).

67   *Ibid.*, Article 10(2)(b).

68   *Playa Larga v. I Congreso del Partido,* [1981] 2 All E.R. 1064 (H.L.) [*I Congreso del Partido*].

69   U.K. *State Immunity Act*, above note 29.

70   See Brownlie, above note 4 at 328; Shaw, above note 2 at 633.

albeit through an undertaking with an outwardly commercial appearance. Clearly such an approach has a subjective element to it, and has the potential to extend immunity to certain transactions that would otherwise be considered commercial in nature. The "purpose of the transaction" test thus tends to be less restrictive.

In *I Congreso del Partido*, the majority in the House of Lords concluded that the act of the Cuban government was commercial and did not attract immunity. The Court's reasoning was based on a review of the common law and therefore, implicitly, of customary international law. Having determined that restrictive immunity applied, Lord Wilberforce rejected exclusive reliance on either the nature or purpose tests in determining whether the transaction was commercial:

> … [I]n considering, under the restrictive theory, whether state immunity should be granted or not, the court must consider the whole context in which the claim against the state is made, with a view to deciding whether the relevant act(s) upon which the claim is based, should, in that context, be considered as fairly within an area of activity, trading or commercial or otherwise of a private law character, in which the state has chosen to engage or whether the relevant act(s) should be considered as having been done outside that area and within the sphere of governmental or sovereign activity.

Ultimately the House of Lords asked whether the act in question could have been performed by a private actor, and concluded that it could: in ordering a halt to the delivery of the cargo, the Cuban government was found to be exercising powers that could have been exercised by any private ship owner, notwithstanding that its motivations were clearly political.[71]

Notwithstanding the outcome in that particular case, the appropriate test to be applied remains a matter of considerable debate, even among states accepting the general concept of restrictive state immunity. This controversy is reflected in the compromise position adopted in the *Jurisdictional Immunities Convention*, which defines commercial transactions as follows:

> 1. For the purposes of the present Convention:
> …
> (c) "commercial transaction" means:
>   (i) any commercial contract or transaction for the sale of goods or supply of services;

---

71 *I Congreso del Partido*, above note 68 at 1075.

(ii) any contract for a loan or other transaction of a financial nature, including any obligation of guarantee or of indemnity
in respect of any such loan or transaction;

(iii) any other contract or transaction of a commercial, industrial, trading or professional nature, but not including a contract of employment of persons.

2. In determining whether a contract or transaction is a "commercial transaction" under paragraph 1(c), reference should be made
primarily to the nature of the contract or transaction, but its purpose should also be taken into account if, ... in the practice of the
State of the forum, that purpose is relevant to determining the
non-commercial character of the contract or transaction.[72]

In essence, this definition gives priority to the nature of the transaction while still permitting reference to its purpose as a secondary
consideration in deciding whether it is commercial and thus ineligible
for immunity. This preference for the "nature of the transaction" test is
also favoured in a majority of recent domestic court decisions.[73] However, such a preference was a source of considerable controversy in the
UN General Assembly prior to adoption of the Convention, which explains the ultimate reference to "the practice of the State of the forum"
in determining the relevance of the purpose of the transaction.[74] This
may, accordingly, be an issue on which customary international law
has yet to develop any firm rules,[75] although the idea that commercial
transactions are to be distinguished in some manner from sovereign
acts for purposes of state immunity is now firmly entrenched in state
practice and *opinio juris*.

There are other subject-matter exceptions to the general rule of
immunity, albeit of somewhat lesser prominence and controversy,
contemplated in the *Jurisdictional Immunities Convention*. In general,
proceedings relating to contracts of employment with a state to be performed in whole or in part in another state do not attract immunity from
the jurisdiction of the courts of that other state, unless the employee's

---

72 *Jurisdictional Immunities Convention*, above note 7, Article 2.

73 See ILC Report (1999), above note 21 at paras. 45–55.

74 Indeed, the debate over whether to prefer the nature or purpose of the transaction in determining whether it falls into the "commercial" category led the
International Law Commission's Working Group on the Draft Articles to recommend at one point that paragraph 2 of Article 2 be dropped in its entirety, leaving it to individual domestic courts to determine on a case by case basis whether
any particular transaction is commercial or not without any *a priori* preference
for the nature or purpose of the transaction tests: see *ibid.* at paras. 56–60.

75 See Shaw, above note 2 at 633–34; Brownlie, above note 4 at 329.

functions include the exercise of governmental authority or the proceeding relates specifically to recruitment, renewal, or reinstatement of employment.[76] Further, and pursuant to well-established customary exceptions, states are not immune from foreign judicial proceedings arising from personal injury or property damage attributable to them and occurring wholly or in part within the forum state.[77] Similarly, no immunity generally arises in actions relating to property interests, including intellectual property rights, in the forum state.[78] Finally,[79] actions arising from participation by a state in a corporate or other "collective" body (such as a partnership) do not attract immunity, assuming that body is organized under the laws of the forum state and has participants other than states or international organizations.[80]

d) Defining the "State"

Given the extension of sovereign immunity to the various organs and manifestations of the modern state, an important issue is the nature and extent of the entities that are eligible for state immunity. In other words, how does one define the full extent of the "state" for purposes of determining whether state immunity attaches to the acts of any particular individual or entity?

Some aspects of this issue are relatively straightforward and are well-settled in customary international law. It is generally recognized, for example, that *ratione materiae* immunity extends to official acts of the state itself; the head of state and members of the government; the organs of government (such as government ministries and departments); and state officials, representatives, agents, and servants acting in such capacities. These aspects of the "state" for purposes of defining state immunity are reflected in the *Jurisdictional Immunities Convention*.[81] Diplomatic personnel, while certainly coming within the ambit of state representatives whose official acts would attract state immunity, also enjoy specialized personal immunities to be reviewed below.

However, more uncertainty exists in the case of constitutive units of federal states and other political subdivisions within states.[82] Doubts are periodically expressed by some unitary states as to whether such

---

76   *Jurisdictional Immunities Convention*, above note 7, Article 11.
77   *Ibid.*, Article 12.
78   *Ibid.*, Articles 13 and 14.
79   With respect to admiralty claims (*Jurisdictional Immunities Convention*, above note 7, Article 16), see above note 65.
80   *Jurisdictional Immunities Convention, ibid.*, Article 15.
81   *Ibid.*, Article 2(1)(b).
82   See, generally, Brownlie, above note 4 at 336–37; Shaw, above note 2 at 654–55.

political subdivisions should be entitled to state immunity in their own right.[83] There is nevertheless considerable state practice supporting the notion that provinces or states within federal states, and other political subdivisions within states, such as municipalities, enjoy state immunity in respect of their sovereign acts. Both "constituent units of a federal State" and "political subdivisions of the State" are accordingly included within the *Jurisdictional Immunities Convention's* definition of the "state."[84]

The basis for this inclusion is generally considered to be that, within their own sphere of domestically-defined jurisdictional competence, such political subdivisions exercise elements of the state's overall sovereign powers of governance. In other words, given that such political subdivisions exercise elements of the state's sovereign authority, such exercises of power should attract state immunity no less than if they came solely within the purview of the state's central government.

This was the approach taken by Lord Denning, M.R. in the English Court of Appeal decision in *Mellenger* v. *New Brunswick Development Corporation*.[85] In that case, two Canadian citizens sought to recover, in the British courts, commissions allegedly owed to them by the New Brunswick Development Corporation, an incorporated body charged with the mandate of fostering economic development in New Brunswick. The corporation claimed state immunity but, being established under New Brunswick legislation, the threshold question to be addressed was whether the province itself enjoyed state immunity from the jurisdiction of the British courts. Lord Denning, observing that "[t]he Crown is sovereign in New Brunswick for provincial powers, just as it is sovereign in Canada for dominion powers,"[86] held that New Brunswick was a sovereign state in its own right, at least with respect to its ability to claim state immunity.

Adopting this rationale for including political subdivisions of states in the concept of the "state" for purposes of state immunity, and in order to assuage some of the concerns of unitary states, the *Jurisdictional Immunities Convention* adds the qualifier "to the extent they are entitled to perform and are actually performing acts in the exercise of sovereign authority of the State" to "constituent units of a federal State or political subdivisions of the State" in its definition of the "state."[87]

---

83 See ILC Report (1999), above note 21 at paras. 11–30.

84 *Jurisdictional Immunities Convention*, above note 7, Article 2(1)(b)(ii).

85 *Mellenger v. New Brunswick Development Corporation*, [1971] 1 W.L.R. 604 (Eng. C.A.).

86 *Ibid.* at 608.

87 *Jurisdictional Immunities Convention*, above note 7, Article 2(1)(b)(ii).

Also uncertain is the extent to which so-called "state agencies" may attract state immunity. At issue here is the status of entities (usually but not necessarily incorporated) which are legally and formally independent from the state, but through which the state nevertheless carries out certain activities. Should the acts of such entities be clothed with state immunity? If so, how does one determine which entities should enjoy such immunity and which are too far removed from the state to warrant such protection? In other words, what is the required relationship between the state and such an entity before the latter is considered a "state agency" and thus entitled to immunity?

State practice and domestic court decisions have not been particularly consistent in this area, giving rise to a degree of uncertainty. In general it appears that the principal factors considered are the nature of the functions the entity is entitled to perform and the degree of state control over the entity.[88] Thus, in the *Mellenger* case,[89] Lord Denning reviewed the New Brunswick statute establishing the defendant corporation, noting in particular the control exercised by the New Brunswick government over the composition of the board of directors. That the corporation's primary function was the promotion of New Brunswick's economy, according to government policy and in much the same way as might be performed by a government department, was also a key factor in leading his Lordship to the conclusion that the corporation was in essence an "alter ego" of the province.[90] It clearly qualified as a state agency and was entitled to immunity.

Without referring to either the function or control tests, the *Jurisdictional Immunities Convention* simply refers to "agencies or instrumentalities of the State or other entities, to the extent that they are entitled to perform and are actually performing acts in the exercise of sovereign authority of the State."[91] This definition has the virtue of focussing on the essential issue, which is whether the entity is in fact acting on behalf of the state as its duly authorized agent, regardless of the lack of a formal or an institutional link between them.

e)   Immunity from Execution

It will be recalled that the initial presumption in the law of state immunity, reflected in the *Jurisdictional Immunities Convention*, is that a state is immune from all stages or phases of foreign court proceedings. In examining the theory of restrictive immunity, we in fact focused on

---

88   See, generally, Brownlie, above note 4 at 337.
89   *Mellenger,* above note 85.
90   *Ibid.* at 609.
91   *Jurisdictional Immunities Convention*, above note 7, Article 2(1)(b)(iii).

only a portion of the overall judicial proceedings that may arise from any given transaction. While considerable inroads have been made into the immunity of states with respect to the merits of a case, states have been considerably more resistant to the retrenchment of their immunities in respect of the enforcement or execution of judgments, or other measures of constraint directed against them or their property. As a result, the restrictive nature of modern state immunity in fact largely extends only to those phases of foreign judicial proceedings that deal with the merits of a claim.

In particular, states have generally resisted the notion that they or their property may be subject to mandatory orders by foreign courts, whether in the nature of interlocutory or injunctive relief or by way of execution. This is so even in those cases where no state immunity exists that would prevent the foreign court from exercising jurisdiction over the merits of the dispute. For example, a court may find itself able to exercise jurisdiction over a dispute arising out of a commercial transaction involving a foreign state and yet not able to: order interlocutory relief in the nature of a preservation order; issue injunctions requiring the foreign state to adopt a certain course of action; or levy execution against the foreign state's assets situated in the jurisdiction, in satisfaction of any judgment on the merits. Recall, too, that waiver, by a state, of immunity on the merits does not entail waiver of immunity in respect of enforcement measures.[92]

While state practice thus remains robustly committed to a general immunity from foreign measures of constraint, considerable scholarly opinion supports parallel developments in this area to those which have taken place with respect to judicial jurisdiction on the merits. In other words, it is generally considered necessary, if for no other reason than legal coherence, that immunity from constraint evolves toward a restrictive stance in keeping with the substantive developments reviewed above.[93]

The *Jurisdictional Immunities Convention* therefore reflects a general rule of immunity against pre-judgment and post-judgment measures of constraint, including attachment, arrest, or execution, subject to a number of exceptions.[94] The first such exception is uncontroversial: it refers to the situation where the state has expressly consented to the relevant measure.[95] The second, closely related exception is where the state has allocated or earmarked property for satisfaction of the claim

92   *Ibid.*, Article 20.
93   See, for example, Brownlie, above note 4 at 338–39.
94   *Jurisdictional Immunities Convention*, above note 7, Articles 18–19.
95   *Ibid.*, Articles 18(a) and 19(a).

in the proceeding.[96] The third exception, however, reminiscent of a restrictive theory of immunity, is predicated on a distinction between commercial and governmental acts. It provides that property specifically intended for other than "government non-commercial" use by a state, having a connection with the entity against which the proceeding is brought and located in the territory of the forum, may be subject to measures of constraint.[97] It is to be noted that this third exception is only applicable to *post*-judgment measures of constraint. However, while the scope of the exception is somewhat narrower than the corresponding restrictive approach to jurisdiction over the merits of proceedings arising from commercial transactions, the intent to limit, to some extent, the virtually absolute state immunity against constraint or execution is evident.

In light of the controversial nature of such an innovation, the *Jurisdictional Immunities Convention* also specifically addresses certain particular categories of state property to which the third exception from immunity against post-judgment execution will not apply.[98] In particular, property used for diplomatic purposes, military property, property of central banks, and heritage, archival, or cultural property are specifically excluded from the category of property used for other than governmental, non-commercial purposes.

While there is some state practice recognizing modest restrictions on immunity from constraint in line with those set out in the *Jurisdictional Immunities Convention*,[99] these provisions of the Convention were controversial and delayed its adoption.[100] It remains to be seen whether similar concerns by states will delay the Convention's coming into force or prompt states to formulate reservations to Article 19(c), or whether states will ultimately embrace a more restrictive approach to their traditional immunities from execution.

---

96 *Ibid.*, Articles 18(b) and 19(b).
97 *Ibid.*, Article 19(c). See also the "Understanding with respect to Article 19" which is annexed to the Convention and "forms an integral part" thereof: *ibid.*, Article 25. In particular, the annex clarifies that the required "connection" is not limited to ownership or possession, and that the expression "entity" means "the State as an independent legal personality, a constituent unit of a federal State, a subdivision of a State, an agency or instrumentality of a State or other entity, which enjoys independent legal personality."
98 *Ibid.*, Article 21.
99 See, for example, the Canadian *State Immunity Act*, R.S.C. 1985, c. S-18, s. 12(1)(b).
100 See ILC Report (1999), above note 21 at paras.108–29.

3) Canada's *State Immunity Act*

While it is anticipated that the *Jurisdictional Immunities Convention* will in time be widely ratified and implemented, in the interim the precise course charted by the line dividing sovereign from commercial and other "private" activities of states nevertheless continues to vary in detail from jurisdiction to jurisdiction.[101] Thus, the exact extent of state immunity from foreign judicial jurisdiction still depends critically on the domestic law of the foreign jurisdiction in question, as informed by customary international law. Before leaving the topic of state immunity, therefore, and by way of illustration, Canada's state immunity legislation, which codifies a restrictive form of state immunity, will be analyzed.

a)   Background

Until relatively recently, Canada applied a theory of absolute state immunity. This approach was developed by the courts in a line of cases usually traced back to the decision of the English Court of Appeal in *The Parlement Belge*, in which the doctrine of absolute immunity was held to form part of the common law due to its status as customary international law.[102] That approach was affirmed periodically thereafter by the Supreme Court of Canada, albeit with growing ambivalence as twentieth-century state practice leaned increasingly towards recognition of a restrictive theory of state immunity.[103] In light of such ambivalence, various lower courts occasionally undertook to apply a restrictive form of immunity.[104] The result was a formal and increasingly outmoded adherence to the theory of absolute immunity coupled with considerable uncertainty as to whether a court would hold true to such theory in any given case or would, in fact, give sovereign immunity a restrictive interpretation.

In order to bring clarity and coherence to this confused state of affairs, and in order to align Canada's approach with the, by then, prevailing approach of most developed states, Parliament enacted the *State Immunity Act* in 1982.[105] The Act affirmed as a general proposition that a foreign state is immune from the jurisdiction of any court in Can-

---

101 See Brownlie, above note 4 at 325–26 and 328–32.

102 *The Parlement Belge*, above note 25.

103 Contrast, for example, the clear endorsement of absolute immunity in *Dessaulles v. Republic of Poland*, [1944] S.C.R. 275 with the ambivalent position of the majority and the forceful dissent of Laskin J. in *Congo v. Venne*, [1971] S.C.R. 997.

104 See, generally, H.M. Kindred, "Foreign Governments before the Courts" (1980) 58 Can. Bar Rev. 602.

105 *State Immunity Act*, above note 99.

ada, subject to certain exceptions expressly set out in the Act.[106] Canada therefore extends a form of restrictive state immunity to foreign states.

While the *State Immunity Act* serves to bring a degree of clarity to Canada's position on the immunities of foreign states in Canadian courts, it is also something of an anomaly in that it is legislation that purported to implement an area of customary international law. The effect of the Act was thus, at least theoretically, to "arrest" the development of the common law as a reflection of evolving customary international law on the issue.[107] There is, therefore, the risk that further developments in the customary international law of state immunity will gradually depart over time from the "frozen" provisions of the Act. This difficulty may be alleviated, however, by judicial interpretation that seeks to reconcile the Act as much as possible with evolving custom,[108] or by future legislative amendment. In any case, the Act will likely have to be reviewed to ensure compliance with the provisions of the *Jurisdictional Immunities Convention*, should Canada choose to become a party to it.[109]

b) General Framework

"Foreign state" is defined broadly in the Act to include political subdivisions (for example, provinces or other sub-national entities within a federal state); heads of state; governments of foreign states, including departments and ministries; and agencies of foreign states (in the sense of organs of the state that are nevertheless separate from the state itself).[110] An agency of a foreign state has been held to include any legal entity or person that is separate from the foreign state but that acts at

---

106 *Ibid.*, s. 3.

107 It should be noted, however, that the Act does not apply to criminal proceedings: *ibid.*, s. 18. Immunities in criminal proceedings therefore continue to be governed by customary international law as incorporated by the common law: see Chapter 6, Section C(2).

108 See *ibid.*

109 As we shall see below, however, the Act is in many respects already consistent with the *Jurisdictional Immunities Convention*.

110 *State Immunity Act*, above note 99, s. 2, definitions of "foreign state," "political subdivision," and "agency of a foreign state." It has been held, however, that nothing in the Act derogates from the prior common law principle that, when acting in pursuit of their duties, officials or employees of foreign states enjoy the benefits of sovereign immunity: *Jaffe v. Miller* (1993), 13 O.R. (3d) 745 (C.A.) [*Jaffe*]; *Ritter v. Donell* (2005), 383 A.R. 280 at para. 24 (Q.B.). The same has been held with respect to functionaries of an agency of a foreign state: see. *P.(R.) v. Westwood*, 2003 BCSC 1279 at para. 19. See also *Parent v. Singapore Airlines Inc.*, [2003] J.Q. No. 18068 at para. 58 (S.C.) [*Parent*] holding that Taiwan, although not a widely recognized state, is entitled to the benefit of state immunity under the Act.

the request of the foreign state in situations where that state would enjoy sovereign immunity.[111] Factors to be considered in determining whether the agency is "separate" from the foreign state include the amount of state control over the organization, whether it can sue or be sued in its own name, and whether it is a separate legal (corporate) entity.[112]

The principal exceptions to the presumptive immunity of a foreign state are proceedings relating to:

1) any commercial activity of the foreign state;[113]

2) death, personal or bodily injury, or damage to property occurring in Canada;[114]

3) maritime proceedings in respect of shipping or cargo owned by the foreign state but intended for use in commercial activity;[115] and

4) an interest of the foreign state in property in Canada that arises by way of succession or gift.[116]

The foreign state may of course also waive its immunity in a number of ways[117] that will be described in greater detail below.[118]

Notwithstanding these exceptions to a foreign state's general immunity from the jurisdiction of Canadian courts, foreign states nevertheless enjoy, under the Act, very broad immunities from virtually all forms of attachment, execution, or other enforcement jurisdiction of Canadian courts.[119] For the most part, such immunities from attachment, execution, or enforcement do not extend to agencies of foreign states.[120] The precise scope of these immunities will be described below,[121] as will other procedural matters peculiar to the participation of foreign states in proceedings before Canadian courts.[122]

---

111 *Walker v. Bank of New York Inc.* (1993), 16 O.R. (3d) 504 (C.A.) [*Walker*]. But see *D & J Coustas Shipping Co. S.A. v. Cia de Navegacao Lloyd Brasileiro* (1990), 48 F.T.R. 161 (T.D.), where it was held that an agency must be an organ or alter ego of the state in the sense of satisfying conditions of function and control. The function and control requirement will not necessarily be met in the case of a corporation merely because the foreign state is the majority shareholder of the corporation.

112 *Ferguson v. Arctic Transportation Ltd.*, [1995] 3 F.C. 656 (T.D.).

113 *State Immunity Act*, above note 99, s. 5; note also the definition of "commercial activity" in s. 2.

114 *Ibid.*, s. 6.

115 *Ibid.*, s. 7.

116 *Ibid.*, s. 8.

117 *Ibid.*, s. 4.

118 See Section B(3)(c)(i), below in this chapter.

119 *State Immunity Act*, above note 99, ss. 11–12.

120 *Ibid.*, ss. 11(3) and 12(2).

121 See Section B(3)(d), below in this chapter.

122 See Section B(3)(e), below in this chapter.

It is important to note that the federal cabinet may, on the recommendation of the minister of foreign affairs, order that any immunity or privileges under the Act be restricted with respect to a foreign state where, in the opinion of the cabinet, such immunity or privileges exceed those accorded by the law of that foreign state.[123] Canada's system of state immunity is thus notionally premised upon the reciprocal extension of immunities to Canada by the courts of foreign states.

c)   Restrictions on State Immunity

i)   Waiver

A state waives its general state immunity if it submits to the jurisdiction of a Canadian court.[124] Such submission may be effected explicitly by written agreement or otherwise, either before or after the court proceedings are commenced, and will extend to any appeal proceedings in the same matter.[125] It has been held that any such submission must be clear and unequivocal and cannot be presumed.[126]

Alternatively, a state may be deemed to have submitted implicitly to the jurisdiction of the court either by initiating proceedings in that court or by intervening or taking any step in proceedings already initiated before the court.[127] A state that initiates or intervenes in a proceeding will also be deemed to have submitted to the jurisdiction of the Canadian courts in any appeal[128] or in respect of any counterclaim or third party actions arising "out of the subject-matter of the proceedings."[129] However, it has been held that the words "out of the subject-matter of the proceedings" indicate a legislative intention to exclude counterclaims that are independent of the original proceeding — that

---

123 *State Immunity Act*, above note 99, s. 15.

124 *Ibid.*, s. 4(1).

125 *Ibid.*, ss. 4(2)(a) and 4(5).

126 *P.S.A.C. v. United States Defence Department* (1988), 74 di 191 (Can. L.R.B.), aff'd (*sub nom. Re Canada Labour Code*) [1990] 1 F.C. 332 (C.A.), rev'd on other grounds [1992] 2 S.C.R. 50 [*Re Canada Labour Code*]; *United States of America v. Friedland* (1999), 46 O.R. (3d) 321 (C.A.) [*Friedland*].

127 *State Immunity Act*, above note 99 at ss. 4(2)(b) & (c). It has been held that a foreign state which requests extradition of a suspect by Canada neither initiates the extradition proceedings subsequently commenced by the Attorney General of Canada in the Canadian courts nor subsequent civil proceedings brought by the suspect against the requesting state: see *Schreiber v. Canada (Attorney General)*, [2002] 3 S.C.R. 269 at para. 24 [*Schreiber*]. However, a defendant who brings a motion for summary judgment on the merits will be deemed to have waived immunity: see *Smith v. Chin* (2006), 31 C.P.C. (6th) 114 at para. 35 (Ont. S.C.J.).

128 *State Immunity Act*, above note 99, s. 4(5). See also *Schreiber, ibid.* at paras. 25–26.

129 *State Immunity Act, ibid.*, s. 4(4).

is, counterclaims that are not merely defensive in nature.[130] Further, merely intervening in a proceeding for the purpose of claiming immunity, or intervening in ignorance of facts entitling the state to immunity, are not deemed submissions to the jurisdiction of the court.[131]

ii)   Commercial Activity

Section 5 of the Act sets out the general rule that a foreign state is not immune from the jurisdiction of Canadian courts in any proceedings relating to the commercial activity of the state. Section 2 of the Act defines "commercial activity" to mean "any particular transaction, act or conduct or any regular course of conduct that by reason of its nature is of a commercial character." The circularity of this definition has meant that the courts have had to provide guidance as to what will or will not in fact constitute "commercial activity" of a foreign state. Echoing the international debate, the focus of this judicial guidance has been on whether the definition of "commercial activity" limits a court to considering the nature of the activity, or whether a court may also have regard to the purpose of the activity, in determining whether it is commercial or not.

The leading case is the 1992 decision of the Supreme Court of Canada in *Re Canada Labour Code*.[132] That case involved a United States naval base located in the Province of Newfoundland and Labrador pursuant to a 1941 lease between the United States and the United Kingdom, which was later incorporated into the terms of Newfoundland's union with Canada. Sixty civilian employees at the base, all Canadian nationals, sought union certification before the Canada Labour Relations Board pursuant to the provisions of the *Canada Labour Code*.[133] These employees were employed as firefighters and tradespersons to do maintenance work on the base, which supported anti-submarine warfare command and tactical forces through the operation of a high-security communications centre. The United States claimed state immunity from the certification proceedings pursuant to sections 2 and 5 of the *State Immunity Act*, but the Canada Labour Relations Board held that such immunity did not exist and the Federal Court of Canada, on appeal, affirmed that decision.

---

130 *Schreiber v. The Federal Republic of Germany* (2001), 52 O.R. (3d) 577 (S.C.J.); Friedland, above note 126.
131 *State Immunity Act*, above note 99, s. 4(3); *Jaffe*, above note 110.
132 *Re Canada Labour Code*, above note 126.
133 *Canada Labour Code*, R.S.C. 1985, c. L-2.

On further appeal the Supreme Court of Canada held, relying on the decision of the House of Lords in *I Congreso del Partido*,[134] that although the section 2 definition of "commercial activity" refers only to the nature of the activity in question, the Act must nevertheless be applied contextually. This means, in effect, that while the nature of the activity in question is to be given primary consideration, the purpose of the activity may also be considered in determining whether it is commercial. This brings the Canadian approach to determining whether an activity is commercial more or less in line with that espoused in Article 2(2) of the *Jurisdictional Immunities Convention*.

Applying this approach to the facts of this case, the Court conceded that a bare contract of employment at the base would for the most part be a simple commercial activity, and that the Canadian employees would generally be entitled to enforce their contracts with the United States in Canadian courts. However, the Court also held that to fall under the commercial activity exception, the proceedings in question must do more than incidentally affect the hiring of civilian labour at the base. They must relate to the activity viewed in its entire context.

Viewed in that context, the Court reasoned that certification proceedings, while relevant to contracts of hiring, also had a direct and substantial impact on the overall management of the naval base which the court viewed, having regard to the dual nature-purpose test, as sovereign and not commercial activity. In particular, it was found that subjecting aspects of base operations to supervision by a domestic Canadian tribunal would create an unacceptable intrusion into the sovereign immunity of the United States in an area critical to its national security. The Court thus allowed the appeal and held that the United States was immune from the certification proceedings.

Subsequent Canadian cases have followed the same dual-nature-purpose approach to determining whether any particular activity is commercial or not, albeit not always recognizing immunity.[135] A recent case emphasizing the predominance of the nature over the purpose tests, however, is the Ontario Court of Appeal decision in *Bouzari* v. *Iran*.[136] As we have seen above, Bouzari sought civil relief against Iran in the Canadian courts for acts of torture committed against him by Iranian agents in Iran. Faced with the *State Immunity Act's* general rule

---

134 *I Congreso del Partido*, above note 68.
135 For example, *Ferguson v. Arctic Transportation Ltd.*, above note 112; *Butcher v. Saint Lucia* (1998), 21 C.P.C. (4th) 236 (Ont. Ct. Gen. Div.), aff'd [1999] O.J. No. 1234 (C.A.); *Collavino Inc. v. Yemen (Tihama Development Authority)*, 2007 ABQB 212 [*Collavino v. Yemen*]; *Smith v. Chin*, above note 127 at paras. 39–46.
136 *Bouzari v. Iran*, above note 47.

of state immunity in civil proceedings, Bouzari argued that the section 5 commercial activity exception applied in the circumstances of his case. In particular, he argued that he was tortured because of his commercial involvement in the exploitation of oil and gas fields in Iran. In other words, Bouzari argued that the acts of torture which he suffered were inflicted for a commercial purpose.

The Ontario Court of Appeal rejected this argument, finding that there was nothing commercial in the nature of acts of torture and that, even accepting an intent by Iran to influence commercial activities by such acts, "that is not enough to turn the acts of torture themselves into the commercial activity of Iran."[137] Adding that the "acts of torture are related only by intention to ... commercial activity," the Court concluded that this was insufficient to bring them within the definition of commercial activity set out in section 2 of the Act.[138] Moreover, as Iran's intent was not strictly relevant to Bouzari's claim for damages, it could not be said that that claim "relate[d]" to commercial activity by Iran, as required by section 5 of the Act.[139]

Bouzari v. *Iran* can thus be seen as placing the emphasis squarely back on the nature of the transaction test, which is not particularly surprising given that only that test is expressly mentioned in section 2 of the Act. It also seems to clarify that the purpose of the transaction only has a contextual role to play, in the *Re Canada Labour Code* sense, where there is some ambiguity as to the nature of the activity in question. Where the activity is unambiguously of a non-commercial nature, as found to be the case in *Bouzari* v. *Iran*, a commercial purpose or intent on the part of the state actor would appear to be irrelevant.

iii) Death, Injury, and Property Damage

A foreign state enjoys no immunity from the jurisdiction of Canadian courts in any proceedings relating to death, personal or bodily injury, or damage to or loss of property occurring in Canada.[140] It has been judicially emphasized that the injuries complained of must have occurred in Canada for the exception to apply.[141]

It has also been held that section 6(a) of the Act does not extend to mental distress or emotional upset that are not linked to physical

---

137 *Ibid.* at para. 53.
138 *Ibid.*
139 *Ibid.* at para. 54.
140 *State Immunity Act*, above note 99, s. 6.
141 *Walker*, above note 111 at 510; *Bouzari* v. *Iran*, above note 47 at para. 47; *P.(R.)* v. *Westwood*, above note 110 at para. 22.

injury.[142] Even in cases of mental suffering linked to physical injury, moreover, the physical injury itself must have occurred in Canada: it is not enough for the mental suffering to be experienced in Canada following a physical injury abroad.[143]

Similarly, section 6(b) of the Act does not extend to pure economic loss not consequent upon some tangible damage to or loss of property.[144]

iv) Maritime Matters

The exception from the general immunity of foreign states in respect of maritime matters[145] is merely an extension of the commercial activity exception. In particular, a foreign state is not immune from the jurisdiction of a Canadian court in any proceedings relating to an action *in rem* against a ship or cargo owned or operated by the foreign state, or an action *in personam* for enforcing a claim in connection with a ship or cargo owned or operated by the foreign state, if at the time the claim arose or the proceedings were commenced the ship or cargo was being used or was intended for use in a commercial activity.[146] "Owned" extends to possession or control by the foreign state, as well as to an interest claimed by a foreign state.[147]

It has been held that, in deciding whether immunity is displaced under this provision, it does not matter whether the subject matter of the proceeding in question is directly or only incidentally connected to the ship or cargo.[148] It has also been held that it is the nature of the activity, and not the activity's purpose from the perspective of the foreign state, that must be considered in assessing whether or not the ship or cargo was being used or intended for use in commercial activity.[149] This last finding

---

142 *Friedland*, above note 126 at para. 39; *Schreiber*, above note 127 at para. 42; *Castle v. United States Department of Justice (Attorney General)* (2006), 218 O.A.C. 53 at para. 4 (C.A.), leave to appeal to S.C.C. refused, [2007] S.C.C.A. No. 55 [*Castle*]; *Ritter v. Donell*, above note 110 at paras. 26–27. Note that in *Schreiber, ibid.*, LeBel J. writing for the Court allowed the possibility that s. 6(a) might also extend to "an overlapping area between physical harm and mental injury, such as mental stress": para. 80. This has been interpreted to require that mental distress and psychological upset "manifest themselves physically, as in nervous shock": *P.(R.) v. Westwood*, above note 110 at para. 21.

143 *Bouzari v. Iran*, above note 47 at para. 47.

144 *Friedland*, above note 126 at para. 27; *Castle*, above note 142 at para. 5.

145 *State Immunity Act*, above note 99, s. 7.

146 As defined in s. 2 of the Act, *ibid.*

147 *Ibid.*, s. 7(3).

148 *Sarafi v. "Iran Afzal" (The)*, [1996] 2 F.C. 954 (T.D.).

149 *Ibid.*

is difficult to reconcile with the Supreme Court of Canada's reasoning in *Re Canada Labour Code*,[150] although it is arguably consistent with the definition of commercial activity given in section 2 of the Act and its interpretation by the Ontario Court of Appeal in *Bouzari v. Iran*.[151]

v) Property in Canada

A foreign state enjoys no immunity from the jurisdiction of Canadian courts in any proceedings relating to an interest in property arising by way of succession or gift. Due to the unqualified use of the term "property" (which presumably includes both real and personal property), this appears to be an extension of the prior common law position that no immunity extended to proceedings relating to land in the forum state.[152]

d) Additional Immunities from Attachment or Execution

i) General Approach

While states have in general relinquished absolute immunity from the process of foreign courts, particularly in commercial matters, they have been considerably more reluctant, as we have seen, to subject themselves to coercive measures of enforcement in foreign jurisdictions. In this sense, therefore, immunities from enforcement (as distinct from mere adjudicative) jurisdiction tend still to be more absolute than restrictive in nature.

ii) Injunctions, Specific Performance, Recovery of Land or Property

In keeping with this general approach in international law, the Canadian *State Immunity Act* provides that injunctions, orders for specific performance, or orders for the recovery of land or other property cannot be imposed by a Canadian court on a foreign state,[153] although this restriction does not apply to an agency of a foreign state.[154]

As with other immunities, the immunity from such injunctions or orders may be waived by the express consent of the foreign state.[155] Mere submission by the foreign state to the jurisdiction of the court, however, is not deemed to be consent to the issuance of an injunction,

---

150 *Re Canada Labour Code*, above note 126.
151 See the text accompanying notes 136–39, above in this chapter.
152 *Jaffe*, above note 110.
153 *State Immunity Act*, above note 99, s. 11(1).
154 *Ibid.*, s. 11(3). "Agency of a foreign state" is defined in s. 2 of the Act to mean "any legal entity that is an organ of the foreign state but that is separate from the foreign state."
155 *Ibid.*, s. 11(1).

an order for specific performance, or an order for the recovery of land or other property.[156]

iii) Attachment and Execution

In general, the property of a foreign state located in Canada is immune from attachment, execution, arrest, detention, seizure, and forfeiture.[157] This general principle is subject to three important exceptions. First, the immunity does not attach if the foreign state has explicitly or by implication waived such immunity.[158] Second, the immunity does not attach if the property is used or is intended for use in a commercial activity as defined in section 2 of the Act,[159] an exception reminiscent of Article 19(c) of the *Jurisdictional Immunities Convention*.[160] Third, the immunity does not attach if the execution relates to a judgment establishing rights in property that have been acquired by succession or gift or in immovable property located in Canada.[161] In general, the immunity is not available to an agency of a foreign state.[162]

A special immunity from attachment, execution, arrest, detention, seizure, and forfeiture applies to military property of a foreign state or property under the control of a military authority or defence agency.[163] This immunity extends to agencies of a foreign state.[164]

Similarly, a special immunity from attachment and execution applies to property of a foreign central bank or monetary authority that is held for its own account and is not used for commercial activity,[165] unless the bank, authority, or foreign government has explicitly waived the immunity.[166]

iv) Procedural Penalties

A Canadian court may not impose a fine or penalty on a foreign state for failing or refusing to produce any document or other information in

---

156 *Ibid.*, s. 11(2).
157 *Ibid.*, s. 12(1).
158 *Ibid.*, s. 12(1)(a). See, for example, *Collavino v. Yemen*, above note 135 at para. 139, holding that agreement to international commercial arbitration will be interpreted as waiver of immunity from execution.
159 *State Immunity Act*, above note 99, s. 12(1)(b).
160 *Jurisdictional Immunities Convention*, above note 7. See also the text accompanying note 97, above in this chapter.
161 *State Immunity Act*, above note 99, s. 12(1)(c).
162 *Ibid.*, s. 12(2).
163 *Ibid.*, s. 12(3).
164 *Ibid.*, s. 12(2).
165 *Ibid.*, s. 12(4).
166 *Ibid.*, s. 12(5).

the course of proceedings before the court.[167] This immunity does not extend to agencies of a foreign state.[168]

e) Other Procedural Provisions

i) General

The Act provides for certain procedures to be followed in proceedings involving foreign states. Generally, however, the usual rules of court apply, except as modified by the Act, to proceedings involving a foreign state.[169]

ii) Service of Originating Documents

With respect to the service of originating documents on a foreign state, such service may be made in a manner agreed to by the foreign state, in accordance with any international convention to which the foreign state is a party, or by delivering a copy of the document, in person or by registered mail, to the Canadian deputy minister of foreign affairs who will transmit it to the foreign state.[170] In the case of service on an agency of a foreign state, such service may be made in a manner agreed to by the agency, in accordance with any international convention applicable to the agency and in accordance with applicable rules of court, or as directed by the court itself.[171] Failure to serve originating documents on the foreign state as required by section 9 of the Act may deprive Canadian courts of jurisdiction to enter judgments against the foreign state,[172] although the requirements of service may be waived by Canadian courts in circumstances where such requirements cannot be fulfilled.[173]

iii) Default Judgment

When service of an originating document has been made on a foreign state or agency and the state has failed to take any step in the matter, default judgment may not be obtained unless a period of at least sixty days has elapsed since service.[174] Default judgment so obtained must be

---

167   *Ibid.*, s. 13(1).

168   *Ibid.*, s. 13(2).

169   *Ibid.*, s. 17. See also *Jaffe*, above note 110.

170   *State Immunity Act*, above note 99, ss. 9(1) & (2).

171   *Ibid.*, ss. 9(3) & (4).

172   See *TMR Energy Inc. v. Ukraine (State Property Fund)* (2004), 245 Nfld. & P.E.I.R. 191 (Nfld. S.C.T.D.); *Softrade Inc. v. United Republic of Tanzania (Ministry of Water and Livestock Development)*, [2004] O.T.C. 482 (S.C.J.).

173   See *Zhang v. Jiang* (2006), 82 O.R. (3d) 306 (S.C.J. Master).

174   *State Immunity Act*, above note 99, s. 10(1). See *Croteau v. United States of America (Federal Trade Commission)* (2006), 22 C.P.C. (6th) 320 at paras. 7–8 (Ont. C.A.).

served on the foreign state or agency in accordance with the Act.[175] The foreign state may then apply, within sixty days of service of the default judgment, to have the default judgment set aside.[176]

iv) Executive Certificates

The Canadian minister of foreign affairs may issue a certificate with respect to three factual matters, namely:

1) whether a country is a foreign state within the meaning of the Act;
2) whether a particular area or territory of a foreign state is a political subdivision of that state; or,
3) whether a person is to be regarded as the head of government of a foreign state or of a political subdivision thereof.

Such a certificate will be deemed by any Canadian court to be conclusive proof of the matter stated in the certificate,[177] but its absence is not conclusive, for example, as to the non-existence of a state.[178]

C. DIPLOMATIC IMMUNITIES

1) Development and Basis of Diplomatic Immunities

In contrast to the evolving scope and extent of state immunity, the law of diplomatic immunities is well settled and largely uncontroversial. In part this is due to its longer history: the practice of exchanging diplomatic envoys stretches to well before the emergence of the Westphalian state, and was intensified with the emergence of the modern state and the resulting need for diplomatic contact between sovereigns. This intensity and frequency of diplomatic contact has meant that customary practices, including, in particular, the extension of special immunities to diplomatic envoys, have been consolidated and refined into well-established, mandatory, and detailed rules of customary international law.

Such well-established customary rules surrounding diplomatic contact have paved the way for the conclusion of a number of highly successful multilateral conventions which, in turn, have added clarity and consistency to the law in the area. By far the most important of these

---

175 *State Immunity Act, ibid.*, s. 10(2).
176 *Ibid.*, s. 10(3).
177 *Ibid.*, s. 14(1).
178 See *Parent*, above note 110 at paras. 37 and 50.

conventions, the 1961 *Vienna Convention on Diplomatic Relations*,[179] is yet another product of the International Law Commission's codification efforts.[180] Since its conclusion, the Convention has attracted near-universal ratification and is the authoritative reference point for most questions relating to the international law of diplomatic relations.[181] Canada ratified the Convention in 1966 and has since implemented it in part in the *Foreign Missions and International Organizations Act*.[182]

As implied by its title, the Convention addresses the rights and obligations of states with respect to the (usually) permanent exchange of diplomatic personnel (ambassadors or high commissioners and other diplomatic representatives) and the establishment of diplomatic missions (embassies or high commissions) abroad. Other conventions cover the related fields of consular relations,[183] the privileges and immunities of the United Nations,[184] the privileges and immunities re-

---

179 *Vienna Convention on Diplomatic Relations*, 18 April 1961, 500 U.N.T.S. 95 (entered into force 24 April 1964) [*Diplomatic Relations Convention*].

180 Although the General Assembly recommended in 1949 that the law of diplomatic immunities be codified, the Commission did not appoint a Special Rapporteur for the topic until 1954. In 1957, the Commission submitted a provisional draft for state comment. Shortly thereafter, the text was revised and a final draft submitted to the General Assembly along with a recommendation that a conference be held for the purpose of concluding a convention: "Report of the International Law Commission on the Work of its Tenth Session, 28 April to 4 July 1958" (UN Doc. A/3859), in *Yearbook of the International Law Commission 1958*, vol. II (New York: United Nations, 1958).

181 As of August, 2007, there were 186 parties and 60 signatories to the *Diplomatic Relations Convention*.

182 *Foreign Missions and International Organizations Act*, S.C. 1991, c. 41.

183 *Vienna Convention on Consular Relations*, 24 April 1963, 596 U.N.T.S. 261 (entered into force 19 March 1967); currently 171 parties and 48 signatories. Consular relations are distinct from diplomatic relations in that they are more limited in scope and generally do not extend to overall political representation of the sending state in the host state. The functions of consuls vary widely but frequently relate to administrative matters, such as the issuance of visas or the performance of services for nationals of the sending state, as well as representing the sending state's interests in cultural, economic, tourism, and other areas.

184 *Convention on the Privileges and Immunities of the United Nations*, 13 February 1946, 1 U.N.T.S. 15 (entered into force 17 September 1946); currently 154 parties. See also Article 19 of the *Statute of the International Court of Justice*, 26 June 1945, Can. T.S. 1945 No. 7 (in force 24 October 1945), which extends diplomatic privileges and immunities to judges of the International Court of Justice.

lating to other international organizations,[185] and the privileges and immunities of special missions.[186]

The basic rationales for the special privileges and immunities of foreign diplomats and diplomatic missions, to be reviewed below, are largely the same as those for state immunity, even though the scope and potency of the two types of immunity are markedly different. The most important of these rationales is clearly the functional objective of permitting diplomatic representatives of foreign states to devote themselves fully to their representative roles without interference or fear of constraint by the host state.[187] The primacy of this objective is explicitly stated in the preamble to the *Diplomatic Relations Convention*:

> The States Parties to the present Convention,
>
> ...
>
> Realizing that the purpose of such privileges and immunities is not to benefit individuals but· to ensure the efficient performance of the functions of diplomatic missions as representing States....[188]

As the establishment of diplomatic relations and the exchange of diplomatic representatives are strictly matters of mutual consent between states,[189] the considerable constraints imposed on a host state's jurisdiction over foreign diplomatic personnel and missions are also fully explicable on the basis of the consent of the host state. Consent to a foreign diplomatic presence in one's territory necessarily entails consent to the protections afforded by customary international law and the Convention as a corollary to that presence. Thus, the territorial sovereignty of the host state is readily reconciled with diplomatic immunities.

---

185 *Vienna Convention on the Representation of States in their Relations with International Organizations of a Universal Character*, 14 March 1975, U.N. Doc. A/DONF.67/16 (not yet in force, thirty-three parties). Other, organization-specific treaties may also provide for immunities in favour of such organizations or their representatives: see, for example, the *Agreement on Privileges and Immunities of the International Criminal Court*, 9 September 2002, ICC-ASP/1/3 at 215 and Corr. 1 (in force 22 July 2004), fifty-two parties. Note that the International Law Commission has recently placed the topic "Immunities of International Organizations" on its long-term programme of work, which may yield further codification of international law in this specialized area.

186 *Convention on Special Missions*, 8 December 1969, 1400 U.N.T.S. 231 (entered into force 21 June 1985); currently thirty-eight parties. Special missions refer to official but temporary delegations to diplomatic conferences and other non-permanent international fora.

187 See, for example, *Boos v. Barry*, 485 U.S. 312 at 323 (1988).

188 *Diplomatic Relations Convention*, above note 179.

189 *Ibid.*, Article 2.

2) Nature and Scope of Diplomatic Immunities

a) General

In very general terms, the overall effect of diplomatic immunities is to subtract foreign diplomatic personnel, premises, and property from the jurisdictional reach of the host state, again with the objective of preserving their ability to serve, in an unfettered manner, the interests of the sending state. The scope of diplomatic immunities is thus much broader than that of state immunity, which is largely focused on immunity from local judicial and enforcement processes. Diplomatic immunities are also in many ways more potent in that they include *ratione personae* and *ratione materiae* elements that are not subject to the many exceptions that characterize the restrictive doctrine of state immunity. Of course, there is an area of overlap between state and diplomatic immunities, in that diplomatic personnel represent states and thus perform acts to which *ratione materiae* state immunity will apply. In addition to such immunity, however, diplomatic personnel enjoy greater personal immunities, and diplomatic property is subject to even greater protections, than those provided by state immunity alone.

b) Inviolability

The cornerstone of diplomatic immunities is the concept of "inviolability," a term not defined in the Convention but which implies immunity from any form of interference, arrest, or detention whatsoever, as well as a duty of protection by the host state.[190]

The premises of the diplomatic mission, its archives, documents, and official communications are all inviolable.[191] This essentially means that the host state cannot enter mission premises without the consent of the head of the mission or interfere with its furnishings, means of transport, other property, documents, and communications in any way whatsoever. This is so regardless of the surrounding circumstances, including the severance of diplomatic relations or even the outbreak of armed conflict between the two states.[192]

In addition, the host state owes a special duty of protection to the mission premises, meaning that it must take all appropriate steps to protect the premises of the mission against intrusion, damage, or dis-

---

190 See, generally, Brownlie, above note 4 at 347, n. 37.
191 *Diplomatic Relations Convention,* above note 179, Articles 22, 24, and 27. The inviolability of official communications extends to the diplomatic courier and the diplomatic bag in which official communications are carried between the mission and the sending state.
192 *Ibid.,* Article 45.

turbance of the peace. This requires the host state to go beyond mere non-interference with the mission and to exercise due diligence in controlling the activities of purely private parties in its territory who may pose a threat to the security of the mission.[193] The same inviolability also extends to the private residence of a diplomatic agent.[194]

Similarly, the persons of diplomatic agents and their families are inviolable, meaning that they are not liable to any form of arrest or detention, and that the host state must take appropriate steps to protect them from attack against their person, freedom, or dignity.[195] The same inviolability extends to members of the administrative and technical staff of the mission and their families, provided they are neither nationals nor permanent residents of the host state.[196] This inviolability must be respected regardless of the surrounding circumstances, including the outbreak of armed conflict, for as long as the protected person occupies his or her position and for a reasonable period of time thereafter necessary for the person to leave the host state.[197] In essence, therefore, the host state is legally powerless to exercise any form of constraint against these persons, even if they are suspected of criminal or other illegal activity.

It is this aspect of diplomatic immunities that most frequently gives rise to controversy, as it appears to grant a licence to foreign diplomatic personnel to break local law with impunity. In fact this is not so. First, the sending state and its diplomatic personnel are under an obligation to respect the laws of the receiving state and to limit their activities and use of the mission to legitimate diplomatic purposes as defined in the Convention.[198] Second, in the event the sending state or its personnel fail to honour these obligations, the host state is not without recourse, although it continues to be under an obligation to respect the inviolability of the foreign mission and its diplomatic personnel.

The host state's principal remedy is, in the case of an offending member of the visiting state's diplomatic personnel, to revoke that individual's diplomatic status and to require the sending state either to recall the individual or to terminate his or her functions with the

---

193 *United States Diplomatic and Consular Staff in Tehran (United States v. Iran)*, [1980] I.C.J. Rep. 3 at paras. 61–68.

194 *Diplomatic Relations Convention*, above note 179, Article 30. Inviolability also extends to the diplomatic agent's papers, correspondence, and property.

195 *Ibid.*, Articles 29 and 37(1). Inviolability does not apply to family members who are nationals of the host state.

196 *Ibid.*, Article 37(2).

197 *Ibid.*, Article 39.

198 *Ibid.*, Articles 3 and 41.

mission. This process is known as declaring the offending diplomatic envoy *persona non grata* and essentially puts the sending state on notice that, if the individual is not recalled or relieved of duty within a reasonable period, the host state will cease to recognize the individual's diplomatic status and, hence, his or her inviolability and other diplomatic immunities.[199] Ultimately, therefore, the host state is in a position to assert jurisdiction over the offending individual if the sending state does not comply with its obligations of recall or termination. However, if the individual in question remains within the premises of the diplomatic mission, *its* continuing inviolability will afford indirect protection against local enforcement jurisdiction.

Of course, in this and other situations where the sending state is itself in violation of its obligations under the Convention, either through its own acts or acts of its diplomatic personnel, the host state also retains its right to bring an international claim in state responsibility against the sending state.[200] Therefore, the true effect of inviolability is not to provide a cloak of impunity to foreign diplomats, but rather to direct the host state toward alternative remedies.

c) Immunities from Local Jurisdiction

In addition to their inviolability, which essentially provides protection from measures of personal constraint, diplomatic agents also enjoy a number of immunities from the legal process of the host state. In particular, diplomatic agents are immune from all local criminal proceedings. They are also immune from local civil and administrative jurisdiction except in respect of actions relating to privately held real property in the jurisdiction, estates actions involving the diplomatic agent personally, and actions relating to private, professional, or commercial activities of the diplomatic agent performed in the host state.[201] These immunities are premised on the assumption that the sending state retains criminal and civil jurisdiction over the diplomatic agent.[202] In the event that the diplomatic agent commits a criminal act while in the host state, the assumption is that the sending state will prosecute the offence in its own courts.

As with state immunity, however, these immunities exempt diplomatic agents from local legal proceedings, but not from the local law

---

199 *Ibid.*, Article 9. In implementing the *Diplomatic Relations Convention*, Canada has defined "reasonable period" in such circumstances to mean ten days: see *Foreign Missions and International Organizations Act*, above note 182, s. 2(2).
200 See further Chapter 12.
201 *Diplomatic Relations Convention*, above note 179, Article 31.
202 *Ibid.*, Article 31(4).

itself. As seen above, diplomatic agents continue to be under a duty to respect local law, even though they are immune from local proceedings seeking to enforce it.[203]

This distinction is significant in that the immunity from local jurisdiction may be waived by the sending state, in which case the local courts gain jurisdiction to apply local law against the diplomatic agent.[204] Unlike state immunity, waiver must generally be express, except insofar as the diplomatic agent initiates his or her own proceedings in the host court. In such a case, immunity is deemed waived in respect of counterclaims directly connected to the principal claim.[205]

The sending state may also waive immunity from measures of execution although, as with state immunity, such waiver is not implied by waiver of immunity from jurisdiction on the merits. Rather, a separate, express waiver is required.[206] Even in the presence of a waiver of immunity from execution, however, the host state must still respect the inviolability of the diplomatic agent's person and residence. For example, execution might be levied against an item of the diplomatic agent's personal property or a personal bank account, but only if this can be done without interfering with his or her person or residence.[207]

d) Limited Immunities from Local Laws

Finally, sending states are immune from the application of certain laws of the host state, mostly of a fiscal nature. For instance, the sending state is exempt from all property or other taxes relating to the premises of its mission, although it must of course pay charges arising from the consumption or use of specific services (such as utilities).[208] Similarly, fees charged by the diplomatic mission (for example, visa or passport application fees) are exempt from local taxation.[209] Diplomatic agents are also exempt from various forms of host state taxation and social security levies, other than indirect taxes incorporated into the price of goods or services, dues and taxes levied on privately held property or investments other than for mission purposes, and charges for specific services, such as utilities.[210] Although this is probably implied in their

---

203 *Ibid.*, Article 41(1).
204 *Ibid.*, Article 32.
205 *Ibid.*, Article 32(3).
206 *Ibid.*, Article 32(4).
207 *Ibid.*, Article 31(3).
208 *Ibid.*, Article 23.
209 *Ibid.*, Article 28.
210 *Ibid.*, Articles 33, 34, and 36.

personal inviolability, diplomatic agents are also exempt from all forms of local public service, including military service.[211]

FURTHER READING

BARKER, J.C., *The Abuse of Diplomatic Privileges and Immunities: A Necessary Evil?* (Burlington: Ashgate Publishing Co., 1996)

BRÖHMER, J., *State Immunity and the Violation of Human Rights* (The Hague: Martinus Nijhoff, 1997)

BROWNLIE, I., *Principles of Public International Law*, 6th ed. (Oxford: Oxford University Press, 2003) c. 16–17

COOPER-HILL. J., *The Law of Sovereign Immunity and Terrorism* (Oxford: Oceana, 2006)

CRAWFORD, J., "International Law and Foreign Sovereigns: Distinguishing Immune Transactions" (1983) 54 Brit. Y.B. Int'l L. 75

DENZA, E., *Diplomatic Law, A Commentary on the Vienna Convention on Diplomatic Relations*, 2nd ed. (Oxford: Clarendon Press, 1998)

FOX, H., *The Law of State Immunity* (Oxford: Oxford University Press, 2002)

HESS, B., "The International Law Commission's Draft Convention on the Jurisdictional Immunities of States and their Property" (1993) 4 Eur J. Int'l L. 269

INSTITUTE OF INTERNATIONAL LAW, "Report on State Immunity" (1992) 64 *Annuaire de l'Institut de droit international* 388

INTERNATIONAL LAW COMMISSION, "Report of the Commission on the Work of its Forty-Third Session" (UN Doc. A/46/10) in Yearbook of the International Law Commission 1991, vol. II, Part 2 (New York: United Nations, 1991)

LAUTERPACHT, H., "The Problem of the Jurisdictional Immunities of Foreign States" (1951) 28 Brit. Y.B. Int'l L. 220

LEWIS, C., *State and Diplomatic Immunity*, 3d ed. (London: Lloyd's of London Press, 1990)

---

211 *Ibid.*, Article 35.

MOLOT, H.L., & JEWETT, M.L., "The *State Immunity Act* of Canada" (1982) Can. Y.B. Int'l L. 79

MORGAN, E., *International Law and the Canadian Courts: Sovereign Immunity, Criminal Jurisdiction, Aliens' Rights and Taxation Powers* (Agincourt: Carswell, 1990)

PINGEL-LENUZZA, I., *Les immunités des États en droit international* (Brussels: Éditions Bruylant, 1997)

SCHREUER, C., *State Immunity: Some Recent Developments* (Cambridge: Cambridge University Press, 1988)

SCOTT, C.M., ed., *Torture as Tort: Comparative Perspectives on the Development of Transnational Human Rights Litigation* (Oxford: Hart Publishing, 2001)

SINCLAIR, I., "The Law of Sovereign Immunity: Recent Developments" (1980-II) 167 Rec. des Cours 113

SORNARAJAH, M., "Problems in Applying the Restrictive Theory of Sovereign Immunity" (1982) 31 Int'l Comp. L.Q. 661

WATTS, A., "The Legal Position in International Law of Heads of State, Heads of Government and Foreign Ministers" (1994-III) 247 Rec. des Cours 13

CHAPTER 10

INTERNATIONAL PROTECTION OF HUMAN RIGHTS

A. INTRODUCTION

The emergence and growth of international human rights law probably ranks, along with the establishment of the United Nations and the prohibition of the unilateral use of force, among the most significant developments in international law since the Peace of Westphalia some three and a-half centuries ago. This is because this relatively new area challenges some of the most fundamental assumptions of traditional international law. Until the twentieth century, chief among these was the assumption that international law only concerned the mutual rights and obligations of states,[1] which in turn were assumed to be its sole subjects.[2]

In contrast, the whole premise of international human rights law is that individuals and, in some cases, groups enjoy certain basic rights that are recognized in international law and are opposable against all states, including their own. The rapid establishment of international human rights law in the twentieth century thus not only fractured the virtually complete monopoly that states had previously held over international legal personality, but it also radically narrowed the concept of "domestic jurisdiction," the protected sphere in which states exercise their sovereignty and in which other states and the international com-

---

1 See Chapter 1, Section B(2).
2 See Chapter 2, Section B(1).

munity must not interfere.[3] In other words, international human rights law displaced the earlier bedrock principles that individuals do not directly enjoy rights at international law and that states are not answerable in that forum for their treatment of their own nationals within their own territory. International human rights law thus emerged as the single most potent "spoiler" of the full sovereignty of the traditional Westphalian state.

Given such deep implications, human rights discourse has come to permeate virtually all modern developments in international law. As we shall see, however, while the concept of human rights protection has gained widespread currency in modern international law, concrete implementation and enforcement measures remain substantially underdeveloped. Thus, the evolution of international human rights protection at once illustrates international law's potential for extraordinary and rapid innovation, but also its frustrating reluctance to develop robust enforcement mechanisms that would interfere with the sovereign interests of states.

In light of the foregoing, a general familiarity with at least the overall international human rights framework that has emerged in the past sixty years or so is essential to understanding the dynamic of modern international law. The goal of this chapter is to introduce readers to that framework. This basic overview can then serve as a basis for further study of what has become a vast and highly specialized field of international law, the full scope of which would be difficult to capture in a large volume, let alone in the present chapter.[4]

---

3   "Nothing contained in the present *Charter* shall authorize the United Nations to intervene in matters which are essentially within the domestic jurisdiction of any state or shall require the Members to submit such matters to settlement under the present *Charter*": *Charter of the United Nations*, 26 June 1945, Can. T.S. 1945 No. 7 (entered into force 24 October 1945) [*UN Charter*], Article 2(7). Article 2(7) goes on to say that "this principle shall not prejudice the application of enforcement measures under Chapter VII."

4   For a more thorough introduction to this area of international law, readers are referred to a companion volume in this series: see M. Freeman & G. van Ert, *International Human Rights Law* (Toronto: Irwin Law, 2004).

B. DEVELOPMENT AND SCOPE OF THE INTERNATIONAL HUMAN RIGHTS FRAMEWORK

1) Precursors to International Human Rights Protection

The concept of human rights is not in itself particularly new, having roots in ancient philosophy. As a legal construct it rose rapidly to prominence during the Enlightenment, mainly in the writings of such legal philosophers as John Locke,[5] Jean-Jacques Rousseau,[6] Montesquieu,[7] and others. Various events, such as the English Civil War and the American and French Revolutions, catalyzed a considerable ferment of ideas about the relationship of the individual to the state and, more particularly, about certain inalienable rights of individuals and concomitant restraints on the power of the state. However, the majority of this rumination concerned the internal relations of states or governments with their own peoples. While what would eventually come to be known as human rights have been a prominent feature of legal discourse for a considerable period, until the twentieth century it was widely considered that such matters concerned only domestic, and not international, law.

A number of early developments, however, may help to explain the astonishing rapidity with which human rights norms entered the mainstream of international law in the mid-twentieth century. For example, the nineteenth century development of international rules for the treatment of foreign nationals (or "aliens") marked an indirect recognition of certain basic standards of conduct required of states *vis-à-vis* certain individuals. However, that area of the law was largely based on mutual obligations of states not to harm one another through mistreatment of one another's nationals, rather than on international legal rights held by individuals themselves. It also provided no protection at all to individuals from mistreatment by their own state.[8]

---

5   See J. Locke (1632–1704), *Second Treatise of Government*, 1690, ed. by C.B. Macpherson (Indianapolis: Hackett, 1980).

6   See J-J. Rousseau (1712–1778), *Social Contract and Other Later Political Writings*, trans. by V. Gourevitch, ed. (Cambridge: Cambridge University Press, 1997).

7   See C. de S. Montesquieu (1689–1755), *De l'esprit des lois* (Paris: Garnier frères, 1941).

8   See further Chapter 8, Section D. And see, generally, R.B. Lillich, *The Human Rights of Aliens in Contemporary International Law* (Manchester: Manchester University Press, 1984).

Other antecedents included a certain penchant by the United States and some European states for foreign military interventions to halt humanitarian atrocities, signalling a nascent conviction that even sovereign states could not be permitted to commit certain acts against their own populations.[9] This idea took on more concrete form in the various peace treaties that followed the First World War, many of which included guarantees protecting racial, ethnic, and religious minorities from persecution. Monitoring for state compliance with such guarantees fell to the Council of the League of Nations and, ultimately, the Permanent Court of International Justice, but only at the instance of states and not the protected groups or individuals themselves.[10]

Perhaps the most significant precursor to the emergence of international human rights law, however, was the establishment by treaty of the International Labour Organization (ILO) in 1919.[11] The work of the ILO extends to such issues as forced labour, freedom of association (including collective bargaining rights), discriminatory practices in employment, and other matters that today are considered questions of human rights. Of particular significance is that the constitution of the ILO contemplates direct participation by employers, workers, and unions, in addition to states, in the workings of the organization. In particular, the ILO constitution establishes a cooperative supervisory system that involves not only governments but also employers' and workers' groups in supervising states' respect for labour standards. In this way, with respect to those standards of conduct that states have

---

9   For a brief overview of the chief instances of such state practice, see W.M. Reisman & M.S. McDougal, "Humanitarian Intervention to Protect the Ibos" in R.B. Lillich, ed., *Humanitarian Intervention and the United Nations* (Charlottesville, VA: University Press of Virginia, 1973) 167 at 179–83. See also I. Brownlie, *International Law and the Use of Force by States* (Oxford: Clarendon Press, 1968) at 338–42.

10 See, generally, I. Brownlie, *Principles of Public International Law*, 6th ed. (Oxford: Oxford University Press, 2003) at 530; M.N. Shaw, *International Law*, 5th ed. (Cambridge: Cambridge University Press, 2003) at 252–53. Early judicial decisions applying these minority group protections include *Rights of Minorities in Upper Silesia (Minority Schools), Advisory Opinion* (1928), P.C.I.J. (Ser. A) No. 15; *Treatment of Polish Nationals and Other Persons of Polish Origin or Speech in the Danzig Territory, Advisory Opinion* (1932), P.C.I.J. (Ser. A/B) No. 44; *Minority Schools in Albania, Advisory Opinion* (1935), P.C.I.J. (Ser. A/B) No. 64.

11 The original ILO Constitution was drafted as Part XIII of the *Treaty of Versailles (Treaty of Peace between the Allied and Associated Powers and Germany)*, 28 June 1919. See further L. Betten, *International Labour Law: Selected Issues* (Boston: Kluwer Law and Taxation Publishers, 1993); V-Y. Ghebali, *The International Labour Organization: A Case Study on the Evolution of U.N. Specialised Agencies* (Dordrecht: M. Nijhoff Publishers, 1989).

accepted by treaty, the ILO constitution holds them accountable to the actual beneficiaries of such standards.[12] Both in recognizing international standards of conduct derived from the rights of individuals and in establishing supervisory mechanisms calling for participation by the holders of such rights, the ILO paved the way for the wider human rights developments that were to follow the Second World War.

2) The *UN Charter*

While the foregoing developments were important in placing the idea of human rights on the international legal agenda, the real catalyst for incorporating human rights protections into international law was public opinion. Abhorrence of the brutalities committed by many states, sometimes against their own populations, during the Second World War led to the incorporation of human rights provisions in early drafts of the *UN Charter*. Initially rather timid, these provisions were ultimately strengthened through the determined efforts of a number of small states and non-governmental organizations.[13] Thus, notwithstanding strong misgivings expressed by many states prior to its conclusion, the *UN Charter* makes numerous references to human rights. Above all, it refers to the protection of human rights in setting out the purposes of the United Nations:

> The Purposes of the United Nations are:
>
>   ...
>
>   To achieve international co-operation in solving international problems of an economic, social, cultural, or humanitarian character, and in promoting and encouraging respect for human rights and for fundamental freedoms for all without distinction as to race, sex, language, or religion ....[14]

---

12   See, generally, L. Swepston, "International Labour Organization Standards and Human Rights" in Y. Danieli, E. Stamatopoulou, & C.J. Dias, eds., *The Universal Declaration of Human Rights: Fifty Years and Beyond* (Amityville, NY: Baywood Publishing, 1999) 37 at 38–41.

13   See J.T.P. Humphrey, *Human Rights and the United Nations: A Great Adventure* (Dobbs Ferry, NY: Transnational, 1984) at 12–13.

14   *UN Charter*, above note 3, Article 1(3). See also *ibid.*, Preamble ("We the peoples of the United Nations, determined ... to reaffirm faith in fundamental human rights, in the dignity and worth of the human person, in the equal rights of men and women...") and Article 55 ("... the United Nations shall promote ... universal respect for, and observance of, human rights and fundamental freedoms for all without distinction as to race, sex, language or religion...").

The inclusion of such a provision in the *UN Charter*, which as we have seen came to be quasi-constitutive of a new legal order in international law following the Second World War, conclusively placed human rights, and thus the interests of individuals, at the centre of the international agenda for the first time. It is important to note, however, the somewhat vague and conditional language employed: the provision speaks of "co-operation" in "promoting and encouraging" respect for human rights, terminology that does not clearly state legal obligations or undertakings. Nevertheless, the *UN Charter's* conferral of legitimacy on the notion that human rights are a matter of international concern was crucial to subsequent developments.

3) The Commission on Human Rights and the *Universal Declaration of Human Rights*

First among these developments was the establishment in 1946 of the Commission on Human Rights. Established by the United Nations Economic and Social Council (ECOSOC),[15] this Commission was charged with the task of preparing a draft instrument defining the nature and extent of human rights that were to receive international protection, as well as the means by which such protection would be promoted and encouraged.[16] However, it quickly became apparent, from the divergent views

---

15 The Economic and Social Council is given primary responsibility for making recommendations for "promoting respect for, and observance of, human rights and fundamental freedoms for all" and has the power to establish commissions to assist it in that task: *UN Charter*, above note 3, Articles 62(2) and 68. Note that the UN General Assembly replaced the Commission, in 2006, with a new Human Rights Council: "Human Rights Council", UNGA Res. 60/251, U.N. Doc. A/RES/60/251 (2006). The Human Rights Council is established as a subsidiary organ of the General Assembly itself, rather than as a "commission" reporting to the Economic and Social Council. In part, this change in structure is meant to give greater prominence to human rights issues dealt with by the Council, as well as to signal a break with the troubled and controversial past of the Commission: see K. Annan, UN Secretary General, *In Larger Freedom: Towards Development, Security and Human Rights for All*, UN GAOR 2005, U.N. Doc. A/59/2005 at paras. 181–83.

16 This was in fact only one of a number of post-war initiatives aimed at addressing various deficiencies in international law that were considered at least partially responsible for events during the Second World War. Others included the formulation of the Nuremberg Principles; the conclusion in 1948 of the *Genocide Convention* and, in 1949, of the four *Geneva Conventions*; and the tortuous attempts to formulate a definition of aggression: see *Affirmation of the Principles of International Law Recognized by the Charter of the Nürnberg Tribunal*, in GA Res. 95(I), UN GAOR, 1st Sess., UN Doc. A/64/Add.1 (1946);

expressed by states and their widespread reluctance to move too rapidly (or in some cases, at all) toward the adoption of binding legal obligations, that the work of the Commission would have to proceed in stages.

The first stage was to draft a declaration that would define in greater detail the concept of human rights referenced in the *UN Charter*. After two years of work, the Commission on Human Rights tabled a draft *Universal Declaration of Human Rights* before the United Nations General Assembly.[17] The *Universal Declaration*, which set out in thirty articles a comprehensive statement of basic human rights and freedoms but did not attempt to articulate corresponding obligations for states, was eventually adopted by the General Assembly with virtually no opposition.[18]

The adoption of the *Universal Declaration* was likely eased by the facts that (1) it did not on its face purport to articulate any obligations for states and (2) General Assembly resolutions do not in any event create binding legal obligations.[19] However, once adopted, the *Universal Declaration* rapidly became the baseline for international dialogue on human rights. Having received almost full support in the General Assembly, it became the authoritative source for interpretation of the various references to human rights contained in the *UN Charter*.[20] It also had a profound influence on several domestic legal orders, either

---

Convention on the Prevention and Punishment of the Crime of Genocide, 9 December 1948, 78 U.N.T.S. 277 (in force 12 January 1951) [*Genocide Convention*]; *Geneva Convention for the Amelioration of the Condition of the Wounded and Sick in Armed Forces in the Field*, 12 August 1949, 75 U.N.T.S. 31; *Geneva Convention for the Amelioration of the Condition of Wounded, Sick and Shipwrecked Members of Armed Forces at Sea*, 12 August 1949, 75 U.N.T.S. 85; *Geneva Convention Relative to the Treatment of Prisoners of War*, 12 August 1949, 75 U.N.T.S. 135; *Geneva Convention Relative to the Protection of Civilian Persons in Time of War*, 12 August 1949, 75 U.N.T.S. 287; *Definition of Aggression*, GA Res. 3314(XXIX), UN GAOR, 29th Sess., Supp. No. 31, UN Doc. A/9631 (1974).

17   The initial draft of the *Universal Declaration*, below note 18, was prepared by John Humphrey, a Canadian professor of international law at McGill University and the first Director of the United Nations Division on Human Rights. His original longhand draft is reproduced in (1995) 33 Can. Y.B. Int'l L. 333.

18   *Universal Declaration of Human Rights*, GA Res. 217(III), UN GAOR, 3rd Sess., Supp. No. 13, UN Doc. A/810 (1948) [*Universal Declaration*]. The *Universal Declaration* was adopted by a vote of forty-eight in favour, none opposed, and eight abstentions. The majority of abstaining states, being from the eastern bloc (as well as South Africa and Saudi Arabia), motivated their abstention principally on the basis that the *Universal Declaration* focused too heavily on western liberal conceptions of individual rights and freedoms and placed inadequate emphasis on collective rights and duties of an economic and social character.

19   See Chapter 3, Section D(2).

20   See H.J. Steiner & P. Alston, *International Human Rights in Context: Law, Politics, Morals*, 2d ed. (Oxford: Oxford University Press, 2000) at 139.

through the enactment of human rights legislation, the constitutional entrenchment of bills of rights, or the decisions of domestic courts.[21] Many of its provisions have since been claimed to constitute customary international law, although this has been controversial, particularly with respect to those rights of an economic or social nature.[22]

These developments led many states to believe that further steps were required; the rights described in the *Universal Declaration* needed to be twinned with formally binding obligations. Thus, notwithstanding continuing objections from some states, the Commission on Human Rights began work on a draft multilateral convention that would enshrine basic human rights protections and obligate states to respect them as a matter of international law.

4) The Debate Over "Generations" of Rights

Again, however, it rapidly became apparent that it would not be possible to accomplish this feat in a single step. Notwithstanding the pioneering work that had led to widespread substantive agreement on the text of the *Universal Declaration*, deep divisions emerged between states when it came to reducing its principles to a set of binding legal obligations. In particular, dissension grew as to the nature of the rights that should be included in a binding treaty and whether states should be subject to the same legal obligations and enforcement mechanisms in respect of all such rights.

The lines along which this debate developed roughly parallel what have been described as different "generations" of human rights.[23] In this scheme, so-called "first generation" human rights include civil and political rights common to most Western, liberal democratic legal and constitutional systems. These comprise the great preponderance of the rights recognized in the *Universal Declaration*.[24] Common examples include freedoms of conscience, expression, peaceful assembly, and association, as well as a number of protections designed to safeguard the liberty and personal integrity of the individual and to suppress discrimination based on personal characteristics. In short, first genera-

---

21   See R. Jennings & A. Watts, eds., *Oppenheim's International Law*, 9th ed., vol. 1 (London: Longman, 1992) at 1002–5.

22   See, for example, H. Hannum, "The Status of the Universal Declaration of Human Rights in National and International Law" (1995–96) 25 Ga. J. Int'l & Comp. L. 287.

23   See K. Vasak & P. Alston, eds., *The International Dimensions of Human Rights* (Westport: Greenwood Press, 1982).

24   *Universal Declaration*, above note 18, Articles 2–21.

tion rights tend to focus on the right of the individual to be free from various forms of interference by the state. Recognition of such rights tends to impose merely "negative" obligations on the state, in the sense that the state is required to refrain from certain acts that would be incompatible with the rights in question.

In contrast, so-called "second generation" rights include rights of an economic, social, and cultural character. In general, such rights seek to protect the entitlement of individuals to a fair share of social and economic benefits, and thus often take the form of a "right to" certain benefits rather than a "freedom from" state interferences. As such, second generation rights are frequently described as "positive" rights in the sense that they would obligate states to take positive steps to ensure that such entitlements are fulfilled. Examples include rights to education, housing, basic standards of living, employment, health care, and so on. Perhaps due to the relative difficulty of defining the precise extent and perceived "cost" of such rights—a contentious point between economically advanced states and their developing counterparts—second generation rights, while present in the *Universal Declaration*, are clearly not preponderant.[25]

"Third generation" rights bear some similarity to second generation rights in that they, too, concern fair entitlements, but differ in that they are framed in terms of collective rather than individual entitlements and are aimed at global and not merely state resources. Third generation rights are cast in much broader terms than the first two generations and concern such collective interests as rights to economic and social development, self-determination, peace, environmental sustainability, and equitable sharing of the resources of the global commons. As we have seen with respect to at least some of these,[26] such widely cast collective rights are difficult to define, let alone implement, with legal precision. It also remains unclear who could effectively be made subject to obligations to ensure their fulfillment. Although principally championed by developing states, there is only an oblique allusion to such rights in the *Universal Declaration*[27] and arguably they do not strictly fall under the rubric of human rights at all.[28]

This way of classifying rights illustrates the potentially broad scope and different implications of recognizing international human rights

---

25   *Ibid.*, Articles 22–27.

26   See, for example, Chapter 2, Section C and Chapter 7, Section C(2)(h).

27   See *Universal Declaration*, above note 18, Article 28: "Everyone is entitled to a social and international order in which the rights and freedoms set forth in this Declaration can be fully realized."

28   See, for example, Brownlie, above note 10 at 540–41.

norms. It also reflects the deep divisions that emerged between various blocs of states as to what international human rights protections could and should stand for. Thus, Western, developed states were the principal proponents of first generation rights, which they perceived as lying at the core of international human rights norms. These same states expressed reluctance over according second generation rights the same status and protections as a matter of international law, and virtually rejected third generation rights out of hand due to their perceived incompatibility with market-based economic models. Socialist and developing states, on the other hand, were largely critical of this preference for first generation rights which, in their view, marginalized equally important obligations of a social, economic, and collective character, and sacrificed communal obligations and responsibilities on the altar of individual freedom.[29]

This debate made it impossible for states, when contemplating a multilateral convention implementing the rights recognized in the *Universal Declaration*, to settle upon a single treaty that would accommodate these conflicting views. As a result, it was decided that the second phase of the Commission on Human Rights' work would itself have to be divided into the elaboration of separate treaties governing different elements of the international human rights equation.

5) The Rise of Universal Treaty Regimes

Even treating the topic in this compartmentalized way still required eighteen years of intense negotiations before the Commission on Human Rights and then the General Assembly adopted the texts of two covenants and one optional protocol, in 1966.[30] The *International Covenant on Civil and Political Rights (ICCPR)*[31] enshrines first generation rights and provides a petition system through which states parties to the *ICCPR* may lodge complaints of non-compliance by other parties. The *Optional Protocol to the International Covenant on Civil and Political Rights (Optional Protocol)*[32] enhances the petition system by providing

---

29 See, generally, Shaw, above note 10 at 249–52.
30 *International Covenant on Economic, Social and Cultural Rights, International Covenant on Civil and Political Rights and Optional Protocol to the International Covenant on Civil and Political Rights*, GA Res. 2200(XXI), UN GAOR, 21st Sess., Supp. No. 16, UN Doc. A/RES/2200(XXI) (1966).
31 *International Covenant on Civil and Political Rights*, 16 December 1966, 999 U.N.T.S. 171 (in force 23 March 1976; Article 41 entered into force 28 March 1979) [*ICCPR*].
32 *Optional Protocol to the International Covenant on Civil and Political Rights*, 16 December 1966, 999 U.N.T.S. 171 (in force 23 March 1976) [*Optional Protocol*].

for direct complaints by individuals, thus matching individual rights with a form of individual remedy. The *International Covenant on Economic, Social and Cultural Rights (ICESCR)*,[33] in contrast, deals with second generation rights and provides for no petition system at all.

Even once adopted, states were so reluctant to ratify the covenants and the *Optional Protocol* that their entry into force was delayed for another decade, until the required number of ratifications (thirty-five) was obtained in 1976. This initial reluctance appears largely to have dissipated with the coming into force of the treaties, however, and the covenants now enjoy broad ratification. At the time of writing, the *ICCPR* had been ratified by 160 states, the *ICESCR* by 157 states, and the *Optional Protocol* by 110 states. Given their widespread ratification, general scope, and modern-day centrality to the international human rights system, these agreements will be described in greater detail in the next two subsections.[34]

Building on the momentum that eventually led to the success of these general treaty regimes, a number of specialized multilateral conventions have also been concluded with a view to expanding and further defining international human rights protections enjoyed by particular groups or in particular circumstances.[35] Among the earliest of these and largely in response to the illegal apartheid regime that had been established in South Africa, was the *International Convention on the Elimination of All Forms of Racial Discrimination*, which was concluded in 1966 and is now ratified by 173 states.[36] Other such broadly ratified but particularized conventions include the *Genocide Convention* (1948, 140 parties);[37] *Convention on the Elimination of All Forms of Discrimination Against Women* (1979, 185 parties);[38] the *Convention*

---

33   *International Covenant on Economic, Social and Cultural Rights*, 16 December 1966, 993 U.N.T.S. 3 (in force 3 January 1976) [*ICESCR*].

34   See Sections B(6) & B(7), below in this chapter.

35   For a review of the substantive content of these specialized multilateral human rights instruments, see J.H. Currie, C. Forcese, & V. Oosterveld, *International Law: Doctrine, Practice and Theory* (Toronto: Irwin Law, 2007) at 554–55 and 580–645.

36   *International Convention on the Elimination of All Forms of Racial Discrimination*, 7 March 1966, 660 U.N.T.S. 195 (in force 4 January 1969). See also *International Convention on the Suppression and Punishment of the Crime of Apartheid*, 30 November 1973, 1015 U.N.T.S. 243 (in force 18 July 1976), 107 parties.

37   *Genocide Convention*, above note 16.

38   *Convention on the Elimination of All Forms of Discrimination against Women*, 18 December 1979, 1249 U.N.T.S. 13 (in force 3 September 1981). See further Steiner & Alston, above note 20 at 158–224.

Against Torture (1984, 145 parties);[39] and the *Convention on the Rights of the Child* (1989, 193 parties).[40] Recently concluded multilateral treaties likely to join this list of widely ratified human rights conventions include the *Convention on the Rights of Persons with Disabilities*[41] and the *International Convention for the Protection of All Persons from Enforced Disappearance.*[42]

6) The *International Covenant on Civil and Political Rights*

a) Nature and Scope of Basic Norms

As suggested above, the terms of the *ICCPR* set out a classical Western, liberal conception of human rights, affirming the essential liberty of the individual and concomitant limitations on the rights of states to trench upon that essential liberty.[43] Its contents, primarily of a first generation character, will thus be quite familiar to most students and practitioners of constitutional law in Western democracies. Many such states have explicitly entrenched most of the same guarantees in their basic constitutional texts or, as in the case of the United Kingdom, have long respected such rights notwithstanding the absence of a constitutionally entrenched bill of rights.[44]

Perhaps because of this affinity with the domestic approach of many states to the protection of human rights, the guarantees in the *ICCPR* are quite specific and detailed. Furthermore, the statement of states' legal obligations is direct and quite strong; although, as treaties traditionally establish rights and obligations between states parties, the oddity of a treaty that defines states' legal obligations to individuals requires some linguistic contortions. Thus, Article 2, the *ICCPR*'s general statement of legal obligation, provides:

---

39 *Convention against Torture and Other Cruel, Inhuman or Degrading Treatment or Punishment,* 10 December 1984, 1465 U.N.T.S. 85 (entered into force 26 June 1987).

40 *Convention on the Rights of the Child,* 20 November 1989, 1577 U.N.T.S. 3 (entered into force 2 September 1990).

41 *Convention on the Rights of Persons with Disabilities,* 13 December 2006, U.N. Doc. A/61/611 (not yet in force). The text of this Convention was adopted by the UN General Assembly in UNGA Res. A/RES/61/106 (2006).

42 *International Convention for the Protection of All Persons from Enforced Disappearance,* 20 December 2006, U.N. Doc. A/61/488 (not yet in force). The text of this Convention was adopted by the UN General Assembly in UNGA Res. A/RES/61/177 (2006).

43 See, generally, Steiner & Alston, above note 20 at 136–236.

44 But see *Human Rights Act 1998* (U.K.), 1998, c. 42.

Article 2

1. Each State Party to the present Covenant undertakes to respect and to ensure to all individuals within its territory and subject to its jurisdiction the rights recognized in the present Covenant, without distinction of any kind, such as race, colour, sex, language, religion, political or other opinion, national or social origin, property, birth or other status.

2. Where not already provided for by existing legislative or other measures, each State Party to the present Covenant undertakes to take the necessary steps, in accordance with its constitutional processes and with the provisions of the present Covenant, to adopt such legislative or other measures as may be necessary to give effect to the rights recognized in the present Covenant.

3. Each State Party to the present Covenant undertakes:
   (a) To ensure that any person whose rights or freedoms as herein recognized are violated shall have an effective remedy...;
   (b) To ensure that any person claiming such a remedy shall have his right thereto determined by competent judicial, administrative or legislative authorities...;
   (c) To ensure that the competent authorities shall enforce such remedies when granted.

The relatively robust nature of Article 2's "respect and ensure" obligations must be juxtaposed, however, with the general "derogation" provisions of Article 4. Those provisions essentially allow states parties to derogate from some of their obligations under the *ICCPR* "in times of emergency which threatens the life of the nation".[45] Some protections under the *ICCPR* are so fundamental, however, that states parties may not fail to respect them even in such times of emergency: these include the rights to life, recognition as a person before the law, and freedom of thought, conscience, and religion; as well as freedom from discrimination, torture, slavery, imprisonment for debt, and retroactive application of criminal law.[46] In addition to this list of "non-derogable" protections explicitly set out in Article 4(2) of the *ICCPR*, the Human Rights Committee[47] has identified other protections that it considers

---

45   *ICCPR*, above note 31, Article 4(1). See discussion in *A and Others v. Secretary of State for the Home Department*, [2005] 3 W.L.R. 1249 (H.L.).

46   *ICCPR*, ibid., Article 4(2).

47   On the nature and functions of the Human Rights Committee, see Section B(6)(b), below in this chapter.

enjoy the same status.[48] Whenever a state in fact derogates from any of the remaining protections provided in the *ICCPR*, this fact is to be immediately notified to other states parties through the intermediary of the UN Secretary General.[49]

Following these general provisions, the *ICCPR* sets out a comprehensive set of provisions defining specific fundamental rights and freedoms,[50] including: the right to life;[51] freedom from cruel, inhuman, or degrading treatment or punishment;[52] a ban on slavery and forced labour;[53] the right to liberty and security of the person, including certain procedural guarantees in cases of arrest or detention;[54] the right to freedom of movement within, and to enter and leave, one's home state;[55] procedural protections for foreign nationals subject to expulsion from a state;[56] procedural protections in judicial proceedings, particularly those of a criminal nature;[57] the right to be recognized as a legal person;[58] rights to privacy and reputation;[59] freedom of thought, conscience, and religion;[60] freedom of opinion and expression;[61] freedom from war propaganda and the dissemination of hatred;[62] freedom

---

48   See UN Human Rights Committee, *General Comment 29: States of Emergency (Article 4)*, U.N. Doc. CCPR/C/21/Rev.1/Add.11 (2001) at paras. 13–16. See also the "Siracusa Principles on the Limitation and Derogation Provisions in the International Covenant on Civil and Political Rights," U.N. Doc. E/CN.4/1985/4, Annex (1985).

49   *ICCPR*, above note 31, Article 4(3).

50   For a convenient overview of the specific human rights guarantees contained in the *ICCPR*, with cross-references to similar protections found in other international instruments, see Currie, Forcese, & Oosterveld, above note 35 at 580–628.

51   *ICCPR*, above note 31, Article 6; this provision includes certain restrictions, albeit not an outright ban, on the imposition of the death penalty. A further optional protocol to the *ICCPR* prohibits the death penalty generally: see *Second Optional Protocol to the International Covenant on Civil and Political Rights, Aiming at the Abolition of the Death Penalty*, GA Res. 44/128, UN GAOR, 44th Sess., Supp. No. 49, Annex, UN Doc. A/44/49 (1989) (in force 11 July 1991) (sixty-four parties at time of writing).

52   *ICCPR, ibid.*, Article 7.

53   *Ibid.*, Article 8.

54   *Ibid.*, Articles 9–11.

55   *Ibid.*, Article 12.

56   *Ibid.*, Article 13.

57   *Ibid.*, Articles 14–15.

58   *Ibid.*, Article 16.

59   *Ibid.*, Article 17.

60   *Ibid.*, Article 18.

61   *Ibid.*, Article 19.

62   *Ibid.*, Article 20.

of peaceful assembly;[63] freedom of association;[64] the right "of men and women" to marry with their consent and to found a family;[65] particular rights of children;[66] the right to participate in the public life of one's state, including the right to universal suffrage;[67] the right to equality before and under the law without discrimination;[68] and certain protections for ethnic, religious, or linguistic minorities.[69]

For the most part, as can be seen from the foregoing list, the rights and freedoms set out in the *ICCPR* merely require the state to refrain from engaging in certain activities or intruding into the affairs of individuals. Thus, notwithstanding the language of Article 2, which might suggest positive obligations for states,[70] in reality most of the *ICCPR*'s substantive provisions are generally construed as negative in character. However, the *ICCPR*'s remedial obligations do indeed require state action "to ensure" the availability and effectiveness of such remedies.[71] This is generally understood to require the establishment of judicial or other remedial recourses for individuals whose rights have been violated.

b)   Compliance Mechanisms

Of the two covenants, the *ICCPR* has by far the strongest compliance regime although, in keeping with the pervasive reluctance of states to match their legal undertakings with firm compliance procedures, that regime is not especially onerous.

At the heart of the *ICCPR* compliance scheme is the establishment of a Human Rights Committee, composed of eighteen members, elected by states parties from among their nationals who are human rights experts.[72] Once elected, these experts do not represent their own governments but are intended to sit as individual experts.[73]

---

63   *Ibid.*, Article 21.
64   *Ibid.*, Article 22.
65   *Ibid.*, Article 23.
66   *Ibid.*, Articles 23(4) and 24.
67   *Ibid.*, Article 25.
68   *Ibid.*, Article 26.
69   *Ibid.*, Article 27.
70   For example, the obligation not only to respect but also "to ensure … the rights recognized in the present Covenant," set out in *ibid.*, Article 2(1), might be construed to impose strict obligations on states to guarantee respect for human rights by all persons, whether or not state representatives: see UN Human Rights Committee, *General Comment 31: Nature of the General Legal Obligations on States Parties to the Covenant*, U.N. Doc. CCPR/C/21/Rev.1/Add.13 (2004) at para. 8 [*General Comment 31*].
71   *ICCPR, ibid.*, Article 2(3). See also *General Comment 31, ibid.* at para. 15.
72   See, generally, Steiner & Alston, above note 20 at 705–78.
73   *ICCPR*, above note 31, Article 28.

The principal role of the Committee is to receive and comment upon reports, periodically submitted by states parties, detailing steps taken by those states to give effect to the rights set out in the *ICCPR*. The Committee determines the frequency with which it requires such reports from states parties. The reporting requirements are quite exacting, and include an overall description of the elements of the reporting state's legal and constitutional framework relevant to the protection of civil and political rights, steps taken to improve that framework, as well as a detailed description of how domestic, legal, and other considerations impact upon the reporting state's compliance with each and every substantive right recognized in the *ICCPR*. The Committee in general responds in writing to the report, highlighting any areas of concern it has identified and making non-binding recommendations for future performance.[74] In short, the reporting system provides for a form of political accountability. Unfortunately, its effectiveness has frequently been marred by some states' uneven compliance with their reporting obligations.[75]

Beyond these basic reporting requirements, the *ICCPR* also provides for a petition system under which the Human Rights Committee may receive and consider complaints from states parties concerning other states parties' non-compliance with their *ICCPR* obligations.[76] This procedure is only available, however, on a strictly reciprocal basis: the state which is the subject of the complaint must have declared that it recognizes the competence of the Committee to receive complaints of this sort against it, and the complaining state must itself have made a similar declaration. In other words, states must expressly opt-in to the *ICCPR*'s petition procedure. Declarations opting-in may be withdrawn by the declaring state at any time.

Even where the states involved in a complaint have made the necessary declarations, moreover, the Committee's jurisdiction to receive the complaint is strictly residual. Remedies available under the domestic legal system of the allegedly offending state must have been exhaust-

---

74   *Ibid.*, Article 40. See also UN Office of the High Commissioner for Human Rights, UN Institute for Training and Research, & UN Staff College, *Manual on Human Rights Reporting Under Six Major International Human Rights Instruments* (Geneva: United Nations, 1997); S. Farrior, "International Reporting Procedures" in H. Hannum, ed., *Guide to International Human Rights Practice*, 4th ed. (Ardsley, NY: Transnational, 2004) 189.

75   See Freeman & van Ert, above note 4 at 387–88; H.M. Kindred, P.M. Saunders *et al.*, eds., *International Law Chiefly as Interpreted and Applied in Canada*, 7th ed. (Toronto: Emond Montgomery, 2006) at 910.

76   *ICCPR*, above note 31, Article 41. See, generally, Freeman & van Ert, *ibid.* at 397.

ed without satisfaction, and direct negotiations between the relevant states aimed at resolving the issue must have failed. The procedure thereafter provides for written and oral submissions by the relevant states, following which the Committee issues a report making findings and non-binding recommendations to the parties. Again, therefore, this mechanism is designed to bring political pressure to bear on non-compliant states. However, the procedure has not been invoked,[77] presumably because most states are unwilling to cast the first stone.

More potent is the scheme whereby individuals (rather than states) may submit complaints directly to the Committee for consideration.[78] Such a system is a step toward granting direct standing to individuals as holders of human rights. Given its radical departure from the long-established rule that only states have standing in international law, however, it was necessary to provide separately for such a mechanism in the *Optional Protocol*. The number of ratifications of the *Optional Protocol*, while respectable, is considerably lower than the number of parties to the *ICCPR* itself, signalling again the reluctance of many states to go beyond formal recognition of international human rights norms.[79]

Access to the individual petition system is limited to individuals who are "subject to [the] jurisdiction" of states parties to the *Optional Protocol*.[80] Complaints must not be anonymous and must be submitted in writing by the alleged victim(s) of abuse, who must have exhausted all local remedies. The Committee forwards the complaint to the relevant state party, which is required to respond in writing within six months, detailing its position on the complaint and any remedies that may have been granted. The Committee then formulates "views" that are communicated to the relevant state and complainant. Again, such views are non-binding and no mechanism is provided for their enforcement against the offending state.[81] Given that they are usually publicized by one or the other party, however, such views may serve as a source of political pressure on states, thus encouraging compliance. In contrast to the petition system for states provided for in Article 41 of the *ICCPR*, the individual complaints system under the *Optional Protocol* is invoked extensively by individuals. In general, moreover, the Committee's recommendations tend to be accepted by the majority of states to which they are directed. This latter pattern may be a reflec-

---

77   See Shaw, above note 10 at 296, n. 277.
78   See, generally, Freeman & van Ert, above note 4 at 393–97.
79   The *Optional Protocol*, above note 32, has 110 parties while the *ICCPR*, above note 31, has 160 parties.
80   *Optional Protocol, ibid.*, Article 1.
81   See *Ahani v. Canada (Attorney General)* (2002), 58 O.R. (3d) 107 at para. 32 (C.A.).

tion of the fact that states that have ratified the *Optional Protocol* are, in general, already committed to compliance with their human rights obligations.

Finally, the Committee also, on occasion, issues general comments setting out its interpretation of various provisions of the *ICCPR*.[82] Such general comments are of course non-binding, but are generally considered authoritative because of the expert composition of the Committee. They are also significant in that they do not emanate from any one state or bloc of states, and therefore encourage universal understandings of the *ICCPR*'s norms. While most of the Committee's general comments have not been controversial,[83] some certainly have been and have failed to attract consensual support from states parties.[84]

7) The *International Covenant on Economic, Social and Cultural Rights*

a) Nature and Scope of Basic Norms
In a complementary fashion to the first generation protections contained in the *ICCPR*, the *ICESCR* recognizes predominantly second generation human rights.[85] As suggested in the title of this covenant, the rights guaranteed are primarily of an economic and social character, and relate to conditions of work, social security, standards of living, health, education, and the like. While, as we have seen, the protection of such rights has mainly been championed by socialist and developing states, many of the guarantees of the *ICESCR* are also quite familiar in the many western, developed states which, in the wake of the Second World War, embraced social welfare programmes of various sorts. However, few of these states have entrenched social welfare schemes in their domestic constitutional orders to the same extent as first genera-

---

82   *ICCPR*, above note 31, Article 40(4).

83   See Shaw, above note 10 at 295.

84   See, for example, UN Human Rights Committee, *General Comment 24: General comment on issues relating to reservations made upon ratification or accession to the Covenant or the Optional Protocols thereto, or in relation to declarations under article 41 of the Covenant*, U.N. Doc. CCPR/C/21/Rev.1/Add.6 (1994) at paras. 8 and 17 [*General Comment 24*], maintaining that provisions of the *ICCPR* that reflect customary international law may not be the subject of valid reservations, and that the Committee has the power to rule on the validity of such reservations (on which see further Chapter 4, Section E(3)); or UN Human Rights Committee, *General Comment 26: Continuity of Obligations*, U.N. Doc. CCPR/C/21/Rev.1/Add.8/Rev.1 (1997) at para. 5 [*General Comment 26*], holding that states parties to the *ICCPR* may not denounce or withdraw from it.

85   See, generally, Steiner & Alston, above note 20 at 237–320.

tion civil liberties. By and large this is because economic and social rights are difficult to define with precision and have the appearance of creating onerous, "positive" obligations for states.

This ambivalence among many states with respect to the recognition of economic and social rights is reflected in the stark differences between the provisions of the two covenants. In contrast to the relatively straightforward general statement of obligation contained in the *ICCPR*,[86] the parallel provision in the *ICESCR* contains considerably more conditional and elliptical language:

1. Each State Party to the present Covenant undertakes to take steps ... to the maximum of its available resources, with a view to achieving progressively the full realization of the rights recognized in the present Covenant by all appropriate means, including particularly the adoption of legislative measures.

   ....

3. Developing countries, with due regard to human rights and their national economy, may determine to what extent they would guarantee the economic rights recognized in the present Covenant to non-nationals.[87]

Obviously, such language conveys the message that the various rights set out in the *ICESCR* need not necessarily be fully respected all at once, but may be implemented on a step-by-step basis.[88] As such, there is a best-efforts quality to the *ICESCR* that arguably does not take its legal guarantees much beyond the general statements of principle contained in Articles 22–27 of the *Universal Declaration*. It is difficult to identify the precise extent of the obligations imposed upon states parties to the *ICESCR*, and more difficult still to label any particular state conduct as a clear breach of such obligations. This "fuzziness" of obligation under the *ICESCR* may therefore explain its broad ratification rate notwithstanding the more controversial nature of the second generation rights it purports to protect.

It should further be noted that the *ICESCR*, in a manner analogous but not identical to the *ICCPR*,[89] contains a general provision that allows states parties to limit the rights it protects "in so far as this may be compatible with the nature of these rights and solely for the purpose of

---

86   *ICCPR*, above note 31, Article 2.

87   *ICESCR*, above note 33, Article 2.

88   See UN Committee on Economic, Social and Cultural Rights, *General Comment 3: The Nature of States Parties Obligations (Article 2, Paragraph 1 of the Covenant)*, U.N. Doc. E/1991/23, annex III at 86 (1990) at paras. 1–2.

89   *ICCPR*, above note 31, Article 4.

promoting the general welfare in a democratic society."[90] Significantly, and unlike Article 4 of the *ICCPR*,[91] this limitation provision is not subject to express exceptions in respect of certain fundamental social, economic, or cultural rights. Rather, the permissibility of any particular limitation hinges on its compatibility with the "nature" of the right limited and alignment of the purpose of the limitation with the "general welfare" criterion, which are likely to be open to a considerable range of interpretations in any given situation.

The *ICESCR* nevertheless brings some further definition to the nature of economic, social, and cultural rights.[92] The *ICESCR* recognizes rights to work and to just and favourable working conditions;[93] to form trade unions and to engage in collective bargaining;[94] to social security;[95] to favourable conditions and support for the family;[96] to an adequate standard of living, including adequate food, clothing, and housing;[97] to physical and mental health;[98] to education;[99] and to participation in cultural life and the benefits of scientific, intellectual, or cultural endeavours.[100] The aspirational character of the *ICESCR* is largely confirmed by the many open-ended, idealistic descriptions of rights and entitlements contained within it.

b) Compliance Mechanisms

The *ICESCR*'s compliance mechanisms are also substantially more modest than those provided under the *ICCPR*. In particular, no petition system at all is envisaged in the *ICESCR*, whether by states or individuals, although a draft optional protocol has been proposed to remedy this gap.[101]

---

90 *ICESCR*, above note 33, Article 4.

91 See the text accompanying notes 45–49, above in this chapter.

92 For a convenient overview of the specific human rights guarantees contained in the *ICESCR*, with cross-references to similar protections found in other international instruments, see Currie, Forcese, & Oosterveld, above note 35 at 628–45.

93 *ICESCR*, above note 33, Articles 6–7.

94 *Ibid.*, Article 8.

95 *Ibid.*, Article 9.

96 *Ibid.*, Article 10.

97 *Ibid.*, Article 11.

98 *Ibid.*, Article 12.

99 *Ibid.*, Articles 13–14.

100 *Ibid.*, Article 15.

101 See the *Revised Draft Optional Protocol to the International Covenant on Economic, Social and Cultural Rights*, U.N. Doc. A/HRC/8/WG.4/3 (2008) prepared by the Chair of the Open-Ended Working Group on an Optional Protocol to the *International Covenant on Economic, Social and Cultural Rights*. The Open-Ended Working Group was established in 2002 by the UN Commission on Human

However, a general reporting requirement is included, under which states parties are obligated to report periodically to the Secretary-General of the United Nations on steps taken to implement the guarantees of the *ICESCR*. These reports have, since 1986, been considered by a Committee on Economic, Social and Cultural Rights, established by the Economic and Social Council for this purpose.[102] As with the general reporting system under the *ICCPR*, that Committee formulates non-binding and unenforceable views and recommendations to states based on the content of such reports.

The Committee also periodically issues general comments, setting out its interpretation of various provisions of the *ICESCR*. Such comments are non-binding but are, as with the comments issued by the Human Rights Committee with respect to the *ICCPR*, generally considered authoritative.

C. REGIONAL HUMAN RIGHTS REGIMES

While the drive to adopt universal human rights regimes has ultimately borne fruit in the form of a number of broadly ratified multilateral conventions as described above, such a result did not always appear likely. Moreover, as will be further explored in the next section,[103] even today there remain substantial difficulties in reconciling regional and cultural differences of approach to international human rights issues. The former explains the emergence, while the latter arguably justifies the retention, of various regional human rights regimes that supplement the universal system we have reviewed above. To date there are three such regimes.

The first to be established was the European system through the conclusion of the *European Convention for the Protection of Human Rights and Fundamental Freedoms* in 1950.[104] It has since been amended by,

---

Rights (now succeeded by the UN Human Rights Council) to carry forward the work already done on the topic by the UN Committee on Social, Economic and Cultural Rights. That Committee had previously proposed such a protocol in 1996: see UN ESCOR, 53rd Sess., Annex, UN Doc. E/CN.4/1997/ 105 (1996). The Open-Ended Working Group is scheduled to consider the Chair's revised draft at its Fifth Session in 2008.

102   *Review of the Composition, Organization and Administrative Arrangements of the Sessional Working Group of Governmental Experts on the Implementation of the International Covenant on Economic, Social and Cultural Rights*, ESC Res. 1985/17, UN ESCOR, 1985, 1st Sess., Supp. No. 1, UN Doc. E/RES/1985/17.

103   See Section D(3), below in this chapter.

104   *Convention for the Protection of Human Rights and Fundamental Freedoms*, 4 November 1950, E.T.S. No. 005 (entered into force 3 September 1953) [*European Convention*].

or supplemented with, fourteen protocols.[105] Originally established amidst frustration over the slow progress towards the establishment of a universal human rights regime under United Nations auspices, the European system was the first to commit its members to certain internationally legally binding human rights norms. In its early incarnation it comprised a commission that was empowered to receive complaints of non-compliance from states parties, although complaints could also be received from individuals or groups with the consent of their home state. The commission could make findings but had no binding powers of enforcement. The commission has since been abolished and replaced by the European Court of Human Rights, which has full jurisdiction to adjudicate upon complaints lodged by states or individuals. Individuals have direct access to the Court, whose determinations are final and binding upon the relevant state. In essence, therefore, the Court operates as a supranational constitutional court with jurisdiction over

---

105 Protocol Nos. 1, 4, and 7 extended the list of protected rights and freedoms under the *European Convention*: *Protocol [No. 1] to the Convention for the Protection of Human Rights and Fundamental Freedoms*, 20 March 1952, E.T.S. No. 009 (entered into force 18 May 1954); *Protocol No. 4 to the Convention for the Protection of Human Rights and Fundamental Freedoms*, 16 September 1963, E.T.S. No. 046 (entered into force 2 May 1968); *Protocol No. 7 to the Convention for the Protection of Human Rights and Fundamental Freedoms*, 22 November 1984, E.T.S. No. 117 (entered into force 1 November 1988). Protocols No. 6 and 13 address abolition of the death penalty: *Protocol No. 6 to the Convention for the Protection of Human Rights and Fundamental Freedoms Concerning the Abolition of the Death Penalty*, 28 April 1983, E.T.S. No. 114 (entered into force 1 March 1985); *Protocol No. 13 to the Convention for the Protection of Human Rights and Fundamental Freedoms Concerning the Abolition of the Death Penalty in All Circumstances*, 3 May 2002, E.T.S. No. 187 (entered into force 1 July 2003). Supplanting Protocol Nos. 2, 3, 5, 8, 9, and 10, Protocol No. 11 transformed the enforcement framework: *Protocol No. 11 to the Convention for the Protection of Human Rights and Fundamental Freedoms, Restructuring the Control Machinery Established Thereby*, 11 May 1994, E.T.S. No. 155 (entered into force 1 November 1998). Protocol No. 12 provided for a different approach to the protection of rights and freedoms. A general prohibition of discrimination, on any ground by any public authority, replaced the guarantee of enumerated rights and freedoms under the treaty: *Protocol No. 12 to the Convention for the Protection of Human Rights and Fundamental Freedoms*, 4 November 2000, E.T.S. No. 177 (entered into force 1 May 2005). Protocol 14, not yet in force, will introduce a number of largely administrative measures designed to streamline the workings of the Convention's enforcement mechanisms: *Protocol No. 14 to the Convention for the Protection of Human Rights and Fundamental Freedoms, Amending the Control System of the Convention*, 13 May 2004, E.T.S. No. 194 (not yet in force). At the time of writing, all member states of the Council of Europe, save the Russian Federation, had ratified Protocol 14. Ratification by the Russian Federation is required before the Protocol can come into force.

issues of basic human rights and freedoms as set out in the *European Convention*.

The European regional human rights regime thus represents a highly evolved system that is readily accessible by individual complainants. It also has a sophisticated judicial enforcement mechanism with the power to issue binding judgments against states parties. However, the human rights protections of the *European Convention* and its various protocols are largely limited to civil and political rights, corresponding roughly to the protections of the *ICCPR*, and do not extend to the economic, social, and cultural rights recognized in the *ICESCR*.[106] To fill this gap, the *European Social Charter* was adopted in 1961[107] and revised in 1996.[108] While the *European Social Charter* extends protections in respect of economic and social rights, its enforcement does not fall within the purview of the European Court of Human Rights. Rather, compliance is encouraged by submission by states parties of periodic reports to the European Committee of Social Rights. In addition, those states parties that have ratified the relevant protocol may be the subject of "collective complaints" lodged with the Committee by non-governmental organizations possessed of "participatory status" before the Council of Europe.[109] That process, however, may only lead to the formulation of non-binding recommendations to the non-compliant state.[110]

The second regional human rights regime to emerge was the Inter-American system established under the *American Declaration of the Rights and Duties of Man (American Declaration)*,[111] the *Charter of the*

---

106 For a further overview of the European human rights system, including mechanisms established by the Organization for Security and Cooperation in Europe and the European Union, see K. Boyle, "Council of Europe, OSCE, and European Union" in Hannum, above note 74 at 143; Freeman & van Ert, above note 4 at 438–42; Steiner & Alston, above note 20 at 786–867.

107 *European Social Charter*, 18 October 1961, E.T.S. No. 35 (in force 26 February 1965).

108 *European Social Charter (Revised)*, 3 May 1996, E.T.S. No. 163 (in force 1 July 1999).

109 *Additional Protocol to the European Social Charter Providing for a System of Collective Complaints*, 11 November 1995, E.T.S. No. 158 (in force 1 July 1998).

110 *Ibid.*, Article 9.

111 *American Declaration of the Rights and Duties of Man*, O.A.S. Res. XXX, adopted by the Ninth International Conference of American States (1948), reprinted in *Basic Documents Pertaining to Human Rights in the Inter-American System*, OEA/Ser.L.V/II.82 doc.6 rev.1 at 17 (1992) [*American Declaration*]. Note that while the adoption of the *American Declaration* in 1948 preceded the adoption of the *European Convention* in 1950 (and even the *Universal Declaration* in 1948), the establishment of the formal legal machinery of the Inter-American system followed that of the European system.

Organization of American States (OAS)[112] and the *American Convention on Human Rights* (*American Convention*).[113] While the *American Convention* focuses essentially on civil and political rights, it is supplemented by a protocol addressing economic, social, and cultural rights.[114]

The Inter-American system's machinery includes: an Inter-American Commission on Human Rights, which receives petitions from individuals against states parties, as well as from states against states parties which accept its jurisdiction in this regard; and, since 1979, the Inter-American Court of Human Rights, to which the Commission and states may submit contentious cases or requests for advisory opinions on issues of interpretation or application of the *American Convention*.

The enforcement mechanisms of the Inter-American system are therefore substantially less developed than those of the European system, even though the rights protected by the *American Convention* are broadly similar in nature to those of the *European Convention* and the *ICCPR*. While the Inter-American Commission may receive and investigate complaints from individuals, it has no power to issue binding judgments or to require compliance. Conversely, the Inter-American Court, the judgments of which are binding upon states that have accepted its jurisdiction, is not directly accessible by individuals. Thus, the intended beneficiaries of rights do not enjoy concomitant direct standing to seek enforcement of such rights.[115]

A third regional system was established in 1981 pursuant to the *African Charter on Human and Peoples' Rights* (*African Charter*).[116] Essentially, that system establishes a Human Rights Commission with the power to give advisory opinions, upon request by a state party, the African Union (AU) or African organizations recognized by the AU, on the interpretation of rights set out in the *African Charter*. It is also em-

---

112 *Charter of the Organization of American States*, 30 April 1948, OAS T.S. 1C and 61, [1990] Can. T.S. No. 23 (entered into force 13 December 1951), as amended by *Protocol of Buenos Aires* (1967), *Protocol of Cartagena de Indias* (1985), *Protocol of Washington* (1992), and *Protocol of Managua* (1993).

113 *American Convention on Human Rights*, 22 November 1969, OAS T.S. No. 36 (entered into force 18 July 1978).

114 *Additional Protocol to the American Convention on Human Rights in the Area of Economic, Social and Cultural Rights*, 17 November 1988, OAS T.S. No. 69 (entered into force 16 November 1999).

115 On the Inter-American system and its compliance mechanisms, see, generally, D.L. Shelton, "The Inter-American Human Rights System" in Hannum, above note 74 at 127; Freeman & van Ert, above note 4 at 425–37; Steiner & Alston, above note 20 at 868–919.

116 *African Charter on Human and Peoples' Rights*, 27 June 1981, (1982) 21 I.L.M. 58 (entered into force 21 October 1986).

powered to investigate complaints made by states parties against other states parties, and may play a conciliatory role between the disputing states. The Commission may also consider complaints lodged by individuals, but has no direct or binding powers of enforcement.

More recently, the African Court on Human and Peoples' Rights was established pursuant to a protocol to the *African Charter* adopted in 1998.[117] The Court has jurisdiction to hear cases referred to it by the Commission, states parties, African intergovernmental organizations, as well as (where the subject state has made a declaration to such effect) non-governmental organizations with observer status before the Commission. While its decisions in contentious cases are to be final and binding, again individuals have no direct standing before it. The Court also has jurisdiction, on request by the AU, member states, or African organizations recognized by the AU, to issue advisory opinions on human rights matters not being considered by the Commission. The Court, whose first members were elected in 2006, has yet to decide a case.[118]

A striking feature of the African regional system is the wide scope of the substantive rights recognized in the *African Charter*. These extend beyond the civil and political rights that dominate the European and Inter-American systems, to include rights of a social, economic, and cultural character, as well as third-generation rights such as collective rights to peace, development, and a healthy environment. The *African Charter* also includes controversial provisions outlining duties of individuals to the state and to their community. In these ways, the *African Charter* appears to present a uniquely African perspective on the nature and meaning of international human rights protections.[119]

Each regional regime plays a role in the definition and protection of human rights that is complementary to that of the United Nations' universal system, while accommodating regional variations in the strength and nature of substantive human rights obligations and their corresponding enforcement mechanisms.

---

117 See the *Protocol to the African Charter on the Establishment of the African Court on Human and Peoples' Rights*, OAU Doc. OAU/LEG/MIN/AFCHPR/PROT.1 rev.2 (1997), (1999) I.H.R.R. 891 (in force 25 January 2005). Following a decision of the AU Assembly in June 2004, the African Court on Human and Peoples' Rights will be administratively merged with the African Court of Justice. At the time of writing, the modalities of that merger continue to be worked out.

118 On the African system and its compliance mechanisms, see, generally, Freeman & van Ert, above note 4 at 447–52; Steiner & Alston, above note 20 at 920–37.

119 See further C. Flinterman & E. Ankumah, "*The African Charter on Human and Peoples' Rights*" in Hannum, above note 74 at 127.

D. CURRENT POINTS OF CONTENTION IN INTERNATIONAL HUMAN RIGHTS LAW

1) Introduction

The overall effect of the adoption of widely ratified universal and regional human rights treaties has been to move the international debate on human rights beyond the desirability or viability of according international legal recognition to such rights. Thus, the existence of human rights as a source of international legal obligations for states is now almost universally accepted. Moreover, there is widespread acceptance of most of the universal human rights recognized in the *Universal Declaration,* the covenants, and the other specialized universal human rights treaties. However, this is not to say that controversy over international human rights has abated. Rather, new points of contention have emerged that threaten to undermine the full realization and implementation of universal human rights protections.

Among the more prominent areas of controversy are the permissibility of reservations to universal or regional human rights treaty regimes; the customary status of human rights norms; whether the concept of universal human rights norms entails universal interpretation and application of these norms, or whether there is room for interpretations and applications sensitive to contextual factors such as local cultural traditions; and whether and how to strengthen enforcement mechanisms by granting individuals, the ostensible beneficiaries of human rights, the necessary standing to ensure compliance.

2) Nature and Status of Universal Human Rights Norms

The first two such areas of debate, the capacity of states to lodge reservations to human rights treaties and the customary status of universal human rights, are in fact interrelated. Both ultimately concern the nature and source of human rights obligations and the relationship of such obligations with other rules of international law. For example, should human rights obligations rank higher than other international legal obligations because of the fundamental interests they protect? Or should they rank lower because they relate to rights of individuals rather than states, which are, after all, the primary subjects of international law? Or should some human rights norms rank higher and some lower, depending on their content? The latter possibility would imply, of course, not only a hierarchy between human rights norms and other international legal norms, but also a hierarchy among human rights norms themselves—in the sense that some would be more "fundamental" than others.

The answers to these questions remain disputed, although some international instruments suggest that certain human rights protections do indeed take precedence over other legal rights and duties of states. For example, the International Law Commission's *Draft Articles on State Responsibility* outlaw countermeasures that would derogate from the protection of "fundamental human rights."[120] Similarly, the *ICCPR* provides that some (but not all) of the rights it protects may not be suspended even in times of public emergency.[121] The *Vienna Convention on the Law of Treaties* also restricts the circumstances in which a treaty "relating to the protection of the human person" may be terminated or suspended.[122] The difficulty, however, is that there appears to be no consistent approach taken to the issue in international law.[123]

A further difficulty is that the notion that at least some human rights norms may take precedence over other international legal obligations is inconsistent with the absence of any general hierarchy among the various sources of international law.[124] In general, international legal obligations owed by states to one another have equal rank. The peculiarity of international human rights law, however, is that it primarily concerns obligations owed by states to individuals, not to other states.[125] In any event, the closest analogue in international law to "super rules," such as those entrenched in many domestic constitutional bills of rights, is the concept of *jus cogens*. While, as we have seen, the notion of *jus cogens* as a category of non-derogable norms is now generally recognized in international law, it has been extremely difficult to achieve consensus on precisely what norms fall within the ambit of the concept.[126]

This has been particularly true in attempting to determine which, if any, human rights norms constitute *jus cogens*. Indeed, given that international human rights law has evolved almost exclusively through the elaboration of multilateral treaties, states have largely been unable

---

120 See below note 138. See further Chapter 12, Section C(3).
121 *ICCPR*, above note 31, Article 4(2). See further the text accompanying notes 45–49, above in this chapter.
122 *Vienna Convention on the Law of Treaties*, 23 May 1969, 1155 U.N.T.S. 331 (entered into force 27 January 1980), Article 60(5); see further Chapter 4, Section J.
123 See, generally, T. Meron, "On a Hierarchy of International Human Rights" (1986) 80 A.J.I.L. 1.
124 See further Chapter 3, Section C(1).
125 See *General Comment 26*, above note 84 at para. 5.
126 See further Chapter 4, Section I(2)(g).

to agree even on the extent to which human rights obligations exist in customary international law. As we have seen elsewhere,[127] the Human Rights Committee established pursuant to the *ICCPR*[128] has nevertheless expressed an opinion on the right of states to enter reservations to the *ICCPR*. In the view of the Committee, reservations are not permissible with respect to human rights provisions that reflect customary international law:[129]

> [P]rovisions in the [*ICCPR*] that represent customary international law (and *a fortiori* when they have the character of peremptory norms) may not be the subject of reservations. Accordingly, a State may not reserve the right to engage in slavery, to torture, to deprive persons of their lives, to arbitrarily arrest and detain persons, to deny freedom of thought, conscience and religion, to presume a person guilty unless he proves his innocence, to execute pregnant women or children, to permit the advocacy of national, racial or religious hatred, to deny to persons of marriageable age the right to marry, or to deny to minorities the right to enjoy their own culture, profess their own religion, or use their own language.[130]

While the Committee's opinion as to the customary nature of the listed human rights obligations is of course persuasive, states continue to be divided on the customary and *jus cogens* status of many human rights provisions.[131] States have also liberally entered reservations when ratifying universal human rights treaties, thereby undermining arguments that the provisions of such treaties can be considered customary by virtue of their widespread ratification, and contradicting the Human Rights Committee's view of the impermissibility of such reservations.[132]

3) Universality vs. Cultural Relativism

Even less consensus exists in the third area of debate identified above, that of accommodating regional or local cultural sensitivities within a

---

127 See Chapter 4, Section E(3).

128 See Section B(6)(b), above in this chapter.

129 This view is open to question, as states are in general free to modify their mutual customary obligations (other than *jus cogens*) by treaty, and there would appear to be no reason in principle to deny the same possibility in the case of a reservation to a treaty: see further on this issue in Chapter 4, Section E.

130 *General Comment 24*, above note 84 at para. 8.

131 See B. Simma & P. Alston, "The Sources of Human Rights Law: Custom, *Jus Cogens* and General Principles" (1992) Aus. Y.B. Int'l L. 82.

132 See, for example, W. Schabas, "Reservations to Human Rights Treaties: Time for Innovation and Reform" (1994) 32 Can. Y.B. Int'l L. 39.

universal human rights framework. This issue was presaged in the disagreements between the Western, developed states, on the one hand, and the Eastern Bloc and many developing states on the other, throughout the elaboration of the *Universal Declaration*, the *ICCPR*, and the *ICESCR*. The latter groups generally considered that the post-war universal human rights agenda was dominated by Western liberal ideologies. This tension has remained, with many developing and Islamic states regarding the main pillars of universal human rights, the *Universal Declaration* and the covenants, as largely Western constructs. As a result, many such states, rather than rejecting outright the concept of universal human rights, have asserted that such rights are to be given an interpretation and an application that is consistent with their local traditions and cultural norms.[133]

On its face, however, there would appear to be a contradiction between the concept of truly universal human rights and the possibility of local interpretation and application of such rights. The language used in the principal instruments refers to "all members of the human family," which does not seem to contemplate local interpretations based on cultural variations. Rather, the universal instruments appear to start from the premise that the rights they enshrine constitute a common baseline of entitlements for all persons, regardless of their background or cultural *milieu*.

In an attempt to reconcile these divergent views, the 1993 United Nations World Conference on Human Rights adopted a *Declaration and Programme of Action* containing the following language:

> 5. All human rights are universal, indivisible and interdependent and interrelated. The international community must treat human rights globally in a fair and equal manner, on the same footing, and with the same emphasis. While the significance of national and regional particularities and various historical, cultural and religious backgrounds must be borne in mind, it is the duty of States, regardless of their political, economic and cultural systems, to promote and protect all human rights and fundamental freedoms.[134]

This language does not so much resolve the debate as restate its essential elements; it moreover reinforces the relevance of each view. The matter has accordingly not been settled and remains one of the most

---

133 On this issue, see, generally, Steiner & Alston, above note 20 at 323–402.

134 World Conference on Human Rights, *Vienna Declaration and Programme of Action*, UN Doc. A/CONF.157/23 (1993) at para. 5.

common sources of tensions between states in the area of international human rights.[135]

4) The Problem of Compliance and Enforcement

It is one thing to undertake to "respect and ensure" civil and political rights, or to "achieve progressively" economic, social, and cultural rights, even as binding legal obligations. It is quite another to provide mechanisms that will effectively ensure that states comply with such undertakings. As we have seen, one of the peculiarities of the international legal system is that, despite reasonably well-developed substantive rules, there is a paucity of effective enforcement mechanisms or institutions that can implement those rules without the consent of the states concerned. As we have also seen, this peculiarity flows from the sovereign nature of the state as the principal subject of international law.

As we have seen illustrated in our discussion of the *ICCPR* and *ICESCR* above, the problem of enforcement is particularly acute in the case of international human rights norms. This may in part be because such norms do not generally implicate rights of states but, rather, rights of individuals. Where a state breaches an obligation owed to another state, the latter at least has the international legal personality required to assert a claim against the former on the international plane.[136] In the case of individuals, however, no such general standing exists in international law. In other words, the recognition of the existence and substance of international human rights does not address the practical issue of how such rights are to be vindicated.

One possible solution to this dilemma is to "co-opt" the well-established international legal personality of states and entrust them with the task of supervising compliance with human rights obligations, and, perhaps, even of pursuing claims in the event of a breach. Such an approach is theoretically awkward as it requires an asymmetry between the identity of the holder of the right (an individual) and the identity of the party seeking to enforce that right (a state); in general, a claim in state responsibility may normally only be advanced by the holder of

---

135 See, generally, W. Schmale, ed., *Human Rights and Cultural Diversity* (Goldbach: Keip, 1993); A. An-Na'im, "Human Rights in the Muslim World: Socio-Political Conditions and Scriptural Imperatives" (1990) 3 Harv. Hum. Rts. J. 13; K. Savell, "Wrestling with Contradiction: Human Rights and Traditional Practices Affecting Women" (1996) 41 McGill L.J. 781.

136 Although, of course, the claimant state must still find an appropriate and competent forum in which to press its claim.

a right that has been violated.[137] Another problem is that, while states may have an interest in pursuing the human rights claims of their own nationals against other states (by way of espousal of the claims of nationals injured by other states), there is usually little incentive to do so in the case of foreign nationals, potentially leaving persons whose rights are abused by their own state with little or no protection at all.

A partial solution to these problems would be to assert that human rights violations not only affect individuals, or even particular states, but affect the entire international community. In this way, a claim against an offending state could potentially be brought by any state on the basis that its interests (as part of the broader interests of the international community) have been affected by the alleged violation. This approach has been adopted in part by the International Law Commission, in its *Draft Articles on State Responsibility*, by providing for limited standing for all states in cases of violations of the "collective interest" or of obligations "owed to the international community as a whole."[138] There is also support in the jurisprudence of the International Court of Justice for the proposition that at least "basic rights of the human person" are owed *erga omnes*—that is, to the international community as a whole—and thus generate standing for all states to pursue claims arising out of breaches of such rights.[139]

However, such a solution remains somewhat unsatisfactory in that, again, it ultimately relies upon the will of states to take up and pursue a claim in which they may have no direct interest and which may well conflict with other pressing concerns, of a political nature for example. Another and more direct approach that would address this weakness would be to give an individual, as the holder of international legal rights, the corresponding standing to pursue such claims directly, even against his or her own state. This obviously would require the creation of a forum in which such standing could be asserted. As we seen above, this is the model that has been adopted under the *European Convention on Human Rights*.[140] As we have also seen, however, such an approach is the exception rather than the rule.

---

137 See further Chapter 12, Section B(1).
138 International Law Commission, *Draft Articles on State Responsibility*, UN Doc. A/CN.4/L.602/Rev. 1 (2001), Article 40. See further Chapter 12, Section B(1).
139 See, for example, *Barcelona Traction, Light and Power Company, Ltd.*, [1970] I.C.J. Rep. 3 at 32 [*Barcelona Traction*]. See also *Case Concerning East Timor (Portugal v. Australia)*, [1995] I.C.J. Rep. 90 at para. 29 [*East Timor*]; and *Legal Consequences of the Construction of a Wall in the Occupied Palestinian Territory, Advisory Opinion*, [2004] I.C.J. Rep. 136 at paras. 155–59 [*Israeli Wall*].
140 See Section C, above in this chapter.

The difficulty, of course, is that such a system would represent a significant incursion into the sovereignty of states and would expose them to unwelcome levels of international scrutiny. States, ever jealous of their prerogatives under international law and still reluctant to limit unduly the scope of what constitutes their "domestic affairs," have so far largely resisted any such developments. On the other hand, as we have also seen above, the *Optional Protocol* to the *ICCPR*, as well as the Commission procedures in the Inter-American and African systems, take some tentative steps in this direction.

In general, however, it remains the case that the development of legal regimes of compliance and enforcement has not kept pace with the elaboration of substantive human rights norms. Beyond the treaty mechanisms such as those contained in the covenants, the *Optional Protocol*, and the regional systems, reviewed above, there is little in the way of machinery that has the power to ensure that the human rights undertakings of states are fulfilled. Rather, those mechanisms that exist rely in large measure on various means of exerting political pressure upon non-compliant states.

In this connection, the work of non-governmental organizations, such as Amnesty International and Human Rights Watch, in bringing human rights abuses to public light has been instrumental. Moreover, notwithstanding its early determination that it had no enforcement powers *per se*,[141] the United Nations Human Rights Commission[142] was authorized by the Economic and Social Council in 1967 to "make a thorough study of situations which reveal a consistent pattern of violations of human rights."[143] Unfortunately, the processes put in place by the Commission to give effect to this mandate, particularly when a specific country was the subject of complaint, tended to be politicized and adversarial.[144] An alternative confidential procedure for the examination of systematic and gross violations of human rights, known as the "1503 procedure," as well as a number of other "special procedures,"

---

141 See Brownlie, above note 10 at 533.

142 Established in 1946 by the Economic and Social Council: see above note 15.

143 *Question of the Violation of Human Rights and Fundamental Freedoms, including Policies of Racial Discrimination and Segregation and of Apartheid, in all Countries, with Particular Reference to Colonial and Other Dependent Countries and Territories*, ESC Res. 1235 (XLII), UN ESCOR, 42nd Sess., Supp. No. 1, UN Doc. E/4393 (1967).

144 See, generally, Freeman & van Ert, above note 4 at 402–3. Dissatisfaction with this process was part of overall dissatisfaction with the functioning of the Commission which ultimately led to its replacement, in 2006, by the UN Human Rights Council: see above, note 15.

are also available.[145] While none of these amount to enforcement mechanisms that provide for individual remedies, such external scrutiny of states' overall human rights record is thought to bring some pressure to bear on non-compliant states to respect at least basic human rights norms.[146] Recent efforts to increase the effectiveness of such scrutiny include the establishment, following the 1993 United Nations World Conference on Human Rights, of the Office of the High Commissioner for Human Rights;[147] and the abolition, in 2006, of the Human Rights Commission and its replacement with the Human Rights Council as a "subsidiary organ" directly answerable to the UN General Assembly.[148]

It nevertheless remains the case that moving from recognition to implementation of human rights is one of the greatest challenges in this area of international law. The steps taken to date towards the establishment of compliance and enforcement mechanisms have been wholly inadequate, prompting Mary Robinson, former United Nations High Commissioner for Human Rights, to lament a "massive failure of implementation [that] shames us all."[149] Progress depends on the willingness of states to further dilute their hold on the privileges of sovereignty and to subject themselves to legal processes designed to give substance to the lofty principles they have espoused in the *Universal Declaration*, the covenants, and other human rights instruments.

E. CONCLUSIONS

By way of summary, we have seen that remarkable progress has been made in the second half of the twentieth century toward the recognition of human rights as a matter of international concern. This has led to the establishment of substantive international legal obligations

---

145 See *Procedure for Dealing with Communications relating to Violations of Human Rights and Fundamental Freedoms*, ESC Res. 1503 (XLVIII), UN ESCOR, 48th Sess., Supp. No. 1A, UN Doc. E/4832/Add.1 (1970); *Question of the Violation of Human Rights and Fundamental Freedoms*, ESC Res. 1235 (XLII), U.N. ESCOR, 42nd Sess., Supp. No. 1, U.N. Doc. E/4393 (1967); and see, generally, Freeman & van Ert, above note 4 at 404–7; Steiner & Alston, above note 20 at 592–704.

146 See, generally, N. Rodley & D. Weissbrodt, "United Nations Non-Treaty Procedures for Dealing with Human Rights Violations" in Hannum, above note 74 at 65.

147 See *High Commissioner for the Promotion and Protection of All Human Rights*, UNGA Res. 48/141, U.N. Doc. A/RES/48/141 (1993).

148 *Human Rights Council*, UNGA Res. 60/251, U.N. Doc. A/RES/60/251 (2006).

149 M. Robinson, "Addressing the Gap between Rhetoric and Reality" in Danieli *et al.*, above note 12, 423 at 426.

for states in the area of human rights. In general, however, the normative force that has been accorded to first generation civil and political rights has been considerably more robust than that accorded to second generation economic, social, and cultural rights. That precedence is particularly reflected in the willingness of states to accept more robust compliance measures with respect to the first category than with respect to the second, although in neither case are enforcement measures particularly potent. Such a preference for legal entrenchment of civil and political rights in international law reflects to some extent the dominance of Western, liberal ideologies that have prevailed in the articulation of international human rights norms, a fact that has created ongoing tensions between states with respect to the shape of the international human rights system.

Ultimately, the root of many of the difficulties still besetting international human rights law, whether in defining the hierarchical relationship between human rights and other rules of international law, addressing cultural relativism, or considering the extent to which substantive human rights must be matched with effective compliance mechanisms, can be traced to the peculiar grounding of international human rights law in a partial revival of natural law theories. Notwithstanding the heavily consent-based nature of modern international law, much of the rhetoric—even by states—that has surrounded the recognition of human rights in international law has focused on such rights as inherent, inalienable, and thus the natural entitlements of individuals.[150] Obviously such concepts are an awkward fit in a legal system premised upon the sovereignty of states and the theory of consent as the principal source of binding obligation. This is clearly illustrated in states' reluctance to follow through with true enforcement measures that would ensure respect for such inherent and inalienable entitlements. States have so far preferred to reserve their legal positions and stand upon their sovereignty rather than agree to effective measures that would ensure compliance. Being also predominantly the product of a particular cultural experience, as were the natural law theories that were first advanced to rationalize the newly emerging system of international law in Europe in the sixteenth and seventeenth centuries,

---

150 Consider, for example, the opening paragraph of the Preamble to the *Universal Declaration*, above note 18: "Whereas recognition of the *inherent* dignity and of the equal and *inalienable* rights of all members of the human family is the foundation of freedom, justice and peace in the world ..." [emphasis added]. See also similar language used in the preambles to the *ICCPR* and the *ICESCR*, above notes 31 and 33.

it is perhaps not surprising that the universality of human rights norms should be challenged.

In short, the impressive and rapid establishment of international human rights law as a central pillar of modern international law is a work-in-progress, as states struggle to reconcile their sovereignty with ever-growing pressures to relinquish aspects thereof for the greater, common good.

FURTHER READING

ALSTON, P., & MÉGRET, F., eds., *The United Nations and Human Rights: A Critical Appraisal*, 2d ed. (Oxford: Oxford University Press, forthcoming in 2008)

BREMS, E., *Human Rights: Universality and Diversity* (The Hague: Kluwer Law International, 2001)

COTLER, I., & ELIADIS, F.P., *International Human Rights Law: Theory and Practice* (Montreal: Canadian Human Rights Foundation, 1992)

DANIELI, Y., STAMATOPOULOU, E., & DIAS, C.J., eds., *The Universal Declaration of Human Rights: Fifty Years and Beyond* (Amityville, NY: Baywood Publishing, 1999)

FREEMAN, M. & VAN ERT, G., *International Human Rights Law* (Toronto: Irwin Law, 2004)

HANNUM, H., ed., *Guide to International Human Rights Practice*, 4th ed. (Ardsley, NY: Transnational Publishers, 2004)

HUMPHREY, J.T.P., *Human Rights and the United Nations: A Great Adventure* (Dobbs Ferry, NY: Transnational, 1984)

LAGOUTTE, S., SANO, H-O., & SCHARFF SMITH, P., *Human Rights in Turmoil: Facing Threats, Consolidating Achievements* (Leiden: Martinus Nijhoff, 2007)

LAUTERPACHT, H., *International Law and Human Rights*, rev. ed. (1950; repr., New York: Garland, 1973)

LILLICH, R.B., *et al.*, eds., *International Human Rights: Problems of Law, Policy, and Practice*, 4th ed. (New York: Aspen, 2006)

MERON, T., ed., *Human Rights in International Law: Legal and Policy Issues* (Oxford: Clarendon Press, 1984)

PROVOST, R., *International Human Rights and Humanitarian Law* (Cambridge: Cambridge University Press, 2002)

ROBERTSON, A., & MERRILLS, J.G., *Human Rights in the World: An Introduction to the Study of the International Protection of Human Rights*, 4th ed. (New York: St. Martin's Press, 1996)

SCHABAS, W.A., "Canada and the Adoption of the Universal Declaration of Human Rights" (1998) 43 McGill L.J. 403

SCHABAS, W.A., *Précis du droit international des droits de la personne, avec une attention particulière au droit du Canada et du Québec* (Cowansville, QC: Éditions Y. Blais, 1997)

SCHABAS, W.A. & BEAULAC, S., *International Human Rights and Canadian Law: Legal Commitment, Implementation and the Charter*, 3d ed. (Toronto: Thomson Carswell, 2007)

STEINER, H.J. & ALSTON, P., *International Human Rights in Context: Law, Politics, Morals*, 2d ed. (Oxford: Oxford University Press, 2000)

VASAK, K., & ALSTON, P., eds., *The International Dimensions of Human Rights*, 2 vols. (Westport: Greenwood Press, 1982)

WATSON, J.S., *Theory and Reality in the International Protection of Human Rights* (Ardsley, NY: Transnational, 1999)

CHAPTER 11

THE USE OF FORCE
IN INTERNATIONAL
RELATIONS

A. INTRODUCTION

In this chapter we consider the international legal rules governing whether, and under what circumstances, states may resort to armed force in their international relations. This area of international law is of relatively recent vintage, and stands, along with the emergence of international human rights law, as one of the most profound twentieth-century innovations in substantive international law. Its emergence is also inextricably entwined with modern international law's most important institutional development, the establishment of the United Nations (UN) and in particular the UN Security Council. However, given that it strikes at the very heart of what historically was considered a sacred prerogative of state sovereignty—the right to make war—international law governing the use of force is a profoundly contentious area. Moreover, as a state's decision to resort to armed force is usually driven by a domestic assessment that some fundamental national interest requires it, important questions arise as to the effectiveness of rules of international law that would seek to constrain such decisions.[1] In short, familiarity with the law governing resort to force is helpful in understanding the modern international legal system more generally, as well as its potential shortcomings.

---

1   See, generally, C. Gray, *International Law and the Use of Force*, 2d ed. (Oxford: Oxford University Press, 2004) c. 1.

Before examining the history, extent, and limits of modern international law's prohibition of the threat or use of force, it is important to underline a fundamental legal distinction. This chapter concerns itself with rules governing whether and when states may resort to armed force. In that sense, the focus of such rules is the threshold issue of whether the use of force is *in principle* legally permissible in any given situation. This is reflected in the expression *jus ad bellum* (literally, "right to war"), which is commonly used to describe this area of international law. These rules are to be distinguished, however, from a closely related yet fundamentally distinct area of international law: the law of armed conflict, sometimes also referred to as international humanitarian law or the *jus in bello* (literally, "law in war"). In contrast to the *jus ad bellum*, the *jus in bello* governs the *manner* in which armed force may be used once it has been resorted to.[2] While there is an important academic debate on the relationship between both bodies of law and how they may or should interact, the preponderance of state, scholarly, and judicial practice is to treat them as rigidly distinct.[3] In this way, violation of the *jus ad bellum* is generally not considered relevant to the ongoing existence of, or assessment of respect for, obligations under the *jus in bello*, and vice versa.[4] While consideration of the *jus in bello*—a vast and important area—is beyond the scope of this chapter and book, the reader is referred to the copious literature addressing the topic.[5]

---

2   Caution is required in thinking of the *jus ad bellum* as solely concerned with "threshold" determinations of the legality of resort to force. Such a characterization should not be mistaken to mean that once a state first uses force, the *jus ad bellum* is spent and becomes irrelevant to assessing the legality of subsequent uses of force by that state in the course of the same conflict. Rather, state practice and scholarly opinion appear to accept that each instance of a state's use of force in an ongoing conflict is subject to legal assessment according to the *jus ad bellum* (in addition, of course, to the *jus in bello*): see C. Greenwood, "The Relationship of *Ius ad Bellum* and *Ius in Bello*" (1983) 9 Rev. Int'l Stud. 221.

3   See C. Greenwood, "Historical Development and Legal Basis" in D. Fleck, ed., *The Handbook of Humanitarian Law in Armed Conflicts* (New York: Oxford University Press, 1995) 1 at 7–8.

4   M. Sassòli & A.A. Bouvier, *How Does Law Protect in War?*, 2d ed. (Geneva: ICRC, 2006) at 102–8.

5   Recent contributions to this literature include Y. Dinstein, *The Conduct of Hostilities Under the Law of International Armed Conflict* (Cambridge: Cambridge University Press, 2004); D. Fleck, ed., *The Handbook of Humanitarian Law in Armed Conflicts*, 2d ed. (Oxford: Oxford University Press, 2008); L.C. Green, *The Contemporary Law of Armed Conflict*, 2d ed. (Manchester: Manchester University Press, 2000); J-M. Henckaerts & L. Doswald-Beck, *Customary International Humanitarian Law* (Cambridge: Cambridge University Press, 2005);

We turn now to our examination of the *jus ad bellum* — that is, the rules of international law governing the threshold issue of whether and when a state may resort to armed force in the first place.

B. HISTORICAL DEVELOPMENT

While it is commonplace to consider the international legal prohibition of the threat or use of force as a post-Second World War development coinciding with adoption of the *UN Charter* and the establishment of the UN, this is a considerable and not-altogether accurate oversimplification. This is relevant because an understanding of the meaning of the *UN Charter*'s provisions on the use of force, and of their relationship with customary international law, turns in part on an appreciation of the pre-1945 international legal context.

In fact, if one takes the long view, attempts to constrain resort to war by the rule of law have an ancient pedigree, and the general liberty to use armed force that characterized eighteenth and nineteenth century international law emerges as a relatively fleeting and aberrant phenomenon. In other words, it is not accurate to think of legal limitations on the use of force as an exclusively mid-twentieth century innovation. Nor does history bear out the sometimes-advanced assertion that war, by its very nature, is beyond the scope of legal control.[6]

Certainly there is clear evidence that several ancient civilizations placed legal constraints on resort to armed force.[7] While assuming many forms, for the most part these constraints required that war only be invoked in response to some prior violation of a right or in some other just cause. Perhaps the best-preserved evidence of such requirements

---

F. Kalshoven & L. Zegveld, *Constraints on the Waging of War*, 3d ed. (Geneva: ICRC, 2001); H. McCoubrey, *International Humanitarian Law*, 2d ed. (Aldershot, UK: Ashgate, 1998); L. Moir, *The Law of Internal Armed Conflict* (Cambridge: Cambridge University Press, 2002); R. Provost, *International Human Rights and Humanitarian Law* (Cambridge: Cambridge University Press, 2002); A.P.V. Rogers, *Law on the Battlefield*, 2d ed. (Manchester: Manchester University Press, 2004); Sassòli & Bouvier, *ibid.*; UK Ministry of Defence, *The Manual of the Law of Armed Conflict* (Oxford: Oxford University Press, 2004).

6   See Y. Dinstein, *War, Aggression and Self-Defence*, 4th ed. (Cambridge: Cambridge University Press, 2005) at 73–75.

7   See, for example, I. Brownlie, *International Law and the Use of Force by States* (Oxford: Clarendon Press, 1963) at 3–5; Dinstein, above note 6 at 63–64; Greenwood, above note 3 at 12–15.

relates to the ancient Roman concept of the *iustum bellum* ("just war").[8] Under this doctrine, a decision to go to war had to be shown to be both substantively and procedurally justified.[9] Compliance with such requirements was vetted by an institution known as the *fetiales*, essentially a college of priests charged with ensuring that adequate substantive grounds were advanced to justify war and that formalities, such as the making of a prior demand for satisfaction or a formal declaration of war, had been respected. While the historical record is somewhat unclear as to whether such legal and institutional mechanisms were always effective, the idea that a political decision to go to war could be both procedurally and substantively fettered by legal rules was to have a profound impact on European thought, and hence international law, several centuries later.

The writings of St. Augustine of the early fifth century are generally credited with reviving and injecting the Roman "just war" theory into early Christian theological doctrine. For St. Augustine, the presumed starting point was that conquest was in principle unlawful, but could be justified on a number of ill-defined bases.[10] This theory was considerably refined some eight centuries later by St. Thomas Aquinas, who opined that "just war" could only be waged under sovereign authority, for an (objectively) just cause, and with (subjective) "right intention."[11]

As we have already seen,[12] in developing their natural-law-inspired theories of the international legal order, the pre-Westphalian European international legal philosophers known as the "primitives" were deeply influenced by both early Roman and Christian teachings. When it came to addressing the role of war in international law, therefore, they naturally espoused and adapted the foregoing just war doctrines. In other words, their assumed starting point was that war was unlawful unless pursued in a legally just cause. Unhappily, there were virtually as many theories of what constituted such just cause as there were

---

8   A. Nussbaum, *A Concise History of the Law of Nations*, rev. ed. (New York: Macmillan, 1962) at 10–11.

9   C. Phillipson, *The International Law and Custom of Ancient Greece and Rome*, vol. II (London: MacMillan & Co., 1911) at 328.

10   Similar approaches to defining conditions for the lawful resort to war emerged in Islam during its spread following the seventh century AD: see Greenwood, above note 3 at 14.

11   See Brownlie, above note 7 at 5–6; Dinstein, above note 6 at 64–65; Greenwood, above note 3 at 15; J. von Elbe, "The Evolution of the Concept of Just War in International Law" (1939) 33 A.J.I.L. 665 at 667.

12   See Chapter 3, Section B(1).

legal philosophers willing to address the topic,[13] so much so that it was also widely held that *both* sides to any given conflict could claim justification for their use of force. Not surprisingly, this rendered the theory all but useless in constraining resort to war. This difficulty was of course merely illustrative of the central shortcomings of natural law theories in general: namely, their propensity to produce widely varying accounts of right and wrong, depending on the (often unexamined and unstated) subjective moral and political persuasions of the writer; and their consequent irrelevance in actually regulating state behaviour.[14]

As we have also already seen,[15] this and other factors eventually led to the emergence of a heavily positivist, consent-based account of international law. By the eighteenth century, writers such as Vattel had consigned natural law's "just war" theories to the status of moral, rather than legal, considerations.[16] International law was reconceived as those rules of international conduct to which states consented, and absent any evidence that states had consented to rules prohibiting the use of armed force, the presumed point of departure became that such uses were, as a general rule, lawful. This eventually led, in the nineteenth and early twentieth centuries, to a near-consensus among (at least European and American) international lawyers and states that every state had an inherent right, protected by international law, to engage in war at its pleasure.[17] In short, international law had been evacuated of

---

13   See Brownlie, above note 7 at 6–7; Dinstein, above note 6 at 65–67. For example, Vitoria (1480–1546), taking the view that Spain's war against the aboriginal peoples of the Americas required just as much justification as war against a Christian nation, nevertheless considered it just because it was in response to violations of Spanish rights to engage in commerce and to convert pagans to Christianity. Suarez (1584–1617) took extremely broad views of what could qualify as just cause for war, including "any grave injury to one's reputation or honour." Gentili (1552–1608) also took a broad approach to just causes, including states of necessity (for example, self-defence) and even expediency, but not religious motivations.

14   See Chapter 3, Section B(1).

15   See Chapter 1, Section B(2) and Chapter 3, Section B(2).

16   E. de Vattel (1714–1767), *The Principles of Natural Law as Applied to the Conduct and to the Affairs of Nations and of Sovereigns*, 1758, trans. by C.G. Fenwick, Classics of International Law Series No. 4, J.B. Scott, ed. (Washington: Carnegie Institution, 1916).

17   The views expressed in leading international legal treatises of the time are instructive on this point: see, for example, J.C. Bluntschli, *Le droit international codifié* (Paris: Guillaumin 1895) at 11 (describing war as a lawful mechanism by which the international community evolves); G.B. Davis, *The Elements of International Law*, 4th ed. by G.E. Sherman (New York: Harper, 1916) at 272 ("With the inherent rightfulness of war international law has nothing to do …"); T.J.

any content that would hinder resort to force by states; it had become "dominated by an unrestricted right of war."[18] In a perversely circular manner, such a doctrine was both confirmed by, and a legitimation of, the conquest and colonization of much of Africa, the Middle East, and Southeast Asia, mainly by European powers. The theoretical incoherence of a system of law that at once advocated the sovereign equality of nations and their right to try to subjugate one another militarily was largely ignored.

By the late nineteenth and early twentieth centuries, however, certain countervailing tendencies began to emerge.[19] Among these was the growing practice among states of concluding (usually bilateral) treaties of friendship, in which the parties mutually promised not to resort to war against one another and to subject any disputes between them to a peaceful dispute resolution process—at least as a first resort.[20] While such agreements tended to confirm (by necessary implication) the general, customary legality of resort to war, they did plant the seed of a "war-as-last-resort" theme in the practice of states that was to bear fruit in the period between the First and Second World Wars. At roughly the same time, with the spread of democratic government, the rise of the middle class, and the increasingly direct effects of war on civilian populations and economic activity, European and American popular

---

Lawrence, *The Principles of International Law*, 4th ed. (Boston: D.C. Heath & Co., 1911) at 333 (the distinctions between just and unjust war "belong to morality and theology, and are as much out of place in a treatise on international law as would be a discussion on the ethics of marriage in a book on the law of personal status ..."); A. Hershey, *The Essentials of International Public Law* (New York: MacMillan, 1912) (war is "a right inherent in sovereignty itself ..."); C.A. Pompe, *Aggressive War: An International Crime* (The Hague: M. Nihjoff, 1953) (summarizing the views of Anzilotti and others: "Law cannot say when, but only how war is to be waged ..."). Considerable support for such views is to be found in European and American state practice during this period, including the Prussian annexation of parts of Denmark; the German annexation of Alsace-Lorraine; the invasion and subsequent annexation/colonization/"protection" of much of Asia and Africa by the United Kingdom, France, Belgium, Germany, Italy, Russia, etc.; the annexation by the United States of Texas, the Philippines, Cuba, and Puerto Rico following wars in 1846 and 1898; and so on: see, generally, Brownlie, above note 7 at 20; Dinstein, above note 6 at 67 and 75–77.

18 Brownlie, *ibid.* at 19.

19 See, generally, *ibid.* at 19–50; Dinstein, above note 6 at 77–79.

20 An early multilateral manifestation of such an undertaking appears in *Hague Convention I (Pacific Settlement of International Disputes)*, 1899/1907. However, its obligations were weak, applying only "as far as circumstances allow," a discretionary judgment apparently left to the parties themselves: *ibid.*, Article 2. See also *Hague Convention II (Limitation of Employment of Force for Recovery of Contract Debts)*, 18 October 1907, Article 1.

opinion became an important political consideration for governments contemplating war. This provided the primary impetus for the development of international humanitarian law in the late and early twentieth centuries, but it also led to an increasing propensity by states, notwithstanding the lack of any international legal requirement that they do so, for publicly justifying their uses of armed force. While formally devoid of international legal significance, "just war" rhetoric was thus resuscitated, again paving the way for post-World War I developments.

One principal such development was the conclusion of the *Covenant of the League of Nations*,[21] by which the League of Nations was established in 1920. In response to widespread public revulsion over the dislocation and bloodshed caused by the "Great War," the *Covenant* amounted essentially to a compulsory peaceful dispute settlement agreement among League members. It required that members "respect and preserve as against external aggression the territorial integrity and existing political independence of all members of the League."[22] It declared "any war or threat of war ... a matter of concern to the whole League."[23] Certain limits were imposed upon members' ability to declare war on one another pending exhaustion of prescribed dispute resolution procedures, violation of which would be deemed an act of war against all other members of the League.[24]

As such, the provisions of the *Covenant* fell well short of a comprehensive repudiation of member states' legal right to resort to armed force. Still less was it an effective deterrent to war. A close reading of Articles 13 to 16 of the *Covenant* reveals that, at best, it amounted to a somewhat complex procedural guide as to *how* to resort to war, serving at best to delay its occurrence. Moreover, its focus on limiting resort to "war"—a formal legal status subject to manipulation[25]—rather than the factual deployment of armed force, left a considerable loophole that could be (and was) liberally exploited by members.[26] And the principal sanctions contemplated for violation of its provisions—a state of war between the offender and all other members, or ejection from the League—were hardly conducive to the general abatement of warfare.[27]

---

21   *Covenant of the League of Nations Adopted by the Peace Conference at Plenary Session, April 28, 1919* (1919) 13 A.J.I.L. Supp. 128. See further Chapter 1, Section B(3).

22   *Ibid.*, Article 10.

23   *Ibid.*, Article 11.

24   *Ibid.*, Articles 12–16.

25   See further the text accompanying notes 74–79, below in this chapter.

26   This was a deliberate choice by the drafters; earlier drafts had used the expression "resort to armed force" rather than "war": see Brownlie, above note 7 at 60.

27   See, generally, Dinstein, above note 6 at 80–82; Brownlie, *ibid.* at 55–65.

These shortcomings, combined with limited sustained membership in the League, ultimately doomed the *Covenant*'s potential effectiveness in constraining states' resort to armed force in their international relations. Nor were the shortcomings inadvertent or accidental: it has been observed that they were the direct result of the reluctance of most states to go much further than to place procedural preconditions on their hitherto unfettered right to go to war.[28] However, it might nevertheless be said that the *Covenant* confirmed, in multilateral legal form, the emerging idea that war, while ultimately legal, should be approached as a last resort rather than as an ubiquitously available and inherently rightful first response; and in any case that war was a matter of international concern rather than a purely bilateral matter of interest only to the belligerents.

The inter-war period also saw attempts at remedying some of the gaps left by the *Covenant* regime.[29] One of the earliest of these was the proposal, in 1920, of the *Geneva Protocol on the Pacific Settlement of Disputes*.[30] Intended as a more ambitious optional protocol to the *Covenant*, the *Geneva Protocol* provided that parties to it would "in no case resort to war," except in self-defence or with the consent of the League.[31] It also went beyond the concept of "war," prohibiting "any act which might constitute a threat of aggression against another state."[32] However, while nineteen League members eventually ratified the *Geneva Protocol*, the various conditions for its coming into force were not fulfilled and it therefore never became legally binding.[33]

A far more successful attempt at bridging some of the gaps left by the *Covenant* was the conclusion in 1928 of the *Kellogg-Briand Pact*,[34] a free-standing treaty concluded outside the League apparatus.[35] Originally proposed in 1927 by the French foreign minister (Aristide Briand) to his American counterpart (Frank B. Kellogg) as a bilateral non-aggression treaty between their two countries, it was instead formulated, at Kellogg's suggestion, as a multilateral agreement open to signature and ratification by all states. Notwithstanding its brevity—it compris-

---

28 Brownlie, *ibid.* at 62.
29 See, generally, *ibid.* at 66–104.
30 *Geneva Protocol on the Pacific Settlement of Disputes*, 2 October 1924.
31 *Ibid.*, Article 2.
32 *Ibid.*, Article 8.
33 *Ibid.*, Article 21. See Brownlie, above note 7 at 69–70.
34 *Treaty Providing for the Renunciation of War as an Instrument of National Policy*, 1928, 94 L.N.T.S. 57 [*Kellogg-Briand Pact*]. The *Kellogg-Briand Pact* is sometimes also referred to as the "*Pact of Paris*."
35 See, generally, Dinstein, above note 6 at 83–85; Brownlie, above note 7 at 74–80.

es a grand total of only three short articles—the *Pact* is an agreement of astonishingly sweeping scope. Its two substantive articles provide as follows:

Article I

The high contracting parties solemnly declare in the names of their respective peoples that they condemn recourse to war for the solution of international controversies, and renounce it as an instrument of national policy in their relations with one another.

Article II

The high contracting parties agree that the settlement or solution of all disputes or conflicts of whatever nature or of whatever origin they may be, which may arise among them, shall never be sought except by pacific means.

Even more astonishing, perhaps, than its brevity and its unconditional repudiation of "war ... as an instrument of national policy," the *Kellogg-Briand Pact* had achieved near-universal ratification by the outbreak of World War II.[36]

This is not to say, however, that the *Pact* resolved all of the difficulties inherent in the League system. For example, it still focused on the legal concept of "war" rather than the factual concept of armed force. Moreover, the renunciation of war "as an instrument of national policy," which was probably intended to preserve the possibility of collective military action by the League of Nations, was instead interpreted by some to preserve a right for states unilaterally to resort to war for "non-national" policy reasons. For example, some argued that waging war to secure respect for international law (such as enforcement of an international arbitral award) was to employ it as an instrument of international, rather than national, policy, and thus not prohibited by the *Pact*.[37] And of course

---

36　By 1938, the *Kellogg-Briand Pact* had been ratified by sixty-three states—that is, by all but four (Bolivia, El Salvador, Uruguay, and Argentina) of the states then in existence: see (1939) 33 A.J.I.L. Supp. 865. Indeed the *Pact* remains in force and binding upon parties to it, although much of the substance of its provisions has been supervened by the arguably broader provisions of the *Charter of the United Nations*, 26 June 1945, Can. T.S. 1945 No. 7 (in force 24 October 1945) [*UN Charter*].

37　See J.H.W. Verzijl, *International Law in Historical Perspective*, vol. VIII (Alphen aan den Rijn: Sijthoff & Noordhoff, 1976) at 109–10 and 600; H. Kelsen, *Principles of International Law* (New York: Rinehart, 1952) at 43. Such arguments necessarily had to downplay the significance of Article II of the *Pact*, which on its face categorically outlaws war as a means of settling disputes.

its periodic violation, both prior to and during the Second World War, underscored its lack of an enforcement regime.[38]

Nevertheless, it has been convincingly argued that the conclusion of the *Kellogg-Briand Pact*, coupled with its near-universal ratification and its frequent invocation by states and the League Assembly to condemn acts of aggression in the run-up to the Second World War, demonstrate that a general prohibition of aggressive war[39] had emerged as a rule of customary international law by 1939 at the latest.[40] Indeed, such a conclusion was an important element of the reasoning of the post-World War II Nuremberg Tribunal, permitting it to convict, under international law, various high-ranking Nazi officials of committing "crimes against peace" prior to 1945. It also appears to have received the tacit endorsement of the UN General Assembly in its subsequent affirmation of the principles of international law applied by the Nuremberg Tribunal.[41] Some forty years later, the International Court of Justice (ICJ) appeared to take the same view.[42]

It is thus against this background—a likely pre-existing customary international legal prohibition of the waging of aggressive war—that the *UN Charter*, with its provisions addressing the threat or use of force by states, was adopted in 1945.[43]

---

38 See Dinstein, above note 6 at 83–85.

39 That is, war other than in self-defence. While not explicitly addressed in the *Kellogg-Briand Pact*, it is clear from contemporaneous exchanges of diplomatic correspondence and from reservations formulated by several states upon ratification of the *Pact*, that its prohibitions did not extend to the use of armed force in self-defence. See Dinstein, above note 6 at 83–84; see also Section D(3), below in this chapter.

40 Brownlie, above note 7 at 107–211; M. Howard, "*Temperamenti Belli*: Can War Be Controlled?" in M. Howard, ed., *Restraints on War* (Oxford: Oxford University Press, 1979) 1 at 11; Dinstein, above note 6 at 83.

41 UNGA Res. 95(I), 11 December 1946.

42 *Case Concerning Military and Paramilitary Activities in and Against Nicaragua (Nicaragua v. United States of America), Merits*, [1986] I.C.J. Rep. 14 [*Nicaragua*] at para. 181: "... so far from having constituted a marked departure from a customary international law which still exists unmodified, the *Charter* gave expression in this field [the use of force] to principles already present in customary international law."

43 For a detailed review of legal developments related to war in the period 1920–45, see Brownlie, above note 7 at 66–111.

C. THE PROHIBITION OF FORCE IN MODERN INTERNATIONAL LAW

1) The Overall *UN Charter* Scheme Relating to the Use of Force

It is generally agreed that the focal point for any discussion of the international use of armed force in the post-Word War II period is the *UN Charter.*[44] As we have seen, the *UN Charter* was concluded immediately following World War II in response to a newly perceived, overriding international imperative—that of preserving international peace and security—that was to rival the traditional imperative of preserving the sovereignty of states.[45] As with the *Covenant of the League of Nations*, therefore, the *UN Charter* was a reactive instrument, spawned by the recent experience of war but also moulded by an appreciation of the shortcomings of the *Covenant* and the *Kellogg-Briand Pact.*[46]

The heart of the *UN Charter*'s scheme relating to the use of force is found in Article 2(4), which provides that UN members "shall refrain in their international relations from the threat or use of force against the territorial integrity or political independence of any state, or in any other manner inconsistent with the Purposes of the United Nations."[47] We will review, below, some of the debates concerning the precise meaning of this provision, but on its face it is a prohibition of sweeping scope. Coupled with Article 2(3), which imposes an obligation on UN members to settle their international disputes by peaceful means, it is a dramatic affirmation of the sea change in international legal thinking that had been presaged by near-universal ratification of the *Kellogg-Briand Pact* several years before.

Article 2(4) tells only part of the story, however; its significance can only be appreciated in the broader context of the other peace and security provisions of the *UN Charter*. It must in particular be read in conjunction with Chapter VII of the *Charter*, which provides for "Action with Respect to Threats to the Peace, Breaches of the Peace, and Acts of Aggression." In very broad terms, Chapter VII legitimizes two types of action involving the use of force. The first of these is military action

---

44 *UN Charter*, above note 36.
45 Note for example the first concern cited in the *UN Charter*'s Preamble ("Determined to save succeeding generations from the scourge of war …") and the first purpose of the United Nations articulated in Article 1(1) ("To maintain international peace and security").
46 Dinstein, above note 6 at 85.
47 *UN Charter*, above note 36, Article 2(4).

taken or authorized by the UN Security Council in order to maintain or restore international peace and security. This is the so-called "collective security" mechanism.[48] The second is the right of states to act, on their own initiative, in self-defence. However, this right only subsists until the Security Council has addressed the situation through the collective security mechanism.[49]

As such, the *Charter's* peace and security provisions are not so much about *eradicating* the use of force in international relations as they are about *centralizing* legal control over it in the hands of a relatively small executive body (the UN Security Council). When combined with the very broad discretion enjoyed by the Council in exercising such power,[50] as well as UN member states' overriding legal obligation to carry out the Council's decisions,[51] the significance of the *UN Charter's* use of force scheme is difficult to overstate. It arguably represents the single greatest formal surrender of sovereignty by states, to an international organization, since the emergence of the Westphalian system of international law in the mid-seventeenth century. Just how far that surrender goes will become clearer following a more detailed review, below, of the scope of the Article 2(4) prohibition and the two Chapter VII exceptions to it.

2) The *UN Charter's* Prohibition of Force and Customary International Law

A curious feature of Article 2(4) of the *UN Charter* is that it prohibits force against "any state," not simply any UN member. Moreover, Article 2(6) obliges the UN to ensure that non-UN-member states act in accordance with its principles, including Article 2(4), "so far as may be necessary for the maintenance of international peace and security." Recalling that the *UN Charter* is a treaty, these provisions, which (at least indirectly) seem to confer benefits and obligations on non-member states, appear somewhat anomalous. Whether that anomaly is relevant, however, depends on whether there are any significant differences between the treaty law stated in Article 2(4) and customary international law concerning the use of force.

---

48 See further Section D(2), below in this chapter.
49 *UN Charter*, above note 36, Article 51. See further Section D(3)(c)(i)(ee), below in this chapter.
50 See further Section D(2)(b), below in this chapter.
51 *UN Charter*, above note 36, Articles 25 and 103; see further Section D(2)(a), below in this chapter.

These considerations, along with the overall brevity of the *UN Charter*'s use of force provisions, raise the question of the relationship between those provisions and customary international law. While the importance of some aspects of this issue is somewhat attenuated now that the *UN Charter* commands universal or near-universal state membership, this was not the case until very recently. In addition and as we have already seen in our examination of treaty law,[52] even as between parties to a treaty, customary international law may fill the interstices between the treaty's provisions, and may even have an impact on interpretation of treaty provisions themselves. Moreover, given that treaty and customary international legal obligations may exist in parallel,[53] it will frequently be necessary to have an understanding of both in order to fully appreciate one's international legal position.

Nowhere has the significance of the relationship between Article 2(4) and customary international law been more vividly illustrated than in the *Nicaragua* case before the International Court of Justice (ICJ).[54] It will be recalled that in that case, in which Nicaragua sought a finding that the United States (US) was responsible for unlawful uses of force against it, the US objected to the jurisdiction of the Court. The basis for this objection was that the US declaration of acceptance of the compulsory jurisdiction of the Court, under Article 36(2) of the *ICJ Statute*, was subject to a reservation in respect of cases involving interpretation or application of a multilateral treaty, unless all parties to the treaty whose rights or obligations were in issue were also parties to the case. As Nicaragua relied in its submissions on the *UN Charter*, but had not included as parties certain other UN member states (El Salvador, Honduras, and Costa Rica) that might be affected by the proceedings, the US contended that the ICJ was without jurisdiction.[55]

The ICJ agreed, but only in part, with the US submission. In particular it agreed that the US multilateral treaty reservation ousted its jurisdiction to apply the *UN Charter* to the dispute.[56] However, this had no impact, ruled the Court, on its jurisdiction to apply customary international law to the issues before it.[57] This in turn led the Court to

---

52   See Chapter 4, Section H(1) and Chapter 5, Section E.

53   See Chapter 5, Section E(3).

54   *Nicaragua*, above note 42.

55   See also *Case Concerning Military and Paramilitary Activities in and against Nicaragua (Nicaragua v. United States of America), Jurisdiction and Admissibility*, [1984] I.C.J. Rep. 392.

56   *Nicaragua*, above note 42 at para. 56.

57   *Ibid.* at paras. 172–82. We have already noted the general significance of this ruling on the issue of the independent, parallel applicability of treaty and cus-

an explicit consideration of the content of customary international law on the use of force and its relation to the prohibition found in Article 2(4) of the *UN Charter*.

Examining state practice and *opinio juris*, the ICJ first had to contend with the fact that several states had, on a number of occasions since adoption of the *UN Charter*, used force against other states. The Court addressed this uncomfortable fact by placing it in its broader context: in fact there was no evidence that the preponderance of states routinely or consistently disregarded the strictures of Article 2(4). Moreover, observed the Court, even those states that did resort to force against other states from time to time invariably affirmed not only the existence of a *prima facie* prohibition of such behaviour, but that their actions were consistent with that prohibition by virtue of recognized exceptions to it (usually some variation on the theme of self-defence).[58] In other words, the significance of state practice invoking the use of force against other states since 1945 lies in its relative rarity, as well as in the attitudes of other states to such actions and even in the attitudes of the actors themselves.[59] All tend to point towards an undoubted and universal conviction by states of the *prima facie* unlawfulness of the unauthorized use of force in international relations.[60]

The Court bolstered this reasoning by referring to the first principle set out in the *Friendly Relations Declaration*, a UN General Assembly resolution adopted on consensus in 1970.[61] In particular, the first "principle of international law" proclaimed in the *Declaration* repeats, virtually verbatim, the prohibition set out in Article 2(4). The one, telling deviation in wording is the *Declaration*'s substitution of the word "states"

---

tomary international law to the relations between states: see Chapter 5, Section E(3).

58 *Ibid.* at para. 186.

59 L. Henkin, "The Reports of the Death of Article 2(4) Are Greatly Exaggerated" (1971) 65 A.J.I.L. 544 at 547 (responding to T.M. Franck, "Who Killed Article 2(4)? Or: Changing Norms Governing the Use of Force by States" (1970) 64 A.J.I.L. 809). For more recent views on this issue by the latter author, see T.M. Franck, *Recourse to Force: State Action against Threats and Armed Attacks* (Cambridge: Cambridge University Press, 2002); T.M. Franck, "What Happens Now? The United Nations After Iraq" (2003) 97 A.J.I.L. 607.

60 See O. Schachter, "In Defense of International Rules on the Use of Force" (1986) 53 U. Chicago L. Rev. 113 at 131: "No state has ever suggested that violations of art. 2(4) have opened the door to free use of force"; Dinstein, above note 6 at 94: "The plea that article 2(4) is dead has never been put forward by any government."

61 *Declaration on Principles of International Law Concerning Friendly Relations and Co-operation among States in Accordance with the Charter of the United Nations*, GA Res. 2625 (XXV), UN GAOR, 25th Sess., Supp. No. 28, UN Doc. A/8028 (1971) [*Friendly Relations Declaration*].

for UN "members" in describing the entities subject to the prohibition. The Court took this as confirmation that the prohibition articulated in Article 2(4) was not limited in its application to parties to the *UN Charter*.[62] In other words, the *Friendly Relations Declaration* reflects a consensus acceptance, in the *opinio juris* of states, of a prohibition of the use of force that transcends the strict applicability of the *UN Charter*. In short, the prohibition also exists in customary international law.[63]

The ICJ was cautious, however, with respect to the parties' submissions that the content of the customary and *Charter* regimes on the use of force were in all respects identical.[64] The Court was not willing to go quite so far, holding that "on a number of points, the areas governed by the two sources of law do not exactly overlap, and the substantive rules in which they are framed are not identical in content."[65] The primary lack of identity that the Court seems to have had in mind had not so much to do with direct inconsistencies between the two regimes. Rather, the Court adverted to the more comprehensive and detailed rules of customary international law on the topic, as compared to the somewhat cursory provisions (particularly those relating to self-defence) of the *UN Charter*.[66] In other words, its cautious refusal to accept complete identity between the two sources of rules appears to have had more to do with differences in the scope of their coverage than with any substantive contradictions between their respective rules. Indeed, the Court emphasized that "both the *Charter* and the customary international law flow from a common fundamental principle outlawing the use of force in international relations"; that the *Charter*'s provisions "gave expression in this field to principles already present in customary international law"; and that customary international law "has in the subsequent four decades developed under the influence of the *Charter*."[67] Given these common origins and mutual influences, it therefore seems safe to assume that the essential content of each regime is more or less the same, or at least consistent.[68] In fact, the ICJ has more recently confirmed this position in much less equivocal terms:

---

62 *Nicaragua*, above note 42 at para. 188.

63 *Ibid*. at paras. 187–90. See also, for example, Dinstein, above note 6 at 95; Gray, above note 1 at 29.

64 *Nicaragua, ibid*. at paras. 175–77. Such a position was important to the US "ouster" argument—i.e. that if the Court had no jurisdiction to apply the provisions of the *UN Charter*, it must also be taken to have no jurisdiction to apply allegedly identical rules found in customary international law.

65 *Ibid*. at para. 175.

66 *Ibid*. at para. 176.

67 *Ibid*.

68 See also *ibid*. at paras. 187–90.

"[T]he principles as to the use of force incorporated in the *Charter* reflect customary international law."[69]

What is more, the International Law Commission has concluded,[70] and the ICJ in *Nicaragua* clearly implied,[71] that the general prohibition of the use of force is not only a universally applicable customary rule, it is also a rule of *jus cogens*, or a peremptory norm of international law[72]—one from which no derogation is permitted.[73] It is, in other words, one of the most fundamental pillars of the post-Second World War international legal order. The implications of this for the future evolution of international law on the use of force, whether customary or treaty-based, will be touched upon below.

3) Scope of the Prohibition of Force

a) The Threat or Use of Force

i)   "Force" versus "War"
It has already been noted that the drafting of the *UN Charter*'s peace and security provisions was heavily influenced by lessons learned from the failings of the League of Nations era. This is most plainly illustrated in the pivotal concept at the heart of Article 2(4): the prohibition of the threat or use of "force," rather than "war."

"War," an international legal concept that emerged in the eighteenth and nineteenth centuries, was a formal legal status that did not necessarily bear any relationship to the factual occurrence of hostil-

---

69   See *Legal Consequences of the Construction of a Wall in the Occupied Palestinian Territory, Advisory Opinion*, [2004] I.C.J. Rep. 136 at para. 87 [*Israeli Wall Case*].

70   International Law Commission, "Commentary to Article 50, Draft Articles on the Law of Treaties" in [1966] II Yearbook of the International Law Commission at 247; International Law Commission, "Commentaries to the Draft Articles on the Responsibility of States for Internationally Wrongful Acts" in [2001] II Yearbook of the International Law Commission at 283–84.

71   *Nicaragua*, above note 42 at para. 190. See also the Separate Opinions of President Singh and Judge Sette-Camara, which explicitly adopted this view.

72   See also American Law Institute, *Restatement (Third) of the Foreign Relations Law of the United States* (St. Paul, MN: The Institute, 1987) §102. On *jus cogens* more generally, see further Chapter 4, Section I(2)(g) and Chapter 5, Section E(1).

73   Non-derogability in this context should not be taken to mean that the prohibition is absolute. Rather, it is the prohibition *as qualified by the Chapter VII exceptions to be reviewed below* that is non-derogable. See, for example, *Legality of the Threat or Use of Nuclear Weapons, Advisory Opinion*, [1996] I.C.J. Rep. 226 at para. 38 [*Nuclear Weapons Advisory Opinion*] ("... [the] prohibition of the use of force is to be considered in the light of other relevant provisions of the Charter ...").

ities.[74] Rather, the existence of a "state of war" in international law required an express or necessarily implied intention on the part of one state to enter into such a legal condition with respect to another.[75] The concept was important for distinguishing between various international legal rights and obligations that applied to relations between states depending on whether they were in a state of war, peace, or neutrality with one another.[76] As the existence of a state of war depended primarily on declared intention rather than actual behaviour, the concept also provided a useful tool for states wishing to manipulate domestic public opinion (either by refraining from declaring war while nevertheless engaging in military action abroad or, conversely, by declaring war while taking no military action at all).[77] It further allowed states to evade international legal proscriptions of "war," such as those contained in the *Covenant of the League of Nations* and the *Kellogg-Briand Pact,* by the simple expedient of not declaring it.

Substitution of the concept of "force" for "war" in the *Charter* scheme was a clear attempt to avoid such artificial distinctions.[78] The important issue, both under the *Charter* and corresponding post-1945 customary international law, is thus the actual behaviour of states rather than their formally declared status. With this change in emphasis in the modern *jus ad bellum*, much of the significance of "war" as a legal concept has faded, and state practice appears now only occasionally to advert to the concept or to imbue it with formal international legal meaning.[79]

ii) Armed Force

A curious feature of Article 2(4)'s focus on "force" is the absence of the qualifier "armed," particularly given its use in several provisions of

---

74   See, generally, Q. Wright, "When Does War Exist?" (1932) 26 A.J.I.L. 362; I. Detter Delupis, *The Law of War,* 2d ed. (Cambridge: Cambridge University Press, 2000) at 5–26; Brownlie, above note 7 at 26–40 and c. XXIII; Dinstein, above note 6 at 9–10 and 30–50.

75   See C. Greenwood, "War, Terrorism, and International Law" (2003) 56 Curr. Legal Probs. 505 at 513–15.

76   For a useful and accessible introduction to the concept of neutrality, see Dinstein, above note 6 at 24–29.

77   Brownlie, above note 7 at 38–39.

78   See, generally, Dinstein, above note 6 at 85; Franck, *Recourse,* above note 59 at 20–21.

79   See C. Greenwood, "The Concept of War in Modern International Law" (1987) 36 I.C.L.Q. 283; F. Mégret, "War? Legal Semantics and the Move to Violence" (2002) 13 E.J.I.L. 361. But see Dinstein, above note 6 at 15, proposing a very wide (and controversial) definition of war that would encompass factual hostilities and thus remain relevant in current international law.

Chapter VII of the *UN Charter*.[80] This has led to an extensive debate, since 1945, as to whether the prohibition of "force" in Article 2(4) was meant to be limited to armed force or rather to extend to other forms of coercion, such as economic coercion.[81] This debate has been mainly carried on between developed and certain developing states, the former insisting that, given the historical context in which Article 2(4) was drafted, it must be understood to refer to armed force only;[82] whereas many of the latter have insisted that economic coercion can pose just as serious a threat to their sovereignty, and hence to international peace and security, as any military action.

While this controversy has never been entirely resolved, it is probably fair to say that the preponderance of scholarly and state opinion favours the view that "force" in Article 2(4) is intended to refer to armed force alone.[83] Rarely are economic measures denounced as violations of Article 2(4), and when they are, such a characterization is not widely endorsed. Moreover, the issue has been considerably defused with the widespread recognition that economic coercion, if not a violation of Article 2(4) *per se*, nevertheless amounts to a violation of the customary international legal principle of non-intervention.[84] It is thus unlawful in its own right, if not as a species of the use of "force" prohibited by Article 2(4).

iii) Direct and Indirect Force

Even if one accepts that "force" in Article 2(4) is to be read as referring exclusively to "armed force," this still leaves open the question of the range of actions that come within the ambit of that concept and hence of the prohibition itself. It is in addressing this question that

80   See, for example, *UN Charter*, above note 36, Articles 41 and 46 (both of which use the expression "armed force") and Article 51 (which refers to "armed attack").

81   See, for example, R.D. Kearney & R.E. Dalton, "The Treaty on Treaties" (1970) 64 A.J.I.L. 495 at 534–35.

82   And note that, while "armed force" is used in some provisions in Chapter VII of the *UN Charter*, above note 36, "force" alone is also used elsewhere (see, for example, Article 44), suggesting an intent on the part of the drafters to use the expressions interchangeably.

83   See M. Virally, "Article 2 Paragraph 4" in J-P. Cot & A. Pellet, eds., *La Charte des Nations Unies* (Montreal: Éditions Y. Blais, 1985) 113 at 120; A. Randelzhofer, "Article 2(4)" in B. Simma, ed., *The Charter of the United Nations: A Commentary*, 2d ed., vol. I (Oxford: Oxford University Press, 2002) 112 at 117–18; H. Wehberg, "L'interdiction du recours à la force: le principe et les problèmes qui se posent" (1951) 78 Rec. des Cours 1 at 69; Dinstein, above note 6 at 85–86.

84   See, for example, *Friendly Relations Declaration*, above note 61, Principle 3. See further Chapter 2, Section B(4).

the importance of the symbiotic, or mutually modifying, relationship of Article 2(4) and customary international law becomes prominent.[85] In particular, two key General Assembly resolutions have been instrumental in clarifying the substantive content of Article 2(4): the *Friendly Relations Declaration*[86] and the *Definition of Aggression*.[87] Both were adopted on consensus following protracted debate and compromise among UN member states and have thus repeatedly been treated by the ICJ as authoritative guides to interpretation of Article 2(4) and its customary analogue.[88]

As we have already seen, the first principle of the *Friendly Relations Declaration* essentially restates the provisions of Article 2(4).[89] However, it also amplifies on the meaning of that prohibition. In addition to such obvious instances of the use of armed force as waging a "war of aggression," forcibly violating international boundaries or international lines of demarcation (such as armistice lines), or militarily occupying the territory of another state, the *Declaration* also includes much less direct actions within the concept of the use of force, in the following terms:

> Every state has the duty to refrain from organizing or encouraging the organization of irregular forces or armed bands, including mercenaries, for incursion into the territory of another State.
>
> Every State has the duty to refrain from organizing, instigating, assisting or participating in acts of civil strife or terrorist acts in another State or acquiescing in organized activities within its territory directed towards the commission of such acts, when the acts referred to in the present paragraph involve a threat or use of force.

These provisions were explicitly applied by the ICJ in *Nicaragua* as a basis for finding that certain US actions in that case amounted to *prima facie* violations of the customary prohibition of the use of force.

---

85 Franck, *Recourse*, above note 59 at 174.

86 *Friendly Relations Declaration*, above note 61.

87 *Definition of Aggression*, GA Res. 3314 (XXIX) UN GAOR, 29th Sess., Supp. No. 31 (14 December 1974) [*Definition of Aggression*]. See also *Declaration on the Enhancement of the Effectiveness of the Principle of Refraining from the Threat or Use of Force in International Relations*, UNGA Res. 42/22, U.N. Doc. A/RES/42/22 (18 November 1987) [*Non-Use of Force*].

88 The *Friendly Relations Declaration*, above note 61, itself underscores the consistency of its use of force provisions and those of *UN Charter*: "Nothing in the foregoing paragraphs [addressing the use of force] shall be construed as enlarging or diminishing in any way the scope of the provisions of the *Charter* concerning cases in which the use of force is lawful." The *Definition of Aggression*, *ibid.*, contains a similarly worded provision in Article 6.

89 See Chapter 2, Section B(4).

Nicaragua claimed that the US had undertaken a campaign to destabil-ize its government by, *inter alia,* supporting and directing the activities of an armed Nicaraguan rebel group known as the "*contras.*" The ICJ concluded, on the evidence before it, that the US had indeed largely financed, trained, equipped, armed, and organized the *contras.*[90] Of these acts, training, arming, and organizing were found by the ICJ to constitute threats or uses of force by the US against Nicaragua,[91] not-withstanding its conclusion that the US had neither given the *contras* "direct and critical combat support," nor directly intervened in Nicar-agua with its own combat forces.[92] On the other hand, the mere act of funding the *contras,* "while undoubtedly an act of intervention in the internal affairs of Nicaragua," was not in itself considered a use of force by the US against Nicaragua.[93]

Also helpful in elucidating the range of actions prohibited by Arti-cle 2(4) is the *Definition of Aggression.* It begins by equating "aggres-sion" with the use of armed force[94] and then sets out the following non-exhaustive enumeration of acts that qualify *prima facie* as acts of aggression:

(a) The invasion or attack by the armed forces of a State of the terri-tory of another State, or any military occupation, however tempor-ary, resulting from such invasion or attack, or any annexation by the use of force of the territory of another State or part thereof;

(b) Bombardment by the armed forces of a State against the territory of another State or the use of any weapons by a State against the territory of another State;

(c) The blockade of the ports or coasts of a State by the armed forces of another State;

(d) An attack by the armed forces of a State on the land, sea or air forces, or marine and air fleets of another State;

(e) The use of armed forces of one State which are within the terri-tory of another State with the agreement of the receiving State, in contravention of the conditions provided for in the agreement or any extension of their presence in such territory beyond the termination of the agreement;

---

90   *Nicaragua,* above note 42 at para. 108.
91   *Ibid.* at para. 228.
92   *Ibid.* at para. 108.
93   *Ibid.* at para. 228.
94   *Definition of Aggression,* above note 87, Article 1: "Aggression is the use of armed force by a State against the sovereignty, territorial integrity or political independence of another State, or in any other manner inconsistent with the *Charter of the United Nations* ...."

(f) The action of a State in allowing its territory, which it has placed at the disposal of another State, to be used by that other State for perpetrating an act of aggression against a third State;

(g) The sending by or on behalf of a State of armed bands, groups, irregulars or mercenaries, which carry out acts of armed force against another State of such gravity as to amount to the acts listed above, or its substantial involvement therein.[95]

Again, in addition to direct acts of armed force against another state such as those contemplated in paragraphs (a) to (e), paragraphs (f) and (g) include less direct means by which states may be deemed to have unlawfully used force. *Nicaragua* illustrates application of the latter concept in particular. The evidence before the Court established that, in addition to the support it had given to the *contras*, the United States had recruited, paid, and directed certain third-party nationals to carry out attacks against various Nicaraguan ports, oil installations, and a naval base. While the Court accepted that no US military personnel "took a direct part in the operations,"[96] its use of third parties to carry out attacks which it planned, directed, and supported constituted a violation of the prohibition of the use of force.[97]

It thus appears that the use of force is an expansive concept, encompassing both the direct and indirect projection of armed force against another state, whether by regular armed forces or otherwise.

iv) *The Threat of Force*

Given that a threat of force may in some circumstances be just as destabilizing to international peace and security as its actual use, it is not surprising that the framers of the *UN Charter* chose to include it explicitly in the Article 2(4) prohibition.[98] Yet this aspect of Article 2(4) has rarely played a pivotal role in the positions taken by states in relation to the prohibition of force, and it has received little in the way of international judicial treatment.

---

95 *Definition of Aggression, ibid.,* Article 3.

96 *Nicaragua,* above note 42 at para. 86.

97 *Ibid.* at para. 227. It should be noted that the ICJ did not explicitly refer to Article 3(g) of the *Definition of Aggression* in reaching this particular conclusion. However, it had earlier observed that Article 3(g) "may be taken to reflect customary international law": *ibid.* at para. 196. It therefore seems reasonable to assume that it had this aspect of the prohibition of the use of force in mind when it found that the sending by the US of third parties to execute attacks on Nicaraguan facilities amounted to a violation of the prohibition of the use of force.

98 See Dinstein, above note 6 at 86.

An early but unedifying exception to this arose in *Nicaragua*. Nicaragua submitted, and the Court accepted,[99] that the US had staged a number of military manoeuvres with Honduras near the Nicaraguan border, as well as a number of naval exercises just outside Nicaraguan waters. In Nicaragua's view, these "war games" were meant to intimidate Nicaragua and thus constituted an unlawful threat of force. The ICJ, without explaining the basis for its conclusion, merely opined that these actions did not "in the circumstances" amount to threats of force, which are "equally forbidden by the principle of non-use of force."[100]

The ICJ was somewhat more forthcoming, however, in its 1996 Advisory Opinion on the *Legality of the Threat or Use of Nuclear Weapons*.[101] In that case, several states argued that the mere possession of nuclear weapons itself constitutes an unlawful threat of force within the meaning of Article 2(4). While the Court accepted that possession of weapons might well imply a preparedness to use them, this in itself is not necessarily contrary to the prohibition of the threat of force.[102] Rather, the legality of such an implied "threat" will turn on the legality of the force threatened.[103] For example, if weapons (nuclear or otherwise[104]) are possessed for purely defensive purposes and their anticipated use would respect international legal limitations on the use of force in self-defence, the only "threat" implied by their possession is that they will be used lawfully. The threat itself is, therefore, lawful. However, if a state acquires weapons for the stated or clearly implied purpose of using them to acquire territory from another state or otherwise interfere in its political independence, both the threatened actions and the threat itself would be unlawful. In short, the legality of a threat of force depends on the legality of the force threatened.[105]

What are the practical consequences of this approach? If the threat is not carried out, its legality is contingent on an assessment of the legality of hypothetical occurrences, proof of which will inevitably be somewhat speculative and hence difficult. If on the other hand the threat is carried out, its legality will be more readily ascertainable. However, it

---

99 *Nicaragua*, above note 42 at para. 92.

100 *Ibid.* at para. 227.

101 *Nuclear Weapons Advisory Opinion*, above note 73.

102 *Ibid.* at para. 48.

103 *Ibid.*

104 The Court had earlier declared that Article 2(4) was "weapons-neutral," in the sense that its prohibition of the threat or use of force did not depend on the nature of the weapon employed: *ibid.* at para. 39. It should be noted, however, that international humanitarian law prohibits the use of certain weapons.

105 See also R. Sadurska, "Threats of Force" (1988) 82 A.J.I.L. 239 at 241; Dinstein, above note 6 at 86.

will also be less significant, as the consequences of the threat are likely to be eclipsed by those of the act itself. Accordingly, whether the inclusion of the threat of force in the Article 2(4) prohibition, as interpreted by the ICJ, is legally meaningful or useful is open to question. On the other hand, it may serve an important hortatory purpose in conveying the seriousness with which modern international law reviles the unauthorized or otherwise unjustified use of force in international relations: so repugnant is such behaviour in modern international society that the mere threat of it is "equally forbidden."[106]

b)   Internal Limitations on the Scope of the Prohibition of Force?

i)   General
In light of the foregoing, Article 2(4) appears to constitute a sweeping repudiation of the legality of the threat or use of force in international relations. This statement masks, however, a series of important and long-standing controversies concerning the proper interpretation of Article 2(4).[107] These arguments, which have largely been carried on between academics, tend not to focus on that portion of Article 2(4) that requires all members to "refrain … from the threat or use of force." Rather, they concentrate on its remaining language. In particular, what is the significance of such additional phrases as "in their international relations" and "against the territorial integrity or political independence of any state, or in any other manner inconsistent with the Purposes of the United Nations"? Most importantly, do such phrases lend emphasis to and strengthen the prohibition of force? Or do they rather condition or limit it?

On one side of this debate are so-called "maximalists," scholars who urge that Article 2(4) must be read as a very broad, unconditional prohibition of the use of force which is subject only to well-defined exceptions expressly provided for in Chapter VII of the UN Charter.[108] On the other are "minimalists," scholars (mainly but not exclusively American) who argue that the additional language found in Article 2(4)

---

106 *Nicaragua*, above note 42 at para. 227.
107 See, generally, T.J. Farer, "Human Rights in Law's Empire: The Jurisprudence War" (1991) 85 A.J.I.L. 117; Gray, above note 1 at 29–31; Dinstein, above note 6 at 88–91.
108 A concise summary of the maximalist argument is found in O. Schachter, "The Legality of Pro-Democratic Invasion" (1984) 78 A.J.I.L. 645. See also, generally, L. Henkin, *How Nations Behave*, 2d ed. (New York: Columbia University Press for the Council on Foreign Relations, 1979); Brownlie, above note 7; Franck, *Recourse*, above note 59; O. Schachter, "The Right of States to Use Armed Force" (1984) 82 Mich. L.R. 1620.

plays an important role in limiting its scope.[109] In this way, they argue, some interstate uses of force are not prohibited by Article 2(4) at all and hence require no justification under Chapter VII or otherwise. In addition to its legal importance as a matter of treaty interpretation, this issue obviously also has enormous practical implications for the comprehensiveness and effectiveness of the *UN Charter*'s use of force regime, as we shall now see.

ii) "In Their International Relations"

It is striking that Article 2(4) expressly prohibits the threat or use of force by UN members "in their international relations." It seems probable that the addition of these words to Article 2(4) was intended to distinguish between, on the one hand, international uses of force of the sort seen in the Second World War and hence central to the aim of the *Charter*'s international peace and security provisions; and, on the other, civil conflict or uses of force by a state within its own borders, arguably of less legitimate concern to the international community (at least at the time of conclusion of the *Charter*).[110] However, this language has on occasion been invoked by certain states to seek to exclude from the ambit of Article 2(4) their uses of force purportedly for purposes of recovering territory they claim to be their own. The essential argument thus made is that force used to recover one's rightful territory is force used in internal, rather than international, relations, and is thus not prohibited by Article 2(4).

Variations on this type of argument were advanced to justify the forcible seizures by Morocco of the Western Sahara (1975), Indonesia of East Timor (1975), Argentina of the Falkland Islands (1982), and Iraq of Kuwait (1990).[111] Tellingly, all such arguments were widely rejected by other states, as evidenced by the strong condemnation of these seizures in either or both the UN General Assembly and Security Council.[112] Thus, while it seems to be widely accepted that purely domestic uses

---

109 A concise summary of the minimalist view is found in M. Reisman, "Coercion and Self-Determination: Construing *Charter* Article 2(4)" (1984) 78 A.J.I.L. 642. See also, generally, D. Bowett, *Self-Defence in International Law* (Manchester: Manchester University Press, 1958); M. Reisman, "Kosovo's Antinomies" (1999) 93 A.J.I.L. 860.

110 Dinstein, above note 6 at 85; Gray, above note 1 at 59. For discussion of the rules governing armed intervention in civil conflict by foreign states, see Gray, *ibid.*, c. 3; L. Doswald-Beck, "The Legal Validity of Military Intervention by Invitation of the Government" (1985) 56 Brit.Y.B. Int'l L. 189.

111 See S. Korman, *The Right of Conquest* (Oxford: Clarendon Press, 1996) at 267, 275, and 292; T.M. Franck, "The Stealing of the Sahara" (1976) 70 A.J.I.L. 694.

112 Gray, above note 1 at 57.

of force do not come within the Article 2(4) prohibition of the threat or use of force in "international relations,"[113] it does not follow that force may be used to seize territory over which one has a claim but not possession.[114]

iii) Territorial Integrity, Political Independence, and UN Purposes

The closing language of Article 2(4) — "against the territorial integrity or political independence of any state, or in any other manner inconsistent with the Purposes of the United Nations" — poses greater challenges. Maximalists tend to argue that these words must be read cumulatively, in the sense that the final clause ("or in any *other* manner inconsistent with the Purposes of the United Nations") subsumes or supplements the earlier references to territorial integrity and political independence — notions that might otherwise be read so as to narrow the scope of the prohibition. This approach appears to be consistent with the UN Charter's *travaux préparatoires*, which show that references to "territorial integrity" and "political independence" did not appear in early drafts, but were later added to give "particular emphasis" to some aspects of the basic test of consistency with the purposes of the UN.[115]

Assuming for the moment that this interpretation of Article 2(4) is correct, where does it lead? For maximalists, the answer lies in a hierarchical understanding of the purposes of the UN. They point to the fact that the "maintenance of international peace and security" and the "suppression of acts of aggression or other breaches of the peace" appear as the very first purposes of the UN in Article 1(1). They also note that the Preamble to the UN Charter refers, first and foremost, to members' determination "to save succeeding generations from the scourge of war," and that Article 2(3) unconditionally requires that all international disputes be settled by peaceful means. All of this signals, for maximalists, that the UN Charter's overriding purpose is the maintenance of peace. It follows, therefore, that the effect of Article 2(4)'s closing reference to the purposes of the UN is to render its prohibition

---

113 Although they may engage other rules of international law, most notably those parts of international humanitarian law applicable to non-international armed conflict: see further sources cited, above note 5.

114 Gray, above note 1 at 57.

115 Dinstein, above note 6 at 86–87; Franck, *Recourse*, above note 59 at 12; J. Stone, *Aggression and World Order: A Critique of United Nations Theories of Aggression* (London: Stevens, 1958) at 43; M. Lachs, "The Development and General Trends of International Law in Our Time" (1980) 169 Rec. des Cours 9 at 162; A. Randelzhofer, "Article 2(4)" in Simma, above note 83, 112 at 123.

of the international use of force virtually absolute, save as expressly permitted in Chapter VII.[116]

Minimalists, on the other hand, prefer to disaggregate the closing phrases of Article 2(4). For example, some have argued that a use of force that does not lead to a permanent loss of territory by a state is not a use of force "against the territorial integrity" of that state.[117] On this theory, the 1981 air strike by Israel against an Iraqi nuclear reactor would not constitute a violation of Article 2(4), as it did not lead to a loss of territory (nor, for that matter, political independence) by Iraq.[118] And yet the attack was soundly condemned, in both the UN General Assembly and Security Council, as a violation of the prohibition of the use of force.[119] Indeed, even Israel did not invoke such an argument in defence of its actions, preferring instead to rely on an alleged right of anticipatory self-defence to excuse its *prima facie* violation of Article 2(4).[120] Similar postures taken by states in other instances—for example, in the case of US air strikes against Libya in 1986 or against Iraqi intelligence headquarters in Baghdad in 1993—suggest that states themselves do not accept that Article 2(4) may be read so narrowly,[121] a view apparently shared by the preponderance of academic opinion.[122]

An alternative minimalist approach focuses more specifically on Article 2(4)'s closing reference to consistency with the purposes of the UN. Even accepting the maximalist view that such consistency is the controlling factor in assessing the legality of international uses of force, minimalists nevertheless contend that there are other UN purposes than simply maintaining the peace at all costs. This set of arguments follows two main currents.

The first such current, which reached full flood during the Cold War, had its source in the virtual paralysis of the Security Council

---

116 See J. Mrazek, "Prohibition of the Use and Threat of Force: Self-Defence and Self-Help in International Law" (1989) 27 Can. Y.B. Int'l L. 81 at 90; Dinstein, above note 6 at 87–88.

117 See, for example, A. D'Amato, "Israel's Air Strike Upon the Iraqi Nuclear Reactor" (1983) 77 A.J.I.L. 584; A. D'Amato, *International Law: Process and Prospect* (Dobbs Ferry, NY: Transnational, 1987) at 58–59.

118 For a description of this incident, see Franck, *Recourse*, above note 59 at 105–107.

119 G.A. Res. 36/27 (13 November 1981); S.C. Res. 487 (19 June 1981).

120 See Gray, above note 1 at 133.

121 See Gray, *ibid.* at 162; Franck, *Recourse*, above note 59 at 89–91 and 94.

122 See, for example, Brownlie, above note 7 at 112; Bowett, above note 109 at 112–13; O. Schachter, *International Law in Theory and Practice* (Boston: M. Nijhoff, 1991) at 110; C. Greenwood, "International Law and the Pre-Emptive Use of Force: Afghanistan, Al-Qaida, and Iraq" (2003) 4 San Diego Int'l L.J. 7 at 10–11.

during that period. In essence, the ideological divide between "East" and "West," each represented on the Security Council by permanent members wielding vetoes over non-procedural matters,[123] crippled the Council's ability to fulfill its collective security responsibilities as contemplated in Chapter VII of the *UN Charter*. In reaction to this, some scholars argued that an important purpose of the United Nations, the maintenance of international security, was not being fulfilled. They therefore argued that states choosing to fill this void by using force in the name of "world public order" would in fact be acting in a manner consistent with the purposes of the UN and thus not run afoul of Article 2(4). In other words, unilateral state uses of force not authorized by the Security Council but nevertheless claimed to be in furtherance of the collective security interests of the international community would not be prohibited.[124]

While the importance of this line of argument has waned with the end of the Cold War and the revival of the Security Council's ability to respond to at least some international crises, it appears never to have been taken seriously by the vast majority of states even at the height of the Cold War. It is true that the United Kingdom invoked a variant of this argument in the 1949 *Corfu Channel* case.[125] In particular it argued that its naval intervention in Albanian territorial waters to sweep for mines was a justifiable attempt to secure evidence in support of subsequent peaceful dispute resolution mechanisms. The ICJ famously rejected such reasoning as a "policy of force such as has in the past given rise to most serious abuses and such as cannot find a place in international law."[126] Similar, isolated arguments advanced (somewhat half-heartedly[127]) by Israel to justify its 1976 raid on Entebbe (Uganda) and by the US to excuse its 1983 invasion of Grenada met with no support in the ensuing Security Council debates.[128] Other instances of

---

123 See further Section D(2)(a), below in this chapter.

124 See, for example, M.S. McDougal & F.P. Feliciano, *Law and Minimum World Public Order: The Legal Regulation of International Coercion* (New Haven: Yale University Press, 1961); Reisman (1984), above note 109; A. D'Amato, "The Invasion of Panama Was a Lawful Response to Tyranny" (1990) 84 A.J.I.L. 516; M. Reisman, "Sovereignty and Human Rights in Contemporary International Law" (1990) 84 A.J.I.L. 866.

125 *Corfu Channel Case (Merits) (United Kingdom v. Albania)*, [1949] I.C.J. Rep. 4 [*Corfu Channel*].

126 *Ibid.* at 35.

127 In the sense that they were only offered as alternative, second- or third-order arguments to bolster more central arguments founded on self-defence or (in the case of the US invasion of Grenada) invitation: see Gray, above note 1 at 30–31.

128 See Gray, *ibid.* at 30–31; Franck, *Recourse*, above note 59 at 82–88.

states advancing such arguments have been exceedingly rare, suggesting that they carry very little legal weight.[129]

Moreover, in *Nicaragua*, in the course of its discussion of the customary prohibition of the use of force, the ICJ observed:

> … The principle of non-use of force … may thus be regarded as a principle of customary international law, not as such conditioned by provisions relating to collective security, or to the facilities or armed contingents to be provided under Article 43 of the *Charter*. It would therefore seem apparent that the attitude referred to [an acceptance of the validity of the rules regarding the use of force stated in the *Friendly Relations Declaration*] expresses an *opinio juris* respecting such rule … to be thenceforth treated separately from the provisions, especially those of an institutional kind, to which it is subject on the treaty-law plane of the *Charter*.[130]

In other words, the customary prohibition of the use of force is not amenable to a restrictive reading based on any alleged malfunctioning of the *Charter*'s collective security mechanism. Presumably the same is true of the prohibition in Article 2(4), given the Court's disavowal of any significant inconsistency between the *UN Charter*'s use of force provisions and their customary analogues.[131]

In short, the minimalist approach to Article 2(4) based on inability of the Security Council to fulfill its collective security functions or other "world public order" concerns has only rarely been invoked by states, has never been widely endorsed by them, and has implicitly been rejected by the ICJ. It is therefore unlikely that it represents a reliable approach to interpretation of Article 2(4).

The second minimalist current flowing from Article 2(4)'s closing reference to the purposes of the UN fixes on UN purposes other than the maintenance of international peace and security. For example, Article 1(2) of the *UN Charter* posits that one of the UN's purposes is "to develop friendly relations among nations based on respect for the principle of equal rights and self-determination of peoples." We have already seen that international law recognizes a right of external self-determination for peoples subject to colonial rule, alien occupation, or, arguably, denial of internal self-determination.[132] The minimalist argument that is therefore put forward is that the use of force to assist a people in fulfilling its international legal right to self-determination

---

129 Gray, *ibid.* at 30.
130 *Nicaragua*, above note 42 at para. 188.
131 See the text accompanying notes 64–69, above in this chapter.
132 See Chapter 2, Section C(3).

is consistent with the purposes of the UN and, hence, not prohibited by Article 2(4).[133]

This argument has met with some, albeit ambivalent and far from universal, support by states. During the decolonization period in particular, newly independent and socialist states used their numerical superiority in the UN General Assembly to adopt a number of resolutions either suggesting or openly declaring that the use of force to support a self-determination or national liberation movement was consistent with the purposes of the United Nations.[134] Most such resolutions failed to garner consensus, however, being consistently opposed by western, developed states. In the case of "declaratory" resolutions such as the *Friendly Relations Declaration* and the *Definition of Aggression*, where achievement of consensus was politically and legally important, deliberately vague language was used to paper over the differences between the two camps on this subject.[135]

Nor is this contradictory and ambiguous stance by states much clarified by their record of actual practice. There are three main contexts in which states have used international force and where arguments based on self-determination might have been deployed in justification thereof: (1) the anti-apartheid struggle in South Africa; (2) Portugal's resistance to ending its colonial rule over various overseas territories; and (3) the Middle East conflict. And yet in none of these situations where states intervened forcibly on the side of self-determination movements did they claim to be doing so on that basis. Rather, they typically *denied*

---

133 See, for example, J. Zourek, "Enfin une définition de l'agression" (1974) 20 Ann. Fr. D.I. 9 at 24; R.E. Gorelick, "Wars of National Liberation: *Jus ad Bellum*" (1979) 11 Case W. Res. J. Int'l L. 71 at 77; G. Abi-Saab, "Wars of National Liberation and the Geneva Conventions and Protocols" (1979) 165 Rec. des Cours 353; A. Grahl-Madsen, "Decolonization: The Modern Version of a Just War" (1979) 22 Ger. Y.B. Int'l L. 255; R. Falk, "Intervention and National Liberation" in H. Bull, ed., *Intervention in World Politics* (New York: Oxford University Press, 1984) 119; H.A. Wilson, *International Law and the Use of Force by National Liberation Movements* (New York: Oxford University Press, 1988) at 130; R. Rosenstock, "The Declaration of Principles of International Law Concerning Friendly Relations: A Survey" (1971) 65 A.J.I.L. 713; J. Dugard, "The OAU and Colonialism: An Inquiry Into the Plea of Self-Defence as a Justification for the Use of Force in the Eradication of Colonialism" (1967) 16 I.C.L.Q. 157.

134 See Gray, above note 1 at 53–56.

135 See the *Friendly Relations Declaration*, above note 61, Principle 4 (referring to the right of peoples seeking self-determination to "seek and receive support in accordance with the purposes and principles of the *Charter*"); *Definition of Aggression*, above note 87, Article 7, (referring to the right of peoples seeking self-determination to "struggle to that end and to seek and receive support, in accordance with the principles of the *Charter* ...").

that this was their legal basis for action, insisting that they were in fact acting in self-defence or on other grounds.[136]

The curious result is that a right to use force in aid of self-determination movements is supported, in some General Assembly resolutions, by considerable (but not general) *opinio juris* divorced from state practice; and, on the ground, by some state practice divorced from *opinio juris*. It would seem exceedingly difficult to conclude, on this basis, that such a right exists in customary international law or is compatible with the prohibition in Article 2(4).[137]

Another UN purpose that has been pressed into service by minimalists seeking to limit the scope of the prohibition in Article 2(4) is the promotion and encouragement of respect for human rights.[138] Some academics, for instance, have argued that democratic governance is a human right and that the use of force to install (or restore) a democratic government in a non-democratic state would therefore be consistent with Article 2(4).[139] Altogether aside from difficulties posed by Article 2(4)'s explicit prohibition of force against the "political independence" of states, this argument again finds little if any support in state practice and *opinio juris*. For example, the US expressly disavowed any such legal basis for its 1989 intervention in Panama, by which it ousted the Noriega government and replaced it with a more democratic one.[140] Strikingly, as noted by the Court, the US also did not advance a legal

---

136 Gray, above note 1 at 56 and 58.

137 Dinstein, above note 6 at 89–90 and 130–31. See also *Nicaragua*, above note 42 at 351 (Schwebel J., dissenting on other points).

138 *UN Charter*, above note 36, Article 1(3).

139 See, for example, T.M. Franck, "The Emerging Right to Democratic Governance" (1992) 86 A.J.I.L. 46; T.M. Franck, *Fairness in International Law and Institutions* (New York: Oxford University Press, 1995); J. Crawford, "Democracy and International Law" (1993) 64 Brit. Y.B. Int'l L. 113; G.H. Fox, "The Right to Political Participation in International Law" (1992) 17 Yale J. Int'l L. 539; B.R. Roth, *Governmental Illegitimacy in International Law* (New York: Oxford University Press, 1999); S.D. Murphy, "Democratic Legitimacy and the Recognition of States and Governments" (1999) 48 I.C.L.Q. 545; M. Reisman, "Allocating Competences to Use Coercion in the Post-Cold War World: Practices, Conditions and Prospects" in L.F. Damrosch & D.J. Scheffer, eds., *Law and Force in the New International Order* (Boulder: Westview Press, 1991) 26 at 36; D'Amato (1990), above note 124.

140 Gray, above note 1 at 50–51, quoting the US statement to the Security Council during the debate on the US invasion of Panama: "I am not here today to claim a right on behalf of the United States to enforce the will of history by intervening in favour of democracy .... We are supporters of democracy but not the gendarmes of democracy .... We acted in Panama for legitimate reasons of self-defence ...."

right of democratic intervention to justify its actions in the *Nicaragua* case.[141] Similarly, when Nigeria intervened (on behalf of ECOWAS) in Sierra Leone in 1997 to restore its elected but recently overthrown government, neither it nor ECOWAS sought to justify the action on the basis of a right to use force in support of democracy.[142] In short, this argument appears to have little traction with states.

Much more contentious, however, is the more general proposition that Article 2(4) does not prohibit the unauthorized use of force to secure respect for fundamental human rights. If a state has an oppressive government that persecutes some or all of its people, should other states have the legal ability to intervene, forcibly if necessary, to provide relief? Proponents of so-called "humanitarian intervention" assert just such a right, arguing that the protection of human rights—at least against serious, widespread, and systematic abuse—ranks at least as highly, among UN purposes, as the preservation of international peace and security.[143]

As a preliminary matter, such an argument encounters the textual difficulty that Article 1(3) of the *UN Charter* does not in fact enunciate,

---

141   "[T]hese justifications [i.e. that Nicaragua had taken 'significant steps towards establishing a totalitarian Communist dictatorship'], advanced solely in a political context …, were not advanced as legal arguments. The [US] has always confined itself to the classic argument of self-defence, and has not attempted to introduce a legal argument derived from a supposed rule of 'ideological intervention,' *which would have been a striking innovation*": *Nicaragua*, above note 42 at para. 266 [emphasis added].

142   Gray, above note 1 at 52.

143   See, for example, J-P.L. Fonteyne, "The Customary International Law Doctrine of Humanitarian Intervention: Its Current Validity under the *U.N. Charter*" (1973–74) 4 Cal. W. Int'l L.J. 203; R.B. Lillich, "Forcible Self-Help by States to Protect Human Rights" (1967–68) 53 Iowa L.R. 325; R.B. Lillich, ed., *Humanitarian Intervention and the United Nations* (Charlottesville: University Press of Virginia, 1973); T.M. Franck, "Interpretation and Change in the Law of Humanitarian Intervention" in J.L. Holzgrefe & R.O. Keohane, eds., *Humanitarian Intervention* (Cambridge: Cambridge University Press, 2003) 204; J. Stromseth, "Rethinking Humanitarian Intervention: The Case for Incremental Change" in Holzgrefe & Keohane, *ibid.* at 232; Franck, *Recourse*, above note 59, c. 9; F.R. Teson, *Humanitarian Intervention: An Inquiry Into Law and Morality*, 2d ed. (Dobbs Ferry: Transnational, 1997); D'Amato (1990), above note 124; D. Kritsiotis, "Reappraising Policy Objections to Humanitarian Intervention" (1998) 19 Mich. J. Int'l L. 1005; D. Kritsiotis, "The Kosovo Crisis and NATO's Application of Armed Force Against the Federal Republic of Yugoslavia" (2000) 49 I.C.L.Q. 330; W. Verwey, "Humanitarian Intervention Under International Law" (1985) 32 Nethl. Int'l L. Rev. 357; J.I. Charney, "Anticipatory Humanitarian Intervention in Kosovo" (1999) 93 A.J.I.L. 834; A. Cassese, "*Ex Injuria Ius Oritur*: Are We Moving Towards International Legitimation of Forcible Humanitarian Countermeasures in the World Community?" (1999) 10 E.J.I.L. 23.

as one of the purposes of the UN, the promotion and encouragement of respect for human rights. Rather, the stated purpose is to *"achieve international cooperation* in ... promoting and encouraging respect for human rights...."[144] It is difficult to appreciate how the unilateral use of force, no matter how laudable the goal or motivation, could ever be consistent with the *cooperative* promotion of human rights.

Be that as it may, here as with other minimalist arguments of this ilk, supportive state practice accompanied by *opinio juris* is rather scanty, particularly if one considers the number of governments accused of gross human rights violations over the past sixty years or so.[145] In order to address this difficulty, some proponents of humanitarian intervention reach back to nineteenth- and early twentieth-century state practice to find support for such a right. This is clearly problematic: it ignores the fundamental normative shift concerning the use of force that took place with, or shortly prior to, adoption of the *UN Charter*. State practice prior to 1945 or, perhaps, 1939 must be understood in its legal context—that of a generally recognized right to use force in international relations on any grounds whatsoever.[146] Instances of alleged humanitarian intervention in that context therefore tell us nothing conclusive about the existence of such a right in the *Charter* era. In other words, the real issue is whether any right of unilateral humanitarian intervention that might have pre-existed the *Charter* survived its adoption and universal ratification, or has since emerged as a matter of customary international law. In either case, it is post-1945 state practice that is most telling.

As suggested above, such post-Second World War practice is quite sparse.[147] Indeed, it is generally recognized that there were only three instances of alleged humanitarian intervention between 1945 and the end of the Cold War, namely (1) India's intervention to end repression and support self-determination in Bangladesh in 1971; (2) Vietnam's invasion of Cambodia to end the brutal Pol Pot regime in 1978; and (3) Tanzania's intervention to end the oppressive rule of Idi Amin in Uganda in 1979.[148] In all three cases, however, the intervening states invoked human rights considerations only as corollary rather than as

---

144 *UN Charter*, above note 36, Article 1(3).
145 See Gray, above note 1 at 31–49.
146 See Section B, above in this chapter.
147 For a review of post-*Charter* state practice, see Franck, *Recourse*, above note 59 at 139–70.
148 See Gray, above note 1 at 31–32; Franck, *Recourse*, ibid. at 139–51; T.M. Franck & N.S. Rodley, "After Bangladesh: The Law of Humanitarian Intervention by Military Force" (1973) 67 A.J.I.L. 275. See also generally J.H. Currie, "NATO's

primary or explicitly legal justifications. All preferred instead to base their legal case on extended notions of self-defence.[149] Moreover, in the case of Vietnam, its intervention was condemned in the UN General Assembly, with states such as France and the United Kingdom expressly denying that even gross human rights violations could justify the use of force without Security Council authorization.[150] Meanwhile, the *Friendly Relations Declaration* and the *Definition of Aggression*, adopted on consensus in the UN General Assembly, declared forcible intervention unlawful in absolute terms.[151] Even the ICJ in *Nicaragua* could be said to have rejected the existence of an alleged right to use force unilaterally in the name of encouraging respect for human rights or humanitarian considerations.[152]

There emerged, however, a number of countervailing signs following the end of the Cold War. First, immediately following the first Gulf War, evidence arose of widespread repression by the central Iraqi authorities of Iraq's northern Kurdish and southern Shi-ite populations. The US, UK, and France responded by imposing and enforcing, without clear Security Council authorization, "no-fly zones" in the north and south of Iraq.[153] Significantly, none of these states at first relied upon a right of humanitarian intervention, arguing rather that they were "implementing" a prior Security Council resolution.[154] However, in a num-

---

Humanitarian Intervention in Kosovo: Making or Breaking International Law?" (1998) 36 Can.Y.B. Int'l L. 303.

149 Gray, above note 1 at 32.

150 *Ibid.* See also the 1984 UK Foreign Office paper expressing considerable doubt as to the existence of such a legal right: G. Marston, "UK Materials on International Law" (1986) 57 Brit. Y.B. Int'l L. 487 at 614.

151 *Friendly Relations Declaration*, above note 61, Principle 3; *Definition of Aggression*, above note 87, Article 5(1).

152 In responding to the US assertion that any uses of force attributable to it were justifiable responses to Nicaraguan violations of its human rights and humanitarian obligations, the Court observed: "... the use of force could not be the appropriate method to monitor or ensure ... respect [for human rights] .... [T]he protection of human rights, a strictly humanitarian objective, cannot be compatible with the mining of ports, the destruction of oil installations, or again with the training, arming and equipping of the *contras*": *Nicaragua*, above note 42 at para. 268.

153 Franck, *Recourse*, above note 59 at 152–55.

154 UN Security Council Resolution 688 had called for an end to the repression and demanded that humanitarian organizations be given access to Iraq's affected regions; however, it contained no authorization for UN member states to take enforcement action to that end. In taking the position they did, the three intervening states were in fact pioneering the concept of "implied" Security Council authorization to use force, a matter considered at greater length below: see Section D(2)(b)(iii), below in this chapter. See further J. Lobel & M. Ratner,

ber of publications issued by the Foreign and Commonwealth Office beginning in 1992, the UK began gradually to shift its position in order to justify its actions on the basis of humanitarian intervention. In particular, it suggested, without clearly explaining how, that the law had changed (seemingly since it had taken the opposite position in 1984) to permit intervention "in cases of extreme humanitarian need" and where there was "no practical alternative" to unilateral action.[155] Its allies, however, were much more cautious. France, for its part, abandoned the operation in 1996 without ever having endorsed the humanitarian intervention rationale, and the US only began to echo the UK rationale for the no-fly zones, somewhat ambivalently, in 1999.[156]

Then came the Kosovo crisis when, in response to Yugoslav repression of ethnic Albanians in the Yugoslav province of Kosovo, NATO states undertook a seventy-eight-day aerial bombing campaign against Yugoslavia in 1999.[157] The ostensible aim of the campaign, according to its participants, was to forestall a humanitarian catastrophe in Kosovo. However, NATO itself took a somewhat ambiguous stance as to the precise legal basis for the action, referring both to humanitarian concerns and the need to support the "political aims of the international community."[158] The ensuing Security Council debates disclosed deep divisions between states as to the legality of the action. Russia, China, India, the Ukraine, Belarus, and Cuba all condemned the bombardment as a clear violation of Article 2(4), while Costa Rica, Brazil, and Mexico expressed concern over the fact that the action had been taken without Security Council authorization. France, the Netherlands, and Slovenia essentially took the position that the action could be consid-

---

"Bypassing the Security Council: Ambiguous Authorization to Use Force, Cease-Fires and the Iraqi Inspection Regime" (1999) 93 A.J.I.L. 124.

155 See G. Marston, "UK Materials on International Law" (1992) 63 Brit. Y.B. Int'l L. 615 at 826–27. This dramatic shift in legal position is all the more remarkable if one accepts (as the ICJ apparently did in *Nicaragua*, above note 42 at para. 190) the premise that the prohibition of the use of force is a *jus cogens* norm. As we have seen, while changes to such norms are possible (*via* the emergence of new rules themselves having *jus cogens* status), it is highly doubtful that such changes had been brought about by the early 1990s (or since, for that matter) given the paucity of state practice or *opinio juris* evidencing such a shift: see Gray, above note 1 at 35, 46.

156 See, generally, Gray, *ibid.* at 33–37; see also C. Gray, "After the Cease-Fire: Iraq, the Security Council and the Use of Force" (1994) 65 Brit. Y.B. Int'l L. 135; C. Gray, "From Unity to Polarization: International Law and the Use of Force Against Iraq" (2002) 13 E.J.I.L. 1.

157 See, for example, Franck, *Recourse*, above note 59 at 163–70; Gray, above note 1 at 37–42.

158 Gray, *ibid.* at 38–39.

ered to have been at least implicitly authorized by prior Security Council resolutions and was thus lawful on that account. The US similarly relied on prior Security Council resolutions as well as, somewhat ambiguously, the need to prevent further threats to peace and stability in the region. Only the UK relied expressly and unambiguously on a purported right of unilateral humanitarian intervention in keeping with its prior position taken in connection with the Iraqi no-fly zones. Outside the Security Council, the action was widely condemned as unlawful by states, including the G77 group of states as well as the 115 member states of the Non-Aligned Movement.[159]

It is well known that the Federal Republic of Yugoslavia brought applications before the ICJ against several participating NATO states alleging violations of Article 2(4) of the *UN Charter*. However, these applications proved inconclusive as they failed on jurisdictional grounds and the ICJ was therefore deprived of the opportunity to address the merits.[160] Nor have other instances of alleged humanitarian intervention since emerged.

Thus, the proponents of an extant right of states to intervene forcibly in another state on human rights or humanitarian grounds have considerable hurdles to overcome. The first such hurdle is found in the quite scant state practice supporting such a right in the Cold War period, coupled with General Assembly resolutions and ICJ *dicta* pointing in the opposite direction. Second is the still limited supportive state practice and *opinio juris* in the post-Cold War period, with the United Kingdom and Belgium seemingly the only states willing clearly to assert such a right without also relying on some form of implied Security Council authorization to justify their actions. This is particularly significant in light of wide acknowledgment that the prohibition of the use of force is a rule of *jus cogens*. If this is so, changes in its scope are only possible through emergence of rules having the same character, which in turn would require very clear and broad-based support. However, the great majority of states remain openly hostile to a right of

---

159 *Ibid.* at 39–42 and 45–46.

160 See *Case Concerning the Legality of the Use of Force (Yugoslavia v. Belgium et al.), Provisional Measures, Order of 2 June 1999*, [1999] I.C.J. Rep. 124; *Case Concerning the Legality of the Use of Force (Serbia and Montenegro v. Belgium et al.), Preliminary Objections*, [2004] I.C.J. Rep. 279. It is, however, perhaps notable that Belgium availed itself of the jurisdictional phase of the proceedings to advance the argument that the NATO action was fully justifiable on the basis of a legal right of humanitarian intervention: *Case Concerning Legality of Use of Force (Yugoslavia v. Belgium), Provisional Measures*, "Oral argument of Mrs. Foucart-Kleynen" (10 May 1999), *I.C.J. Pleadings* (CR/99/15); see also Gray, above note 1 at 43–44.

unauthorized humanitarian intervention, and even many NATO states maintain that the Kosovo intervention was exceptional and should not be considered law-making or precedent-setting.[161]

Finally, notwithstanding further UK efforts to promote its position by better defining the circumstances that would justify unilateral humanitarian intervention,[162] the shape of the debate has shifted considerably since the Kosovo crisis. In particular, the emergence of the so-called "responsibility to protect" doctrine has shifted the focus away from an alleged *right* of states to use force unilaterally in the name of protecting human rights, to a *responsibility* borne by the international community to protect civilian populations from gross human rights violations.[163] As the Security Council has apparently emerged as the focal point for the discharge of this responsibility, through exercise of its collective security responsibilities,[164] any momentum that might have existed in favour of a *unilateral* right of humanitarian intervention, as a use of force not prohibited by Article 2(4), has largely dissipated.

In light of the foregoing, therefore, it would be difficult to conclude that the scope of the Article 2(4) prohibition is limited by a right of states to use force unilaterally in the name of promoting or encouraging respect for human rights.

---

161 See Gray, *ibid.* at 45–48. See also generally B. Simma, "NATO, the UN and the Use of Force: Legal Aspects" (1999) 10 E.J.I.L. 1; P. Hilpold, "Humanitarian Intervention: Is There a Need for a Legal Reappraisal?" (2001) 12 E.J.I.L. 437; M. Byers & S. Chesterman, "Changing the Rules About Rules? Unilateral Humanitarian Intervention and the Future of International Law" in Holzgrefe & Keohane, above note 143 at 177; S. Chesterman, *Just War or Just Peace? Humanitarian Intervention and International Law* (Oxford: Oxford University Press, 2001); N. Krisch, "Legality, Morality and the Dilemma of Humanitarian Intervention after Kosovo" (2002) 13 E.J.I.L. 323.

162 See G. Marston, "UK Materials on International Law" (2000) 71 Brit. Y.B. Int'l L. 517 at 646.

163 See Department of Foreign Affairs and International Trade, *The Responsibility to Protect: Report of the International Commission on Intervention and State Sovereignty* (Ottawa: International Development Research Centre, 2001).

164 *A More Secure World: Our Shared Responsibility*, Report of the UN Secretary-General's High-Level Panel on Threats, Challenges and Change, U.N. GAOR, 59th Sess., UN Doc A/59/565 (2004) at paras. 193–209 (see particularly para. 203); *In Larger Freedom: Towards Development, Security and Human Rights for All*, Report of the Secretary-General, U.N. GAOR, 59th Sess., UN Doc. A/59/2005 (2005) at para. 126; *2005 World Summit Outcome*, U.N. GAOR, 60th Sess., UN Doc. A/RES/60/1 (2005) at paras. 138–39; *Protection of Civilians*, SC Res. 1674, U.N. SC 2006, UN Doc. S/RES/1674 at para. 4.

D. EXCEPTIONS TO THE PROHIBITION

1) Introduction

As indicated above, the very broad scope of the Article 2(4) prohibition and its customary analogue must be understood in the context of other *UN Charter* provisions that qualify it. While there is some academic debate on the full range of those qualifications or "exceptions" to the general rule, the preponderance of judicial, academic, and state opinion is that they are essentially two in number:[165]

1) the international threat or use of armed force is permissible when authorized or directed by the Security Council acting under Chapter VII of the *UN Charter* to maintain or restore international peace and security; and

2) even in the absence of Security Council authorization, states may use armed force, individually or collectively, in self-defence; albeit only in certain circumstances and subject to strict legal limits, as we shall see.[166]

Indeed it is arguable that the comprehensive nature of the *prima facie* prohibition asserted in Article 2(4) is only viable in light of these exceptions.[167] It is therefore essential to have a clear understanding of their scope so that the true extent of the limitations placed on states' ability to use force in international relations may be fully appreciated.

---

165 See, for example, *Nuclear Weapons Advisory Opinion*, above note 73 at para. 38; Greenwood, above note 122 at 11; Franck, *Recourse*, above note 59 at 180; Dinstein, above note 6 at 88.

166 It should be noted that the identification of these two exceptions to the general prohibition of the threat or use of force is without prejudice to the availability of potential defences, under the law of state responsibility, which might preclude the wrongfulness of what might otherwise constitute a breach of Article 2(4) or its customary analogue. For example, the presence of one's troops on another state's territory may be considered a threat or use of force contrary to Article 2(4), which will nevertheless not be considered wrongful if that other state genuinely consents to such presence. See further Chapter 12, Section A(5)(b); see also discussion of consent as a justification to the presence of foreign troops in *Case Concerning Armed Activities on the Territory of the Congo (Democratic Republic of the Congo v. Uganda)*, [2005] I.C.J. Rep. 5 at paras. 42–54 and 92–105 [*DRC v. Uganda*]; Dinstein, above note 6 at 112–16; D. Brown, "Use of Force against Terrorism after September 11th: State Responsibility, Self–Defence and Other Responses" (2003) 11 Cardozo J. Int'l & Comp. L. 1 at 30.

167 See, generally, Franck, *Recourse*, above note 59 at 2–5.

2) Collective Security Measures under Chapter VII of the *UN Charter*

a) General

As suggested above, it is common to characterize Security Council authorization to use force under Chapter VII of the *UN Charter* as one of two exceptions to the general prohibition of the use of force in international relations.[168] This should not, however, be taken to mean that there is some fundamental incongruity or opposition between the Chapter VII collective security mechanism and the basic principle articulated in Article 2(4). Rather, the two are mutually complementary and interdependent. The notion of collective security (coupled with a limited right to use force in self-defence) is what makes a general prohibition of the use of force feasible. In a world where armed aggression continues to be a reality, it would not have been possible to convince states to relinquish the lion's share of their right unilaterally to use military force without also providing for some means of keeping or restoring international peace and security.

As we shall see, an understanding of the functioning of the Chapter VII system of collective security requires two levels of inquiry. The first concerns the originally intended design and functioning of the system, as articulated in Chapter VII. The second requires an examination of the way that system has been implemented in practice, which in some ways bears very little resemblance to the apparent intentions of the *Charter*'s drafters.[169]

Before examining the particular provisions of Chapter VII, however, it is necessary to recall some of the *Charter*'s other provisions relating to the composition, role, and functioning of the Security Council. The starting point here is Article 24. That article provides that responsibility for the accomplishment of the chief purpose of the UN, the maintenance of international peace and security, is primarily vested in the Security Council, which as we have seen is a form of executive organ of the UN.[170] Article 24 is also the provision by which UN members expressly acknowledge that the Security Council acts on their behalf

---

168 See above note 165.

169 See Franck, *Recourse*, above note 59 at 21–31; Gray, above note 1 at 195; Dinstein, above note 6, c. 10; J.A. Frowein & N. Krisch, "Article 42" in Simma, above note 83 at 729.

170 The UN General Assembly also has a residual role in this regard, although not one that includes the power to authorize the use of force against states: see *Certain Expenses of the United Nations (Art. 17, Para. 2 of the Charter), Advisory Opinion*, [1962] I.C.J. Rep. 151 at 163; "Uniting for Peace," UNGA Res. 377 (V) (1950).

in fulfilling that responsibility. In other words, the Security Council's powers are delegated to it by member states "up front," and are thus not contingent on subsequent or renewed expressions of consent by members in individual cases.

The complement of Article 24 is Article 25, which adds that UN members agree to accept and carry out the "decisions" of the Security Council.[171] This obligation is in turn bolstered by Article 103, a form of supremacy clause that provides that the obligations of UN members under the *Charter* (including, of course, those set out in Article 25) supersede any obligations they may have under any other international agreement. Thus, it is not legally possible for member states to seek, in other treaties, to derogate from their *Charter* commitments, in particular their delegation of authority to the Security Council in matters of international peace and security.

These provisions, taken together, represent a truly breathtaking surrender of sovereignty by states, unparalleled since the emergence of the modern nation-state in the mid-seventeenth century. They amount to a relinquishment, in unequivocal and irrevocable terms, of decision-making power on issues traditionally considered to be at the very heart of sovereign status, coupled moreover with an unconditional obligation of cooperation and obedience. The enormity of such a relinquishment is all the more astounding when one considers (1) the relative non-representativity of the body to which such powers are delegated and (2) the broad scope of the powers thus surrendered.

On the first of these, it will be recalled that the Security Council is made up of representatives of only fifteen states at any one time, including five permanent members[172] as well as ten additional members, elected on a rotational basis by the UN General Assembly for two-year terms.[173] At first blush this may not seem so unrepresentative after all. However, the voting requirements stipulated in Article 27 provide that "decisions" of the Security Council on non-procedural matters require the "affirmative" votes of nine members, including the "concurring" votes of the five permanent members.[174] The latter requirement is the source of the

---

171 See also *UN Charter*, above note 36, Articles 48 & 49.

172 China, France, Russia, the United Kingdom, and the United States of America.

173 See *UN Charter*, above note 36, Article 23.

174 In the practice of the Council, a failure to vote or an abstention by a permanent member is considered a concurring vote: see *Legal Consequences for States of the Continued Presence of South Africa in Namibia (South West Africa) Notwithstanding Security Council Resolution 276 (1970), Advisory Opinion*, [1971] I.C.J. Rep. 16 at 22; C.A. Stavropoulos, "The Practice of Voluntary Abstentions by Permanent Members of the Security Council Under Article 27, Paragraph 3 of the *Charter of*

well-known "veto" power held by each permanent member. If any one of them votes against a non-procedural resolution, it cannot be adopted. The effect, of course, is that even one permanent member may obstruct the will of all other Security Council members as well as, by extension, that of the broader UN membership on behalf of which they act. Each permanent member, in other words, individually wields disproportionate power in the UN system of peace and security.

It should also be noted that Article 27(3) provides that a Security Council member who is a party to a dispute being considered by the Council shall abstain from voting on resolutions related to that dispute. Significantly, however, this only applies when the vote pertains to recommendations regarding the peaceful settlement of disputes[175] and does not prevent a Security Council member who is a party to a dispute from voting on Chapter VII measures related to that dispute. The upshot of this is that a permanent member may single-handedly veto a Chapter VII resolution that may be targeted at it. In other words, the Security Council is effectively powerless to act against one of its own permanent members in order to maintain or restore international peace and security.[176]

As for the scope of the powers delegated to the Security Council for purposes of maintaining international peace and security, these are set out in Chapter VII, to which we now turn.

b)   Article 39 Determinations, Recommendations, and Decisions

i)   *General*
The key to the Security Council's powers under Chapter VII is Article 39, which provides first for a power of determination of the existence of any "threat to the peace," "breach of the peace," or "act of aggression." Once it has been determined that any one of these three situations exists, Article 39 provides for two consequential powers. First, the

---

the *United Nations*" (1967) 61 A.J.I.L. 737 at 742–44; S.D. Bailey & S. Daws, *The Procedure of the UN Security Council*, 3d ed. (New York: Oxford University Press, 1998) at 257.

175 That is, recommendations adopted under Chapter VI or para. 52(3): see *UN Charter*, above note 36, Article 27(3).

176 This may go some way towards explaining how the extraordinary surrender of sovereignty evidenced in the *UN Charter*'s collective security mechanism came about: The five most significant military powers at the time of its adoption — that is, those with the most to lose through centralization of the right to use force in international relations — did not, in reality, participate in that act of surrender. Rather, they were to be its beneficiaries, while at the same time being protected, by the veto, against any diminution of their own sovereignty.

Security Council may *recommend* measures, to member states, for the maintenance or restoration of international peace and security. Second, it may *decide* upon measures that *shall* be taken, in accordance with Articles 41 (non-forcible measures) or 42 (forcible measures), in order to maintain or restore international peace and security.

ii) Article 39 Determinations

The consequential powers contemplated in Article 39 suggest that a great deal depends on the Council's threshold determination that there exists either a threat or breach of the peace or an act of aggression. This is significant because it is generally agreed that an Article 39 determination is a "decision" within the meaning of Article 25, which UN members are obliged to accept.[177] And while the Appeals Chamber of the International Criminal Tribunal for the Former Yugoslavia (ICTY) has opined that an Article 39 determination by the Security Council is "not a totally unfettered discretion" but must remain "within the legal limits of the Purposes and Principles of the *Charter*,"[178] it is unclear whether this a meaningful constraint. In particular, there are no clearly entrenched legal criteria, other than the wording of the *Charter* itself, that define the Security Council's power to make such determinations.[179] Thus, even assuming the existence of a process or forum in which a state might challenge such a determination,[180] the legal basis upon which it would do so is entirely unclear, particularly given the breadth and ambiguity of the "Purposes and Principles of the

---

177 See Dinstein, above note 6 at 285 and 290; F.L. Kirgis, "The Security Council's First Fifty Years" (1995) 89 A.J.I.L. 506 at 516 and 527.

178 *Prosecutor v. Tadic*, Case No. IT-94-1-A, (1996) 35 I.L.M. 32 at para. 29.

179 See, for example, H. Kelsen, *The Law of the United Nations: A Critical Analysis of Its Fundamental Problems* (New York: F.A. Praeger, 1951) at 727; R. Kolb, *Ius contra bellum: Le droit international relatif au maintien de la paix* (Bâle: Helbing & Lichtenhahn, 2003) at 68; P. Malanczuk, *Akehurst's Modern Introduction to International Law*, 7th ed. (London, New York: Routledge, 1997) at 387–89.

180 At this stage it remains an open question whether the decisions of the Security Council may be subject to any type of judicial review, for example by the International Court of Justice: see, for example, the differing opinions expressed by Judge (*ad hoc*) Lauterpacht in *Application of the Convention on the Prevention and Punishment of the Crime of Genocide (Bosnia and Herzegovina v. Yugoslavia (Serbia and Montenegro)), Order of 13 September 1993*, [1993] I.C.J. Rep. 325 at 407 (Separate Opinion of Lauterpacht J.) (see especially paras. 98–104); and by President Schwebel in *Questions of Interpretation and Application of the 1971 Montreal Convention Arising from the Aerial Incident at Lockerbie (Libyan Arab Jamahiriya v. United Kingdom), Preliminary Objections*, [1998] I.C.J. Rep. 9 (Dissenting Opinion of Schwebel J.).

Charter."[181] Beyond this, it is also generally accepted that the Security Council is not limited to legal considerations at all in assessing the existence of threats to or breaches of the peace. As the ICJ has explicitly recognized on a number of occasions, the Security Council is primarily a political rather than a judicial body, and it may therefore base its Article 39 determinations on political as well as legal factors.[182]

In short, therefore, the Security Council's threshold power to determine the existence of threats to or breaches of the peace or acts of aggression is extremely broad, apparently subject to few if any substantive or procedural fetters. This is not accidental. The Charter itself underscores that the basic reason for the conferral of broad powers on the Security Council is "to ensure prompt and effective action" by the United Nations in peace and security matters.[183] That the Security Council has not always been able to realize that goal has nothing to do with any inadequacy of its powers. Rather, it is the result of the only true fetter on its otherwise extensive authority: the Charter's stipulation that it may only make decisions (including Article 39 determinations) with the consent of a supermajority of its members, including at least the acquiescence of every one of its permanent members.[184]

It is this requirement in particular that explains the Council's dismal record of making Article 39 determinations during the Cold War. During that period, the Security Council only formally determined the existence of three each of threats to the peace, breaches of the peace, and acts of aggression.[185] With the fall of the iron curtain, however, and the consequent dramatic decline of exercise of the veto by permanent

---

181 See UN Charter, above note 36, Articles 1, 2.
182 See, for example, United States Diplomatic and Consular Staff in Tehran (United States of America v. Iran), [1980] I.C.J. Rep. 3 at 21–22; Case Concerning Armed Activities on the Territory of the Congo (Democratic Republic of the Congo v. Uganda), Provisional Measures, Order of 1 July 2000, [2000] I.C.J. Rep. 111 at para. 36; Case Concerning Military and Paramilitary Activities in and against Nicaragua (Nicaragua v. United States of America) Jurisdiction and Admissibility, Judgment, above note 55 at para. 95; Case Concerning Application of the Convention on the Prevention and Punishment of the Crime of Genocide (Bosnia and Herzegovina v. Yugoslavia (Serbia and Montenegro)), Provisional Measures, Order of 8 April 1993, [1993] I.C.J. Rep. 3 at para. 33; Case Concerning Questions of Interpretation and Application of the 1971 Montreal Convention Arising from the Aerial Incident at Lockerbie (Libyan Arab Jamahiriya v. United Kingdom), Provisional Measures, Order of 14 April 1992, [1992] I.C.J Rep. 114 at para. 40. See also Dinstein, above note 6 at 285.
183 UN Charter, above note 36, Article 24(1).
184 See the discussion accompanying notes 172–76, above in this chapter.
185 See Gray, above note 1 at 197; Dinstein, above note 6 at 292–94.

members, Article 39 determinations have been made by the Security Council with remarkable regularity.[186]

iii) Article 39 Recommendations and the "Authorization" of Force

Once the Security Council determines the existence of either a threat to or breach of the peace or an act of aggression, Article 39 contemplates that it may make "recommendations." This power of recommendation is apparently unlimited: as long as Article 39 recommendations are purportedly directed towards maintaining or restoring international peace and security, nothing in Article 39 or Chapter VII more generally defines or limits their substantive content, nor indeed the range of entities to which they may be addressed. They may be directed specifically at states responsible for or affected by the relevant threat to or breach of the peace or act of aggression, or to all states. They may concern non-forcible or (as we shall see) forcible measures.[187]

One explanation for the virtually unlimited scope of the Security Council's power of recommendation under Article 39 is that recommendations are not "decisions" within the meaning of Article 25. They are accordingly not binding on UN member states and otherwise carry no mandatory weight. This means, essentially, that states will not generally be in breach of their obligations under the *UN Charter* merely because they choose not to accept or act upon recommendations made by the Security Council under Article 39.[188]

This is not to say, however, that such recommendations carry no legal weight. Quite the contrary: it is generally accepted in UN practice that the effect of a Security Council recommendation under Article 39 is to raise a presumption of legality in respect of the actions of states

---

186 Dinstein records more than two dozen such instances since 1990, compared with the handful that had been made by the Council in the preceding forty-five years: see Dinstein, *ibid.* at 300–2.

187 See, generally, Dinstein, *ibid.* at 283–89; I. Osterdahl, *Threat to the Peace: The Interpretation by the Security Council of Article 39 of the UN Charter* (Uppsala: Iustus, 1998) at 28; A. Orakhelashvili, "The Legal Basis of the United Nations Peace-Keeping Operations" (2002–2003) 43 Va. J. Int'l L. 485 at 492–93.

188 See Dinstein, *ibid.* at 280–81, 289; Gray, above note 1 at 196–97; G. Schwarzenberger, *International Law as Applied by International Courts and Tribunals, Volume III: International Constitutional Law* (London: Stevens, 1976) at 204–5; O. Schachter, "Legal Aspects of the Gulf War of 1991 and Its Aftermath" in W. Kaplan & D.M. McRae, eds., *Law, Policy and International Justice: Essays in Honour of Maxwell Cohen* (Montreal: McGill-Queen's University Press, 1993) 5 at 20. Of course, such a failure may ultimately lead to the adoption of a "decision" imposing mandatory measures; however, it is only at that point that positive obligations of compliance arise for member states.

complying with that recommendation.[189] While the theoretical basis for such a presumption is not clear and nothing in the *UN Charter* expressly provides for it, it has been argued that it derives from the Security Council's binding power of determining threats to or breaches of the peace or acts of aggression, which is invariably exercised prior to the making of Article 39 recommendations.[190]

Indeed it is this effect of an Article 39 recommendation that grounds the legality of a state's use of force pursuant to Security Council authorization under Chapter VII. While, as we shall see below, Chapter VII elsewhere contemplates that the Security Council may "decide" that measures involving the use of force *shall* be taken, it has never in fact invoked that particular power.[191] Rather, it has only ever *authorized* states to take military enforcement action for purposes of maintaining or restoring international peace and security. The preferable view is that such authorizations effectively amount to recommendations under Article 39 — which, therefore, do not *require* states to use force but merely *permit* them to do so.[192] And if they do so, it is generally accepted that their use of force, as long as it complies with the terms of the Security Council's authorization, is protected by the mantle of legality.[193]

In practice, the authorization of force by the Security Council has been an almost exclusively post-Cold War phenomenon. The principal Cold War exception to this was the 1950 Korean crisis.[194] Following

---

189 Dinstein, *ibid.* at 281.

190 *Ibid.* at 290.

191 See "An Agenda for Peace: Preventive Diplomacy, Peacemaking and Peace-keeping," Report of the Secretary-General, U.N. Doc. A/47/277 (17 June 1992) at para. 42 ["An Agenda for Peace"]; Dinstein, *ibid.* at 304 and 310.

192 See the convincing argument to this effect by Dinstein, *ibid.* at 310. It should, however, be noted that there is some debate as to the precise *locus* of the Security Council's power to authorize, as opposed to require, the use of force by states, with some arguing that such a power is a lesser but included aspect of the Security Council's power to take direct military action under Article 42: see, for example, Franck, *Recourse*, above note 59 at 26–27; Frowein & Krisch, above note 169 at 756–58. Uncertainty here is exacerbated by the general failure of the Council's resolutions to articulate expressly the provisions of the *Charter* pursuant to which they are adopted: see Gray, above note 1 at 199–200. In any case it would appear that very little turns on the precise source of the Council's power to authorize (as opposed to require) the use of force as it is clear that UN member states have acquiesced in its existence and consider such authorizations to be non-binding: see Dinstein, *ibid.* at 310; E.V. Rostow, "Until What? Enforcement Action or Collective Self-Defense?" (1991) 85 A.J.I.L. 506 at 509.

193 See above note 189.

194 For a review of the facts surrounding the crisis, see Franck, *Recourse*, above note 59 at 24–25; Gray, above note 1 at 199–200; Dinstein, above note 6 at 153–56 and 292–93.

North Korea's attack against South Korea, the Security Council first determined the existence of a breach of the peace and then recommended "such assistance to South Korea as may be necessary to repel the armed attack and to restore international peace and security."[195] While this formulation does not expressly refer to the use of force, this was clearly implied in a subsequent resolution recommending that states provide the necessary "assistance" by making armed forces available to a unified command acting under US leadership.[196]

This use of euphemistic language to refer indirectly to an authorization to use force has become a persistent feature of the much more active Chapter VII practice of the Security Council following the Cold War. Perhaps most notably, the Security Council in 1990 authorized UN member states to use "all necessary means" to secure the withdrawal of Iraqi troops from Kuwait and to restore international peace and security to the area.[197] Similar formulations have subsequently been used by the Security Council to authorize forcible measures to secure delivery of humanitarian aid in conflict zones, to protect safe havens and enforce no-fly zones, to restore democratically elected governments, to protect refugee camps, to enforce embargoes, and to maintain order and effectively impose peace-building measures in transitional and post-conflict situations.[198] As a result, a Security Council authorization to use "all necessary means" (or substantially similar language) has become synonymous, in UN practice, with an authorization to use force.[199]

---

195 UNSC Res. 82 (1950), U.N. Doc. S/1501 (25 June 1950); UNSC Res. 83 (1950), U.N. Doc. S/1511 (27 June 1950). Note that the adoption of these resolutions was probably only made possible by the fact that China's seat on the Security Council was occupied by the government-in-exile of Chiang Kai-Shek (rather than the mainland communist Chinese government), as well as by the USSR's boycott of the Council's debate on the issue in protest over this fact.

196 UNSC Res. 84 (1950), U.N. Doc. S/1588 (7 July 1950).

197 UNSC Res. 678, U.N. Doc. S/RES/678 (29 November 1990) at para. 2.

198 See Gray, above note 1 at 204–205 and 252–64; Dinstein, above note 6 at 303–4. It should be noted that "peace-building," "peace-making," or "peace enforcement" must be distinguished from "peacekeeping". While detailed treatment of the latter is beyond the scope of this chapter, the legal basis for the presence of foreign peacekeeping troops (usually under UN auspices) on the territory of parties to a conflict is, traditionally, the consent of those parties. By contrast, peace-building, peace-making or peace enforcement missions are typically undertaken prior to the end of a conflict and without the consent of all parties to it. The legal basis for the presence of such forces on the territory of parties to the conflict is usually found in Security Council authorization under Chapter VII. See further Gray, ibid. at 210–51.

199 Gray, ibid. at 205; H. Duffy, The "War on Terror" and the Framework of International Law (Cambridge: Cambridge University Press, 2005) at 175.

While perhaps inconsequential in itself, this Security Council practice (that is, authorizing force without explicitly saying so) has ultimately led to a new and troubling phenomenon: the invocation, by some states, of so-called "implied Security Council authorization."[200] Under this doctrine, even where the Security Council has not expressly authorized "all necessary means," *patterns* of Security Council resolutions are nevertheless interpreted as "implying" such an authorization. The first inklings of such an approach emerged in arguments made by the United States and the United Kingdom to justify their establishment and enforcement of no-fly zones over northern and southern Iraq from 1993 onwards. Security Council Resolution 688 had previously demanded that Iraq stop its repression of its northern Kurdish and southern Shi'ite communities and that it grant access to the affected areas by humanitarian organizations.[201] Although that resolution was not adopted under Chapter VII and did not authorize any means for its enforcement (let alone "all necessary means"), both the US and UK argued that the no-fly zones they subsequently established were "in support of" the resolution and thus justified.[202]

This approach was taken further in the run-up to the Kosovo intervention by NATO in 1999. The Security Council had previously adopted a series of resolutions under Chapter VII in which it demanded certain actions by the central Yugoslav authorities, failing which it would consider further measures to address the situation.[203] In the debates preceding the adoption of these resolutions, Russia made it clear that it was abstaining (rather than exercising its veto) only because the resolutions did not, directly or indirectly, authorize states to use force to address the situation. When in the end NATO went ahead with its aerial bombing campaign of Yugoslav territory in the absence of a further Security Council resolution authorizing "all necessary means," a number of NATO states justified their actions in part on the basis that the preceding Security Council resolutions, taken as a whole, implicitly authorized such a use of force.[204]

---

200 See, generally, C. Scott, "Interpreting Intervention" (2001) 39 Can. Y.B. Int'l L. 333; Gray (2002), above note 156 at 8–13; J.H. Currie, "The Continuing Contributions of Ronald St. J. Macdonald to UN Charter and Peace and Security Issues" (2002) 40 Can. Y.B. Int'l L. 265 at 272–84; Gray, above note 1 at 264–81.
201 UNSC Res. 688, U.N. Doc. S/RES/688 (5 April 1991) at paras. 2–3.
202 See Gray, above note 1 at 264–67.
203 UNSC Res. 1160, U.N. Doc. S/RES/1160 (31 March 1998); UNSC Res. 1199, U.N. Doc. S/RES/1199 (23 September 1998); UNSC Res. 1203, U.N. Doc. S/RES/1203 (24 October 1998). For a review of the facts, see Franck, *Recourse*, above note 59 at 163–70.
204 See Gray, above note 1 at 267–70.

It has also been argued that the wording of Security Council Resolution 1373,[205] which was adopted in the aftermath of the September 11, 2001 terrorist attacks against the World Trade Centre and the Pentagon, provided authorization for the US- and UK-led actions in Afghanistan that followed. In particular, the Security Council's decision that "all States shall ... [t]ake the necessary steps to prevent the commission of terrorist acts" was said to constitute a potentially unlimited authorization to use force in combating terrorism, notwithstanding its departure from the usual "all necessary means" formulation.[206] It should be noted, however, that the US was reluctant to adopt this interpretation, preferring instead to rely on its inherent right of self-defence, which was itself "recognized," "reaffirmed," and "reiterated" in Resolution 1373 and its predecessor, Resolution 1368.[207]

Resort to implied Security Council authorization has most recently been invoked to justify the forcible toppling of the Saddam Hussein regime in Iraq in 2003. In particular, the US and UK resurrected Security Council Resolutions 678[208] and 687,[209] in combination with Resolution 1441,[210] in order to provide a mantle of implied Security Council authorization for military action that plainly could not have been obtained explicitly.[211] The essential gist of the argument put forward by the US and UK was that Resolution 678 had, in 1990, authorized "all necessary means" to eject Iraq from Kuwait and to restore international peace and security in the area. Following the ejection of Iraqi forces from Kuwait, Resolution 687 declared a ceasefire in the area and imposed comprehensive disarmament obligations on Iraq. The US and UK thus argued that, if the disarmament obligations of Resolution 687 were not respected, the ceasefire imposed by the same resolution was

---

205 UNSC Res. 1373, U.N. Doc. S/RES/1373 (28 September 2001).
206 See M. Byers, "Terrorism, the Use of Force and International Law after 11 September" (2002) 51 Int'l & Comp. L.Q. 401 at 401–3. Byers refers to several such interpretations given to Resolution 1373, including by British Prime Minister Tony Blair (at 402, n. 8).
207 UNSC Res. 1368, U.N. Doc. S/RES/1368 (12 September 2001). See also Byers, *ibid.* at 403.
208 UNSC Res. 678, above note 197.
209 UNSC Res. 687, U.N. Doc. S/RES/687 (8 April 1991).
210 UNSC Res. 1441, U.N. Doc. S/RES/1441 (8 November 2002).
211 "Plainly" because the required votes endorsing such action could not be mustered by the sponsors of a resolution setting out such an explicit authorization; that draft resolution was consequently withdrawn: see Gray, above note 1 at 273. Further, France had made plain its intention of vetoing any such authorization: see, for example, "Chirac Says France Will Veto U.N. Resolution on Iraq," PBS Online Newshour (10 March 2003), online: www.pbs.org/newshour/updates/iraq_03-10-03.html.

automatically suspended and the authorization to use force in Resolution 678 reactivated—albeit in a radically different context than originally contemplated by the Security Council.[212]

One potential difficulty with this automatic revival argument was that paragraph 34 of Resolution 687 explicitly provided that the Security Council remained "seized of the matter … to take such further steps as may be required for the implementation of the present resolution."[213] That seemed to suggest that further steps, in the case of a violation of Resolution 687, could only be taken by the Security Council in a subsequent resolution. The US and UK therefore also relied on Resolution 1441, which warned of "serious consequences" in the event that Iraq did not avail itself of its "final opportunity to comply with its disarmament obligations."[214] This additional warning, while again not explicitly authorizing any use of force, was interpreted by the US and UK as a "further step" within the meaning of paragraph 34 of Resolution 687. And while Resolution 1441 itself provided for further *consideration* of the matter by the Security Council should Iraq continue to fail to honour its obligations, this, it was argued, did not require further *authorization* before the authorization to use all necessary means previously provided in Resolution 678 was revived.

While it is true that many states condemned the 2003 invasion of Iraq as illegal, what remains unclear is whether they did so on the basis that the particular implied authorization argument advanced by the US and UK was flawed on the facts, or because they reject the notion of implied authorization in principle. In any case, the arguments put forward by the US and UK clearly show that at least these permanent members of the Security Council consider the practice sound.

The principal difficulty posed by the doctrine of implied authorization, of course, is that it injects substantial uncertainty into the

---

212 For the clearest and most explicit articulation of this argument, see the legal opinion tabled by Lord Goldsmith, the UK Attorney General, in the British House of Commons on 18 March 2003, in answer to a question concerning the legality of military action in Iraq: (UK) Foreign and Commonwealth Office, "Iraq: Legal Basis for the Use of Force" (17 March 2003), (2003) 52 I.C.L.Q. 812. See also the much more nuanced legal opinion given by the UK Attorney General to Prime Minister Blair on 7 March 2003, online: www.number-10.gov.uk/output/Page7445.asp, as well as an after-the-fact statement of the American position given by W.H. Taft & T.F. Buchenwald, "Pre-emption, Iraq and International Law" (2003) 97 A.J.I.L. 557.

213 UNSC Res. 687, above note 209 at para. 34. See M. Byers, "The Shifting Foundations of International Law: A Decade of Forceful Measures against Iraq" (2002) 13 E.J.I.L. 21 at 24.

214 UNSC Res. 1441, above note 210 at paras. 2 and 13.

Security Council's collective security practice and, in particular, the determination of the circumstances in which states are in fact authorized to use force.[215] Whereas traditional UN practice, mindful of the profound legal and real-world ramifications of a Chapter VII authorization to use force, has sensibly required that such authorization be clear and unambiguous, reliance on implied authorization, which shows signs of becoming endemic, does not.

But the implications in fact go much further. First, implied authorization has the potential to move much of the power to decide on appropriate responses to threats to international peace and security out of the Security Council's hands altogether. Rather than requiring clear endorsement by the Security Council, states can unilaterally read an authorization to use force into ambiguous language previously used by the Council, sometimes in entirely different contexts. In other words, it is a vehicle by which the Security Council's authority to determine and manage threats to international peace and security may be usurped by individual states.

Second, all of the procedural guarantees set out in the *UN Charter* to govern the Security Council's exercise of its extensive peace and security powers—including those requiring a conclusive and readily ascertainable decision (an explicit resolution), reached through the participation of a defined set of participants (all members of the Security Council wielding their duly delegated authority), in a known and relatively transparent process (the voting requirements of Article 27)—are entirely lost. The indispensable constraint upon the powers of the Security Council—the need to achieve consensus among, or at least acquiescence of, a significant cross-section of states, including all of the Council's permanent members—is effectively evaded.

Third, in the case of reliance by a permanent member of the Security Council on supposed implied authorization, the Council's ability to contradict such an interpretation and assert its authority over the situation is effectively neutered. No resolution contradicting the position taken by the US or the UK in 2003, for example, could ever have been adopted by the Council, as each would surely have used its veto to prevent the passage of such a resolution.

Finally, if language falling short of an authorization to use force can subsequently be unilaterally interpreted to have exactly that effect, the willingness of some members of the Security Council to use robust language in dealing with threats to the peace is likely to be eroded. Such a "chilling" effect is not likely to be conducive to the Council's

---

215 Scott, above note 200 at 339–40.

ability effectively to fulfill its role of maintaining international peace and security.

iv) Article 39 Decisions and Article 42 Measures

It was noted above that, in addition to its Article 39 power to make recommendations, the Security Council may also "decide" upon measures that shall be taken in accordance with Articles 41 or 42. Such a decision will, of course, give rise to mandatory obligations for member states pursuant to Article 25. While Article 41 concerns measures "not involving the use of armed force," and is therefore not within the scope of this chapter, Article 42 specifically contemplates armed action. As indicated above, the Security Council has never decided that measures *shall* be taken in accordance with Article 42. However, as it is theoretically possible that it might do so in the future, at least a brief review of its features is in order.

First, Article 42 appears to establish an additional threshold before its provisions may be invoked by the Security Council; namely, that the Council determine that measures under Article 41 — that is, measures not involving the use of force — would be inadequate. Assuming such a determination has been made, resort may then be had to "such action by air, sea or land forces as may be necessary to maintain or restore international peace and security." Curiously, however, Article 42 contemplates that it is the Security Council itself that shall take such action, albeit using forces provided by UN member states. To understand this unusual formulation, one must also refer to Article 43.

In Article 43, UN members undertake to make elements of their armed forces available to the Security Council, "on its call," in accordance with agreements to be negotiated with it. The apparent purpose of requiring the conclusion of such agreements was to avoid, as far as possible, any delays in equipping the Security Council to deal with threats to the peace as they emerge.[216] The idea, in other words, was to have pre-identified, standing units available to the Security Council so that it could react swiftly to international crises. In short, the Security Council was to have the equivalent of a standing army at its disposal, which could then be deployed rapidly pursuant to Article 42.

---

216 See Franck, *Recourse*, above note 59 at 21–23; Dinstein, above note 6 at 305–6. Similarly, Articles 45 (requiring members to keep ready air-force contingents for rapid deployment at the call of the Security Council) and 46–47 (establishment of and planning by a Military Staff Committee to assist the Security Council in taking military measures) were intended to permit the Security Council to react swiftly to threats to international peace and security.

In fact, no Article 43 agreements have ever been negotiated, and Cold War tensions prevented the effective establishment of the contemplated Military Staff Committee.[217] There has been some academic debate as to whether the conclusion of Article 43 agreements are a necessary prerequisite to the ability of the Security Council to decide that force shall be deployed by states pursuant to Article 42, but that issue has never been resolved in the practice of the Security Council because the mandatory measures of Article 42 have never been invoked.[218] And while, in 1992, the UN Secretary-General called for the negotiation of Article 43 agreements in order to reinvigorate the Security Council's Chapter VII functions in the wake of the Cold War,[219] in fact the Council has continued to *authorize* states to use force under Article 39, rather than *require* them to do so under Article 42.[220]

v)   Conclusions

In the result, the collective security mechanism established in Chapter VII, by which force may lawfully be used under the authority of the Security Council, has not been implemented in quite the manner originally contemplated by the framers of the UN Charter. By and large this has been due to the deep ideological divide that emerged between East and West almost immediately upon adoption of the *Charter* and that persisted throughout the Cold War. The result was that the Security Council was never equipped with the forces with which it was intended to police international peace and security under Article 42. Nor was it even able, in most situations requiring it, to unlock its considerable remaining Chapter VII powers by making threshold determinations, under Article 39, of the existence of threats to or breaches of the peace or acts of aggression.

With the end of the Cold War, however, the Security Council has much more frequently invoked this power and developed the practice of authorizing, rather than requiring, the use of force by member states when necessary to maintain or restore international peace and security. The legal cover thus provided to states responding to such authorizations has therefore emerged as an important qualification to the general prohibition of the use of force in Article 2(4). It remains to be seen whether the mantle of legality thus afforded to states will remain under

---

217 See Franck, *Recourse*, *ibid*. at 24–26; Dinstein, *ibid*. at 305–6.
218 Contrast the views expressed by Dinstein, *ibid*. at 305 and Franck, *Recourse*, *ibid*. at 26–27. See also Gray, above note 1 at 199–200.
219 See "An Agenda for Peace," above note 191 at para. 43.
220 See Dinstein, above note 6 at 310; Gray, above note 1 at 252–64; Franck, *Recourse*, above note 59 at 27–31.

the strict control of the Security Council, or whether the emergence of the doctrine of implied authorization will allow states in fact acting without authorization to nevertheless claim its protection.

3) Self-Defence

a) Introduction

We turn now to the law of self-defence, probably the most controversial area of the *jus ad bellum*. It is a topic on which academics and states sharply disagree in a number of key areas, and where the rules are prone to abuse.[221] In some sense this is not at all surprising, as self-defence is the only clearly surviving vestige of states' earlier, unfettered discretion to use force against one another without authorization. It is therefore natural that its limits should be tested and occasionally transgressed. Part, too, of the explanation for such disagreements and abuses is that this is an area of the law that essentially attempts to regulate resort to a form of self-help.[222] Elsewhere in this book it is explained that self-help has long been a prevalent feature of the international legal system, particularly given the absence, until relatively recently, of effective international dispute resolution mechanisms.[223] It is, in other words, a type of "extra-legal" remedy that does not easily lend itself to detailed or effective legal regulation. This is exacerbated by the fact that the imperative for immediate and effective remedies is nowhere so keenly felt by states as where their territorial integrity or even survival is threatened. In such circumstances, most other considerations, including those of an international legal character, may become secondary.

The problems for the international lawyer in this area extend, however, beyond the mere fact that self-defence as a form of self-help tends, by its very nature, to be self-serving. In addition, assessment of the legality of a use of force in alleged self-defence is usually heavily dependent on the availability and reliability of the surrounding facts. These in turn are not often objectively or conclusively tested or established, but tend to be "interpreted" by various parties to suit their own particular needs.[224] Moreover, it is often the case that *all* parties to a given conflict claim to be acting in self-defence, which suggests considerable relativity as to either the content or application of the relevant rules. Consider, too, that neither the *Friendly Relations Declaration*[225] nor the *Definition*

---

221 See, generally, Gray, *ibid.* at 95.
222 See Dinstein, above note 6 at 175–76.
223 See Chapter 12, Section C(3).
224 See, generally, Gray, above note 1 at 96–97; Dinstein, above note 6 at 211–16.
225 *Friendly Relations Declaration*, above note 61.

of Aggression[226] attempts to codify the law relating to the use of force in self-defence. This is a reflection of the inability of UN member states to reach consensus on certain elements of that law.[227] The international lawyer is therefore left without key sources of guidance that have otherwise proven instrumental in fleshing out the details of the post–Second World War legal regime concerning the use of force.

It is important, however, not to let the admitted areas of controversy or uncertainty eclipse the fact that there is a generally agreed core to the law of self-defence, one that in fact suffices to address the vast majority of situations that arise between states. In other words, most of the contentious issues — for instance, whether there is a right of anticipatory or pre-emptive self-defence, or a right to use force in self-defence against non-state actors — tend to arise or be determinative in very few cases and to be of direct interest to very few states. Thus, the areas of uncertainty must be kept in perspective: in fact, the near-universal invocation of self-defence, as a legal right, by states using force attests to widespread *opinio juris* as to the existence of important international legal rules on the subject. Moreover, it must be remembered that many invocations of self-defence are contentious not because of any fundamental doctrinal disagreement but because well-settled and generally recognized rules are being applied to disputed facts.[228]

In this section, we will begin by outlining some of the theoretical debates that have surfaced concerning the right of states to use force in self-defence since 1945. We will then review the generally agreed "core" of the law of self-defence, before finally turning to consider some of the main controversies that continue to cloud the outer limits of the doctrine.

b)   Theoretical Debates: The Source and Scope of the Right of Self-Defence

As with the prohibition of the threat or use of force itself, the *UN Charter* provides the usual starting point for an examination of the legal bounds of the use of force in self-defence. In particular, Article 51 stipulates that "[n]othing in the present *Charter* shall impair the inherent right of individual or collective self-defence if an armed at-

---

226 *Definition of Aggression*, above note 87.

227 See Gray, above note 1 at 95. Note, too, that the General Assembly's 1987 *Declaration on the Non-Use of Force* only repeats the *UN Charter*'s rather cursory Article 51 reference to the right of self-defence, without attempting to elaborate upon the content or limits of that right: see *Non-Use of Force*, above note 87.

228 Gray, *ibid.* at 95–99.

tack occurs against a Member of the United Nations, until the Security Council has taken measures necessary to maintain international peace and security." Other than adding that resort to this right shall immediately be reported to the Security Council and shall not affect the Security Council's prerogatives, the *UN Charter* fails to provide any further guidance as to the nature, scope, or limitations of the right of self-defence.

This curious approach to setting out an extremely significant exception to the prohibition articulated in Article 2(4)[229] has given rise to a long-standing academic debate between two main schools of thought on the meaning of Article 51.

One such school, championed mainly by scholars advocating an expansive right to use force in self-defence,[230] focuses on the fact that Article 51 seems to be drafted as a sort of "saving" clause rather than as a provision establishing a legal right. It refers to an "inherent" right of self-defence (rather than one created by Article 51 itself) and states that this right is not "impaired" by the *UN Charter* (rather than being defined by it). These features are taken to mean that Article 51 should not be treated as a codification of the circumstances in which self-defence may be invoked by states. Rather, Article 51 merely refers to another body of law, customary international law, which defines those circumstances.

But therein lies the rub: according to most proponents of this first school of thought, the relevant customary rules to which reference is thus made are those that existed immediately prior to adoption of the *Charter*, in 1945. Given that constraints on the use of force were significantly less stringent at that time, they conclude that the right of self-defence thus preserved by Article 51 is very broad indeed. A necessary addendum to this line of argument, given that there is very little support in post-1945 state practice or *opinio juris* for such an expansive right of self-defence, is that Article 51 either froze the development of the customary right of self-defence in its pre-1945 state, or trumps, at least as between UN member states, any subsequent customary developments.

---

229 The right to use force in self-defence has repeatedly been characterized by the ICJ as an exception to the general prohibition set out in Article 2(4) of the *UN Charter* and its customary analogue: see, for example, *Nicaragua*, above note 42 at paras. 50 and 193; and, *semble*, *DRC v. Uganda*, above note 166 at para. 304.

230 See, for example, Bowett, above note 109; S.M. Schwebel, "Aggression, Intervention and Self-Defense in Modern International Law" (1972-II), 136 Rec. des Cours 463; McDougal & Feliciano, above note 124. It should come as no surprise that proponents of an expansive right of self-defence tend also to be minimalists when it comes to interpretation of Article 2(4), and *vice versa*.

On the other hand, Article 51 *does* appear to stipulate at least some of the conditions that must be present for exercise of the right of self-defence. For example, it refers to the right of self-defence "if an armed attack occurs"; it contemplates that the inherent right of self-defence remains unimpaired only until the Security Council has taken necessary measures to maintain international peace and security; and it requires that actions in self-defence be reported to the Security Council.

These features, which on their face go beyond a mere referral to customary international law, have led to a competing view of the meaning of Article 51. According to champions of this second school of thought, Article 51 is not simply a clause that preserves pre-1945 customary international law relating to self-defence.[231] Rather, they argue that it in fact codifies at least some of the conditions and circumstances which must obtain before self-defence may validly be invoked by a state. They reason that it would be meaningless to include such stipulations in Article 51 if its intent and effect were merely to preserve a much broader customary right that is not subject to them. In other words, why should the use of "inherent" in Article 51 control the meaning to be attributed to its remaining provisions? Finally, they reject the "frozen law" approach espoused by the former school of thought, arguing that treaties must be interpreted in light of the evolving practice of states parties to them. And such state practice, since 1945, has largely been consistent with a relatively restrictive right of self-defence, in line with the language of Article 51.[232]

While a great deal may seem to turn on which of these competing schools of thought has it right, in fact this is a debate that has been almost wholly confined to academic circles. In particular, states purporting to use force in self-defence rarely provide such elaborate doctrinal analyses of the effects of Article 51 or of its relationship with customary international law. Rather, they tend to take shelter in the least controversial aspects of the doctrine.[233] A concrete manifestation of this predilection is that states invariably invoke Article 51 when purporting to act in self-defence, but only exceptionally invoke customary international law explicitly. Still less do they expressly seek to

---

231   It should be noted that most proponents of this school of thought also challenge the open-ended characterization of the pre-1945 right of self-defence advanced by those of the first school.

232   See, for example, Brownlie, above note 7, c. 13; Dinstein, above note 6 at 179–82; Gray, above note 1 at 98–99 and 133–34. See also (albeit taking a more expansive view of the right of self-defence in light of post-1945 state practice) Franck, *Recourse*, above note 59 at 45–51.

233   See Gray, *ibid.* at 95–96.

justify their actions according to pre-1945 standards of international conduct. It is of course possible to read this particular pattern of behaviour in two ways: it either signals that states consider that Article 51 itself defines the right of self-defence; or, rather, that it incorporates customary international law (whether pre- or post-1945) by reference. It does not, therefore, conclusively favour one school of thought over the other. On the other hand and as we shall see below, overall state practice, *opinio juris*, and international jurisprudence in the area of self-defence since 1945 is more readily reconciled with the second school of thought—that is, one advocating a relatively narrow right of self-defence that is consistent with the express terms of Article 51.

c)   Traditional Self-Defence Against Armed Attacks

i)   *Individual Self-Defence*

aa. "Armed Attacks" vs. "Mere Frontier Incidents"
Perhaps the most striking feature of Article 51 is its apparent limitation of states' inherent right of self-defence to situations where an "armed attack" occurs. Particularly troubling for the lawyer is that this language does not mirror the "threat or use of force" formulation found in Article 2(4). Nor does Article 51 otherwise posit a violation of Article 2(4) by an aggressor state as a sufficient condition for the lawful use of force in self-defence. This raises the prospect of a legal asymmetry between the scope of Articles 2(4) and 51 respectively; that is, that not all violations of Article 2(4) will necessarily amount to an "armed attack" and thus ground a lawful, forcible response by way of self-defence pursuant to Article 51.

This was in fact precisely the conclusion reached by the ICJ in the *Nicaragua* case.[234] Having first found that the right of self-defence described in Article 51 also exists as a matter of customary international law,[235] the Court addressed the US contention that any uses of force attributable to it were justifiable exercises of a right of collective self-defence on behalf of El Salvador, Honduras, and Costa Rica.[236] In particular, the US claimed that Nicaragua had supplied arms to armed opposition groups in El Salvador, and had mounted a number of armed transborder incursions of its own into neighbouring Costa Rica and Honduras. This, the US claimed, gave the target states as well as the US

---

234   *Nicaragua*, above note 42.
235   *Ibid.* at para. 193.
236   We will return to the collective aspect of self-defence in Section D(3)(c)(ii), below in this chapter.

(acting collectively with them) the right to respond forcibly by way of self-defence.

The Court accepted that arms had indeed been routed through Nicaragua's territory to an armed rebel group in El Salvador (although it was not satisfied that Nicaragua was itself responsible for this supply), and that Nicaragua was responsible for a number of direct military incursions into Costa Rica and Honduras.[237] The issue, however, was whether any of these occurrences could be characterized as an "armed attack" giving rise to a right of self-defence. On this point, the Court found it "necessary to distinguish the most grave forms of the use of force (those constituting an armed attack) from other less grave forms."[238] It accordingly drew a distinction between an operation which "because of its scale and effects, would [be] classified as an armed attack rather than as a mere frontier incident."[239] Moreover, the Court held that while the provision of weapons or logistical or other support to rebels may constitute a threat or use of force, it will not as a general rule amount to an armed attack.[240]

In other words, "armed attack" as used in Article 51 is a narrower legal concept than a "threat or use of force" as used in Article 2(4). Or, thinking of it from a slightly different angle, only a subset of "threats or uses of force" contrary to Article 2(4) also rise, by virtue of their gravity or "scale and effects," to the level of "armed attacks" justifying resort to self-defence under Article 51. The remainder are "mere frontier incidents"—perhaps violations of Article 2(4), but not sufficiently grave to warrant a forcible self-help response by the victim state.

The distinction thus drawn by the ICJ in *Nicaragua* has been heavily criticized by a number of commentators on various policy grounds.[241] It has been pointed out that the dividing line between armed attacks and mere frontier incidents is vague and thus not particularly helpful

---

237 *Nicaragua*, above note 42 at para. 164.

238 *Ibid.* at para. 191.

239 *Ibid.* at para. 195.

240 *Ibid.*

241 See, for example, T.M. Franck, "Some Observations on the ICJ's Procedural and Substantive Innovations" (1987) 81 A.J.I.L. 116; R. Higgins, *Problems and Process: International Law and How We Use It* (Oxford: Clarendon Press, 1994) at 251; N. Moore, "The *Nicaragua* Case and the Deterioration of World Order" (1987) 81 A.J.I.L. 151; R. St. J. Macdonald, "The *Nicaragua* Case: New Answers to Old Questions" (1986) 24 Can. Y.B. Int'l L. 127; Dinstein, above note 6 at 194–96; O. Schachter, "In Defense of International Rules on the Use of Force" (1986) 53 U. Chicago L. Rev. 113; J.L. Hargrove, "The *Nicaragua* Judgment and the Future of the Law of Force and Self-Defense" (1987) 81 A.J.I.L. 135; Reisman, above note 139.

in a self-help context. Some have argued that there is no need for such a distinction, given that it is well-established that only necessary and proportionate force may be used in self-defence in any event. Moreover, Article 51 itself contains no hint of a distinction between more or less grave armed attacks. It has even been suggested that the distinction effectively authorizes sustained, low-level uses of force which, taken singly, would not constitute armed attacks and thus could not be met with any effective response.[242]

On the other hand, it has been observed that as self-defence is prone to abuse, its availability should be strictly limited to circumstances that truly warrant it.[243] Some have also pointed out that the ICJ did not invent the distinction between grave and less grave uses of force, but that such a distinction clearly already existed in customary international law. For example, Article 2 of the *Definition of Aggression* clearly includes a *de minimis* element in excluding acts which are "not of sufficient gravity" from the concept of aggression. And while it might be argued that there is no necessary correlation between the concepts of aggression and armed attack, in fact the General Assembly debates leading to adoption of Article 2 reveal quite extensive discussion of the distinction between serious armed attacks and "frontier incidents," as well as a general consensus among participants that the latter should not trigger a right of forcible, unilateral response on the part of the target state.[244]

Unfortunately, beyond the above brief references to "most grave" and "less grave" uses of force, the ICJ in *Nicaragua* did not elaborate on the nature of the threshold that separates armed attacks from mere frontier incidents.[245] Similarly, it did not clearly identify factors, other than an attack's "scale and effects," that might be considered in assessing whether that threshold has been exceeded in any particular case.[246]

---

242 It should be noted, however, that the Court in *Nicaragua* did contemplate cumulative assessment of small-scale attacks in deciding whether the Nicaraguan actions amounted to an armed attack: see *Nicaragua*, above note 42 at para. 231. See also *Case Concerning Oil Platforms (Islamic Republic of Iran v. United States of America)*, [2003] I.C.J. Rep. 161 at para. 64 [*Oil Platforms*].

243 *Nicaragua, ibid.* at 543, Jennings J. (dissenting), addressing collective self-defence in particular.

244 See Gray, above note 1 at 148–51.

245 In subsequent cases, the ICJ has merely repeated the nature and importance of the distinction in the same terms as it used in *Nicaragua*: see, for example, *Oil Platforms*, above note 242 at para. 51; *DRC v. Uganda*, above note 166 at paras. 165 and 304.

246 See *Nicaragua*, above note 42 at para. 195. Note however the Court's cryptic association of armed attacks with operations on a "significant scale": see *ibid.*

However, in reaching its conclusions, the Court did make a passing, unexplained reference to the potential relevance of an alleged aggressor state's "motivations" in deciding whether its actions amounted to an armed attack.[247] While no more was said on that point in *Nicaragua*, precisely such a consideration proved pivotal in the later *Oil Platforms* case between Iran and the US.[248]

The *Oil Platforms* case arose from events occurring in the Persian Gulf during the Iran-Iraq war of 1980-88. In the course of that conflict, both Iran and Iraq regularly attacked shipping in the Gulf, including merchant oil tankers sailing under the flags of neutral states. Some such states therefore sought greater protection for their ships by having them reflagged to powerful naval states (such as the US), which in turn sent naval task forces to the Gulf to guarantee their safety. Two incidents in particular gave rise to the proceedings in this case. First, in October 1987, a Kuwaiti-owned oil tanker sailing under the US flag in Kuwaiti waters was hit by a surface-to-surface missile, which caused damage to the ship and injury to six crew-members. Second, in April 1988, a US warship struck a mine in international waters, sustaining serious damage and injuries to ten of its crew-members. Within a few days of each incident, the US, attributing both the missile attack and the presence of the mine to Iran, responded by attacking and either destroying or very seriously damaging a number of Iranian oil platforms. In the Security Council and in the subsequent proceedings before the ICJ, the US claimed that Iranian military authorities had used the platforms either to stage or support the attacks on its vessels as well as other attacks against neutral shipping in the Gulf.

On the critical issue of whether the actions attributed by the US to Iran could, either singly or cumulatively, be considered "armed attacks" justifying self-defence, the Court placed particular emphasis on whether it had been established that Iran *intended* to attack the US specifically. The Court in particular noted that the distance from which the missile had apparently been fired, in the first incident, was too great to have been aimed at a US vessel specifically, rather than "some target in Kuwaiti waters."[249] Similarly, it stressed that there was no evidence that any mines laid by Iran had been "aimed specifically" at the

---

247   *Ibid.* at para. 231: "Very little information is however available to the Court as to the circumstances of these incursions [by Nicaragua into the territory of Costa Rica and Honduras] *or their possible motivations*, which renders it difficult to decide whether they may be treated for legal purposes as amounting, singly or collectively, to an 'armed attack' ..." [emphasis added].

248   *Oil Platforms*, above note 242.

249   *Ibid.* at para. 64.

US or laid with the "specific intention of harming ... United States ves-sels."[250] On this basis, the Court concluded that "these incidents do not seem to the Court to constitute an armed attack on the United States, of the kind that the Court, in [*Nicaragua*], qualified as a 'most grave' form of the use of force...."[251]

It would therefore appear that only an attack intentionally aimed at a specific state can amount to an armed attack against that state en-titling it to use force by way of self-defence. This may be sensible in that one state's accidental or unintended uses of force against another should not furnish grounds for a military escalation of the situation. However, the ICJ's ruling in *Oil Platforms* seems to go further. It implies that a use of force by one state aimed intentionally but indiscriminately at a number of others ("some target in Kuwaiti waters") cannot be charac-terized as an armed attack against any one of them—even an affected one—justifying the use force in self-defence. The Court did not explain why this should be so. That intention to strike a state should be relevant in assessing the gravity of a use of force seems self-evident;[252] why that intention must relate to a *specific* state, rather than *any* state, does not.

In summary, it appears that a legal distinction exists between a "most grave" and "less grave" breach of Article 2(4). In particular, only the former may constitute an "armed attack" within the meaning of Article 51 justifying a responsive use of force in self-defence.[253] Less certain, however, is how precisely one distinguishes between the two categories of use of force. Certainly, the specific intentions of the at-tacker, as well as the scale and effects of the attack, will be relevant considerations. However, it remains unclear whether an intentional but indiscriminate attack, even one on a massive scale causing devastating effects, can ever amount to a "most grave" use of force. Similarly, there is uncertainty as to the point at which an attack's scale and effects suf-fice to make it "most grave," as opposed to "less grave." On the latter point, it has plausibly been suggested that a sufficiently grave use of force for these purposes is one that causes human casualties or serious

---

250 *Ibid.*

251 *Ibid.*

252 Indeed, during the UN General Assembly debates that led to adoption of the *Definition of Aggression*, many states took the position that an act of aggression could only be committed intentionally: see B.B. Ferencz, *Defining International Aggression, the Search for World Peace: A Documentary History and Analysis*, vol. 2 (Dobbs Ferry, NY: Oceana Publications, 1975) at 31; Dinstein, above note 6 at 128.

253 Remedies for less grave breaches of Article 2(4) must therefore be pursued by other, peaceful, means, unless the Security Council authorizes a forcible response pursuant to Chapter VII of the *UN Charter*, above note 36.

destruction of property.[254] However, it must be admitted that there is little by way of authoritative guidance on this particular aspect of the issue and it is likely that each case will turn on its own particular facts. Coupled with *dicta* by the ICJ in *Nicaragua* to the effect that "it is the State which is the victim of an armed attack which must form and declare the view that it has been so attacked,"[255] this likely means that the occurrence of an armed attack in any particular situation will often be in the eye of the beholder.

bb. Attributability

A constant theme that runs throughout the cases addressing the use of force in self-defence is the requirement that the armed attack being defended against be attributable to the state against which force in self-defence is directed. At some level this is mere logical necessity: it would make little sense to assert a right to use force in self-defence against a state that is not responsible for the armed attack to which one is responding. In what sense would such a use of force be defensive? Moreover, such a right, were it to exist, would be a prescription for the rapid and uncontrollable spread of international armed conflict. The prohibition in Article 2(4) of the *UN Charter* would effectively be gutted almost as soon as even one state mounted an armed attack against another.

It may be that the self-evident nature of these considerations explains why Article 51 does not explicitly set out such a requirement of attributability. In any case, the requirement appears to be firmly anchored in customary international law. States invariably, when purporting to use force in self-defence against other states, allege that they have been the victim of an armed attack by the state or states against which they, in response, are using force. They rarely, if ever, assert a right to use force against a state not responsible for an armed attack against them.[256]

Moreover, as suggested above, the ICJ has consistently insisted that a state invoking a right of self-defence against another state adduce evidence that an armed attack is attributable to the latter. For example, in *Nicaragua*, the availability to the US of the plea of self-defence against Nicaragua turned critically on whether the cross-border flow of arms into El Salvador, or military incursions into Honduras and Costa Rica, were imputable to Nicaragua.[257] In *Oil Platforms*, the Court rejected the

---

254 Dinstein, above note 6 at 193.
255 *Nicaragua*, above note 42 at para. 195.
256 The distinct issue of the purported use of force in self-defence against a non-state actor is addressed in Section D(3)(d)(ii), below in this chapter.
257 See *Nicaragua*, above note 42 at paras 155, 160, 164, and 230–231.

US claim that its attacks on the Iranian oil platforms were acts of self-defence primarily on the basis that the US could not prove that Iran specifically was responsible for the firing of the missile or the laying of the mine that damaged the US vessels. In doing so, the Court expressly formulated the burden of proof borne by the US in terms of "proof of the existence of an armed attack *by Iran*."[258] Most recently, in *DRC v. Uganda*,[259] where Uganda sought to justify its unauthorized military presence on the territory of the Democratic Republic of the Congo (DRC) as an act of self-defence, the Court rejected the argument on the basis that Uganda had failed to show that it had been the subject of an armed attack specifically attributable to the DRC.[260]

The usual question in this area, therefore, is not whether an armed attack must be attributable to a state before force may be used against it in self-defence. Rather, the issue is the basis upon which an armed attack may or may not be attributed to any given state. The general approach taken by the ICJ to this question has been to rely on general principles of attributability derived from the law of state responsibility.[261] As we shall see in the next chapter, these principles provide that a state may be held responsible, not only for the acts of its own organs and agencies, but also, in certain circumstances, for acts committed by persons or entities with no official ties to it.[262]

It should however be noted that, in addition to such extended notions of attributability found in the general law of state responsibility, the *Friendly Relations Declaration*[263] and the *Definition of Aggression*[264] also proscribe a number of state activities that only indirectly involve the use of force. For example, the *Friendly Relations Declaration* includes, as a prohibited use of force, "organizing or encouraging the organization of irregular forces or armed bands, including mercenaries, for incursion into the territory of another state," as well as "organizing, instigating, assisting or participating in acts of civil strife or terrorist acts in another state or acquiescing in organized activities within its

---

258 See *Oil Platforms*, above note 242 at para. 61 [emphasis added]. See also *ibid.* at paras. 57, 64, and 72.
259 *DRC v. Uganda*, above note 166.
260 *Ibid.* at paras. 131–35, 146, 301, and 303–4.
261 For a critique of the application of these principles in the specific context of self-defence against terrorist acts, see Tal Becker, *Terrorism and the State: Rethinking the Rules of State Responsibility* (Oxford: Hart, 2006).
262 For detailed discussion of these principles, including their application by the Court to the availability of the plea of self-defence in *Nicaragua*, see further below, Chapter 12, Section A(4)(b).
263 *Friendly Relations Declaration*, above note 61.
264 *Definition of Aggression*, above note 87.

territory directed towards the commission of such acts, when the acts referred to in the present paragraph involve a threat or use of force."[265] Similarly, the *Definition of Aggression* includes the following in its non-exhaustive enumeration of acts of aggression: "The sending by or on behalf of a State of armed bands, groups, irregulars or mercenaries, which carry out acts of armed force against another State of such gravity as to amount to the acts listed above, or its substantial involvement therein."[266] These provisions have been found by the ICJ to be declaratory of customary international law.[267] However they do not, strictly speaking, set out rules of attributability, but rather include, *within* the concepts of the use of force and aggression, a number of state actions that in themselves involve no use of force at all (organizing, instigating, assisting, sending, acquiescing). Classifying such actions as forcible is nevertheless justifiable because of their connection to the use of force (incursion, acts of civil strife, terrorist acts, acts of armed force) by non-state actors.

Thus a state may, in certain circumstances, be found to have committed, or to be responsible for, an armed attack even if it or its armed forces have not in fact directly used force against another state at all. As a result, it may lawfully be the object of the use of force, in self-defence, by the attacked state. In short, the requirement that an armed attack be attributable to the state against which force in self-defence is directed does not necessarily act as a legal shield against such force merely because that state did not itself directly participate in the armed attack.

cc. Necessity and Proportionality

To date we have been focusing on the legal characteristics of an "armed attack" that justifies the use of force in self-defence. We now turn to a consideration of the legal characteristics of the attacked state's lawful response to such an attack.

Article 51 does not explicitly set out any legal requirements pertaining to the permissible nature or scope of actions that may be taken in self-defence. However, it is universally accepted by states and commentators alike that customary international law requires that all acts in self-defence be (1) necessary to one's defence and (2) proportionate to the armed attack against which one is defending oneself.[268]

---

265 *Friendly Relations Declaration*, above note 61, Principle 1.
266 *Definition of Aggression*, above note 87, Article 3(g).
267 See, for example, *Nicaragua*, above note 42 at para. 195; *DRC v. Uganda*, above note 166 at paras. 162 and 300.
268 See, generally, Dinstein, above note 6 at 208–11; Gray, above note 1 at 120–26.

These requirements are sometimes traced to correspondence exchanged between the United States and the United Kingdom in connection with the so-called *Caroline* incident of 1837. In 1837, Canada (then under British sovereignty) was the scene of rebellion, which was being fomented in part by a number of American nationals. The *Caroline* was an American ship being used to supply the rebels and American volunteers. In late 1837, the British Navy decided to put a stop to this activity. While the *Caroline* was docked in American waters, British forces boarded her, set her alight and sent her over Niagara Falls, killing two American citizens in the process. The American government protested these actions to the British Government. In doing so it laid out what it deemed at the time to be the conditions controlling the legality of a state's resort to force in self-defence. According to the American diplomatic note, the right to use force in self-defence only arose if the need to do so was "instant, overwhelming, leaving no choice of means and no moment for deliberation." It added that any actions taken in such circumstances must not be "unreasonable or excessive."[269] Significantly, the British agreed with the American statement of the applicable legal principles, although they did differ on their application to the facts of the case.[270]

The requirements thus set out—that a use of force in self-defence must be necessary and proportionate if it is to be considered lawful—have been repeatedly asserted and applied by the ICJ.[271] The ICJ stated these conditions particularly forcefully in the *Nuclear Weapons Advisory Opinion*.[272]

> The submission of the exercise of the right of self-defence to the conditions of necessity and proportionality is a rule of customary international law. As the Court stated in [*Nicaragua*]: 'there is a specific rule whereby self-defence would warrant only measures which are proportional to the armed attack and necessary to respond to it, a rule well established in customary international law.' This dual condition applies equally to Article 51 of the *Charter* whatever the means of force employed.[273]

It seems relatively uncontroversial that necessity in this context means that force used in self-defence must not be retaliatory or punitive.

---

269 Letter from Mr. Webster to Mr. Fox, 24 April 1841, reproduced in *The Caroline* (1837), 2 Moore 409.
270 Letter from Lord Ashburton to Mr. Webster, 28 July 1842, reproduced in *ibid*.
271 See, for example, *Nicaragua*, above note 42 at para. 176, *Oil Platforms*, above note 242 at para. 76, *DRC v Uganda*, above note 166 at para. 147.
272 *Nuclear Weapons Advisory Opinion*, above note 73.
273 *Ibid*. at para. 41.

In other words, the necessity requirement limits the permissible aims of force used in self-defence to halting or repelling an armed attack. Similarly, it is generally agreed that proportionality does not require a precise tabulation or balancing of targets, weapons, or means of warfare. Rather, the overall operation undertaken in self-defence must be in reasonable proportion to the overall threat being met.[274] Beyond these very general considerations, however, there is very little clear guidance as to the substantive content of each requirement. Indeed, the articulation of clear legal standards often appears to be eschewed in favour of an assessment of the necessity and proportionality of a state's actions in self-defence on the specific facts and circumstances of each case.[275]

The ICJ has occasionally been more forthcoming, however. For example, in *Nicaragua*,[276] the Court considered whether US actions in 1981 could be considered necessary responses to alleged support by Nicaragua of an armed rebel group in El Salvador. In concluding they could not, the Court underlined that the armed insurgency in El Salvador was no longer a serious threat by 1981.[277] In other words, a considerable lapse of time between an armed attack and a responsive use of force will tend to cast doubt on the necessity of the latter. On the question of proportionality, however, the Court merely concluded, without further explanation, that the US attacks on Nicaraguan ports and oil installations "could not" be proportionate to Nicaraguan support to the El Salvadoran rebels, whatever its scale.[278]

In *Oil Platforms*,[279] the ICJ elaborated somewhat further on the approach to be taken in assessing necessity. In particular, it rejected the US suggestion that the state invoking self-defence should be accorded a "measure of discretion" in deciding whether force in self-defence is a necessary response to an armed attack. Rather, the Court held that the necessity requirement is both strict and objective, in the sense that the subjective views of the attacked state regarding the necessity of force in self-defence are not determinative.[280] This is not to say, however,

---

274 See, generally, Gray, above note 1 at 121; Dinstein, above note 6 at 209–10; C. Forcese, *National Security Law* (Toronto: Irwin Law, 2007) at 149–51.

275 For example, the ICJ in the *Nuclear Weapons Advisory Opinion* refused to find that the use of nuclear weapons in self-defence would necessarily be disproportionate, suggesting rather that such an assessment will always depend on the surrounding circumstances: *Nuclear Weapons Advisory Opinion*, above note 73 at para. 43.

276 *Nicaragua*, above note 42.

277 *Ibid.* at para. 237.

278 *Ibid.*

279 *Oil Platforms*, above note 242.

280 *Ibid.* at para. 73.

that its views are entirely irrelevant. Indeed the Court considered such views, expressed contemporaneously with the actions taken in self-defence, to be highly significant. In particular, the Court noted that the US had not complained to Iran about military activities emanating from the platforms before or at the time it attacked them, which tended to undermine its claim that their near-destruction was a measure necessary to its defence. Moreover, the US was on record as having attacked at least one of the platforms as a "target of opportunity," further undermining its claim that such an attack was a strictly necessary act of self-defence.[281]

These findings tend to underline not only the importance of one's contemporaneous statements to subsequent assessments of the necessity of one's actions. They seem also to suggest that necessity must be demonstrated in connection with the specific targets or measures chosen. An important question, in other words, is whether either the nature of the force used or the target against which it is directed advances the only permissible goals of self-defence; that is, to end or repel an armed attack.

The ICJ's analysis of proportionality in *Oil Platforms* was, by contrast, quite conclusory. In particular, the Court suggested that the destruction of several oil platforms might be considered proportional to the missile attack attributed by the US to Iran. On the other hand, it found that the same type of response to the mining of a US warship could not be proportional. This was so notwithstanding that in both cases the attacks being responded to involved damage and injuries but the loss neither of the vessels nor of life. No explanation for these seemingly contradictory conclusions was offered, other than a cryptic reference to "the circumstances of this case."[282] This again seems to underline that the determination of the proportionality of the use of force in self-defence in any given situation will almost always, ultimately, be a heavily fact-dependent exercise.

dd. The Duty to Report to the Security Council

Article 51 sets out a notable procedural requirement: that "[m]easures taken by Members in the exercise of this right of self-defence ... be immediately reported to the Security Council." This provision prompts a number of questions. Does the legality of one's use of force in self-defence depend on the making of such a report? Or does the failure to re-

---

281 *Ibid.* at para. 76.
282 *Ibid.* at para. 77.

port simply give rise to a breach of a procedural treaty obligation rather than an unlawful use of force? What is the purpose of such a report?

At least on the first of these—the substantive legal consequences of a failure to report to the Security Council—the ICJ has provided some guidance. In *Nicaragua*, the Court adopted a middle line between deeming such a failure to vitiate the lawfulness of one's actions in self-defence, on the one hand, and deeming it a mere technical breach of no significance to the legality of one's use of force, on the other. The Court's starting point was that, because the reporting requirement relates to an institution (the Security Council) established by treaty (the *UN Charter*), it is not a requirement of customary international law. It follows, therefore, that in customary international law "it is not a condition of the lawfulness of the use of force in self-defence" that such a report be made.[283]

However, this does not mean that a failure to report in accordance with Article 51 is wholly irrelevant to the legality of one's actions in self-defence. In particular, such a failure may provide indirect evidence of whether the acting state in fact considered itself to be acting in self-defence. In support of this position, the Court noted that the US had itself in other contexts relied upon a state's failure to report to the Security Council as evidence of its lack of *bona fides* in invoking self-defence. The fact that the US had not in this case reported its activities against Nicaragua to the Security Council pursuant to Article 51 was thus considered relevant by the Court in assessing whether the US itself considered such activities to be necessary in self-defence.[284]

This same approach was taken by the ICJ in *DRC v. Uganda*.[285] It will be recalled that Uganda justified, as self-defence, its continued military presence on the territory of the DRC following the latter's withdrawal of its consent to such presence. The Court, in weighing Uganda's motivations (in particular whether it considered itself to be the subject of an armed attack), drew a negative inference from Uganda's failure to make the requisite report to the Security Council of actions taken in self-defence.[286]

In short, while the Article 51 reporting requirement is a formality, in the sense that its breach does not in itself vitiate the legality of one's actions in self-defence, such a breach may nevertheless have an indirect effect on the substantive evaluation of a state's claim that it was acting in self-defence.

---

283 *Nicaragua*, above note 42 at para. 235.
284 *Ibid.*
285 *DRC v. Uganda*, above note 166.
286 *Ibid.* at paras. 145–47.

The impact of the Court's reasoning on this point has been dramatic. States have become scrupulous in reporting their military actions in purported self-defence to the Security Council, so much so that some commentators have suggested that such reports have become merely ritualistic incantations meant to cloak military actions with the outward appearance of legality.[287] They may have lost, therefore, much of their probative value. By the same token, such uniform state practice may in fact have caused the requirement to become, since the *Nicaragua* decision, an element of the customary international law of self-defence.

ee. "Until the Security Council Has Taken Measures...."
A final significant element of Article 51 is its apparent indication that states' inherent right of self-defence only subsists "until the Security Council has taken measures necessary to maintain international peace and security." A series of questions arise when considering the effect of this clause. Among them: what are "measures necessary to maintain international peace and security"? Who determines whether they have been taken? What if the Security Council takes some measures but does not fully address a state's perceived security or defence needs? Does the right of self-defence come to an end when the Security Council first begins to take measures, or only after international peace and security have been "maintained"?

The answers to many of these questions will depend on whether one views Article 51 as consecrating an inalienable right for states to act unilaterally in self-help; or, rather, as preserving self-defence as a merely residuary, stop-gap necessity within the *UN Charter*'s broader scheme of the collectivization of the use of force in international relations.[288] The views of commentators are divided on this issue.[288] Some contend that both the overall structure of the *Charter*—which is geared towards the centralization of the use of force—as well as the

---

287 See Gray, above note 1 at 101–4.
288 Contrasting arguments are put forward, for example, by A. Chayes, "The Use of Force in the Persian Gulf" in Damrosch & Scheffer, above note 139 at 3; K.S. Elliott, "The New World Order and the Right of Self-Defense in the *United Nations Charter*" (1991–92) 15 Hast. Int'l & Comp. L. Rev. 55; O. Schachter, "United Nations Law in the Gulf Conflict" (1991) 85 A.J.I.L. 452; E.V. Rostow, "Until What? Enforcement Action or Collective Self-Defense?" (1991) 85 A.J.I.L. 506; C.H.M. Waldock, "The Regulation of the Use of Force by Individual States in International Law" (1952-II) 81 Rec. des Cours 451 at 496; R. Higgins, *The Development of International Law Through the Political Organs of the United Nations* (London: University Press, 1963) at 198 and 206; T.M. Franck & F. Patel, "UN Police Action in Lieu of War: 'The Old Order Changeth'" (1991) 85 A.J.I.L. 63.

express wording of Article 51 itself—which clearly suggests that the right to act in self-defence is temporary ("until")—lead to the conclusion that the intent was to limit resort to unauthorized force in self-defence as far as possible. In other words, Article 51 only preserves a right for states to use force in self-defence on an urgent basis, pending mobilization of an effective collective security response by the Security Council. Further, in order to forestall potential abuses that may result from a state's unilateral assessment of the situation, they argue that the Security Council itself must have the ultimate authority to determine whether it has taken sufficient measures and that the right of unilateral self-defence in any given case is accordingly at an end.

However, the practice of states and of the Security Council is not so clear. It certainly seems incontrovertible that if the Security Council decides to impose a ceasefire or other measures that clearly indicate that a state's right to use force in self-defence is at an end, the state in question would be legally obliged to comply and would be acting outside Article 51 if it failed to do so.[289] The difficulty, however, is that the Security Council is very rarely explicit as to whether a state's right to use force in self-defence has arisen in the first place, much less whether it continues or has rather come to an end in light of measures taken by the Security Council.[290] This has given rise to a number of instances where states continue to act in self-defence notwithstanding the fact that the Security Council has taken at least some measures to address the same situation.[291]

---

289 See Dinstein, above note 6 at 214–15.

290 *Ibid.* A rare example to the contrary is Security Council Resolution 661, which explicitly preserved Kuwait's right of self-defence (against Iraq) notwithstanding the imposition by the Security Council of economic sanctions on Iraq in response to the latter's invasion of Kuwait: see UNSC Res. 661 (1991), U.N. Doc. S/RES/661 (6 August 1990) at para. 9.

291 For example, during the Falklands crisis in 1982, the United Kingdom continued to act in its own defence notwithstanding that the Security Council had adopted Resolution 502 pursuant to Chapter VII. Resolution 502 determined that there had been a breach of the peace, demanded a cessation of hostilities, and demanded withdrawal of Argentine forces from the Falkland Islands: see UNSC Res. 502 (1982), U.N. Doc. S/RES/502 (3 April 1982). The United Kingdom nevertheless took the view that, as long as the islands remained under Argentine occupation, its right of self-defence persisted. Similarly, during the Iran-Iraq War of 1980–88, the Security Council adopted (*inter alia*) Resolution 598, calling for a ceasefire between the belligerents: see UNSC Res. 598 (1987), U.N. Doc. S/RES/598 (20 July 1987). Iran nevertheless persisted in using force, alleging that it was acting pursuant to its continuing right of self-defence. See, generally, Gray, above note 1 at 104–5.

The conclusion to be drawn from such state practice is likely that, unless the Security Council *specifically* determines that sufficient measures have been taken by it and that a state's right of self-defence is therefore spent, a state's right to act in otherwise lawful self-defence does not come to an end merely because the Security Council has taken *some* measures. It should be remembered, however, that even in the face of silence from the Security Council as to the cessation of a state's right to use force in self-defence, the requirement of necessity considered above will likely have a role to play in determining the lawfulness of further such actions.

ii) Collective Self-Defence

So far, we have been focusing on rules applicable to the right of individual self-defence; that is, the right of a state, which is itself the subject of an armed attack, to use force to defend itself. Article 51, however, also refers to an inherent right of "collective self-defence." This should not be confused with the *UN Charter*'s quite distinct "collective security" mechanism, which involves a collective use of force authorized by the Security Council. Rather, "collective self-defence" refers to the right of states, which have not themselves been attacked, to come to the aid of one which has—even in the absence of Security Council authorization.

The impetus for including such a concept in Article 51 came mainly from Latin American states which, under an earlier, regional peace and security arrangement, could call upon one another for assistance in repelling acts of aggression. Its inclusion in the *UN Charter* was much-debated at the time of negotiation of the text of Article 51, given fears that it would either be incompatible with the collective security functions of the Security Council, or would be particularly prone to abuse.[292] That such debate occurred suggests that a right of collective self-defence may not have existed in pre-1945 customary international law.[293] Be that as it may, it appears to have been embraced in state practice and *opinio juris* since 1945,[294] such that by the time of the *Nicaragua* judgment, the ICJ affirmed its existence in customary international law.[295]

---

292 See Franck, *Recourse*, above note 59 at 48–49; Gray, *ibid.* at 137–38.

293 See *Nicaragua*, above note 42, Separate Opinion of Judge Oda at paras. 90–97. But see Bowett, above note 109 at 200–48; I. Brownlie, *Principles of Public International Law*, 6th ed. (Oxford: Oxford University Press, 2003) at 702.

294 The notion of collective self-defence is at the heart, for example, of the NATO regional defence system: see *North Atlantic Treaty*, 34 U.N.T.S. 243 (4 April 1949), Articles 5 and 11.

295 *Nicaragua*, above note 42 at para. 193.

What remained substantially uncertain prior to *Nicaragua*, however, were the precise requirements for valid exercise of the right of collective self-defence. Did states have an autonomous right to come to the aid of a state which had been attacked, or did they have to be invited? Or in the further alternative, would it suffice if a state wishing to come to the assistance of another shared some common interest with the latter? If so, would it have to be shown that that interest was jeopardized by the armed attack before the state wishing to act "collectively" had a right to do so? Perhaps most critically, would a state purporting to act in collective self-defence of another have a right to use force in the territory of the latter? *Nicaragua* definitively resolved all of these issues, and while the ICJ was much criticized in some quarters for taking some liberties with what it found to be settled law, state practice and *opinio juris* have since largely aligned themselves with the judgment's legal findings on collective self-defence.

The essential starting point in *Nicaragua* was that all of the legal requirements we have already reviewed pertaining to the right of individual self-defence under Article 51—the occurrence of an armed attack, attributability, necessity, proportionality, and immediate reporting to the Security Council—apply equally to exercises of the right of collective self-defence. There are, however, additional legal requirements when the state invoking the right of self-defence has not itself been the subject of the armed attack.

In *Nicaragua*, the US did not allege that it had been the victim of an armed attack by Nicaragua. Rather, it alleged that Nicaragua was responsible for armed attacks on El Salvador, Costa Rica, and Honduras, and that US actions against Nicaragua were justified acts of collective self-defence "on behalf of" those states. On this submission, the Court found that a collective right of self-defence can only arise if the state which has been the subject of an armed attack (1) declares that it has been so attacked;[296] and (2) requests the assistance of the third party state which purports to act in its defence.[297] The judgment suggests, in other words, that there is an element of "privity" to the right of self-defence: it arises only as between the victim and perpetrator of an armed attack, unless the former chooses to "share" the right with third parties, by invitation.

As suggested above, these additional requirements of declaration and invitation were widely criticized by many writers in the aftermath

---

296 *Ibid.* at para. 195.

297 *Ibid.* at para. 199. This requirement seemingly applies regardless of whether the acts of purported collective self-defence involve access to the territory of the attacked state. But see Dinstein, above note 6 at 269–70.

of the case.[298] Essentially, the criticisms were threefold. First, however desirable they might be from a policy perspective, the Court offered virtually no authority or support for its conclusion that these requirements existed as a matter of customary international law. Second, it was contended that the requirements were overly formalistic and unrealistic in a conflict situation. Third, by treating the right of collective self-defence as purely derivative of the attacked state's right of individual self-defence, the Court failed to recognize that a third party state might in fact have some interest of its own, or in common with the attacked state, that might justify its intervention without an express invitation.

It seems, however, that most of these objections are either misplaced or exaggerated. First, while it is true that very little authority for its legal conclusions were offered by the Court, in fact they were consistent with the bulk of state practice and *opinio juris* since 1945. The requirement of a request for assistance is a common element of many collective self-defence arrangements in the post-World War II period. Moreover, in virtually every case where a state has invoked a right of collective self-defence since 1945, it has done so on the basis of an express request for assistance from an attacked state.[299]

Second, the ICJ was clearly alive to the fact that excessive formalism could not be expected in times of conflict. In particular, it characterized the requirements of declaration and invitation as being "likely" and "normally" necessary, signalling that extenuating circumstances might have to be taken into account in particular cases. Moreover, in applying the law in this case the Court looked to the conduct of El Salvador, Honduras, and Costa Rica to determine if the requirements had been fulfilled implicitly, rather than insisting on express, formal compliance.[300]

In addition, state practice and *opinio juris* in fact reveal that states invoking collective self-defence almost never claim to be acting to protect some interest of their own, but rather invariably rely on requests for assistance, in one form or another, by states which have been the victim of an armed attack.[301] In other words, the behaviour of states themselves appears to confirm the purely derivative nature of the right

---

298 See the review of the criticisms levelled at this aspect of the Court's decision in Gray, above note 1 at 138–41 and 151–54; and Dinstein, above note 6 at 268–70. Judges Schwebel and Jennings, dissenting, were also critical of the majority's assertion of these requirements.

299 See Gray, *ibid.* at 152–54.

300 See *Nicaragua*, above note 42 at para. 232.

301 See Gray, above note 1 at 154–55.

of collective self-defence. Moreover, nothing prevents an "assisting" state from having mixed or even purely selfish motivations in so acting, as long as its assistance has been invited by the state which has suffered an armed attack.[302]

In general, therefore, whatever its formal defects, the judgment in *Nicaragua* can fairly be said to reflect the requirements of collective self-defence under Article 51 and in customary international law. In short, a third-party state wishing to use force in collective self-defence—that is, to defend a state that has been the subject of an armed attack—may only do so if the latter declares that such an attack has occurred and requests the assistance of the former.

d)   Controversial Aspects of the Right of Self-Defence

i)   *Anticipatory and Pre-emptive Self-Defence*

Having addressed the relatively uncontroversial and generally well-settled aspects of the right of self-defence, we turn now to consider some of its more divisive dimensions. Chief among these is whether the right of self-defence is a strictly reactive one—that is, whether it only arises after an armed attack has already occurred—or whether in some circumstances a state may seek to defend itself by striking first.

In part the issue of whether and in what circumstances states may take proactive military measures to defend themselves from potential attacks is a well-worn issue, a topic of debate since at least the first half of the twentieth century when the unauthorized use of force was generally forbidden in international law. However, the debate has been rekindled in recent years, especially following the September 11, 2001 terrorist attacks on the United States and in light of renewed fears that rogue states and perhaps even terrorists may acquire nuclear weapons or other weapons of mass destruction. These developments have prompted renewed calls by some for recognition of a right to "anticipate" an armed attack before it actually occurs.[303] Others have claimed that an even broader right should exist to use force not only to prevent armed attacks from being carried out, but also to "pre-empt" the emergence of such threats in the first place.[304]

In fact the question whether the use of force in self-defence is permissible before an armed attack has actually occurred takes us back to the (largely academic) debate over the correct interpretation of Article

---

302 See *Nicaragua*, above note 42 at para. 127.

303 See, for example, Franck, *Recourse*, above note 59, c. 7.

304 George W. Bush, "The National Security Strategy of the United States of America" (17 September 2002), online: www.whitehouse.gov/nsc/nss.html at 15.

51 of the *UN Charter* and its relationship to customary international law.[305] It will be recalled that on one side of this debate are scholars who characterize Article 51 as a mere savings clause and argue that the substantive scope of the right of self-defence is found in customary international law.[306] These writers also argue that customary international law recognizes a right of "anticipatory" self-defence in the face of an "imminent" armed attack. They point primarily to the correspondence in the *Caroline* incident,[307] and interpret it as authority for the legality of anticipatory action in the face of a threat that is "instant, overwhelming, leaving no choice of means, and no moment for deliberation."[308] They then rely on a number of instances of state practice since 1945 which they interpret as consistent with such a doctrine and which, they contend, support the continuing existence of a right of anticipatory self-defence in parallel to the more restrictive self-defence doctrine articulated in Article 51.[309]

It will also be recalled that on the other side of this debate are a number of scholars[310] who consider that the effect of Article 51 is not to preserve pre-existing customary international law but rather to supplant it and/or to shape its content since 1945. To the extent that the word "inherent" in Article 51 preserves or imports customary rules on self-defence, they argue that it does so only insofar as such rules are consistent with its other express terms. In particular they focus on the words "if an armed attack occurs." Taken at face value, these words clearly contemplate only a reactive right of self-defence, not one that arises when an armed attack is about to occur or is anticipated. Why would such words have been included in Article 51 if a much broader right was to continue to exist as a matter of customary international law? Finally, they interpret pre-1945 state practice as either irrelevant (in light of the adoption of the *UN Charter*) or inconclusive, and post-

---

305 A useful summary of the main arguments is provided by Gray, above note 1 at 98–99.

306 See Section D(3)(b), above in this chapter; see also authorities cited, above note 230.

307 See the text accompanying notes 269–70, above in this chapter.

308 It seems doubtful, however, that the *Caroline* incident involved an anticipatory use of force, as British forces were responding to prior incursions both by the *Caroline* and American volunteers: see Dinstein, above note 6 at 184–85.

309 See, for example, Waldock, above note 288 at 496–98; Bowett, above note 109 at 187–92; Greenwood, above note 122 at 12–15; Franck, *Recourse*, above note 59 at 99–108.

310 See authorities cited, above note 232.

1945 state practice as wholly insufficient to demonstrate the continuing existence of a right of anticipatory self-defence.[311]

One of the major difficulties in assessing the merits of these differing approaches, or the extent to which they correspond to the actual state of international law, is that the ICJ has never authoritatively addressed the issue of anticipatory self-defence.[312] Moreover, disagreement among states on this very question prevented any clarification of the issue in either the *Friendly Relations Declaration*[313] or the *Definition of Aggression*.[314] Thus, a return to first principles seems to be required and the question therefore turns on one's appreciation of state practice and *opinio juris*. How do states approach Article 51 in this regard? Do they assert and act on a right of anticipatory self-defence notwithstanding its apparent requirement of an armed attack that "occurs"?

Here it must be admitted that the record in favour of a right of anticipatory self-defence is neither clear nor strong.[315] It is true that a number of states (particularly nuclear weapons states) assert, as part of their defence policy, that they reserve the right to use force in anticipatory self-defence.[316] This may be taken as evidence of *opinio juris* which is, however, far from universally or even generally shared. Remarkably, moreover, even states asserting such a policy virtually never act upon it — or, if they do, they tend to deny strenuously that such is the basis for their actions. Consider, for example, the following instances of state practice which are usually put forward by proponents of a right of anticipatory self-defence:

- the US naval blockade of Cuba during the 1962 Cuban missile crisis;
- Israel's strike in 1967 against Egypt, in response to the massing of Egyptian forces along the Israeli border and other Egyptian actions deemed threatening by Israel;
- Iraq's initial strike against Iran which sparked the 1980–88 Iran-Iraq War;
- the 1981 Israeli air strike against an Iraqi nuclear reactor in order to forestall Iraq's development of nuclear weapons;

---

311 See, for example, Brownlie, above note 7 at 257–76; Henkin, above note 108 at 141–49; Gray, above note 1 at 129–33; Dinstein, above note 6 at 182–87.

312 The Court in *Nicaragua* set the issue to one side, as it did not arise on the facts: see *Nicaragua*, above note 42 at para 194. The issue has not squarely been raised in subsequent ICJ cases dealing with the use of force.

313 *Friendly Relations Declaration*, above note 61.

314 *Definition of Aggression*, above note 87.

315 See, generally, Gray, above note 1 at 129–33.

316 See Franck, *Recourse*, above note 59 at 98; Greenwood, above note 122 at 12–14.

- US engagement, while patrolling the Persian Gulf during the 1980–88 Iran-Iraq War, of aircraft and vessels showing "hostile intent," which led to the (erroneous) July 1988 downing by the *USS Vincennes* of a civilian airliner;
- the 1999 extension, by the United States and the United Kingdom, of their air forces' rules of engagement in order to permit anticipatory targeting of Iraqi air defences while enforcing no-fly zones in the north and south of Iraq prior to 2003.[317]

Altogether aside from their rather sparse number, reliance on these examples to support the existence of a customary right of anticipatory self-defence is problematic. During the Cuban missile crisis, the US justified its actions on the basis that it was acting in a regional peacekeeping role, rather than on a right of anticipatory self-defence. In the case of the 1967 Six Days' War between Israel and Egypt, Israel strenuously argued that while it was the first to open fire, it was in fact reacting to a number of Egyptian actions that cumulatively amounted to a prior armed attack. In the case of Iraq's first strike against Iran, while it initially claimed to have acted pursuant to a right of anticipatory self-defence, it rapidly changed its position and insisted that it had been the victim of a prior armed attack by Iran to which it was responding.[318] With respect to Israel's 1981 attack against the Iraqi nuclear reactor, it is true that Israel clearly asserted, for the first time, a right to use force against another state in anticipation of a future armed attack. However, its actions were strongly condemned in the UN General Assembly[319] and unanimously so in the Security Council.[320] In the case of the *Vincennes* incident, the US studiously avoided reliance on any right of anticipatory self-defence in justifying its actions, preferring instead to rely on a somewhat strained argument based on a "pattern" of prior attacks that, cumulatively, justified *responsive* actions in self-defence. Finally, neither the US nor the UK, in justifying their "anticipatory targeting" policy while patrolling Iraqi no-fly zones between 1999 and 2003, clearly relied upon a right to use unauthorized force in anticipatory self-defence. Rather, they argued that they were defending themselves while acting pursuant to Security Council authorization, suggesting that it was the latter that justified any anticipatory action

---

317 See Gray, above note 1 at 130–33; Franck, *Recourse, ibid.* at 99–107.
318 *Contra* the findings of the UN Secretary General: see [1980] United Nations Yearbook at 312.
319 UN General Assembly Resolution 36/27, 13 November 1981, UN Doc. A/RES/36/27 (adopted by a vote of 109 in favour, 2 against and 34 abstentions).
320 UNSC Res. 487, U.N. Doc. S/RES/487 (19 June 1981).

rather than customary international law.[321] Moreover, they both took the position that "radar locks" on their aircraft by Iraqi air defence installations in fact constituted the commencement of an armed attack justifying *responsive* force in self-defence.[322]

What is striking about all of this—with the exception of Israel's stance against Iraq in 1981—is that it at best evidences *opinio juris* divorced from state practice, or state practice divorced from *opinio juris*. Given that customary international law is formed or evidenced by *general and consistent* state practice *accompanied* by *opinio juris*, it must be admitted that the evidence supporting a customary right of anticipatory self-defence is very scanty indeed.

Before leaving this topic, mention should also be made of a new twist in the academic debate over anticipatory self-defence prompted by the US National Security Policy[323] announced in the wake of the September 11, 2001 attacks on the World Trade Center and the Pentagon. Two aspects of that Policy are particularly germane here. First, it asserts that "for centuries, international law recognized that nations need not suffer an armed attack before they can lawfully take action to defend themselves against forces that present an imminent danger of attack." On its face, this is an assertion of the classic anticipatory self-defence doctrine, in line with the stringent *Caroline* criteria noted above. In itself, this is not a new element of US defence policy but rather a reiteration of long-standing US *opinio juris* on the matter—albeit *opinio juris* as yet unimplemented in its own post-1945 state practice, as seen above.

What is new, however, is the call for "adaptation" of the imminence requirement to permit uses of force in self-defence to "pre-empt emerging threats," even if uncertainty remains as to the "time and place of the enemy's attack." In other words, the Policy calls for a right of "pre-emptive self-defence" that would go beyond anticipation of an immin-

---

321 The *UN Charter*, in setting out the Security Council's Chapter VII powers, explicitly contemplates an anticipatory element to those powers. In particular, Article 39 grants to the Security Council the power to determine the existence of not only breaches of the peace, but also *threats* to the peace. Similarly, Article 42, the provision by which the Security Council may decide upon measures involving the use of force, allows it to do so for purposes not only of restoring international peace and security but also of *maintaining* it. In other words, the Security Council may authorize forcible measures before any breach of the peace has occurred but where one is merely threatened: see Dinstein, above note 6 at 283–84.

322 See, generally, Gray, above note 1 at 130–33.

323 See above note 304.

ent attack and allow states to use force against one another to prevent threats from emerging in the first place.

It is important to underscore that the Policy does not claim that such a right currently exists. It would be surprising if it did, as the pre-emptive doctrine it advocates is essentially the one put forward by Israel to justify its attack against Iraq in 1981 and that was so widely condemned at the time (including by the United States).[324] Rather, the Policy calls for adaptation of the law along such lines, which necessarily implies that pre-emptive action of the sort contemplated remains illegal under current international law.[325]

Significantly, even traditional US allies responded coolly to this call for reform; other states have reacted with open hostility.[326] This was evident in the developments that immediately preceded the 2003 invasion of Iraq by the US, the UK, and their allies. Among the arguments advanced by the US to galvanize support for the invasion was the need to deprive Iraq of weapons of mass destruction — that is, to pre-empt a threat that might become imminent if left unchecked. Many states openly rejected this as an inadequate justification for the invasion, and even NATO members were so deeply split on the issue that NATO failed to endorse the use of force against Iraq, on a pre-emptive or any other basis.[327] Moreover, even those states supporting the invasion carefully avoided relying on any doctrine of pre-emptive (or, for that matter, anticipatory) self-defence as the legal basis for such action. In particular, both the UK and Australia (the only states, other than the US, contributing forces at the outset of Operation Iraqi Freedom) relied exclusively on alleged prior authorization of the use of force by the Security Council as their sole legal basis for acting.[328] Even the United States in the end chose to rely primarily on implied Security Council authorization as the legal basis for its actions, adding only a cursory and ambiguous assertion of a right to defend itself "from the threat posed by Iraq."[329]

---

324 See above note 320.

325 For discussion of the current existence of a right of pre-emptive self-defence, see W.M. Reisman & A. Armstrong, "The Past and Future of the Claim of Preemptive Self-Defence" (2006) 100 A.J.I.L. 525; J.T. Gathii, "Assessing Claims of a New Doctrine of Pre-emptive War under the Doctrine of Sources" (2005) 43 Osgoode Hall L.J. 67; M. Bothe, "Terrorism and the Legality of Pre-Emptive Force" (2003) 14 E.J.I.L. 227.

326 See Gray, above note 1 at 177–84.

327 *Ibid.* at 181.

328 *Ibid.* at 182–83.

329 Letter dated 20 March 2003 from the Permanent Representative of the United States of America to the United Nations Addressed to the President of the Se-

Even assuming an international legal right exists to use force in self-defence before the occurrence of an armed attack, therefore, it seems extremely unlikely that it extends to anything more remote than an imminent attack. The question, however, is whether the call by the US for a more extensive right of "pre-emptive self-defence" will, if sustained, serve in time to make the doctrine of "anticipatory self-defence" against imminent attacks more palatable to states. If it does, and states choose (contrary to their practice to date) to assert and act upon such a right, it may be that the ICJ will at last have an opportunity to address, and provide some legal guidance on, the issue.

ii)   A Right of Self-Defence Against Non-State Actors?

The traditional law on the use of force that we have been reviewing to date is exclusively directed at states. As made plain by the language used in the *UN Charter*,[330] the *Friendly Relations Declaration*,[331] the *Definition of Aggression*,[332] and the relevant jurisprudence, its sole *raison-d'être* is to constrain and, exceptionally, to authorize or excuse resort to armed force by states against other states.

This essentially state-centred focus of the *jus ad bellum* of course flows from its keystone: Article 2(4) of the *UN Charter*, which is explicitly addressed to UN members (that is, states) alone and just as explicitly limits the scope of its prohibition to the threat or use of force against states. For added measure it explicitly addresses only the use of force by states "in their international relations." Similarly, Article 51 only speaks of an inherent right of self-defence enjoyed by UN members (that is, states).[333] Interestingly, however, while self-defence within the meaning of Article 51 may only be exercised by states, Article 51 does not expressly stipulate that it may only be invoked *against* states. Nevertheless, as Article 51 does not exhaustively define the right of self-defence—as evidenced, for example, by its failure to advert to the universally recognized requirements of necessity and proportionality reviewed above—this omission cannot be taken as proof that there is no such limitation.

This issue has assumed new prominence in the wake of the September 11, 2001 terrorist attacks against the United States. As those attacks were perpetrated by a non-state entity, the Al Qaeda terrorist organization, having its base of operations in Afghanistan, the question

---

curity Council, UN Doc. S/2003/351 (21 March 2003).
330 *UN Charter*, above note 36.
331 *Friendly Relations Declaration*, above note 61.
332 *Definition of Aggression*, above note 87.
333 See *Nicaragua*, above note 42 at para. 193.

that arose was whether the United States and its allies could lawfully use force against Al Qaeda in Afghanistan in the exercise of their inherent right of individual or collective self-defence. The answer immediately and overwhelmingly given by states to that question was "yes."[334] The US, the UK, and many other states that played a supporting role in the invasion of Afghanistan following the September 11, 2001 attacks expressly justified their actions as an exercise of self-defence. General Assembly Resolutions 1368[335] and 1373,[336] in condemning the September 11 attacks, expressly referred to the inherent right of self-defence, implicitly but clearly suggesting that that right in fact arose in those circumstances. NATO, the Organization of American States, and the European Union, along with many states, explicitly endorsed the existence of a right of self-defence in the circumstances.[337]

None of this is surprising or novel in itself. Ever since the adoption of the *Friendly Relations Declaration*, it has been clear that a terrorist attack from abroad can give rise to a classic right of self-defence under Article 51. In particular, the *Friendly Relations Declaration*, in elaborating on the content of the prohibition of the use of force by states, asserts that "every state has the duty to refrain from organizing, instigating, assisting or participating in ... terrorist acts in another state or acquiescing in organized activities within its territory directed towards the commission of such acts...."[338] In other words, as long as there is some state complicity—amounting at minimum to "acquiescence in organized activities within its territory"—in a terrorist organization's attack against another state, and that attack amounts to an "armed attack" because of its scale or effects, the traditional law of self-defence allows the attacked state to use force in and against the territory of the complicit state in order to counter the terrorist threat.[339]

This was precisely the situation in the particular case of Al Qaeda and Afghanistan in 2001. It was widely known that the Taliban government of Afghanistan had at least acquiesced in, and probably supported, Al Qaeda's activities within its borders. In its Article 51 letter to the Security Council reporting its use of force in and against Afghanistan in self-defence, the US explicitly claimed that the Taliban had "supported" Al Qaeda, and that the September 11 attacks had been "made possible" by the Taliban's decision to allow Al Qaeda to use Afghan

---

334 See Gray, above note 1 at 164–65.
335 UNSC Res. 1368 (2001), above note 207.
336 UNSC Res. 1373 (2001), above note 205.
337 See Dinstein, above note 6 at 207–8; Gray, above note 1 at 164–71.
338 *Friendly Relations Declaration*, above note 61, Principle 1.
339 See further Section D(3)(c)(i)(bb), above in this chapter.

territory as a base of operations.[340] Similarly, in its Article 51 letter to the Security Council, the UK relied on the "close alliance" between Al Qaeda and the Taliban, and asserted that the latter had "supported" the former.[341] In short, the invocation of the right of self-defence to justify the invasion of Afghanistan in response to the armed attack by Al Qaeda against the United States was consistent with long-established rules concerning the use of force and state responsibility.[342]

Some commentators, however, have gone much further.[343] They interpret the Afghan case as either evidencing or establishing a right for states to use force in self-defence against a terrorist organization itself, a right that can be exercised in the territory of another state *regardless* of any complicity between that state and the organization. They argue that all that is required to give rise to such a right is that the state from whose territory a terrorist attack originates fails, for whatever reason, to prevent it. In such a case, the "host" state must acquiesce in the use of force, in its territory, by the attacked state against the terrorist organization.

This, to put it mildly, would be a radical rewriting of the law governing the use of force in general and self-defence in particular. It requires acceptance of at least three novel propositions of international law; namely, that (1) there exists an international legal right to use force in self-defence against non-state actors themselves, rather than against states which may be supporting them; (2) this right may be exercised without consent in the territory of another state without amounting to an unlawful use of force against that state; and/or (3) the minimum "acquiescence" requirement referred to in the *Friendly Relations Declaration* no longer applies, or can be interpreted to include mere failure to prevent, for whatever reason, the terrorist organization from acting.

Of these, the first proposition is arguably the least sustainable. While it is surprisingly difficult to find explicit, authoritative statements to the effect that the use of force by states in self-defence may

---

340 Letter dated 7 October 2001 from the Permanent Representative of the United States of America to the United Nations Addressed to the President of the Security Council, UN Doc. S/2001/946 (7 October 2001).

341 Letter dated 7 October 2001 from the Chargé d'Affaires a.i. of the Permanent Mission of the United Kingdom of Great Britain and Northern Ireland to the United Nations Addressed to the President of the Security Council, UN Doc. S/2001/947 (7 October 2001).

342 But see Becker, above note 261 at 217; Duffy, above note 199 at 189.

343 See, for example, Dinstein, above note 6 at 204–8; E. Gross, *The Struggle of Democracy Against Terrorism* (Charlottesville, VA: University Press of Virginia, 2006) at 42; Becker, *ibid.*

only be directed at other states,[344] this may be because it follows as a simple matter of logical necessity. Self-defence operates as an excuse or exception that legalizes, under certain conditions, one state's use of force against another. As international law contains no general prohibition of the use of armed force by states against non-state actors in the first place (as it does in the case of armed force by states against states), an exception or excuse "permitting" such a use of force in self-defence is simply not required or even meaningful. Asserting the existence of such an international legal right is, quite simply, a legal *non sequitur.*

The second proposition is similarly untenable. We have already seen that the preponderance of state practice and *opinio juris* does not cleave to the minimalist view that a non-consensual use of force in the territory of another state is consistent with Article 2(4) simply because it does not lead to the permanent loss of all or part of that territory.[345] The *Friendly Relations Declaration* explicitly asserts that states have a duty not to use force to "violate ... international boundaries" or to subject the territory of another state to "military occupation." The *Definition of Aggression* condemns, as acts of aggression, "invasion or attack ... of the territory of another state, or any military occupation, however temporary, resulting from such invasion or attack," as well as the "use of armed forces of one State ... within the territory of another State" without or in excess of the consent of the latter.[346] Moreover, in *DRC v. Uganda,* the ICJ flatly rejected Uganda's argument that it was entitled to use force in the territory of the DRC, without the latter's consent, in order to defend itself against rebel or terror groups operating therefrom.[347]

Nor does the third proposition fare any better. The carefully negotiated and consensually agreed "complicity" requirements set out in the

---

344 See, however, the ICJ's assertion, in response to Israel's invocation of an inherent right of self-defence against terrorist attacks to justify the construction of a security wall in the Occupied Palestinian Territory, that Article 51 recognizes a right of self-defence "in the case of armed attack *by one State* against another State": *Israeli Wall Case,* above note 69 at para. 139 [emphasis added]. That the right of self-defence may only be invoked against a state responsible for an armed attack also seems to be implicit in the ICJ's vain search, in *Nicaragua,* for evidence that Nicaragua was responsible for the flow of arms through Nicaraguan territory to rebel groups in El Salvador (see *Nicaragua,* above note 42 at paras. 160 and 230); or in its insistence on the requirement of state attributability in *Oil Platforms* (see *Oil Platforms,* above note 242 at paras. 57, 61, 64, and 72) and *DRC v. Uganda* (see *DRC v. Uganda,* above note 166 at paras. 131–35, 146, 301, and 303–4).

345 See the text accompanying notes 117–22, above in this chapter.

346 *Definition of Aggression,* above note 87, Articles 3(a) and (e).

347 See *DRC v. Uganda,* above note 166 at paras. 301–4.

Friendly Relations Declaration have never been generally interpreted by states to impose a form of absolute liability on states for the acts of every terror group that manages successfully to launch an attack from their territory against another state. Certainly the post-September 11, 2001 invasion by coalition forces of Afghanistan provides no support for such a proposition given that, as described above, states participating in that action uniformly asserted active support and even close collaboration between Al Qaeda and the government of Afghanistan.

Moreover, when just such a proposition was advanced by Uganda in *DRC v. Uganda* to justify its military activities within the DRC, it was rejected outright by the ICJ. The Court found "no satisfactory proof of involvement, direct or indirect," by the DRC in attacks mounted by rebels within its territory against Uganda.[348] It held that the "absence of action by the [DRC] government against rebel groups in the border area is not tantamount to 'tolerating' or 'acquiescing' in their activities."[349] It flowed, rather, from the DRC's inability to control those activities in such remote areas with the limited resources at its disposal. Given that Uganda had "failed to provide conclusive evidence of actual support for anti-Ugandan rebels by the DRC," the Court therefore rejected Uganda's argument that it was entitled to use force in self-defence either against the DRC or against the rebels operating from DRC territory.[350] In the result, the key test is whether there has been tolerance of or acquiescence in the activities of terror or rebel groups within one's territory, which in turn requires proof of some "involvement" or "actual support," not mere passive failure or inability to do anything about such activities.

It therefore seems highly implausible that there exists a right to use unauthorized force in self-defence, in or against the territory of another state, merely because one has been the subject of an armed attack by a non-state actor located there. Current international law clearly requires more, in the form of some actual support or involvement by the host state in the non-state actor's activities, before such a right arises.[351]

Whether this *should* be the law is of course another matter, one for states to decide through general and uniform state practice and *opinio juris* or, perhaps, through conclusion of a multilateral treaty addressing the issue. At present there seems to be little if any evidence of the former and no serious suggestion of the latter. As for whether this leaves a

---

348   *Ibid.* at para. 146.
349   *Ibid.* at para. 301.
350   *Ibid.* at para. 303.
351   See discussion in Forcese, above note 274 at 194–98; J. Paust, "Use of Armed Force Against Terrorists in Iraq, Afghanistan and Beyond" (2002) 35 Cornell Int'l L.J. 533 at 540; Duffy, above note 199 at 161.

"gap" in modern international law's protection of the security interests of states in the face of transnational terrorism, the ICJ has perhaps put it best:

> Article 51 of the *Charter* may justify a use of force in self-defence only within the strict confines there laid down. It does not allow the use of force by a state to protect perceived security interests beyond these parameters. Other means are available to a concerned state, including, in particular, recourse to the Security Council.[352]

To the extent that the Security Council fails or is unable to fulfill its responsibilities in this regard, it may be more constructive to address the reasons for such shortcomings than to attempt to dismantle or erode the carefully designed limits that have been erected, in modern international law, around states' right to use unauthorized force in the name of self-defence.

FURTHER READING

ALEXANDROV, S., *Self-Defense Against the Use of Force in International Law* (The Hague: Kluwer Law International, 1996)

AREND, A., & BECK, R., *International Law and the Use of Force* (London: Routledge, 1993)

BECKER, T., *Terrorism and the State: Rethinking the Rules of State Responsibility* (Oxford: Hart, 2006)

BEST, G., *War and Law Since 1945* (New York: Oxford University Press, 1997)

BOWETT, D., *Self-Defence in International Law* (Manchester: Manchester University Press, 1958)

BROWNLIE, I., *International Law and the Use of Force by States* (Oxford: Clarendon Press, 1963)

BYERS, M., *War Law: Understanding International Law and Armed Conflict* (Vancouver: Douglas & McIntyre, 2005)

CANNIZZARO, E., & PALCHETTI, P., eds., *Customary International Law on the Use of Force* (Leiden: Martinus Nijhoff, 2005)

---

352 *DRC v. Uganda*, above note 166 at para. 148.

CHESTERMAN, S., *Just War or Just Peace? Humanitarian Intervention and International Law* (Oxford: Oxford University Press, 2001)

DETTER DELUPIS, I., *The Law of War*, 2d ed. (Cambridge: Cambridge University Press, 2000)

DINSTEIN, Y., *War, Aggression and Self-Defence*, 4th ed. (Cambridge: Cambridge University Press, 2005)

FRANCK, T.M., *Recourse to Force: State Action Against Threats and Armed Attacks* (Cambridge: Cambridge University Press, 2002)

GRAY, C., *International Law and the Use of Force*, 2d ed. (Oxford: Oxford University Press, 2004)

NEFF, S.C., *War and the Law of Nations: A General History* (Cambridge: Cambridge University Press, 2005)

SAROOSHI, D., *The United Nations and the Development of Collective Security* (Oxford: Clarendon Press, 1999)

SIMMA, B., ed., *The Charter of the United Nations: A Commentary*, 2d ed. (Oxford: Oxford University Press, 2002)

CHAPTER 12

STATE RESPONSIBILITY

A. GENERAL PRINCIPLES

1) Concept and Development of State Responsibility

In international law, state responsibility is an area of general application, meaning that it is of potential relevance in virtually all substantive international legal contexts. Broadly speaking, the topic governs the legal consequences of a state's breach of its international legal obligations. It may therefore be useful to think of state responsibility as akin to the legal principles of liability for wrongful acts found in most domestic legal systems. It is also the international equivalent of a law of remedies.[1]

Some authors and jurists prefer to think in terms of a body of "secondary" legal obligations that arise only upon breach of "primary" obligations. The latter would be substantive legal obligations (such as the duty to perform a treaty undertaking in good faith, to refrain from the use of force contrary to the *UN Charter*, or to respect the freedom of the high seas) whereas the former would be legal obligations (such as the duty to make reparations) that only arise for any particular state when it has breached a primary obligation. Of course, breach of a secondary

---

1   See, generally, J.G. Starke & I.A. Shearer, *Starke's International Law*, 11th ed. (London: Butterworths, 1994) at 264.

obligation may in turn generate yet further secondary obligations or consequences.

While analogies between state responsibility and domestic principles of liability and remedies may be useful in a general sense, caution is required before presuming too great a correlation. This is because the principles of state responsibility are relatively rudimentary when compared to the much more sophisticated conceptions of liability found in most domestic systems. For example, state responsibility draws no clear distinctions between the legal consequences that flow from breaches of different types of primary obligation. For example, breaches of treaty obligations, arguably "contractual" in character, are in principle treated no differently in terms of state responsibility than breaches of customary obligations, arguably "tortious" in nature.[2] Nor is there even a clearly developed distinction between the consequences for states of criminal behaviour and lesser, "delictual" forms of wrongdoing.[3]

This lack of sophistication can be understood by considering the relatively recent development of a general theory of state responsibility. European states have long engaged in the practice of making reparations *inter se*, usually pursuant to treaty undertakings. The practice of paying compensation for personal or property damages suffered by foreign nationals also developed relatively early. Outside these contexts, however, a state suffering some wrong by another state had until fairly recently to rely on a number of self-help remedies, such as direct reprisals, or authorizing one's nationals to carry out reprisals against nationals of the offending state.[4]

Obviously such a crude system of enforcement is undesirable if the goal is to establish a mature legal system based on conceptions of the rule of law rather than the use of force. However, a tension arises between the interests of individual states, for whom the development of a law of secondary obligations further fetters their sovereignty, and the interests of the international community as a whole, which are best served by fostering a rules-based system of dispute settlement. This tension, and the predominant role played by states in the development

---

2   See *Rainbow Warrior Arbitration (New Zealand v. France)*, (1990) 82 I.L.R. 499 at 551 [*Rainbow Warrior*].

3   See further the text accompanying notes 23–34, below in this chapter. The term "delictual" denotes a category of wrongs roughly corresponding to the concept of "civil wrongs" in domestic legal systems. It therefore refers to a breach of obligations owed by one state to another, rather than obligations owed to the community of states as a whole.

4   See, generally, I. Brownlie, *Principles of Public International Law*, 6th ed. (Oxford: Oxford University Press, 2003) at 420.

of international law, may explain why it was not until the nineteenth century that substantial progress was made in establishing the basic principle that most international legal actors now take for granted: that breach of a primary obligation necessarily entails a corresponding obligation to make right the wrong.

The development of this area of the law has been mainly customary, such that the general principles of state responsibility can be taken to be universally applicable. Many of these principles have been explained and applied by international tribunals, adding a degree of certainty to such customary international law.

However, it is also important to acknowledge the International Law Commission's (ILC) major contribution to the process of codifying and progressively developing the rules of state responsibility. The Commission began working on the topic in 1949[5] and, although the going was at times slow and problematic, in 1996 it succeeded in adopting, on first reading, a complete set of *Draft Articles*.[6] Immediately following this, a new Special Rapporteur was appointed and the *Draft Articles* were substantially reworked in light of comments received from governments.[7] In 2001, a revised set of *Draft Articles* was thus adopted on second reading by the Commission and thereafter referred to the UN General Assembly for further action by states.[8] The General As-

5   Approved by the UN General Assembly in 1953: *Request for the Codification of the Principles of International Law Governing State Responsibility*, GA Res. 799(VIII), UN GAOR, 8th Sess., Supp. No. 17, UN Doc. A/RES/799(VII) (1953).

6   *Draft Articles on State Responsibility* in "Report of the International Law Commission on the Work of its Forty-Eighth Session" (UN Doc. A/51/10) in *Yearbook of the International Law Commission 1996*, vol. II (New York: United Nations, 1996) 58 [*Draft Articles 1996*].

7   See J. Crawford, Special Rapporteur on State Responsibility, International Law Commission, *First Report on State Responsibility*, UN GAOR, 50th Sess., UN Doc. A/CN.4/490 (1998); J. Crawford, Special Rapporteur on State Responsibility, International Law Commission, *Second Report on State Responsibility*, UN GAOR, 51st Sess., UN Doc. A/CN.4/498 (1999); J. Crawford, Special Rapporteur on State Responsibility, International Law Commission, *Third Report on State Responsibility*, UN GAOR, 52nd Sess., UN Doc. A/CN.4/507 (2000); J. Crawford, Special Rapporteur on State Responsibility, International Law Commission, *Fourth Report on State Responsibility*, UN GAOR, 53rd Sess., UN Doc. A/CN.4/517 (2001).

8   *Draft Articles on State Responsibility* in "Report of the International Law Commission on the Work of its Fifty-Third Session", UN GAOR, 56th Sess., Supplement No. 10 (A/56/10), c. IV.E.1, UN Doc. A/CN.4/L. 602/Rev. 1 (2001) [*Draft Articles*]. See also the *Commentaries to the Draft Articles on Responsibility of States for Internationally Wrongful Acts* in ibid., c. IV.E.2 [*Commentaries*]. The *Draft Articles* and the ILC *Commentaries* accompanying them are also conveniently reproduced in J. Crawford, *The International Law Commission's Articles on State*

sembly has taken note of the *Draft Articles*, commended them to the attention of governments,[9] and solicited the views of governments as to future action on them.[10] Among the possibilities are the adoption, by the General Assembly, of the *Draft Articles* as a multilateral treaty on state responsibility, or the convening of a diplomatic conference at which the *Draft Articles* would form the basis for negotiation of such a multilateral treaty. Given that the *Draft Articles* have generally been embraced as a useful restatement of customary international law on the topic, however, it is also possible that the General Assembly will simply allow them to stand in their current form.[11]

For present purposes, the *Draft Articles* will be referred to as they provide valuable guidance as to the current state of the customary international law of state responsibility. However, the reader is reminded that the *Draft Articles* and the work of the International Law Commission generally, while of persuasive authority, are not binding *per se* or definitive statements of the law. Moreover, as with all customary international law, the law of state responsibility is susceptible to change in accordance with the evolving practice of states. Accordingly, any areas of uncertainty or controversy that have arisen in respect of the *Draft Articles* will be highlighted in the following sections.

2) Basic Principle of the Responsibility of States

The fundamental principle of state responsibility was articulated by the Permanent Court of International Justice in the *Chorzów Factory Case*:

> … [I]t is a principle of international law, and even a general conception of law, that any breach of an engagement involves an obligation to make reparation.[12]

Responsibility: Introduction, Text and Commentaries (Cambridge: Cambridge University Press, 2002). It should be noted that the ILC is now considering the related topic of the "Responsibility of International Organizations": see "Report of the International Law Commission on the Work of its Fifty-Ninth Session," UN GAOR, 62nd Sess., Supplement No. 10 (A/62/10) c. VIII [ILC Report (2007)].

9   See "Responsibility of States for Internationally Wrongful Acts," UNGA Res. 56/83, UN GAOR, 56th Sess., UN Doc. A/RES/56/83 (2001) at para. 3.

10 See "Responsibility of States for Internationally Wrongful Acts," UNGA Res. 59/35, UN GAOR, 59th Sess., UN Doc. A/RES/59/35 (2004) at para. 2. See also UNGA Res. 62/61, UN GAOR, 62nd Sess., U.N. Doc. A/RES/62/61 (2008) at para 2.

11 The General Assembly is scheduled to consider this issue during its sixty-fifth session, in 2010 or 2011: see UNGA Res. 62/61, *ibid.* at para. 4.

12 *Case Concerning the Factory at Chorzów (Claim for Indemnity) (Merits)* (1928), P.C.I.J., (Ser. A), No. 17 at 29 [*Chorzów Factory Case*].

This basic principle has been repeated in many judgments[13] and is succinctly restated by the International Law Commission in its first draft article:

Article 1
Responsibility of a State for its Internationally Wrongful Acts

Every internationally wrongful act of a State entails the international responsibility of that State.[14]

The *Draft Articles* go on to clarify that the cumbersome expression "internationally wrongful act" means "a breach of an international obligation of the State."[15]

Thus, it is a universal principle of international law that responsibility to make reparation is a necessary corollary of a breach of an international obligation.[16] Such a broad principle, which seems uncontroversial if not self-evident, in fact masks a number of problematic issues.

For example, the key or central concept is an "internationally wrongful act," an expression of very general application that apparently encompasses breaches of all forms of international obligation, whether customary, treaty-based, or otherwise.[17] This is so even though certain areas of international law have developed their own, "built-in" remedial rules in case of breach. An obvious example is the law of treaties, which provides for certain legal consequences and remedies in the case of a material breach by one of the parties to a treaty.[18] In casting such a wide net, the basic rule of responsibility for breach of any and all international legal obligations will apply in addition to any particularized

---

13 See, for example, *Spanish Zone of Morocco Claims* (1923), 2 R.I.A.A. 615 at 641; *Corfu Channel Case (Merits) (United Kingdom v. Albania)*, [1949] I.C.J. Rep. 4 at 23–24 [*Corfu Channel*]; *Case Concerning Military and Paramilitary Activities in and Against Nicaragua (Nicaragua v. United States of America)*, [1986] I.C.J. Rep. 14 at 142–43 [*Nicaragua*]; *Case Concerning the Arrest Warrant of 11 April 2000 (Democratic Republic of the Congo v. Belgium)*, [2001] I.C.J. Rep. 3 at paras. 75–77 [*DRC v. Belgium*]; *Case Concerning Armed Activities on the Territory of the Congo (Democratic Republic of the Congo v. Uganda)*, [2005] I.C.J. Rep. 5 at para. 259 [*DRC v. Uganda*].

14 *Draft Articles*, above note 8, Article 1.

15 *Ibid.*, Article 2.

16 Barring, of course, the availability of some justification or defence under international law: see further Section A(5), below in this chapter.

17 See *Draft Articles*, above note 8, Article 12.

18 For example, the right of other parties in certain circumstances to terminate, withdraw from, or suspend the treaty: see further Chapter 4, Section J. And see, generally, P. Reuter, *Introduction to the Law of Treaties*, 2d ed., trans. by J. Mico & P. Haggenmacher (London: Kegan Paul International, 1995).

remedies.[19] In the case of conflict between the particularized remedial regime and the general principles of state responsibility, however, the *Draft Articles* provide that the former will prevail.[20]

A closely related issue is that the *Draft Articles* contemplate a single regime of responsibility for breach of an international obligation, regardless of the nature or source of the primary obligation breached.[21] The primary focus of that responsibility regime is a duty of "reparation," again regardless of the nature of the primary obligation breached. While the meaning and various forms of "reparation" will be explored further below,[22] the concept clearly suggests that responsibility in international law is essentially delictual in nature. In other words, the secondary obligation to make reparation is very similar to the secondary obligations owed in most domestic legal systems upon commission of a civil, as opposed to a criminal or public, wrong.

Such a conception of universally applicable delictual responsibility leaves little room for meaningful development of primary obligations for states of a "criminal" or "public order" character. While there have been controversial attempts by the international community to brand certain conduct of states[23] as criminal and thus, arguably, of a different order of wrongfulness than lesser breaches,[24] a system of responsibility

---

19   See *Rainbow Warrior,* above note 2 at 551; *Case Concerning the Gabčíkovo-Nagymaros Project (Hungary v. Slovakia),* [1997] I.C.J. Rep. 7 at 38 [*Gabčíkovo-Nagymaros*].

20   *Draft Articles,* above note 8, Article 55.

21   *Ibid.,* Article 12. The ILC commentary accompanying this article asserts: "As far as the obligation breached is concerned, there is a single general regime of State responsibility": see *Commentaries,* above note 8 at 127.

22   See Section C, below in this chapter.

23   As distinct from the international criminal liability of individuals, a concept recognized and applied, for example, by the International Military Tribunal at Nuremberg. The texts of the Nuremberg Trials may be found in the *Trial of the Major War Criminals before the International Military Tribunal,* Nuremberg, 14 November 1945–1 October 1946, Official Documents (1947) [*Nuremberg Trials*]. See also "Report of the International Law Commission on the Work of its Twenty-Eighth Session" (UN Doc. A/31/10) in *Yearbook of the International Law Commission 1976,* vol. II, Part 2 (New York: United Nations, 1976) at 119. The most recent and authoritative application of the concept of the international criminal liability of individuals is the *Rome Statute of the International Criminal Court,* 17 July 1998, 2187 U.N.T.S. 90, entered into force 1 July 2002, Article 27 [*Rome Statute*]. See further A. Cassese, *International Criminal Law* (New York: Oxford University Press, 2003).

24   For example, the condemnation of acts of aggression, colonial domination, slavery, genocide, and the like: see the *Draft Code of Crimes Against the Peace and Security of Mankind* in "Report of the International Law Commission on the Work of its Forty-Eighth Session" (UN Doc. A/51/10) in *Yearbook of the International Law Commission 1996,* vol. II (New York: United Nations, 1996) 17.

that ultimately reduces the consequences of all wrongdoing to a duty of reparation does little to support such a concept.

Aware of this conundrum, the International Law Commission introduced in its *Draft Articles 1996* a highly controversial distinction between "international crimes" and other international wrongs committed by states ("international delicts").[25] Aside from the difficulty of defining the concept of an international crime committed by a state[26] and the potential for confusion with the very different field of individual criminal responsibility,[27] the *Draft Articles 1996* provided for little substantive difference in the legal consequences that would flow from the distinction.[28]

This distinction between crimes and delicts was removed, however, from the *Draft Articles* adopted by the International Law Commission in 2001.[29] This reflects the fact that there is little support in state practice or *opinio juris* for recognizing, at least for purposes of state responsibility, a separate category of criminal acts of states.[30] The *Draft Articles* never-

---

25 *Draft Articles 1996*, above note 6, Article 19.

26 The *Draft Articles 1996* defined an international crime in a particularly circular way as "an international obligation so essential for the protection of fundamental interests of the international community that its breach is recognized as a crime by that community," although it included an illustrative list of acts from which an international crime "may result": see *ibid.*, Articles 19(2)–(3).

27 See above note 23 and Chapter 2, Section E(1). Note, however, that Article 58 of the *Draft Articles*, above note 8, expressly reserves questions of the individual responsibility of persons "acting on behalf of a State."

28 *Draft Articles 1996*, above note 6, Article 51. The principal differences contemplated were wider standing for "injured states" (Article 40(3)), less flexibility in terms of the form and extent of reparation due (Article 52), and an obligation on all states not to recognize or assist in the criminal conduct (Article 53).

29 *Draft Articles*, above note 8. But note that Article 33 provides that international obligations may be owed to the international community as a whole, and that the *Draft Articles* are without prejudice to individual (presumably criminal) responsibility in international law.

30 The ILC Commentary accompanying Article 12 of the *Draft Articles* states simply: "Nor does any distinction exist between the 'civil' and 'criminal' responsibility as is the case in internal legal systems": *Commentaries*, above note 8 at 127. In the ILC Report (2000), it was noted that the inclusion of state crimes in the *Draft Articles 1996* had moved "beyond codification": see "Report of the International Law Commission on the Work of its Fifty-Second Session" (UN Doc. A/CN.4/L.600) in *Yearbook of the International Law Commission 2000*, vol. II (New York: United Nations, 2000) at 18, 42, 58, and 104 [*ILC Report (2000)*]. See also, for example, the *Case Concerning the Application of the Convention for the Prevention and Punishment of the Crime of Genocide (Bosnia and Herzegovina v. Serbia and Montenegro)* (26 February 2007), General List No. 91 (I.C.J.) [*Genocide Convention Case*]: while the ICJ in that case found that genocide is a "crime under international law" that states parties to the *Genocide Convention*

theless retain the concept of a "serious breach by a State of an obligation arising under a peremptory norm of general international law,"[31] as well as of an obligation owed "to the international community as a whole."[32] Again, the principal difficulties with such categories of wrongdoing are their lack of clear definition, basis in state practice, and meaningful consequences. For example, the only additional consequences contemplated in the *Draft Articles* for a serious breach of a peremptory norm are not directed at the breaching state at all. Rather, the *Draft Articles* require that *other* states cooperate to bring the breach to an end and that they not "recognize as lawful a situation created by a serious breach … nor render aid or assistance in maintaining that situation."[33] In a similar vein, the principal significance of breach of an obligation owed to the international community as a whole is procedural: it grants standing to any state to seek certain remedies for the breach.[34]

3) Basis of Responsibility: Objective or Subjective?

A further issue that is not explicitly addressed in the basic proposition that all breaches of obligation entail state responsibility and a duty of reparation is the degree of fault required, if any, to give rise to such a breach. The silence of the *Draft Articles* as to any fault requirement in defining an internationally wrongful act would tend to suggest that the basis of liability in international law is objective or strict, in the sense

---

are bound not to commit, it was careful to specify that they were bound not to do so "through the actions of their organs or persons or groups whose actions are attributable to them": *ibid.* at para. 167. Moreover, both parties were agreed that international law does not recognize the criminal responsibility of states, a position seemingly accepted by the Court in reaching its conclusion that the obligations imposed on states parties to the *Genocide Convention* "are not of a criminal nature": *ibid.* at para. 170. See further the judgment of the Nuremberg Tribunal which held that "crimes against international law are committed by men, not by abstract entities": *Nuremberg Trials*, above note 23, vol. 1 at 222.

31   *Draft Articles*, above note 8, Article 40.

32   *Ibid.*, Articles 33(1) and 48(1)(b). The concept of *erga omnes* obligations, that is, obligations owed to the international community as a whole rather than to individual states, was recognized by the International Court of Justice in the *Case Concerning the Barcelona Traction, Light and Power Company, Ltd. (Belgium v. Spain)*, [1970] I.C.J. Rep. 3 at 32 [*Barcelona Traction*]; *Case Concerning East Timor (Portugal v. Australia)*, [1995] I.C.J. Rep. 90 at para. 29 [*East Timor*]; and *Legal Consequences of the Construction of a Wall in the Occupied Palestinian Territory, Advisory Opinion*, [2004] I.C.J. Rep. 136 at paras. 155–59 [*Israeli Wall*].

33   *Draft Articles, ibid.*, Article 41. See also *Israeli Wall, ibid.* at para. 159.

34   *Draft Articles, ibid.*, Article 48. See further Section B(1), below in this chapter.

that it does not generally depend on a state's subjective and culpable state of "mind."[35] Thus, responsibility would merely require an act or omission causally linked to the breach of an international obligation.

Many, and perhaps the preponderance of, writers support this view.[36] It is also implicitly supported by the majority of the cases, which generally appear to resolve issues of state responsibility without expressly inquiring into issues of intention, negligence, or other forms of fault on the part of the offending state. Unfortunately, however, some judgments are also open to a contrary interpretation and so some writers take the opposite view. State practice does not conclusively resolve the matter. There thus remains some uncertainty as to whether some degree of fault—intention or negligence, for example—is required before a state can be said to have breached an international obligation, giving rise to state responsibility and a duty to make reparation.

Some of the difficulty here may result from a failure to distinguish between a fault requirement as a general matter of state responsibility, and various duties of care or diligence that may attach to or form an integral part of the particular *primary* legal obligation that has been breached.[37] It would be difficult in light of the jurisprudence to sustain an argument that fault must be demonstrated in all cases before international liability will attach.[38] However, there may be exceptional cases where fault becomes relevant because of the particular nature of the substantive, primary obligation under consideration. For example, a state is under a general obligation to exercise due diligence in protecting the security of foreign diplomatic premises and personnel within its territory.[39] Establishing a breach of that obligation will require a demonstration of a culpable lack of diligence on the part of the host

---

35 See *Commentaries*, above note 8 at 69–70.

36 See, for example, Brownlie, above note 4 at 423–25; M.N. Shaw, *International Law*, 5th ed. (Cambridge: Cambridge University Press, 2003) at 698–700; Starke & Shearer, above note 1 at 280–82; A. Cassese, *International Law*, 2d ed. (Oxford: Oxford University Press, 2005) at 250–51.

37 See Brownlie, above note 4 at 424–25.

38 See, for example, *Estate of Jean-Baptiste Caire (France)* v. *Mexico* (1929), 5 R.I.A.A. 516 at 529 [*Caire*], where President Verzjil of the Franco-Mexican Claims Commission applied "lesdits principes dans le sens de la doctrine qui professe, en cette matière, la 'responsabilité objective' de l'État, c'est-à-dire une responsabilité pour les actes commis par ses fonctionnaires ou organes, qui peut lui incomber malgré l'absence de toute 'faute' de sa part." See also *L.F.H. Neer and P. Neer Claim (United States of America v. United Mexican States)* (1926), 4 R.I.A.A. 60; *Roberts Claim (United States of America v. United Mexican States)* (1926), 4 R.I.A.A. 77.

39 See Chapter 9, Section C.

state, not because of any general fault requirement in the law of state responsibility but because the primary obligation itself requires a certain level of care or diligence.[40] The difference is between fault as a general requirement of liability in all cases, and fault required only in the exceptional case where it is a necessary, integral component of the primary obligation or its breach.

The distinction, and the ease with which it can be confounded, is well illustrated in the *Corfu Channel* case.[41] That dispute arose as a result of damage sustained by British warships transiting the Corfu Channel, an international strait passing through Albanian territorial waters.[42] During transit, the British vessels struck several mines, killing a number of British seamen and seriously damaging the vessels. There was no direct evidence that Albania was responsible for laying the mines and the issue became whether Albania bore responsibility for failing to warn international shipping of the existence of the minefield. Before giving a positive answer, however, the Court found it necessary to consider whether it could conclude, on the basis of circumstantial evidence, that Albania knew of the existence of the minefield. This was relevant, wrote the Court, in determining whether Albania had breached "every State's obligation not to allow knowingly its territory to be used for acts contrary to the rights of other states."[43] In the end, the Court found that Albania must have had such knowledge and was responsible.

While some authors have interpreted the case as support for a general fault requirement in state responsibility,[44] clearly the Court's search for evidence of knowledge was driven by the substantive content of the primary obligation under consideration. In other words, the requirement of subjective knowledge was built into the primary obligation not to allow one's territory to be used in such a way as to injure other states,

---

40 See, for example, *United States Diplomatic and Consular Staff in Tehran* (*United States v. Iran*), [1980] I.C.J. Rep. 3 at 32 [*Tehran Hostages*]. See also, in the context of a state's duty to exercise due diligence in protecting foreign nationals from acts of violence by mobs or rebels, *Home Missionary Society Claim* (*United States of America v. United Kingdom*) (1920), 6 R.I.A.A. 42 at 44.

41 *Corfu Channel*, above note 13.

42 On this aspect of the case, see further Chapter 7, Section C(2)(b)(v).

43 *Corfu Channel Case*, above note 13 at 20. It has been pointed out that the French version of the judgment omits the word "knowingly," with potential ramifications for the judgment's meaning for the theory of objective state responsibility: see H.M. Kindred, P.M. Saunders *et al.*, eds., *International Law Chiefly as Interpreted and Applied in Canada*, 7th ed. (Toronto: Emond Montgomery, 2006) at 638, n. 4.

44 For example, H. Lauterpacht, *The Development of International Law by the International Court* (London: Stevens, 1958) at 88.

not superimposed by the theory of state responsibility as a condition of liability.[45]

A general rule of objective responsibility, subject to exceptions dictated by the substance of primary obligations, is generally, albeit not unanimously, endorsed. It is consistent with the majority of the judgments and the *Draft Articles*, and widely accepted by states. Moreover, it advances sound policy considerations, such as the encouragement of strict standards of state conduct and effective reparation even in cases where states have inadvertently breached their duties to one another. As a practical matter, moreover, it avoids difficult and largely artificial issues of proof when it comes to establishing the state of "mind" of states which are, after all, artificial legal entities.

4) Attributability

Before a state can be held internationally responsible for a breach of an international obligation, the act or omission giving rise to that breach must of course be attributable to it.[46] This idea, while uncontroversial and even self-evident in itself, is difficult to apply in many situations. For the most part this is because states, being artificial legal persons, cannot in reality perform acts directly at all. Rather, states act through or are represented by various officials, ministries, organizations, and even corporations. Hence, many international obligations focus not so much on what a state must or must not do itself, but rather on its duty to control or regulate the conduct of non-state actors. Both factors combine to pose difficult problems in deciding precisely what and whose conduct may give rise to state responsibility. In practice, different approaches apply depending on whether one is dealing with state representatives or non-state actors.

a) State Organs and Representatives
As a general rule, the acts of all state organs, officials, public servants, and so on are attributable to the state and may give rise to state responsibility.[47] This is so regardless of the rank, position, or role of the organ, official, public servant, *et cetera* within the governmental structure.[48] Thus, a state will bear responsibility for the acts of its armed

---

45   See Brownlie, above note 4 at 425.
46   *Draft Articles*, above note 8, Article 2(a). This is also sometimes referred to as the requirement of "imputability."
47   *Ibid.*, Article 4(1).
48   *Ibid.* See also *Commentaries*, above note 8 at 87–88.

personnel,[49] law enforcement officials,[50] executive or administrative organs,[51] judiciary,[52] legislatures,[53] and other such representatives that contravene the state's international obligations.[54] It makes no difference whether the governmental organ or representative involved is at the federal, provincial, or municipal level—the acts of state representatives at all levels or orders of government may give rise to responsibility on the part of the state.[55]

Two issues arise. The first is how to determine if a given entity or person is indeed an organ or official in the service of or representing the state. On this matter the *Draft Articles* defer primarily to domestic law. If an entity is an organ of the state (in the extended sense seen above) according to the internal law of the state in question, it will be treated as such for purposes of the international law of state responsibility.[56]

Such an approach avoids difficult problems of identifying general criteria by which a state organ or representative could be identified as a matter of international law. Possible criteria might include the nature of the entity's powers, the manner in which they are conferred, the degree of control or supervision by the state over the representative, and so on.[57] The difficulty in establishing such criteria, however, is that certain judgments must be made as to the role of the state and the means by which it organizes its internal affairs. This would appear to be incompatible with the basic right of non-interference in domestic affairs enjoyed by all states.

---

49 See, for example, *Spanish Zone of Morocco Claims*, above note 13 at 645, Huber, Commissioner.

50 See, for example, *Gertrude Parker Massey (United States) v. Mexico* (1927), 4 R.I.A.A. 155.

51 *Ibid.* at 159, Nielsen, Commissioner; see also Brownlie, above note 4 at 432–33.

52 For example, a failure of a domestic court to apply a binding treaty obligation of the state, or to apply a minimum international standard of treatment to a foreign national: see A. McNair, *The Law of Treaties* (Oxford: Clarendon Press, 1961) at 346. On the international responsibility of states for "denial of justice" see C.F. Amerasinghe, *Local Remedies in International Law* (Cambridge: Grotius Publications, 1990) c. 2.

53 For example, a legislative failure to give effect to a treaty or other international legal obligation: see McNair, *ibid.* at 547–50; G. Schwarzenberger, *International Law*, 3d ed., vol. 1 (London: Stevens and Sons, 1957) at 604–5.

54 *Draft Articles*, above note 8, Article 4(1).

55 *Ibid.* See also *Commentaries*, above note 8 at 88–90; Schwarzenberger, above note 53 at 625–27; *Thomas H. Youmans (United States) v. Mexico* (1926), 4 R.I.A.A. 110 [*Youmans Claim*].

56 *Draft Articles*, above note 8, Article 4(2).

57 ILC Report (2000), above note 30 at para. 73.

On the other hand, deferring wholly to domestic law to define which entities or persons constitute organs or representatives of the state may invite abuse. States may be tempted to enact domestic legislation effectively limiting the range of agencies for whose acts they can be held responsible in international law.[58] This in turn would be incompatible with the fundamental principle that domestic law provides no excuse for breach of an international legal obligation.[59]

In an effort to reconcile these competing concerns, the *Draft Articles* in fact provide for a non-conclusive reference to domestic law.[60] In other words, domestic law may be conclusive when it confers the status of state organ on an entity or person, but the converse does not necessarily follow: when domestic law does not confer such status, it is not the end of the matter. This of course raises the issue, not addressed in the *Draft Articles*, of the basis upon which the law of state responsibility will deem an entity to be an organ of the state, notwithstanding its lack of such status under internal law.

That question was recently addressed by the International Court of Justice (ICJ) in the *Genocide Convention Case*.[61] At issue in that case was whether the Federal Republic of Yugoslavia (FRY) could be held responsible for acts of genocide committed at Srebrenica in Bosnia in July 1995. The facts established that, after seizing Srebrenica, units of the Bosnian Serb army (VRS) had massacred thousands of Bosnian Muslim men from the town. The question was whether, given the close ties between the armed forces of the FRY and the VRS (as well as the latter's political master, the "Republika Srpska"), the massacre was attributable to the FRY. Bosnia and Herzegovina argued that the VRS and Republika Srpska were organs of the FRY. However, it was clear that the internal law of the FRY provided for no such formal status.

---

58 See, for example, the comments of the United Kingdom on Article 5 of the *Draft Articles 1996: State Responsibility: Comments and Observations Received from Governments*, UN GAOR, 50th Sess., UN Doc. A/CN.4/488 (1998) at 37.

59 We have already seen a particularized aspect of this general rule in Article 27 of the *Vienna Convention on the Law of Treaties*, which provides that domestic legal impediments provide no excuse for a failure to perform treaty obligations: *Vienna Convention on the Law of Treaties*, 23 May 1969, 1155 U.N.T.S. 331 (entered into force 27 January 1980) [*Vienna Convention*]. See further Chapter 4, Section G(1) and authorities cited, below note 67.

60 *Draft Articles*, above note 8, Article 4(2): "… [a state] organ *includes* any person or entity which has that status in accordance with the internal law of the State" [emphasis added].

61 *Genocide Convention Case*, above note 30.

In addressing this issue, the ICJ confirmed that domestic law was not conclusive. Rather, referring to its earlier decision in *Nicaragua*,[62] the ICJ stated the rule thus:

> 392. ... [A]ccording to the Court's jurisprudence, persons, groups of persons or entities may, for purposes of international responsibility, be equated with State organs even if that status does not follow from internal law, provided that in fact the persons, groups or entities act in "complete dependence" on the State, of which they are merely an instrument. In such a case, it is appropriate to look beyond legal status alone, in order to grasp the reality of the relationship between the person taking action, and the State to which he is so closely attached as to appear to be nothing more than its agent: any other solution would allow States to escape their international responsibility by choosing to act through persons or entities whose supposed independence would be purely fictitious.

> 393. However, so to equate persons or entities with State organs when they do not have that status under internal law must be exceptional, for it requires proof of a particularly great degree of State control over them ....[63]

Applying this test to the relationship between the FRY and the VRS and Republika Srpska, the ICJ concluded that the necessary "complete dependence" did not exist at the relevant time, notwithstanding "powerful" political, military, and logistical relations between them and "very important support" given by the FRY to Republika Srpska "without which it could not have 'conduct[ed] its crucial or most significant military and paramilitary activities.'"[64] This clearly illustrates that the circumstances in which "complete dependence" will exist, sufficient to deem an entity a state organ notwithstanding its lack of such status under domestic law, will be highly exceptional indeed. In other words, the situations in which domestic law will not in fact be conclusive as to the non-organ status of an entity will be extremely rare.

A somewhat related circumstance in which the conduct of an entity that is not a state organ will nevertheless be attributed to the state is when such an entity is "empowered by the law of the State to exercise elements of ... governmental authority."[65] This article is meant to cap-

---

62   *Nicaragua*, above note 13 at 62–64.
63   *Genocide Convention Case*, above note 30 at paras. 392–93.
64   *Ibid.* at para. 394.
65   *Draft Articles*, above note 8, Article 5. A closely related provision is found in Article 6, "Conduct of organs placed at the disposal of a State by another State".

ture the phenomenon of "privatization" that has swept much of the developed world, in which functions formerly carried out by governmental organs or agencies are delegated to private or semi-private entities or corporations.[66] As long as such entities are in fact exercising governmental authority duly conferred upon them by domestic law, their actions in that capacity will be attributable to the conferring state. This can be seen as another instance of privileging substance over form: the decision by a state to delegate elements of governmental authority to a private entity will not permit it to escape international responsibility for internationally wrongful acts committed by such an entity in the course of exercising that authority.

This brings us to the second issue arising from attribution to a state of the acts of its organs or of entities empowered by it to exercise elements of governmental authority: How is one to deal with *ultra vires* acts of state organs or representatives? Should a state be held internationally responsible for the conduct of an official acting outside the scope of his or her authority? The apparent unfairness of an affirmative answer to this question must be balanced against the general rule that respect for international legal obligations transcends requirements of domestic law—at least from the perspective of international law.[67] Obviously one can only judge the *vires* of an official's conduct by referring to domestic law establishing the parameters of the official's authority. Thus, if domestic law is no excuse for a failure to respect an international legal obligation, the problem posed is whether it can permit a state to escape responsibility for the unauthorized acts of its agents.

The rule generally adopted here is that even the unauthorized or *ultra vires* acts of state representatives engage the state's responsibility, as long as they are acting in their official capacity at the relevant time.[68] In other words, as long as state representatives act within the general scope of their apparent (as opposed to actual) authority, their acts will be attributable to the state.[69] For example, law enforcement or security personnel may abuse their powers in direct contravention of their assigned duties or domestic law, but as long as such abuse is carried out in their apparent capacity as law enforcers, such conduct will be

---

66 See *Commentaries*, above note 8 at 92–95.

67 See, for example, *Treatment of Polish Nationals and Other Persons of Polish Origin or Speech in the Danzig Territory* (1932), P.C.I.J., Ser. A/B, No. 44 at 4; *Reparation for Injuries Suffered in the Service of the United Nations, Advisory Opinion*, [1949] I.C.J. Rep. 174 at 180 [*Reparations Case*]. See also *Draft Articles*, above note 8, Article 3; *Commentaries*, above note 8 at 75–79 and 99.

68 *Draft Articles, ibid.*, Article 7.

69 See *Commentaries*, above note 8 at 102.

attributable to the state.[70] On the other hand, an assault on a foreign diplomat in a grocery queue by a person who just happens to be an off-duty public servant would not likely be characterized as an act attributable to the host state, given that such an act would not be in apparent execution of any official capacity.

This rule, loosely akin to the domestic legal concept of employers' vicarious liability for the acts of their employees,[71] illustrates the general "strictness" or "objectivity" of state responsibility. It is probably justifiable in international law on the basis that states should be permitted to rely on the appearance of official capacity of another state's representatives.[72] States are thereby encouraged to act diligently in overseeing and controlling the conduct of their representatives.

b) Non-State Actors

Beyond the wide net cast by the broad definition of state organs and entities empowered to exercise elements of governmental authority, the question that arises is whether and in what circumstances a state can be held responsible for the acts of persons having no official capacity as state representatives at all. The matter can be complicated because states have various duties in international law to control events in their territory which may cause prejudice to the rights or interests of other states.[73] It is easy to confuse state responsibility in such cases (which flows from the failure of the state to control the conduct of non-state actors, rather than the attributability of such private conduct to the state) with cases where the conduct of non-state actors is itself directly imputed to the state.

As a general rule it can be said that a state will not be held responsible for the conduct of private persons[74] not acting on its behalf.[75] For example, a state will not generally be held responsible for acts of individuals or corporations, even its nationals, merely because these occur in its territory. Something more is generally required before a state will bear responsibility for such private conduct.

---

70 See, for example, the *Youmans Claim*, above note 55, where troops sent to protect foreign nationals in fact participated in attacking and killing them. See also *Caire*, above note 38 at 531; *Velásquez Rodríguez Case* (1988), Inter-Am. Ct. H.R. (Ser. C) No. 4 at para. 170.

71 See, for example, *Bazley v. Curry*, [1999] 2 S.C.R. 534.

72 See *Commentaries*, above note 8 at 99–100.

73 See *Corfu Channel*, above note 13 at 20. See also, for example, Chapter 8, Section D.

74 That is, persons with no official capacity as state representatives within the meaning of Articles 4, 5, and 6 of the *Draft Articles*, above note 8.

75 See *Commentaries*, above note 8 at 80–81, 103.

This was illustrated by the judgment of the International Court of Justice in the *Tehran Hostages* case.[76] In 1979, the American embassy in Tehran was overrun, ransacked, and occupied by a group of "militants." Most of the American diplomatic personnel were taken hostage and held for several months. In the absence of any evidence that the militants were in the service of or otherwise officially connected to the Iranian government at the time of the initial occupation, the Court found that Iran could not be held responsible for their acts.[77]

There are, however, a number of exceptional situations in which the conduct of private persons will be attributed to a state.[78] One of these, again illustrated in the *Tehran Hostages* case, is where a state acknowledges and adopts otherwise private conduct as its own.[79] In *Tehran Hostages*, after finding that Iran was not responsible for the initial occupation of the American embassy by private actors, the Court went on to hold that subsequent endorsements and statements of approval and support by the Iranian government for the acts of the militants, while the hostage crisis was ongoing, eventually made them *de facto* agents of the state of Iran. As such, and notwithstanding the absence of any official link between Iran and the militants, their continuing occupation became conduct imputable to the state of Iran for which it was held internationally responsible.[80]

A second circumstance where the conduct of private actors will be attributed to a state is where that conduct is carried out on the instructions of, or under the direction or control of, that state.[81] This rule in fact conceals two different situations. The first, where a state instructs a private actor to carry out specific acts, is fairly straightforward. Its application merely requires evidence of such instructions and does not

---

76 *Tehran Hostages*, above note 40.
77 However, the Court did find that Iranian officials had breached Iran's duty to take effective measures to provide adequate security for foreign diplomatic premises and personnel: *ibid.* at 29–33.
78 In addition to the situations discussed in the following paragraphs, there are two highly specialized cases of attribution to a state of the conduct of non-state actors: see *Draft Articles*, above note 8, Article 9, "Conduct carried out in the absence or default of the official authorities" (dealing with situations where private persons exercise elements of governmental authority where there are no official authorities, for example in disaster or emergency situations); and Article 10, "Conduct of an insurrectional movement or other movement" (dealing with situations where an insurrectional or other movement subsequently becomes the government of a state).
79 *Draft Articles, ibid.*, Article 11.
80 *Tehran Hostages*, above note 40 at 33–35.
81 *Draft Articles*, above note 8, Article 8.

otherwise require that any further relationship, either legal or factual, be established between the state and the private actor.[82] By contrast, the second situation, where the private actor acts under the "direction or control" of a state, is more complex. This is because being "under the direction or control" of a state suggests a relationship transcending discrete instructions to commit specific acts. The question, of course, is: what are the necessary elements of such a relationship?

This question has been considered on a number of occasions by the ICJ. For example, in *Nicaragua*,[83] Nicaragua claimed that the United States had undertaken a campaign to destabilize its government by supporting and directing the activities of an armed rebel group known as the "*contras*." The ICJ found the United States responsible for the acts of its own agents in fomenting instability and the use of force against the Nicaraguan government. However, the issue also arose as to whether the United States could be held responsible for the acts of the *contras* themselves. Having first found that the *contras* were not so completely dependent on the United States that they could be considered one of its organs or agents,[84] the ICJ went on to consider whether they could nevertheless be considered to be acting under the direction or control of the United States. On this the Court articulated a particularly stringent standard:

> ... United States participation, even if preponderant or decisive, in the financing, organizing, training, supplying and equipping of the *contras*, the selection of its military or paramilitary targets, and the planning of the whole of its operation, is still insufficient in itself ... for the purpose of attributing to the United States the acts committed by the *contras* in the course of their military or paramilitary operations in Nicaragua.... [E]ven the general control by the respondent state over a force with a high degree of dependency on it, would not in [itself] mean ... that the United States directed or enforced the perpetration of the acts.... Such acts could well be committed by members of the *contras* without the control of the United States. For this conduct to give rise to legal responsibility of the United States, *it would in principle have to be proved that that State had effective control of the military or paramilitary operations in the course of which the alleged violations were committed.*[85]

---

82   See *Commentaries*, above note 8 at 104.
83   *Nicaragua Case*, above note 13.
84   *Ibid.* at paras. 109–110.
85   *Ibid.* at 64–65, para. 115 [emphasis added].

This test was also applied in the *Genocide Convention Case*.[86] Recall that in that case, the ICJ found, in applying the "complete dependence" test, that the VRS and Republika Srpska were not *de facto* organs of the FRY.[87] Bosnia and Herzegovina nevertheless urged that the actions of the VRS and Republika Srpska could be attributed to the FRY on the basis that they were acting under its direction or control. This argument gave the ICJ an opportunity, first, to reaffirm the *Nicaragua* "effective control" test, and, second, to distinguish this test from the "complete dependence" attribution test for *de facto* state organs:

> 400. The [*Nicaragua* effective control] test just formulated differs in two respects from the test … to determine whether a person or entity may be equated with a State organ even if not having that status under internal law. First, in this context it is not necessary to show that the persons who performed the acts alleged to have violated international law were in general in a relationship of "complete dependence" on the respondent State; it has to be proved that they acted … under its "effective control." It must however be shown that this "effective control" was exercised … in respect of each operation in which the alleged violations occurred, not generally in respect of the overall actions taken by the persons or groups of persons having committed the violations.[88]

The latter holding is particularly significant, for it appears to be the crux of the distinction between attributability of the conduct of *de facto* state organs (on the basis of the "complete dependence" test) and that of private actors acting under state direction or control (on the basis of the "effective control" test). Both the "complete dependence" and "effective control" tests appear ultimately to come down to a very high degree of control by the state in question.[89] The distinction between them, however, lies in control of *what*: for purposes of the "complete dependence" test, control has to be shown over the *entity*; for purposes of the "effective control" test, control has to be shown over the *operation* in which the breach of international law occurred.[90] The former

---

86 *Genocide Convention Case*, above note 30 at para. 399.

87 See the text accompanying notes 61–64, above in this chapter.

88 *Genocide Convention Case*, above note 30 at para. 400.

89 Recall that in explaining the "complete dependence" test, the ICJ indicated that it "requires proof of a particularly great degree of State control": *ibid.* at para. 393.

90 Note that in upholding this distinction, the ICJ explicitly overruled a contrary opinion expressed by the Appeals Chamber of the International Criminal Tribunal for the Former Yugoslavia in international criminal proceedings arising out of the same events in *Prosecutor v. Tadic*, Case No. IT-94-1-A, (1995) 35

justifies treating the entity as a representative of the state, whereas the latter only justifies holding the state responsible for private activity that it in fact controls.

In any event, the stringency of both tests illustrates the overall reluctance of international tribunals to attribute responsibility to states for the conduct of entities not formally associated with them.

5) Defences

a) General

As a complement to the general theory of objective or strict state responsibility for violations of international legal obligations, the law of state responsibility provides for certain generally applicable defences or justifications. The *Draft Articles* use the expression "circumstances precluding wrongfulness" for this category of defences, conveying the idea that such a defence, if applicable, does not merely excuse some wrongdoing but rather means that no wrongdoing has been committed at all.[91]

These defences are in addition to any specific defences or justifications developed under a particular legal regime. However, in the case of conflict, the rules applicable in the particular regime would prevail over the general defences provided in the law of state responsibility.[92]

Two general rules should be noted before reviewing the defences articulated by the ILC in its *Draft Articles*. The first is that compliance with domestic law is no excuse for a failure to observe an international legal obligation.[93] The rationale for such a rule has already been considered in its application to the requirement for states to perform treaty undertakings in good faith.[94]

Second is the effect of invoking a "circumstance precluding wrongfulness." The *Draft Articles* clarify that the existence of such a circumstance at one point in time does not thereafter relieve the state from complying with its obligations should the circumstance cease to exist.[95] In other words, the defences to state responsibility do not as such affect the existence or enforceability of a legal obligation. Rather, they serve to excuse non-compliance with the obligation only for so long as the

---

,I.L.M. 32 at paras. 116–37: see *Genocide Convention Case*, above note 30 at paras. 402–6.

91   *Draft Articles*, above note 8, Part I, Chapter V, "Circumstances Precluding Wrongfulness."

92   *Ibid.*, Article 55.

93   *Ibid.*, Article 3. See also authorities cited, above note 67.

94   *Vienna Convention*, above note 59, Article 27; see further Chapter 4, Section G(1).

95   *Draft Articles*, above note 8, Article 27(a).

circumstances giving rise to the defence subsist.[96] The *Draft Articles* also provide that the existence of a circumstance precluding wrongfulness is "without prejudice to"[97] the issue of compensation for any harm actually caused by one state to another. This tentative language reflects the uncertainty surrounding the nature and even existence of any requirement of compensation for lawful acts.[98]

We turn now to a brief review of the defences or justifications provided for in the *Draft Articles*.

b) Consent

In light of the sovereignty of states and their right to consent freely to binding legal obligations,[99] it is obvious that they may consent to acts by other states that would otherwise constitute breaches of international law. It is a right of states to derogate from universally applicable rules of customary international law in their particular relations with other states, whether by treaty or some other binding expression of intent.[100] For example, the presence of foreign troops on a state's territory might be a breach of the territorial state's sovereignty. If, however, such troops are present pursuant to an agreement between the territorial and sending state, no breach of international law has occurred.

As such, this category of justification provides little difficulty in practice. The only real issues, which can be problematic from an evidentiary perspective, are related to the establishment of true and valid consent as well as its scope. In general, the law governing the formation and interpretation of treaties or other binding expressions of intention will be invoked to resolve such difficulties.[101]

Limitations imposed by international law on the *ability* of states to give valid consent are more problematic because of their indeterminate scope. In particular, we have already seen that states may not conclude

---

96 See *Commentaries*, above note 8 at 169. See also *Gabčíkovo-Nagymaros*, above note 19 at para. 48.

97 *Draft Articles*, above note 8, Article 27(b).

98 See Brownlie, above note 4 at 429–30. See also the International Law Commission's *Draft Principles on the Allocation of Loss in the Case of Transboundary Harm Arising Out of Hazardous Activities*, adopted by the ILC on second reading (see ILC Report (2006), above note 8, c. V(E)) and commended by the UN General Assembly to the attention of governments: UNGA Res. 61/36, UN GAOR, Sixty-First Sess., UN Doc. A/RES/61/36 (2006), para. 2. The General Assembly is scheduled to consider the *Draft Principles* during its 65th session in 2010–2011: UNGA Res. 62/68, UN GAOR, 62nd Sess., UN Doc. A/RES/62/68 (2007), para. 6.

99 See further Chapter 3.

100 For example by way of unilateral declaration: see further Chapter 3, Section D(1).

101 See *Commentaries*, above note 8 at 174.

treaties that conflict with a norm of *jus cogens* (that is, a peremptory norm of international law).[102] Such a treaty is invalid from the outset.[103] This is but a particular application of the general rule that no derogation in any form is permitted from a *jus cogens* norm, which is in fact simply the definition of a peremptory, "non-derogable" norm.[104]

It is therefore not surprising that the *Draft Articles* provide expressly that none of the defences recognized therein justifies any state act that is not in conformity with peremptory norms.[105] This stipulation is in fact highlighted, in the case of the defence of consent, by the express requirement that consent be "valid" in order to constitute a circumstance precluding wrongfulness.[106]

c) Countermeasures

Countermeasures are a form of self-help remedy of ancient vintage and dubious modern legality. In essence, they comprise acts that would otherwise be illegal at international law but for the fact that they are committed in response to a prior act of illegality by the state against which they are directed. This prior act of illegality is the "circumstance precluding wrongfulness" that makes countermeasures a category of justification.[107]

The advent in post-Second World War international law of duties to refrain from acts of international force and to seek peaceful settlement of disputes has dramatically narrowed the number of situations in which a valid exercise of countermeasures may occur. The modern limits on the availability of the doctrine, and hence of this justification, will be reviewed in greater detail below in examining remedies and, in particular, self-help remedies.

d) *Force Majeure*

Force majeure refers to an unforeseen event or irresistible force, beyond the control of the state, which makes it materially impossible for the state to respect an international obligation. The *Draft Articles* provide that such an occurrence precludes state responsibility for the resulting failure to respect the obligation.[108] The notion is similar to that of

---

102 See Chapter 4, Section I(2)(g).
103 *Vienna Convention,* above note 59, Article 53.
104 See *Commentaries,* above note 8 at 207.
105 *Draft Articles,* above note 8, Article 26.
106 *Ibid.,* Article 20. See also *Commentaries,* above note 8 at 175.
107 *Draft Articles, ibid.,* Article 22.
108 *Ibid.,* Article 23(1).

supervening impossibility of performance of a treaty obligation[109] in that what is contemplated is true and complete impossibility, rather than difficulty or more onerous circumstances resulting from performance of the obligation.[110]

The conditions that must be met in order to qualify for the justification are therefore strictly defined. First, the requirement of impossibility clearly requires that the state have no option but to breach its international obligation.[111] Examples would include the disappearance or destruction of objects or geographical features indispensable to the performance of an obligation. Alternatively, insurrection or civil war leading to the loss of effective governmental control by a state over portions of its territory or population might make performance of legal obligations impossible.[112] Second, the state must not have contributed to the occurrence of the situation of impossibility.[113] Thus, a state's failure to take reasonably available steps to contain an insurrection would disentitle it from justifying its breach of international obligations by relying upon *force majeure*. Third, the situation must have been truly unforeseen or not "of an easily foreseeable nature."[114] In other words, if the state foresaw or ought to have foreseen the possibility of such an occurrence, it ought also to have provided for the consequences of its failure to respect any obligations it could not perform in such event.[115] Such foresight, coupled with a failure to provide for consequences in this way, is tantamount to an assumption of the risk of the occurrence and will bar a claim of justification based on *force majeure*.[116]

e) Distress

This highly specialized justification refers specifically to the situation where an act attributable to a state and in breach of the state's international obligations is the only reasonable means of saving the life of the actor or of persons under his or her care.[117] Such a situation differs from *force majeure* in that the breach of obligation is the result of a choice (that of saving life) rather than an inevitable outcome.[118] An ex-

---

109 See further Chapter 4. Section J(2)(c).
110 See *Commentaries,* above note 8 at 184.
111 *Ibid.* at 183.
112 See, for example, the *Russian Indemnity Case* (1912), 11 R.I.A.A. 421 at 443.
113 *Draft Articles,* above note 8, Article 23(2)(a).
114 See *Commentaries,* above note 8 at 184.
115 *Draft Articles*, above note 8, Article 23(1).
116 *Ibid.*, Article 23(2)(b).
117 *Ibid.*, Article 24(1).
118 See *Commentaries,* above note 8 at 189.

ample of distress would be trespass by a member of one state's air force into the airspace or onto the territory of another state in a situation of mechanical failure or other distress requiring an emergency landing. Of course, if the situation of distress has been brought about or contributed to by conduct attributable to the state invoking it, the act will not be justified.[119] Similarly, if the act in question is likely to create a situation of comparable or greater danger to the lives of others, it will also not be justified.[120]

f) Necessity

By far the most controversial and problematic justification provided for in the *Draft Articles* is that of necessity.[121] The dangers of indeterminacy and abuse arising from such a defence may be appreciated by juxtaposing it with the other circumstances considered by the ILC to preclude a finding of wrongful conduct, including *force majeure* and distress. The question that arises is whether there is any place for a further justification of necessity outside of these circumstances.

In general, judicial and academic opinion is unreceptive to the concept,[122] a fact reflected in the negative language used by the ILC in describing the limited availability of the justification.[123] That language describes necessity as a highly exceptional defence only available to safeguard an "essential interest against a grave and imminent peril." Even in this narrow sense, moreover, a state cannot invoke necessity if its breach of obligation would seriously impair an essential interest of the state or states to which it is owed or would violate a norm of *jus cogens*. Further still, the defence will be unavailable if the state has contributed to the situation of necessity or if the defence is specifically disallowed by the law establishing the relevant legal obligation itself.

An illustration of judicial affirmation of the existence, but also the exceptional availability, of this justification can be found in *Gabčíkovo-Nagymaros*,[124] the facts of which have been described in an earlier chap-

---

119 *Draft Articles*, Article 24(2)(a).
120 *Ibid.*, Article 24(2)(b).
121 *Ibid.*, Article 25.
122 See, for example, *Rainbow Warrior*, above note 2 at 554–55, describing the existence of the defence as "controversial." See also Brownlie, above note 4 at 448: "… necessity as an omnibus category probably does not exist, and its availability as a defence is circumscribed by fairly strict conditions"; Shaw, above note 36 at 712, n. 116: "The doctrine [of necessity] has been controversial in academic writings"; and *Commentaries*, above note 8 at 201, although the ILC ultimately found "substantial authority" for the concept (*ibid.* at 195–200).
123 *Draft Articles*, above note 8, Article 25(1).
124 *Gabčíkovo-Nagymaros*, above note 19 at 40.

ter.[125] Hungary argued, *inter alia*, that its abandonment and termination of an agreement between it and Slovakia (as successor to Czechoslovakia) for joint development of the Danube was justified by a state of necessity. In particular it argued that grave danger to its environment would be posed by continuation of the project.

The International Court of Justice, although recognizing that the natural environment is an "essential interest" of the state, nevertheless found that the added requirement of a grave and imminent peril was not met. The Court stressed that the criterion of imminence required more than an apprehension of risk, although it did not necessarily require immediacy of harm. Rather, the Court held that "grave and imminent peril" required grave danger that was inevitable or certain to occur, even if its certain and inevitable occurrence might be delayed beyond the short term.[126] In this case, the evidence available did not suffice to establish the inevitability of the anticipated harm. Nor had Hungary's behaviour been consistent with an apprehension of certain environmental damage.

It can thus be seen that speculation as to potential damage, even to a vital state interest, will be insufficient to ground recourse to the doctrine of necessity in order to escape state responsibility. Only persuasive evidence of grave and inevitable harm to such an interest will satisfy the stringent requirements of this justification.

g) Self-Defence

An act involving the use or threat of force against a state, and therefore otherwise in breach of one of the most fundamental duties of states in international law,[127] will be lawful if taken in accordance with the requirements of the *UN Charter* related to self-defence.[128] The ILC chose to include this general principle in its *Draft Articles* as a circumstance precluding wrongfulness,[129] although the justification for doing so is far from clear.[130] Given near universal adherence to the *UN Charter* and

---

125 See above Chapter 2, Section B(5)(b)(ii)(bb).

126 *Gabčíkovo-Nagymaros*, above note 19 at 40–42.

127 See Chapter 2, Section B(4), and Chapter 11.

128 *Charter of the United Nations*, 26 June 1945, Can. T.S. 1945 No. 7 (entered into force 24 October 1945), Article 51 [*UN Charter*].

129 *Draft Articles*, above note 8, Article 21.

130 The *Commentaries* offer little by way of explanation other than the observation that "Article 21 simply reflects the basic principle [of self-defence] for the purposes of chapter V [of the *Draft Articles*], leaving questions of the extent and application of self-defence to the applicable primary rules referred to in the *Charter*": *Commentaries*, above note 8 at 180.

the fact that the *Draft Articles* already make provision for "special rules of international law,"[131] it is doubtful that much is added by doing so.

B. STANDING AND THE ESPOUSAL OF CLAIMS

1) Standing of States to Invoke State Responsibility

To date we have been examining the circumstances in which states may be considered to have committed a breach of their international legal obligations and may thus be made the subject of a claim in state responsibility. Here we examine international claims from the opposite perspective: Rather than ask which states may be subject to a claim in state responsibility, we ask which states may *bring* such a claim. In other words, which states have standing to invoke the responsibility of other states?

The primary basis upon which a state may claim standing to invoke the responsibility of another state is that the latter's breach of an international legal obligation has "injured" the former. A state may be considered injured in a number of ways. In the most straightforward situation, if the obligation breached is owed to a state individually, that state is simply deemed injured by the fact of the breach alone.[132]

Somewhat more complex is the situation where the obligation breached is owed collectively to a group of states, or even *erga omnes* — that is, to the international community as a whole.[133] In such cases, a potential claimant state will be considered injured (and hence have standing) if the breach "specially affects" it[134] or radically changes the position of all states to which the obligation is owed.[135] The first of these contemplates particular injury that is not suffered by other states

---

131   See *Draft Articles*, above note 8, Article 55.

132   *Ibid.*, Article 42(a).

133   See *Barcelona Traction*, above note 32 at 32–34, where the ICJ noted that *erga omnes* obligations were of a special nature in that all states have a legal interest in their protection, and identified the prohibitions of aggression, genocide and violations of fundamental human rights, including slavery and racial discrimination, as having such an *erga omnes* character. See also *Israeli Wall*, above note 32 at paras. 155–62, where the ICJ recognized that certain rules of international humanitarian law, and the right of self-determination of peoples, were of an *erga omnes* character. See further discussion of the nature of *erga omnes* obligations in Chapter 10, Section D(4).

134   *Draft Articles*, above note 8, Article 42(b)(i).

135   *Ibid.*, Article 42(b)(ii).

concerned. In other words, the claimant state has been affected differently or more seriously than the other states to which the collective obligation is owed.[136] The second contemplates that all states to which the obligation is owed are equally but "radically" affected, either in their enjoyment of rights under, or in their performance of, the obligation breached.[137] Due to the radical change in position of all states to which the obligation is owed, each is considered "injured" and thus to have standing to seek a remedy.

Of course, it may be that several states are injured in the sense of being "specially affected" or having their positions "radically changed" as the result of a breach of an obligation owed to them collectively. In such circumstances, each such injured state may separately bring a claim against the breaching state.[138] Similarly, a breach of obligation attributable to more than one state may be pursued against each such state.[139]

While standing thus hinges primarily on being an injured state, it is also possible, in two exceptional cases, for a state to bring a claim against another even when the former has not been injured within the meaning of Article 42 of the *Draft Articles*. The first such case is where the obligation breached is owed collectively to a group of states "for the protection of a collective interest of the group."[140] These latter words are the distinguishing feature between such an obligation and a collective obligation referred to in Article 42(b), which is focused on protecting the individual interests of the various states to which it is owed. An example of a collective obligation in the more restrictive sense of Article 48(1)(a), one that is not only collectively owed but that also protects a collective interest, might be a treaty protecting a common environmental interest, such as the sustainability of a high seas fish stock.[141]

The second situation in which standing may be claimed by a state not injured by the breach of an international obligation is where that obligation is owed to the international community as a whole.[142] Significantly, there is no additional requirement of being specially affected or having one's position radically changed as a result of such a breach, as in the case of Article 42(b). Recall that the rule in Article 48(1)(b) grants standing to a state that specifically has *not* been injured in one

---

136 See *Commentaries*, above note 8 at 299–300.
137 *Ibid.* at 300.
138 *Draft Articles*, above note 8, Article 46.
139 *Ibid.*, Article 47.
140 *Ibid.*, Article 48(1)(a).
141 See *Commentaries*, above note 8 at 320–21.
142 *Draft Articles*, above note 8, Article 48(1)(b).

of these ways; it therefore suffices merely that the obligation be owed *erga omnes*.

It might be wondered why Article 42(b) adds such additional requirements if standing in respect of the breach of an *erga omnes* obligation can be gained more simply through Article 48(1)(b). Similarly, there is overlap between the concept of an obligation owed collectively to a group of states (Article 42(b)), and such an obligation that specifically protects a collective interest of the group (Article 48(1)(a)), in that the former clearly subsumes the latter. As the boundaries between the situations covered by, and the requirements of, Articles 42 (standing by "injured" states) and 48 (standing by "non-injured" states) are therefore not watertight, what is the significance of distinguishing between them in the first place?

The answer to this query is contained in Article 48(2). Essentially, the standing granted to a non-injured state, in the sense of Article 48(1), is limited to claiming cessation of the breach (if ongoing), assurances and guarantees of non-repetition, and reparation *on behalf of an injured state or beneficiary of the obligation breached.*[143] By contrast, an injured state within the meaning of Article 42 is entitled to claim, *on its own behalf,* any of the forms of redress provided for in the *Draft Articles,*[144] and may also resort to lawful countermeasures.[145] In other words, the standing of a non-injured state under Article 48 is limited to the assertion of claims on behalf of others, including non-state actors such as a people denied its right of self-determination.[146] Given its essentially benevolent nature, it is perhaps not surprising that such standing is rarely invoked in practice. In any case, it is the considerably different range of remedies that may be sought that motivates the distinctions between standing as an injured state under Article 42 and standing as a non-injured state under Article 48.

2) State Espousal of Individual or Corporate Claims

a) Introduction
As a general rule and as we have seen earlier,[147] only states (and to a limited extent some international organizations) have the legal person-

---

143 This limited range of potential remedies that may be sought pursuant to Article 48 is to be considered exhaustive: *Commentaries*, above note 8 at 322.

144 See Section C, below in this chapter.

145 See *Commentaries*, above note 8 at 295.

146 See, for example, *East Timor*, above note 32 at para. 29; *Israeli Wall*, above note 32 at para. 155.

147 See Chapter 2.

ality necessary to assert claims on the international plane and to seek reparation for the international wrongs of other international legal persons. However, states and international organizations are not the only entities that may suffer harm as a result of such wrongs. For example, a state may breach its international legal obligation to respect certain standards of conduct in its treatment of foreign nationals.[148] While this may, depending on the circumstances, give rise to a direct claim by the state whose nationals have been mistreated for its own injury arising from such mistreatment, it may also result in damages to those nationals themselves for which they have no direct capacity to bring a claim in international law.

The mechanism by which such claims are in fact pursued in the international legal system is known as "espousal of claims."[149] Just as a state may be held responsible in certain limited circumstances for the acts of private persons, so too may it adopt or "espouse" the claims of private persons who would otherwise have no standing in international law to pursue a claim against a state that has wronged them. Whether a state espouses such a claim or not is, from the perspective of international law, entirely a discretionary matter for it to decide on whatever basis it deems relevant, provided it respects the two requirements outlined below.[150] Moreover, if a state decides to espouse a private person's claim, this does not grant standing to that person to pursue the claim. Rather, the espousing state assumes all aspects of the conduct of the claim, including the choice of forum.[151] In the eyes of international law, therefore, the espoused claim becomes for all practical intents and purposes that of the espousing state. The person whose claim is espoused, as well as their damages, become merely the subject matter of the claim.[152]

While a state's decision whether or not to espouse a claim is entirely discretionary, this is not to say that there are no international rules limiting *which* individuals' or corporations' claims may be so espoused by any given state. In general, there are two requirements before a state's

---

148 On the topic of mistreatment of "aliens," see Chapter 8, Section D.

149 Sometimes also referred to as the exercise or extension by states of "diplomatic protection."

150 *Barcelona Traction*, above note 32 at 44. See also R.B. Lillich, *The Human Rights of Aliens in Contemporary International Law* (Manchester: Manchester University Press, 1984) at 9. This is without prejudice to any constraints that may be imposed upon a state in the exercise of this discretion as a result of its internal legal order.

151 Whether diplomatic, arbitral, judicial, or other.

152 See Brownlie, above note 4 at 459.

purported espousal of a claim will be deemed "admissible": first, there must be a national link between the claimant and the espousing state, and second, the claimant must have exhausted local remedies in the state against which the claim is to be brought. While the *Draft Articles* only mention such requirements in passing,[153] the ILC completed, in 2006, another set of draft articles specifically addressing this topic.[154] These again appear to closely reflect the customary international rules governing the espousal of claims. Reference will therefore be made to the relevant provisions of the *Diplomatic Protection Articles* in describing those rules in the next two subsections.

b) Nationality Requirement

The right of states to espouse claims rests almost exclusively on the existence of a link of nationality between the espousing state and the person whose claim is being adopted.[155] The theoretical basis for the espousal of the claims of one's nationals is somewhat unclear. Some of the early judgments of the Permanent Court of International Justice suggested that, in espousing a claim on behalf of one of its nationals, "a State is in reality asserting its own right, the right to ensure in the person of its nationals respect for the rules of international law."[156] On the other hand, an espoused claim may result in an order for reparation that is conceptually distinct from that due directly to the claiming state

---

153 *Draft Articles*, above note 8, Article 44.

154 See *Draft Articles on Diplomatic Protection* in "Report of the International Law Commission on the work of its 58th Session", UN GAOR, 61st Sess., Supplement No. 10 (A/61/10), c. IV.E.1 (2006) [*Diplomatic Protection Articles*]. See also *Commentaries to the Draft Articles on Diplomatic Protection* in *ibid.*, c. IV.E.1 [*Diplomatic Protection Commentaries*]. The UN General Assembly has taken note of the *Diplomatic Protection Articles* and invited comments from governments as to whether they should form the basis for negotiation of a multilateral convention on the topic.: UNGA Res. 61/35, UN GAOR, 61st Sess., UN Doc. A/RES/61/35 (2006). The General Assembly is scheduled to consider the matter again during its sixty-fifth session in 2010–2011: see UNGA Res. 62/67, UN GAOR, 62nd Sess., UN Doc. A/RES/62/67 (2007), para 4.

155 *Diplomatic Protection Articles*, *ibid.*, Articles 1, 3, 5–7, and 10. This general requirement applies to both individuals and corporations. On the attribution of nationality to individuals and corporations, see Chapter 8, Section C(3).

156 See, for example, the *Panevezys-Saldutiskis Railway Case* (*Estonia v. Lithuania*) (1939), P.C.I.J., (Ser. A/B), No. 76 at 16; or the *Mavrommatis Palestine Concessions Case* (*Greece v. United Kingdom*) (1924), P.C.I.J., (Ser. A), No. 2 at 12. See also E. de Vattel, *The Law of Nations or the Principles of Natural Law Applied to the Conduct and to the Affairs of Nations and Sovereigns*, 1758, trans. by C.G. Fenwick, vol. III (Washington: Carnegie Institution, 1916) at 136.

for a breach of its own rights,[157] which has led the ILC to characterize the "assertion of a state's own right" rationale as a "fiction."[158] In any case, the presentation by states of the claims of their nationals against other states preserves the formality of "a claim between two political entities, equal in law, similar in form, and both the direct subjects of international law."[159]

As a general rule, the national link must exist both at the time of the acts or omissions giving rise to the claim and at the time the claim is made.[160] In the case of a person who has the nationality of the espousing state at the time the claim is made but not at the time of the injury, an exception to this "continuous nationality" requirement is made if the person's previous nationality was lost and current nationality acquired for reasons unconnected to the bringing of the claim.[161] However, a claim cannot be espoused against a former state of nationality if the claimant had that former—but not the present—nationality at the time of the injury.[162] Similarly, if the claimant acquires, after a claim is made, the nationality of the state against which that claim has been espoused, the claim can no longer proceed.[163]

The growing propensity of individuals to have more than one state of nationality, a result of increased migration and more flexible domestic nationality laws, might be thought to give rise to difficulties in applying the continuous nationality rule. With respect to the espousal of claims of dual or multiple nationals against a state of which the claimant is not a national (a so-called "third state"), no such difficulty in fact arises: the rule is simply that any or all of the states of nationality may espouse the claim against the third state.[164]

The situation is more complicated, however, in the case of espousal by one state of nationality against another state of nationality. Earlier

---

157 See, for example, *SS I'm Alone* (1935), 3 R.I.A.A. 1609 [*The I'm Alone*] where separate awards were made to the Canadian government in its own right, and on behalf of the victims of the illegal sinking of the *I'm Alone* by the United States Coast Guard.
158 See *Diplomatic Protection Commentaries*, above note 154 at 25.
159 *Reparations Case*, above note 67 at 177–78.
160 *Diplomatic Protection Articles*, above note 154, Articles 5(1) and 10(1). See also E.B. Wang, "Nationality of Claims and Diplomatic Intervention" (1965) 43 Can. Bar Rev. 136.
161 *Diplomatic Protection Articles*, above note 154, Article 5(2).
162 *Ibid.*, Article 5(3).
163 *Ibid.*, Articles 5(4) and 10(2).
164 *Ibid.*, Article 6.

international law appeared to prohibit espousal in such a case.[165] More recent and widespread practice is, however, to allow espousal in such a case as long as the nationality of the espousing state is "predominant," both at the date of the injury and at the time of making the claim.[166] This is therefore the position adopted in the *Diplomatic Protection Articles*.[167] The nationality of the espousing state will be predominant if the claimant has stronger ties with it than with the state against which the claim is to be espoused.[168] Factors that have been considered by tribunals in applying this test include:

> ... habitual residence, the amount of time spent in each country of nationality, date of naturalization (i.e., the length of the period spent as a national of the protecting State before the claim arose); place, curricula and language of education; employment and financial interests; place of family life; family ties in each country; participation in social and public life; use of language; taxation, bank account, social security insurance; visits to the other State of nationality; possession and use of passport of the other State; and military service.[169]

Application of the predominant nationality rule remains difficult in practice, however, as several states continue to insist on the former rule.[170]

Finally, the *Diplomatic Protection Articles* contemplate two exceptional circumstances in which a link of nationality will not be required as a condition of valid espousal of a claim. First, where a person has no nationality, the state in which the person is habitually resident at the time of the injury and at the time of making the claim may espouse that

---

165 See, for example, the *Hague Convention on Certain Questions Relating to the Conflict of Nationality Laws*, 1930, Can. T.S. 1937 No. 7; *Harvard Draft Convention of Responsibility of States for Damage Done in Their Territory to the Person or Property of Foreigners* (1929) 23 A.J.I.L. Sp. Supp. 133, Article 16(a); *Harvard Draft Convention on the International Responsibility of States for Injuries to Aliens*, (1961) 55 A.J.I.L. 548, Article 23(5); *Reparations Case*, above note 67 at 186.

166 See authorities collected in the *Diplomatic Protection Commentaries*, above note 154 at 44–46.

167 *Diplomatic Protection Articles*, above note 154, Article 7.

168 *Diplomatic Protection Commentaries*, above note 154 at 46.

169 *Ibid.*

170 As illustrated, for example, in the continuing dispute between Canada and Iran over Canada's attempt to extend diplomatic protection in respect of Zahra Kazemi, a journalist of dual Canadian-Iranian nationality who was beaten to death by Iranian interrogators over allegations of espionage in July 2003. Iran continues to contest Canada's standing to exercise diplomatic protection in the case: see Department of Foreign Affairs and International Trade News Release No. 76, "Statement by Minister MacKay on the Death of Zahra Kazemi" (10 July 2006).

person's claim.[171] The same rule applies with respect to a person who, although having a nationality, is considered a refugee by the state in which he or she is habitually resident.[172] This latter rule will not apply, however, in the case of a claim against the refugee's state of nationality.[173] Given that many refugees have such status as a result of violations of their fundamental human rights by their state of nationality, such a limitation goes a considerable distance towards rendering the rule in Article 8(2) meaningless.

c) Requirement of Exhaustion of Local Remedies

In addition to the national link requirement, it is a general rule that a state may not validly advance the claim of one of its nationals until that national has exhausted, without satisfaction, all remedies locally available in the allegedly offending state.[174] Such a requirement does not exist in the case of a breach of international legal obligations owed directly by one state to another,[175] but is confined to claims against a state by foreign nationals, which of course require espousal. The theory behind the distinction may be that, in the former case, it would be inconsistent with the sovereign equality of states to require the injured state to subject itself to the remedial jurisdiction of the other. It is also unlikely that effective or acceptable remedies could be provided by the domestic legal system of the offending state.

On the other hand, in claims arising from a state's treatment of a foreign national, that treatment is deemed to include any remedial mechanisms provided by that state's legal system. Theoretically, therefore, there can be no "injury" to the foreign national until such procedures have been pursued and have failed to provide redress. The validity of this rationale for the requirement of the exhaustion of local remedies may depend, however, on the nature of the obligation breached and other circumstances.[176] Some judicial pronouncements, for example, have regarded the doctrine as a purely procedural requirement not connected to the substantive breach of an obligation.[177] It may nevertheless

---

171 *Diplomatic Protection Articles*, above note 154, Article 8(1).

172 *Ibid.*, Article 8(2).

173 *Ibid.*, Article 8(3).

174 *Ibid.*, Article 14; *Case Concerning Ahmadou Sadio Diallo (Republic of Guinea v. Democratic Republic of the Congo), Preliminary Objections* (24 May 2007), General List No. 103 (I.C.J.) at para. 42 [*Ahmadou Sadio Diallo*].

175 *Diplomatic Protection Articles*, above note 154, Article 14(3).

176 See Brownlie, above note 4 at 472–81.

177 See, for example, *Phosphates in Morocco Case (Preliminary Objections)* (1938), P.C.I.J., (Series A/B), No. 74 at 27; *Elettronica Sicula S.p.A. (ELSI) Case (United States of America v. Italy)*, [1989] I.C.J. Rep. 15 at 46–48.

play a useful role in ensuring that the majority of claims of private persons are resolved in a domestic legal system, arguably a more suitable forum than international tribunals.[178]

Exhaustion of local remedies requires that the claim be pursued completely in the domestic legal system of the allegedly offending state, including available appeal routes.[179] However, it is generally recognized that obviously ineffective remedies, or appeals that would clearly be futile, need not be pursued.[180] Nor is there any requirement to pursue purely discretionary remedies, such as appeals for executive mercy, as these do not as a general rule represent legal entitlements.[181] Further, if there is no effective legal system at all or if it does not provide for timely redress, a state may espouse and assert its national's claim notwithstanding the national's failure to try to obtain such redress.[182] Moreover, the *Diplomatic Protection Articles* provide for an exception if it would be unreasonable in the circumstances to expect a claimant to exhaust local remedies, as in the case where there is no relevant connection between the claimant and the offending state.[183] It is unclear, however, whether this represents a well-established rule of customary international law or represents "progressive development" by the ILC.[184]

Finally, the state against which a claim is made may waive the exhaustion of local remedies requirement and permit the matter to proceed directly on a state-to-state basis in an international forum.[185]

---

178 See Brownlie, above note 4 at 473; I. Head, "A Fresh Look at the Local Remedies Rule" (1967) 5 Can. Y.B. Int'l L. 142 at 155.

179 See *Diplomatic Protection Commentaries*, above note 154 at 72.

180 *Diplomatic Protection Articles*, above note 154, Article 15(a). See, for example, *The Ambatielos Claim (Greece v. United Kingdom)* (1956), 12 R.I.A.A. 93 at 119.

181 See *Diplomatic Protection Commentaries*, above note 154 at 72; *Ahmadou Sadio Diallo*, above note 174 at para. 47; *Case Concerning Avena and Other Mexican Nationals (Mexico v. United States of America)*, [2004] I.C.J. Rep. 12 at paras. 135–43.

182 *Diplomatic Protection Articles*, above note 154, Articles 15(b) and (d).

183 *Ibid.*, Article 15(c). For example, an individual or business might be injured by the unlawful behaviour of a state without ever having been present in its territory; in such cases, it would seem unreasonable to require the injured person to take steps within that state's territory to obtain redress: see *Diplomatic Protection Commentaries*, above note 154 at 80–81.

184 See the somewhat tentative description of the authorities supporting this rule in the *Diplomatic Protection Commentaries*, *ibid.* at 81–83.

185 *Diplomatic Protection Articles*, above note 154, Article 15(e).

C. REMEDIES

1) General Principles

In general, breach of an international obligation entails two further, broad secondary obligations. The first, which is self-explanatory, is cessation of the wrongful conduct, if it is ongoing, and resumed compliance with the international obligation.[186] The second is to make what is known in international law as full "reparation" for the breach of obligation to the aggrieved state or states.[187] While reparation may take many forms, to be reviewed below, it should be noted at the outset that a breach of an international obligation is wrongful *per se*. In other words, and as a general rule, no material damage need be caused to another state before the breaching state may be held responsible for the breach.[188] The failure to respect the obligation is in itself considered injurious to the state to which the obligation is owed and is sufficient to establish a secondary duty of reparation.[189] Again, this approach is in keeping with the generally strict tenor of state responsibility.

2) Reparation

While analogies to the domestic law of remedies seem almost inevitable in this area of international law, it must be noted that the domestic law of the parties is technically irrelevant to the process of determining the appropriate remedy for a breach of an international obligation.[190] In other words, international law itself prescribes a range of generally applicable remedies and determines the priority of their application in any individual case. This is in addition to particularized remedies that may be prescribed by specific international legal regimes, such as a right of termination of a treaty in response to a material breach by another party.[191]

---

186 *Draft Articles*, above note 8, Articles 29 & 30. Article 30(b) also refers to the possibility of seeking "assurances and guarantees of non-repetition."

187 *Ibid.*, Article 31. And see the *Chorzów Factory Case*, above note 12 at 29: "The Court observes that it is a principle of international law … that any breach of an engagement involves an obligation to make reparation."

188 See *Commentaries*, above note 8 at 225–26.

189 *Chorzów Factory Case*, above note 12 at 29.

190 *Draft Articles*, above note 8, Article 32.

191 See Chapter 4, Section J(2)(b).

The archetypal statement of the overall purpose of reparation is still that of the Permanent Court of International Justice in the *Chorzów Factory Case*:

> The essential principle contained in the actual notion of an illegal act—a principle which seems to be established by international practice and in particular by the decisions of arbitral tribunals—is that reparation must, as far as possible, wipe out all the consequences of the illegal act and reestablish the situation which would, in all probability, have existed if that act had not been committed. Restitution in kind, or, if this is not possible, payment of a sum corresponding to the value of which a restitution in kind would bear; the award, if need be, of damages for loss sustained which would not be covered by restitution in kind or payment in place of it—such are the principles which should serve to determine the amount of compensation due for an act contrary to international law.[192]

Thus, the objective is to undo the consequences of the international wrong to the fullest extent possible. While there are inconsistencies of usage and nomenclature, it can be said that there are essentially three forms of reparation, each serving a different function in the overall attempt to erase the consequences of an internationally wrongful act. Each of these—restitution, compensation, and satisfaction—will be described in turn below.

a)   Restitution

Restitution, as suggested by the Permanent Court in the passage reproduced above, is the preferred remedial option in international law, as it will normally present the greatest chance of truly restoring the parties to the situation they would have occupied had the breach of obligation never occurred. A classic example would be the return of a wrongfully seized vessel or the restoration of secure diplomatic premises.[193]

The *Draft Articles* therefore give priority to restitution.[194] Indeed, the injured state has the option in international law of demanding restitution in kind, in preference to other forms of reparation. The exercise of such a preference is limited only by two considerations. The first, of course, is that restitution in kind must be materially possible; meaning, for example, that the object to be restored still exists. Second, requiring

---

192 *Chorzów Factory Case*, above note 12 at 47.

193 Another example is an order that an unlawful arrest warrant be cancelled: see *DRC v. Belgium*, above note 13 at para. 76.

194 *Draft Articles*, above note 8, Article 35.

restitution over compensation must not impose a burden on the wrong-doer that is "out of all proportion" to the benefit gained thereby.[195]

Aside from these requirements, however, restitution is clearly the remedy of choice, sometimes in combination with others, in seeking to erase all consequences of the breach of an obligation.

b) Compensation

A state that causes damage through its failure to respect its international obligations must pay compensation for any damage not made good by way of restitution.[196] This is obviously a second-best alternative to restitution in that it attempts to provide a monetary substitute for the interest that has been damaged rather than to restore it in kind. Generally, such a remedy can only ever place the parties in a position that imperfectly approximates that which they would have occupied had the wrong not occurred. For this reason it is not the preferred remedial option in international law, but is resorted to out of necessity.

A duty of compensation will extend to any financially assessable damage not otherwise made whole and will include lost profits where these can be established.[197] Interest will also be payable on an award of damages from the date of the award until the date of payment.[198] In practice, for purposes of assessing damages, international tribunals tend to borrow from better-developed domestic legal principles relating to such assessment under the rubric of "general principles of law."[199]

c) Satisfaction

Beyond material reparation by way of restitution and the payment of compensation, there is in international law a general theory of "non-material" damage caused by one state to another upon breach of an international obligation. This notion is bound up with the principle of the sovereign equality of states and roughly translates to interference with the dignitary interest that comes with such sovereign status. It is

---

195 *Ibid.*, Article 35(b). The *Draft Articles 1996*, above note 6, further stipulated that requiring restitution must not jeopardize the political independence or economic stability of the wrongdoing state if the aggrieved state would not be similarly jeopardized in the absence of restitution. This element has been omitted from the 2001 *Draft Articles*, presumably on the basis that it comes within the scope of the concept of disproportionate burden.

196 *Draft Articles*, above note 8, Article 36.

197 *Ibid.*, Article 36(2).

198 *Ibid.*, Article 38.

199 See further Chapter 3, Section C(4). For examples of the types of compensation awarded and methods of quantification employed by various international tribunals, see *Commentaries*, above note 8 at 248–58.

generally considered that such non-material damage must also be the subject of reparation if the parties are truly to be placed in the position they would have occupied had the breach not occurred. This form of reparation is known as "satisfaction."[200]

The forms satisfaction may take are dictated by the intangible nature of the dignitary interests sought to be repaired. In practice, formal acknowledgments of wrongdoing, expressions of regret, formal apologies, guarantees of non-repetition, and declaratory judgments are all common forms of satisfaction.[201] There are also instances where nominal damages have been awarded by way of satisfaction for violation of a state's sovereignty.[202] However, forms of satisfaction that would themselves impair the dignity of or humiliate the wrongdoing state may not be required.[203]

3) Self-Help: Countermeasures

As indicated above,[204] international law has a long history of self-help remedies, dating from a time when there were few international fora of a judicial or quasi-judicial nature. In the absence of readily available and effective (peaceful) dispute resolution mechanisms, states often took matters into their own hands and exacted reprisals or countermeasures against states they considered to have breached obligations owed to them.[205]

Despite the vastly improved conditions of international relations and the proliferation of peaceful dispute settlement options in the post-Second World War period, it nevertheless remains the case that the international legal system is not always perceived as effective. The reasons for this range from a lack of peaceful law enforcement mechanisms that do not depend for their jurisdiction on the consent of all parties involved in the dispute, to continued perceptions of self-interest by some states in pursuing unilateral remedial options. The challenge for inter-

---

200 *Draft Articles*, above note 8, Article 37.

201 *Ibid.*, Article 37(2).

202 See, for example, *The I'm Alone*, above note 157 at 1618, where the United States was ordered to formally acknowledge and apologize for its illegal conduct in sinking, on the high seas, a vessel sailing under the Canadian flag. In addition, the United States was ordered to pay $25,000 to the Canadian government "as a material amend in respect of the wrong." See also the *Rainbow Warrior*, above note 2 at 575.

203 *Draft Articles*, above note 8, Article 37(3).

204 See the text accompanying note 4, above in this chapter.

205 The concept of countermeasures has been introduced earlier in this chapter: see Section A(5)(c), above in this chapter.

national law, therefore, is to reconcile the modern obligations of states to refrain from acts of armed force and to seek peaceful settlement of disputes, on the one hand, with their residual sovereignty and persistent state practice still clearly entitling them to resort to certain remedial measures of self-help, on the other.[206] This is no mean feat given the inherent flavour of retribution or reprisal that runs through the concept of countermeasures, and the potential for violence, or at least of escalation of tensions, posed by resort to such self-help remedies.

The solution, according to the *Draft Articles*, is to precisely delimit the permissible objectives and scope of countermeasures. Thus, the only permissible objective of countermeasures, according to the *Draft Articles*, is to induce compliance by an offending state with its obligations and to make full reparation for wrongful conduct that has already occurred.[207] Countermeasures may only involve suspending the performance of obligations owed to the offending state, albeit in such a manner that does not, to the extent possible, inhibit the resumption of their performance in due course.[208] Further, countermeasures cannot involve the suspension of certain fundamental state obligations—such as the duty to refrain from the use of force or to respect fundamental human rights—certain obligations of a humanitarian character, and other rules of *jus cogens*.[209] In addition, in the interests of maintaining channels of communication between the parties as well as opportunities for peaceful dispute resolution, rules concerning the inviolability of foreign diplomatic premises, documents, and agents, as well as relevant obligations relating to dispute settlement, may not be suspended as a countermeasure.[210]

As such, permissible countermeasures would appear to be limited to the suspension of performance of legal obligations of a largely economic or political character. Within these limits and in all cases, proportionality of response is to be observed.[211] Further, the *Draft Articles* prescribe complex procedural requirements that must be exhausted before a state may resort to countermeasures.[212] Such requirements are designed to bring the dispute to an early end by resort to peaceful dispute resolution mechanisms.

---

206 See, for example, the *Air Services Agreement Case* (1978), 18 R.I.A.A. 417.
207 *Draft Articles*, above note 8, Article 49(1).
208 *Ibid.*, Articles 49(2) & (3).
209 *Ibid.*, Article 50(1).
210 *Ibid.*, Article 50(2). See also *Commentaries*, above note 8 at 333 and 338.
211 *Draft Articles*, *ibid.*, Article 51.
212 *Ibid.*, Article 52.

The restrictive view of permissible countermeasures taken by the ILC is at least partially supported by the duties of states, already mentioned and clearly established in post-Second World War international law, to refrain from the use or threat of force and to resolve disputes peacefully. It is doubtful, however, that the full range of procedural restrictions, contemplated in Article 52 of the *Draft Articles*, has yet been sufficiently integrated into state practice to constitute general customary international law.[213] For the time being, therefore, at least some of the procedural aspects of the *Draft Articles'* provisions on countermeasures may reflect an attempt at the progressive development of international law rather than its codification.

FURTHER READING

ALLOTT, P., "State Responsibility and the Unmaking of International Law" (1988) 29 Harv. Int'l L.J. 1

AMERASINGHE, C.F., *Local Remedies in International Law* (Cambridge: Grotius Publications, 1990)

BECKER, T., *Terrorism and the State: Rethinking the Rules of State Responsibility* (Oxford: Hart, 2006)

BOWETT, D., "Crimes of States and the 1996 Report of the International Law Commission on State Responsibility" (1998) 9 Eur. J. Int'l L. 163

BROWNLIE, I., *System of the Law of Nations: State Responsibility*, Part 1 (Oxford: Clarendon Press, 1983)

CRAWFORD, J., *The International Law Commission's Articles on State Responsibility: Introduction, Text and Commentaries* (Cambridge: Cambridge University Press, 2002)

DUMBERRY, P., *State Succession to International Responsibility* (Leiden: Martinus Nijhoff, 2007)

---

213 See, for example, the *Air Services Agreement Case*, above note 206; and the views of the Legal Bureau of the Canadian Department of Foreign Affairs and International Trade recorded in a memorandum dated 24 November 1989 and reported at (1990) 28 Can. Y.B. Int'l L. 494. It is probably also significant that the ILC *Commentaries* make no reference to international or arbitral decisions supporting the procedural obligations set out in Article 52, other than the obligation to call upon an offending state to fulfill its obligations before resorting to countermeasures (Article 52(1)): see *Commentaries*, above note 8 at 346–49.

ELAGAB, O.Y., *The Legality of Non-Forcible Counter-Measures in International Law* (Oxford: Clarendon Press, 1988)

GRAY, C., *Judicial Remedies in International Law* (Oxford: Clarendon Press, 1987)

HEAD, I., "A Fresh Look at the Local Remedies Rule" (1967) 5 Can. Y.B. Int'l L. 142

JENNINGS, R.Y. & WATTS, A.D., *Oppenheim's International Law*, 9th ed., vol. 1 (London: Longman, 1992) c. 4

LAW, C.H.P., *The Local Remedies Rule in International Law* (Genève: E. Droz, 1961)

LILLICH, R.B., ed., *International Law of State Responsibility for Injuries to Aliens* (Charlottesville: University Press of Virginia, 1983)

OKOWA, P.N., *State Responsibility for Transboundary Air Pollution in International Law* (Oxford: Oxford University Press, 2000)

PROVOST, R., ed., *State Responsibility in International Law* (Aldershot, UK: Ashgate, 2002)

SIMMA, B., "Bilateralism and Community Interest in the Law of State Responsibility" in Y. Dinstein & M. Tabory, eds., *International Law at a Time of Perplexity: Essays in Honour of Shabtai Rosenne* (Dordrecht: M. Nijhoff, 1989) 821

VERHEYEN, R., *Climate Change Damage and International Law: Prevention, Duties and State Responsibility* (Leiden: M. Nijhoff, 2005) c. 5

WEILER, J.H., CASSESE, A., & SPINEDI, M., eds., *International Crimes of State: A Critical Analysis of the ILC's Draft Article 19 on State Responsibility* (New York: W. de Gruyter, 1989)

GLOSSARY

Abandonment The lapse of a state's sovereignty over territory, causing the territory to become a *res nullius*.

Absolute state immunity A theory of state immunity that does not differentiate between commercial (or "private") and sovereign acts of states in extending immunity to them from the judicial process of foreign domestic courts; contrast with **restrictive state immunity**.

Accession The process by which a state that has not participated in the negotiation of the text of a treaty nevertheless expresses its consent to be bound by and become a party to that treaty.

Accretion A natural process, such as the extension of a river delta, by which the land territory of a state is gradually enlarged.

Acquiescence Tacit or implied acceptance or recognition of another state's claim or right, often in relation to territory.

Adoption The process by which the text of a treaty is agreed to or finalized by negotiating states.

Adoptionist An approach to the domestic reception of international law that presumes that international law (in particular, customary international law) is part of domestic law (in particular, the common law); see also **incorporationist**.

Alien A foreign national; a national of another state.

Annexation The formal act by which a state that has conquered the territory of another state asserts its sovereignty over such territory; see also **conquest**.

Anticipatory self-defence A controversial doctrine that would permit states to use force in self-defence prior to the occurrence of an **armed attack**, provided however that an **armed attack** is imminent; see also **self-defence, pre-emptive self-defence**.

Archipelagic state A state composed entirely of islands or of one or more archipelagoes.

Archipelagic waters The marine waters enclosed by straight baselines joining the outer points of the outer islands of an archipelagic state.

Armed attack A use of force intentionally directed at a state which, by virtue of its scale and effects, is of such gravity as to justify a responsive use of force by that state in self-defence; contrast with **mere frontier incident**.

Attributability The required relationship between the acts of a non-state actor and a state for purposes of engaging the state responsibility of, or justifying the use of force in self-defence against, the latter; see also **imputability**.

Authentication The process by which states verify that the official text of a treaty corresponds to the terms negotiated, usually by initialling or signing the official text.

Baseline The line from which the seaward extent of a coastal state's maritime zones is measured; the default baseline corresponds to the low-water line along the coast, but straight baselines enclosing fringes of coastal islands or deeply indented coastlines are also permissible.

Bay An indentation in a coast that is sufficiently pronounced that its area is equal to or greater than that of a semi-circle with a diameter equal to the width of the mouth of the indentation.

Bilateral treaty A treaty between two subjects of international law.

Binding intent The intent of a party to a treaty to be bound by that treaty as a matter of international law.

Calvo clause A clause sometimes inserted by states into a concession contract with foreign investors by which the latter agree not to seek the protection of their national state but to submit to local law and jurisdiction with respect to all matters or disputes arising under the contract.

Cession The transfer of sovereignty over territory from one state to another by agreement.

Clean slate doctrine In connection with state succession, a rule by which a successor state generally does not inherit the prior treaty rights or obligations of a predecessor state.

Collective security The mechanism provided for in Chapter VII of the *Charter of the United Nations* by which the Security Council may take or authorize necessary measures, on behalf of the international community, to maintain or restore international peace and security.

Collective self-defence, Right of An exception to the general prohibition of the use of force among states permitting one state to use force in response to an **armed attack** against another, provided that the latter declares that it has been the victim of an armed attack and requests the assistance of the former; compare with **self-defence**.

Colonized people, colony People or state that has been subject to colonial rule by a foreign, metropolitan power.

Common heritage of humankind A legal regime said to apply to the resources of the deep seabed, and perhaps of celestial bodies, which prevents their unilateral appropriation, use, or exploitation by states; exploitation of an area designated as the common heritage of humankind is reserved for the benefit of all states; also designated in some instruments as the "common heritage of mankind."

Concession contract A contract between a state and a private legal entity governed by domestic rather than international law.

Conflict of laws An area of domestic law governing the manner in which domestic courts deal with transactions having one or more foreign elements (e.g., an event or transaction occurring abroad or involving foreign nationals); also **private international law**.

Conquest The military occupation of the territory of one state by another with the intent of transferring sovereignty over the territory from the former to the latter by way of **annexation**.

Consent to be bound The essential ingredient in the formation of binding treaty obligations, consisting of the expression by a state or other subject of international law of its intent to fulfill the obligations stipulated in the treaty as a matter of international law.

Consular protection The discretionary extension by a state of various services to its nationals detained by a foreign state. Services usually include visits by consular officials to ensure lawful conditions of detention, as well as facilitation of retainer of local legal representation.

Contiguity, Principle of A rebuttable presumption that the legal status of territory should follow that of territory to which it is adjacent or proximate; often invoked in support of claims to sovereignty over territory.

Contiguous zone A maritime zone commencing immediately beyond a coastal state's territorial sea and extending to a maximum of twenty-four nautical miles from the coastal state's baselines; the coastal state enjoys limited enforcement jurisdiction within the contiguous zone with respect to its customs, fiscal, immigration, and sanitary laws.

Continuity, Principle of A rebuttable presumption that the legal status of territory should follow that of territory to which it is connected; often invoked in support of claims to sovereignty over territory.

Continuity, State The doctrine by which a state's identity as an international legal person persists notwithstanding unconstitutional or even violent changes in its government. As a result, a state generally continues to owe and accrue international legal obligations notwithstanding such changes.

Convention A treaty.

Countermeasures A self-help remedy which permits states to commit certain acts that would be illegal at international law but for the fact that they are committed in response to prior acts of illegality by the states against which they are directed; also a defence against a claim in state responsibility.

Customary international law A source of international law predicated upon general state practice accompanied by the conviction that such practice is required as a matter of international law.

Decolonization The process by which a colonizing state withdraws its sovereign control over a colony, typically resulting in the colony's accession to statehood.

Deep seabed The seabed extending beyond the continental shelves of coastal states; corresponds roughly to the seabed beneath the **high seas**.

Denunciation The repudiation by one party of a **bilateral treaty**.

Diplomatic immunity A category of immunity from local jurisdiction extended to the diplomatic premises, correspondence and personnel of a foreign state.

Diplomatic protection The discretionary extension by a state of its protection (legal, diplomatic, or otherwise) to one of its nationals, usually in connection with a claim by the latter against a foreign state.

Distress A justification advanced to counter a claim of state responsibility on the basis that the acts alleged to be internationally wrongful constituted the only reasonable means of saving human life.

Domestic affairs Matters coming within the sole purview of a state's sovereign domestic authority, and thus not amenable to interference by other states or the international community generally; also **internal affairs**.

Domestic law/legal system The law or legal system established within a state to govern events, transactions, and persons within or having a connection to that state; also **internal**, **municipal**, **national**, or **local law/legal system**.

Dualism A theoretical model emphasizing the distinct nature of the international legal system and domestic legal systems; contrast with **monism**.

Effects doctrine A doctrine, developed mainly by the American courts in anti-trust cases, asserting jurisdiction over acts of foreign nationals committed abroad but having effects in the American marketplace; an extended form of the **objective territorial principle**.

Enforcement jurisdiction The power of a state to investigate, arrest, prosecute, punish, or otherwise enforce the law against persons present within its territory or aboard vessels or aircraft bearing its nationality.

Erga omnes In respect of international legal obligations, obligations owed to the community of nations as a whole rather than to any individual state or person.

Espousal of claim An exercise of diplomatic protection in which a state formally asserts an international claim on behalf of one of its nationals against another state.

Estoppel A general principle of law preventing a party which has, by act or omission, asserted a statement of fact from resiling from that assertion where to do so would cause prejudice to another party relying upon it; occasionally invoked in territorial disputes to prevent a state from disavowing its prior recognition of another state's sovereignty.

Estrada doctrine A policy, named after the Mexican foreign minister who first propounded it in 1930, under which a state abstains from taking any position on the validity of a new government in another state, on the basis that taking such a position would constitute an unjustified interference in the domestic affairs of that other state.

Exclusive economic zone A maritime zone extending seaward from the outer limit of a coastal state's territorial sea to a maximum distance of 200 nautical miles from the state's **baselines**.

Exhaustion of local remedies The requirement that a foreign national pursue, without satisfaction, all available domestic legal remedies before the foreign national's claim may be espoused and asserted against the local state by the foreign national's state.

Extradition The process by which one state, having custody of a suspected offender, transfers such custody to another state wishing to prosecute the suspected offender; a transfer of enforcement jurisdiction, often pursuant to a bilateral extradition treaty.

First generation human rights Human rights of a civil or political character, focused principally on rights and freedoms of the individual.

Fisheries zone A maritime zone declared under customary international law by some coastal states and extending seaward from the outer limit of the coastal state's territorial sea to a maximum distance of 200 nautical miles from the state's **baselines**.

Flag state The state of nationality or registration of a ship, under whose flag it navigates on the **high seas**.

Force majeure A justification advanced to counter a claim of state responsibility on the basis that the alleged internationally wrongful act of a state is due to an unforeseen event or irresistible force, beyond the control of the state, which makes it materially impossible for the state to respect an international obligation.

Full powers In the context of treaty negotiations, documents or other proof attesting to a state representative's authority to negotiate on behalf of, or to bind, his or her government or state.

Fundamental change of circumstances A basis for termination or suspension of treaty obligations based on a radical transformation of the extent of such obligations brought about by an unforeseen change of circumstances which constituted an essential basis of the party's consent to the treaty; see also *rebus sic stantibus*.

General Assembly An organ of the United Nations in which all member states are represented and have a vote; discusses and makes recommendations on any matter within the scope of the *Charter of the United Nations*.

General principles of law A formal source of international law, identified in Article 38(1)(c) of the *Statute of the International Court of Justice*, based on legal principles generally found in domestic legal systems.

Hard law Binding law; law emanating from a recognized, formal source of law; see also *lex lata*.

High seas The maritime zone lying beyond coastal states' territorial seas or, where declared, exclusive economic zones.

Historic waters Marine waters that are subject to a claim of sovereignty by a state based on historic occupation or usage.

Hot pursuit Pursuit of a foreign vessel commenced by a coastal state within one of its maritime zones and extending in an uninterrupted fashion onto the high seas.

Humanitarian intervention, Right of unilateral A controversial doctrine that would excuse a *prima facie* violation of the prohibition of the use of force among states on the basis that such force was necessary to halt or forestall a humanitarian crisis or gross human rights violations.

Implementation The process of transforming a treaty obligation into a domestic rule of law, usually through the enactment of legislation implementing the treaty obligation.

Implied authorization Alleged UN Security Council (UNSC) authorization to use force under Chapter VII of the *UN Charter*, based on language found in prior UNSC resolutions which does not expressly provide for the use of "all necessary means" or similar formulations. Notoriously invoked by Australia, the United Kingdom, and the United States to justify their invasion of Iraq in 2003.

Imputability The required relationship between the acts of a non-state actor and a state for purposes of engaging the state responsibility of, or justifying the use of force in self-defence against, the latter; see also **attributability**.

In force The quality of a treaty that has become binding upon and enforceable by parties to it, often through the achievement of a threshold number of ratifications or accessions.

Incorporationist An approach to the domestic reception of international law that presumes that international law (in particular, customary international law) is part of domestic law (in particular, the common law); see also **adoptionist**.

Independence Freedom from control by foreign states, but not from the strictures of international law.

Innocent passage, Right of A right of passage without prior authorization enjoyed by the vessels of all states through the territorial sea of a coastal state; to be innocent, passage must constitute a direct transit through the territorial sea punctuated only by temporary layovers that are incidental to passage in accordance with standard navigational practices.

Intergovernmental organization As a subject of international law, a permanent association of states with international legal rights and obligations distinct from those of its members and equipped with permanent organs or institutions; see also **international organization**.

Internal affairs Matters coming within the sole purview of a state's sovereign domestic authority, and thus not amenable to interference by other states or the international community generally; see also **domestic affairs**.

Internal law/legal system The law or legal system established within a state to govern events, transactions, and persons within or having a connection to that state; see also **domestic**, **municipal**, **national**, or **local law/legal system**.

Internal waters Coastal waters lying landward of a coastal state's baselines, including harbours, bays, the mouths of rivers, etc.

International claim A claim arising from an alleged breach of an international legal obligation.

International Court of Justice (ICJ) The principal judicial organ of the United Nations enjoying general subject-matter jurisdiction; its contentious jurisdiction depends upon consent of the parties to the dispute before it; the successor to the Permanent Court of International Justice of the League of Nations era.

International Law Commission (ILC) An international commission of jurists established in 1947 by the United Nations General Assembly with a mandate to undertake "the progressive development of international law and its codification."

International legal person An entity having rights, obligations, and standing under international law.

International minimum standard A minimum standard of treatment to be accorded by all states to foreign nationals, particularly in the context of law enforcement and judicial proceedings.

International organization As a subject of international law, a permanent association of states with international legal rights and obligations distinct from those of its members and equipped with permanent organs or institutions; see also **intergovernmental organization**.

International strait A narrow sea passage, bordered by opposite coasts, connecting two parts of the high seas, and used for international navigation.

Intertemporal rule A doctrine requiring interpretation or assessment of the legal effects of past transactions in the light of international law as it existed at the time of such transactions.

Invalidity In relation to treaties, a basis for vitiating a treaty *ab initio*.

Inviolability A potent form of immunity forbidding all physical interference with foreign diplomatic premises, communications, and personnel.

Isobath A contour line of constant depth on the seabed.

Jure gestionis In relation to restrictive state immunity, state acts of a commercial or non-sovereign or non-governmental character; contrast with *jure imperii*.

Jure imperii In relation to restrictive state immunity, state acts of a sovereign or governmental character; contrast with *jure gestionis*.

Jurisdiction The various forms of power exercised by a state over persons, property, events, and territory.

Jurisdictional immunity A rule of international law blocking the exercise of jurisdiction by a state over persons, property, or events.

Jus ad bellum The body of international law governing the circumstances in which states may lawfully resort to armed force against one another; contrast with *jus in bello*.

Jus cogens Rules of international law so fundamental to the international legal order that they cannot be set aside or suspended, even upon the express consent of states; see also **peremptory** or **non-derogable norms of international law**.

Jus in bello The body of international law governing the manner in which states and individuals may engage in armed conflict; contrast with *jus ad bellum*.

Jus sanguinis A ground for the granting of nationality on the basis of the nationality of one or both of a person's parents.

Jus solis A ground for the granting of nationality on the basis that the person was born in the territory of the granting state.

Law of nations International law.

Law-making treaty A multilateral treaty that purports to codify generally applicable, substantive rules of international law, and which is designed to attract as many parties as possible.

League of Nations An international organization established between the First and Second World Wars in an early attempt to foster international peace and cooperation.

Lex ferenda "Soft" law; non-binding or emerging norms which may or may not eventually harden into binding law; rules not yet grounded in a recognized, formal source of law.

Lex lata "Hard" law; binding law; law emanating from a recognized, formal source of law.

Local customary international law Customary international law that arises from state practice and *opinio juris* of a discrete and limited number of states; as it departs from generally applicable customary international law, it is only binding upon and opposable against those states participating in its formation; see also **regional** or **special customary international law**; contrast with **customary international law** without qualification.

Local law/legal system The law or legal system established within a state to govern events, transactions, and persons within or having a connection to that state; see also **domestic**, **internal**, **municipal**, or **national law/legal system**.

Material breach A repudiation of a treaty, or a breach of a treaty provision essential to the accomplishment of its object or purpose; a basis for termination or suspension of a treaty.

Mere frontier incident In connection with the law of self-defence, a use of force against a state which, by virtue of its limited scale and effects, is not of such gravity as to justify a responsive use of force by that state in self-defence; contrast with **armed attack**.

Metropolitan power A state that exercises sovereignty over colonies or that has established a colonial empire.

Monism A theoretical model positing the essential continuity of the international legal system and domestic legal systems; contrast with **dualism**.

Multilateral treaty A treaty between three or more subjects of international law.

Municipal law/legal system The law or legal system established within a state to govern events, transactions and persons within or having a connection to that state; see also **domestic, internal, national,** or **local law/legal system.**

National law/legal system The law or legal system established within a state to govern events, transactions and persons within or having a connection to that state; see also **domestic, internal, municipal,** or **local law/legal system.**

National treatment The extension by a state to foreign nationals of the same standards of treatment that are accorded to its own nationals, particularly with respect to law enforcement and judicial proceedings.

Nationality principle A basis for the exercise of prescriptive jurisdiction by a state over persons that have its nationality.

Nautical mile A unit of measure commonly used in the law of the sea and corresponding approximately to 1.15 land miles or 1.85 kilometres.

Necessity A justification advanced to counter a claim of state responsibility on the basis that the alleged internationally wrongful act of a state was necessary to protect an essential interest of that state against a grave and imminent peril.

Nemo dat quod non habet A general principle of law meaning that one cannot give more than one has; applied in territorial disputes in tracing the root of a state's claim of title to territory.

Newly-independent state A state which has relatively recently achieved independence and recognition as a sovereign state; usually reserved for former colonies.

Non-derogable norm of international law A rule of international law so fundamental to the international legal order that it cannot be set aside or suspended, even upon the express consent of states; see also *jus cogens* or **peremptory norm of international law.**

Non-intervention, Principle of The basic obligation of states not to interfere in the domestic affairs of other states.

Objection to reservation An assertion by a party to a treaty that it rejects the validity of a reservation entered by another party to the treaty, with the effect either that no treaty relations are established between the reserving and the objecting parties or that the provision to which the reservation and objection relate does not apply as between the reserving and objecting parties.

Objective regime In connection with state succession to treaty rights and obligations, a treaty regime creating or governing rights and obligations relating to the use of territory. Generally such treaty regimes are exempted from the operation of the **clean slate doctrine**.

Objective territorial principle A basis for the exercise of jurisdiction by a state over an event that terminates or has effects in its territory.

Occupation Peaceful and effective exercise of sovereign control over territory; frequently invoked as a basis of sovereign title to territory.

Opinio juris The subjective conviction by states that their actions are required as a matter of law; short form of *opinio juris sive necessitatis* (Latin for "opinion that an act is necessary by rule of law").

Opposable In relation to international legal obligations, the quality of obligations binding upon, and that can therefore be asserted against, a state or other subject of international law.

Pacta sunt servanda The most fundamental rule of treaty law: legal undertakings by international legal subjects must be performed by them in good faith.

Party In the law of treaties, a state or other subject of international law that has expressed its consent to be bound by a treaty.

Passive personality principle A basis for the exercise of prescriptive jurisdiction by a state over acts committed abroad by foreign nationals, but which adversely affect its nationals.

Peremptory norm of international law A rule of international law so fundamental to the international legal order that it cannot be set aside or suspended, even upon the express consent of states; see also *jus cogens* or a **non-derogable norm of international law**.

Permanent Court of International Justice (PCIJ) The principal judicial organ of the League of Nations and predecessor to the International Court of Justice.

Persistent objector A state that clearly and consistently manifests its objection to a rule of customary international law since its inception, thereby escaping its universally binding effect.

Piracy An international crime consisting of acts of violence or depredation committed by private persons for private ends or profit on the high seas or in areas beyond national jurisdiction.

Pre-emptive self-defence A controversial doctrine proposed in the 2002 National Security Policy of the United States that would permit states to use force in self-defence to counter a threat which is not yet imminent; see also **self-defence, anticipatory self-defence**.

Prescription The process by which sovereignty over territory is transferred from one state to another as a result of adverse effective occupation of the territory by the latter.

Prescriptive jurisdiction The power of a state to regulate people, property, and transactions or to prescribe conduct, usually through the passage of laws or regulations.

Private international law An area of domestic law governing the manner in which domestic courts deal with transactions having one or more foreign elements (e.g., an event or transaction occurring abroad or involving foreign nationals); see also **conflict of laws**.

Protective principle A basis for the exercise of prescriptive jurisdiction by a state over acts committed abroad by foreign nationals, but which adversely affect the state's security interests.

Protocol A treaty; frequently used to designate a secondary or consequential treaty augmenting or modifying elements of a primary treaty.

Publicist A scholarly expert in international law.

Ratification The process by which a state that has participated in the negotiation and adoption of the text of a treaty subsequently expresses its consent to be bound by that treaty.

Ratione materiae **immunity** Immunity that attaches to actions due to their substantive subject matter as official state acts.

Ratione personae **immunity** Immunity that attaches to the person of an office-holder, such as a head of state.

Rebus sic stantibus A basis for termination or suspension of treaty obligations based on a radical transformation of the extent of such obligations brought about by an unforeseen change of circumstances which constituted an essential basis of the party's consent to the treaty; see also **fundamental change of circumstances**.

Recognition Expression of consent to or acceptance of a claim made by another state; frequently invoked in territorial disputes as a basis for precluding subsequent objections to a claim of sovereignty which has been recognized. Also, an act by which a state acknowledges the emergence of a new state or, less frequently, the legitimacy of a new government within an existing state.

Regional customary international law Customary international law that arises from state practice and *opinio juris* of a discrete and limited number of states; as it departs from generally applicable customary international law, it is only binding upon and opposable against those states participating in its formation; contrast with **general** or **universal customary international law**, or simply **customary international law** without qualification.

Regional human rights Human rights protections that have been articulated at a regional (e.g. European, African, or American) level; contrast with **universal human rights**.

Renunciation The transfer of sovereignty over territory from one state to another by the unilateral act of the former.

Reparation A secondary obligation flowing from the commission of an internationally wrongful act giving rise to state responsibility; the required remedy aimed at eliminating to the extent possible the consequences of an internationally wrongful act, usually through restitution, compensation, and/or satisfaction.

Res communis Areas beyond, and not subject to incorporation into, state territory; thus available for unilateral use and exploitation by all states; examples include the high seas.

Res nullius Territory not currently under the sovereignty of any state but subject to potential incorporation into state territory.

Reservation A unilateral statement made by a state when signing, ratifying, or acceding to a treaty, which purports to exclude or modify the legal effect of certain provisions of the treaty in their application to that state.

Responsibility to protect An emerging doctrine positing a responsibility, borne by the international community, to protect civilian populations from gross human rights violations. The focal point for discharge of this responsibility appears at present to be the UN Security Council.

Restitution A remedy calling for the restoration of the situation that existed prior to the commission of an internationally wrongful act; frequently takes the form of the return of territory or of an object.

Restrictive state immunity A theory of state immunity that differentiates between commercial (or "private") and sovereign acts of states, extending immunity from the judicial process of foreign domestic courts in respect of the latter but not the former; contrast with **absolute state immunity**.

Satisfaction A remedy aimed at repairing "moral," non-material damage suffered by a state which has been the victim of an internationally wrongful act; often takes such non-material forms as an apology or a guarantee of non-repetition, but may also assume a material (e.g., monetary), symbolic form of reparation.

Second generation human rights Human rights of a social, economic, or cultural character.

Sector theory A controversial basis for claiming sovereignty over territory coming within a "sector" formed by drawing longitudinal lines to either the North or South Pole from points located in a state's territory; invoked only with respect to claims of sovereignty in Arctic and Antarctic regions.

Security Council (SC) An organ of the United Nations composed of permanent and elected members and having primary responsibility for the maintenance and restoration of international peace and security.

Self-defence, Right of An exception to the general prohibition of the use of force among states permitting one state to use force in response to an **armed attack** attributable to another; see also **anticipatory self-defence**, **collective self-defence**, **pre-emptive self-defence**.

Signatory A state or other subject of international law that has expressed its agreement with the text of a treaty and a future intent to become bound by it; in contrast to a party to the treaty, a signatory is not presently bound to perform the treaty, although it is required to refrain from acts that would defeat the object and purpose of the treaty or its coming into force.

Signature The act of signing a draft treaty text; may have differing legal effects, depending on the intent of the parties negotiating the treaty text, including authentication or the expression of consent to be bound.

Soft law Non-binding or emerging norms which may or may not eventually harden into binding law; rules not yet grounded in a recognized, formal source of law; see also *lex ferenda*.

Sovereignty The full range of powers and privileges enjoyed by a state over its territory and population to the exclusion of all other states but subject to international law.

Special customary international law Customary international law that arises from state practice and *opinio juris* of a discrete and limited number of states; as it departs from generally applicable customary international law, it is only binding upon and opposable against those states participating in its formation; also referred to as **regional** or **local customary international law**; contrast with **customary international law** without qualification.

Stare decisis A common law doctrine requiring courts to abide by prior decisions in future cases disclosing the same facts; a rule of binding precedent elevating judicial decisions to a source of law; specifically *not* applicable in international law, such that international judicial decisions are not a formal source of international law.

State A stable, independent political community comprising a government exercising exclusive, sovereign jurisdiction over a given territory and population and capable of entering into international legal relations with other states.

State immunity An immunity enjoyed by states from the jurisdiction of foreign domestic courts.

State practice A pattern of behaviour by states which, if accompanied by a conviction by those states that their behaviour is required as a matter of law, may give rise to customary international law.

State responsibility The area of international law governing the liabilities of states for their internationally wrongful acts.

Subject of international law An entity having rights and obligations under international law.

Subjective territorial principle A basis for the exercise of jurisdiction by a state over an event which originates in its territory.

Succession, State A change in the international legal identity of the state enjoying sovereignty over a given piece of territory.

Supervening impossibility of performance A ground for terminating or suspending treaty obligations based on physical impossibility brought about by the disappearance or destruction of an object indispensable to the performance of the treaty.

Supranational Beyond or outside the state.

Suspension The process by which performance of treaty obligations is suspended for a period of time, subject to its revival at some subsequent point in time.

Termination The process by which treaty obligations are ended.

Territorial principle A basis for the exercise of state jurisdiction over persons/events due to their presence/occurrence within a state's territory.

Territorial sea A maritime zone extending from a coastal state's baselines to a maximum breadth of 12 nautical miles.

Third generation human rights A broadly-defined category of human rights corresponding primarily to rights of a collective or communal nature, such as rights to a healthy environment, economic development, self-determination, etc.

Transformationist An approach to the domestic reception of international law that requires that international law (in particular, treaty law) be transformed into domestic law by a domestic law-making process (usually by way of implementing legislation) in order to have domestic legal effect.

Transit passage, Right of A right of passage without prior authorization through international straits recognized in the 1982 *United Nations Convention on the Law of the Sea*; such right of passage may not be suspended nor may passage of a foreign vessel be stopped by a coastal state bordering the strait.

Travaux préparatoires Drafts and other documents relating to the negotiation of the text of a treaty.

Treaty An agreement between two or more subjects of international law that is intended to be legally binding and governed by international law.

Unilateral declaration An undertaking given unilaterally by a state with the intent of creating binding legal obligations for itself.

United Nations (UN) An international organization established by treaty (the *Charter of the United Nations*) in 1945 and enjoying near-universal membership by states; its principal objectives include the maintenance of international peace and security, the promotion of respect for human rights, and the development of international cooperation.

Universal human rights Human rights protections that have been articulated at a universal or global level; contrast with **regional human rights**.

Universal principle A basis for the exercise of state jurisdiction over an individual in respect of a criminal act regardless of the location of the act or the nationality of the individual or victim; invoked only in connection with serious international crimes such as piracy, genocide, war crimes, etc.

Uti possidetis A doctrine by which internal, administrative boundaries between colonial units governed by a single metropolitan power achieve the status of international boundaries upon decolonization.

Withdrawal The repudiation by one party of a multilateral treaty.

TABLE OF CASES

INDEX

ABOUT THE AUTHOR

John H. Currie is a law professor in the Faculty of Law at the University of Ottawa, where he teaches international law, the use of force by states, the law of armed conflict, torts, and constitutional law. He has degrees from the Universities of Toronto, Ottawa, and Cambridge, and litigated for several years with Lang Michener LLP in Toronto and Ottawa. From 2004 to 2006, Professor Currie was Scholar in Residence in the Legal Affairs Bureau of Canada's Department of Foreign Affairs and International Trade where he worked primarily on international criminal and humanitarian law issues. In that capacity, he represented Canada before a number of UN and other bodies, including the International Criminal Tribunal for the Former Yugoslavia. An Assistant Editor of the Canadian Yearbook of International Law and Past-President of the Canadian Council on International Law, Professor Currie is the author or co-author of seven books, including (with Professors Craig Forcese and Valerie Oosterveld) *International Law: Doctrine, Practice, and Theory* (Irwin Law, 2007). His research interests include the use of force by states, international humanitarian law, extraterritorial jurisdiction, the domestic reception of international law, maritime boundary delimitation, and international criminal law.